THE
CELEBRITY
BIRTHDAY
BOOK

Researched and Compiled
by
Robert Brett Bronaugh

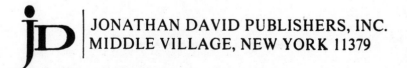

JONATHAN DAVID PUBLISHERS, INC.
MIDDLE VILLAGE, NEW YORK 11379

THE CELEBRITY BIRTHDAY BOOK
Copyright © 1981
by
Robert Brett Bronaugh
All rights reserved.

Jonathan David Publishers, Inc.
68-22 Eliot Avenue
Middle Village, New York 11379

Library of Congress Cataloging in Publication Data

Bronaugh, Robert Brett, 1947-
  The celebrity birthday book

  1. Biography—20th century. 2. Biography.
3. Birthday books. I. Title.
CT120.B74   920'.009'04   80-14221
ISBN 0-8246-0253-6

CONTENTS

This book is dedicated to the celebrities listed in this volume, who have given and who continue to give the public enjoyment, entertainment, excitement and thrills, inventions, knowledge and wisdom, leadership, and record-setting achievements.

ACKNOWLEDGMENTS

The author wishes to express his sincere appreciation to the following celebrities who have contributed to this volume:

Sharon Acker
Nancy Ames*
Senator Howard Baker
Senator Dewey Bartlett
Nelson Benton
Meredith Baxter Birney*
Lloyd Bochner
Pat Boone
Ed Bradley
David Brenner
Tom Brokaw
Foster Brooks
Georg Stanford Brown*
Victor Buono
Myron Cohen
Hans Conried
"Professor" Irwin Corey
Don Cornell
Norm Crosby*
Scatman Crothers*
Rodney Dangerfield*
Cesare Danova
Morton Dean
Elinor Donahue
Jessica Dragonette
Steffi Duna
Marj Dusay
Robert Duvall*

Jack Elam
Morgan Fairchild
Marty Feldman
Totie Fields*
Fannie Flagg
Bill Flemming
Eva Gabor
Crystal Gayle*
Phyllis George*
Frank Glieber
Gogi Grant
Karen Grassle*
Shecky Greene
Dabbs Greer
Christina Hart
Peter Haskell
Alexandra Hay
Senator Ernest Hollings
Bo Hopkins*
Susan Howard
Kate Jackson
Tom Jarriel
Jimmy The Greek
Senator J. Bennett Johnston
Charlie Jones
Phil Jones
Bernard Kalb
Ted Knight

Nancy Kovack
Senator Paul Laxalt
Michael Learned
Ruta Lee*
Lennon Sisters
Mort Lindsey
Rue McClanahan
Anne Meara*
Larry Merchant
Donna Mills
Bruce Morton
Nick Nolte*
Ike Pappas
Jane Pauley
Pat Paulsen*
Honorable Claude Pepper
Roger Perry
Robert Pierpoint

Harve Presnell*
Lee Purcell
Jay Randolph
Raymond St. Jacques
Chris Schenkel
Bob Schieffer
Senator William L. Scott
Tina Sinatra
Tom Snyder
Julie Sommars
David Soul*
Laurette Spang
Jackie Stewart
Jerry Stiller*
Woody Strode*
Lesley Ann Warren*
Betty White
Morgan Woodward

Included in the list below are the family members and representatives who have contributed to this book in behalf of those celebrities whose names are marked with an asterisk above.

The author also gratefully acknowledges the following individuals and businesses who have contributed, either directly or indirectly, to this volume:

Mrs. Victor Ricardo Alfaro
Barbara Best, Inc.
Ms. Lou Bressler, Public Information Secretary,
    PGA Tour-Professional Golfers' Association
Bernie Brillstein Co. Personal Management
Broadcasting Magazine/Broadcasting Publications Inc.
David Capell & Company/Howard Hinderstein Productions, Inc.
Kingsley Colton, Executive Director, Irene Ryan Foundation
Kingsley Colton & Associates, Inc., Artists' Manager
Richard Connelly, Vice President, Public Information, ABC Television
Donald Davidson, Statistician, USAC-United States Auto Club
Mrs. William H. Duvall
Estelle Endler Publicity-Public Relations
Jack Fields & Associates, Artists' Manager
Phyllis Friedman, Rogers & Cowan, Inc. Public Relations
J. Bret Garwood, Executive Coordinator, Spelling-Goldberg Productions
Mrs. J. Robert George

Nathaniel J. Hyland, Assistant Secretary, The Jockey Club
Howard Kercheval, Manager, NASCAR News Bureau—
   National Association For Stock Car Auto Racing, Inc.
LPGA-Ladies Professional Golf Association
Frank Liberman & Associates
Jeff Mackler, AMPR Public Relations
Ron Mason, Neil Rosen & Sons Personal Management
Janey Messmore
Janice S. Morgan Public Relations
Irene Pinn, Inc.
Mrs. Veeva Hamblen Presnell
Barrie Richardson, Vice President, Press Information, CBS Television
Sharr Enterprises, Inc.
Paul Shefrin, The Shefrin Company Public Relations
WBAL-TV
WTOP-TV (now WDVM-TV)
Ed Walker, WMAL-AM & WJLA-TV

Press Offices of:
Baltimore Colts
Cleveland Browns
Dallas Cowboys
Denver Broncos
Green Bay Packers
Los Angeles Rams
Minnesota Vikings
San Francisco Forty Niners
Washington Redskins

Press Offices of:
Senator James Abourezk
Senator Carl Curtis
Senator Robert Dole
Senator Floyd Haskell
Senator Henry Jackson
Senator Lee Metcalf
Senator Harrison Schmitt
Senator Malcolm Wallop

   The author extends a very special note of thanks to Alfred Jacob
Kolatch, President & Editor-in-Chief of Jonathan David Publishers,
for his expertise, support and patience.

PREFACE

The Celebrity Birthday Book includes the greatest array of celebrities ever listed within the pages of a single volume. This definitive reference work is highly contemporary, yet equally nostalgic, as well as historic. Not only are most celebrities of the twentieth century included, but additionally celebrities of previous centuries who have made a significant impact on our lives today are listed. Readers who are fascinated with astrology, numerology, and biorhythms will find this book especially entertaining. It represents a comprehensive cross-section of individuals who have received recognition in such fields of endeavor as art, broadcasting, business and industry, civil rights, cosmetics, education, entertainment, exploration and navigation, fashion design, government, literature, medicine, military service, music, philosophy, politics, religion, science, sports, and women's rights.

The reader will soon discover that this book contains much more than just a list of birthdays. In addition to the celebrity's birthdate, for each person included the following information is provided: his or her professional name; the full, middle, real, and maiden name of the celebrity, where applicable; and the field or fields of endeavor with which the individual is identified. I have made very effort to give the celebrities' full birth dates. However, in certain instances only the month and day of birth have been given, and in several cases only the year of birth has been listed, where the complete information is either unknown or unavailable.

For convenience, *The Celebrity Birthday Book* is divided into two sections: alphabetical and chronological. The first allows the reader to randomly look up a celebrity of his or her choice; the second enables the reader to look under any day of the year and discover which famous people were born on that particular day.

This volume goes far beyond the usual stars and superstars who are commonly found in most other books. VIPs and prominent social figures, who are sometimes inadvertently and incorrectly labeled as celebrities, are not included. However, there are some Very Important People and socialites who are indeed classed as celebrities, and they are listed in this book.

Only individual celebrities have been included. Groups who have achieved fame—for example, music and comedy groups— have not been incorporated into this book, since the group as a unit is the celebrity, rather than the individuals who comprise the group. In cases where individuals left famous groups to become stars in their own right, they have been selected for inclusion.

What is a celebrity? It would, of course, be extremely difficult to arrive at an authoritative and universally accepted definition. It has been said that one man's celebrity is another man's nobody. Since neither I nor anyone else can claim to be the final authority in each and every field in which an individual can distinguish himself or herself, I extend my apologies to anyone who feels that he or she is a celebrity worthy of inclusion in this volume, but was somehow overlooked and omitted.

The information presented in *The Celebrity Birthday Book* has been gathered from thousands of sources, including directly from the celebrities themselves; their families, employers, agents, managers, and personal representatives; network and studio biographies; sports press guides and team yearbooks; as well as from previously published sources. All information has been checked, double-checked and cross-checked.

Each celebrity listed in this volume is identified by one word which best describes the field of endeavor with which he or she is most readily associated. In instances where celebrities are equally well known in more than one field, they are identified as being recognized in each field.

Most one word identifications are self-explanatory; however, for the sake of simplicity, celebrities are acknowledged by general delineations rather than specific ones. In order to avoid confusion the following is a partial list of specific categories of celebrities who have been combined into general categorical descriptions:

Broadway show singers, country, western & bluegrass singers, folk singers, gospel singers, jazz singers, opera singers, pop singers, rhythm & blues singers, rock singers, rock n' roll singers, and soul singers are all identified simply as *singers*.

Band leaders, composers, lyricists, orchestra leaders, musicians, songwriters, and symphony conductors are all identified by the general term *music*.

Stage, motion picture, and television producers and directors are identified simply as *producers* and *directors*.

Network news anchorpersons, commentators, correspondents, and reporters are all identified as *newscasters*.

Print media columnists, critics, editorial writers, and feature writers are all identified as *journalists*.

Governors, senators, mayors, speakers of the U.S. House of Representatives, and congressmen are all identified as *politicians*.

Presidential Cabinet officers, U.S. ambassadors to the United Nations, government bureau chiefs, White House staff members, and U.S. presidential advisors and aides are all identified by the word *government*.

The words *dramatist* and *playwright* are used interchangeably throughout this volume.

Unlike many publications, *The Celebrity Birthday Book* does not provide death dates. Consequently, this volume will never become outdated, only incomplete as new people achieve celebritydom in the coming years.

Robert Brett Bronaugh

Chevy Chase, Maryland
Spring 1981

Alphabetical Listing
of Celebrities

A

Aandahl, Fred George (politician)	April 9, 1897
Aaron, Hank; born Henry Louis Aaron (baseball)	February 5, 1934
Aaron, Tommy; born Thomas Dean Aaron (golf)	February 22, 1937
Abbott, Bud; born William Alexander Abbott (actor/comedian)	October 2, 1895
Abbott, George Francis (playwright/producer/director)	June 25, 1887
Abbott, Philip; born Philip Abbott Alexander (actor)	March 20, 1924
Abdul-Aziz, Zaid; born Donald A. Smith (basketball)	April 7, 1946
Abdul-Jabbar, Kareem; born Ferdinand Lewis Alcindor, Jr. (basketball/actor)	April 16, 1947
Abdul-Rahman, Mahdi; born Walt Hazzard (basketball)	April 15, 1942
Abel, Elie (newscaster)	October 17, 1920
Abel, Sid; born Sidney Gerald Abel (hockey)	February 22, 1918
Abel, Taffy; born Clarence John Abel (hockey)	May 28, 1900
Abel, Walter Charles (actor)	June 6, 1898
Abernathy, Ralph David (civil rights leader)	March 11, 1926
Abourezk, James G. (politician)	February 24, 1931
Abramowicz, Dan; born Daniel Abramowicz (football)	July 13, 1945
Abrams, Creighton Williams (army officer)	September 15, 1914
Abzug, Bella; born Bella Savitsky (politician)	July 24, 1920
Acheson, Dean Gooderham (government)	April 11, 1893
Acker, Sharon Eileen (actress)	April 2, 1935
Acker, Tom; born Thomas James Acker (baseball)	March 7, 1930
Ackerman, Bettye Louise (actress)	February 28, 1928
Acuff, Roy Claxton (singer/music)	September 15, 1903
Adair, Jerry; born Kenneth Jerry Adair (baseball)	December 17, 1936
Adam, Noelle Huguette (actress)	December 24, 1933
Adams, Abigail Smith; born Abigail Smith (First Lady)	November 23, 1744
Adams, Alva Blanchard (politician)	October 29, 1875
Adams, Bobby; born Robert Henry Adams (baseball)	December 14, 1921
Adams, Brock; born Brockman Adams (politics/government)	January 13, 1927
Adams, Buster; born Elvin Clark Adams (baseball)	June 24, 1915
Adams, Charles Francis (government)	August 2, 1866
Adams, Don (actor)	April 19, 1927
Adams, Don (basketball)	November 27, 1947
Adams, Edie, born Elizabeth Edith Enke, (actress/singer)	April 16, 1927

3

Adams, Franklin Pierce (journalist/author)	November 15, 1881
Adams, Jack, born John James Adams (hockey)	June 14, 1895
Adams, Joey; born Joseph Abramowitz (comedian)	January 6, 1911
Adams, John (President)	October 30, 1735
Adams, John Quincy (President)	July 11, 1767
Adams, Julie; born Betty May Adams (actress)	October 17, 1926
Adams, Louisa Catherine Johnson; born Louisa Catherine Johnson (First Lady)	February 12, 1775
Adams, Maude; born Maude Kiskadden (actress)	November 11, 1872
Adams, Nick; born Nicholas Aloysius Adamshock (actor)	July 10, 1931
Adams, Samuel (statesman/patriot)	September 27, 1722
Adams, Sherman; born Llewellyn Sherman Adams (politician)	January 8, 1899
Adams, Sparky; born Earl John Adams (baseball)	August 26, 1894
Adams, William Herbert (politician)	February 15, 1861
Adamson, Joy; born Joy-Friederike Victoria Gessner (naturalist/writer)	January 20, 1910
Adcock, Joe; born Joseph Wilbur Adcock (baseball)	October 30, 1927
Addams, Charles Samuel (cartoonist)	January 7, 1912
Addams, Dawn (actress)	September 21, 1930
Addams, Jane (humanitarian/social worker)	September 6, 1860
Adderley, Cannonball; born Julian Edwin Adderley (music)	September 15, 1928
Adderley, Herb; born Herbert Anthony Adderley (football)	June 8, 1939
Adenauer, Konrad (German government)	January 5, 1876
Adkins, Homer Martin (politician)	October 15, 1890
Adler, Larry; born Lawrence Cecil Adler (music)	February 10, 1914
Adler, Luther; born Lutha Adler (actor)	May 4, 1903
Adler, Richard (music/producer)	August 3, 1921
Adrian, Iris; born Iris Adrian Hostetter (actress)	May 29, 1913
Agar, John George (actor)	January 31, 1921
Agee, James (author)	November 27, 1909
Agee, Tommie Lee (baseball)	August 9, 1942
Agnew, Spiro Theodore "Ted" (Vice President)	November 9, 1918
Agronsky, Martin Zama (journalism/broadcasting)	January 12, 1915
Agutter, Jenny (actress)	December 20, 1952
Ahern, Kathy; born Kathleen Ahern (golf)	May 7, 1949
Aherne, Brian de Lacy (actor)	May 2, 1902
Ahn, Philip (actor)	March 29, 1911
Aidman, Charles L. (actor)	January 31, 1925
Aiken, Conrad Potter (poet/author)	August 5, 1889
Aiken, George David (politician)	August 20, 1892
Ailey, Alvin (dancer/choreographer)	January 5, 1931
Aimée, Anouk; born Francoise Sorya (actress)	April 27, 1932
Ainsmith, Eddie; born Edward Wilbur Ainsmith (baseball)	February 4, 1890
Akins, Claude (actor)	May 25, 1918
Akins, Zoë (playwright/poet)	October 30, 1886
Albanese, Licia (singer)	July 22, 1913
Albee, Edward Franklin (playwright)	March 12, 1928
Alberghetti, Anna Maria (actress/singer)	May 15, 1936
Albert, Carl Bert (politician)	May 10, 1908
Albert, Eddie; born Edward Albert Heimberger (actor/singer)	April 22, 1908
Albert, Edward (actor)	February 20, 1951

Albert, Frankie; born Frank Culling Albert (football)	January 27, 1920
Albertson, Jack (actor)	June 16, 1910
Albright, Hardie; born Hardy Albrecht (actor)	December 16, 1903
Albright, Lola Jean (actress/singer)	July 20, 1925
Albright, Tenley Emma (ice skating)	July 18, 1935
Alcott, Amy (golf)	February 22, 1956
Alcott, Louisa May (author)	November 29, 1832
Alda, Alan (actor/writer)	January 28, 1936
Alda, Robert; born Alphonso Giovanni Guiseppe Roberto D'Abruzzo (actor)	February 26, 1914
Alderman, Grady C. (football)	December 10, 1938
Aldrich, Chester Hardy (politician)	November 10, 1862
Aldridge, Lionel (football)	February 14, 1941
Aldridge, Vic; born Victor Eddington Aldridge (baseball)	October 25, 1893
Aldrin, Buzz; born Edwin Eugene Aldrin, Jr. (astronaut)	January 20, 1930
Aletter, Frank (actor)	January 14, 1926
Alexander, Ben; born Nicholas Benton Alexander (actor)	May 26, 1911
Alexander, Dale; born David Dale Alexander (baseball)	April 26, 1903
Alexander, Grover Cleveland (baseball)	February 26, 1887
Alexander, Jane; born Jane Quigley (actress)	October 28, 1939
Alexander, Katherine (actress)	September 22, 1901
Alexander, Kermit J. (football)	January 4, 1941
Alexander, Moses (politician)	November 13, 1853
Alexander, Shana; born Shana Ager (journalist/author)	October 6, 1925
Alger, Horatio (author)	January 13, 1834
Algren, Nelson (author)	March 28, 1909
Ali, Muhammad; born Cassius Marcellus Clay, Jr. (boxing/actor)	January 17, 1942
Alioto, Joseph Lawrence (politician)	February 12, 1916
Allan, Elizabeth (actress)	April 9, 1908
Allbritton, Louise (actress)	July 3, 1920
Allen, Bernie; born Bernard Keith Allen (baseball)	April 16, 1939
Allen, Chuck; born Charles R. Allen (football)	September 7, 1939
Allen, Elizabeth, born Elizabeth Ellen Gillease (actress)	January 25, 1934
Allen, Ethan (soldier)	January 10, 1738
Allen, Ethan Nathan (baseball)	January 1, 1904
Allen, Frank Gilman (politician)	October 6, 1874
Allen, Fred; born John Florence Sullivan (comedian)	May 31, 1894
Allen, George Herbert (football/sportscaster/author)	April 29, 1922
Allen, George Trenholme (hockey)	July 27, 1914
Allen, Gracie; born Grace Ethel Cecile Rosalie Allen (comedienne/actress)	July 26, 1899
Allen, Henry Justin (politician)	September 11, 1868
Allen, Irwin (producer/director)	June 12, 1916
Allen, James Browning (politician)	December 28, 1912
Allen, Johnny; born John Thomas Allen (baseball)	September 30, 1904
Allen, Judith; born Marie Elliott (actress)	January 28, 1913
Allen, Lucius Oliver, Jr. (basketball)	September 26, 1947
Allen, Mel; born Melvin Allen Israel (sportscaster)	February 14, 1913
Allen, Oscar Kelly (politician)	August 8, 1882
Allen, Rex E. (actor/singer)	December 31, 1920

Allen, Richard Anthony "Dick" or "Richie" (baseball)	March 8, 1942
Allen, Steve; born Stephen Valentine Patrick William Allen (comedian/actor/singer/TV host/music/author)	December 26, 1921
Allen, Woody; born Allen Stewart Konigsberg (actor/ director/writer)	December 1, 1935
Alley, Gene; born Leonard Eugene Alley (baseball)	July 10, 1940
Allgood, Sara (actress)	October 31, 1883
Allin, Brian (golf)	October 13, 1944
Allison, Bob; born William Robert Allison (baseball)	July 11, 1934
Allison, Bobby; born Robert Arthur Allison (auto racing)	December 3, 1937
Allison, Donnie Joseph (auto racing)	September 7, 1939
Allison, Fran (actress)	—————1924
Allison, Wilmer Lawson (tennis)	December 8, 1902
Allott, Gordon Llewellyn (politician)	January 2, 1907
Allred, James V. (politician)	March 29, 1899
Allwyn, Astrid (actress)	November 27, 1909
Allyson, June; born Ella Geisman (actress)	October 7, 1917
Almada, Mel; born Baldomero Melo Almada (baseball)	February 7, 1913
Almeida, Laurindo (music)	September 2, 1917
Almond, James Lindsay, Jr. (politician)	June 15, 1898
Alomar, Sandy; born Conde Santos Alomar (baseball)	October 19, 1943
Alonso, Alicia; born Alicia Ernestina de la Caridad del Cobre Marinez Hoyo (dancer)	December 21, 1921
Alou, Felipe Rojas (baseball)	May 12, 1935
Alou, Jesus Maria Rojas (baseball)	March 24, 1943
Alou, Matty; born Mateo Rojas Alou (baseball)	December 22, 1938
Alpert, Herb (music)	March 31, 1935
Alsop, Joseph Wright, Jr. (journalist)	October 11, 1910
Alsop, Stewart Johonnot Oliver (journalist)	May 17, 1914
Alston, Mack (football)	April 27, 1947
Alston, Walter Emmons (baseball)	December 1, 1911
Altman, George Lee (baseball)	March 20, 1933
Altman, Robert (director/producer/writer)	February 20, 1922
Alvis, Max; born Roy Maxwell Alvis (baseball)	February 2, 1938
Alworth, Lance D. (football)	August 3, 1940
Alzado, Lyle Martin (football)	April 3, 1949
Amalfitano, Joe; born John Joseph Amalfitano (baseball)	January 23, 1934
Amaro, Ruben Mora (baseball)	January 6, 1936
Ambler, Eric (author)	June 28, 1909
Ameche, Alan D.; born Lino Dante Ameche (football)	June 1, 1933
Ameche, Don; born Dominic Felix Amici (actor/singer)	May 31, 1908
Ames, Adrienne; born Adrienne Ruth McClure (actress)	August 3, 1907
Ames, Ed (singer/actor—Ames Brothers)	July 9, 1927
Ames, Gene (singer—Ames Brothers)	February 13, 1925
Ames, Joe (singer—Ames Brothers)	May 3, 1924
Ames, Leon; born Leon Waycoff (actor)	January 20, 1903
Ames, Nancy; born Nancy Hamilton Alfaro (singer/actress)	September 30, 1937
Ames, Vic (singer—Ames Brothers)	May 20, 1926
Amies, Hardy; born Edwin Hardy Amies (fashion designer)	July 17, 1909
Amis, Kingsley William (author)	April 16, 1922
Ammons, Elias Milton (politician)	July 28, 1860

Ammons, Teller (politician) — December 3, 1895
Amon, Chris; born Christopher Arthur Amon (auto racing) — July 20, 1943
Amory, Cleveland (writer/conservationist) — September 2, 1917
Amos; born Freeman Fisher Gosden (actor—Amos 'n Andy) — May 5, 1896
Amos, John (actor) — December 27, 1942
Ampère, André Marie (physicist/mathematician) — January 22, 1775
Amsterdam, Morey (comedian/actor/music) — December 14, 1912
Anders, William Alison (astronaut) — October 17, 1933
Andersen, Elmer Lee (politician) — June 17, 1909
Andersen, Hans Christian (author) — April 2, 1805
Anderson, Bill (singer/music) — November 1, 1937
Anderson, Bill, born Walter W. Anderson (football) — July 16, 1936
Anderson, C. Elmer (politician) — March 16, 1912
Anderson, Clinton Presba (politics/government) — October 23, 1895
Anderson, Cowboy; born Thomas Linton Anderson (hockey) — July 9, 1911
Anderson, Dick; born Richard Paul Anderson (football) — February 10, 1946
Anderson, Donny; born Gary Don Anderson (football) — May 16, 1943
Anderson, Forrest Howard (politician) — January 30, 1913
Anderson, Gilbert M. "Broncho Billy"; born Max Aronson — March 21, 1882
(actor/producer/director)
Anderson, Jack Northman (journalist) — October 19, 1922
Anderson, John Jr. (politician) — May 8, 1917
Anderson, Dame Judith; born Frances Margaret Anderson — February 10, 1898
(actress)
Anderson, Ken; born Kenneth A. Anderson (football) — February 15, 1949
Anderson, Lindsay Gordon (director) — April 17, 1923
Anderson, Liz; born Elizabeth Jane Haaby (singer/music) — March 13, 1930
Anderson, Lynn Rene (singer/actress) — September 26, 1947
Anderson, Marian (singer) — February 17, 1902
Anderson, Maxwell (playwright) — December 15, 1888
Anderson, Melissa Sue (actress) — September 26, 1962
Anderson, Mike; born Michael Allen Anderson (baseball) — June 22, 1951
Anderson, Richard Norman (actor) — August 8, 1926
Anderson, Robert Bernerd (government) — June 4, 1910
Anderson, Robert Woodruff (playwright) — April 28, 1917
Anderson, Sherwood (author) — September 13, 1876
Anderson, Sigurd (politician) — January 22, 1904
Anderson, Sparky; born George Lee Anderson (baseball) — February 22, 1934
Anderson, Victor Emanuel (politician) — March 30, 1902
Anderson, Wendell Richard (politician) — February 1, 1933
Andersson, Bibi; born Birgitta Andersson (actress) — November 11, 1935
Andes, Keith; born John Charles Andes (actor) — July 12, 1920
Andre, Lona; born Laura Anderson (actress) — March 12, 1915
Andress, Ursula (actress) — March 19, 1936
Andretti, Mario Gabriel (auto racing) — February 28, 1940
Andrews, Billy; born William D. Andrews, Jr. (football) — June 14, 1945
Andrews, Charles Oscar (politician) — March 7, 1877
Andrews, Dana; born Carver Dana (or Daniel) Andrews (actor) — January 1, 1909
Andrews, Edward (actor) — October 9, 1914
Andrews, Harry (actor) — November 10, 1911
Andrews, Julie; born Julia Elizabeth Wells (singer/actress) — October 1, 1935

Andrews, LaVerne (singer—Andrew Sisters)	July 6, 1915
Andrews, Maxene (singer—Andrews Sisters)	January 3, 1918
Andrews, Mike; born Michael Jay Andrews (baseball)	July 9, 1943
Andrews, Patty (singer—Andrews Sisters)	February 16, 1920
Andrews, Tige; born Tiger Androwaous (actor)	March 19, 1923
Andrie, George J. (football)	April 20, 1940
Andrus, Cecil Dale (politics/government)	August 25, 1931
Andy; born Charles James Correll (actor—Amos 'n Andy)	February 1, 1890
Angel, Heather (actress)	February 9, 1909
Angeles, Victoria de los; born Victoria Gamez Cima (singer)	November 1, 1924
Angeli, Pier; born Anna Maria Pierangeli (actress)	June 19, 1932
Angotti, Louis Frederick (hockey)	January 16, 1938
Anka, Paul Albert (singer/actor/music)	July 30, 1941
Ankers, Evelyn (actress)	August 17, 1918
Ann-Margret; born Ann Margaret Olsson (actress/singer/ dancer)	April 28, 1941
Annabella, born Suzanne Georgette Charpentier (actress)	July 14, 1909
Anne, Princess; born Anne Elizabeth Alice Louise Mountbatten (British Royalty)	August 15, 1950
Anouilh, Jean (playwright)	June 23, 1910
Ansara, Michael George (actor)	April 15, 1922
Anson, Cap; born Adrian Constantine Anson (baseball)	April 17, 1851
Anspach, Susan (actress)	———1939
Anthony, Ray; born Raymond Antonini (music)	January 20, 1922
Anthony, Susan B.; born Susan Brownell Anthony (reformer/suffragist)	February 15, 1820
Anthony, Tony (actor)	October 16, 1937
Anton, Susan (singer/actress)	October 12, 1950
Antonelli, Johnny; born John August Antonelli (baseball)	April 12, 1930
Antonio, Lou; born Louis Demetrious Antonio (actor/director)	January 23, 1934
Antonioni, Michelangelo (director)	September 29, 1912
Antwine, Houston (football)	April 11, 1939
Aparicio, Luis Ernesto Monteil (baseball)	April 29, 1934
Apodaca, Jerry (politician)	October 3, 1934
Appling, Luke; born Lucius Benjamin Appling (baseball)	April 2, 1907
Apps, Syl; born Joseph Sylvanus Apps (hockey)	January 18, 1915
Arbanas, Fred; born Frederick V. Arbanas (football)	January 14, 1939
Arbour, Al; born Alger Arbour (hockey)	November 1, 1932
Arbuckle, Fatty; born Roscoe Conkling Arbuckle (actor/director)	March 24, 1887
Arcaro, Eddie; born George Edward Arcaro (jockey/sportscaster)	February 19, 1916
Archer, Anne (actress)	August 25, 1947
Archer, George William (golf)	October 1, 1939
Archer, John; born Ralph Shipwith Bowman (actor)	May 8, 1915
Archerd, Army; born Armand Archerd (journalist/actor)	January 13, 1919
Archibald, Nate (basketball)	April 18, 1948
Ard, Jim (basketball)	September 19, 1948
Arden, Elizabeth, born Florence Nightingale Graham (cosmetics)	December 31, 1884

Arden, Eve; born Eunice Quedens (actress)	April 30, 1912
Ardrey, Robert (author)	October 16, 1908
Arendt, Hannah (historian)	October 14, 1906
Ariyoshi, George Ryoichi (politician)	March 12, 1926
Arizin, Paul (basketball)	April 9, 1928
Arkin, Alan Wolf (actor/director)	March 26, 1934
Arledge, Roone Pickney (broadcasting)	July 8, 1931
Arlen, Harold; born Hyman Arluck (music)	February 15, 1905
Arlen, Richard; born Cornelius van Mattemore (actor)	September 1, 1898
Arliss, George; born George Augustus Andrews (actor)	April 10, 1868
Armetta, Henry (actor)	July 4, 1888
Armour, Tommy; born Thomas Dickson Armour (golf)	September 24, 1895
Armstrong, Bess; born Elizabeth Armstrong (actress)	December 11, 1953
Armstrong, Chief; born George Edward Armstrong (hockey)	July 6, 1930
Armstrong, Louis; born Daniel Louis Armstrong (music/singer/actor)	July 4, 1900
Armstrong, Murray Alexander (hockey)	January 1, 1916
Armstrong, Neil Alden (astronaut)	August 5, 1930
Armstrong, Otis (football)	November 15, 1950
Armstrong, R.G. (actor)	————1920
Armstrong, Robert (actor)	November 20, 1890
Armstrong, Robert Richard (hockey)	April 7, 1931
Arn, Edward F. (politician)	May 19, 1906
Arnall, Ellis Gibbs (politician)	March 20, 1907
Arnaz, Desi, Sr.; born Desiderio Alberto Arnaz y de Acha, III (actor/singer/music/producer/author)	March 2, 1917
Arnas, Desi, Jr. (actor/singer/music)	January 19, 1953
Arnaz, Lucie Désirée (actress/singer)	July 17, 1951
Arness, James King; born James King Aurness (actor)	May 26, 1923
Arnett, Jon Dwane (football)	April 20, 1935
Arno, Peter (cartoonist)	January 8, 1904
Arno, Sig; born Siegfried Aron (actor)	December 27, 1895
Arnold, Benedict (soldier/traitor)	January 14, 1741
Arnold, Eddy; born Richard Edward Arnold (singer/music)	May 15, 1918
Arnold, Edward; born Guenther Schneider (actor)	February 18, 1890
Arnovich, Morrie; born Morris Arnovich (baseball)	January 20, 1910
Aronson, John Hugo (politician)	September 1, 1891
Arrau, Claudio (music)	February 6, 1903
Arrington, Buddy (auto racing)	July 26, 1938
Arroyo, Martina (singer)	February 2, 1937
Arthur, Beatricé; born Bernice Frankel (actress)	May 13, 1924
Arthur, Chester Alan (President)	October 5, 1830
Arthur, Ellen Lewis Herndon; born Ellen Lewis Herndon (First Lady)	August 30, 1837
Arthur, Harold John (politician)	February 9, 1904
Arthur, Jean; born Gladys Georgianna Greene (actress)	October 17, 1905
Arthur, Robert; born Robert Arthaud (actor)	June 18, 1925
Ascari, Alberto (auto racing)	July 13, 1918
Ash, Roy Lawrence, (government)	October 20, 1918
Ashburn, Richie; born Don Richie Ashburn (baseball)	March 19, 1927
Ashe, Arthur Robert, Jr. (tennis)	July 10, 1943

Asher, Jane (actress)	April 5, 1946
Ashley, Elizabeth; born Elizabeth Ann Cole (actress)	August 30, 1939
Ashley, John; born John Atchley (actor)	December 25, 1934
Ashurst, Henry Fountain (politician)	September 13, 1874
Asimov, Isaac (author)	January 2, 1920
Askew, Reubin O'Donovan (politician)	September 11, 1928
Asner, Edward (actor)	November 15, 1929
Aspromonte, Bob; born Robert Thomas Aspromonte (baseball)	June 19, 1938
Aspromonte, Ken; born Kenneth Joseph Aspromonte (baseball)	September 22, 1932
Astaire, Adele; born Adele Marie Austerlitz (dancer/actress)	September 10, 1897
Astaire, Fred; born Frederick Austerlitz (dancer/actor/singer)	May 10, 1899
Asther, Nils (actor)	January 17, 1897
Astin, John Allen (actor)	March 30, 1930
Astor, John Jacob (financier)	July 17, 1763
Astor, Mary; born Lucille Vasconcellos Langhanke (actress)	May 3, 1906
Astrologes, Maria (golf)	August 10, 1951
Athas, Pete; born Peter G. Athas (football)	September 15, 1947
Atherton, William; born William Atherton Knight (actor)	July 30, 1947
Atkins, Chet; born Chester Burton Atkins (music)	June 20, 1924
Atkins, Doug; born Douglas L. Atkins (football)	May 8, 1930
Atkins, Eileen (actress)	June 16, 1934
Atkinson, Brooks; born Justin Brooks Atkinson (journalist)	November 28, 1894
Atkinson, George Henry (football)	January 4, 1947
Atkinson, Ted; born Theodore Francis Atkinson (jockey)	June 17, 1916
Atlas, Charles (body builder)	October 30, 1893
Attenborough, Sir Richard Samuel (actor/director)	August 29, 1923
Attlee, Clement Richard (British government)	January 3, 1883
Attles, Alvin (baseketball)	November 7, 1936
Atwill, Lionel (actor)	March 1, 1885
Atwood, Donna (ice skating)	February 14, 1923
Auberjonois, René Murat (actor)	June 1, 1940
Aubrey, Skye; born Susan Schuyler Aubrey (actress)	December 20, 1945
Auchincloss, Louis Stanton (author)	September 27, 1917
Auden, W.H.; born Wystan Hugh Auden (poet)	February 21, 1907
Audubon, John James (ornithologist/artist)	April 26, 1785
Auer, Mischa; born Mischa Ounskowsky (actor)	November 17, 1905
Auerbach, Red; born Arnold Jacob Auerbach (basketball)	September 20, 1917
Auger, Claudine (actress)	April 26, 1942
Auker, Elden LeRoy (baseball)	September 21, 1910
Aumont, Jean-Pierre; born Jean-Pierre Salomons (actor)	January 5, 1909
Aurie, Harry Lawrence (hockey)	February 8, 1905
Austen, Jane (author)	December 16, 1775
Austin, Bill; born William Austin (football)	October 18, 1928
Austin, Debbie; born Deborah E. Austin (golf)	February 1, 1948
Austin, Pamela (actress)	December 20, 1941
Austin, Stephen F.; born Stephen Fuller Austin (colonizer/statesman)	November 3, 1793
Austin, Tracy (tennis)	December 2, 1962
Austin, Warren Robinson (politician)	November 12, 1877
Autry, Gene; born Orvon Gene Autry (actor/singer/ business executive)	September 29, 1907

Avalon, Frankie, born Francis Thomas Avallone (actor/singer) — September 18, 1939
Avellini, Bob; born Robert H. Avellini (football) — August 28, 1953
Averill, Earl; born Howard Earl Averill (baseball) — May 21, 1902
Averill, Earl Douglas (baseball) — September 9, 1931
Avery, Ken; born Kenneth Avery (football) — May 23, 1944
Avery, Milton Clark (artist) — March 7, 1893
Avery, Phyllis (actress) — November 14, 1924
Avery, Val (actor) — July 14, 1924
Avery, William Henry (politician) — August 11, 1911
Avila, Bobby; born Roberto Francisco Avila (baseball) — April 2, 1924
Awrey, Donald William (hockey) — July 18, 1943
Awtrey, Dennis (basketball) — February 22, 1948
Axelrod, George (playwright/author) — June 9, 1922
Axton, Hoyt Wayne (singer/music) — March 25, 1938
Aycock, Charles Brantley (politician) — November 1, 1859
Ayers, Roy Elmer (politician) — November 9, 1882
Aykroyd, Dan; born Daniel Edward Aykroyd (actor/comedian/ singer) — July 1, 1952
Aylmer, Felix; born Felix Edward Aylmer-Jones (actor) — February 21, 1889
Ayres, Lew; born Lewis Frederick Ayer, III (actor) — December 28, 1908
Azcue, Joe; born Jose Joaquin Azcue (baseball) — August 18, 1939
Aznavour, Charles; born Varenagh Aznavourian (singer/actor) — May 22, 1924

B

Babcock, Tim (politician) — October 27, 1919
Babich, Bob; born Robert Babich (football) — May 5, 1947
Bacall, Lauren; born Betty Joan Perske (actress) — September 16, 1924
Bach, Barbara (actress) — August 27, 1949
Bach, Johann Sebastian (music) — March 21, 1685
Bacharach, Burt F. (music) — May 12, 1928
Bachman, Nathan Lynn (politician) — August 2, 1878
Backstrom, Ralph (hockey) — September 18, 1937
Backus, Jim; born James Gilmore Backus (actor) — February 25, 1913
Baclanova, Olga (dancer/actress) — August 19, 1899
Bacon, Coy; born Lander McCoy Bacon (football) — August 30, 1942
Bacon, Francis (philosopher/writer) — January 22, 1561
Bacon, Irving (actor) — September 6, 1892
Bacon, Walter W. (politician) — January 20, 1880
Baddeley, Hermione; born Hermione Clinton-Baddeley (actress) — November 13, 1906
Baer, Max, Sr.; born Maximilian Adelbert Baer (boxing) — February 11, 1909
Baer, Max, Jr.; born Maximilian Adelbert Baer, Jr. (actor/producer) — December 4, 1937
Baez, Joan (singer/music) — January 9, 1941
Baeza, Braulio (jockey) — March 26, 1940
Bagnold, Enid Algerine (author) — October 27, 1889
Bahnsen, Stan; born Stanley Raymond Bahnsen (baseball) — December 15, 1944
Bailey, Ace; born Irvine Wallace Bailey (hockey) — July 3, 1903
Bailey, Bob; born Robert Sherwood Bailey (baseball) — October 13, 1942
Bailey, Carl Edward (politican) — October 8, 1894

Bailey, Ed; born Lonas Edgar Bailey (baseball)	April 15, 1931
Bailey, F. Lee; born Francis Lee Bailey (attorney)	June 10, 1933
Bailey, Jim; born James Randall Bailey (football)	June 9, 1948
Bailey, Josiah William (politician)	September 14, 1873
Bailey, Pearl Mae (singer/actress)	March 29, 1918
Bailey, Thomas Lowry (politician)	January 6, 1888
Bailey, Willis Joshua (politician)	October 12, 1854
Bain, Barbara; born Millie Fogel (actress)	September 13, 1934
Bain, Conrad Stafford (actor)	February 4, 1923
Bainter, Fay Okell (actress)	December 7, 1892
Baird, Bil; born William Britton Baird (puppeteer)	August 15, 1904
Baird, Butch; born Fred Baird (golf)	July 20, 1936
Baker, Buck; born Elzie Wylie Baker, Sr. (auto racing)	March 4, 1919
Baker, Buddy; born Elzie Wylie Baker, Jr. (auto racing)	January 25, 1941
Baker, Carrol (actress)	May 28, 1931
Baker, Diane (actress)	February 25, 1938
Baker, Dusty; born Johnnie B. Baker, Jr. (baseball)	June 15, 1949
Baker, Frank; born John Franklin Baker (baseball)	March 13, 1886
Baker, Floyd Wilson (baseball)	October 10, 1916
Baker, Howard Henry, Jr. (politician)	November 15, 1925
Baker, Joe Don (actor)	February 12, 1936
Baker, Josephine (singer/actor)	June 3, 1906
Baker, Kenny; born Kenneth Lawrence Baker (singer/actor)	September 30, 1912
Baker, Newton Diehl (government)	December 3, 1871
Baker, Sam; born Loris H. Baker (football)	November 12, 1929
Baker, Samuel Aaron (politician)	November 7, 1874
Baker, Stanley (actor)	February 28, 1927
Baker, Tony; born Vernon Baker (football)	February 16, 1945
Bakken, Jim; born James Leroy Bakken (football)	November 2, 1940
Balanchine, George; born Gyorgi Melitonovitch	January 9, 1904
Balanchivadze (choreographer)	
Balboa, Vasco Nuñez de (explorer)	———— 1475
Baldridge, H. Clarence (politician)	November 24, 1868
Baldwin, Faith (writer)	October 1, 1893
Baldwin, James Arthur (writer)	August 2, 1924
Baldwin, Raymond Earl (politician)	August 31, 1893
Baldwin, Simeon Eben (politician)	February 5, 1840
Balenclaga, Cristóbal (fashion designer)	————1895
Balfour, Murray (hockey)	August 24, 1936
Balin, Ina; born Ina Sandra Rosenberg (actress)	November 12, 1937
Ball, George Wildman (government)	December 21, 1909
Ball, Joseph Hurst (politician)	November 3, 1905
Ball, Kenny (music)	May 22, 1937
Ball, Lewis Heisler (politician)	September 21, 1861
Ball, Lucille Désirée (comedienne/actress/singer/producer)	August 6, 1910
Ballard, Kaye; born Catherine Gloria Balotta	November 20, 1926
(comedienne/actress/singer)	
Ballman, Gary J. (football)	July 6, 1940
Balmain, Pierre (fashion designer)	May 18, 1914
Balon, David Alexander (hockey)	August 2, 1937
Balsam, Martin Henry (actor)	November 4, 1919

Balzar, Frederick Bennett (politician)	June 15, 1880
Bamberger, Simon (politician)	February 27, 1847
Banaszak, Pete; born Peter Banaszak (football)	July 21, 1944
Banaszek, Cas; born Casmir J. Banaszek, II (football)	December 24, 1945
Bancroft, Anne; born Anna Maria Luisa Italiano (actress)	September 17, 1931
Bancroft, Dave; born David James Bancroft (baseball)	April 20, 1891
Bancroft, George (actor)	September 30, 1882
Bando, Sal; born Salvatore Leonard Bando (baseball)	February 13, 1944
Bankhead, John Hollis, Sr. (politician)	September 13, 1842
Bankhead, John Hollis, Jr. (politician)	July 8, 1872
Bankhead, Tallulah Brockman (actress)	January 31, 1902
Bankhead, William Brockman (politician)	April 12, 1874
Banks, Ernie, born Ernest Banks (baseball)	January 31, 1931
Banks, Henry (auto racing)	June 14, 1913
Banks, Tom; born Thomas S. Banks (football)	August 20, 1948
Bankston, Warren (football)	July 22, 1947
Banky, Vilma; born Vilma Lonchit (actress)	January 9, 1898
Bannen, Ian (actor)	June 29, 1928
Bara, Theda; born Theodosia Goodman (actress)	July 20, 1890
Barbeau, Adrienne (actress/singer)	June 11, 1945
Barber, Jerry; born Carl Jerome Barber (golf)	April 25, 1916
Barber, Miller (golf)	March 31, 1931
Barber, Red; born Walter Lanier Barber (sportscaster)	February 17, 1908
Barber, Samuel (music)	March 9, 1910
Barber, Steve; born Stephen David Barber (baseball)	February 22, 1939
Barbour, William Warren (politician)	July 31, 1888
Bardot, Brigitte, born Camille Javal (actress)	September 28, 1933
Bare, Bobby (singer/music)	April 7, 1935
Barenboim, Daniel (music)	November 15, 1942
Bari, Lynn; born Marjorie Bitzer (or Marjorie Schuyler Fisher) (actress)	December 18, 1913
Barker, Bob; born Robert William Barker (TV host)	December 12,———
Barker, Lex; born Alexander Crichlow Barker (actor)	May 8, 1919
Barker, Sue; born Susan Barker (tennis)	April 19, 1956
Barkley, Alben William (Vice President)	November 24, 1877
Barkum, Jerome Phillip (football)	July 18, 1950
Barnard, Christiaan N. (medicine)	October 8, 1922
Barnes, Binnie; born Gertrude (or Gitelle) Maude Barnes (actress)	March 25, 1905
Barnes, Clive Alexander (journalist)	May 13, 1927
Barnes, Erich (football)	July 4, 1935
Barnes, Jesse Lawrence (baseball)	August 26, 1892
Barnes, Jim (basketball)	April 13, 1941
Barnes, Joanna (actress/author)	November 15, 1934
Barnes, Margaret Ayer; born Margaret Ayer (author)	April 8, 1886
Barnes, Pete; born Peter Barnes (football)	August 31, 1945
Barnet, Charlie; born Charles Daly Barnet (music)	October 26, 1913
Barnett, Dick; born Richard Barnett (basketball)	April 5, 1936
Barnett, Jim (basketball)	July 7, 1944
Barnett, Pam; born Pamela Barnett (golf)	March 2, 1944
Barnett, Ross Robert (politician)	January 22, 1898

Barney, Lem; born Lemuel Jackson Barney (football)	September 8, 1945
Barnhill, John (basketball)	March 30, 1938
Barnum, P.T.; born Phineas Taylor Barnum (showman)	July 5, 1810
Baron, Sandy; born Sandy Beresofsky (comedian/actor)	May 5, 1937
Barrett, Frank, A. (politician)	November 10, 1892
Barrett, Rona; born Rona Burstein (journalist)	October 8, 1936
Barrie, Barbara; born Barbara Ann Berman (actress)	May 23, 1931
Barrie, Sir James Matthew (author/dramatist)	May 9, 1860
Barrie, Mona; born Mona Smith (actress)	December 18, 1909
Barrie, Wendy; born Marguerite Wendy Jenkins (actress)	April 18, 1912
Barron, Herman (golf)	December 23, 1909
Barron, William Wallace (politician)	December 8, 1911
Barrows, Lewis Orin (politician)	July 8, 1876
Barry, Don "Red"; born Donald Barry de Acosta (actor)	January 11, 1912
Barry, Gene; born Eugene Klass (actor/singer)	June 14, 1919
Barry, Jack (TV host)	March 20, 1918
Barry, Martin J. (hockey)	December 8, 1905
Barry, Patricia (actress)	November 16,———
Barry, Rick; born Richard Francis Barry, III (basketball/sportscaster)	March 28, 1944
Barrymore, Diana; born Diana Blanche Blythe (actress)	March 3, 1921
Barrymore, Ethel; born Ethel Mae Blythe (actress)	August 15, 1879
Barrymore, Georgie, born Georgianna Emma Drew (actress)	July 11, 1854
Barrymore, John; born John Sidney Blythe (actor)	February 15, 1882
Barrymore, John Blyth "John, Jr.", now John Drew Barrymore (actor)	June 4, 1932
Barrymore, Lionel; born Lionel Blythe (actor)	April 28, 1878
Barrymore, Maurice; born Herbert Maurice Blythe (actor)	———1847
Bartell, Dick, born Richard William Bartell (baseball)	November 22, 1907
Barth, John Simmons (author)	May 27, 1930
Barthelme, Donald (author)	April 7, 1931
Barthelmess, Richard (actor)	May 9, 1895
Bartholomew, Freddie; born Frederick Llewellyn Bartholomew (actor)	March 28, 1924
Bartkowski, Steve (football)	November 12, 1952
Bartlett, Dewey Follett (politician)	March 28, 1919
Bartlett, Edward Louis (politician)	April 20, 1904
Bartlett, John Henry (politician)	March 15, 1869
Bartók, Béla (music)	March 25, 1881
Bartok, Eva; born Eva Martha Szöke (or Sjoke) (actress)	June 18, 1926
Barton, Clara; born Clarissa Harlowe Barton (founder of American Red Cross)	December 25, 1821
Barton, James (actor)	November 1, 1890
Baruch, Bernard Mannes (financier/statesman)	August 19, 1870
Baryshnikov, Mikhail Nikolayevich (dancer)	January 27, 1948
Basehart, Richard (actor)	August 31, 1914
Basie, Count; born William Basie (music)	August 21, 1904
Basilio, Carmen (boxing)	April 2, 1927
Basinger, Kim (actress)	December 8, 1953
Basquette, Lina; born Lena Baskette (actress)	April 19, 1907
Bass, Dick; born Richard Lee Bass (football)	March 15, 1937

Bass, Mike; born Michael T. Bass (football)	March 31, 1945
Bass, Robert Perkins (politician)	September 1, 1873
Bass, Ross (politician)	March 17, 1918
Bassen, Hank; born Henry Bassen (hockey)	December 6, 1932
Basserman, Albert (actor)	September 7, 1865
Bassey, Shirley (singer)	January 8, 1937
Bassler, Johnny; born John Landis Bassler (baseball)	June 3, 1895
Batchelor, Clarence Daniel (cartoonist)	April 1, 1888
Bateman, John Alvin (baseball)	July 21, 1942
Bateman, Marv (football)	April 5, 1950
Bates, Alan Arthur (actor)	February 17, 1930
Bates, Blanche (actress)	August 25, 1873
Bates, John Lewis (politician)	September 18, 1859
Bathgate, Andy; born Andrew James Bathgate (hockey)	August 28, 1932
Batista, Fulgencio; born Fulgencio Batista y Zaldivar (Cuban government)	January 16, 1901
Battey, Earl Jesse (baseball)	January 5, 1935
Battle, John Stewart (politician)	July 11, 1890
Battles, Cliff; born Clifford Franklin Battles (football)	May 1, 1910
Bauer, Bobby; born Robert Theodore Bauer (hockey)	February 16, 1915
Bauer, Hank; born Henry Albert Bauer (baseball)	July 31, 1922
Bauer, Jaime Lyn (actress)	March 8———
Baugh, Laura Zonetta (golf)	May 31, 1955
Baugh, Sammy; born Samuel Adrian Baugh (football)	March 17, 1914
Baughan, Maxie C., Jr. (football)	August 3, 1938
Baumholtz, Frankie, born Frank Conrad Baumholtz (baseball)	October 7, 1918
Baun, Robert T. (hockey)	September 9, 1936
Baur, Elizabeth (actress)	December 11, 1947
Bavier, Frances; born Franceo Bavier (actress)	January 14, 1905
Baxley, Barbara (actress)	January 1, 1925
Baxter, Anne (actress)	May 7, 1923
Baxter, Percival Proctor (politician)	November 22, 1876
Baxter, Warner (actor)	March 29, 1889
Bay, Howard (designer/director)	May 3, 1912
Bayard, Thomas Francis (politician)	June 4, 1868
Bayh, Birch Evans, Jr. (politician)	January 22, 1928
Baylor, Don; born Donald Edward Baylor (baseball)	June 28, 1949
Baylor, Elgin Gay (basketball)	September 16, 1934
Bayne, Beverly Pearl (actress)	November 22, 1895
Beal, John; born J. Alexander Bliedung (actor)	August 13, 1909
Beall, J. Glenn, Sr.; born James Glenn Beall, Sr. (politician)	June 5, 1894
Beall, J. Glenn, Jr.; born James Glenn Beall, Jr. (politician)	June 19, 1927
Beame, Abraham David (politician)	March 20, 1906
Bean, Alan L. (astronaut)	March 15, 1932
Bean, Andy (golf)	March 13, 1953
Bean, Orson; born Dallas Frederick Burrows (actor)	July 22, 1928
Beard, Butch (basketball)	May 4, 1947
Beard, Frank (golf)	May 1, 1939
Beardsley, William Shane (politician)	May 13, 1901

Beasley, John Michael (basketball)	February 5, 1944
Beathard, Pete; born Peter F. Beathard (football)	March 7, 1942
Beatty, Clyde R. (circus)	June 10, 1903
Beatty, Morgan (newscaster)	September 6, 1902
Beatty, Ned (actor)	July 6, 1937
Beatty, Robert (actor)	October 19, 1909
Beatty, Warren; born Henry Warren Beaty (actor/producer/	March 30, 1937
director)	
Beaty, Zelmo (basketball)	October 25, 1941
Beauchamp, Al; born Alfred Beauchamp (football)	June 25, 1944
Beauchamp, Joe; born Joseph Beauchamp (football)	April 11, 1944
Beaumont, Hugh (actor)	February 16, 1909
Beauvoir, Simone Lucie Ernestine Marie Bertrand de (author)	January 9, 1908
Beavers, Louise (actress)	March 8, 1898
Beck, Byron (basketball)	January 25, 1945
Beck, Ernie (basketball)	December 11, 1931
Beckert, Glenn Alfred (baseball)	October 12, 1940
Beckett, Samuel Barclay (playwright)	April 13, 1906
Beckham, John Crepps Wickliffe (politician)	August 5, 1869
Beckley, Jake; born Jacob Peter Beckley (baseball)	August 4, 1867
Bedelia, Bonnie; born Bonnie Culkin (actress)	March 25, 1946
Bedford, Brian Anthony (actor)	February 16, 1935
Bednarik, Chuck; born Charles Phillip Bednarik (football)	May 1, 1925
Bee, Molly; born Molly Beachboard (singer/actress)	August 18, 1939
Beebe, William; born Charles William Beebe	July 29, 1877
· (naturalist/explorer/author)	
Beecher, Henry Ward (clergyman)	June 24, 1813
Beecher, Janet; born Janet B. Meysenburg (actress)	October 21, 1884
Beeckman, Robert Livingston (politician)	April 15, 1866
Beene, Geoffrey (fashion designer)	August 30, 1927
Beerbohm, Sir Max (author)	August 24, 1872
Beery, Noah, Sr. (actor)	January 17, 1883
Beery, Noah Jr. (actor)	August 10, 1913
Beery, Wallace (actor)	April 1, 1881
Beethoven, Ludwig van (music)	December 16, 1770
Begin, Menachem (Israeli government)	August 16, 1913
Begley, Ed; born Edward James Begley (actor)	March 25, 1901
Behra, Jean (auto racing)	February 16, 1921
Beirne, Jim; born James Beirne (football)	October 15, 1946
Beisler, Randy; born Randall Beisler (football)	October 24, 1944
Belafonte, Harry; born Harold George Belafonte, Jr.	March 1, 1927
(singer/actor)	
Belanger, Mark Henry (baseball)	June 8, 1944
Belasco, David (playwright/producer/actor)	July 25, 1854
Belford, Christine (actress)	January 14————
Bel Geddes, Barbara; born Barbara Geddes (actress)	October 31, 1922
Bel Geddes, Norman; born Norman Geddes (producer/	April 27, 1893
director/designer)	
Beliveau, Jean Marc (hockey)	August 31, 1931
Bell, Alexander Graham (inventor)	March 3, 1847
Bell, Bob; born Robert Francis Bell (football)	January 25, 1948

Bell, Bobby; born Robert Lee Bell (football)	June 17, 1940
Bell, Charles James (politician)	March 16, 1845
Bell, Ed; born Edward Allen Bell (football)	September 13, 1947
Bell, Gary (baseball)	November 17, 1936
Bell, Griffin Boyette (government)	October 31, 1918
Bell, Gus; born David Russell Bell (baseball)	November 15, 1928
Bell, Les; born Lester Rowland Bell (baseball)	December 14, 1901
Bellamy, Madge; born Madge Philpott (actress)	June 30, 1900
Bellamy, Ralph Rexford (actor)	June 17, 1904
Bellamy, Walt; born Walter Bellamy (basketball)	July 24, 1939
Bellinni, Giovanni (artist)	circa 1430
Bellmon, Henry L. (politician)	September 3, 1921
Bellow, Saul (writer)	June 10, 1915
Bellson, Louis; born Louis Balassoni (music)	July 26, 1924
Belmondo, Jean-Paul (actor)	April 9, 1933
Beltoise, Jean-Pierre (auto racing)	April 26, 1937
Belushi, John (actor/comedian/singer)	January 24, 1950
Beman, Deane Randolph (golf)	April 22, 1938
Benaderet, Bea (actress)	April 4, 1906
Bench, Johnny Lee (baseball)	December 7, 1947
Benchley, Peter Bradford (author)	May 8, 1940
Benchley, Robert Charles (humorist)	September 15, 1889
Bender, Chief; born Charles Albert Bender (baseball)	May 5, 1883
Bendix, William (actor)	January 14, 1906
Benedict, Dirk; born Dirk Niewoehner (actor)	March 1, 1946
Beneke, Tex; born Gordon Beneke (music)	February 12, 1914
Benét, Stephen Vincent (poet/author)	July 22, 1898
Benét, William Rose (poet/author)	February 2, 1886
Ben-Gurion, David; born David Green (Israeli government)	December 16, 1886
Benjamin, Richard (actor)	May 22, 1938
Bennett, Arnold; born Enoch Arnold Bennett (author/dramatist)	May 27, 1867
Bennett, Bruce; born Herman Brix (actor)	May 19, 1906
Bennett, Constance Campbell (actress)	October 22, 1904
Bennett, Jill (actress)	December 24, 1930
Bennett, Joan (actress)	February 27, 1910
Bennett, Robert Frederick (politician)	May 23, 1927
Bennett, Robert Russell (music)	June 15, 1894
Bennett, Tony; born Antonio Dominick Benedetto (singer)	August 3, 1926
Bennett, Wallace Foster (politician)	November 13, 1898
Benny, Jack; born Benjamin Joseph Kubelsky (or Joseph Benjamin Kubelsky) (comedian/actor/music)	February 14, 1894
Benson, Duane (football)	August 5, 1945
Benson, Elmer Austin (politician)	September 22, 1895
Benson, Ezra Taft (government)	August 4, 1899
Benson, Frank Williamson (politician)	March 20, 1858
Benson, George (singer/music)	March 22, 1943
Benson, Robby; born Robert Segal (actor)	January 21, 1956
Bentley, Doug; born Douglas Wagner Bentley (hockey)	September 3, 1916
Bentley, Eric Russell (writer)	September 14, 1916
Bentley, Max; born Maxwell Lloyd Bentley (hockey)	March 1, 1920

Benton, Barbi (singer/actress)	January 28, 1950
Benton, Brook; born Benjamin Franklin Peay (singer)	September 19, 1931
Benton, James (football)	September 25, 1916
Benton, Larry; born Lawrence James Benton (baseball)	November 20, 1897
Benton, Nelson; born Joseph Nelson Benton, Jr. (newscaster)	September 16, 1924
Benton, Thomas Hart (artist)	August 15, 1889
Benton, William (politician)	April 1, 1900
Bentsen, Lloyd Millard, Jr. (politician)	February 11, 1921
Benvenuti, Nino (boxing)	April 26, 1938
Benzell, Mimi; born Miriam Ruth Benzell (singer/actress)	April 6, 1924
Berardino, John (baseball/actor)	May 1, 1917
Berenson, Marisa (actress)	February 15, 1947
Berenson, Red; born Gordon Berenson (hockey)	December 8, 1939
Berg, Gertrude; born Gertrude Edelstein (actress)	October 3, 1899
Berg, Patty; born Patricia Jane Berg (golf)	February 13, 1918
Bergen, Candice (actress/photo-journalist)	May 9, 1946
Bergen, Edgar; born Edgar John Bergren (or Berggren) (ventriloquist)	February 16, 1903
Bergen, Polly; born Nellie Paulina Burgin (actress/ singer/cosmetics)	July 14, 1929
Berger, Senta (actress)	May 13, 1941
Berger, Wally; born Walter Antone Berger (baseball)	October 10, 1905
Bergerac, Jacques (actor)	May 26, 1927
Bergey, Bill; born William Earl Bergey (football)	February 9, 1945
Bergland, Robert Selmer (government)	July 22, 1928
Bergman, Gary Gunnar (hockey)	October 7, 1938
Bergman, Ingmar; born Ernst Ingmar Bergman (director/writer)	July 14, 1918
Bergman, Ingrid (actress)	August 29, 1915
Bergner, Elisabeth; born Elizabeth Ettel (actress)	August 22, 1898
Berkeley, Busby; born William Berkeley Enos (choreographer/director/actor)	November 29, 1895
Berle, Milton; born Milton Berlinger (comedian/actor)	July 12, 1908
Berlin, Irving; born Isador Baline (music)	May 11, 1888
Berlin, Jeannie (actress)	November 1, 1949
Berlinger, Warren (actor)	August 31, 1937
Berlioz, Hector; born Louis Hector Berlioz (music)	December 11, 1803
Berman, Shelley; born Sheldon Leonard Berman (comedian/actor)	February 3, 1924
Bernardi, Herschel (actor)	October 20, 1923
Bernhardt, Sarah; born Henriette Rosine Bernard (actress)	October 22, 1844
Berning, Susie Maxwell; born Susie Maxwell (golf)	July 22, 1941
Bernstein, Elmer (music)	April 4, 1922
Bernstein, Leonard (music)	August 25, 1918
Berra, Yogi; born Lawrence Peter Berra (baseball)	May 12, 1925
Berry, Bob; born Robert Berry (football)	March 10, 1942
Berry, Charlie; born Charles Francis Berry (baseball)	October 18, 1902
Berry, Chuck; born Charles Edward Anderson Berry (singer/music)	October 18, 1926
Berry, Ken (actor/dancer/singer)	November 3, 1933
Berry, Ken; born Allen Kent Berry (baseball)	May 10, 1941

Berry, Raymond (football)	February 27, 1933
Berry, Tom (politician)	April 23, 1879
Bertelsen, Jim; born James Bertelsen (football)	February 26, 1950
Bertinelli, Valerie Anne (actress)	April 23, 1960
Bertoia, Reno Peter (baseball)	January 8, 1935
Bertolaccini, Silvia (golf)	January 30, 1950
Bessell, Ted (actor)	————1936
Bessemer, Sir Henry (inventor)	January 19, 1813
Best, Edna (actress)	March 3, 1900
Best, James (actor)	July 26, 1926
Bethea, Elvin (football)	March 1, 1946
Benthune, Zina (actress/dancer/singer)	February 17, 1945
Betjeman, Sir John (poet)	August 28, 1906
Bettenhausen, Gary (auto racing)	November 18, 1941
Bettenhausen, Tony; born Melvin Eugene Bettenhausen (auto racing)	September 12, 1916
Bettger, Lyle (actor)	February 13, 1915
Betz, Carl (actor)	March 9, 1920
Betz, Pauline M. (tennis)	August 6, 1919
Beveridge, William S. (hockey)	July 1, 1909
Beymer, Richard; born George Richard Beymer, Jr. (actor)	February 21, 1939
Bianchi, Al; born Alfred Bianchi (basketball)	March 26, 1932
Bianchi, Daniela (actress)	————1942
Bibby, Henry (basketball).	November 24, 1949
Bibeault, Paul (hockey)	April 13, 1919
Bible, Alan Harvey (politician)	November 20, 1909
Bickett, Thomas Walter (politician)	February 28, 1869
Bickford, Charles Ambrose (actor)	January 1, 1889
Biddle, Francis Beverly (government)	May 9, 1886
Biden, Joseph Robinette, Jr. (politician)	November 20, 1942
Bielski, Dick; born Richard Bielski (football)	September 7, 1932
Bies, Don; born Donald Bies (golf)	December 10, 1937
Bigbee, Carson Lee (baseball)	March 31, 1895
Biggs, Verlon (football)	March 16, 1943
Bikel, Theodore (actor/singer)	May 2, 1924
Bilbo, Theodore Gilmore (politician)	October 13, 1877
Bilentnikoff, Fred; born Frederick Bilentnikoff (football)	February 23, 1943
Bilko, Steve; born Stephen Bilko (baseball)	November 13, 1928
Billingham, Jack; born John Eugene Billingham (baseball)	February 21, 1943
Billings, Franklin Swift (politician)	May 11, 1862
Billy The Kid; born William H. Bonney (outlaw)	November 23, 1859
Bing, Dave (basketball)	November 29, 1943
Bingham, George Caleb (artist)	March 20, 1811
Binns, Edward (actor)	September 12, 1916
Birdwell, Dan; born Daniel L. Birdwell (football)	October 14, 1940
Birney, David Edwin (actor)	April 23, 1939
Birney, Meredith Baxter; born Meredith Baxter (actress)	June 21, 1947
Bishop, Jim; born James Alonzo Bishop (journalist/author)	November 21, 1907
Bishop, Joey; born Joseph Abraham Gottlieb (comedian/actor/TV host)	February 3, 1918
Bishop, Julie; born Jacqueline Wells (actress)	August 30, 1914

Bishop, Max Frederick (baseball)	September 5, 1899
Bismark-Schönhausen, Otto Eduard Leopold von (German statesman)	April 1, 1815
Bissell, Whit (actor)	———1914
Bisset, Jacqueline Fraser (actress)	September 13, 1944
Bixby, Bill; born Wilfred Bailey Bixby (actor/director)	January 22, 1934
Bizet, Georges; born Alexandre César Léopold Bizet (music)	October 25, 1838
Black, Cilla; born Priscilla Maria Veronica White (singer)	May 27, 1943
Black, Hugo La Fayette (jurist)	February 27, 1886
Black, Karen; born Karen Blanche Ziegler (actress)	July 1, 1942
Blackman, Honor (actress)	August 22, 1926
Blackmer, Sidney Alderman (actor)	July 13, 1895
Blackmun, Harry Andrew (jurist)	November 12, 1908
Blackwell, Ewell (baseball)	October 23, 1922
Blackwood, Ibra Charles (politician)	November 21, 1878
Blades, Ray; born Francis Raymond Blades (baseball)	August 6, 1896
Blaeholder, George Franklin (baseball)	January 26, 1904
Blaine, John James (politician)	May 4, 1875
Blaine, Vivian; born Vivienne Stapleton (actress/singer)	November 21, 1921
Blair, Andrew Dryden (hockey)	February 27, 1908
Blair, Betsy; born Elizabeth Boger (actress)	December 11, 1923
Blair, Frank (newscaster)	May 30, 1915
Blair, James Thomas, Jr. (politician)	March 15, 1902
Blair, Janet; born Martha Janet Lafferty (actress/singer)	April 23, 1921
Blair, Linda Denise (actress)	January 22, 1959
Blair, Matt; born Albert Matthew Blair (football)	September 20, 1951
Blair, Paul L. D. (baseball)	February 1, 1944
Blake, Amanda; born Beverly Louise Neill (actress)	February 20, 1929
Blake; Eubie; born James Hubert Blake (music)	February 7, 1883
Blake, Marie; born Blossom MacDonald (actress)	August 21, 1896
Blake, Robert; born Michael James Vijencio Gubitosi (actor)	September 18, 1933
Blake, Sheriff; born John Frederick Blake (baseball)	September 17, 1899
Blake, Toe; born Hector Blake (hockey)	August 21, 1912
Blake, William (poet/artist)	November 28, 1757
Blakely, Colin (actor)	September 23, 1930
Blakely, Susan (actress)	———1949
Blakley, Ronee (actress/singer/music)	———1946
Blalock, Jane B. (golf)	September 19, 1945
Blanc, Mel; born Melvin Jerome Blanc (cartoon voice/actor)	May 30, 1908
Blancas, Homero (golf)	March 7, 1938
Blanchard, Johnny; born John Edwin Blanchard (baseball)	February 26, 1933
Blanchard, Mari; born Mary Blanchard (actress)	April 13, 1927
Blanchard, Newton Crain (politician)	January 29, 1849
Blanchard, Tom; born Thomas R. Blanchard (football)	May 28, 1948
Blanda, George Frederick (football)	September 17, 1927
Blandick, Clara (actress)	June 4, 1880
Blane, Marcie (singer)	May 21, 1944
Blane, Sally; born Elizabeth Jane Young (actress)	July 11, 1910
Blanton. L. Ray; born Leonard Ray Blanton (politician)	April 10, 1930
Blasingame, Don Lee (baseball)	March 16, 1932

Blasingame, Wade Allen (baseball)	November 22, 1943
Blass, Bill (fashion designer)	June 22, 1922
Blass, Steve; born Stephen Robert Blass (baseball)	April 18, 1942
Blatty, William Peter (writer/producer)	January 7, 1928
Blease, Coleman Livingston (politician)	October 8, 1868
Blefary, Curt; born Curtis LeRoy Blefary (baseball)	July 5, 1943
Bleier, Rocky; born Robert Patrick Bleier (football)	March 5, 1946
Bliss, Aaron Thomas (politician)	May 22, 1837
Bloch, Ernest (music)	July 24, 1880
Bloch, Ray; born Raymond A. Bloch (music)	August 3, 1902
Blocker, Chris (golf)	November 10, 1939
Blocker, Dan (actor)	————1927
Blondell, Joan (actress)	August 30, 1909
Blood, Henry Hooper (politician)	October 1, 1872
Blood, Robert Oscar, (politician)	November 10, 1887
Bloodworth, Jimmy; born James Henry Bloodworth (baseball)	July 26, 1917
Bloom, Claire; born Patricia Claire Blume (actress)	February 15, 1931
Bloom, Verna (actress)	August 7————
Bloomgarden, Kermit (producer)	December 15, 1904
Blore, Eric (actor)	December 23, 1887
Blount, Mel; born Melvin Cornell Blount (football)	April 10, 1948
Blount, Winton Malcolm (government)	February 1, 1921
Blue, Ben; born Benjamin Bernstein (comedian/actor)	September 12, 1901
Blue, Forrest M., Jr. (football)	September 7, 1945
Blue, Lu; born Luzerne Atwell Blue (baseball)	March 5, 1897
Blue, Monte (actor)	January 11, 1890
Blue, Robert Donald (politician)	September 24, 1898
Blue, Vida Rochelle (baseball)	July 28, 1949
Bluege, Ossie; born Oswald Louis Bluege (baseball)	October 24, 1900
Blumenthal, W. Michael; born Werner Michael Blumenthal (government)	January 3, 1926
Blyden, Larry; born Ivan Lawrence Blieden (actor/singer/TV host)	June 23, 1925
Blyleven, Bert; born Rik Aalbert Blyleven (baseball)	April 6, 1951
Blythe, Ann Marie (actress/singer)	August 16, 1928
Blythe, Betty; born Elizabeth Blythe Slaughter (actress)	September 1, 1893
Boardman, Eleanor (actress)	August 19, 1898
Bochner, Lloyd (actor)	July 29, 1924
Bock, Jerry; born Jerrold Lewis Bock (music)	November 23, 1928
Bockhorn, Bucky; born Arlen Bockhorn (basketball)	July 8, 1933
Bodnar, Gus; born August Bodnar (hockey)	August 24, 1925
Boe, Nils Andreas (politician)	September 10, 1913
Boerwinkle, Tom (basketball)	August 23, 1945
Bogarde, Dirk; born Derek Niven van de Bogaerde (actor)	March 28, 1920
Bogart, Humphrey DeForest (actor)	December 25, 1899
Bogdanovich, Peter (director/producer/writer/actor)	July 30, 1939
Boggs, James Caleb (politician)	May 15, 1909
Böhm, Karl (music)	August 28, 1894
Bohr, Niels Henrik David (atomic physicist)	October 7, 1885
Boivin, Leo Joseph (hockey)	August 2, 1932
Boland, Mary (actress)	January 28, 1880

Boles, John (actor)	October 27, 1895
Bolger, Ray; born Raymond Wallace Bolger (actor/dancer)	January 10, 1904
Bolin, Bobby Donald (baseball)	January 29, 1939
Bolin, Wesley H. (politician)	July 1, 1908
Bolivar, Simón (South American liberator)	July 24, 1783
Boll, Buzz; born Frank Thurman Boll (hockey)	March 6, 1911
Bolling, Frank Elmore (baseball)	November 16, 1931
Bolling, Milt; born Milton Joseph Bolling, III (baseball)	August 9, 1930
Bolling, Tiffany Royce (actress)	———1949
Bolt, Robert Oxton (playwright)	August 15, 1924
Bolt, Tommy; born Thomas Bolt (golf)	March 31, 1918
Bolton, Guy; born St. George Guy Reginald Bolton (playwright)	November 23, 1884
Bombeck, Erma; born Erma Louise Fiste (writer)	February 21, 1927
Bonaparte, Charles Joseph (government)	June 9, 1851
Bonaparte, Napoleon (French Emperor)	August 15, 1769
Bonavena, Oscar (boxing)	September 25, 1942
Bond, Christopher Samuel (politician)	March 6, 1939
Bond, Derek (actor)	January 26, 1919
Bond, Lilian (actress)	January 18, 1910
Bond, Ward (actor)	April 9, 1903
Bondi, Beulah; born Beulah Bondy (actress)	May 3, 1892
Bonds, Bobby Lee (baseball)	March 15, 1946
Bonerz, Peter (actor)	August 6, 1938
Bonham, Ernie; born Ernest Edward Bonham (baseball)	August 16, 1913
Bonnier, Jo (auto racing)	January 31, 1930
Bono, Sonny; born Salvatore Phillip Bono (singer/actor)	February 16, 1935
Bonura, Zeke; born Henry John Bonura (baseball)	September 20, 1908
Booke, Sorrell (actor)	January 4, 1926
Boone, Bob; born Robert Raymond Boone (baseball)	November 19, 1947
Boone, Cherry; born Cheryl Lynn Boone (singer—Boone Family)	July 7, 1954
Boone, Daniel (frontiersman)	November 2, 1734
Boone, Debby; born Deborah Ann Boone (singer—Boone Family)	September 22, 1956
Boone, Ike; born Isaac Morgan Boone (baseball)	February 17, 1897
Boone, Laury; born Laura Gene Boone (singer—Boone Family)	January 30, 1958
Boone, Lindy; born Linda Lee Boone (singer—Boone Family)	October 11, 1955
Boone, Pat; born Charles Eugene Boone (singer/actor/author)	June 1, 1934
Boone, Ray; born Raymond Otis Boone (baseball)	July 27, 1923
Boone, Richard Allen (actor)	June 18, 1916
Boone, Ron (basketball)	September 6, 1946
Boone, Shirley; born Shirley Lee Foley (singer—Boone Family /author)	April 24, 1934
Booth, Edwin Thomas (actor)	November 13, 1833
Booth, John Wilkes (actor/assassin)	August 26, 1838
Booth, Shirley; born Thelma Booth Ford (actress/singer)	August 30, 1907
Boozer, Bob; born Robert Boozer (basketball)	April 26, 1937
Boozer, Emerson Jr. (football/sportscaster)	July 4, 1943

Borah, William Edgar (politician)	June 29, 1865
Borchers, Cornell; born Cornelia Bruch (actress)	March 16, 1925
Borden, Lizzie Andrew (alleged murderess)	July 19, 1860
Bordoni, Irene (actress/singer)	January 16, 1895
Boren, David Lyle (politician)	April 21, 1941
Börg, Bjorn (tennis)	June 6, 1956
Borg, Veda Ann (actress)	January 11, 1915
Borge, Victor; born Borge Rosenbaum (music/comedian/actor)	January 3, 1908
Borgnine, Ernest; born Ermes Effron Borgnino (actor)	January 24, 1915
Borman, Frank (astronaut)	March 14, 1928
Boros, Julius Nicholas (golf)	March 3, 1920
Boros, Steve; born Stephen Boros (baseball)	September 3, 1936
Borowy, Hank; born Henry Ludwig Borowy (baseball)	May 12, 1916
Boryla, Mike; born Michael J. Boryla (football)	March 6, 1951
Boryla, Vince (basketball)	March 11, 1921
Bosley, Bruce L. (football)	November 5, 1933
Bosley, Tom; born Thomas Edward Bosley (actor)	October 1, 1927
Bosman, Dick; born Richard Allen Bosman (baseball)	February 17, 1944
Bostwick, Barry (actor)	February 24, 1945
Boswell, Connee (singer/actress)	December 3, 1907
Boswell, Ken; born Kenneth George Boswell (baseball)	February 23, 1946
Botticelli, Sandro; born Alessandro di Mariano dei Filipepi (artist)	———1445
Bottolfsen, Clarence A. (politician)	October 10, 1891
Bottomley, Jim; born James LeRoy Bottomley (baseball)	April 23, 1900
Bottoms, Joseph (actor)	April 22, 1954
Bottoms, Timothy (actor)	August 30, 1951
Bouchard, Butch; born Emile Joseph Bouchard (hockey)	September 11, 1920
Boucher, Frank (hockey)	October 7, 1901
Bouchet, Barbara; born Barbara Gutscher (actress)	August 15, 1943
Boudreau, Lou; born Louis Boudreau (baseball)	July 17, 1917
Boulez, Pierre (music)	March 26, 1925
Bourassa, Jocelyn (golf)	May 30, 1947
Bourne, Jonathan, Jr. (politician)	February 23, 1855
Bouton, Jim; born James Alan Bouton (baseball/author/ actor)	March 8, 1939
Bow, Clara Gordon (actress)	July 29, 1904
Bowa, Larry; born Lawrence Robert Bowa (baseball)	December 6, 1945
Bowen, Otis Ray (politician)	February 26, 1918
Bower, Johnny; born John William Bower (hockey)	November 8, 1924
Bowie, David; born David Robert Jones (singer/music)	January 8, 1947
Bowles, Chester Bliss (politics/government)	April 5, 1901
Bowman, Joe; born Joseph Emil Bowman (baseball)	June, 17, 1910
Bowman, Lee; born Lucien Lee Bowman, Sr. (actor)	December 28, 1910
Boyd, Alan Stephenson (government)	July 20, 1922
Boyd, Bill; born William Lawrence Boyd (actor)	June 5, 1895
Boyd, Bob; born Robert D. Boyd (football)	December 3, 1937
Boyd, Bob; born Robert Richard Boyd (baseball)	October 1, 1925
Boyd, Fred (basketball)	June 13, 1950
Boyd, Stephen; born William Millar (actor)	July 4, 1928
Boyer, Charles (actor)	August 28, 1899

Boyer, Clete; born Cletis Leroy Boyer (baseball)	February 8, 1937
Boyer, Ken; born Kenton Lloyd Boyer (baseball)	May 20, 1931
Boyington, Pappy; born Gregory Boyington (aviator)	December 4, 1912
Boyle, Emmet Derby (politician)	July 26, 1879
Boyle, Peter (actor)	————1933
Braase, Ordell (football)	March 13, 1932
Brabham, Jack; born John Arthur Brabham (auto racing)	April 2, 1926
Bracken, Eddie; born Edward Vincent Bracken (actor/singer)	February 7, 1920
Bradbury, Ray Douglas (writer)	August 22, 1920
Braddock, Jim; born James J. Braddock (boxing)	December 6, 1905
Bradford, Buddy; born Charles William Bradford (baseball)	July 25, 1944
Bradford, Robert Fiske (politician)	December 15, 1902
Bradley, Bill; born William Warren Bradley (basketball)	July 28, 1943
Bradley, Bill; born William Bradley (football)	January 2, 1947
Bradley, Ed; born Edward R. Bradley, Jr. (newscaster)	June 22, 1941
Bradley, Grace (actress)	September 21, 1913
Bradley, Omar Nelson (army officer))	February 12, 1893
Bradley, Pat; born Patricia Ellen Bradley (golf)	March 24, 1951
Bradley, Thomas (politician)	December 29, 1917
Bradna, Olympe (actress)	August 12, 1920
Bradshaw, Terry Paxton (football)	September 2, 1948
Brady, Alice (actress)	November 2, 1892
Brady, James Henry (politician)	June 12, 1862
Brady, Michael J. (golf)	April 15, 1887
Brady, Pat; born Robert Patrick Brady (actor/singer)	December 31, 1914
Brady, Scott; born Gerard Kenneth Tierney (actor)	September 13, 1924
Bragan, Bobby; born Robert Randall Bragan (baseball)	October 30, 1917
Bragg, Mike; born Michael E. Bragg (football)	September 26, 1946
Brahms, Johannes (music)	May 7, 1833
Braille, Louis C. (teacher of blind)	January 4, 1809
Branca, Ralph Theodore Joseph (baseball)	January 6, 1926
Branch, Cliff; born Clifford Branch (football)	August 1, 1948
Brand, Neville (actor)	August 13, 1920
Brand, Oscar (music)	February 7, 1920
Brandeis, Louis Dembitz (jurist)	November 13, 1856
Brando, Jocelyn (actress)	November 18, 1919
Brando, Marlon (actor)	April 3, 1924
Brandon, Michael (actor)	April 20, 1945
Brandon, William Woodward (politician)	June 5, 1868
Brandt, Ed; born Edward Arthur Brandt (baseball)	February 17, 1905
Brandt, Jackie; born John George Brandt (baseball)	April 28, 1934
Brandt, Willy; born Herbert Ernst Karl Frahm (German government)	December 18, 1913
Branigin, Roger Douglas (politician)	July 26, 1902
Brann, Louis Jefferson (politician)	July 8, 1876
Brannan, Charles Franklin (government)	August 23, 1903
Brasselle, Keefe; born Keefe Brusselle (actor/singer)	February 7, 1923
Bratkowski, Zeke; born Edmund R. Bratkowski (football)	October 20, 1931
Braun, Carl (basketball)	September 25, 1927
Braun, Steve; born Stephen Russell Braun (baseball)	May 8, 1948

Brazle, Al; born Alpha Eugene Brazle (baseball)	October 19, 1913
Brazzi, Rossano (actor)	September 18, 1916
Breathitt, Edward Thompson, Jr. (politician)	November 26, 1924
Brecheen, Harry David (baseball)	October 14, 1914
Brecht, Bertolt; born Eugen Berthold Friedrich Brecht (playwright)	February 10, 1898
Breck, Peter (actor)	March 13, 1930
Breckinridge, John Cabell (Vice President)	January 21, 1821
Breedlove, Craig Norman (auto racing)	March 23, 1938
Breer, Murle Mackenzie; born Murle Mackenzie Lindstrom (golf)	January 20, 1939
Brel, Jacques (singer/music)	April 8, 1929
Bremer, Lucille (actress)	February 21, 1922
Brennan, Eileen; born Verla Eileen Brennan (actress)	September 3, 1935
Brennan, Peter J. (government)	May 24, 1918
Brennan, Walter Andrew (actor)	July 25, 1894
Brennan, William Joseph, Jr. (jurist)	April 25, 1906
Brenner, David (comedian)	February 4, 1945
Brent, Evelyn "Eve"; born Mary Elizabeth Riggs (actress)	October 20, 1899
Brent, George; born George B. Nolan (actor)	March 15, 1904
Breslin, Jimmy (journalist/author)	October 17, 1930
Bresnahan, Roger Philip (baseball)	June 11, 1879
Bressler, Rube; born Raymond Bloom Bressler (baseball)	October 23, 1894
Bressoud, Eddie; born Edward Francis Bressoud (baseball)	May 2, 1932
Brett, George Howard (baseball)	May 15, 1953
Brett, Ken; born Kenneth Alven Brett (baseball)	September 18, 1948
Brewer, Albert Preston (politician)	October 26, 1928
Brewer, Carl Thomas (hockey)	October 21, 1938
Brewer, Earl LeRoy (politician)	August 11, 1869
Brewer, Gay (golf)	March 19, 1932
Brewer, Jim; born James Thomas Brewer (baseball)	November 17, 1937
Brewer, Teresa; born Theresa Breuer (singer)	May 7, 1931
Brewer, Tom; born Thomas Austin Brewer (baseball)	September 3, 1931
Brewster, Daniel Baugh (politician)	November 23, 1923
Brewster, Ralph Owen (politician)	February 22, 1888
Brezhnev, Leonid Ilyich (Russian government)	December 16, 1906
Brezina, Greg; born Gregory Brezina (football)	January 7, 1946
Brian, David (actor)	August 5, 1914
Brian, Mary; born Louise Byrdie Dantzler (actress)	February 17, 1908
Brice, Fanny; born Frances Borach (actress/singer)	October 29, 1891
Brickell, Beth (actress)	November 13———
Bricker, John William (politician)	September 6, 1893
Bridges, Beau; born Lloyd Vernet Bridges, III (actor)	December 9, 1941
Bridges, Bill (basketball)	April 4, 1939
Bridges, Henry Styles (politician)	September 9, 1898
Bridges, Jeff (actor)	December 4, 1949
Bridges, Lloyd Vernet, Jr. (actor)	January 15, 1913
Bridges, Rocky; born Everett Lamar Bridges (baseball)	August 7, 1927
Bridges, Tommy; born Thomas Jefferson David Bridges (baseball)	December 28, 1906
Briggs, Johnny; born John Edward Briggs (baseball)	March 10, 1944

Briles, Nelson Kelly (baseball)	August 5, 1943
Brimsek, Frank; born Francis Charles Brimsek (hockey)	September 26, 1915
Brinegar, Claude Stout (government)	December 16, 1926
Brinkley, David McClure (newscaster)	July 10, 1920
Brinkman, Eddie; born Edwin Albert Brinkman (baseball)	December 8, 1941
Briscoe, Dolph, Jr. (politician)	April 23, 1923
Briscoe, Marlin O. (football)	September 10, 1945
Brisson, Frederick; born Carl Frederick Brisson (producer)	March 17, 1917
Bristow, Joseph Little (politician)	July 22, 1861
Britt, May; born Maybritt Wilkens (actress)	March 22, 1933
Britten, Benjamin; born Edward Benjamin Britten (music)	November 22, 1913
Britton, Barbara; born Barbara Brantingham (actress)	September 26, 1919
Brock, Lou; born Louis Clark Brock (baseball)	June 18, 1936
Brock, William Emerson, III (politician)	November 23, 1930
Brockington, John Stanley (football)	September 7, 1948
Broda, Turk; born Walter Broda (hockey)	May 15, 1914
Broderick, Helen (actress)	August 11, 1891
Broderick, James Joseph (actor)	March 7, 1927
Brodie, John Riley (football/sportscaster)	August 14, 1935
Brodie, Steve; born Johnny Stevens (actor)	November 25, 1919
Broglio, Ernie; born Ernest Gilbert Broglio (baseball)	August 27, 1935
Brokaw, Tom; born Thomas John Brokaw (newscaster/TV host)	February 6, 1940
Brolin, James; born James Bruderlin (actor)	July 18, 1940
Bromfield, John; born Farron Bromfield (actor)	June 11, 1922
Bromfield, Louis (author)	December 27, 1896
Bromley, Sheila (actress)	October 31, 1911
Bromwich, Jack; born John Edward Bromwich (tennis)	November 14, 1918
Bronson, Betty; born Elizabeth Ada Bronson (actress)	November 17, 1906
Bronson, Charles; born Charles Dennis Buchinsky (actor)	November 3, 1921
Brontë, Anne (author/poet)	January 17, 1820
Brontë, Charlotte (author/poet)	April 21, 1816
Brontë, Emily Jane (author/poet)	July 30, 1818
Brook, Clive; born Clifford Brook (actor)	June 1, 1886
Brooke, Edward William (politician)	October 26, 1919
Brooke, Hillary; born Beatrice Sofia Mathilda Peterson (actress)	September 8, 1914
Brookhart, Smith Wildman (politician)	February 2, 1869
Brooks, Bryant Butler (politician)	February 5, 1861
Brooks, C. Wayland; born Charles Wayland Brooks (politician)	March 8, 1897
Brooks, Dick; born Richard Brooks (auto racing)	April 14, 1942
Brooks, Foster Murrell (comedian/actor)	May 11, 1912
Brooks, Geraldine; born Geraldine Stroock (actress)	October 29, 1925
Brooks, Gwendolyn (poet)	June 7, 1917
Brooks, Leo; born Leonard Leo Brooks (football)	December 7, 1947
Brooks, Louise (actress)	November 14, 1900
Brooks, Mel; born Melvyn Kaminsky (actor/director/producer/writer)	June 28, 1926
Brooks, Phyllis; born Phyllis Weiler (or Seiler) (or Steiller) (actress)	July 18, 1914
Brooks, Ralph Gilmour (politician)	July 6, 1898

Brooks, Richard (writer/director)   May 18, 1912
Brooks, Tony; born Charles Anthony Brooks (auto racing)   February 25, 1932
Brookshier, Tom; born Thomas Brookshier   December 16, 1931
  (football/sportscaster)
Brosch, Red; born Alfred Brosch (golf)   November 8, 1911
Brothers, Joyce; born Joyce Diana Bauer (psychologist)   October 20, 1928
Brough, Charles Hillman (politician)   July 9, 1876
Brough, Louise; born Althea Louise Brough (tennis)   March 11, 1923
Broughton, Melville; born Joseph Melville Broughton   November 17, 1888
  (politician)
Broun, Heywood Hale; born Heywood Hale Brown   March 10, 1918
  (sportscaster/actor)
Brouthers, Dan; born Dennis Joseph Brouthers (baseball)   May 8, 1858
Broward, Napoleon Bonaparte (politician)   April 19, 1857
Brown, Aaron L., Jr. (football)   November 16, 1943
Brown, Adam (hockey)   February 4, 1920
Brown, Albert Oscar (politician)   July 18, 1852
Brown, Arnie; born Stewart Arnold Brown (hockey)   January 28, 1942
Brown, Bill; born William Dorsey Brown (football)   June 29, 1938
Brown, Bob; born Robert Eddie Brown (football)   February 23, 1940
Brown, Bob; born Robert Stanford Brown (football)   December 8, 1941
Brown, Clint; born Clinton Harold Brown (baseball)   July 8, 1903
Brown, Dick; born Richard Ernest Brown (baseball)   January 17, 1935
Brown, Ed; born Charles Edward Brown (football)   October 26, 1928
Brown, Eddie; born Edward William Brown (baseball)   July 17, 1891
Brown, Fred (basketball)   July 7, 1948
Brown, Fred Herbert (politician)   April 12, 1879
Brown, Gates; born William James Brown (baseball)   May 2, 1939
Brown, Georg Stanford (actor/director)   June 24, 1943
Brown, Georgia; born Lillian Claire Laizer Getel Klot   October 21, 1933
  (actress/singer)
Brown, Hal; born Hector Harold Brown (baseball)   December 11, 1924
Brown, Harold (government)   September 19, 1927
Brown, Helen Gurley; born Helen Gurley (author/editor)   February 18, 1922
Brown, James (singer/music)   May 3, 1928
Brown, Jerry; born Edmund Gerald Brown, Jr. (politician)   April 7, 1938
Brown, Jim; born James Nathaniel Brown (football/actor/   February 17, 1935
  sportscaster)
Brown, Jimmy; born James Roberson Brown (baseball)   April 25, 1910
Brown, Joe E.; born Joe Evan Brown (comedian)   July 28, 1891
Brown, John (abolitionist)   May 9, 1800
Brown, Johnny Mack (actor)   September 1, 1904
Brown, Joseph Mackey (politician)   December 28, 1851
Brown, Larry; born Lawrence Brown, Jr. (football)   September 19, 1947
Brown, Larry Lesley (baseball)   March 1, 1940
Brown, Les; born Lester Raymond Brown (music)   March 14, 1912
Brown, Lloyd Andrew (baseball)   December 25, 1904
Brown, Ollie Lee (baseball)   February 11, 1944
Brown, Pamela Mary (actress)   July 8, 1917
Brown, Pat; born Edmund Gerald Brown, Sr. (politician)   April 21, 1905
Brown, Paul (football)   July 9, 1908

Brown, Pete (golf)	February 2, 1935
Brown, Peter (actor)	October 5———
Brown, Roger L. (football)	May 1, 1937
Brown, Roosevelt (football)	October 20, 1932
Brown, Ruth (singer)	January 30, 1928
Brown, Terry (football)	January 9, 1947
Brown, Three Fingers; born Mordecai Peter Centennial Brown (baseball)	October 19, 1876
Brown, Tim; born Thomas Allen Brown (football)	May 24, 1937
Brown, Tom; born Thomas Edward Brown (actor)	January 6, 1913
Brown, Vanessa; born Smylla Brind (actress)	March 24, 1928
Brown, Walter Folger (government)	May 31, 1869
Brown, Willie; born William Ferdie Brown (football)	December 2, 1940
Browne, Coral (actress)	July 23, 1913
Browne, Irene (actress)	June 29, 1891
Browne, Jackson (singer/music)	October 9, 1950
Browne, Kathie (actress)	October 19———
Browne, Roscoe Lee (actor/director/writer)	———1925
Brownell, Herbert Jr. (government)	February 20, 1904
Browning, Elizabeth Barrett; born Elizabeth Moulton (poet)	March 6, 1806
Browning, Gordon (politician)	November 22, 1889
Browning, Robert (poet)	May 7, 1812
Broyles, Frank; born John Franklin Broyles (football/ sportscaster)	December 26, 1924
Brubeck, David Warren (music)	December 6, 1920
Bruce, Carol (actress/singer)	November 15, 1919
Bruce, Lenny; born Leonard Alfred Schneider (comedian)	October 13, 1925
Bruce, Nigel; born William Nigel Bruce (actor)	February 4, 1895
Bruce, Virginia; born Helen Virginia Briggs (actress)	September 29, 1910
Brucker, Wilber Marion (politician)	June 23, 1894
Brueghel (or Bruegel) (or Breughel), Pieter (the Elder) (artist)	circa 1520
Bruhn, Erik Belton Evers (dancer)	October 3, 1928
Brumbaugh, Martin Grove (politician)	April 14, 1862
Brumm; Don; born Donald D. Brumm (football)	October 4, 1941
Brundige, Bill; born William G. Brundige (football)	November 13, 1948
Bruneteau Mud; born Modere Bruneteau (hockey)	November 28, 1914
Brunsdale, Clarence Norman (politician)	July 9, 1891
Bruton, Bill; born William Haron Bruton (baseball)	December 22, 1929
Bryan, Charles Wayland (politician)	February 10, 1867
Bryan, Jane; born Jane O'Brian (or O'Brien) (actress)	June 11, 1918
Bryan, Jimmy; born James Ernest Bryan (auto racing)	January 28, 1927
Bryan, William Jennings (orator/writer/politics/ government)	March 19, 1860
Bryant, Anita Jane (singer)	March 25, 1940
Bryant, Bear; born Paul William Bryant (football)	September 11, 1913
Bryant, Bobby Lee (football)	January 24, 1944
Bryant, Bonnie (golf)	October 5, 1943
Bryant, Cullen; born William Cullen Bryant (football)	May 20, 1951
Bryant, Farris; born Cecil Farris Bryant (politician)	July 26, 1914
Bryant, William Cullen (poet)	November 3, 1749

Brydson, Glenn (hockey)	November 7, 1910
Brynner, Yul; born Youl Bryner (or Taidje Khan, Jr.) (actor/singer)	July 11, 1915
Brzezinski, Zbigniew Kazimierz (government)	March 28, 1928
Bubbles, John; born John William Sublett (actor)	February 19, 1902
Buber, Martin (philosopher/theologian)	February 8, 1878
Buchanan, Buck; born Junious Buchanan (football)	September 10, 1940
Buchanan, Edgar (actor)	March 21, 1902
Buchanan, James (President)	April 23, 1791
Buchanon, Willie James (football)	November 4, 1950
Buchholz, Horst Werner (actor)	December 4, 1933
Buchtel, Henry Augustus (politician)	September 30, 1847
Buchwald, Art; born Arthur Buchwald (journalist/humorist/ author)	October 20, 1925
Buck, Clayton Douglass (politician)	March 21, 1890
Buck, Pearl Sydenstricker (author)	June 26, 1892
Buckley, Betty (actress)	July 3, 1947
Buckley, James Lane (politician)	March 9, 1923
Buckley, William F.; born William Frank Buckley, Jr.(journalist)	November 24, 1925
Buckner, Bill; born William Joseph Buckner (baseball)	December 14, 1949
Bucyk, Johnny; born John Paul Bucyk (hockey)	May 12, 1935
Budde, Ed; born Edward Budde (football)	November 2, 1940
Buddin, Don; born Donald Thomas Buddin (baseball)	May 5, 1934
Budge, Don; born John Donald Budge (tennis)	June 13, 1915
Buehler, George (football)	August 10, 1947
Bueno, Maria Ester Audion (tennis)	October 11, 1939
Buffalo Bill; born William Frederick Cody (frontier scout)	February 26, 1846
Buffett, Jimmy (singer/music)	December 25, 1946
Buffone, Doug; born Douglas John Buffone (football)	June 27, 1944
Buford, Don; born Donald Alvin Buford (baseball)	February 2, 1937
Bugatti, Ettore (auto manufacturer)	September 15, 1881
Buhl, Bob; born Robert Ray Buhl (baseball)	August 12, 1928
Bujold, Geneviève (actress)	July 1, 1942
Bukich, Rudy; born Rudolph A. Bukich (football)	December 15, 1932
Bulaich, Norm; born Norman B. Bulaich (football)	December 25, 1946
Bulow, William John (politician)	January 13, 1869
Bumbry, Al; born Alonza Benjamin Bumbry (baseball)	April 21, 1947
Bumbry, Grace Ann (singer)	January 4, 1937
Bumpers, Dale Leon (politician)	August 12, 1925
Bunche, Ralph Johnson (government)	August 7, 1904
Buncom, Frank J., Jr. (football)	November 2, 1939
Bundy, Brooke (actress)	August 8————
Bundy, McGeorge (government)	March 30, 1919
Bunker, Ellsworth (government)	May 11, 1894
Bunning, Jim; born James Paul David Bunning (baseball)	October 23, 1931
Buñuel, Luis (director)	February 22, 1900
Buoniconti, Nick, born Nicholas Anthony Buoniconti (football/sportscaster/attorney)	December 15, 1940
Buono, Victor Charles (actor)	February 3, 1938
Burbank, Luther (naturalist/horticulturist)	March 7, 1849
Burdett, Winston M. (newscaster)	December 12, 1913

Burdette, Lou; born Selva Lewis Burdette (baseball)   November 22, 1926
Burdick, Quentin Northrop (politician)   June 19, 1908
Burfeindt, Betty (golf)   July 20, 1945
Burford, Chris; born Christopher W. Burford (football)   May 31, 1938
Burger, Warren Earl (jurist)   September 17, 1907
Burgess, Dorothy (actress)   March 4, 1907
Burgess, Smoky; born Forrest Harrill Burgess (baseball)   February 6, 1927
Burgess, Thornton Waldo (author)   January 14, 1874
Burghoff, Gary (actor)   May 24, 1943
Burke, Arleigh Albert (naval officer)   October 19, 1901
Burke, Billie; born Mary William Ethelbert Appleton Burke   August 7, 1884
    (comedienne/actress)
Burke, Billy; born William Burke (golf)   December 14, 1902
Burke, Edmund (politicial philosopher/statesman/orator)   January 21, 1729
Burke, Edward Raymond (politician)   November 28, 1880
Burke, Jack Jr. (golf)   January 29, 1923
Burke, John (politician)   February 25, 1859
Burke, Martin Alphonsos (hockey)   January 28, 1903
Burke, Paul (actor)   July 21, 1926
Burkemo, Walter (golf)   October 9, 1918
Burkett, Jesse Cail (baseball)   December 4, 1868
Burleson, Albert Sidney (government)   June 7, 1863
Burnett, Carol Creighton (comedienne/actress/singer)   April 26, 1933
Burnette, Smiley; born Lester Alvin Burnette (actor)   March 18, 1911
Burney, Dwight Willard (politician)   January 7, 1892
Burnquist, Joseph Alfred Arner (politician)   July 21, 1879
Burns, Arthur Frank (government)   April 27, 1904
Burns, Bob (comedian/actor)   August 2, 1893
Burns, Catherine (actress)   September 25, 1945
Burns, Charles Frederick (hockey)   February 14, 1936
Burns, David (actor)   June 22, 1902
Burns, George; born Nathan Birnbaum (comedian/actor/singer)   January 20, 1896
Burns, George III (golf)   July 29, 1949
Burns, George Henry (baseball)   January 31, 1893
Burns, Haydon; born William Haydon Burns (politician)   March 17 1912
Burns, Jack; born John Irving Burns (baseball)   August 31, 1907
Burns, James MacGregor (author)   August 3, 1918
Burns, John Anthony (politician)   March 30, 1909
Burns, Robert (poet)   January 25, 1759
Burr, Aaron (Vice President)   February 6, 1756
Burr, Raymond William Stacey (actor)   May 21, 1917
Burrough, Ken; born Kenneth O. Burrough (football)   June 14, 1948
Burroughs, Edgar Rice (author)   September 1, 1875
Burroughs, Jeff; born Jeffrey Allan Burroughs (baseball)   March 7, 1951
Burroughs, John (politician)   April 7, 1907
Burrow, Ken; born Kenneth Burrow (football)   March 29, 1948
Burrows, Abe; born Abram Solman Borowitz   December 18, 1910
    (playwright/director)
Burrud, Bill (actor/producer)   January 12, 1925
Burstyn, Ellen; born Edna Rae Gillooly (actress)   December 7, 1932
Burton, Harold Hitz (jurist)   June 22, 1888

Burton, LeVar; born Levardis Robert Martyn Burton, Jr. — February 16, 1957
   (actor)
Burton, Richard; born Richard Walter Jenkins, Jr. (actor) — November 10, 1925
Busbee, George Dekle (politician) — August 7, 1927
Busby, Jim; born James Franklin Busby (baseball) — January 8, 1927
Busch, August Anheuser, Jr.(beer magnate/sportsman) — March 28, 1899
Busch, Mae (actress) — January 20, 1891
Bush, Bullet Joe; born Leslie Ambrose Bush (baseball) — November 27, 1892
Bush, George Herbert Walker (government) — June 12, 1924
Bush, Guy Terrell (baseball) — August 23, 1901
Bush, Prescott Sheldon (politician) — May 15, 1895
Bushfield, Harlan John (politician) — August 6, 1882
Bushman, Francis X.; born Francis Xavier Bushman (actor) — January 10, 1883
Bushmiller, Ernie (cartoonist) — August 23, 1905
Butcher, Max; born Albert Maxwell Butcher (baseball) — September 21, 1910
Butkus, Dick; born Richard John Butkus (football/actor) — December 9, 1942
Butler, Hugh Alfred (politician) — February 28, 1878
Butler, John Marshall (politician) — July 21, 1897
Butler, Pierce (jurist) — March 17, 1866
Butler, Skip; born William Foster Butler (football) — October 21, 1947
Butterfield, Alexander Porter (government) — April 6, 1926
Buttons, Red; born Aaron Chwatt (or Schwatt) — February 5, 1918
   (actor/comedian/singer)
Buttram, Pat (actor/comedian) — June 19,———
Butz, Earl Lauer (government) — July 3, 1909
Buzhardt, John William (baseball) — August 15, 1936
Buzzi, Ruth Ann (comedienne/actress/singer) — July 24, 1936
Byington, Spring (actress) — October 17, 1892
Byrd, Butch; born George E. Byrd (football) — September 20, 1941
Byrd, Charlie; born Charles Lee Byrd (music) — September 16, 1925
Byrd, Harry Flood, Sr. (politician) — June 10, 1887
Byrd, Harry Flood, Jr. (politician) — December 20, 1914
Byrd, Richard Evelyn (naval officer/polar explorer) — October 25, 1888
Byrd, Robert Carlyle (politician) — January 15, 1918
Byrne, Brendan Thomas (politician) — April 1, 1924
Byrne, Frank M. (politician) — October 23, 1858
Byrne, Jane Margaret; born Jane Margaret Burke (politician) — May 24, 1934
Byrne, Tommy; born Thomas Joseph Byrne (baseball) — December 31, 1919
Byrnes, Edd; born Edward Breitenberger (actor) — July 30, 1933
Byrnes, James Francis (politics/government) — May 2, 1879
Byrns, Joseph Wellington, Sr. (politician) — July 20, 1869
Byron, Lord; born George Gordon Byron (poet) — January 22, 1788
Byron, Red; born Robert Byron (auto racing) — ———1916

C

Caan, James (actor) — March 26, 1939
Cabot, Bruce; born Etienne Pelissier Jacques de Bujac — April 20, 1904
   (actor)
Cabot, Sebastian (actor) — July 6, 1918
Cabot, Susan (actress) — July 6, 1927

Cadmus, Paul (artist)	December 17, 1904
Caesar, Irving; born Isidore Irving Caesar (music)	July 4, 1895
Caesar, Sid; born Isaac Sidney Caesar (comedian/actor)	September 8, 1922
Caffey, Lee Roy (football)	June 3, 1941
Cagney, James Francis, Jr. (actor)	July 17, 1899
Cagney, Jeanne Carolyn (actress)	March 25, 1919
Cahan, Lawrence Louis (hockey)	December 25, 1933
Cahill, William Thomas (politician)	June 25, 1912
Cahn, Sammy; born Samuel Cohen (music)	June 18, 1913
Cain, Harry Pulliam (politician)	January 10, 1906
Cain, Herbert (hockey)	December 24, 1913
Cain, J.V.; born James Victor Cain (football)	July 22, 1951
Caine, Michael; born Maurice Joseph Micklewhite (actor)	March 14, 1933
Calder, William Musgrave (politician)	March 3, 1869
Calder-Marshall, Anna (actress)	January 11, 1947
Caldwell, Erskine Preston (author)	December 17, 1903
Caldwell, Joe (basketball)	November 1, 1941
Caldwell, Millard Fillmore, Jr. (politician)	February 6, 1897
Caldwell, Taylor; born Janet Taylor Caldwell (author)	September 7, 1900
Caldwell, Zoë Ada (actress)	September 14, 1933
Calhern, Louis; born Carl Henry Vogt (actor)	February 19, 1895
Calhoun, John Caldwell (Vice President)	March 18, 1782
Calhoun, Rory; born Francis Timothy Durgin (actor)	August 8, 1922
Califano, Joseph Anthony, Jr. (government)	May 15, 1931
Calisher, Hortense (author)	December 20, 1911
Callaghan, James; born Leonard James Callaghan (British government)	March 27, 1912
Callan, Michael; born Martin Calinieff (actor/singer/ dancer)	November 22, 1935
Callas, Charlie (comedian/actor/music)	December 20———
Callas, Maria Meneghini; born Cecilia Sophia Anna Maria Kalogeropoulou (singer)	December 3, 1923
Calleia, Joseph; born Joseph Spurin-Calleja (actor)	August 4, 1897
Callison, Johnny; born John Wesley Callison (baseball)	March 12, 1939
Calloway, Cab; born Cabell Calloway, III (music/singer/actor)	December 25, 1907
Calvert, Phyllis; born Phyllis Bickle (actress)	February 18, 1915
Calvet, Corinne; born Corinne Dibos (actress)	April 30, 1925
Calvin, John; born Jean Chauvin (religious reformer)	July 10, 1509
Calvin, Mack (basketball)	July 27, 1949
Cambridge, Godfrey MacArthur (comedian/actor)	February 26, 1933
Cameron, JoAnna (actress)	September 20,———
Cameron, Ralph Henry (politician)	October 21, 1863
Cameron, Rod; born Roderick Cox (actor)	December 7, 1910
Camilli, Dolf; born Adolf Louis Camilli (baseball)	April 23, 1907
Campanella, Joseph Mario (actor)	November 21, 1927
Campanella, Roy (baseball)	November 19, 1921
Campaneris, Bert; born Blanco Dagoberto Campaneris (baseball)	March 9, 1942
Campbell, Archie (singer/comedian)	November 17, 1914
Campbell, Bruce Douglas (baseball)	October 20, 1909

Campbell, Earl (football)	March 29, 1955
Campbell, Glen Travis (singer/actor/music)	April 22, 1936
Campbell, Jack M. (politician)	September 10, 1916
Campbell, Thomas Edward (politician)	January 18, 1878
Campbell, Thomas Mitchell (politician)	April 22, 1856
Camus, Albert (author)	November 7, 1913
Canadeo, Tony; born Anthony Robert Canadeo (football)	May 5, 1919
Caniff, Milton Arthur (cartoonist)	February 28, 1907
Cannizzaro, Chris; born Christopher John Cannizzaro (baseball)	May 3, 1938
Cannon, Billy; born William Abb Cannon (football)	August 2, 1937
Cannon, Dyan; born Samille Diane Friesen (actress)	January 4, 1929
Cannon, Freddy; born Frederick Anthony Picariello (singer)	December 4, 1940
Cannon, Howard Walter (politician)	January 26, 1912
Cannon, J.D.; born John Donovan Cannon (actor)	April 24, 1922
Cannon, Joseph Gurney (politician)	May 7, 1836
Canova, Diana; born Diana Canova Rivero (actress)	June 2, 1953
Canova, Judy; born Juliet Canova (comedienne/actress /singer)	November 20, 1916
Cantinflas; born Mario Moreno-Reyes (comedian/actor)	August 12, 1911
Cantor, Eddie; born Edward Israel "Izzie" Iskowitz (actor/singer)	January 31, 1892
Cantrell, Lana (singer)	August 7, 1944
Cantwell, Ben; born Benjamin Caldwell Cantwell (baseball)	April 13, 1902
Capehart, Homer Earl (politician)	June 6, 1897
Capone, Al; born Alfonso (or Alphonse) Capone (gangster)	January 17, 1899
Capote, Truman; born Truman Streckfus Persons (author/actor)	September 30, 1924
Capp, Al; born Alfred Gerald Caplin (cartoonist)	September 28, 1909
Cappelletti, Gino (football)	March 26, 1934
Cappelletti, John Raymond (football)	August 9, 1952
Capper, Arthur (politician)	July 14, 1865
Capra, Frank (director/producer)	May 18, 1897
Capucine; born Germaine Lefebvre (actress)	January 6, 1933
Caracciola, Rudi; born Rudolph Caracciola (auto racing)	January 30, 1901
Caravaggio, Michelangelo Amerighi da; born Michelangelo Merisi (artist)	September 28, 1573
Caraway, Hattie Wyatt (politician)	February 1, 1878
Caraway, Thaddeus Horatius (politician)	October 17, 1871
Carbo, Bernie; born Bernardo Carbo (baseball)	August 5, 1947
Cardenal, Jose Rosario Domec (baseball)	October 7, 1943
Cardenas, Leo; born Leonardo Lazaro Cardenas (baseball)	December 17, 1938
Cardin, Pierre (fashion designer)	July 7, 1922
Cardinale, Claudia (actress)	April 15, 1939
Cardozo, Benjamin Nathan (jurist)	May 24, 1870
Cardwell, Don; born Donald Eugene Cardwell (baseball)	December 7, 1935
Carew, Rod; born Rodney Cline Carew (baseball)	October 1, 1945
Carey, Andy; born Andrew Arthur Carey (baseball)	October 18, 1931
Carey, Bob (auto racing)	September 24, 1905
Carey, Harry; born Henry DeWitt Carey, II (actor)	January 16, 1878
Carey, Harry, Jr. (actor)	May 16, 1921

Carey, Hugh Leo (politician)	April 11, 1919
Carey, Joseph Maull (politician)	January 19, 1845
Carey, Macdonald; born Edward Macdonald Carey (actor)	March 15, 1913
Carey, Max George; born Maximilan Carnarius (baseball)	January 11, 1890
Carey, Philip (actor)	July 15, 1922
Carey, Robert Davis (politician)	August 12, 1878
Cargo, David Francis (politician)	January 13, 1929
Carle, Frankie; born Francis Carlone (music)	March 25, 1903
Carleton, Tex; born James Otto Carleton (baseball)	August 19, 1906
Carlin, George Denis (comedian/actor)	May 12, 1938
Carlisle, Kitty; born Catherine Conn (or Holzman) (actress/singer)	September 3, 1914
Carlisle, Mary (actress)	February 3, 1912
Carlson, Frank (politician)	January 23, 1893
Carlson, George Alfred (politican)	October 23, 1876
Carlson, Hal; born Harold Gust Carlson (baseball)	May 17, 1894
Carlson, Richard (actor/director/writer)	April 29, 1912
Carlton, Doyle Elam (politician)	July 6, 1885
Carlton, Steve; born Stephen Norman Carlton (baseball)	December 22, 1944
Carlyle, Thomas (writer/historian)	December 4, 1795
Carmel, Roger C. (actor)	———1929
Carmichael, Al; born Albert R. Carmichael (football)	November 10, 1929
Carmichael, Harold; born Lee H. Carmichael (football)	September 22, 1949
Carmichael, Hoagy; born Hoagland Howard Carmichael (music/actor)	November 22, 1899
Carmichael, Ian (actor/singer)	June 18, 1920
Carmichael, Stokely (civil rights leader)	June 29, 1941
Carne, Judy; born Joyce Botterill (actress/singer)	April 27, 1939
Carnegie, Andrew (industrialist)	November 25, 1835
Carnegie, Dale (lecturer/author)	November 24, 1888
Carner, JoAnne Gunderson; born JoAnne Gunderson (golf)	April 4, 1939
Carnera, Primo (boxing)	October 26, 1906
Carney, Art; born Arthur William Matthew Carney (actor)	November 4, 1918
Carnovsky, Morris (actor)	September 5, 1897
Carol, Sue; born Evelyn Lederer (actress)	October 30, 1907
Caron, Leslie Claire Margaret (actress/dancer)	July 1, 1931
Carpenter, Carleton Upham, II (actor)	July 10, 1926
Carpenter, Karen Anne (singer)	March 2, 1950
Carpenter, Malcolm Scott (astronaut)	May 1, 1925
Carpenter, Richard Lynn (singer/music)	October 15, 1945
Carr, Austin G., Jr. (basketball)	March 10, 1948
Carr, Darlene; born with surname Farnon (actress/singer)	December 12, ———
Carr, Lorne Bell (hockey)	July 2, 1910
Carr, Ralph L. (politician)	December 11, 1887
Carr, Roger (football)	July 1, 1952
Carr, Vikki; born Florencia Bisenta De Casillas Martinez Cardona (singer)	July 19, 1942
Carradine, David (actor)	December 8, 1936
Carradine, John; born Richmond Reed Carradine (actor)	February 5, 1906
Carradine, Keith Ian (actor/singer/music)	August 8, 1949
Carrasquel, Chico; born Alfonso Colon Carrasquel (baseball)	January 23, 1928

Carrillo, Leo (actor)	August 6, 1881
Carroll, Beryl F. (politician)	March 15, 1860
Carroll, Clay Palmer (baseball)	May 2, 1941
Carroll, Diahann; born Carol Diahann Johnson (singer/actress)	July 17, 1935
Carroll, John; born Julian la Faye (actor/singer)	July 17, 1905
Carroll, John Albert (politician)	July 30, 1901
Carroll, Julian Morton (politician)	April 16, 1931
Carroll, Leo G. (actor)	October 25, 1892
Carroll, Lewis; born Charles Lutwidge Dodgson (author/mathematician)	January 27, 1832
Carroll, Madeleine; born Marie Madeleine Bernadette O'Carroll (actress)	February 26, 1906
Carroll, Nancy; born Ann Veronica La Hiff (actress)	November 19, 1904
Carroll, Pat; born Patricia Ann Carroll (comedienne/actress)	May 5, 1927
Carson, Jack; born John Elmer Carson (actor)	October 27, 1910
Carson, Jeannie; born Jean Shufflebottom (actress/comedienne/singer)	May 28, 1929
Carson, Johnny; born John William Carson (comedian/TV host)	October 23, 1925
Carson, Kit; born Christopher Carson (frontiersman)	December 24, 1809
Carson, Mindy (singer)	July 16, 1926
Carson, Rachel Louise (biologist/author)	May 27, 1907
Carson, Sunset; born Michael Harrison (actor)	November 12, 1922
Carter, Amy Lynn (First family)	October 19, 1967
Carter, Billy; born William Alton Carter, III (President's brother)	March 29, 1937
Carter, Chip; born James Earl Carter (First family)	April 12, 1950
Carter, Duane (auto racing)	May 5, 1913
Carter, Fred (basketball)	February 14, 1945
Carter, Jack; born Jack Chakrin (comedian/actor)	June 24, 1923
Carter, Jack; born John William Carter (First family)	July 3, 1947
Carter, Jeff; born Donnel Jeffrey Carter (First family)	August 18, 1952
Carter, Jimmy; born James Earl Carter, Jr. (President)	October 1, 1924
Carter, June (singer)	June 23, 1929
Carter, Lillian; born Bessie Lillian Gordy (President's mother)	August 15, 1898
Carter, Lynda (Miss World-USA/actress/singer)	July 24, 1951
Carter, Mother Maybelle; born Maybelle Addington (singer)	May 10, 1909
Carter, Rosalynn; born Eleanor Rosalynn Smith (First Lady)	August 18, 1927
Cartier, Jacques (explorer)	December 31, 1491
Cartwright, Angela (actress)	September 9, 1952
Carty, Rico; born Ricardo Adolfo Jacobo Carty (baseball)	September 1, 1939
Caruso, Anthony (actor)	————1913
Caruso, Enrico (singer)	February 25, 1873
Caruthers, Jimmy; born James Douglas Caruthers, Jr. (auto racing)	January 18, 1945
Carvel, Elbert Nostrand (politician)	February 9, 1910
Carver, George Washington (botanist)	July 12, 1861
Carveth, Joseph Gordon (hockey)	March 21, 1918
Carville, Edward Peter (politician)	May 14, 1885

Cary, Joyce; born Arthur Joyce Lunel Cary (author)	December 7, 1888
Casals, Pablo; born Pablo Pau Carlos Salvador Defillo de Casals (music)	December 29, 1876
Casals, Rosemary (tennis)	September 16, 1948
Casanova, Tom; born Thomas R. Casanova (football)	July 29, 1950
Casanova de Seingalt, Giovanni Jacopo (adventurer)	April 2, 1725
Casares, Rick; born Ricardo Jose Casares (football)	July 4, 1931
Case, Clifford Philip (politician)	April 16, 1904
Case, Francis Higbee (politician)	December 9, 1896
Case, George Washington (baseball)	November 11, 1915
Case, Norman Stanley (politician)	October 11, 1888
Casey, Bernie; born Bernard Casey (football/actor)	June 8, 1939
Cash, Dave; born David Cash (baseball)	June 11, 1948
Cash, Johnny; born John Ray Cash (singer/actor)	February 26, 1932
Cash, Norm; born Norman Dalton Cash (baseball)	November 10, 1934
Casper, Billy; born William Earl Casper, Jr. (golf)	June 24, 1931
Casper, Dave; born David John Casper (football)	September 26, 1951
Cass, Peggy; born Mary Margaret Cass (actress)	May 21, 1925
Cassady, Howard (football)	March 2, 1934
Cassatt, Mary (artist)	May 22, 1845
Cassavetes, John (actor/director)	December 9, 1929
Cassidy, David Bruce (singer/actor)	April 12, 1950
Cassidy, Jack; born John Edward Joseph Cassidy (actor/singer)	March 5, 1927
Cassidy, Shaun Paul (singer/actor)	September 27, 1958
Cassini, Oleg; born Oleg Loiewski-Cassini (fashion designer)	April 11, 1913
Castellano, Richard (actor)	September 3, 1934
Caster, George Jasper (baseball)	August 4, 1907
Caster, Richard (football)	October 16, 1948
Castle, Irene; born Irene Foote (dancer/actress)	April 7, 1893
Castle, Peggie; born Peggie Blair (actress)	December 22, 1927
Castle, Vernon; born Vernon Castle Blythe (dancer/actor)	May 2, 1887
Castles, Soapy; born Neil Castles (auto racing)	January 10, 1934
Castro, Raul Hector (politician)	June 12, 1916
Castro Ruz, Fidel (Cuban government)	August 13, 1927
Cater, Danny Anderson (baseball)	February 25, 1940
Catherine the Great; born Ekaterina Alekseevna (Russian Empress)	May 2, 1729
Cather, Willa Sibert (author)	December 7, 1876
Catt, Carrie Lane Chapman; born Carrie Lane (suffragist)	January 9, 1859
Catton, Bruce; born Charles Bruce Catton (author)	October 9, 1899
Catts, Sidney Johnston (politician)	July 31, 1863
Caulfield, Henry Stewart (politician)	December 9, 1873
Caulfield, Joan; born Beatrice Joan Caulfield (actress)	June 1, 1922
Causey, Wayne; born James Wayne Causey (baseball)	December 26, 1936
Cauthen, Steve; born Stephen Mark Cauthen (jockey)	May 1, 1960
Cavallaro, Carmen (music)	May 6, 1913
Cavarretta, Phil; born Philip Joseph Cavarretta (baseball)	July 19, 1916
Cavendish, Henry (chemist/physicist)	October 10, 1731
Cavett, Dick; born Richard Cavett (TV host/actor)	November 19, 1936
Cedeno, Cesar Eugenito (baseball)	February 25, 1951

Celebrezze, Anthony J.; born Anthony Giuseppe Cilibrizzi   September 4, 1910
   (government)
Celi, Adolfo (actor)   July 27, 1922
Celler, Emanuel (politician)   May 6, 1888
Cepeda, Orlando Manuel (baseball)   September 17, 1937
Cerf, Bennett Alfred (publisher/journalist)   May 25, 1898
Cernan, Eugene Andrew (astronaut)   March 14, 1934
Cerrudo, Ron; born Ronald Cerrudo (golf)   February 4, 1945
Cerv, Bob; born Robert Henry Cerv (baseball)   May 5, 1926
Cervantes Saavedra, Miguel de (author)   ————1547
Cevert, Francois; born Albert Francois Cevert   February 25, 1944
   (auto racing)
Cey, Ron; born Ronald Charles Cey (baseball)   February 15, 1948
Cézanne, Paul (artist)   January 19, 1839
Chabot, Lorne (hockey)   October 5, 1900
Chabrol, Claude (director)   June 24, 1930
Chafee, John Hubbard (politician)   October 22, 1922
Chagall, Marc (artist)   July 7, 1887
Chakiris, George (actor/dancer)   September 16, 1933
Chamberlain, Abiram (politician)   December 7, 1837
Chamberlain, George Earle (politician)   January 1, 1854
Chamberlain, Murph; born Erwin Groves Chamberlain   February 14, 1915
   (hockey)
Chamberlain, Neville; born Arthur Neville Chamberlain   March 18, 1869
   (British government)
Chamberlain, Richard; born George Richard Chamberlain (actor) March 31, 1935
Chamberlain, Wilt; born Wilton Norman Chamberlain   August 21, 1936
   (basketball)
Chambers, Wally; born Wallace Chambers (football)   May 15, 1951
Chambliss, Chris; born Carroll Christopher Chambliss   December 26, 1948
   (baseball)
Champion, Gower (dancer/actor/choreographer/director)   June 22, 1920
Champion, Marge; born Marjorie Celeste Belcher   September 2, 1919
   (dancer/actress)
Chance, Dean; born Wilmer Dean Chance (baseball)   June 1, 1941
Chance, Frank Leroy (baseball)   September 9, 1877
Chancellor, John William (newscaster)   July 14, 1927
Chandler, Don; born Donald G. Chandler (football)   September 9, 1934
Chandler, Happy; born Albert Benjamin Chandler   July 14, 1898
   (politics/baseball)
Chandler, Helen (actress)   February 1, 1906
Chandler, Jeff; born Ira Grossel (actor)   December 15, 1918
Chandler, Raymond Thornton (author)   July 23, 1888
Chandler, Spud; born Spurgeon Ferdinand Chandler (baseball) September 12, 1907
Chanel, Coco; born Gabrielle Bonheur (fashion designer)   August 19, 1883
Chaney, Don (basketball)   March 22, 1946
Chaney, Lon Sr.; born Alonso Chaney (actor)   April 1, 1883
Chaney, Lon, Jr.; born Creighton Tull Chaney (actor)   February 10, 1906
Channing, Carol Elaine (actress/singer)   January 31, 1921
Chapin, Harry Forster (singer/music)   December 7, 1942
Chapin, Lauren (actress)   May 23, 1945

Chaplin, Sir Charlie; born Charles Spencer Chaplin   April 16, 1889
   (actor/director)
Chaplin, Geraldine (actress)   July 31, 1944
Chaplin, Sydney Earl (actor/singer)   March 31, 1926
Chapman, Arthur V. (hockey)   May 29, 1907
Chapman, Ben; born William Benjamin Chapman (baseball)   December 25, 1908
Chapman, Judith (actress)   November 15———
Chapman, Lonny; born Lon Leonard Chapman   October 1, 1920
   (actor/director/playwright)
Chapman, Oscar Littleton (government)   October 22, 1896
Chapman, Sam; born Samuel Blake Chapman (baseball)   April 11, 1916
Chapman, Virgil Munday (politician)   March 15, 1895
Chappell, Len (basketball)   January 31, 1941
Charisse, Cyd; born Tula Ellice Finklea (dancer/actress)   March 8, 1921
Charles, Bob; born Robert James Charles (golf)   March 14, 1936
Charles, Ezzard; born Charles Ezzard (boxing)   July 7, 1921
Charles, Prince; born Charles Philip Arthur   November 14, 1948
   George Mountbatten (British Royalty)
Charles, Ray (music)   September 13, 1918
Charles, Ray; born Ray Charles Robinson (singer/music)   September 23, 1930
Charleson, Leslie A. (actress)   February 22———
Charo, born Maria Rosario Pilar Martinez Molina Baeza   ———1945
   (singer/dancer/actress)
Chase, Barrie (dancer)   October 20, 1934
Chase, Charlie; born Charles Parrott (comedian/actor)   October 20, 1893
Chase, Chevy; born Cornelius Crane Chase (comedian/actor) October 8, 1943
Chase, Ilka (actress/author)   April 8, 1903
Chase, Mary Coyle (playwright)   February 25, 1907
Chase, Samuel (jurist/revolutionary leader)   April 17, 1741
Chase, Stuart (writer)   March 8, 1888
Chase, Sylvia (newscaster)   February 23, 1938
Chatterton, Fenimore (politician)   July 21, 1860
Chatterton, Ruth (actress/author)   December 24, 1893
Chaucer, Geoffrey (poet)   circa 1340
Chavez, Carlos Antonio de Padua (music)   June 13, 1899
Chavez, Cesar (labor leader)   March 31, 1927
Chavez, Dennis (politician)   April 8, 1888
Chayefsky, Paddy; born Sidney Chayefsky (playwright)   January 29, 1923
Checker, Chubby; born Ernest Evans (singer)   October 3, 1941
Cheever, John (author)   May 27, 1912
Cheevers, Gerald (hockey)   December 2, 1940
Chekhov, Anton Pavlovich (playwright)   January 17, 1860
Chenier, Phil (basketball)   October 30, 1950
Chennault, Anna Chan; born Anna Chan (author)   June 23, 1925
Chennault, Claire Lee (army force officer)   September 6, 1890
Cher; born Cherilyn Sarkisian (or Sakisian) (or Cherilyn   May 20, 1946
   La Piere) (singer/actress)
Cherrill, Virginia (actress)   April 12, 1908
Cherry, Don; born Donald Cherry (golf/singer)   January 11, 1924
Cherry, Francis Adams (politician)   September 5, 1908
Cherry, Robert Gregg (politician)   October 17, 1891

Cherubini, Maria Luigi Carlo Zenobio Salvatore (music)	September 14, 1760
Chesbro, Jack; born John Dwight Chesbro (baseball)	June 5, 1874
Chester, Raymond (football)	June 28, 1948
Chesterton, Gilbert Keith (journalist/author)	May 29, 1874
Chevalier, Maurice Auguste (actor)	September 12, 1888
Chevrefils, Real (hockey)	May 2, 1932
Chevrolet, Louis Joseph (auto racing & manufacturer)	December 25, 1878
Cheyunski, Jim; born James M. Cheyunski (football)	December 29, 1945
Chiang Kai-shek (Chinese government)	October 31, 1887
Child, Julia; born Julia McWilliams (cook/author/TV personality)	August 15, 1912
Childress, Richard Reed (auto racing)	September 21, 1945
Childs, Marquis William (journalist)	March 17, 1903
Chiles, Lawton Mainor (politician)	April 3, 1930
Chirico, Giorgio de (artist)	July 10, 1888
Chisholm, Shirley; born Shirley Anita St. Hill (politician)	November 30, 1924
Chiti, Harry (baseball)	November 16, 1932
Chopin, Frederic-Francois (music)	February 22, 1810
Chou En-lai (Chinese communist leader)	———1898
Christian, Linda; born Blanca Rosa Welter (actress)	November 13, 1923
Christians, Mady; born Margarethe Marie Christians (actress)	January 19, 1900
Christiansen, Jack L. (football)	December 20, 1928
Christianson, Theodore (politician)	September 12, 1883
Christie, Agatha; born Agatha Mary Clarissa Miller (author)	September 15, 1890
Christie, Audrey (actress)	June 27, 1911
Christie, Julie (actress)	April 14, 1941
Christine, Virginia (actress)	March 5, 1917
Christman, Mark; born Marquette Joseph Christman (baseball)	October 21, 1913
Christman, Paul C. (football/sportscaster)	March 5, 1918
Christy, June (singer)	November 20, 1925
Chrysler, Walter Percy (auto manufacturer)	April 2, 1875
Church, Frank Forrester (politician)	July 25, 1924
Churchill, Marguerite (actress)	December 25, 1909
Churchill, Sarah (actress)	October 7, 1914
Churchill, Sir Winston Leonard Spencer (British government)	November 30, 1874
Chuvalo, George (boxing)	September 12, 1937
Cilento, Diane (actress)	October 5, 1933
Cimoli, Gino Nicholas (baseball)	December 18, 1929
Cioffi, Charles (actor)	October 31, 1935
Cissell, Bill; born Chalmer William Cissell (baseball)	January 3, 1904
Clair, René; born René-Lucien Chomette (director)	November 11, 1898
Claire, Ina; born Ina Fagan (actress)	October 15, 1892
Clancy, King; born Francis Michael Clancy (hockey)	February 25, 1903
Clapper, Dit; born Aubrey Victor Clapper (hockey)	February 9, 1907
Clark, Alonzo Monroe (politician)	August 13, 1868
Clark, Barzilla Worth (politician)	December 22, 1881
Clark, Bennett Champ (politician)	January 8, 1890

Clark, Boobie; born Charles L. Clark (football)	November 8, 1950
Clark, Champ; born James Beauchamp Clark (politician)	March 7, 1850
Clark, Chase Addison (politician)	August 21, 1883
Clark, Dane; born Bernard Zanville (actor)	February 18, 1913
Clark, David Worth (politician)	April 2, 1902
Clark, Dick; born Richard Wagstaff Clark	November 30, 1929
(TV host/actor/producer)	
Clark, Dutch; born Earl Clark (football)	October 11, 1906
Clark, Fred; born Frederic Leonard Clark (actor)	March 9, 1914
Clark, Jim; born James Clark, Jr. (auto racing)	March 4, 1936
Clark, Joseph Sill, Jr. (politician)	October 21, 1901
Clark, Mark Wayne (army officer)	May 1, 1896
Clark, Mike; born Michael V. Clark (football)	November 7, 1940
Clark, Monte (football)	January 24, 1937
Clark, Petula Sally Olwen (singer/actress)	November 15, 1932
Clark, Ramsey (government)	December 18, 1927
Clark, Richard Clarence (politician)	September 14, 1929
Clark, Roy Linwood (singer/music)	April 15, 1933
Clark, Susan Nora Gouding (actress)	March 8, 1944
Clark, Tom (or Thomas) Campbell (government/jurist)	September 23, 1899
Clark, Watty; born William Watson Clark (baseball)	May 16, 1902
Clark, William (explorer)	August 1, 1770
Clarke, Bobby; born Robert Earle Clarke (hockey)	August 13, 1949
Clarke, Fred Clifford (baseball)	October 3, 1872
Clarke, George W. (politician)	October 24, 1852
Clarke, Horace Meredith (baseball)	June 2, 1940
Clarke, John Hessin (jurist)	September 18, 1857
Clarke, Mae; born Violet Mary Klotz (actress)	August 16, 1907
Clary, Robert; born Robert Widerman (actor)	March 1, 1926
Clay, Henry (statesman)	April 12, 1777
Clay, Lucius DuBignon (army officer)	April 23, 1897
Clayburgh, Jill (actress)	April 30, 1944
Clayton, Jan; born Jane Byral Clayton (actress/singer)	August 26, 1917
Cleamons, Jim (basketball)	September 13, 1949
Cleaver, Eldridge; born Leroy Eldridge Cleaver	August 31, 1935
(civil rights leader)	
Clemenceau, Georges Eugène Benjamin (French government)	September 28, 1841
Clemens, Barry (basketball)	May 1, 1943
Clement, Frank Goad (politician)	June 2, 1920
Clement, Percival Wood (politician)	July 7, 1846
Clemente, Roberto Walker (baseball)	August 18, 1934
Clements, Earle C. (politician)	October 22, 1896
Clements, Stanley (actor)	July 16, 1926
Clendenon, Donn Alvin (baseball)	July 15, 1935
Cleveland, Frances Folsom; born Frances Folsom (First Lady)	July 21, 1864
Cleveland, Grover; born Stephen Grover Cleveland	March 18, 1837
(President)	
Cliburn, Van; born Harvey Lavan Cliburn, Jr. (music)	July 12, 1934
Clifford, Clark McAdams (government)	December 25, 1906
Clift, Harlond Benton (baseball)	August 12, 1912
Clift, Montgomery; born Edward Montgomery Clift (actor)	October 17, 1920

Clifton, Nat; born Nathaniel Clifton (basketball)	October 13, 1922
Cline, Patsy; born Virginia Patterson Hensley (singer)	September 8, 1932
Cline, Tony; born Anthony Cline (football)	July 25, 1948
Cline, Ty; born Tyrone Alexander Cline (baseball)	June 15, 1939
Clines, Gene; born Eugene Anthony Clines (baseball)	October 6, 1946
Clinton, George (Vice President)	July 26, 1739
Cloninger, Tony Lee (baseball)	August 13, 1940
Clooney, Rosemary (singer/actress)	May 23, 1928
Clower, Jerry (comedian)	September 28, 1926
Clurman, Harold Edgar (director/author)	September 18, 1901
Clyde, George Dewey (politician)	July 21, 1898
Clyde, June (actress)	December 2, 1909
Coan, Gil; born Gilbert Fitzgerald Coan (baseball)	May 18, 1922
Cobb, Lee J.; born Leo Jacob (or Lee Jacoby) (actor)	December 9, 1911
Cobb; Ty; born Tyrus Raymond Cobb (baseball)	December 18, 1886
Cobb, William Titcomb (politician)	July 23, 1857
Coburn, Charles Douville (actor)	June 19, 1877
Coburn, James (actor)	August 31, 1928
Coca, Imogene; born Imogene Fernandez y Coca (comedienne/actress)	November 18, 1908
Cochet, Henri (tennis)	December 14, 1901
Cochran, Robert Leroy (politician)	January 28, 1886
Cochran, Steve; born Robert Alexander Cochran (actor)	May 25, 1917
Cochrane, Mickey; born Gordon Stanley Cochrane (baseball)	April 6, 1903
Cocker, Joe; born John Robert Cocker (singer/music)	May 20, 1944
Cockroft, Don; born Donald L. Cockroft (football)	February 6, 1945
Coco, James Emil (actor)	March 21, 1929
Cocteau, Jean (poet/dramatist/author/director/artist)	July 5, 1889
Cody, Lew; born Louis Joseph Coté (actor)	February 22, 1884
Coffey, Junior Lee (football)	March 21, 1942
Coffman, Dick; born Samuel Richard Coffman (baseball)	December 18, 1906
Cogdill, Gail R. (football)	April 7, 1937
Cohan, George M.; born George Michael Cohan(actor/ dancer/singer/producer/director/playwright/music)	(real) July 3, 1878 (adopted) July 4, 1878
Cohen, Alexander H. (producer)	July 24, 1920
Cohen, Myron (comedian)	July 1, 1902
Colavito, Rocky; born Rocco Demenico Colavito (baseball)	August 10, 1933
Colbert, Claudette; born Lily Chauchoin (actress)	September 13, 1905
Colbert, Jim; born James Colbert (golf)	March 9, 1941
Colbert, Nate; born Nathan Colbert (baseball)	April 9, 1946
Colbert, Robert (actor)	July 16, ——
Colby, Anita; born Anita Katherine Counihan (actress)	August 5, 1914
Colby, William Egan (government)	January 4, 1920
Cole, Bobby; born Robert Cole (golf)	May 11, 1948
Cole, Buddy; born Edwin Le Mar Cole (music)	December 15, 1916
Cole, Cozy; born William R. Cole (music)	October 17, 1909
Cole, Dennis (actor)	July 19, 1943
Cole, George (actor)	April 22, 1925
Cole, Larry; born Lawrence R. Cole (football)	November 15, 1946
Cole, Michael (actor)	July 3, 1945
Cole, Nat King; born Nathaniel Adams Coles (singer/actor)	March 17, 1919

Cole, Natalie; born Stephanie Natalie Maria Cole (singer) — February 6, 1949
Cole, Tina (singer/actress) — August 4, 1943
Coleman, Cy; born Seymour Kaufman (music) — June 14, 1929
Coleman, Dabney (actor) — January 3, ————
Coleman, Gary (actor) — February 8, 1968
Coleman, Gordy; born Gordon Calvin Coleman (baseball) — July 5, 1934
Coleman, Jack (basketball) — May 23, 1924
Coleman, James Piemon (politician) — January 9, 1914
Coleman, Jerry; born Gerald Francis Coleman (baseball) — September 14, 1924
Coleman, Joe; born Joseph Howard Coleman (baseball) — February 3, 1947
Coleman, William Thaddeus, Jr. (government) — July 7, 1920
Coleridge, Samuel Taylor (poet) — October 21, 1772
Coleridge-Taylor, Samuel (music) — August 15, 1875
Colfax, Schuyler (Vice President) — March 23, 1823
Colicos, John (actor) — December 10, 1928
Collett, Elmer; born Charles Elmer Collett (football) — November 7, 1944
Collier, Constance; born Laura Constance Hardie (actress) — January 22, 1875
Collingwood, Charles Cummings (newscaster) — June 4, 1917
Collins, Bill; born William Collins (golf) — September 23, 1928
Collins, Dorothy; born Marjorie Chandler (singer) — November 18, 1926
Collins, Eddie; born Edward Trowbridge Collins (baseball) — May 2, 1887
Collins, Gary (actor) — April 30, 1938
Collins, Gary J. (football) — August 20, 1940
Collins, Jimmy; born James Joseph Collins (baseball) — January 16, 1870
Collins, Joan (actress) — May 23, 1933
Collins, Joe; born Joseph Edward Kollonige (baseball) — December 3, 1922
Collins, Judy Marjorie (singer/music) — May 1, 1939
Collins, LeRoy (politician) — March 10, 1909
Collins, Michael (astronaut) — October 31, 1930
Collins, Pat; born Patricia Colinaka Allan (performer) — May 7, 1935
Collins, Peter (auto racing) — November 8, 1931
Collins, Phil; born Philip Eugene Collins (baseball) — August 27, 1901
Collins, Ray (actor) — December 10, 1889
Collins, Rip; born Harry Warren Collins (baseball) — February 26, 1896
Collins, Ripper; born James Anthony Collins (baseball) — March 30, 1904
Collins, Shano; born John Francis Collins (baseball) — December 4, 1885
Collyer, Bud; born Clayton Collyer (TV host) — June 18, 1908
Collyer, June; born Dorothea Heermance (actress) — August 19, 1907
Colman, Ronald Charles (actor) — February 9, 1891
Colonna, Jerry; born Gerard Colonna (comedian/actor/music) — September 17, 1904
Colquitt, Oscar Branch (politician) — December 16, 1861
Colson, Chuck; born Charles Wendell Colson (government) — October 16, 1931
Colter, Jessi; born Miriam Johnson (singer/music) — May 25, 1947
Coltrane, John William (music) — September 23, 1926
Columbo, Russ; born Ruggiero de Rudolpho Columbo (singer/music/actor) — January 14, 1908
Columbus, Christopher; born Christoforo Colombo (explorer) — circa 1451
Colville, Mac; born Mathew Lamont Colville (hockey) — January 8, 1916
Colville, Neil Macneil (hockey) — August 4, 1914
Colzie, Neal; born Cornelius C. Colzie (football) — February 28, 1953
Comaneci, Nadia (gymnast) — November 12, 1961

Combs, Bert Thomas (politician)	August 13, 1911
Combs, Earle Bryan (baseball)	May 14, 1899
Comden, Betty; born Betty Cohen (writer)	May 3, 1919
Comer, Anjanette (actress)	August 7, 1942
Comer, Braxton Bragg (politician)	November 7, 1848
Comiskey, Charlie; born Charles Albert Comiskey (baseball)	August 15, 1859
Commager, Henry Steele (historian)	October 25, 1902
Como, Perry; born Pierino Roland Como (singer)	May 18, 1912
Comorosky, Adam Anthony (baseball)	December 9, 1904
Compson, Betty; born Eleanor Lucicime Compson (actress)	March 18, 1897
Compton, Ann Woodruff (newscaster)	January 19, 1947
Compton, Joyce; born Eleanor Hunt (actress)	January 27, 1907
Compton, Karl Taylor (physicist)	September 14, 1887
Comstock, William Alfred (politician)	July 2, 1877
Conacher, Charlie; born Charles William Conacher, Jr. (hockey)	December 10, 1909
Conacher, James (hockey)	May 5, 1921
Conacher, Lionel Pretoria (hockey)	May 24, 1901
Conacher, Roy Gordon (hockey)	October 5, 1916
Concannon, Jack; born John J. Concannon, Jr. (football)	February 25, 1943
Concepcion, Dave; born David Ismael Bonitez Concepcion (baseball)	June 17, 1948
Condon, Eddie; born Albert Edwin Condon (music)	November 16, 1905
Cone, Frederick Preston (politician)	September 28, 1871
Conerly, Charlie; born Charles A. Conerly (football)	September 19, 1921
Conigliaro, Billy; born William Michael Conigliaro (baseball)	August 15, 1947
Conigliaro, Tony; born Anthony Richard Conigliaro (baseball)	January 7, 1945
Conklin, Chester; born Jules Cowles (actor)	January 11, 1888
Conklin, Peggy; born Margaret Eleanor Conklin (actress)	November 2, 1910
Conley, Gene; born Donald Eugene Conley (baseball/basketball)	November 10, 1930
Conley, William Gustavus (politician)	January 8, 1866
Conn, Billy; born William David Conn (boxing)	October 8, 1917
Connally, John Bowden, Jr. (politics/government)	February 27, 1917
Connally, Thomas Terry (politician)	August 19, 1877
Connelly, Christopher (actor)	September 8. 1941
Connelly, Marc; born Marcus Cook Connelly (playwright)	December 13, 1890
Connelly, Wayne Francis (hockey)	December 16, 1939
Conner, Martin Sennett (politician)	August 31, 1891
Conners, Dan; born Daniel Conners (football)	February 6, 1941
Connery, Sean; born Thomas Connery (actor)	August 25, 1930
Conniff, Ray (music)	November 6, 1916
Connolly, Maureen Catherine (tennis)	September 17, 1934
Connolly, Walter (actor)	April 8, 1887
Connor, George (football)	January 1, 1925
Connor, Roger (baseball)	July 1, 1857
Connor, John Thomas (government)	November 3, 1914
Connors, Chuck; born Kevin Joseph Connors (actor)	April 10, 1921
Connors, Jimmy; born James Scott Connors (tennis)	September 2, 1952

Connors, Mike; born Krekor Ohanian (actor)	August 15, 1925
Conrad, Bobby Joe; born Robert Joseph Conrad (football)	November 17, 1935
Conrad, Joseph; born Jozef Teodor Konrad Nalecz Korzeniowski (author)	December 3, 1857
Conrad, Michael (actor)	October 16, ————
Conrad, Pete; born Charles Conrad, Jr. (astronaut)	June 2, 1930
Conrad, Robert; born Conrad Robert Falk (actor/singer)	March 1, 1935
Conrad, William (actor/director/producer/singer)	September 27, 1920
Conried, Hans (actor)	April 15, 1917
Considine, Tim (actor)	————, 1940
Consolo, Billy; born William Angelo Consolo (baseball)	August 18, 1934
Constable, John (artist)	June 11, 1776
Constantine, Michael; born Michael Efstration (or Constantine Joanides) (actor)	May 22, 1927
Conte, Richard; born Nicholas Peter Conte (actor)	March 24, 1914
Converse, Frank (actor)	May 22, 1938
Convy, Bert; born Bernard Whalen Patrick Convy (actor/singer/TV host)	July 23, 1934
Conway, Shirl; born Shirley Elizabeth Crosman (actress)	June 13, 1916
Conway, Tim; born Thomas Daniel Conway (comedian/actor)	December 15, 1933
Conway, Tom; born Thomas Charles Sanders (actor)	September 15, 1904
Coody, Charles (golf)	July 13, 1937
Coogan, Jackie; born John Leslie Coogan, Jr. (actor)	October 26, 1914
Cook, Barbara Nell (actress/singer)	October 25, 1927
Cook, Bill; born William Osser Cook (hockey)	October 9, 1896
Cook, Bun; born Frederick Joseph Cook (hockey)	September 18, 1903
Cook, Donald (actor)	September 26, 1901
Cook, Elisha, Jr. (actor)	December 26, 1902
Cook, James (navigator)	October 28, 1728
Cook, Marlow Webster (politician)	July 27, 1926
Cook, Peter Edward (comedian/actor/writer)	November 17, 1937
Cooke, Alistair; born Alfred Alistair Cooke (journalist/broadcaster/author/TV host)	November 20, 1908
Cooke, Sam (singer)	January 22, 1931
Cooley, Denton Arthur (medicine)	August 22, 1920
Coolidge, Calvin; born John Calvin Coolidge (President)	July 4, 1872
Coolidge, Grace Anne Goodhue; born Grace Anne Goodhue (First Lady)	January 3, 1879
Coolidge, Rita (singer/music)	May 1, 1944
Cooney, Frank H. (politician)	December 31, 1872
Cooper, Alice; born Vincent Furnier (singer)	February 4, 1948
Cooper, Ben (actor)	September 30, 1930
Cooper, Earl (auto racing)	————, 1886
Cooper, Gary; born Frank James Cooper (actor)	May 7, 1901
Cooper, Gladys Constance (actress)	December 18, 1888
Cooper, Harry E. (golf)	August 4, 1904
Cooper, Henry (boxing)	May 3, 1934
Cooper, Jackie; born John Cooper, Jr. (actor/director)	September 15, 1921
Cooper, James Fenimore (author)	September 15, 1789
Cooper, John Sherman (politician)	August 23, 1901
Cooper, Joseph (hockey)	December 14, 1914
Cooper, Leroy Gordon, Jr. (astronaut)	March 6, 1927

Cooper, Mort; born Morton Cecil Cooper (baseball)	March 2, 1913
Cooper, Myers Young (politician)	November 25, 1873
Cooper, Prentice (politician)	September 28, 1895
Cooper, Robert Archer (politician)	June 12, 1874
Cooper, Walker; born William Walker Cooper (baseball)	January 8, 1915
Coote, Robert (actor)	February 4, 1909
Copeland, Royal Samuel (politician)	November 7, 1868
Copernicus, Nicolaus; born Mikolaj Kopernik (astronomer)	February 19, 1473
Copland, Aaron (music)	November 14, 1900
Copley, John Singleton (artist)	July 3, 1738
Coppola, Francis Ford (producer/director)	April 7, 1939
Corbett, Glenn; born Glenn Rothenburg (actor)	August 17, 1929
Corbett, Gretchen (actress)	August 13, 1947
Corby, Ellen Hansen; born Ellen Hansen (actress)	June 13, 1914
Corcoran, Donna (actress)	September 29, 1942
Corcoran, Kevin (actor)	June 10, 1945
Corcoran, Noreen (actress)	October 20, 1943
Cord, Alex; born Alexander Viespi (actor)	August 3, 1931
Corday, Mara; born Marilyn Watts (actress)	January 3, 1932
Cordero, Angel Tomas, Jr. (jockey)	May 8, 1942
Cordon, Guy (politician)	April 24, 1890
Corelli, Franco (singer)	April 8, 1923
Corey, Irwin "Professor" (comedian/actor)	July 29, 1912
Corey, Jeff (actor/director)	August 10, 1914
Corey, Jill; born Norma Jean Speranza (singer)	September 30, 1935
Corey, Wendell Reid (actor)	March 20, 1914
Corio, Ann (actress)	———, 1914
Cornelius, Kathy; born Katharine McKinnon (golf)	October 27, 1932
Cornell, Don; born Louis F. Varlaro (singer)	April 21, 1919
Cornell, Katherine (actress)	February 16, 1893
Cornwallis, Charles (English soldier)	December 31, 1738
Cornwell, John Jacob (politician)	July 11, 1867
Corot, Jean Baptiste Camille (artist)	July 17, 1796
Corri, Adrienne; born Adrienne Riccoboni (actress)	November 13, 1930
Corrigan, Crash; born Ray Bernard (actor)	February 14, 1902
Corrigan, Wrong Way; born Douglas Corrigan (aviator)	———, 1907
Cortelyou, George Bruce (government)	July 26, 1862
Cortes, Hernando (explorer)	———, 1485
Cortesa, Valentina (actress)	January 1, 1924
Cortéz, Ricardo; born Jacob Krantz (actor)	September 19, 1899
Corwin, Norman Lewis (writer)	May 3, 1910
Cosby, Bill; born William Henry Cosby, Jr. (comedian/actor)	July 12, 1937
Cosell, Howard; born Howard Cohen (sportscaster/attorney)	March 25, 1920
Costa, Dave; born David J. Costa (football)	October 27, 1941
Costa, Mary (singer/actress)	April 5, 1930
Costello, Dolores (actress)	September 17, 1904
Costello, Helene (actress)	June 21, 1903
Costello, Larry; born Lawrence Ronald Costello (basketball)	July 2, 1931
Costello, Lou; born Louis Francis Cristillo (comedian/actor)	March 6, 1906
Costigan, Edward Prentiss (politician)	July 1, 1874

Cotsworth, Staats Jennings, Jr. (actor)	February 17, 1908
Cotten, Joseph Cheshire (actor)	May 15, 1905
Cotten, Norris (politician)	May 11, 1900
Cotton, Baldy; born Harold Cotton (hockey)	November 5, 1902
Coulter, Art; born Arthur Edmund Coulter (hockey)	May 31, 1909
Counts, Mel (basketball)	October 16, 1941
Courage, Piers Raymond (auto racing)	May 27, 1942
Courbet, Gustave (artist)	June 10, 1819
Cournoyer, Yvan Serge (hockey)	November 22, 1943
Courregès, André (fashion designer)	March 9, 1923
Court, Hazel (actress)	————, 1926
Court, Margaret; born Margaret Smith (tennis)	July 16, 1942
Courtenay, Tom; born Thomas Daniel Courtenay (actor)	February 25, 1937
Courtland, Jerome; born Courtland Jourolman, Jr. (actor/singer/producer)	December 27, 1926
Courtney, Chuck; born Charles Courtney (golf)	October 11, 1940
Courtney, Clint; born Clinton Dawson Courtney (baseball)	March 16, 1927
Cousins, Norman (journalist)	June 24, 1912
Cousteau, Jacques-Yves (marine explorer)	June 11, 1910
Cousy, Bob; born Robert Joseph Cousy (basketball)	August 9, 1928
Couture, Gerald Joseph Wilfred Arthur (hockey)	August 6, 1925
Couzens, James (politician)	August 26, 1872
Coveleski, Stanley Anthony "Stan"; born Stanislaus Kowalewski (baseball)	July 13, 1889
Covington, Wes; born John Wesley Covington (baseball)	March 27, 1932
Cowan, Billy Rolland (baseball)	August 28, 1938
Cowan, Charlie; born Charles Cowan (football)	June 19, 1938
Cowan, Jerome Palmer (actor)	October 6, 1897
Coward Sir Noel Pierce (playwright/actor/director/music)	Deceember 16, 1899
Cowens, Dave; born David William Cowens (basketball)	October 25, 1948
Cowles, Gardner (publisher)	January 31, 1901
Cowley, Bill; born William M. Cowley (hockey)	June 12, 1912
Cox, Archibald (attorney)	May 17, 1912
Cox, Billy; born William Richard Cox (baseball)	August 29, 1919
Cox, Channing Harris (politician)	February 28, 1879
Cox, Fred; born Frederick W. Cox (football)	December 11, 1938
Cox, James Middleton (politician)	March 31, 1870
Cox, John Isaac (politician)	November 23, 1855
Cox, Wally; born Wallace Maynard Cox (actor)	December 6, 1924
Cozzens, James Gould (author)	August 19, 1903
Crabbe, Buster; born Clarence Linden Crabbe (swimmer/actor)	February 7, 1907
Craft, Harry Francis (baseball)	April 19, 1915
Craig, George North (politician)	August 6, 1909
Craig, James; born James Henry Meador (actor)	February 4, 1912
Craig, Locke (politician)	August 16, 1860
Craig, Roger Lee (baseball)	February 17, 1931
Craig, Yvonne (actress/dancer)	May 16, 1941
Crain, Jeanne (actress)	May 25, 1925
Cramer, Doc; born Roger Maxwell Cramer (baseball)	July 22, 1905
Cramer, Floyd (music)	October 27, 1933
Crampton, Bruce Sidney (golf)	September 28, 1935
Crandall, Del; born Delmar Wesley Crandall (baseball)	March 5, 1930

Crane, Arthur Griswold (politician)	September 1, 1877
Crane, Bob Edward (actor)	July 13, 1928
Crane, Stephen (writer)	November 1, 1871
Crane, Winthrop Murray (politician)	April 23, 1853
Cranston, Alan MacGregor (politician)	June 19, 1914
Crawford, Broderick; born William Broderick Crawford (actor)	December 9, 1911
Crawford, Cheryl (producer)	September 24, 1902
Crawford, Coe Isaac (politician)	January 14, 1858
Crawford, Jack; born John Shea Crawford (hockey)	October 26, 1916
Crawford, Joan; born Lucille Fay Le Suer (actress)	March 23, 1904
Crawford, Katherine; born Katherine Huggins (actress)	March 2———
Crawford, Sam; born Samuel Earl Crawford (baseball)	April 18, 1880
Crawford, Willie Murphy (baseball)	September 7, 1946
Creed, Clifford Ann (golf)	September 23, 1938
Creighton, David Theodore (hockey)	June 24, 1930
Crenna, Richard (actor/director)	November 30, 1927
Crenshaw, Ben; born Benjamin Daniel Crenshaw (golf)	January 11, 1952
Crews, Laura Hope (actress)	December 12, 1879
Crichton, Michael; born John Michael Crichton (author/director)	October 23, 1942
Crisp, Donald (actor)	July 27, 1880
Crist, Judith; born Judith Klein (journalist)	May 22, 1922
Cristal, Linda; born Marta Victoria Moya Burges (actress)	February 24, 1936
Cristofer, Michael (playwright/actor)	January 22, 1945
Critz, Hughie; born Hugh Melville Critz (baseball)	September 17, 1900
Croce, Jim (singer/music)	January 10, 1942
Crocker,Mary Lou; born Mary Lou Daniel (golf)	September 17, 1944
Crockett, Davy; born David Crockett (frontiersman)	August 17, 1786
Cromwell, Oliver (lord protector of England)	April 25, 1599
Cromwell, Richard; born Roy M. Radabaugh (actor)	January 8, 1910
Cronin, A.J.; born Archibald Joseph Cronin (author)	July 19, 1896
Cronin, Joe; born Joseph Edward Cronin (baseball)	October 12, 1906
Cronkite, Walter Leland, Jr. (newscaster)	November 4, 1916
Cronyn, Hume; born Hume Blake (actor/director)	July 18, 1911
Crosby; Bing; born Harry Lillis Crosby (singer/actor)	May 2, 1901
Crosby, Bob; born George Robert Crosby (music)	August 23, 1913
Crosby, Cathy Lee (actress)	———1949
Crosby, Gary Evan (actor)	June 27, 1933
Crosby, Kathryn; born Olive Kathryn Grandstaff (actress)	November 25, 1933
Crosby, Mary Frances (actress)	September 14, 1959
Crosby, Norm; born Norman Lawrence Crosby (comedian)	September 15, 1927
Crosby, Robert Berkey (politician)	March 26, 1911
Crosetti, Frank Peter Joseph (baseball)	October 4, 1910
Crosman, Henrietta (actress)	September 2, 1861
Cross, Burton Melvin (politician)	November 15, 1902
Cross, Irv; born Irvin Cross (football/sportscaster)	July 27, 1939
Cross, Wilbur Lucius (politician)	April 10, 1862
Crothers, Austin L. (politician)	May 20, 1860
Crothers, Scatman; born Benjamin Sherman Crothers (actor/comedian/singer/music)	May 23, 1910
Crouse, Russel (playwright)	February 20, 1893

Crow, John David (football)	July 8, 1935
Crow, Lindon (football)	April 4, 1933
Crowder, General; born Alvin Floyd Crowder (baseball)	January 11, 1899
Crowley, Kathleen (actress)	———1931
Crowley, Pat; born Patricia Crowley (actress)	September 17, 1929
Crozier, Roger Alan (hockey)	March 16, 1942
Cruce, Lee (politician)	July 8, 1863
Cruickshank, Bobby; born Robert Allan Cruickshank (golf)	November 16, 1894
Cruz, Jose Dilan (baseball)	August 8, 1947
Crystal, Billy (actor/comedian)	March 14, 1949
Csonka, Larry; born Lawrence Richard Csonka (football)	December 25, 1946
Cuccinello, Tony; born Anthony Francis Cuccinello (baseball)	November 8, 1907
Cude, Wilfred (hockey)	July 4, 1910
Cueller, Mike; born Miguel Angel Cueller (baseball)	May 8, 1937
Cugat, Xavier; born Francisco De Asis Javier Cugat Mingall De Bru y Deulofeo (music/actor/artist)	January 1, 1900
Cukor, George Dewey (director)	July 7, 1899
Cullen, Betsy; born Mary Elizabeth Cullen (golf)	August 14, 1938
Cullen, Bill; born William Lawrence Cullen (actor/TV host)	February 18, 1920
Cullen, Brian Joseph (hockey)	November 11, 1933
Cullenbine, Roy Joseph (baseball)	October 18, 1915
Cullum, John (actor/singer)	March 2, 1930
Culp, Curley (football)	October 10, 1946
Culp, Ray; born Raymond Leonard Culp (baseball)	August 6, 1941
Culp, Robert (actor/director)	August 16, 1930
Culver, John Chester (politician)	August 8, 1932
Cummings, Bob; born Charles Clarence Robert Orville Cummings (actor)	June 9, 1908
Cummings, Constance; born Constance Halverstadt (actress)	May 15, 1910
Cummings, E.E.; born Edward Estlin Cummings (author)	October 14, 1894
Cummings, Homer Stillé (government)	April 30, 1870
Cummings, Quinn (actress)	August 13, 1967
Cummins, Albert Baird (politician)	February 15, 1850
Cummins, Peggy (actress)	December 18, 1925
Cunningham, Billy (basketball/sportscaster)	June 3, 1943
Cunningham, Cecil (actress/singer)	August 2, 1888
Cunningham, Joe; born Joseph Robert Cunningham (baseball)	August 27, 1931
Cunningham, R. Walter (astronaut)	March 16, 1932
Cunningham; Sam; born Samuel Lewis Cunningham, Jr. (football)	August 15, 1950
Cuozzo, Gary (football)	April 26, 1941
Cupit, Jacky (golf)	February 1,1938
Curie, Marie; born Marja Sklodowski (physical chemist)	November 7, 1867
Curl, Rod (golf)	January 9, 1943
Curley, James Michael (politician)	November 20, 1874
Curran, Pat; born Patrick M. Curran (football)	September 21, 1945
Current, Mike; born Michael W. Current (football)	September 17, 1945
Currie, Dan; born Daniel Currie (football)	June 27, 1935
Currie, Finlay; born Finlay Jefferson (actor)	January 20, 1878
Currier, Nathaniel (lithographer)	March 27, 1813

Curry, Busher; born Floyd James Curry (hockey)	August 11, 1925
Curtin, Jane Therese (actress/comedienne/singer)	September 6, 1947
Curtin, Phyllis; born Phyllis Smith (singer)	December 3, 1922
Curtis, Carl Thomas (politician)	March 15, 1905
Curtis, Charles (Vice President)	January 25, 1860
Curtis, Isaac Fisher (football)	October 20, 1950
Curtis, Jamie Lee (actress)	November 22, 1958
Curtis, Keene Holbrook (actor)	February 15, 1923
Curtis, Ken; born Curtis Gates (actor)	July 12, 1916
Curtis, Kenneth Merwin (politician)	February 8, 1931
Curtis, Mike; born James Michael Curtis (football)	March 27, 1943
Curtis, Oakley Chester (politician)	March 29, 1865
Curtis, Tony; born Bernard Schwartz (actor/author)	June 3, 1925
Curzon, Clifford (music)	May 18, 1907
Cusack, Cyril (actor)	November 26, 1910
Cushing, Peter (actor)	May 26, 1913
Custer, George Armstrong (military officer)	December 5, 1839
Cutler, John Christopher (politician)	February 5, 1846
Cutting, Bronson Murray (politician)	June 23, 1888
Cuyler, Kiki; born Hazen Shirley Cuyler (baseball)	August 30, 1899
Cypher, Jon (actor)	January 13, 1932
Cyrano De Bergerac, Savinien de (French soldier/poet)	March 6, 1619

D

Dagmar, born Virginia Ruth Egnor (actress)	———1926
Dahl, Arlene Carol (actress)	August 11, 1924
Dahlgren, Babe; born Ellsworth Tenney Dahlgren (baseball)	June 15, 1912
Dahlstrom, Cully; born Carl Dahlstrom (hockey)	July 3, 1913
Dailey, Dan (actor/dancer)	December 14, 1917
Dailey, Irene (actress)	September 12, 1920
Dale, Carroll W. (football)	April 24, 1938
Dale, Charles Milby (politician)	March 8, 1893
Dale, Esther (singer/actress)	November 10, 1885
Dale, Porter Hinman (politician)	March 1, 1867
Daley, Cass; born Catherine Dailey (comedienne/actress)	July 17, 1915
Daley, Richard Joseph (politician)	May 15, 1902
Dali, Salvador Felipe Jacinto (artist)	May 11, 1904
Dallas, George Mifflin (Vice President)	July 10, 1792
Dallenbach, Wally; born Wallace J. Dallenbach (auto racing)	December 12, 1936
Dalrymple, Clay; born Clayton Errol Dalrymple (baseball)	December 3, 1936
Dalton, Abby (actress)	August 15, 1935
Dalton, Audrey (actress)	January 21, 1934
Dalton, John Montgomery (politician)	November 9, 1900
Dalton, John Nichols (politician)	July 11, 1931
Daly, James Firman (actor)	October 23, 1918
Daly, John Charles, Jr. (newscaster/TV host)	February 20, 1914
Daly, Tyne; born Ellen Tyne Daly (actress)	———1944
d'Amboise, Jacques Joseph (dancer)	July 28, 1934
Damita, Lili; born Liliane-Marie-Madeleine Carré (actress)	July 19, 1901

Damon, Cathryn (actress)	September 11———
Damon, Mark; born Alan Harris (actor)	April 22, 1933
Damone, Vic; born Vito Farinola (singer/actor)	June 12, 1928
Dampier, Louie (basketball)	November 20, 1944
Damrosch, Walter Johannes (music)	January 30, 1862
Dana, Bill (comedian/actor)	October 5, 1924
Dana, Vic (dancer/singer)	August 26, 1942
Dana, Viola; born Viola Flugrath (actress)	June 28, 1897
Danaher, John Anthony (politician)	January 9, 1899
Dandridge, Bob (basketball)	November 15, 1947
Dandridge, Dorothy (actress)	November 9, 1922
Dane, Karl; born Karl Daen (actor)	October 12, 1886
Danforth, John Claggett (politician)	September 5, 1936
Dangerfield, Rodney (comedian/actor/author)	November 22, 1921
Daniel, Clifton; born Elbert Clifton Daniel, Jr. (journalist)	September 19, 1912
Daniel, Price; born Marion Price Daniel (politician)	October 10, 1910
Daniels, Bebe; born Virginia Daniels (actress)	January 14, 1901
Daniels, Clem; born Clemon Daniels (football)	July 9, 1937
Daniels, Josephus (government/journalism)	May 18, 1862
Daniels, William David (actor)	March 31, 1927
Danilova, Alexandra (dancer)	January 20, 1904
Dankworth, John (music)	September 20, 1927
Danner, Blythe Katharine (actress)	———1943
Danning, Harry (baseball)	September 6, 1911
Dano, Royal Edward (actor)	November 16, 1922
Danova, Cesare Deitinger (actor)	March 1, 1926
Dantine, Helmut (actor/director)	October 7, 1917
Danton, Ray (actor/director)	September 19, 1931
Darby, Kim; born Deborah Elias Zerby (actress)	July 8, 1948
Darcel, Denise; born Denise Billecard (actress)	September 8, 1925
Darden, Colgate Whitehead, Jr. (politician)	February 11, 1897
Darden, Severn Teackle (actor)	———1937
Darin, Bobby; born Walden Robert Cassotto (singer/actor)	May 14, 1936
Dario, Ruben; born Felix Ruben Garcia-Sarmiento (poet/author)	January 18, 1867
Dark, Al; born Alvin Ralph Dark (baseball)	January 7, 1922
Darling, Jean; born Dorothy Jean LeVake (actress/singer)	August 23, 1925
Darling, Joan; born Joan Kugell (actress/director)	April 14, 1935
Darnell, Linda; born Monetta (or Manetta) Eloyse (or Eloisa) Darnell (actress)	October 16, 1921
Darren, James; born James William Ercolani (singer/actor)	June 8, 1936
Darrieux, Danielle (actress)	May 1, 1917
Darro, Frankie; born Frank Johnson (actor)	December 22, 1917
Darrow, Clarence Seward (attorney)	April 18, 1857
Darrow, Henry; born Henry Thomas Delgado (actor)	September 15, 1933
Darvas, Lili (actress)	April 10, 1902
Darwell, Jane; born Patti Woodward (actress)	October 15, 1879
Darwin, Bobby; born Arthur Bobby Lloyd Darwin (baseball)	February 16, 1943
Darwin, Charles Robert (naturalist)	February 12, 1809
Da Silva, Howard; born Howard Silverblatt (actor)	May 4, 1909

Dassin, Jules (director)   December 18, 1911
Daugherty, Duffy; born Hugh Daugherty   September 8, 1915
   (football/sportscaster)
Daugherty, Harry Micajah (government)   January 26, 1860
Dauphin, Claude; born Claude Franc-Nohain (actor)   August 19, 1903
Davalillo, Vic; born Victor Jose Davalillo (baseball)   July 31, 1936
Davenport, Jim; born James Houston Davenport (baseball)   August 17, 1933
Davenport, Nigel (actor)   May 23, 1928
Davey, Martin Luther (politician)   July 25, 1884
David, Hal (music)   May 25, 1921
David, Thayer (actor)   March 4, 1927
Davidson, Ben; born Benjamin Earl Davidson   June 14, 1940
   (football/actor)
Davidson, James Ole (politician)   February 10, 1854
Davidson, John Hamilton (singer/actor)   December 13, 1941
Davidson, Robert (hockey)   February 10, 1912
Davies, Bob; born Robert Edris Davies (basketball)   January 15, 1920
Davies, Marion; born Marion Cecelia Douras (actress)   January 3, 1897
Davis, Angela Yvonne (civil rights leader)   January 26, 1944
Davis, Ann B.; born Ann Bradford Davis (actress)   May 5, 1926
Davis, Bette; born Ruth Elizabeth Davis (actress)   April 5, 1908
Davis, Billy, Jr. (singer)   June 26, 1940
Davis, Clarence Eugene (football)   June 28, 1949
Davis, Clifton D. (actor/singer)   October 4, 1945
Davis, Curt; born Curtis Benton Davis (baseball)   September 7, 1903
Davis, Danny; born George Joseph Nowlan (music)   April 29, 1925
Davis, David William (politician)   April 23, 1873
Davis, Deane Chandler (politician)   November 7, 1900
Davis, Dwight Filley (government)   July 5, 1879
Davis, Gail; born Betty Jeanne Grayson (actress)   October 5, 1925
Davis, Harold Lenoir (author)   October 18, 1896
Davis, Harry Lyman (politician)   January 25, 1878
Davis, James John (politics/government)   October 27, 1873
Davis, Jefferson (President of the Confederacy)   June 3, 1808
Davis, Jefferson (politician)   May 6, 1862
Davis, Jim (actor)   August 26, 1915
Davis, Jimmie; born James Houston Davis (politician/singer)   September 11, 1902
Davis, Joan; born Madonna Josephine Davis (actress)   June 29, 1907
Davis, John Edward (politician)   April 18, 1913
Davis, Jonathan McMillan (politician)   April 26, 1871
Davis, Mac (singer/music)   January 21, 1942
Davis, Miles Dewey, Jr. (music)   May 25, 1926
Davis, Nancy; born Anne Frances Robbins (actress/governor's wife)   July 6, 1921
Davis, Ossie (actor/director/writer)   December 18, 1917
Davis, Owen (playwright)   January 29, 1874
Davis, Sam; born Samuel Davis (football)   July 4, 1944
Davis, Sammy, Jr. (singer/actor/dancer)   December 8, 1925
Davis, Skeeter, born Mary Frances Penick (singer)   December 30, 1931
Davis, Spud; born Virgil Lawrence Davis (baseball)   December 20, 1904
Davis, Tom; born Thomas R. Davis (football)   October 13, 1934
Davis, Tommy; born Herman Thomas Davis (baseball)   March 21, 1939

Davis, Westmoreland (politician)	August 21, 1859
Davis, Willie; born William D. Davis (football)	July 24, 1934
Davis, Willie; born William Henry Davis (baseball)	April 15, 1940
Dawber, Pam (actress/singer)	October 18, 1951
Dawes, Charles Gates (Vice President)	August 27, 1865
Dawkins, Joe (football)	January 27, 1948
Dawn, Hazel; born Hazel Dawn La Tout (actress/singer)	March 23, 1891
Dawson, Lenny; born Leonard Ray Dawson	June 20, 1935
(football/sportscaster)	
Dawson, Richard (actor/TV host)	November 20, 1932
Dawson, William Mercer Owens (politician)	May 21, 1853
Day, Dennis; born Eugene Dennis McNulty (singer/actor)	May 21, 1917
Day, Doris; born Doris von Kappelhoff (actress/singer)	April 3, 1924
Day, Happy; born Clarence Henry Day (hockey)	June 14, 1901
Day, J. Edward; born James Edward Day (government)	October 11, 1914
Day, Laraine; born La Raine Johnson (actress)	October 13, 1917
Day, William Rufus (government/jurist)	April 17, 1849
Dayan, Moshe (Israeli government)	May 20, 1915
Dea, William Fraser (hockey)	April 3, 1933
Deacon, Richard (actor)	May 14, 1922
Dean, Dizzy; born Jay Hanna Dean (baseball/sportscaster)	January 16, 1911
Dean, James Byron (actor)	February 8, 1931
Dean, Jimmy Ray (singer/music)	August 10, 1928
Dean, John Wesley, III (government)	October 14, 1938
Dean, Morton (newscaster)	August 22, 1935
Dean, Priscilla (actress)	September 16, 1896
Dearie, Blossom (singer)	April 28, 1926
De Bakey, Michael Ellis (medicine)	September 7, 1908
Debs, Eugene Victor (Socialist leader)	November 5, 1855
De Busschere, Dave; born David Albert De Busschere	October 16, 1940
(basketball)	
Debussy, Claude; born Achille Claude Debussy (music)	August 22, 1862
De Camp, Rosemary (actress)	November 14, 1914
De Carlo, Yvonne; born Peggy Yvonne Middleton (actress)	September 1, 1922
Decatur, Stephen (naval officer)	January 5, 1779
Deconcini, Dennis (politician)	May 8, 1937
Dee, Frances; born Jean Dee (actress)	November 26, 1907
Dee, Ruby; born Ruth Ann Wallace (actress)	October 27, 1924
Dee, Sandra; born Alexandra Zuck (actress)	April 23, 1942
Defoe, Daniel; born Daniel Foe (author)	———1659
Defore, Don J. (actor)	August 25, 1917
Degas, Edgar; born Hilaire Germain Edgar Degas (artist)	July 19, 1834
De Gaulle, Charles André Joseph Marie (French government)	November 22, 1890
De Haven, Gloria Mildred (actress)	July 23, 1924
De Havilland, Olivia Mary (actress)	July 1, 1916
Dehner, John (actor)	November 23, 1915
DeJordy, Denis (hockey)	November 12, 1938
Dekker, Albert (actor)	December 20, 1905
de Kooning, Willem (artist)	April 24, 1904
Delacroix, Ferdinand Victor Eugene (artist)	April 26, 1798
Delahanty, Ed; born Edward James Delahanty (baseball)	October 30, 1867
DeLamielleure, Joe; born Joseph DeLamielleure (football)	March 16, 1951

Delaplane, Stan; born Stanton Hill Delaplane (journalist)	October 12, 1907
De La Renta, Oscar (fashion designer)	July 22, 1932
De Laurentiis, Dino; born Agostino De Laurentiis (producer)	August 8, 1919
Del Greco, Bobby; born Robert George Del Greco (baseball)	April 7, 1933
Dell, Dorothy; born Dorothy Goff (actress)	January 30, 1915
Dell, Gabriel; born Gabriel del Vecchio (actor)	October 7, 1919
Delock, Ike; born Ivan Martin Delock (baseball)	November 11, 1929
Delon, Alain (actor)	November 8, 1935
Del Rio, Dolores; born Lolita Dolores Martinez Asunsolo Lopez Negrette (actress)	August 3, 1904
Del Sesto, Christopher (politician)	March 10, 1907
Delsing, Jim; born James Henry Delsing (baseball)	November 13, 1925
Delugg, Milton (music)	December 2, 1918
Deluise, Dom (comedian/actor)	August 1, 1933
Delvecchio, Alex born Alexander Peter Delvecchio (hockey)	December 4, 1931
DeMaestri, Joe; born Joseph Paul DeMaestri (baseball)	December 9, 1928
DeMarco, Bob; born Robert A. DeMarco (football)	September 16, 1938
Demaree, Frank; born Joseph Franklin Dimaria (baseball)	June 10, 1910
Demarest, William (actor)	February 27, 1892
Demaret, Jimmy; born James Newton Demaret (golf)	May 10, 1910
Demarie, John (football)	August 28, 1945
Demeter, Don; born Donald Lee Demeter (baseball)	June 25, 1935
de Mille, Agnes George (choreographer/dancer)	———1905
De Mille, Cecil B.; born Cecil Blount De Mille (director)	August 12, 1881
De Mille, Katherine; born Katherine Lester (actress)	June 29, 1911
Dempsey, Jack; born William Harrison Dempsey (boxing)	June 24, 1895
Dempsey, John Joseph (politician)	June 22, 1879
Dempsey, John Noel (politician)	January 3, 1915
Dempsey, Tom; born Thomas Dempsey (football)	January 12, 1947
Dempster, Carol (actress)	———1902
Denby, Edwin (government)	February 18, 1870
Deneen, Charles Samuel (politician)	May 4, 1863
Denenberg, Gail (golf)	January 17, 1947
Deneuve, Catherine; born Catherine Dorléac (actress)	October 22, 1943
Den Herder, Vern; born Vernon W. Den Herder (football)	November 28, 1948
De Niro, Robert (actor)	August 17, 1943
Denison, Michael (actor)	November 1, 1915
Denney, William du Hamel (politician)	March 31, 1873
Denning, Richard; born Louis Albert Denninger (actor)	March 27, 1914
Dennis, Sandy; born Sandra Dale Dennis (actress)	April 27, 1937
Dennison, Doug; born William D. Dennison (football)	December 18, 1951
Denny, Martin (music)	April 10, 1911
Denny, Reginald; born Reginald Leigh Dugmore (or Daymore) (actor)	November 20, 1891
Dent, Frederick Baily (government)	August 17, 1922
Dent, Jim; born James Dent (golf)	May 11, 1942
Denton, Randy (basketball)	February 18, 1949
Denver, Bob (actor)	January 9, 1935
Denver, John; born Henry John Deutschendorf, Jr. (singer/actor)	December 31, 1943
DePalma, Ralph (auto racing)	———1883

De Paolo, Peter (auto racing)	————1898
Derain, André (artist)	June 10, 1880
Derek, John; born Derek Harris (actor)	August 12, 1926
Dern, Bruce MacLeish (actor)	June 4, 1936
Dern, George Henry (politics/government)	September 8, 1872
Derringer, Paul; born Samuel Paul Derringer (baseball)	October 17, 1906
De Santis, Joe; born Joseph V. De Santis (actor)	June 15, 1909
Desautels, Gene; born Eugene Abraham Desautels (baseball)	June 13, 1907
Descartes, René (philosopher/mathematician)	March 31, 1596
DeShannon, Jackie (singer)	August 21, 1944
De Sica, Vittorio (director/actor)	July 7, 1902
Desmond, Johnny; born Giovanni Alfredo de Simone (singer/actor)	November 14, 1921
De Soto, Hernando (explorer)	circa 1500
Devane, William (actor)	September 5, 1937
Dever, Paul Andrew (politician)	January 15, 1903
DeVicenzo, Roberto (golf)	April 14, 1923
Devine, Andy; born Jeremiah Schwartz (actor)	October 7, 1905
Devine, Dan; born Daniel John Devine (football)	December 23, 1924
Devlin, Bernadette Josephine (Irish civil rights leader)	April 23, 1947
Devlin, Bruce (golf/sportscaster)	October 10, 1937
De Vries, Peter (author/journalist)	February 27, 1910
Dewey, George (naval officer)	December 26, 1837
Dewey, Thomas Edmund (politician)	March 24, 1902
Dewhurst, Colleen (actress)	June 3, 1926
de Wilde, Brandon; born Andre Brandon de Wilde (actor)	April 9, 1942
DeWitt, Joyce (actress/singer)	April 23, 1949
de Wolfe, Billy; born William Andrew Jones (actor)	February 18, 1907
Dewsbury, Albert Percy (hockey)	April 12, 1926
Dexter, Brad (actor)	April 9, 1917
Dey, Susan Hallock (actress)	December 10, 1952
Dhiegh, Khigh (actor)	————1910
Diamond, Neil Leslie (singer/music)	January 24, 1941
Dibbs, Eddie; born Edward George Dibbs (tennis)	February 23, 1951
Dick, Charles William Frederick (politician)	November 3, 1858
Dickens, Charles John Huffam (author)	February 7, 1812
Dickerson, Denver Sylvester (politician)	January 24, 1872
Dickey; Bill; born William Malcolm Dickey (baseball)	June 6, 1907
Dickey, James (poet)	February 2, 1923
Dickey, Lynn; born Clifford Lynn Dickey (football)	October 19, 1949
Dickinson, Angie; born Angeline Brown (actress)	September 30, 1931
Dickinson, Emily Elizabeth (poet)	December 10, 1830
Dickinson, Gardner, Jr. (golf)	September 27, 1927
Dickinson, Luren Dudley (politician)	April 15, 1859
Dickson, Gloria; born Thais Dickerson (actress)	August 13, 1916
Dickson, Murry Monroe (baseball)	August 21, 1916
Diddley, Bo; born Ellas McDaniels (singer/music)	December 30, 1928
Didion, Joan (author/journalist)	December 5, 1934
Diefenbacker, John George (Canadian government)	September 18, 1895
Diegel, Leo (golf)	April 27, 1899
Diener, Joan (actress/singer)	February 24, 1934

Dierdorf, Dan; born Daniel Lee Dierdorf (football)	June 29, 1949
Dieringer, Darel Eugene (auto racing)	June 1, 1926
Dierker, Larry; born Lawrence Edward Dierker (baseball)	September 22, 1946
Dierking, Connie (basketball)	October 21, 1936
Dieterich, William Henry (politician)	March 31, 1876
Dietrich, Bill; born William John Dietrich (baseball)	March 29, 1910
Dietrich, Dena (actress)	December 4, 1928
Dietrich, Marlene; born Maria Magdalena Dietrich, adopted Maria Magdalena von Losch (actress)	December 27, 1901
Dietrick, Coby (basketball)	July 23, 1948
Dietz, Howard (music)	September 8, 1896
Dill, Clarence Cleveland (politician)	September 21, 1884
Diller, Phyllis; born Phyllis Driver (comedienne/actress/author)	July 17, 1917
Dillinger, John (criminal)	June 22, 1903
Dillman, Bradford (actor)	April 14, 1930
Dillon, Bobby; born Robert Dillon (football)	February 23, 1930
Dillon, C. Douglas; born Clarence Douglas Dillon (government)	August 21, 1909
Dillon, Cecil Graham (hockey)	April 26, 1908
Dillon, Richard Charles (politician)	June 24, 1877
Di Maggio, Dom; born Dominic Paul Di Maggio (baseball)	February 12, 1917
Di Maggio, Joe; born Joseph Paul Di Maggio (baseball)	November 25, 1914
Di Maggio, Vince; born Vincent Paul Di Maggio (baseball)	September 6, 1912
Dine, Jim (artist)	June 16, 1935
Dion; born Dion DiMucci (singer/music)	July 18, 1939
Dior, Christian (fashion designer)	January 21, 1905
Dirksen, Everett McKinley (politician)	January 4, 1896
Di Salle, Michael Vincent (politician)	January 6, 1908
Dischinger, Terry (basketball)	November 21, 1940
Disney, Walt; born Walter Elias Disney (producer)	December 5, 1901
Disraeli, Benjamin; born Benjamin D'Israeli (statesman/author)	December 21, 1804
Ditka, Mike; born Michael Keller Dyzcko (football)	October 18, 1939
Ditmar, Art; born Arthur John Ditmar (baseball)	April 3, 1929
Dix, Dorothea Lynde (reformer/philanthropist)	April 4, 1802
Dix, Dorothy; born Elizabeth Meriwether (journalist/author)	November 18, 1861
Dix, John Alden (politician)	December 25, 1860
Dix, Richard; born Ernest Carlton Brimmer (actor)	July 18, 1894
Dixon, Frank Murray (politician)	July 25, 1892
Dixon, Hewritt Frederick, Jr. (football)	January 8, 1940
Dixon, Ivan N., III (actor/director)	April 6, 1931
Dixon, Jean; born Marie Jacques (actress)	July 14, 1894
Dixon, Jeane Pinckert (seer)	———1918
Dixon, Joseph Moore (politician)	July 31, 1867
Doak, William Nuckles (government)	December 12, 1882
Dobler, Conrad Francis (football)	October 1, 1950
Dobrynin, Anatoly Fedorovich (Russian government)	November 16, 1919
Dobson, Chuck; born Charles Thomas Dobson (baseball)	January 10, 1944
Dobson, Joe; born Joseph Gordon Dobson (baseball)	January 20, 1917

Dobson, Kevin (actor)   March 18————
Dobson, Pat; born Patrick Edward Dobson, Jr. (baseball)   February 12, 1942
Doby, Larry; born Lawrence Eugene Doby (baseball)   December 13, 1923
Dockery, Alexander Monroe (politician)   February 11, 1845
Docking, George (politician)   February 23, 1904
Docking, Robert Blackwell (politician)   October 9, 1925
Doctorow, E.L; born Edgar Laurence Doctorow (author)   January 6, 1931
Dodd, Claire (actress)   December 29, 1908
Dodd, Thomas Joseph (politician)   May 15, 1907
Dodge, Mary Mapes; born Mary Elizabeth Mapes (author)   January 26, 1831
Doeg, John Hope (tennis)   December 7, 1908
Doerr, Bobby; born Robert Pershing Doerr (baseball)   April 7, 1918
Dole, Robert Joseph (politician)   July 22, 1923
Dolin, Anton; born Patrick Healey-Kay   July 27, 1904
    (dancer/choreographer)
Dolliver, Jonathan Prentiss (politician)   February 6, 1858
Domenici, Pete Vichi (politician)   May 7, 1932
Domergue, Faith (actress)   June 16, 1925
Domingo, Placido (singer)   January 21, 1941
Dominick, Peter Hoyt (politician)   July 7, 1915
Domino, Fats; born Antoine Domino (singer/music)   February 26, 1928
Domres, Marty; born Martin F. Domres (football)   April 17, 1947
Donaghey, George W. (politician)   July 1, 1856
Donahey, Vic; born Alvin Victor Donahey (politician)   July 7, 1873
Donahue, Elinor; born Mary Eleanor Donahue (actress)   April 19, 1937
Donahue, Phil; born Phillip John Donahue (TV host)   December 21, 1935
Donahue, Troy; born Merle Johnson, Jr. (actor)   January 27, 1937
Donaldson, Jesse Monroe (government)   August 17, 1885
Donaldson, Sam; born Samuel Andrew Donaldson (newscaster) March 11, 1934
Donat, Peter; born Pierre Collingwood Donat (actor)   January 20, 1928
Donat, Robert (actor)   March 18, 1905
Donlevy, Brian; born Grosson Brian Boru Donlevy (actor)   February 9, 1899
Donnell, Forrest C. (politician)   August 20, 1884
Donnell, Jeff; born Jean Marie Donnell (actress)   July 10, 1921
Donnelly, Phil Matthew (politician)   March 6, 1891
Donnelly, Ruth (actress)   May 17, 1896
Donohue, Mark Jr. (auto racing)   March 18, 1937
Donohue, Pete; born Peter Joseph Donohue (baseball)   November 5, 1900
Donovan, Art; born Arthur Donovan Jr. (football)   June 5, 1925
Donovan, Dick; born Richard Edward Donovan (baseball)   December 7, 1927
Dooley, Jim; born James Dooley (football)   February 8, 1930
Doolittle, Hilda "H. D." (poet)   September 10, 1886
Doolittle, James Harold (army air force officer)   December 14, 1896
Doran, Ann (actress)   July 28, 1913
Dorati, Antol (music)   April 9, 1906
Dorn, Philip; born Hein Van Der Niet (or Fritz van Dungen) September 30, 1901
    (actor)
Dors, Diana; born Diana Fluck (actress)   October 23, 1931
d'Orsay, Fifi; born Yvonne Lussier (actress)   April 16, 1904
Dorsett, Tony Drew (football)   April 7, 1954
Dorsey, Hugh Manson (politician)   July 10, 1871

Dorsey, Jimmy; born James Francis Dorsey (music)	February 29, 1904
Dorsey, Tommy; born Thomas Francis Dorsey (music)	November 19, 1905
Dos Passos, John Roderigo (author)	January 14, 1896
Dostoyevsky, Fyodor Mikhailovich (author)	November 11, 1821
Doubleday, Abner (inventor of baseball)	June 26, 1819
Doucet, Catharine; born Catharine Green (actress)	June 20, 1875
Doughty, Glenn Martin (football)	January 30, 1951
Douglas, Donna; born Doris Smith (actress)	September 26, 1939
Douglas, Helen Gahagan; born Helen Mary Gahagan (actress/singer/politician)	November 25, 1900
Douglas, Kirk; born Issur Danielovitch, changed to Isidore Demsky (actor/producer/actor)	December 9, 1916
Douglas, Melvyn; born Melvyn Edouard Hesselberg (actor)	April 5, 1901
Douglas, Michael (actor/producer)	September 25, 1944
Douglas, Mike; born Michael Delaney Dowd, Jr. (TV host/singer)	August 11, 1925
Douglas, Paul (actor)	April 11, 1907
Douglas, Paul Howard (politician)	March 28, 1892
Douglas, Stephen Arnold (politician)	April 23, 1813
Douglas, William Orville (jurist)	October 16, 1898
Douglass, Bobby; born Robert G. Douglass (football)	June 22, 1947
Douglass, Dale (golf)	March 5, 1936
Douthit, Taylor Lee (baseball)	April 22, 1901
Dove, Billie; born Lillian Bohny (actress)	May 14, 1900
Dowler, Boyd H. (football)	October 18, 1937
Dowling, Eddie; born Joseph Nelson Goucher (actor)	December 11, 1894
Down, Lesley-Anne (actress)	March 17, 1954
Downey, Morton (singer)	November 14, 1901
Downey, Sheridan (politician)	March 11, 1884
Downing, Al; born Alphonso Erwin Downing (baseball)	June 28, 1941
Downs, Hugh Malcolm (TV host)	February 14, 1921
Downs, Johnny (actor/singer)	October 10, 1913
Doyle, Sir Arthur Conan (author)	May 22, 1859
Doyle, David Fitzgerald (actor)	December 1, 1929
Drabowsky, Moe; born Myron Walter Drabowsky (baseball)	July 21, 1935
Dragon, Carmen (music)	July 28, 1914
Dragon, Daryl (music)	August 27, 1942
Dragonette, Jessica Valentina (singer)	February 14———
Drake, Alfred; born Alfredo Capurro (actor/singer)	October 7, 1914
Drake, Betsy (actress)	September 11, 1923
Drake, Charles; born Charles Ruppert (actor)	October 2, 1914
Drake, Frances; born Frances Dean (actress)	October 22, 1908
Drake, Sir Francis (navigator)	circa 1540
Drake, Tom; born Alfred Alderice (or Alderdeiss) (actor)	August 5, 1918
Draper, Eben Sumner (politician)	June 17, 1858
Dreier, Alex (newscaster/actor)	June 26, 1916
Dressen, Chuck; born Charles Walter Dressen (baseball)	September 20, 1898
Dresser, Louise; born Louise Kerlin (actress)	October 5, 1878
Dressler, Marie; born Leila Marie Von Koerber (actress)	November 9, 1868
Drew, Elizabeth Brenner; born Elizabeth Brenner (journalist)	November 16, 1935

Drew, Ellen; born Terry Parker (or Terry Ray) (actress)	November 23, 1915
Dreyfus, Rene (auto racing)	May 6, 1905
Dreyfuss, Richard Stephan (actor)	October 29, 1947
Drillon, Gordie; born Gordon Arthur Drillon (hockey)	October 23, 1914
Drinan, Robert Frederick (priest/politician)	November 15, 1920
Driscoll, Alfred Eastlack (politician)	October 25, 1902
Drivas, Robert Chris; born Robert Choromokos (actor)	October 7, 1938
Dropo, Walt; born Walter Dropo (baseball)	January 30, 1923
Dru, Joanne; born Joanne Letitia La Cock (actress)	January 31, 1923
Drury, Allen Stuart (author/journalist)	September 2, 1918
Drury, James (actor)	———1934
Dryden, John (poet)	August 9, 1631
Dryden, Ken; born Kenneth Wayne Dryden (hockey)	August 8, 1947
Dryer, Fred; born John Fred Dryer (football)	July 6, 1946
Drysdale, Cliff; born E. Clifford Drysdale (tennis)	May 26, 1941
Drysdale, Don; born Donald Scott Drysdale (baseball/sportscaster)	July 23, 1936
Dubbins, Don (actor)	June 28, 1929
Dubcek, Alexander (Czechoslovakian government)	November 27, 1921
Dubenion, Elbert (football)	February 16, 1933
Dubinsky, David; born David Dobniervski (labor leader)	February 22, 1892
Duchin, Eddy; born Edwin Frank Duchin (music)	April 1, 1909
Duchin, Peter Oelrichs (music)	July 28, 1937
Dudley, Bill; born William M. Dudley (football)	December 24, 1921
Dudley, Edward Bishop (golf)	February 10, 1902
Duff, Howard (actor)	November 24, 1917
Duff, James Henderson (politician)	January 21,1883
Duff, Richard (hockey)	February 18, 1936
Duffy, Hugh (baseball)	November 26, 1866
Duffy, Patrick Garfield (actor)	March 17, 1949
Dugan, Joe; born Joseph Anthony Dugan (baseball)	May 12, 1897
Duggan, Andrew (actor)	December 28, 1923
Dukakis, Michael Stanley (politician)	November 3, 1933
Duke, Patty; born Anna Maria Patricia Duke (actress)	December 14, 1946
Dukes, Walter (basketball)	June 23, 1930
Dullea, Keir (actor)	May 30, 1936
Dulles, Allen Welsh (government)	April 7, 1893
Dulles, John Foster (government)	February 25, 1888
Dumart, Woody; born Woodrow Wilson Clarence Dumart (hockey)	December 23, 1916
Dumas, Alexander (the Elder); born Davy De La Pailleterie (author)	July 24, 1802
Du Maurier, Daphne (writer)	May 13, 1907
Du Maurier, George Louis Palmella Busson (author/artist)	March 6, 1834
Dumbrille, Douglas (actor)	October 13, 1889
Dumont, Margaret; born Margaret Baker (actress)	October 20, 1889
Duna, Steffi; born Stephanie Berindey (dancer/actress)	February 8, 1913
Dunaway, Faye; born Dorothy Faye Dunaway (actress)	January 14, 1941
Dunbar, Dixie; born Christina Elizabeth Dunbar (actress)	January 19, 1919
Duncan, Dave; born David Edwin Duncan (baseball)	September 26, 1945
Duncan, Isadora (dancer)	May 27, 1877

Duncan, Mary (actress)	August 13, 1903
Duncan, Sandy; born Sandra Kay Duncan (actress/singer/ dancer)	February 20, 1946
Duncan, Speedy; born Leslie H. Duncan (football)	August 10, 1942
Dunn, Bryant Winfield Culberson (politician)	July 1, 1927
Dunn, James Howard (actor)	November 2, 1901
Dunn, Josephine; born Mary Josephine Dunn (actress)	May 1, 1906
Dunn, Michael; born Gary Neil Miller (actor)	October 20, 1934
Dunne, Edward Fitzsimons (politician)	October 12, 1853
Dunne, Irene Marie (actress/singer)	December 20, 1901
Dunnock, Mildred Dorothy (actress)	January 25, 1906
du Pont, Margaret Osborne; born Margaret Osborne (tennis)	March 4, 1918
du Pont, Pierre Samuel (industrialist)	January 15, 1870
du Pont, Pierre Samuel, IV (politician)	January 22, 1935
DuPree, Billy Joe (football)	March 7, 1950
Dupree, Minnie (actress)	January 19, 1873
Durant, Ariel; born Ariel Kaufman (philosopher/author)	May 10, 1898
Durant, Will; born William James Durant (philosopher/author)	November 5, 1885
Durante, Jimmy; born James Francis Durante (comedian/actor/singer)	February 10, 1893
Durbin, Deanna; born Edna Mae Durbin (actress)	December 4, 1921
Durbin, Winfield Taylor (politician)	May 4, 1847
Dürer, Albrecht (artist)	May 21, 1471
Durkin, John Anthony (politician)	March 29, 1936
Durnan, Bill; born William Ronald Durnan (hockey)	January 22, 1915
Durning, Charles (actor)	February 28, 1933
Durocher, Leo; born Leon Ernest Durocher (baseball)	July 27, 1906
Durr, Francois (tennis)	December 25, 1942
Durrell, Lawrence George (author)	February 27, 1912
Duryea, Dan; born Daniel Edwin Duryea (actor)	January 23, 1907
Dusay, Marj; born Marjorie E. Mahoney (actress)	February 20,————
Dusek, Brad; born John Bradley Dusek (football)	December 13, 1950
Dussault, Nancy Elizabeth (actress/singer/TV host)	June 30, 1936
Dutra, Olin (golf)	January 17, 1901
Dutton, Red; born Mervyn Dutton (hockey)	July 23, 1898
Duvall, Robert Selden (actor)	January 5, 1931
Duvall, Shelley (actress)	————1949
Dvorak, Ann; born Ann McKim (actress)	August 2, 1912
Dvorak, Antonin (music)	September 8, 1841
Dwinell, Lane (politician)	November 14, 1906
Dworshak, Henry Clarence (politician)	August 29, 1894
Dye, Babe; born Cecil Dye (hockey)	May 13, 1898
Dyer, Duffy; born Don Robert Dyer (baseball)	August 15, 1945
Dykes, Jimmy; born James Joseph Dykes (baseball)	November 10, 1896
Dylan, Bob; born Robert Allen Zimmerman (singer/music)	May 24, 1941

E

Eagles, Jeanne (actress)	June 26, 1890
Eagleton, Thomas Francis (politician)	September 4, 1929

Eakins, Thomas (artist)	July 25, 1844
Earhart, Amelia Mary (aviator)	July 24, 1897
Earle, George Howard, III (politician)	December 5, 1890
Early, Jake; born Jacob Willard Early (baseball)	May 19, 1917
Earnshaw, George Livingston (baseball)	February 15, 1900
Earp, Wyatt (frontier marshall & gunfighter)	March 19, 1848
Easterling, Ray; born Charles R. Easterling (football)	September 3, 1949
Eastland, James Oliver (politician)	November 28, 1904
Eastman, George (inventor/philanthropist)	July 12, 1854
Eastwood, Clint; born Clinton Eastwood, Jr.	May 31, 1930
(actor/director)	
Eaton, Shirley (actress)	————1936
Eban, Abba (Israeli government)	February 2, 1915
Ebb, Fred (music)	April 8, 1932
Eberhart, Adolph Olson (politician)	June 23, 1870
Eberly, Bob (singer)	July 24, 1915
Ebersole, John Joel (football)	November 5, 1948
Ebsen, Buddy; born Christian Rudolph Ebsen, Jr.	April 2, 1908
(actor/dancer)	
Eckstine, Billy; born William Clarence Eckstine (singer)	July 8, 1914
Economaki, Chris; born Christopher Constantine	October 15, 1920
Economaki (sportscaster/journalist)	
Ecton, Zales Nelson (politician)	April 1, 1898
Eddy; Duane (music)	April 26, 1938
Eddy; Mary Baker, born Mary Morse Baker (religious leader)	July 16, 1821
Eddy, Nelson (singer/actor)	June 29, 1901
Edelman, Herb; born Herbert Edelman (actor)	November 5, 1933
Eden, Sir Anthony; born Robert Anthony Eden	June 12, 1897
(British government)	
Eden, Barbara; born Barbara Moorhead (actress/singer)	August 23, 1934
Edge, Walter Evans (politician)	November 20, 1873
Edison, Thomas Alva (inventor)	February 11, 1847
Edmondson, James Howard (politician)	September 27, 1925
Edwards, Blake; born William Blake McEdwards (director)	July 26, 1922
Edwards, Dave; born David Edwards (football)	December 14, 1939
Edwards, Douglas (newscaster)	July 14, 1917
Edwards, Earl (football)	March 17, 1946
Edwards, Edward Irving (politician)	December 1, 1863
Edwards, Edwin Washington (politician)	August 7, 1927
Edwards, Glen (football)	July 31, 1947
Edwards, Hank; born Henry Albert Edwards (baseball)	January 29, 1919
Edwards, James Burrows (politician)	June 24, 1927
Edwards, Johnny; born John Alban Edwards (baseball)	June 10, 1938
Edwards, Penny; born Millicent Edwards (actress)	August 24, 1919
Edwards, Ralph Livingstone (TV host/producer)	June 13, 1913
Edwards, Turk; born Albert Glen Edwards (football)	September 28, 1907
Edwards, Vince; born Vincento Eduardo Zoino (actor)	July 7, 1928
Egan, John (basketball)	January 31, 1939
Egan, Pat; born Martin Joseph Egan (hockey)	April 25, 1918
Egan, Richard (actor)	July 29, 1921
Egan, William Allen (politician)	October 8, 1914

Eggar, Samantha; born Victoria Louise Samantha Marie Elizabeth Therese Eggar (actress)	March 5, 1939
Eglevsky, André Eugenovitch (dancer)	December 21, 1917
Ehman, Gerald Joseph (hockey)	November 3, 1932
Ehmke, Howard Jonathan (baseball)	April 24, 1894
Ehret, Gloria Jean (golf)	August 23, 1941
Ehringhaus, John Christoph Blucher (politician)	February 5, 1882
Ehrlich, Paul (bateriologist)	March 14, 1854
Ehrlichman, John Daniel (government)	March 20, 1925
Eichelberger, Dave; born Martin Davis Eichelberger, Jr. (golf)	September 3, 1943
Eichmann, Adolf; born Otto Adolf Eichmann (Nazi official)	March 19, 1906
Eilers, Sally; born Dorethea Sallye Eilers (actress)	December 11, 1908
Einstein, Albert (theoretical physicist)	March 14, 1879
Eischeid, Mike; born Michael D. Eischeid (football)	September 29, 1940
Eisele, Donn Fulton (astronaut)	June 23, 1930
Eisenhower, Dwight David; born David Dwight Eisenhower (President)	October 14, 1890
Eisenhower, John Sheldon Doud (First family)	August 3, 1922
Eisenhower, Mamie; born Mamie Geneva Doud (First Lady)	November 14, 1896
Eisenhower, Milton Stover (educator)	September 15, 1899
Ekberg, Anita (actress/singer)	September 29, 1931
Ekland, Britt (actress)	October 6, 1942
Elam, Cleveland (football)	April 5, 1952
Elam, Jack (actor)	November 13,1916
Elcar, Dana; born Ibson Dana Elcar (actor)	October 10, 1927
Elder, Lee; born Robert Lee Elder (golf)	July 14, 1934
Eldridge, Florence; born Florence McKechnie (actress)	September 5, 1901
Elg, Taina (actress/dancer)	March 9, 1931
Elgar, Sir Edward (music)	June 2, 1857
Elgart, Larry (music)	March 20, 1922
Elgart, Les (music)	August 3, 1918
El Greco; born Domenikos Theotokopoulos (artist)	————1541
Eliot, George; born Mary Ann (or Marian) Evans (author)	November 22, 1819
Eliot, T.S.; born Thomas Stearns Eliot (poet)	September 26, 1888
Elizabeth I, Queen of England	September 7, 1533
Elizabeth II, Queen of England; born Elizabeth Alexandra Mary	April 21, 1926
Elkin, Stanley Lawrence (author)	May 11, 1930
Elkins, Hillard (producer)	October 18, 1929
Ellender, Allen Joseph (politician)	September 24, 1891
Eller, Carl (football)	January 25, 1942
Elliman, Yvonne (singer/actress)	December 29, 1953
Ellington, Buford (politician)	June 27, 1907
Ellington, Duke; born Edward Kennedy Ellington (music)	April 29, 1899
Ellington, Mercer Kennedy (music)	March 11, 1919
Elliot, Cass ("Mama Cass") born Ellen Naomi Cohen (singer)	September 19, 1941
Elliott, Bob; born Robert B. Elliott (comedian)	March 26, 1923
Elliott, Bob; born Robert Irving Elliott (baseball)	November 26, 1916
Elliott, Denholm Mitchell (actor)	May 31, 1922
Elliott, Lenvil (football)	September 2, 1951

Elliott, Sam (actor)	————1944
Ellis, Dock Phillip (baseball)	March 11, 1945
Ellis, Jimmy (boxing)	February 24, 1940
Ellis, Leroy (basketball)	March 10, 1940
Ellis, Patricia; born Patricia Gene O'Brien (actress)	May 20, 1916
Ellis, Ronald John Edward (hockey)	January 8, 1945
Ellison, Ralph Waldo (author)	March 1, 1914
Ellison, Willie; born William H. Ellison (football)	November 1, 1945
Ellsberg, Daniel (government)	April 7, 1931
Ellsworth, Dick; born Richard Clark Ellsworth (baseball)	March 22, 1940
Elman, Mischa (music)	January 20, 1891
Elmendorf, Dave; born David C. Elmendorf (football)	June 20, 1949
Elrod, Samuel Harrison (politician)	May 1, 1856
Elsom, Isobel; born Isobel Reed (actress)	March 15, 1893
Elthon, Leo (politician)	June 9, 1898
Ely, Joseph Buell (politician)	February 22, 1881
Ely, Ron; born Ronald Pierce (actor)	June 21, 1938
Embry, Wayne Richard (basketball)	March 26, 1937
Emerson, Faye Margaret (actress)	July 8, 1917
Emerson, Lee Earl (politician)	December 19, 1898
Emerson, Ralph Waldo (writer/philosopher)	May 25, 1803
Emerson, Roy (tennis)	November 3, 1936
Emhardt, Robert (actor)	July 16, 1901
Emmerson, Louis Lincoln (politician)	December 27, 1863
Emms, Happy; born Leighton Emms (hockey)	January 16, 1905
Enberg, Dick (sportscaster)	January 9————
Enesco, Georges (music)	August 19, 1881
Engel, Georgia Bright (actress)	July 28, 1948
Engle, Clair (politician)	September 21, 1911
Englehorn, Shirley Ruth (golf)	December 12, 1940
Engles, Friedrich (socialist writer)	November 28, 1820
English, Woody; born Elwood George English (baseball)	March 2, 1907
Ennis, Del; born Delmer Ennis (baseball)	June 8, 1925
Ennis, Ethel (singer)	November 28, 1934
Entremont, Philippe (music)	June 7, 1934
Epstein, Mike; born Michael Peter Epstein (baseball)	April 4, 1943
Erasmus, Desiderius; born Gerhard Gerhards (scholar)	October 28, 1467
Erbe, Norman Arthur (politician)	October 25, 1919
Erdman, Richard (actor/director)	June 1, 1925
Erhard, Ludwig (German government)	February 4, 1897
Erickson, John Edward (politician)	March 14, 1863
Erickson, Keith (basketball/sportscaster)	April 19, 1944
Erickson, Leif; born William Wycliffe Anderson (actor)	October 27, 1911
Ericson, Devon (actress)	December 20————
Ericson, John; born Joseph Meibes (actor)	September 25, 1926
Ernst, Max (artist)	April 2, 1891
Ernst, Richard Pretlow (politician)	February 25, 1858
Errol, Leon (actor)	July 3, 1881
Erskine, Carl Daniel (baseball)	December 13, 1926
Ervin, Sam; born Samuel James Ervin, Jr. (politician)	September 27, 1896
Erving, Julius Winfield "Dr. J." (basketball)	February 22, 1950

Erwin, Stu; born Stuart Philip Erwin (actor)	February 14, 1903
Esmond, Carl (actor)	June 14, 1906
Esposito, Phil; born Philip Anthony Esposito (hockey)	February 20, 1942
Esposito, Tony; born Anthony James Esposito (hockey)	April 23, 1943
Essex, David; born David Albert Cook (singer/actor)	July 23, 1947
Estabella, Bobby; born Robert Estabella (baseball)	April 25, 1911
Estrada, Erik; born Enrique Estrada (actor)	March 16, 1949
Etchebarren, Andy; born Andrew Auguste Etchebarren (baseball)	June 20, 1943
Etten, Nick; born Nicholas Raymond Thomas Etten (baseball)	September 19, 1913
Etting, Ruth (singer)	November 23, 1897
Evans, Al; born Alfred Hubert Evans (baseball)	September 28, 1916
Evans, Bergen Baldwin (writer)	September 19, 1904
Evans, Chick; born Charles Evans, Jr. (golf)	July 18, 1890
Evans, Dale; born Frances Octavia Smith (actress)	October 31, 1912
Evans, Daniel Jackson (politician)	October 16, 1925
Evans, Darrell Wayne (baseball)	May 26, 1947
Evans, Dame Edith (actress)	February 8, 1888
Evans, Gene (actor)	July 11, 1922
Evans, Jack; born William John Evans (hockey)	April 21, 1928
Evans, Joan; born Joan Eunson (actress)	July 18, 1934
Evans, John Victor (politician)	January 18, 1925
Evans, Linda (actress)	November 18, 1942
Evans, Madge; born Margherita Evans (actress)	July 1, 1909
Evans, Maurice Herbert (actor)	June 3, 1901
Evans, Norm; born Norman Earl Evans (football)	September 28, 1942
Everett, Chad; born Raymond Lee Cramton (actor)	June 11, 1936
Everly, Don (singer—Everly Brothers)	February 1, 1937
Everly, Phil (singer—Everly Brothers)	January 19, 1939
Evers, Hoot; born Walter Arthur Evers (baseball)	February 8, 1921
Evers, Jason (actor)	January 2, 1927
Evert, Chris; born Christine Marie Evert (tennis)	December 21, 1954
Evigan, Greg; born Gregory Ralph Evigan (actor)	October 14, 1953
Ewbank, Weeb; born Wilbur Charles Ewbank (football)	May 6, 1907
Ewell, Tom; born Yewell Tompkins (actor)	April 29, 1909
Exon, John James (politician)	August 9, 1921
Eyck, Jan van (artist)	circa 1390
Ezinicki, William (hockey)	March 11, 1924

F

Fabares, Shelley; born Michele Marie Fabares (actress/singer)	January 19, 1944
Faber, Red; born Urban Clarence Faber (baseball)	September 6, 1888
Fabian; born Fabiano Anthony Forte (singer/actor)	February 6, 1940
Fabian, Francoise; born Michèle Cortès de Leone y Fabianera (actress)	May 10, 1935
Fabray, Nanette; born Ruby Bernadette Nanette Fabares (actress/singer)	October 27, 1920
Face, Roy; born Elroy Leon Face (baseball)	February 20, 1928
Factor, Max, Jr. (cosmetics)	August 18, 1904

Fadiman, Clifton Paul (literary critic) — May 15, 1904
Fahrenheit, Gabriel Daniel (physicist) — May 14, 1686
Fain, Ferris Roy (baseball) — March 29, 1921
Fain, Sammy; born Samuel Feinberg (music) — June 17, 1902
Fairbairn, Bruce (actor) — February 19, 1947
Fairbanks, Charles Warren (Vice President) — May 11, 1852
Fairbanks, Chuck; born Charles Leo Fairbanks (football) — June 10, 1933
Fairbanks, Douglas; born Julius Ullman (actor) — May 23, 1883
Fairbanks, Douglas Elton, Jr. (actor) — December 9, 1909
Fairchild, Barbara (singer/music) — November 12, 1950
Fairchild, Morgan; born Patsy Ann McClenny (actress) — February 3, 1950
Fairly, Ron; born Ronald Ray Fairly (baseball) — July 12, 1938
Faith, Adam; born Terence Neilhams (singer/actor) — June 23, 1940
Faith, Percy (music) — April 7, 1908
Falana, Lola (singer/actress) — September 11, 1943
Falk, Bibb August (baseball) — January 27, 1899
Falk, Peter Michael (actor) — September 16, 1927
Falkenburg, Jinx; born Eugenia Lincoln Falkenburg (actress) — January 21, 1919
Fall, Albert Bacon (politics/government) — November 26, 1861
Falla, Manuel de; born Manuel Maria de Falla y Matheu (music) — November 23, 1876
Fangio, Juan Manuel (auto racing) — June 24, 1911
Fannin, Paul Jones (politician) — January 29, 1907
Faraday, Michael (chemist/physicist) — September 22, 1791
Farentino, James (actor) — February 24, 1938
Fargo, Donna; born Yvonne Vaughan (singer/music) — November 10, 1949
Farina, Nino; born Giuseppe Farina (auto racing) — October 30, 1908
Farkas, Andy; born Andrew Farkas (football) — May 2, 1916
Farley, James Aloysius (government) — May 30, 1888
Farmer, George Thaxton (football) — April 19, 1948
Farmer, Frances (actress) — September 19, 1910
Farmer, Mike (basketball) — August 26, 1936
Farouk I (King of Egypt) — February 11, 1920
Farr, Derek (actor) — February 7, 1912
Farr, Felicia (actress) — October 4, 1932
Farr, Jamie; born Jameel Joseph Farah (actor) — July 1, 1934
Farr, Mel; born Melvin Farr (football) — November 3, 1944
Farr, Miller, Jr. (football) — April 8, 1943
Farragut, David Glasgow; born James Glasgow Farragut (naval officer) — July 5, 1801
Farrar, Frank Leroy (politician) — April 2, 1929
Farrell, Charles (actor) — August 9, 1901
Farrell, Dick; born Richard Joseph Farrell (baseball) — April 8, 1934
Farrell, Eileen (singer) — February 13, 1920
Farrell, Glenda (actress) — June 30, 1904
Farrell, James Thomas (author) — February 27, 1904
Farrell, Johnny; born John J. Farrell (golf) — April 1, 1901
Farrell, Mike (actor) — February 6, 1939
Farrell, Suzanne; born Roberta Sue Ficker (dancer) — August 16, 1945
Farrow, Mia; born Maria de Lourdes Villiers Farrow (actress) — February 9, 1945

Fasanella, Ralph (artist)	September 2, 1914
Fassbinder, Rainer Werner (director)	May 31, 1946
Fast, Howard Melvin (author)	November 11, 1914
Faubus, Orval Eugene (politician)	January 7, 1910
Faulk, Mary Lena (golf)	April 15, 1926
Faulkner, William Harrison; born William Harrison Falkner (author)	September 25, 1897
Fawcett-Majors, Farrah; born Mary Farrah Leni Fawcett (actress)	February 2, 1947
Fay, Frank; born Francis Anthony Fay (actor)	November 17, 1894
Faye, Alice; born Alice Jeanne Leppert (actress/singer)	May 5 ,1912
Faye, Joey; born Joseph Anthony Palladino (comedian/actor)	July 12, 1910
Fazenda, Louise (comedienne/actress)	July 17, 1889
Fears, Tom; born Thomas Jesse Fears (football)	December 3, 1923
Feiffer, Jules (cartoonist/writer)	January 26, 1929
Feininger, Lyonel Charles Adrian (artist)	July 17, 1871
Feinstein, Alan (actor)	September 8, 1941
Feinstein, Dianne; born Dianne Goldman (politician)	June 22, 1933
Feld, Fritz (actor)	October 15, 1900
Feldman, Marty (comedian/actor/director)	July 8, 1933
Feldon, Barbara; born Barbara Hall (actress)	March 12, 1939
Feldshuh, Tovah; born Terri Sue Feldshuh (actress)	December 27, 1951
Feliciano, José (singer/music)	September 10, 1945
Felix, Ray (basketball)	December 10, 1930
Felker, Clay S. (editor/publisher)	October 2, 1925
Felker, Samuel Demeritt (politician)	April 16, 1859
Fell, Norman (actor)	March 24, 1925
Feller, Bob; born Robert William Andrew Feller (baseball)	November 3, 1918
Fellini, Federico (director)	January 20, 1920
Fellows, Edith Marilyn (actress)	May 20, 1923
Felton, Verna (actress)	July 20, 1890
Fender, Freddy; born Baldemar G. Huerta (singer/music)	June 4, 1937
Fenneman, George (announcer)	November 10, 1919
Ferber, Edna (author)	August 15, 1887
Ferguson, Homer (politician)	February 25, 1889
Ferguson, James Edward (politician)	August 31, 1871
Ferguson, Joe; born Joseph Vance Ferguson (baseball)	September 19, 1946
Ferguson, Joe (football)	April 23, 1950
Ferguson, John Bowie (hockey)	September 5, 1938
Ferguson, Lorne Robert (hockey)	May 26, 1930
Ferguson, Maynard (music)	May 4, 1928
Ferguson, Miriam Amanda (politician)	June 13, 1875
Fermi, Enrico (physicist)	September 29, 1901
Fernald, Bert Manfred (politician)	April 3, 1858
Fernandel; born Fernand Joseph Désiré Contandin (actor)	May 8, 1903
Fernandez, Chico; born Humberto Fernandez (baseball)	March 3, 1932
Fernandez, Manny; born Manuel J. Fernandez (football)	July 3, 1946
Ferrari, Enzo (auto racing & manufacturer)	February 18, 1898
Ferraris, Jan; born Janis Jean Ferraris (golf)	June 2, 1947
Ferrell, Rick; born Richard Benjamin Ferrell (baseball)	October 12, 1905
Ferrell, Wes; born Wesley Cheek Ferrell (baseball)	February 2, 1908

Ferrer, José; born José Vincente Ferrer Otero y Cintron (actor/director)	January 8, 1909
Ferrer, Mel; born Melchior Gaston Ferrer (actor/director)	August 25, 1917
Ferrier, James (golf)	February 24, 1915
Ferrigno, Lou (body builder/actor)	November 9, 1951
Ferris, Barbara Gillian (actress)	October 3, 1940
Ferris, Woodridge Nathan (politician)	January 6, 1853
Ferry, Bob; born Robert Dean Ferry (basketball)	May 31, 1937
Fess, Simeon Davison (politician)	December 11, 1861
Fetchit, Stepin; born Lincoln Theodore Monroe Andrew Perry (actor)	May 30, 1892
Feuer, Cy; born Seymour Arnold Feuer (producer/director)	January 15, 1911
Fezler, Forrest (golf)	September 23, 1949
Fiedler, Arthur (music)	December 17, 1894
Fiedler, James Fairman (politician)	February 26, 1867
Field, Betty (actress)	February 8, 1918
Field, Eugene (poet/journalist)	September 2, 1850
Field, Sally Margaret (actress)	November 6, 1946
Field, Virginia; born Margaret Cynthia St. John Field (actress)	November 4, 1917
Fielding, Henry (author)	April 22, 1707
Fields, Dorothy (music)	July 15, 1905
Fields, Gracie; born Gracie Stansfield (comedienne/actress/singer)	January 9, 1898
Fields, Totie; born Sophie Feldman (comedienne)	May 7, 1930
Fields, W.C.; born William Claude Dukinfield (comedian/actor)	January 29, 1879
Fields, William Jason (politician)	December 29, 1874
Fillmore, Abigail Powers; born Abigail Powers (First Lady)	March 13, 1798
Fillmore, Millard (President)	January 7, 1800
Finch, Cliff; born Charles Clifton Finch (politician)	April 4, 1927
Finch, Peter; born William Peter Ingle-Finch (actor)	September 28, 1916
Finch, Robert Hutchinson (government)	October 9, 1925
Fine, John Sidney (politician)	April 10, 1893
Fingers, Rollie; born Roland Glen Fingers (baseball)	August 25, 1946
Finley, Charles Oscar (baseball)	February 22, 1918
Finney, Albert (actor)	May 9, 1936
Finney, Lou; born Louis Klopsche Finney (baseball)	August 13, 1910
Finnie, Roger (football)	November 6, 1945
Finnigan, Frank (hockey)	July 9, 1903
Finsterwald, Dow (golf)	September 6, 1929
Firestone, Eddie; born Edward William Firestone (actor)	December 11, 1920
Firkusny, Rudolph (music)	February 11, 1912
Fischer, Pat; born Patrick Fischer (football)	January 2, 1940
Fischer-Dieskau, Dietrich (singer)	May 28, 1925
Fisher, Carrie Frances (actress)	October 21, 1956
Fisher, Eddie; born Edwin Jack Fisher (singer)	August 10, 1928
Fisher, Eddie Gene (baseball)	July 16, 1936
Fisher, Gail Ann (actress)	August 18, 1935
Fisher, Jack; born John Howard Fisher (baseball)	March 4, 1939
Fisher, John Stuchell (politician)	May 25, 1867

Fisk, Carlton Ernest (baseball)	December 26, 1948
Fiske, Minnie Maddern; born Marie Augusta Davey (actress)	December 19, 1865
Fiss, Galen R. (football)	July 10, 1931
Fitch, John Cooper (auto racing)	August 4, 1917
Fittipaldi, Emerson (auto racing)	December 12, 1946
Fitzgerald, Barry; born William Joseph Shields (actor)	March 10, 1888
Fitzgerald, Ed; born Edward Raymond Fitzgerald (baseball)	May 21, 1924
Fitzgerald, Ella (singer)	April 25, 1918
Fitzgerald, Frank Dwight (politician)	January 27, 1885
Fitzgerald, F. Scott; born Francis Scott Key Fitzgerald (author)	September 24, 1896
Fitzgerald, Geraldine (actress)	November 24, 1912
Fitzsimmons, Freddie; born Frederick Landis Fitzsimmons (baseball)	July 28, 1901
Fix, Paul; born Paul Fix Morrison (actor)	March 13, 1902
Flack, Roberta (singer)	February 10, 1939
Flagg, Fannie; born Frances Carlton Flagg (comedienne/actress)	September 21, 1944
Flagstad, Kirsten Malfred (singer)	July 12, 1895
Flagstead, Ira James (baseball)	September 22, 1893
Flaherty, Pat; born George Francis Patrick Flaherty (auto racing)	January 6, 1926
Flaman, Fern; born Ferdinand Charles Flaman (hockey)	January 25, 1927
Flanagan, Ed; born Edward Flanagan (football)	February 23, 1944
Flanagan, Fionnula (or Fionnuala) Manon (actress)	December 10, 1941
Flanders, Ed; born Edward Paul Flanders (actor)	December 29, 1934
Flanders, Ralph Edward (politician)	September 28, 1880
Flannery, Susan (actress)	July 31, 1943
Flatt, Ernest Orville (dancer/choreographer)	October 30, 1918
Flatt, Lester Raymond (singer/music)	June 28, 1914
Flaubert, Gustave (author)	December 12, 1821
Flavin, Martin Archer (author/playwright)	November 2, 1883
Fleck; Jack (golf)	November 8, 1921
Fleckman, Marty; born Martin A. Fleckman (golf)	April 23, 1944
Fleming, Sir Alexander (bateriologist)	August 6, 1881
Fleming, Ian Lancaster (author)	May 28, 1908
Fleming, Les; born Leslie Harvey Fleming (baseball)	August 7, 1915
Fleming, Marv; born Marvin Fleming (football)	January 2, 1942
Fleming, Peggy Gale (ice skating)	July 27, 1948
Fleming, Reginald Stephen (hockey)	April 21, 1936
Fleming, Rhonda; born Marilyn Louis (actress)	August 10, 1922
Fleming, Susan (actress)	February 19, 1909
Flemming, Arthur Sherwood (government)	June 12, 1905
Flemming, Bill; born William Norman Flemming (sportscaster)	September 3, 1926
Flemyng, Robert; born Benjamin Arthur Flemyng (actor)	January 3, 1912
Fletcher, Allen Miller (politician)	September 25, 1853
Fletcher, Chris; born Christopher Fletcher (football)	December 25, 1948
Fletcher, Duncan Upshaw (politician)	January 6, 1859
Fletcher, Elbie; born Elburt Preston Fletcher (baseball)	March 18, 1916
Fletcher, Louise (actress)	July ———1934

Flick, Elmer Harrison (baseball)	January 11, 1876
Flippen, Jay C. (actor)	March 6, 1898
Flock, Fonty; born Truman Fontell Flock (auto racing)	March 21, 1921
Flock, Tim; born Julius Timothy Flock (auto racing)	May 11, 1924
Flockhart, Ron; born William Ronald Flockhart (auto racing)	June 16, 1923
Flood, Curt; born Curtis Charles Flood (baseball)	January 18, 1938
Floren, Myron (music)	November 5———
Flores, Tom; born Thomas R. Flores (football)	March 21, 1937
Floyd, Charles Miller (politician)	June 5, 1861
Floyd, Marlene (golf/sportscaster)	April 2, 1944
Floyd, Ray; born Raymond Floyd (golf)	September 4, 1942
Flynn, Errol Leslie (actor)	June 20, 1909
Flynn, Joe; born Joseph Anthony Flynn (actor)	November 8, 1924
Flynn, William Smith (politician)	August 14, 1885
Foch, Nina; born Nina Consuelo Maud Fock (actress)	April 20, 1924
Fodor, Eugene Nicholas (music)	March 5, 1950
Fogolin, Lee; born Lidlo John Fogolin (hockey)	February 27, 1926
Foiles, Hank; born Henry Lee Foiles (baseball)	June 10, 1929
Foley, Dave; born David Foley (football)	October 28, 1947
Foley, Red; born Clyde Julian Foley (singer)	June 17, 1910
Foley, Tim; born Thomas Foley (football)	January 22, 1948
Folk, Joseph Wingate (politician)	October 28, 1869
Folley, Zora (boxing)	May 27, 1932
Follmer, George (auto racing)	January 27, 1934
Folsom, James Elisha (politician)	October 9, 1908
Folsom, Marion Bayard (government)	November 23, 1893
Fonda, Henry Jaynes (actor)	May 16, 1905
Fonda, Jane Seymour (actress)	December 21, 1937
Fonda, Peter Henry (actor/producer/director)	February 23, 1939
Fondy, Dee Virgil (baseball)	October 31, 1924
Fong, Hiram Leong (politician)	October 1, 1907
Fong, Kam (actor)	May 27———
Fonseca, Lew; born Lewis Albert Fonseca (baseball)	January 21, 1899
Fontaine, Frank (comedian/actor/singer)	April 19, 1920
Fontaine, Joan; born Joan de Beauvoir De Havilland (actress)	October 22, 1917
Fontanne, Lynn; born Lillie Louise Fontanne (actress)	December 6, 1887
Fonteyn, Dame Margot; born Margaret Hookham (dancer)	May 18, 1919
Fonteyne, Valere Ronald (hockey)	December 2, 1933
Fontinato, Louis (hockey)	January 20, 1932
Foran, Dick; born John Nicholas Foran (actor)	June 18, 1910
Forbes, Brenda; born Brenda Forbes Taylor (actress)	January 14, 1909
Forbes, Malcolm Stevenson (publisher/sportsman)	August 19, 1919
Ford, Betty; born Elizabeth Bloomer (First Lady)	April 8, 1918
Ford, Constance (actress)	July 1, 1929
Ford, Doug; born Douglas Ford (golf)	August 6, 1922
Ford, Gerald Rudolph, Jr.; born Leslie King, Jr. (President)	July 14, 1913
Ford, Glenn; born Gwyllyn Samuel Newton Ford (actor)	May 1, 1916
Ford, Henry (auto manufacturer)	July 30, 1863
Ford, Henry, II (auto manufacturer)	September 4, 1917

Ford, Hod; born Horace Hills Ford (baseball)	July 23, 1897
Ford, Jack; born John Gardner Ford (First family)	March 16, 1952
Ford, John; born Sean O'Feeney (or O'Fearna) (director)	February 1, 1895
Ford, Len; born Leonard Ford (football)	February 18, 1926
Ford, Mary; born Irene Colleen Summers (singer)	July 7, 1924
Ford, Michael Gerald (First family)	March 14, 1950
Ford, Paul; born Paul Ford Weaver (actor)	November 2, 1901
Ford, Ruth Elizabeth (actress)	July 7, 1915
Ford, Samuel Clarence (politician)	November 7, 1882
Ford, Steve; born Steven Meigs Ford (First family)	May 19, 1956
Ford, Susan Elizabeth (First family)	July 6, 1957
Ford, Tennessee Ernie; born Ernest Jennings Ford (singer)	February 13, 1919
Ford, Wallace; born Samuel Jones (or Sam Grundy) (actor)	February 12, 1898
Ford, Wendell Hampton (politician)	September 8, 1924
Ford, Whitey; born Edward Charles Ford (baseball)	October 21, 1928
Foreman, Chuck; born Walter Eugene Foreman (football)	October 26, 1950
Foreman, George (boxing)	January 22, 1948
Foreman, Milos (director)	February 18, 1932
Forrest, Steve; born William Forrest Andrews (actor)	September 29, 1924
Forrestal, James Vincent (government)	February 15, 1892
Forster, Robert (actor)	July 13, 1941
Forsyth, Rosemary (actress)	July 6, 1944
Forsythe, John; born John Lincoln Freund (actor)	January 29, 1918
Fort, John Franklin (politician)	March 20, 1852
Fortmann, Danny; born Daniel John Fortmann (football)	April 11, 1916
Fortunato, Joe; born Joseph F. Fortunato (football)	March 28, 1931
Fosdick, Harry Emerson (clergyman)	May 24, 1878
Foss, Eugene Noble (politician)	September 24, 1858
Foss, Joe; born Joseph Jacob Foss (politician)	April 17, 1915
Fosse, Bob; born Robert Louis Fosse (director/choreographer/dancer/actor)	June 23, 1927
Fosse, Ray; born Raymond Earl Fosse (baseball)	April 4, 1947
Foster, Bob (boxing)	April 27, 1942
Foster, George Arthur (baseball)	December 1, 1948
Foster, Jodie (actress)	November 19, 1962
Foster, Meg (actress)	————1949
Foster, Murphy James (politician)	January 12, 1849
Foster, Phil; born with surname Feldman (comedian/actor)	March 29, 1914
Foster, Preston S. (actor)	August 24, 1901
Foster, Stephen Collins (music)	July 4, 1826
Foster, Susanna; born Suzanne DeLee Flanders Larson (actress)	December 6, 1924
Fortas, Abe (jurist)	June 19, 1910
Fothergil, Bob; born Robert Roy Fothergil (baseball)	August 16, 1897
Fountain, Pete; born Peter Dewey Fountain, Jr. (music)	July 3, 1930
Fournier, Jack; born Jacques Frank Fournier (baseball)	September 28, 1892
Foust, Larry (basketball)	June 24, 1928
Fouts, Dan; born Daniel Francis Fouts (football)	June 10, 1951
Fowler, Henry Hamill (government)	September 5, 1908
Fox, Jim (basketball)	April 7, 1943
Fox, Nellie; born Jacob Nelson Fox (baseball)	December 25, 1927

Fox, Pete; born Ervin Fox (baseball)	March 8, 1909
Fox, Virgil Keel (music)	May 3, 1912
Foxworth, Robert (actor)	November 1, 1941
Foxx, Jimmie; born James Emory Foxx (baseball)	October 22, 1907
Foxx, Redd; born John Elroy Sanford (comedian/actor)	December 9, 1922
Foy, Eddie, Sr.; born Edward Fitzgerald (actor)	March 9, 1854
Foy, Eddie, Jr.; born Edwin Fitzgerald Foy (actor)	February 4, 1905
Foyt, A.J.; born Anthony Joseph Foyt (auto racing)	January 16, 1935
Foytack, Paul Eugene (baseball)	November 16, 1930
Fra Angelico; born Guido Di Pietro, changed to Giovanni da Fiesole (artist)	———1387
Fracci, Carla (dancer)	August 20, 1936
Fragonard, Jean-Honoré (artist)	April 5, 1732
Frampton, Peter Kenneth (singer/music)	April 22, 1950
France, Anatole; born Jacques Anatole Francois Thibault (writer)	April 16, 1844
Francescatti, Zino; born René Francescatti (music)	August 9, 1905
Franciosa, Anthony; born Anthony George Papaleo (actor)	October 25, 1928
Francis, Anne (actress)	September 16, 1930
Francis, Arlene; born Arlene Francis Kazanjian (actress)	October 20, 1908
Francis, Connie; born Concetta Franconero (singer/actress)	December 12, 1938
Francis, Emile Percy (hockey)	September 13, 1926
Francis, Kay; born Katherine Edwina Gibbs (actress)	January 13, 1899
Francis, Russ; born Russell R. Francis (football)	April 3, 1953
Franciscus, James Grover (actor)	January 31, 1934
Franck, César Auguste (music)	December 10, 1822
Franco, Francisco; born Francisco Paulino Hermenegildo Teodulo Franco-Bahamonde (Spanish government)	December 4, 1892
Francona, Tito; born John Patsy Francona (baseball)	November 4, 1933
Frank, Larry S. (auto racing)	April 29, 1931
Frankenheimer, John Michael (director)	February 19, 1930
Frankfurter, Felix (jurist)	November 15, 1882
Frankhouse, Fred; born Frederick Meloy Frankhouse (baseball)	April 9, 1904
Franklin, Aretha (singer)	March 25, 1942
Franklin, Benjamin (statesman/philosopher/scientist)	January 17, 1806
Franklin, Bonnie Gail (actress/singer)	January 6, 1944
Franklin, Pamela (actress)	February 4, 1950
Frann, Mary (actress)	February 27———
Franz, Arthur (actor)	February 29, 1920
Franz, Eduard (actor)	October 31, 1902
Fraser, Neale Andrew (tennis)	October 3, 1933
Frawley, William (actor)	February 26, 1887
Frazee, Jane; born Mary Jane Frashe (or Freshe) (actress)	July 18, 1918
Frazer, Dan (actor)	November 20———
Frazier, Charles Douglas (football)	August 12, 1939
Frazier, James Beriah, Sr. (politician)	October 18, 1856
Frazier, Joe; born Joseph Frazier (boxing)	January 12, 1944
Frazier, Lynn Joseph (politician)	December 21, 1874
Frazier, Walt (basketball)	March 29, 1945
Frazier, Willie (football)	June 19, 1942
Frear, J. Allen, Jr.; born Joseph Allen Frear, Jr. (politician)	March 7, 1903

Freberg, Stan; born Stanley Victor Freberg (comedian)   August 7, 1926
Frederick, Johnny; born John Henry Frederick (baseball)   January 26, 1901
Frederick, Pauline; born Beatrice Pauline Libbey (actress)   August 12, 1883
Frederick, Pauline (journalist/newscaster/author)   February 13, 1908
Frederickson, Tucker; born Ivan Charles Frederickson   January 12, 1943
    (football)
Freed, Bert (actor)   November 3, 1919
Freehan, Bill; born William Ashley Freehan (baseball)   November 29, 1941
Freeman, Don (basketball)   July 18, 1944
Freeman, Mona; born Monica Elizabeth Freeman (actress)   June 9, 1926
Freeman, Orville Lothrop (politics/government)   May 9, 1918
Freese, Gene; born Eugene Lewis Freese (baseball)   January 8, 1934
Fregosi, Jim; born James Louis Fregosi (baseball)   April 4, 1942
Freitas, Rockne (football)   September 7, 1945
Frelinghuysen, Joseph Sherman (politician)   March 12, 1869
Frémont, John Charles (explorer/soldier/politician)   January 31, 1813
French, Larry; born Lawrence Herbert French (baseball)   November 1, 1907
French, Valerie; born Valerie Harrison (actress)   March 11, 1931
French, Victor (actor/director)   December 5, ————
Frere, Paul (auto racing)   January 30, 1917
Freud, Sigmund (psychiatry)   May 6, 1856
Frey, Leonard (actor)   September 4, 1938
Frey, Lonny; born Linus Reinhard Frey (baseball)   August 23, 1910
Friberg, Barney; born Augustaf Bernhardt Friberg   August 18, 1899
    (baseball)
Frick, Ford Christopher (baseball)   December 19, 1894
Friebus, Florida (actress)   October 10, 1909
Friedan, Betty; born Betty Naomi Goldstein (feminist)   February 4, 1921
Friedkin, William (director)   August 29, 1939
Friend, Bob ; born Robert Bartmess Friend (baseball)   November 24 1930
Friml, Rudolf; born Charles Rudolf Friml (music)   December 7, 1879
Frings, Ketti; born Katharine Hartley (playwright)   February 28, 1915
Frisch, Frankie; born Frank Francis Frisch (baseball)   September 9, 1898
Frisch, Max Rudolph (playwright/author)   May 15, 1911
Fröbe, Gert (actor)   February 25, 1913
Froman, Jane; born Ellen Jane Froman (singer)   November 10, 1907
Fromholtz, Dianne Lee (tennis)   August 10, 1956
Fromm, Erich (psychoanalyst)   March 23, 1900
Frost, David Paradine (TV host)   April 7, 1939
Frost, Robert Lee (poet)   March 26, 1875
Fry, Christopher; born Christopher Fry Harris   December 18, 1907
    (dramatist/poet)
Fry, Shirley J. (tennis)   June 30, 1927
Frye, David; born David Shapiro (impressionist)   ————1934
Fryman, Woodie; born Woodrow Thompson Fryman (baseball)   April 15, 1940
Fudge, Alan (actor)   February 27, 1944
Fuentes, Tito; born Rigoberto Peat Fuentes (baseball)   January 4, 1944
Fugett, Jean S., Jr. (football)   December 16, 1951
Fulbright, J. William; born James William Fulbright   April 9, 1905
    (politician)
Fulks, Joe; born Joseph Fulks (basketball)   October 26, 1921
Fuller, Alvin Tufts (politician)   February 27, 1878

Fuller, Frances (actress)	October 4, 1907
Fuller, Johnny; born John Fuller (football)	March 3, 1946
Fuller, Melville Weston (jurist)	February 11, 1833
Fuller, Penny (actress)	———1940
Fuller, R. Buckminster; born Richard Buckminster Fuller, Jr.	July 12, 1895
architect/engineer/educator/philosopher/author/poet)	
Fuller, Robert (actor)	July 29, 1934
Fullmer, Gene (boxing)	July 21, 1931
Fulton, Eileen; born Margaret Elizabeth McLarty (actress)	September 13, 1934
Fulton, Robert (inventor)	November 14, 1765
Funicello, Annette (actress)	October 22, 1942
Funseth, Rod (golf)	April 3, 1933
Funt, Allen (producer/TV host)	September 16, 1914
Fuqua, Henry Luce (politician)	November 8, 1865
Fuqua, John William (football)	September 12, 1946
Furcolo, Foster (politician)	July 29, 1911
Furgol, Ed; born Edward Furgol (golf)	March 22, 1917
Furillo, Carl Anthony (baseball)	March 8, 1922
Furness, Betty; born Elizabeth Mary Furness	January 3, 1916
(actress/consumer advocate)	
Furth, George (actor)	December 14, 1932
Futrell, Junius Marion (politician)	August 14, 1872

G

Gabel, Martin (actor)	June 19, 1912
Gabin, Jean; born Alexis Moncourge (actor)	May 17, 1904
Gable, Clark; born William Clark Gable (actor)	February 1, 1901
Gabor, Eva (actress)	February 11, 1921
Gabor, Jolie born Jancsi Tilleman (actress/mother)	September 29, 1896
Gabor, Magda (actress)	July 10, 1917
Gabor, Zsa Zsa; born Sari Gabor (actress)	February 6, 1919
Gabriel, Roman (football)	August 5, 1940
Gabrielson, Len; born Leonard Gary Gabrielson (baseball)	February 14, 1940
Gadsby, Bill; born William Alexander Gadsby (hockey)	August 8, 1927
Gage, Jack Robert (politician)	January 13, 1899
Gagliano, Phil; born Philip Joseph Gagliano (baseball)	December 27, 1941
Gagon, John (hockey)	June 8, 1905
Gain, Bob; born Robert Gain (football)	June 21, 1929
Gainsborough, Thomas (artist)	May 14, 1727
Galan, Augie; born August John Galan (baseball)	May 25, 1912
Galbraith, John Kenneth (economist)	October 15, 1908
Gale, Zona (playwright/author)	August 26, 1874
Galehouse, Denny; born Dennis Ward Galehouse (baseball)	December 7, 1911
Galilei, Galileo (physicist/astronomer)	February 14, 1564
Galimore, Willie Lee (football)	March 30, 1935
Gallagher, Helen (actress/dancer/singer)	July 19, 1926
Gallatin, Harry (basketball)	April 26, 1928
Gallico, Paul William (author/journalist)	July 26, 1897
Galloway, Chick; born Clarence Edward Galloway (baseball)	August 4, 1896
Galloway, Don (actor)	July 27, 1937

Gallup, George Horace (pollster) — November 18, 1901
Galsworthy, John (author) — August 14, 1867
Gam, Rita; born Rita Eleanore MacKay (actress) — April 2, 1928
Gama, Vasco da (explorer) — circa 1460
Gambee, Dave (basketball) — April 16, 1937
Gamble, Bruce George (hockey) — May 24, 1938
Gamble, Oscar Charles (baseball) — December 20, 1949
Gamble, Robert Jackson (politician) — February 7, 1851
Gandhi, Indira; born Indira Priyadarshini Nehru (Indian government) — November 19, 1917
Gandhi, Mahatma; born Mohandas Karamchand Gandhi (Hindu leader) — October 2, 1869
Ganley, Howden; born James Howden Ganley (auto racing) — December 24, 1941
Gann, Ernest Kellogg (author) — October 13, 1910
Gant, Reuben Charles (football) — April 12, 1952
Garagiola, Joe; born Joseph Henry Garagiola (baseball/sportscaster) — February 12, 1926
Garbo, Greta; born Greta Lovisa Gustafsson (actress) — September 18, 1905
Garcia, Mike; born Edward Miguel Garcia (baseball) — November 17, 1923
Gardenia, Vincent; born Vincenzio Scognamiglio (actor) — January 7, 1922
Gardiner, Chuck; born Charles Robert Gardiner (hockey) — December 31, 1904
Gardiner, Reginald; born William Reginald Gardiner (actor) — February 27, 1903
Gardiner, William Tudor (politician) — June 12, 1892
Gardner, Ava Lavinnia; born Lucy Johnson (actress) — December 24, 1922
Gardner, Billy; born William Frederick Gardner (baseball) — July 19, 1927
Gardner, Calvin Pearly (hockey) — October 30, 1924
Gardner, Erle Stanley (author) — July 17, 1889
Gardner, Frank (auto racing) — October 1, 1932
Gardner, Frederick Dozier (politician) — November 6, 1869
Gardner, Hy (journalist) — December 2, 1904
Gardner, John William (government) — October 8, 1912
Gardner, Oliver Max (politician) — March 22, 1882
Garfield, Allen; born Allen Goorwitz (actor) — November 22, 1939
Garfield, James Abram (President) — November 19, 1831
Garfield, John; born Julius Garfinkle (actor) — March 4, 1913
Garfield, Lucretia Rudolph; born Lucretia Rudolph (First Lady) — April 19, 1832
Garfunkel, Art; born Arthur Garfunkel (singer/actor) — October 13, 1941
Gargan, William Dennis (actor) — July 17, 1905
Garibaldi, Giuseppe (Italian patriot) — July 4, 1807
Garland, Beverly Lucy; born Beverly Lucy Fessenden (actress) — October 17, 1926
Garland, Judy; born Frances Ethel Milne Gumm (actress/singer) — June 10, 1922
Garlington, John (football) — June 5, 1946
Garmaker, Dick (basketball) — October 29, 1932
Garn, Jake; born Edwin Jacob Garn (politician) — October 12, 1932
Garner, Erroll Louis (music) — June 15, 1921
Garner, James; born James Scott Baumgarner (actor) — April 7, 1928
Garner, John Nance (Vice President) — November 22, 1868

Garner, Peggy Ann (actress)	February 3, 1932
Garns, Debs C. (baseball)	June 26, 1908
Garr, Ralph Allen (baseball)	December 12, 1945
Garrahy, John Joseph (politician)	November 26, 1930
Garrett, Betty (actress/singer/dancer)	May 23, 1919
Garrett, Carl (football)	August 31, 1947
Garrett, Kelly (singer/actress)	March 25, 1948
Garrett, Leif (singer/actor)	November 8, 1961
Garrett, Mike; born Michael Lockett Garrett (football)	April 12, 1944
Garrett, Wayne; born Ronald Wayne Garrett (baseball)	December 3, 1947
Garrison, Gary Lynn (football)	January 21, 1944
Garrison, Lindley Miller (government)	November 28, 1864
Garrison, Sean (actor)	October 19, 1937
Garrison, Walt; born Walter Benton Garrison (football)	July 3, 1944
Garrison, William Lloyd (abolitionist/reformer)	December 10, 1805
Garron, Larry; born Lawrence Garron, Jr. (football)	May 23, 1937
Garroway, Dave; born David Cunningham Garroway (TV host)	July 13, 1913
Garson, Greer (actress)	September 29, 1908
Garver, Kathy; born Kathleen Marie Garver (actress)	December 13, 1947
Garver, Ned Franklin (baseball)	December 25, 1925
Garvey, Dan E. (politician)	June 19, 1886
Garvey, Steve; born Steven Patrick Garvey (baseball)	December 22, 1948
Garvin, Lucius Fayette Clark (politician)	November 13, 1841
Gary, John; born John Gary Strader (singer)	November 29, 1932
Gary, Raymond Daniel (politician)	January 21, 1908
Gassman, Vittorio (actor)	September 1, 1922
Gaston, Clarence Edwin (baseball)	March 17, 1944
Gaston, Milt; born Nathaniel Gaston (baseball)	January 27, 1896
Gates, Charles Winslow (politician)	January 12, 1856
Gates, Larry; born Lawrence Wheaton Gates (actor)	September 24, 1915
Gates, Ralph Felser (politician)	February 24, 1893
Gates, Thomas Sovereign, Jr. (government)	April 10, 1906
Gateson, Marjorie Augusta (actress)	January 17, 1891
Gatlin, Larry Wayne (singer/music)	May 2, 1948
Gauguin, Paul; born Eugène Henri Paul Gauguin (artist)	June 7, 1848
Gauthier, Jean Phillipe (hockey)	April 29, 1937
Gautier, Dick (actor/singer)	October 30, 1931
Gavin, John; born John Anthony Golenor (actor)	April 8, 1928
Gaye, Marvin (singer/music)	April 2, 1939
Gayle, Crystal; born Brenda Gail Webb (singer)	January 9, 1951
Gaynor, Janet; born Laura Gainor (actress)	October 6, 1906
Gaynor, Mitzi; born Francesca Mitzi Marlene de Charney von Gerber (dancer/singer/actress)	September 4, 1930
Gazzara, Ben; born Biago Anthony Gazzara (actor)	August 28, 1930
Gazzo, Michael V.; born Michael Vincente Gazzo (actor/director/playwright)	April 5, 1923
Gee, George (hockey)	June 28, 1922
Geer, Ellen Ware (actress)	August 29, 1941
Geer, Will; born William Aughe Ghere (actor)	March 9, 1902
Geeson, Judy Amanda (actress)	September 10, 1948
Gehrig, Lou; born Henry Louis Gehrig (baseball)	June 19, 1903

Gehringer, Charlie; born Charles Leonard Gehringer (baseball)	May, 11, 1903
Geiberger, Al; born Allen L. Geiberger (golf)	September 1, 1937
Geiger, Gary Merle (baseball)	April 4, 1937
Gelbert, Charley; born Charles Magnus Gelbert (baseball)	January 26, 1906
Gendebien, Olivier (auto racing)	January 12, 1924
Gendron, Smitty; born Jean Guy Gendron (hockey)	August 30, 1934
Genet, Jean (playwright)	December 19, 1910
Genevieve; born Ginette Marguerite Auger (entertainer)	April 17, 1930
Genewich, Joe; born Joseph Edward Genewich (baseball)	January 15, 1897
Genn, Leo (actor)	August 9, 1905
Gennaro, Peter (dancer/choreographer)	————1924
Gentile, Jim; born James Edward Gentile (baseball)	June 3, 1934
Gentry, Bobbie; born Roberta Streeter (singer)	July 27, 1944
Geoffrion, Boom-Boom; born Bernard Geoffrion (hockey)	February 14, 1931
George, Anthony (actor)	January 29,————
George, Bill; born William George (football)	October 27, 1930
George, Chief Dan; born Geswanouth Slaholt (actor)	June 24, 1899
George, Christopher (actor)	————1929
George, Gladys; born Gladys Clare (actress)	September 13, 1900
George, Jack (basketball)	November 13, 1928
George, Lynda Day; born Lynda Day (actress)	December 11, 1946
George, Phyllis Ann (Miss America/sportscaster/TV host)	June 25, 1949
George, Susan (actress)	July 26, 1950
George, Walter Franklin (politician)	January 29, 1878
Gerber, Wally; born Walter Gerber (baseball)	August 18, 1891
Gerela, Roy (football)	April 2, 1948
Gericault, Jean Louis André Théodore (artist)	September 26, 1791
Gernert, Dick; born Richard Edward Gernert (baseball)	September 28, 1928
Gernreich, Rudi (fashion designer)	August 8, 1922
Geronimo; born Goyathlay (Indian chief)	circa 1829
Geronimo, Cesar Francisco (baseball)	March 11, 1948
Gerry, Elbridge (Vice President)	July 17, 1749
Gerry, Peter Goelet (politician)	September 18, 1879
Gersbach, Carl (football)	January 8, 1947
Gershwin, George; born Jacob Gershvin (music)	September 26, 1898
Gershwin, Ira; born Israel Gershvin (music)	December 6, 1896
Gerulaitis, Vitas Kevin (tennis)	July 26, 1954
Gervin, George (basketball)	April 27, 1952
Gethin, Peter Kenneth (auto racing)	February 21, 1940
Getliffe, Raymond (hockey)	April 3, 1914
Getty, J. Paul; born Jean Paul Getty (oil magnate)	December 15, 1892
Getz, Stan; born Stanley Getz (music)	February 2, 1927
Ghezzi, Victor (golf)	October 19, 1912
Ghostley, Alice Margaret (actress)	August 14, 1926
Giacomin, Ed; born Edward Giacomin (hockey)	June 6, 1939
Giardello, Joey; born Carmine Orlando Tilelli (boxing)	July 16, 1930
Gibbon, Edward (historian)	April 27, 1737
Gibbs, Georgia; born Fredda Lipson (actress)	August 26, 1926
Gibron, Abe; born Abraham Gibron (football)	September 22, 1925
Gibson, Althea (tennis/golf)	August 25, 1927

Gibson, Bob; born Robert Gibson (baseball/sportscaster)	November 9, 1931
Gibson, Don (singer/music)	April 3, 1928
Gibson, Ernest Willard (politician)	December 29, 1872
Gibson, Ernest William (politician)	March 6, 1901
Gibson, Henry; born Henry Bateman (comedian/actor/poet)	September 21, 1935
Gibson, Hoot; born Edmund Richard Gibson (actor)	August 6, 1892
Gibson ,Wynne; born Winifred Gibson (actress)	July 3, 1899
Gide, André (author)	November 22, 1869
Gielgud, Sir John; born Arthur John Gielgud (actor)	April 14, 1904
Gifford, Frances; born Mary Frances Gifford (actress)	December 7, 1920
Gifford, Frank; born Francis Newton Gifford (football/sportscaster/actor)	August 16, 1930
Giftos, Elaine (actress)	January 24, 1945
Gilbert, Gibby; born C.L. Gilbert (golf)	January 14, 1941
Gilbert, John; born John Pringle (actor)	July 10, 1895
Gilbert, Melissa (actress)	May 8, 1964
Gilbert, Rod; born Rodrigue Gilbert (hockey)	July 1, 1941
Gilbert, Sir William Schwenck (dramatist)	November 18, 1836
Gilberto, Astrud (singer)	————1940
Gilchrist, Albert Walker (politician)	January 15, 1858
Gilchrist, Connie; born Rose Gilchrist (actress)	February 2, 1901
Gilchrist, Cookie; born Carlton Chester Gilchrist (football)	May 25, 1935
Gilder, Bob; born Robert Gilder (golf)	December 31, 1950
Giles, Warren Crandall (baseball)	May 28, 1896
Gilford, Jack; born Jacob Gellman (actor)	July 25, 1907
Gillespie, Dizzy; born John Birks Gillespie (music)	October 21, 1917
Gillett, Frederick Huntington (politician)	October 16, 1851
Gillett, James Norris (politician)	September 20, 1860
Gillette, Anita; born Anite Lee Luebben (actress)	August 16, 1936
Gillette, Guy Mark (politician)	February 3, 1879
Gillette, Walker (football)	March 16, 1947
Gilliam, Herman (basketball)	May 5, 1946
Gilliam, Jim "Junior"; born James William Gilliam (baseball)	October 17, 1928
Gilliam, John Rally (football)	August 7, 1945
Gilligan, John Joyce (politician)	March 22, 1921
Gillingham, Gale (football)	February 3, 1944
Gillis, Anne; born Alma Mabel O'Connor (actress)	February 12, 1927
Gillman, Sid; born Sidney Gillman (football)	October 26, 1911
Gillmore, Margalo (actress)	May 31, 1897
Gilmer, Harry (football)	April 14, 1926
Gilmore, Artis (basketball)	September 21, 1949
Gilmore, Virginia; born Virginia Sherman Poole (actress)	July 26, 1919
Gilroy, Frank Daniel (playwright)	October 13, 1925
Gimbel, Bernard Feustman (merchant)	April 10, 1885
Ging, Jack L. (actor)	November 30————
Gingold, Hermione Ferdinanda (actress/singer)	December 9, 1897
Ginn, Hubert (football)	January 4, 1947
Ginsberg, Allen (poet)	June 3, 1926
Ginsberg, Joe; born Myron Nathan Ginsberg (baseball)	October 11, 1926

Ginther, Richie; born Paul Richard Ginther (auto racing)   August 5, 1930
Giotto; born Giotto Di Bondone (artist)   circa 1266
Giovanni, Nikki; born Yolande Cornelia Giovanni, Jr.   June 7, 1943
    (poet)
Gish, Dorothy; born Dorothy Elizabeth de Guiche (actress)   March 11, 1898
Gish, Lillian Diana; born Lillian Diana de Guiche (actress)   October 14, 1896
Giusti, Dave; born David John Giusti, Jr. (baseball)   November 27, 1939
Givenchy, Hubert James Taffin de (fashion designer)   February 21, 1927
Gladstone, William Ewart (statesman/author)   December 29, 1809
Glaser, Paul Michael; born Paul Manfred Glaser (actor)   March 25, 1943
Glasgow, Ellen Anderson Gholson (author)   April 22, 1874
Glaspell, Susan (playwright/author)   July 1, 1882
Glass, Bill; born William S. Glass (football)   August 16, 1935
Glass, Carter (politics/government)   January 4, 1858
Glasscock, William Ellsworth (politician)   December 13, 1862
Gleason, Jackie; born Herbert John Clarence Gleason   February 26, 1916
    (comedian/actor/music)
Gleason, James (actor)   May 23, 1886
Glenn, John Herschel, Jr. (astronaut/politician)   July 18, 1921
Glenn, Robert Brodnax (politician)   August 11, 1854
Gless, Sharon (actress)   May 31———
Glick, Fred; born Frederick C. Glick (football)   February 25, 1937
Glieber, Frank John (sportscaster)   April 5, 1934
Glotzbach, Charlie (auto racing)   June 19, 1938
Gluck, Christoph Willibald (music)   July 2, 1714
Glynn, Martin Henry (politician)   September 27, 1871
Goalby, Bob; born Robert George Goalby (golf/sportscaster)   March 14, 1929
Gobel, George Leslie (comedian/actor)   May 20, 1919
Godard, Jean Luc (director)   December 3, 1930
Goddard, Paulette; born Pauline Marion Levee (actress)   June 3, 1911
Goddard, Samuel Pearson, Jr. (politician)   August 8, 1919
Godfrey, Arthur Michael (entertainer)   August 31, 1903
Godfrey, Rocky; born Warren Edward Godfrey (hockey)   March 23, 1931
Godwin, Mills, Edwin, Jr. (politician)   November 19, 1914
Goegan, Peter John (hockey)   March 6, 1934
Goethe, Johann Wolfgang von (writer)   August 28, 1749
Goff, Nathan (politician)   February 9, 1843
Gogh, Vincent van (artist)   March 30, 1853
Gogolak, Charley; born Charles Gogolak (football)   December 29, 1944
Gogolak, Pete; born Peter Gogolak (football)   April 18, 1942
Gola, Tom; born Thomas Joseph Gola (basketball)   January 13, 1933
Golan, Gila, previous adopted name Miriam Goldenburg   ———1940
    (actress)
Goldberg, Arthur Joseph (government/jurist)   August 8, 1908
Golden, Harry; born Harry Goldhurst (author)   May 6, 1902
Goldham, Bob; born Robert John Goldham (hockey)   May 12, 1922
Goldoni, Carlo (playwright)   February 25, 1707
Goldsboro, Bobby (singer/music)   January 18, 1941
Goldsborough, Phillips Lee (politician)   August 6, 1865
Goldsmith, Oliver (writer)   November 10, 1728
Goldsmith, Paul (auto racing)   October 2, 1927

Goldsworthy, Bill "Goldy"; born William Alfred Goldsworthy (hockey)	August 24, 1944
Goldsworthy, Leroy D. (hockey)	October 18, 1908
Goldwater, Barry Morris (politician)	January 1, 1909
Goldwyn, Samuel; born Samuel Goldfish (producer)	August 27, 1882
Golonka, Arlene Leanore (actress)	January 23, 1936
Gombell, Minna (actress)	May 28, 1892
Gomez, Lefty; born Vernon Louis Gomez (baseball)	November 26, 1908
Gomez, Ruben Colon (baseball)	July 13, 1927
Gomez, Thomas; born Sabino Tomas Gomez, Jr. (actor)	July 10, 1905
Gompers, Samuel (labor leader)	January 27, 1850
Gonsoulin, Austin (football)	June 7, 1938
Gonzales, Pancho; born Richard Alonzo Gonzales (tennis)	May 9, 1928
Gonzalez, Mike; born Miguel Angel Cordero Gonzalez (baseball)	September 24, 1890
Gonzalez, Tony; born Andres Antonio Gonzalez (baseball)	August 28, 1936
Gooch, Johnny; born John Beverly Gooch (baseball)	November 9, 1897
Goodell, Charles Ellsworth, Jr. (politician)	March 16, 1926
Goodfellow, Ebbie; born Ebenezer Ralston Goodfellow (hockey)	April 9, 1907
Goodfriend, Lynda (actress)	October 31, 1950
Gooding, Frank Robert (politician)	September 16, 1859
Goodland, Walter Samuel (politician)	December 22, 1862
Goodman, Benny; born Benjamin David Goodman (music)	May 30, 1909
Goodman, Billy; born William Dale Goodman (baseball)	March 22, 1926
Goodman, Dody; born Dolores Goodman (comedienne/actress)	October 28, 1929
Goodman, Ival Richard (baseball)	July 23, 1908
Goodrich, Gail (basketball)	April 23, 1943
Goodrich, James Putnam (politician)	February 18, 1864
Goodson, Mark (producer)	January 24, 1915
Goolagong, Evonne Fay (tennis)	July 31, 1951
Gorcey, Leo Bernard (actor)	June 3, 1915
Gordon, Cecil Owen (auto racing)	June 20, 1941
Gordon, Gale; born Charles T. Aldrich, Jr. (actor)	February 2, 1906
Gordon, Joe; born Joseph Lowell Gordon (baseball)	February 18, 1915
Gordon, Max; born Mechel Salpeter (producer)	June 28, 1892
Gordon, Richard Francis, Jr. (astronaut)	October 5, 1929
Gordon, Ruth; born Ruth Gordon Jones (actress)	October 30, 1896
Gordon, Sid; born Sidney Gordon (baseball)	August 13, 1917
Gordone, Charles (playwright)	October 12, 1925
Gore, Albert Arnold (politician)	December 26, 1907
Gore, Howard Mason (politics/government)	October 12, 1887
Gore, Lesley (singer) .	May 2, 1946
Gore, Thomas Pryor (politician)	December 10, 1870
Gorki (or Gorky), Maxim (or Maksim); born Alexei (or Aleksei) Maximovitch (or Maksimovich) Petrov (or Peshkov) (playwright)	March 14, 1868
Gorman, Cliff (actor)	October 13, 1936
Gorman, Tom; born Thomas Warner Gorman (tennis)	January 19, 1946
Gormé, Eydie (singer)	August 16, 1931
Gorshin, Frank John (impressionist/actor)	April 5, 1934
Gortner, Marjoe; born Hugh Marjoe Ross Gortner (actor)	January 14, 1944

Gosger, Jim; born James Charles Gosger (baseball)	November 6, 1942
Goslin, Goose; born Leon Allen Goslin (baseball)	October 16, 1900
Gossett, Bruce; born Daniel Bruce Gossett (football)	November 9, 1941
Gossett, Lou; born Louis Gossett, Jr. (actor)	May 27, 1936
Gottfried, Brian Edward (tennis)	January 27, 1952
Gottselig, Johnny; born John P. Gottselig (hockey)	June 25, 1906
Goudal, Jetta (actress)	July 18, 1898
Gould, Chester (cartoonist)	November 20, 1900
Gould, Elliot; born Elliott Goldstein (actor)	August 29, 1938
Gould, Glenn Herbert (music)	September 25, 1932
Gould, Harold (actor)	December 10, 1923
Gould, Morton (music)	December 10, 1913
Goulding, Ray; born Raymond Walter Goulding (comedian)	March 20, 1922
Goulet, Robert Gerard (singer/actor)	November 26, 1933
Gounod, Charles Francois (music)	June 17, 1818
Gowdy, Curt; born Curtis Gowdy (sportscaster)	July 31, 1919
Goya y Lucientes, Francisco José de (artist)	March 30, 1746
Goyette, Phil; born Philippe Goyette (hockey)	October 31, 1933
Grable, Betty; born Elizabeth Ruth Grasle (actress)	December 18, 1913
Grabowski, Jim; born James S. Grabowski (football)	September 9, 1944
Grabowski, Joe (basketball)	January 15, 1930
Gracie, Robert J. (hockey)	November 8, 1911
Gradishar, Randy Charles (football)	March 3, 1952
Grady, Don (actor/singer/music)	June 8, 1944
Graham, Billy; born William Franklin Graham (evangelist)	November 7, 1918
Graham, David Anthony (golf)	May 23, 1946
Graham, Fred Patterson (newscaster/author/attorney)	October 6, 1931
Graham, Horace French (politician)	February 7, 1862
Graham, Lou (golf)	January 7, 1938
Graham, Martha (dancer/choreographer)	May 11, 1894
Graham, Otto Everett (football)	July 6, 1925
Graham, Ronny (actor/singer/music)	August 26, 1919
Graham, Sheilah; born Lily Sheil (writer)	September————1908
Graham, Virginia; born Virginia Komiss (TV host/actress)	July 4, 1912
Grahame, Gloria; born Gloria Grahame Hallward (actress)	November 28, 1924
Grammas, Alex; born Alexander Peter Grammas (baseball)	April 3, 1927
Granatelli, Andy; born Antonio Granatelli (auto racing)	March 18, 1923
Grange, Red; born Harold E. Grange (football)	June 13, 1903
Granger, Farley Earle, II (actor)	July 1, 1925
Granger, Stewart, born James Lablache Stewart (actor)	May 6, 1913
Grant, Bud; born Harry Peter Grant (football)	May 20, 1927
Grant, Cary; born Archibald Alexander Leach (actor)	January 18, 1904
Grant, Danny; born Daniel Frederick Grant (hockey)	February 21, 1946
Grant, Frank (football)	February 15, 1950
Grant, Gogi; born Audrey Brown (singer)	September 20, 1924
Grant, Julia Boggs Dent; born Julia Boggs Dent (First Lady)	January 26, 1826
Grant, Kirby; born Kirby Grant Hoon, Jr. (actor)	November 24, 1911
Grant, Lee; born Lyova Haskell Rosenthal (actress)	October 31, 1929
Grant, Mudcat; born James Timothy Grant (baseball)	August 13, 1935
Grant, Ulysses Simpson; born Hiram Ulysses Grant (President)	April 27, 1822

Grantham, George Farley (baseball)	May 20, 1900
Grantham, Larry; born James Larry Grantham (football)	September 16, 1938
Granville, Bonita (actress/producer)	February 2, 1923
Grass, Günter Wilhelm (author)	October 16, 1927
Grassle, Karen Gene (actress)	February 25———
Grasso, Ella Tambussi (politician)	May 10, 1919
Grau, Shirley Ann (author)	July 8, 1929
Grauer, Ben; born Bennett Franklin Grauer (radio & TV announcer)	June 2, 1908
Gravel, Mike; born Maurice Robert Gravel (politician)	May 13, 1930
Graves, David Bibb (politician)	April 1, 1873
Graves, Peter; born Peter Aurness (actor/director)	March 18, 1926
Graves, Teresa (actress)	January 10, 1938
Gray, Billy; born William Thomas Gray (actor)	January 13, 1938
Gray, Coleen; born Doris Jensen (actress/singer)	October 23, 1922
Gray Dolores (actress/singer)	June 7, 1924
Gray, Harold Lincoln (cartoonist)	January 20, 1894
Gray, Linda (actress)	September 12, 1941
Gray, Mel; born Melvin Dean Gray (football)	September 28, 1948
Gray, Sam; born Samuel David Gray (baseball)	October 15, 1897
Gray, Thomas (poet)	December 26, 1716
Grayson, Dave; born David L. Grayson (football)	June 6, 1939
Grayson, Kathryn; born Zelma Kathryn Hedrick (actress)	February 9, 1923
Graziano, Rocky; born Rocco Barbella (boxing)	January 1, 1921
Greco, Buddy; born Armando Greco (singer/music)	August 14, 1926
Greco, José; born Costanzo Greco (dancer)	December 23, 1918
Greeley, Horace (journalist/politician)	February 3, 1811
Green, Adolph (writer)	December 2, 1915
Green, Al (singer/music)	April 13, 1946
Green, Bobby Joe; born Robert Joseph Green (football)	May 7, 1936
Green, Cornell (football)	February 10, 1940
Green, Dick; born Richard Larry Green (baseball)	April 21, 1941
Green, Donnie; born Donald Green (football)	July 12, 1948
Green, Dwight Herbert (politician)	January 9, 1897
Green, Fred Warren (politician)	October 20, 1872
Green, Hubie; born Hubert Myatt Green (golf)	December 28, 1946
Green, John (basketball)	December 8, 1933
Green, Johnny; born John W. Green (music)	October 10, 1908
Green, Lenny; born Leonard Charles Green (baseball)	January 6, 1934
Green, Mitzi; born Elizabeth Keno (actress)	October 22, 1920
Green, Paul Eliot (playwright)	March 17, 1894
Green, Ted; born Edward Joseph Green (hockey)	March 23, 1940
Green, Theodore Francis (politician)	October 2, 1867
Green, Warren Everett (politician)	March 10, 1870
Greenberg, Hank; born Henry Benjamin Greenberg (baseball)	January 1, 1911
Greene, Bert (golf)	February 11, 1944
Greene, Frank Lester (politician)	February 10, 1870
Greene, Graham; born Henry Graham Greene (author)	October 2, 1904
Greene, Jack (singer/music)	January 7, 1930
Greene, Joe (football)	September 24, 1946
Greene, Lorne (actor)	February 12, 1915

Greene, Richard (actor)	August 25, 1918
Greene, Shecky; born Fred Sheldon Greenfield (comedian)	April 8, 1926
Greene, Tony; born Anthony Greene (football)	August 29, 1949
Greenstreet, Sydney Hughes (actor)	December 27, 1879
Greenwood, Charlotte; born Frances Charlotte Greenwood (actress/dancer)	June 25, 1893
Greenwood, Joan (actress)	March 4, 1919
Greenwood, L.C. (football)	September 8, 1946
Greer, Dabbs; born Robert William Greer (actor)	April 2, 1917
Greer, Germaine (feminist)	January 29, 1939
Greer, Hal (basketball)	June 26, 1936
Greer, Jane; born Bettyjane Greer (actress)	September 9, 1924
Gregg, Forrest; born Alvin Forrest Gregg (football)	October 18, 1933
Gregg, Julie (actress)	January 24, 1944
Gregory, Dick; born Richard Claxton Gregory (comedian/civil rights leader)	October 12, 1932
Gregory, Jack; born Earl Gregory (football)	October 3, 1944
Gregory, James (actor)	December 23, 1911
Gregory, Thomas Watt (government)	November 6, 1861
Gregory, William (politician)	August 3, 1849
Gremminger, Henry (football)	September 1, 1934
Gresham, Bob; born Robert Gresham (football)	July 9, 1948
Grey, Joel; born Joel Katz (actor/singer)	April 11, 1932
Grey, Nan; born Eschol Miller (actress)	July 25, 1918
Grey, Virginia (actress)	March 22, 1917
Grey, Zane (author)	January 31, 1875
Grich, Bobby; born Robert Anthony Grich (baseball)	January 15, 1949
Grieg, Edvard Hagerup (music)	June 15, 1843
Grier, Rosey; born Roosevelt Grier (football/actor)	July 14, 1932
Griese, Bob; born Robert Allan Griese (football)	February 3, 1945
Griffin, Merv; born Mervyn Edward Griffin (TV host/singer)	July 6, 1925
Griffin, Robert Paul (politician)	November 6, 1923
Griffin, Samuel Marvin (politician)	September 4, 1907
Griffith, Andy; born Andrew Samuel Griffith (actor)	June 1, 1926
Griffith, Cal; born Calvin Robertson Griffith (baseball)	December 1, 1911
Griffith, Clark Calvin (baseball)	November 20, 1869
Griffith, Corinne (actress)	November 24, 1896
Griffith, D.W.; born David Lewelyn Wark Griffith (producer/director)	January 22, 1874
Griffith, Emile Alphonse (boxing)	February 3, 1938
Griffith, Hugh Emrys (actor)	May 30, 1912
Grillparzer, Franz (dramatist)	January 15, 1791
Grim, Bob; born Robert Lee Grim (football)	May 8, 1945
Grimes, Burleigh Arland (baseball)	August 18, 1893
Grimes, Gary (actor)	June 2, 1955
Grimes, Tammy Lee (actress/singer)	January 30, 1934
Grimm, Charlie; born Charles John Grimm (baseball)	August 28, 1898
Grimm, Jacob Ludwig Carl (fairy tale author)	January 4, 1875
Grimm, Wilhelm Carl (fairy tale author)	February 24, 1876
Grimsley, Ross Albert, II (baseball)	January 7, 1950
Grissom, Marv; born Marvin Edward Grissom (baseball)	March 31, 1918

Grissom, Virgil Ivan (astronaut)	April 3, 1926
Griswold, Dwight Palmer (politician)	November 27, 1893
Griswold, Morley (politician)	October 10, 1890
Grizzard, George Cooper Jr. (actor)	April 1, 1928
Groat, Dick; born Richard Morrow Groat (baseball)	November 4, 1930
Grodin, Charles (actor)	April 21, 1935
Groesbeck, Alexander Joseph (politician)	November 7, 1873
Grogan, Steve; born Steven James Grogan (football)	July 24, 1953
Groh, David Lawrence (actor)	May 21, 1939
Groh, Gary (golf)	October 11, 1944
Gromek, Steve; born Stephen Joseph Gromek (baseball)	January 15, 1920
Gromyko, Andrei Andreyevich (Russian government)	July 6, 1909
Gronna, Asle Jorgenson (politician)	December 10, 1858
Gronouski, John Austin (government)	October 26, 1919
Grosso, Count; born Donald Grosso (hockey)	April 12, 1915
Grote, Jerry; born Gerald Wayne Grote (baseball)	October 6, 1942
Groth, Johnny; born John Thomas Groth (baseball)	July 23, 1926
Grove, Lefty; born Robert Moses Grove (baseball)	March 6, 1900
Groza, Lou; born Louis Groza (football)	January 25, 1924
Gruening, Ernest Henry (politician)	February 6, 1887
Guardino, Harry; born Harold Vincent Guardino (actor)	December 23, 1925
Gubbrud, Archie M. (politician)	December 31, 1910
Guerin, Richie (basketball)	May 29, 1932
Guerra, Mike; born Fermin Romero Guerra (baseball)	October 11, 1912
Guevara, Che; born Ernesto Guevara Serna (Cuban guerrilla leader)	June 14, 1928
Guffey, Joseph Finch (politician)	December 29, 1870
Guggenheim, Simon (philanthropist/financier/politician)	December 30, 1867
Guidolin, Bep; born Armand Guidolin (hockey)	December 9, 1925
Guild, Curtis, Jr. (politician)	February 2, 1860
Guillaume, Robert; born Robert Peter Williams (actor)	November 30, 1937
Guiness, Sir Alec (actor)	April 2, 1914
Gulager, Clu (actor)	November 16, 1935
Guldahl, Ralph (golf)	November 22, 1912
Gullett, Don; born Donald Edward Gullett (baseball)	January 6, 1951
Gumbert, Harry Edward (baseball)	November 5, 1909
Gunderson, Carl (politician)	June 20, 1864
Gunn, Moses (actor)	October 2, 1929
Gunter, Julius Caldeen (politician)	October 31, 1858
Gunter, Nancy Richey; born Nancy Richey (tennis)	August 23, 1942
Gunther, John Joseph (author)	August 3, 1910
Gurie, Sigrid; born Sigrid Gurie Haukelid (actress)	May 18, 1911
Gurney, Chan; born John Chandler Gurney (politician)	May 21, 1896
Gurney, Dan; born Daniel Sexton Gurney (auto racing)	April 13, 1931
Gurney, Edward John (politician)	January 12, 1914
Gustine, Frankie; born Frank William Gustine (baseball)	February 20, 1920
Guthrie, A.B.; born Alfred Bertram Guthrie, Jr. (author)	January 13, 1901
Guthrie, Arlo (singer/music)	July 10, 1947
Guthrie, Janet (auto racing)	March 7, 1938
Guthrie, Sir Tyrone; born William Tyrone Guthrie (director)	July 2, 1900

Guthrie, Woody; born Woodrow Wilson Guthrie (singer/music)   July 14, 1912
Gutteridge, Don; born Donald Joseph Gutteridge (baseball)   June 19, 1912
Guy, Ray; born William Ray Guy (football)   December 22, 1949
Guy, William Lewis (politician)   September 30, 1919
Gwenn, Edmund (actor)   September 26, 1875
Gwynne, Anne; born Marguerite Gwynne Trice (actress)   December 10, 1918
Gwynne, Fred (actor)   July 10, 1926

H

Haas, Bert; born Berthold John Haas (baseball)   February 8, 1914
Haas, Mule; born George William Haas (baseball)   October 15, 1903
Haber, Joyce (journalist)   December 28, 1932
Hack, Stan; born Stanley Camfield Hack (baseball)   December 6, 1909
Hackbart, Dale L. (football)   July 7, 1938
Hackel, Stella Bloomberg (politician)   December 27, 1926
Hackett, Bobby; born Robert Leo Hackett (music)   January 31, 1915
Hackett, Buddy; born Leonard Hacker (comedian/actor)   August 31, 1924
Hackett, Joan Ann (actress)   March 1, 1927
Hackman, Gene; born Eugene Alden Hackman (actor)   January 30, 1931
Haddix, Harvey (baseball)   September 18, 1925
Haden, Pat; born Patrick Capper Haden (football)   January 23, 1953
Haden, Sara (actress)   November 17, 1897
Hadfield, Victor Edward (hockey)   October 4, 1940
Hadl, John Willard (football)   February 15, 1940
Hadley, Bump; born Irving Darius Hadley (baseball)   July 5, 1904
Hadley, Herbert Spencer (politician)   February 20, 1872
Hafey, Chick; born Charles James Hafey (baseball)   February 12, 1903
Hagaman, Frank Lester (politician)   June 1, 1894
Hagan, Cliff (basketball)   December 9, 1931
Hagen, Halvor (football)   February 4, 1947
Hagen, Jean; born Jean Shirley VerHagen (actress)   August 3, 1924
Hagen, Uta Thyra (actress)   June 12, 1919
Hagen, Walter Charles (golf)   December 21, 1892
Haggard, Merle Ronald (singer/music)   April 6, 1937
Hagge, Marlene Bauer; born Marlene Bauer (golf)   February 16, 1934
Haggerty, Dan (actor/animal trainer)   November 19, 1941
Hagman, Larry Martin (actor)   September 21, 1931
Haig, Alexander Meigs, Jr. (military/government)   December 2, 1924
Haile Selassie; born Ras Taffari Makonnen (Ethiopian   July 17, 1891
     Emperor)
Hailey, Arthur (author)   April 5, 1920
Haines, Jesse Joseph (baseball)   July 22, 1893
Haines, John Michener (politician)   January 1, 1863
Haines, William (actor)   January 1, 1900
Haines, William T. (politician)   August 7, 1854
Hainsworth, George (hockey)   June 26, 1895
Hairston, Happy; born Harold Hairston (basketball)   May 31, 1942
Haise, Fred Wallace, Jr. (astronaut)   November 14, 1933
Halas, George Stanley (football)   February 2, 1895
Halberstam, David (journalist/author)   April 10, 1934

Haldeman, H.R. "Bob" born Harry Robbins Haldeman (government)	October 27, 1926
Hale, Alan, Sr.; born Rufus Alan McKahan (actor)	February 10, 1892
Hale, Alan, Jr. (actor)	March 8, 1918
Hale, Barbara (actress)	April 18, 1922
Hale, Binnie; born Beatrice Mary Hale-Monro (actress/comedienne/singer/dancer)	May 22, 1899
Hale, Edward Everett (clergyman/author)	April 3, 1822
Hale, Frederick (politician)	October 7, 1874
Hale, Monte (actor/singer)	June 8, 1919
Hale, Nathan (military officer)	June 6, 1775
Hale, Odell; born Arvel Odell Hale (baseball)	August 10, 1908
Hale, Sammy; born Samuel Douglas Hale (baseball)	September 10, 1896
Hale, Sonnie; born John Robert Hale-Monro (actor/comedian/singer/director)	May 1, 1902
Haley, Alex Palmer (author)	August 11, 1921
Haley, Jack, Sr.; born John Joseph Haley (actor/comedian/singer)	August 10, 1899
Hall, Charley; born Charles Val Hall, Jr. (football)	March 31, 1948
Hall, Charlie; born Charles Leslie Hall (football)	December 2, 1948
Hall, David (politician)	October 20, 1930
Hall, Dick; born Richard Wallace Hall (baseball)	September 27, 1930
Hall, Glenn Henry (hockey)	October 3, 1931
Hall, James; born James Brown (actor)	October 22, 1900
Hall, Jimmie Randolph (baseball)	March 17, 1938
Hall, John Hubert (politician)	February 7, 1899
Hall, Jon; born Charles Hall Locher (actor)	February 23, 1913
Hall, Juanita; born Juanita Long (actress/singer)	November 6, 1901
Hall, Luther Egbert (politician)	August 30, 1869
Hall, Monty; born Morton Halparin (TV host/actor)	August 25, 1923
Hall, Tom T. (singer/music)	May 25, 1936
Hallahan, Wild Bill; born William Anthony Hallahan (baseball)	August 4, 1902
Halleck, Charles Abraham (politician)	August 22, 1900
Haller, Tom; born Thomas Frank Haller (baseball)	June 23, 1937
Hals, Franz (artist)	circa 1580
Halsey, Brett (actor)	June 20, 1933
Halsey, William Frederick Jr. (naval officer)	October 30, 1882
Halston; born Roy Halston Frowick (fashion designer)	April 23, 1932
Halverson, Dean (football)	August 24, 1946
Ham, Jack; born John Raphael Ham (football)	December 23, 1948
Hamer, Rusty; born Russell Hamer (actor)	February 15, 1947
Hamill, Dorothy Stuart (ice skating)	————1956
Hamill, Mark (actor)	September 25, 1951
Hamill, Pete; born William Peter Hamill (journalist/author)	June 24, 1935
Hamill, Red; born Robert George Hamill (hockey)	January 11, 1917
Hamilton, Alexander (statesman)	January 11, 1757
Hamilton, Billy; born William Robert Hamilton (baseball)	February 16, 1866
Hamilton, Bob; born Robert Hamilton (golf)	January 10, 1916
Hamilton, George Stevens (actor)	August 12, 1939
Hamilton, George, IV (singer/music)	July 19, 1937

Hamilton, Margaret Brainàrd (actress)	December 9, 1902
Hamilton, Murray (actor)	————1923
Hamilton, Neil; born James Neil Hamilton (actor)	September 9, 1899
Hamilton, Pete; born Peter Goodwill Hamilton (auto racing)	July 20, 1942
Hamilton, Reginald (hockey)	April 29, 1914
Hamilton, Roy (singer)	April 16, 1929
Hamlin, Hannibal (Vice President)	August 27, 1809
Hamlin, Luke Daniel (baseball)	July 3, 1904
Hamlin, Shelley (golf)	May 28, 1949
Hamlisch, Marvin Frederick (music)	June 2, 1944
Hammarskjold, Dag Hjalmar Agne Carl (United Nations)	July 29, 1905
Hammer, Granny; born Granville Wilbur Hammer (baseball)	April 26, 1927
Hammerstein, Oscar (music/playwright/producer)	May 8, 1847
Hammerstein, Oscar, II; born Oscar Greeley Clenndenning Hammerstein (music/playwright/producer/director)	July 12, 1895
Hammett, Dashiell; born Samuel Dashiell Hammett (author)	May 27, 1894
Hammill, John (politician)	October 14, 1875
Hammond, Jay Sterner (politician)	July 21, 1922
Hampden, Walter Dougherty (actor)	June 30, 1879
Hampshire, Susan (actress)	May 12, 1938
Hampson, Ted; born Edward George Hampson (hockey)	December 11, 1936
Hampton, Dave; born David Hampton (football)	May 7, 1947
Hampton, James Wade (actor)	July 9, 1936
Hampton, Lionel Leo (music)	April 20, 1913
Hanburger, Chris; born Christian Hanburger (football)	August 13, 1941
Hancock, Herbie; born Herbert Jeffrey Hancock (music)	April 12, 1940
Hancock, John (statesman)	January 23, 1737
Hand, Larry; born Lawrence Thomas Hand (football)	July 10, 1940
Hand, Learned; born Billings Learned Hand (jurist)	January 27, 1872
Handel, George Frideric; born Georg Friedrich Handel (music)	February 23, 1685
Handley, Harold Willis (politician)	November 27, 1909
Handley, Lee Elmer (baseball)	July 31, 1913
Hands, Bill; born William Alfred Hands, Jr. (baseball)	May 6, 1940
Handy, W.C.; born William Christopher Handy (music)	November 16, 1873
Haney, Carol (dancer/actress/choreographer)	December 24, 1924
Haney, Fred Girard (baseball)	April 25, 1898
Hanks, Sam; born Samuel Dwight Hanks (auto racing)	July 13, 1914
Hanley, Bridget Anne Elizabeth (actress)	February 3, 1943
Hanly, J. Frank; born James Franklin Hanly (politician)	April 4, 1863
Hanna, Louis Benjamin (politician)	August 9, 1861
Hannegan, Robert Emmet (government)	June 30, 1903
Hannett, Arthur Thomas (politician)	February 17, 1884
Hannum, Alex (basketball)	July 19, 1923
Hanratty, Terry; born Terrence H. Hanratty (football)	January 19, 1948
Hansen, Clifford Peter (politician)	October 16, 1912
Hansen, Don; born Donald Hansen (football)	August 20, 1944
Hansen, Ron; born Ronald Lavern Hansen (baseball)	April 5, 1938
Hanson, Howard Harold (music)	October 28, 1896
Harbert, Chick; born Melvin R. Harbert (golf)	February 20, 1915
Harburg, E.Y. "Yip"; born Edgar Y. Harburg (music)	April 8, 1898

Hard, Darlene R. (tennis)	January 6, 1936
Hardee, Cary Augustus (politician)	November 13, 1876
Hardeen, Theodore, Sr. "Theo"; born Theodore Weiss (magician)	February 29, 1876
Harder, Mel; born Melvin LeRoy Harder (baseball)	October 15, 1909
Harder, Pat; born Marlin M. Harder (football)	May 6, 1922
Hardin, Clifford Morris (government)	October 9, 1915
Hardin, Ty; born Orison (or Orton) Whipple Hungerford, II (actor)	——1930
Harding, Ann; born Dorothy Walton Gatley (actress)	August 17, 1901
Harding, Florence Kling; born Florence Kling (First Lady)	August 15, 1860
Harding, Warren Gamaliel (President)	November 2, 1865
Harding, William Lloyd (politician)	October 3, 1877
Hardman, Cedrick Ward (football)	October 4, 1948
Hardman, Lamartine Griffin (politician)	April 14, 1856
Hardwick, Thomas William (politician)	December 9, 1872
Hardwicke, Sir Cedric Webster (actor)	February 19, 1893
Hardy, Joseph (actor)	August 10, 1918
Hardy, Oliver Norvell (comedian/actor)	January 18, 1892
Hardy, Thomas (writer)	June 2, 1840
Hargan, Steve; born Steven Lowell Hargan (baseball)	September 8, 1942
Hargrave, Bubbles; born Eugene Franklin Hargrave (baseball)	July 15, 1892
Hargrave, Pinky; born William McKinley Hargrave (baseball)	January 31, 1896
Harkness, Richard Long (newscaster)	September 29, 1907
Harlan, John Marshall (jurist)	May 20, 1899
Harley, Joseph Emile (politician)	September 14, 1880
Harlow, Jean; born Harlean Carpentier (actress)	March 3, 1911
Harmon, Claude (golf)	June 14, 1916
Harmon, David Glen (hockey)	January 2, 1921
Harmon, Judson (politician)	February 3, 1846
Harmon, Tom; born Thomas Dudley Harmon (football/sportscaster)	September 28, 1919
Harnell, Joe; born Joseph Harnell (music)	August 2, 1924
Harney, Paul (golf)	July 11, 1929
Harnick, Sheldon Mayer (music)	April 30, 1924
Harper, Chandler (golf)	March 10, 1914
Harper, George Washington (baseball)	June 24, 1892
Harper, Ron (actor)	January 12, 1936
Harper, Terrance Victor (hockey)	January 27, 1940
Harper, Tommy (baseball)	October 14, 1940
Harper, Valerie Cathryn (actress)	August 22, 1940
Harreld, John William (politician)	January 24, 1872
Harrelson, Bud; born Derrel McKinley Harrelson (baseball)	June 6, 1944
Harrelson, Ken; born Kenneth Smith Harrelson (baseball)	September 4, 1941
Harriman, W. Averill; born William Averill Harriman (politics/government)	November 15, 1891
Harrington, Emerson Columbus (politician)	March 26, 1864
Harrington, Pat; born Daniel Patrick Harrington, Jr. (actor)	August 13, 1929
Harris, Andrew Linter (politician)	November 17, 1835
Harris, Barbara; born Sandra Markowitz (actress/singer)	——1935

ALPHABETICAL LISTING 87

Harris, Bucky; born Stanley Raymond Harris (baseball)	November 8, 1896
Harris, Cliff; born Clifford Allen Harris (football)	November 12, 1948
Harris, Emmylou (singer)	April 2, 1949
Harris, Franco (football)	March 7, 1950
Harris, Fred Roy (politician)	November 13, 1930
Harris, James L. (football)	July 20, 1947
Harris, Jo Ann (actress)	May 27———
Harris, Joe; born Joseph Harris (baseball)	May 20, 1891
Harris, Joel Chandler (author/journalist)	December 8, 1848
Harris, Julie; born Julia Ann Harris (actress)	December 2, 1925
Harris, Labron , Jr. (golf)	September 27, 1941
Harris, Louis (pollster)	January 6, 1921
Harris, Nathaniel Edwin (politician)	January 21, 1846
Harris, Patricia Roberts; born Patricia Roberts (government)	May 31, 1924
Harris, Phil (music/comedian/actor)	June 24, 1906
Harris, Richard D. (football)	January 21, 1948
Harris, Richard St. John (actor)	October 1, 1930
Harris, Rosemary Ann (actress)	September 19, 1930
Harris, Roy Ellsworth (music)	February 12, 1898
Harris, Ted; born Edward Alexander Harris (hockey)	July 18, 1936
Harris, William Edward (hockey)	July 29, 1935
Harris, William Julius (politics/government)	February 3, 1868
Harrison, Albertis Sydney, Jr. (politician)	January 11, 1907
Harrison, Anna Tuthill Symmes; born Anna Tuthill Symmes (First Lady)	July 25, 1775
Harrison, Benjamin (President)	August 20, 1833
Harrison, Caroline Scott; born Caroline Scott(first wife of Benjamin Harrison/First Lady)	October 1, 1832
Harrison, Dutch; born Ernest Joseph Harrison (golf)	March 29, 1910
Harrison, Dwight (football)	October 12, 1948
Harrison, George (singer/music)	February 25, 1943
Harrison, Noel (actor)	January 29, 1936
Harrison, Pat; born Byron Patton Harrison (politician)	August 29, 1881
Harrison, Rex; born Reginald Carey Harrison (actor)	March 5, 1908
Harrison, William Henry (President)	February 9, 1773
Harriss, Slim; born William Jennings Bryan Harriss (baseball)	December 11, 1896
Hart, Christina; born Bonnie Ann Hartzell (actress)	July 21———
Hart, Dolores; born Dolores Hicks (actress) now Mother Dolores (nun)	October 20, 1938
Hart, Doris J. (tennis)	June 20, 1925
Hart, Freddie (singer)	December 22, 1928
Hart, Gary Warren (politician)	November 28, 1937
Hart, Jim; born James Warren Hart (football)	April 29, 1944
Hart, Jim Ray; born James Raymond Hart (baseball)	October 30, 1941
Hart, Lorenz Milton (music)	May 2, 1895
Hart, Louis Folwell (politician)	January 4, 1862
Hart, Moss (playwright/producer/director)	October 24, 1904
Hart, Philip Aloysius (politician)	December 10, 1912

Hart, Tommy; born Thomas Lee Hart (football)	November 7, 1944
Hart, William S.; born William Surrey Hart (actor/director)	December 6, 1862
Hartack, Willie; born William John Hartack, Jr. (jockey)	December 9, 1932
Harte, Bret; born Francis Brett Hart (author)	August 25, 1836
Hartford, Huntington; born George Huntington Hartford, II (heir)	April 18, 1911
Hartke, Vance; born Rupert Vance Hartke (politician)	May 31, 1919
Hartley, Mariette (actress)	June 20, 1940
Hartley, Roland Hill (politician)	June 26, 1864
Hartman, David Downs (actor/TV host)	May 19, 1935
Hartman, Elizabeth (actress)	December 23, 1941
Hartman, Paul William (actor/dancer/comedian)	March 1, 1904
Hartness, James (politician)	September 3, 1861
Hartnett, Gabby; born Charles Leo Hartnett (baseball)	December 20, 1900
Harvey, Doug; born Douglas Norman Harvey (hockey)	December 19, 1924
Harvey, Laurence; born Larushka Mischa Skikne (actor)	October 1, 1928
Harvey, Lilian; born Helene Lilian Muriel Pape (actress)	January 19, 1906
Harvey, Paul (newscaster/journalist/author)	September 4, 1918
Harvey, William (medicine)	April 1, 1578
Haskell, Charles Nathaniel (politician)	March 13, 1860
Haskell, Floyd Kirk (politician)	February 7, 1916
Haskell, Peter Abraham (actor)	October 15, 1934
Haskins, Clem (basketball)	August 11, 1944
Hassett, Buddy; born John Aloysius Hassett (baseball)	September 5, 1911
Hasso, Signe; born Signe Eleonora Cecilia Larsson (actress)	August 15, 1910
Hatch, Carl Atwood (politician)	November 27, 1889
Hatch, Orrin Grant (politician)	March 22, 1934
Hatch, Richard Lawrence (actor)	May 21, 1946
Hatfield, Henry Drury (politician)	September 15, 1875
Hatfield, Hurd; born William Rukard Hurd Hatfield (actor)	December 7, 1918
Hatfield, Mark Odom (politician)	July 12, 1922
Hathaway, Stanley K. (politics/government)	July 19, 1924
Hathaway, William Dodd (politician)	February 21, 1924
Hatton, Grady Edgebert (baseball)	October 7, 1922
Haubiel, Charles Trowbridge (music)	January 30, 1892
Hauss, Len; born Leonard Moore Hauss (football)	July 11, 1942
Havens, Richie (singer/music)	January 21, 1941
Haver, June; born June Stovenour (actress)	June 10, 1926
Havig, Dennis Eugene (football)	May 6, 1949
Havlicek, John (basketball/sportscaster)	April 8, 1940
Havoc, June; born Ellen Evangeline Hovick (actress)	November 8, 1916
Hawes, Harry Bartow (politician)	November 15, 1869
Hawkes, Albert Wahl (politician)	November 20, 1878
Hawkes, John Clendennin Burne, Jr. (author)	August 17, 1925
Hawkins, Alex; born Chilton Alex Hawkins (football/sportscaster)	July 2, 1937
Hawkins, Coleman (music)	November 21, 1904
Hawkins, Connie (basketball)	July 17, 1942

Hawkins, Jack (actor)	September 14, 1910
Hawkins, Tom; born Thomas Jerome Hawkins (basketball)	December 22, 1936
Hawks, Howard Winchester (director/producer)	May 30, 1896
Hawley, James H. (politician)	January 17, 1847
Hawn, Goldie; born Goldie Jean Btudlendgehawn (actress/comedienne/singer/dancer)	November 21, 1945
Haworth, Jill (actress/singer)	August 15, 1945
Hawthorn, Mike; born John Michael Hawthorn (auto racing)	April 10, 1929
Hawthorne, Nathaniel (author)	July 4, 1804
Hay, Alexandra Lynn (actress)	July 24, 1948
Hay, John Milton (statesman)	October 8, 1838
Hay, Marion E. (politician)	December 9, 1865
Hay, Red; born William Charles Hay (hockey)	December 8, 1935
Hayakawa, S.I.; born Samuel Ichiye Hayakawa (educator/politician)	July 18, 1906
Hayakawa, Sessue; born Kintaro Hayakawa (actor)	June 10, 1886
Hayden, Carl Trumbull (politician)	October 2, 1877
Hayden, Melissa; born Mildred Herman (dancer)	April 25, 1928
Hayden, Russell; born Hayden Michael Lucid (actor)	June 10, 1912
Hayden, Sterling; born John Hamilton (or Sterling Relyea Walter) (actor/author)	March 26, 1916
Haydn, Franz Joseph (music)	March 31, 1732
Haydon, Julie; born Donella Donaldson (actress)	June 10, 1910
Hayes, Bill; born William Foster Hayes (actor/singer)	June 5, 1925
Hayes, Bob; born Robert Lee Hayes (olympic athlete /football)	December 20, 1942
Hayes, Elvin (basketball)	November 17, 1945
Hayes, Frankie; born Franklin Witman Hayes (baseball)	October 13, 1914
Hayes, Gabby; born George Hayes (actor)	May 7, 1885
Hayes, Helen; born Helen Hayes Brown (actress)	October 10, 1900
Hayes, Isaac (music/actor)	August 20, 1942
Hayes, Jackie; born Minter Carney Hayes (baseball)	July 19, 1906
Hayes, Lucy Ware Webb; born Lucy Ware Webb (First Lady)	August 28, 1831
Hayes, Margaret "Maggie"; born Dana Dale (actress)	December 5, 1924
Hayes, Mark Stephen (golf)	July 12, 1949
Hayes, Peter Lind; born Joseph Conrad Lind, Jr. (actor/comedian)	June 25, 1915
Hayes, Roland (singer)	June 3, 1887
Hayes, Rutherford Birchard (President)	October 4, 1822
Hayes, Susan Seaforth; born Susan Seaforth (actress)	July 11———
Hayes, Tom; born Thomas Hayes (football)	April 18, 1946
Hayes, Woody; born Wayne Woodrow Hayes (football)	February 14, 1913
Hayman, Richard (music)	March 27, 1920
Haymes, Dick; born Richard Benjamin Haymes (singer/actor)	September 13, 1916
Haymes, Paul (hockey)	March 1, 1910
Haymond, Alvin H. (football)	August 31, 1942
Haynes, Abner (football)	September 19, 1937
Haynes, Lloyd; born Samuel Lloyd Haynes (actor)	October 19, 1935
Haynie, Sandra J. (golf)	June 4, 1943
Hays, George Washington (politician)	September 23, 1863
Hays, Kathryn; born with surname Piper (actress)	July 26———

Hayward, Leland (producer)	September 13, 1902
Hayward, Louis; born Seafield Grant (actor)	March 19, 1909
Hayward, Susan; born Edythe Marrener (actress)	June 30, 1918
Haywood, Spencer (basketball)	April 22, 1949
Hayworth, Ray; born Raymond Hall Hayworth (baseball)	January 29, 1904
Hayworth, Rita; born Margarita Carmen Cansino (actress)	October 17, 1918
Hazeltine, Matt; born Matthew Hazeltine (football)	August 2, 1933
Head, Edith (costume designer)	October 28, 1907
Heafner, Clayton, (golf)	July 20, 1914
Healy, Mary (actress/singer)	April 14, 1918
Heard, Gar (basketball)	May 3, 1948
Heard, Jerry Michael (golf)	May 1, 1947
Heard William Wright (politician)	April 28, 1853
Hearn, Jim; born James Tolbert Hearn (baseball)	April 11, 1921
Hearnes, Warren Eastman (politician)	July 23, 1923
Hearst, David Whitmire (publishing)	December 2, 1915
Hearst, Patty; born Patricia Campbell Hearst	February 20, 1954
(fugitive heiress)	
Hearst, Randolph Apperson (publishing)	December 2, 1915
Hearst, William Randolph (publishing)	April 29, 1863
Hearst, William Randolph, Jr. (publishing)	January 27, 1908
Heath, Edward (British government)	July 9, 1916
Heath, Jeff; born John Geoffrey Heath (baseball)	April 1, 1915
Heathcote, Cliff; born Clifton Earl Heathcote (baseball)	January 24, 1898
Heatherton, Joey; born Davenie Johanna Heatherton	September 14, 1944
(actress/dancer/singer)	
Hebenton, Andy; born Andrew Alex Hebenton (hockey)	October 3, 1929
Hebert, Jay; born Junius Joseph Hebert (golf)	February 14, 1923
Hebert, Lionel Paul (golf)	January 20, 1928
Hebner,Richie; born Richard Joseph Hebner (baseball)	November 26, 1947
Hecht, Ben (writer)	February 28, 1894
Hecht, Harold (producer)	June 1, 1907
Heckart, Eileen; born Anna Eileen Heckart (actress)	March 29, 1919
Hedison, David; born Albert David Hedison, Jr.	May 20, 1928
(or Ara Heditsian) (actor)	
Hedren, Tippi; born Nathalie Kay Hedren (actress)	January 19, 1931
Heffner, Don; born Donald Henry Heffner (baseball)	February 8, 1911
Heflin, James Thomas (politician)	April 9, 1869
Heflin, Van; born Emmet Evan Heflin, Jr. (actor)	December 13, 1910
Hefner, Hugh Marston (publisher)	April 9, 1926
Hegan, Jim; born James Edward Hegan (baseball)	August 3, 1920
Hegan, Mike; born James Michael Hegan (baseball)	July 21, 1942
Hegyes, Robert (actor)	May 7, 1951
Heidt, Horace Murray (music)	May 21, 1901
Heifetz, Jascha (music)	February 2, 1901
Heil, Julius Peter (politician)	July 24, 1876
Heilmann, Harry Edwin (baseball)	August 3, 1894
Hein, Mel; born Melvin John Hein (football)	August 22, 1909
Heinemann, Gustav Walter (German government)	July 23, 1899
Heinlein, Robert Anson (author)	July 7, 1907
Heinsohn, Tom; born Thomas William Heinsohn (basketball)	August 26, 1934

Heinz, H. John, III; born Henry John Heinz, III (politician) — October 23, 1938
Heiss, Carol Elizabeth (ice skating) — January 20, 1940
Held, Woodie, born Woodson George Held (baseball) — March 25, 1932
Heller, Joseph (author) — May 1, 1923
Heller, Ott; born Ehrhardt Henry Heller (hockey) — June 2, 1910
Hellman, Lillian Florence (playwright) — June 20, 1905
Helm, Anne (actress) — September 12, 1938
Helmond, Katherine (actress) — July 5, 1933
Helms, Jesse Alexander, Jr. (politician) — October 18, 1921
Helms, Richard McGarrah (government) — March 30, 1913
Helms, Tommy Van (baseball) — May 5, 1941
Hemingway, Ernest Miller (author) — July 21, 1898
Hemingway, Margaux (actress/model) — February ———1955
Hemmings, David (actor) — November 18, 1938
Hemsley, Rollie; born Ralston Burdett Hemsley (baseball) — June 24, 1907
Hemsley, Sherman (actor) — February 1, 1938
Hemus, Solly; born Solomon Joseph Hemus (baseball) — April 17, 1923
Henderson, Charles (politician) — April 26, 1860
Henderson, Florence (actress/singer) — February 14, 1934
Henderson, Ken; born Kenneth Joseph Henderson (baseball) — June 15, 1946
Henderson, Marcia (actress) — July 22, 1930
Henderson, Moe; born John Murray Henderson (hockey) — September 5, 1921
Henderson, Paul Garnet (hockey) — January 28, 1943
Henderson, Skitch; born Lyle Russell Cedric Henderson (music) — January 27, 1918
Hendrick, Harvey Lee (baseball) — November 9, 1897
Hendricks, Elrod Jerome (baseball) — December 22, 1940
Hendricks, Ted; born Theodore Paul Hendricks (football) — November 1, 1947
Hendricks, Thomas Andrews (Vice President) — September 7, 1819
Hendrickson, Robert Clymer (politician) — August 12, 1898
Hendrix, Jimi; born James Marshall Hendrix (singer) — November 27, 1942
Hendrix, Wanda; born Dixie Wanda Hendrix (actress) — November 3, 1928
Henie, Sonja (ice skating/actress) — April 8, 1910
Henline, Butch; born Walter John Henline (baseball) — December 20, 1894
Henning, Doug (magician/actor) — May 3, 1947
Henning, Linda Kaye (actress/singer) — September 16, 1944
Hennings, Thomas Carey, Jr. (politician) — June 25, 1903
Henreid, Paul; born Paul Georg Julius von Hernreid Ritter von Wasel-Waldingau (actor/director) — January 10, 1908
Henrich, Tommy; born Thomas David Henrich (baseball) — February 20, 1913
Henry VIII (King of England) — June 28, 1491
Henry, Buck; born with surname Zuckerman (actor/writer) — ———1931
Henry, Camille Wilfrid (hockey) — January 31, 1933
Henry, Charlotte (actress) — March 3, 1913
Henry, O.; born William Sydney Porter (author) — September 11, 1862
Henry, Patrick (patriot) — May 29, 1736
Henry, Sugar Jim; born Samuel James Henry (hockey) — October 23, 1920
Hensley, Pamela Gail (actress) — October 3, 1950
Henson, Jim; born James Maury Henson (muppeteer) — September 24, 1936
Hepburn, Audrey; born Audrey Hepburn-Ruston (actress) — May 4, 1929

Hepburn, Katharine Houghton (actress)	November 8, 1907
Herber, Arnold (football)	April 2, 1910
Herbert, Ray; born Raymond Ernest Herbert (baseball)	December 15, 1929
Herbert, Thomas John (politician)	October 28, 1894
Herbert, Victor (music)	February 1, 1859
Herblock; born Herbert Lawrence Block (cartoonist)	October 13, 1909
Hergesheimer, Walter Edgar (hockey)	January 8, 1927
Herlihy, James Leo (actor/writer)	February 27, 1927
Herman, Babe; born Floyd Caves Herman (baseball)	June 26, 1903
Herman, Billy; born William Jennings Bryan Herman (baseball)	July 7, 1909
Herman, Jerry; born Gerald Herman (music)	July 10, 1932
Herman, Woody; born Woodrow Charles Herman (music)	May 16, 1913
Hermeling, Terry (football)	April 25, 1946
Herreid, Charles N. (politician)	October 20, 1857
Herrick, Myron Timothy (politician)	October 9, 1854
Herring, Clyde LaVerne (politician)	May 3, 1879
Herrmann, Don; born Donald Herrmann (football)	June 5, 1947
Herrmann, Ed; born Edward Martin Herrmann (baseball)	August 27, 1946
Herrmann, Edward Kirk (actor)	July 21, 1943
Herschler, Ed C. (politician)	October 27, 1918
Herseth, Ralph (politician)	July 2, 1909
Hersey, John Richard (author)	June 17, 1914
Hershberger, Mike; born Norman Michael Hershberger (baseball)	October 9, 1939
Hershey, Barbara; born Barbara Herzstein (actress)	February 5, 1948
Hershey, Lewis Blaine (army officer)	September 12, 1893
Hershfield, Harry (humorist/journalist/cartoonist)	October 3, 1885
Hersholt, Jean (actor)	July 12, 1886
Herter, Christian Archibald (politics/government)	March 28, 1895
Hervey, Irene; born Irene Herwick (actress)	July 11, 1910
Herzog, Whitey; born Dorrel Norman Elvert Herzog (baseball)	November 9, 1931
Heston, Charlton; born Charlton Carter (actor)	October 4, 1922
Hetzel, Fred (basketball)	July 21, 1942
Hewitt, Alan Everett (actor)	January 21, 1915
Hewitt, Bill; born William Ernest Hewitt (football)	October 8, 1909
Hextall, Bryan Aldwyn, Sr. (hockey)	July 31, 1913
Heyburn, Weldon Brinton (politician)	May 23, 1852
Heyerdahl, Thor (ethnologist/explorer)	October 6, 1914
Heyward, Duncan Clinch (politician)	June 24, 1864
Heywood, Anne; born Violet Pretty (actress)	December 11, 1931
Hicke, William Lawrence (hockey)	March 31, 1938
Hickel, Walter Joseph (politics/government)	August 18, 1919
Hickenlooper, Bourke Blakemore (politician)	July 21, 1896
Hickey, John Joseph (politician)	August 22, 1911
Hickman, Darryl Gerard (actor)	July 28, 1931
Hickman, Dwayne, (actor)	May 18, 1934
Hickman, Jim; born James Lucius Hickman (baseball)	May 10, 1937
Hickok, Wild Bill; born James Butler Hickok (frontier marshall)	May 27, 1837

Higbe, Kirby; born Walter Kirby Higbe (baseball)	April 8, 1915
Higgins, James Henry (politician)	January 22, 1876
Higgins, Mike "Pinky"; born Michael Franklin Higgins (baseball)	May 27, 1909
Higgins, Pam; born Pamela Sue Higgins (golf)	December 5, 1945
High, Andy; born Andrew Aird High (baseball)	November 21, 1897
Higuchi, Chako; born Hisako Higuchi (golf)	October 13, 1945
Hildegarde; born Hildegarde Loretta Sell (singer)	February 1, 1906
Hildreth, Horace Augustus (politician)	December 2, 1902
Hilgenberg, Wally; born Walter Hilgenberg (football)	July 19, 1942
Hill, Arthur Edward Spence (actor)	August 1, 1922
Hill, Calvin (football)	January 2, 1947
Hill, Dave; born David Hill (golf)	May 20, 1937
Hill, George Roy (director)	December 20, 1922
Hill, Graham; born Norman Graham Hill (auto racing)	February 15, 1929
Hill, Harlon (football)	May 4, 1932
Hill, J.D. (football)	October 30, 1948
Hill, James Webster (football)	October 21, 1946
Hill, Jerry; born Gerald A. Hill (football)	October 12, 1939
Hill, John Fremont (politician)	October 29, 1855
Hill, John Melvin (hockey)	February 15, 1914
Hill, Lister (politician)	December 29, 1894
Hill, Mike; born Michael Hill (golf)	January 27, 1939
Hill, Phil; born Philip Toll Hill (auto racing)	April 20, 1927
Hill, Steven; born Solomon Berg (actor)	February 24, 1922
Hill, Winston Cordell (football)	October 23, 1941
Hillaire, Marcel (actor)	April 23, 1908
Hillary, Sir Edmund Percival (apiarist/mountain climber)	July 20, 1919
Hiller, Arthur (director)	November 22, 1923
Hiller, Chuck; born Charles Joseph Hiller (baseball)	October 1, 1935
Hiller, Dutch; born Wilbert Carl Hiller (hockey)	May 11, 1915
Hiller, Wendy Margaret (actress)	August 15, 1912
Hillman, Darnell (basketball)	August 8, 1949
Hillman, Larry Morley (hockey)	February 5, 1937
Hillman, Wayne James (hockey)	November 13, 1938
Hills, Carla Anderson; born Carla Anderson (government)	January 3, 1934
Hilton, Conrad Nicholson (hotel magnate)	December 25, 1887
Hilton, Roy (football)	March 21, 1941
Himes, Chester Bomar (author)	July 29, 1909
Himes, Dick; born Richard Dean Himes (football)	May 25, 1946
Himes, Norman (hockey)	April 13, 1903
Hindemith, Paul (music)	November 16, 1895
Hindenburg, Paul Ludwig Hans Anton von Beneckendorff und von (German military & government)	October 2, 1847
Hines, Duncan (author/publisher/traveler)	March 26, 1880
Hines, Fatha; born Earl Kenneth Hines (music)	December 28, 1905
Hines, Jerome; born Jerome Heinz (singer)	November 8, 1921
Hines, Mimi (comedienne/actress/singer)	July 17, 1933
Hingle, Pat; born Martin Patterson Hingle (actor)	July 19, 1923
Hinkle, Clarke; born William Clarke Hinkle (football)	April 10, 1910
Hinkle, James Fielding (politician)	October 20, 1864
Hinkle, Lon (golf)	July 17, 1949

Hinson, Larry (golf)	August 5, 1944
Hinton, Chuck; born Charles Edward Hinton (baseball)	May 3, 1934
Hirohito (Japanese Emperor)	April 29, 1901
Hirsch, Elroy L. (football)	June 17, 1923
Hirsch, Judd (actor)	March 15, 1935
Hirschfeld, Al; born Albert Hirschfeld (cartoonist/artist)	June 21, 1903
Hirschhorn, Joseph Herman (financier/art collector)	August 11, 1899
Hirt, Al; born Alois Maxwell Hirt (music)	November 7, 1922
Hiskey, Babe; born Bryant Hiskey (golf)	November 21, 1938
Hisle, Larry Eugene (baseball)	May 5, 1947
Hiss, Alger (government/attorney)	November 11, 1904
Hitchcock, Alfred Joseph (producer/director/actor)	August 13, 1899
Hitchcock, Billy; born William Clyde Hitchcock (baseball)	July 31, 1916
Hitchcock, Frank Harris (government)	October 5, 1867
Hitchcock, Gilbert Monell (politician)	September 18, 1859
Hitler, Adolf (German government)	April 20, 1889
Ho, Don (singer/actor)	August 13, 1930
Hoad, Lew; born Lewis A. Hoad (tennis)	November 23, 1934
Hoag, Myril Oliver (baseball)	March 9, 1908
Hoaglin, Fred; born George Frederick Hoaglin (football)	January 28, 1944
Hoak, Dick; born Richard John Hoak (football)	December 8, 1939
Hoak, Don; born Donald Albert Hoak (baseball)	February 5, 1928
Hobart, Garret Augustus (Vice President)	June 3, 1844
Hobart, Rose; born Rose Kefer (actress)	May 1, 1906
Hobbes, Thomas (philosopher/writer)	April 5, 1588
Hobbs, David Wishart (auto racing)	June 9, 1939
Hobby, Oveta Culp; born Oveta Culp (government/journalism)	January 19, 1905
Hobby, William Pettus (politician)	March 26, 1878
Hoblitzell, John Dempsey, Jr. (politician)	December 30, 1912
Hobson, Valerie (actress)	April 14, 1917
Ho Chi Minh (North Vietnamese government)	May 19, 1890
Hoch, Edward Wallis (politician)	March 17, 1849
Hockenhull, A.W.; born Andrew Walter Hockenhull (politician)	January 6, 1877
Hodge, Charles Edward (hockey)	July 28, 1933
Hodge, Ken; born Kenneth Hodge (hockey)	June 23, 1944
Hodges, Eddie (actor/singer)	March 5, 1947
Hodges, George Hartshorn (politician)	February 6, 1866
Hodges, Gil; born Gilbert Raymond Hodges (baseball)	April 4, 1924
Hodges, Luther Hartwell (politics/government)	March 9, 1898
Hodgson, James Day (government)	December 3, 1915
Hodiak, John (actor)	April 16, 1914
Hoeft, Billy; born William Frederick Hoeft (baseball)	May 17, 1932
Hoegh, Leo Arthur (politician)	March 30, 1908
Hoernschemeyer, Hunchy; born Robert J. Hoernschemeyer (football)	September 24, 1925
Hoey, Clyde Roark (politician)	December 11, 1877
Hoff, Philip Henderson (politician)	June 29, 1924
Hoffa, Jimmy; born James Riddle Hoffa (labor leader)	February 14, 1913
Hoffman, Abbie; born Abbott Hoffman (politicial activist)	November 30, 1936

Hoffman, Dustin (actor)	August 8, 1937
Hoffman, Harold Giles (politician)	February 7, 1896
Hoffman, Paul (basketball)	April 12, 1922
Hofmann, Hans (artist)	March 21, 1880
Hogan, Ben; born William Benjamin Hogan (golf)	August 13, 1912
Hogan, Robert (actor)	September 27———
Hogan, Shanty; born James Francis Hogan (baseball)	March 21, 1906
Hogarth, William (artist)	November 10, 1697
Holbein, Hans (the Elder) (artist)	circa 1465
Holbein, Hans (the Younger) (artist)	———1497
Holbrook, Hal; born Harold Rowe Holbrook, Jr. (actor)	February 17, 1925
Holcomb, Marcus Hensey (politician)	November 28, 1844
Holden, Fay; born Dorothy Fay Hammerton (actress)	September 26, 1894
Holden, Gloria (actress)	September 5, 1908
Holden, William; born William Franklin Beedle, Jr. (actor)	April 17, 1918
Holder, Geoffrey Lamont (dancer/actor/singer/director)	August 1, 1930
Holiday, Billie; born Eleanor Gough McKay (singer)	April 7, 1915
Holke, Walter Henry (baseball)	December 25, 1892
Holland, Spessard Lindsey (politician)	July 10, 1892
Holland, Vernon (football)	June 27, 1948
Hollander, Lorin (music)	July 19, 1944
Hollett, Bill; born William Frank Hollett (hockey)	April 13, 1912
Holliday, Judy; born Judith Tuvin (actress)	June 21, 1921
Holliday, Polly Dean (actress)	July 2, 1937
Holliman, Earl; born Anthony Numkena (actor)	September 11, 1928
Hollings, Ernest Frederick (politician)	January 1, 1922
Hollingsworth, Al; born Albert Wayne Hollingsworth (baseball)	February 25, 1908
Holloway, Stanley Augustus (actor)	October 1, 1890
Holloway, Sterling (actor)	January 4, 1905
Holloway, William Judson (politician)	December 15, 1888
Holly, Buddy; born Charles Hardin Holley (singer/music)	September 7, 1936
Holm, Celeste (actress/singer)	April 29, 1919
Holman, Libby; born Elizabeth Holtzman (actress/singer)	May 23, 1906
Holman, Rufus Cecil (politician)	October 14, 1877
Holmes, Ernie; born Ernest Lee Holmes (football)	July 11, 1948
Holmes, Larry (boxing)	November 3, 1949
Holmes, Oliver Wendell (author)	August 29, 1809
Holmes, Oliver Wendell (jurist)	March 8, 1841
Holmes, Phillips (actor)	July 22, 1907
Holmes, Robert (football)	October 5, 1945
Holmes, Robert Denison (politician)	May 11, 1909
Holmes, Tommy; born Thomas Francis Holmes (baseball)	March 29, 1917
Holshouser, James Eubert, Jr. (politician)	October 8, 1934
Holt, Homer Adams (politician)	March 1, 1898
Holt, Tim; born John Charles Holt, Jr. (actor)	February 5, 1918
Holt, W. Elmer; born William Elmer Holt (politician)	October 14, 1884
Holton, Linwood; born Abner Linwood Holton, Jr. (politician)	September 21, 1923
Holtz, Lou (comedian/actor)	April 11, 1893
Holtzman, Ken; born Kenneth Dale Holtzman (baseball)	November 3, 1945
Holtzman, Red; born William Holtzman (basketball)	August 10, 1920

Homeier, Skip; born George Vincent Homeier (actor)	October 5, 1930
Homer, Winslow (artist)	February 24, 1836
Homer; born Henry D. Haynes (singer—Homer & Jethro/ comedian/music)	July 27, 1917
Homolka, Oscar (actor)	August 12, 1898
Honegger, Arthur (music)	March 10, 1892
Hooks, Robert Dean (actor)	April 18, 1937
Hooper, Ben Walter (politician)	October 13, 1870
Hooper, Harry Bartholomew (baseball)	August 24, 1887
Hooton, Burt Carlton (baseball)	February 7, 1950
Hoover, Herbert Clark (President)	August 10, 1874
Hoover, J. Edgar; born John Edgar Hoover (government)	January 1, 1895
Hoover, Lou Henry; born Lou Henry (First Lady)	March 29, 1875
Hope, Bob; born Leslie Townes Hope (comedian/actor)	May 29, 1903
Hopkin, Mary Elizabeth Blowen (singer)	May 3, 1950
Hopkins, Albert Jarvis (politician)	August 15, 1846
Hopkins, Anthony (actor)	December 31, 1937
Hopkins, Bo (actor)	February 2———
Hopkins, Miriam; born Ellen Miriam Hopkins (actress)	October 18, 1902
Hopkins, Telma Louise (singer)	October 28, 1948
Hopp, Johnny; born John Leonard Hopp (baseball)	July 18, 1916
Hopper, Dennis (actor/director)	May 17, 1936
Hopper, Hedda; born Elda Furry (journalist/actress)	June 2, 1890
Hopper, William DeWolf (actor)	January 26, 1915
Horeck, Peter (hockey)	June 15, 1923
Horlen, Joe; born Joel Edward Horlen (baseball)	August 14, 1937
Horn, Ted; born Eylard Theodore Horn (auto racing)	February 27, 1910
Horne, Lena Calhoun (singer/actress)	June 30, 1917
Horne, Marilyn B. (singer)	January 16, 1934
Horner, Henry (politician)	November 30, 1878
Horner, Red; born George Reginald Horner (hcokey)	May 29, 1909
Hornsby, Rogers (baseball)	April 27, 1896
Hornung, Paul Vernon (football/sportscaster)	December 23, 1935
Horowitz, Vladimir (music)	October 1, 1904
Horton, Edward Everett (actor)	March 18, 1886
Horton, Henry Hollis (politician)	February 17, 1866
Horton, Johnny (singer)	April 30, 1925
Horton, Robert; born Meade Howard Horton, Jr. (actor)	July 29, 1924
Horton, Tim; born Myles Gilbert Horton (hockey)	January 12, 1930
Horton, Willie Wattison (baseball)	October 18, 1942
Horvath, Bronco Joseph (hockey)	March 12, 1930
Hoskins, Bob; born Robert Juan Hoskins (football)	September 16, 1945
Hottelet, Richard C.; born Richard Curt Hottelet (newscaster)	September 22, 1917
Houdini, Harry; born Erik Weisz, changed to Erich Weiss (magician)	(real)March 24, 1874 (adopted)April 6, 1874
Houghton, Katharine; born Katharine Grant (actress)	March 10, 1945
Houk, Ralph George (baseball)	August 9, 1919
House, Frank; born Henry Franklin House (baseball)	February 18, 1930
Houseman, John; born Jacques Haussmann (actor/producer/ director/writer)	September 22, 1902

Houser, Jerry (actor)	July 14, 1952
Housman, A.E.; born Alfred Edward Houseman (poet)	March 26, 1859
Houston, David (singer/music)	December 9, 1938
Houston, David Franklin (government)	February 17, 1866
Houston, Jim; born James E. Houston (football)	November 3, 1937
Houston, Ken; born Kenneth Ray Houston (football)	November 12, 1944
Houston, Sam (soldier/statesman)	March 2, 1793
Houx, Frank L. (politician)	December 12, 1860
Howard, Bob; born Robert L. Howard (football)	December 24, 1944
Howard, Clint (actor)	April 20, 1959
Howard, Elston Gene (baseball)	February 23, 1929
Howard, Frank Oliver (baseball)	August 8, 1936
Howard, Jan (singer)	March 13, 1932
Howard, John; born John Cox (actor)	April 14, 1913
Howard, Ken; born Kenneth Joseph Howard, Jr. (actor)	March 28, 1944
Howard, Leslie; born Leslie Howard Stainer (actor)	April 24, 1890
Howard, Ron (actor/director)	March 1, 1954
Howard, Sidney Coe (playwright)	June 26, 1891
Howard, Susan; born Jeri Lynn Mooney (actress)	January 28, 1943
Howard, Trevor Wallace (actor)	September 29, 1916
Howe, Bob; born Robert N. Howe (tennis)	August 3, 1925
Howe, Elias (inventor)	July 9, 1819
Howe, Gordie; born Gordon Howe (hockey)	March 31, 1928
Howe, Julia Ward; born Julia Ward (author/reformer)	May 27, 1819
Howe, Quincy (journalist/newscaster/author)	August 17, 1900
Howe, Syd; born Sydney Harris Howe (hockey)	September 18, 1911
Howell, Bailey (basketball)	January 20, 1937
Howell, Delles Ray (football)	August 22, 1948
Howell, Harry; born Henry Vernon Howell (hockey)	December 29, 1932
Howell, Jim Lee; born James Lee Howell (football)	September 14, 1914
Howells, Ursula (actress)	September 17, 1922
Howells, William Dean (author)	March 1, 1837
Howes, Sally Ann (singer/actress)	July 20, 1930
Howland, Beth; born Elizabeth Howland (actress)	May 28, 1941
Howley, Chuck; born Charles L. Howley (football)	June 28, 1936
Howser, Dick; born Richard Dalton Howser (baseball)	May 14, 1937
Howton, Billy; born William Harris Howton (football)	July 3, 1930
Hoyt, Waite Charles (baseball)	September 9, 1899
Hruska, Roman Lee (politician)	August 16, 1904
Hubbard, Marv; born Marvin Hubbard (football)	May 7, 1946
Hubbell, Carl Owen (baseball)	June 22, 1903
Hubley, Season; born Susan Shelbey Brooks Hubley (actress)	—————1951
Huddleston, Walter Darlington (politician)	April 15, 1926
Hudlin, Willis; born George Willis Hudlin (baseball)	May 23, 1906
Hudson, Bill; born William Louis Hudson, II (music/singer/actor/comedian— Hudson Brothers)	October 17, 1949
Hudson, Brett Stuart Patrick (music/singer/actor/comedian— Hudson Brothers)	January 18, 1953

Hudson, Mark Jeffrey Anthony (music/singer/actor/comedian—Hudson Brothers)	August 23, 1951
Hudson, Rochelle (actress)	March 6, 1914
Hudson, Rock; born Roy Scherer, adopted name Roy Fitzgerald (actor/singer)	November 17, 1925
Hudson, Sid; born Sidney Charles Hudson (baseball)	January 3, 1917
Huff, Gary Earl (football)	April 27, 1951
Huff, Sam; born Robert Lee Huff (football)	October 4, 1934
Huggins, Miller James (baseball)	March 27, 1879
Hughes, Barnard (actor)	July 16, 1915
Hughes, Charles Evans (politician/jurist/government)	April 11, 1862
Hughes, Harold Everett (politician)	February 10, 1922
Hughes, Hatcher (playwright)	February 12, 1881
Hughes, Howard Robard, Jr. (industrialist)	December 24, 1905
Hughes, James Hurd (politician)	January 14, 1867
Hughes, Kathleen; born Betty von Gerlean (actress)	November 14, 1928
Hughes, Langston; born James Langston Hughes (writer)	February 1, 1902
Hughes, Pat; born William Patrick Hughes (football)	June 2, 1947
Hughes, Richard Joseph (politician)	August 10, 1909
Hughes, Roy John (baseball)	January 11, 1911
Hughes, William (politician)	April 3, 1872
Hughson, Tex; born Cecil Carlton Hughson (baseball)	February 9, 1916
Hugo, Victor Marie (author)	February 26, 1802
Hull, Bobby; born Robert Marvin Hull, Jr. (hockey)	January 3, 1939
Hull, Cordell (politics/government)	October 2, 1871
Hull, Dennis William (hockey)	November 19, 1944
Hull, Josephine; born Josephine Sherwood (actress)	January 3, 1884
Hulme, Denis Clive (auto racing)	June 18, 1936
Humbard, Rex; born Alpha Rex Emmanuel Humbard (evangelist)	August 13, 1919
Hume, Benita (actress)	October 14, 1906
Hume, David (philosopher)	April 26, 1711
Hummer, John (basketball)	May 5, 1948
Humperdinck, Engelbert (music)	September 1, 1854
Humperdinck, Engelbert; born Arnold George Dorsey (singer)	May 3, 1936
Humphrey, Claude B. (football)	June 29, 1944
Humphrey, George Magoffin (government)	March 8, 1890
Humphrey, Hubert Horatio (Vice President)	May 27, 1911
Humphrey, Muriel; born Muriel Fay Buck (Vice President's wife)	February 20, 1912
Hundley, Randy; born Cecil Randolph Hundley (baseball)	June 1, 1942
Hundley, Rod; born Rodney Hundley (basketball)	October 26, 1934
Hunn, John (politician)	June 23, 1849
Hunnicutt, Arthur (actor)	February 17, 1911
Hunnicutt, Gayle (actress)	February 6, 1943
Hunt, E. Howard; born Everett Howard Hunt Jr. (government)	October 9, 1918
Hunt, Frank W. (politician)	December 16, 1861
Hunt, George Wylie Paul (politician)	November 1, 1859
Hunt, H.L.; born Haroldson Lafayatte Hunt (industrialist)	February 17, 1889
Hunt, James (auto racing)	August 29, 1947
Hunt, James Baxter, Jr. (politician)	May 16, 1937

Hunt, Lester Callaway (politician)	July 8, 1892
Hunt, Marsha; born Marcia Virginia Hunt (actress)	October 17, 1917
Hunt, Ron; born Ronald Kenneth Hunt (baseball)	February 23, 1941
Hunter, Art; born Arthur Hunter (football)	April 24, 1933
Hunter, Billy; born Gordon William Hunter (baseball)	June 4, 1928
Hunter, Catfish; born James Augustus Hunter (baseball)	April 8, 1946
Hunter, Ian (actor)	June 13, 1900
Hunter, Jeffrey; born Henry Herman McKinnies (actor)	November 25, 1925
Hunter, Kermit Houston (playwright)	October 3, 1910
Hunter, Kim; born Janet Cole (actress)	November 12, 1922
Hunter, Ross; born Martin Fuss (producer/actor)	May 6, 1921
Hunter, Tab; born Arthur Andrew Kelm (or Arthur Gelien) (actor/singer)	July 11, 1931
Huntley, Chet; born Chester Robert Huntley (newscaster)	December 10, 1911
Hurley, Charles Francis (politician)	November 24, 1893
Hurley, Patrick Jay (government)	January 8, 1883
Hurley, Robert Augustine (politician)	August 25, 1895
Hurok, Sol; born Solomon Hurok (producer)	April 9, 1888
Hurst, Don; born Frank O'Donnell Hurst (baseball)	August 12, 1905
Hurst, Fannie (author)	October 18, 1889
Husky, Ferlin (singer/comedian)	December 3, 1927
Hussein I; born Hussein ibn Talal ibn Abdullah el Hashim (King of Jordan)	November 14, 1935
Hussey, Ruth Carol (actress)	October 30, 1913
Huston, John (director/actor/writer)	August 5, 1906
Huston, Walter; born Walter Houghston (actor)	April 6, 1884
Hutcherson, Dick; born Richard Leon Hutcherson (auto racing)	November 30, 1931
Hutchins, Mel (basketball)	November 22, 1928
Hutchins, Will (actor)	May 5, 1932
Hutchinson, Fred; born Frederick Charles Hutchinson (baseball)	August 12, 1919
Hutchinson, Josephine (actress)	October 9, 1898
Hutchison, Chuck; born Charles Hutchison (football)	November 17, 1948
Hutchison, Jock (golf)	June 6, 1884
Hutson, Don; born Donald Montgomery Hutson (football)	January 31, 1913
Hutton, Barbara (heiress)	November 14, 1912
Hutton, Betty; born Elizabeth June Thornburg (actress)	February 26, 1921
Hutton, Ina Ray (music/singer/dancer)	March 13, 1916
Hutton, Jim (actor)	May 31, 1938
Hutton, Lauren; born Mary Hutton (actress)	November 17, 1943
Hutton, Marion; born Marion Thornburg (singer/actress)	———1920
Hutton, Robert; born Robert Bruce Winne (actor)	June 11, 1920
Huxley, Aldous Leonard (author)	July 26, 1894
Huxman, Walter A. (politician)	February 16, 1887
Hyams, Leila (actress)	May 1, 1905
Hyde, Arthur Mastick (politics/government)	July 12, 1877
Hyde-White, Wilfrid (actor)	May 12, 1903
Hyer, Martha (actress)	August 10, 1924
Hyland, Bob; born Robert Joseph Hyland (football)	July 21, 1945
Hyland, Brian (singer)	November 12, 1943
Hyland, Diana; born Joan Diana Gentner (actress)	January 25, 1936
Hylton, James Harvey (auto racing)	August 26, 1935

I

Ian, Janis (singer/music)	May 7, 1950
Ibsen, Henrik Johan (playwright)	March 20, 1828
Ickes, Harold LeClaire (government)	March 15, 1874
Ickx, Jacky; born Jacques-Bernard Ickx (auto racing)	January 1, 1945
Ike, Reverend; born Frederick Joseph Eikerenkoetter, II (evangelist)	June 1, 1935
Inescort, Frieda; born Frieda Wightman (actress)	June 28, 1901
Ingarfield, Earl Thompson (hockey)	October 25, 1934
Inge, William Motter (playwright)	May 3, 1913
Ingels, Marty; born Marty Ingerman (actor)	March 9, 1936
Ingram, Rex (actor)	October 20, 1895
Ingram, Rex; born Reginald Ingram Montgomery Hitchcock (actor/director/producer/writer)	January 15, 1892
Ingres, Jean Auguste Dominique (artist)	August 29, 1780
Inman, Joe (golf)	November 29, 1947
Inness, George (artist)	May 1, 1825
Inouye, Daniel Ken (politician)	September 7, 1924
Ionesco, Eugene (playwright)	November 26, 1912
Ireland, Innes; born Robert McGregor Innes Ireland (auto racing)	June 12, 1930
Ireland, Jill Dorothy (actress/singer)	April 24, 1936
Ireland, John Benjamin (actor)	January 30, 1914
Irons, Gerald Dwayne (football)	May 2, 1947
Irvine, George (basketball)	February 1, 1948
Irvine, Ted; born Edward Amos Irvine (hockey)	December 8, 1944
Irving, Washington (author)	April 3, 1783
Irwin, Hale S., Jr. (golf)	June 3, 1945
Irwin, James Benson (astronaut)	March 17, 1930
Isaac, Bobby; born Robert Vance Isaac (auto racing)	August 1, 1934
Isabella I (Queen of Spain)	April 22, 1451
Isherwood, Christopher William (author/playwright)	August 26, 1904
Isley, O'Kelly (singer—Isley Brothers)	December 25, 1937
Isley, Ronald (singer—Isley Brothers)	May 2, 1941
Isley, Rudolph (singer—Isley Brothers)	April 1, 1939
Issel, Dan (basketball)	October 25, 1948
Iturbi, José (music)	November 28, 1895
Iverson, Don; born Donald Iverson (golf)	October 28, 1945
Ives, Burl Icle Ivanhoe (actor/singer)	June 14, 1909
Ives, Charles Edward (music)	October 20, 1874
Ives, Irving McNeil (politician)	January 24, 1896

J

Jacklin, Tony; born Anthony Jacklin (golf)	July 7, 1944
Jackson, Al; born Alvin Neal Jackson (baseball)	December 25, 1935
Jackson, Andrew (President)	March 15, 1767
Jackson, Anne; born Anna June Jackson (actress)	September 3, 1926
Jackson, Arthur (hockey)	December 15, 1915
Jackson, Busher; born Harvey Jackson (hockey)	January 17, 1911
Jackson, Chuck; born Charles Jackson (singer)	July 22, 1937

Jackson, Edward L. (politician)	December 27, 1873
Jackson, Freda (actress)	December 29, 1909
Jackson, Glenda (actress)	May 9, 1936
Jackson, Grant Dwight (baseball)	September 28, 1942
Jackson, Harold (football)	January 6, 1946
Jackson, Harold Russell (hockey)	August 1, 1918
Jackson, Henry Martin "Scoop" (politician)	May 31, 1912
Jackson, Jesse Louis (civil rights leader)	October 8, 1941
Jackson, Kate (actress)	October 29, 1948
Jackson, Keith MacKenzie (sportscaster)	October 18, 1928
Jackson, Larron (football)	August 26, 1949
Jackson, Larry; born Lawrence Curtis Jackson (baseball)	June 2, 1931
Jackson, Luke; born Lucious Jackson (basketball)	October 31, 1941
Jackson, Mahalia (singer)	October 26, 1911
Jackson, Maynard Holbrook, Jr. (politician)	March 23, 1938
Jackson, Phil (basketball)	September 17, 1945
Jackson, Rachel; born Rachel Donelson (First Lady)	June 15, 1767
Jackson, Randy; born Ransom Joseph Jackson (baseball)	February 10, 1926
Jackson, Reggie; born Reginald Martinez Jackson (baseball/sportscaster)	May 18, 1946
Jackson, Robert Houghwout (government/jurist)	February 13, 1892
Jackson, Sherry; born Sharon Diane Jackson (actress)	February 15, 1947
Jackson, Sonny; born Roland Thomas Jackson (baseball)	July 9, 1944
Jackson, Stonewall; born Thomas Jonathan Jackson (military officer)	January 21, 1824
Jackson, Stonewall (singer/music)	November 6, 1932
Jackson, Travis Calvin (baseball)	November 2, 1903
Jackson, Wanda (singer/music)	October 20, 1937
Jacobi, Lou; born Louis Harold Jacobi (actor)	December 28, 1913
Jacobs, Helen Hull (tennis)	August 6, 1908
Jacobs, Lawrence-Hilton (actor)	September 4, 1953
Jacobs, Tommy; born K. Thomas Jacobs (golf)	February 13, 1935
Jacobson, Baby Doll; born William Chester Jacobson (baseball)	August 16, 1890
Jacoby, Scott (actor)	November 26, 1955
Jaeckel, Richard Hanley (actor)	October 10, 1926
Jaffe, Sam; born Samuel Jaffe (actor)	March 8, 1893
Jagger, Dean; born Dean Jeffries (actor)	November 7, 1903
Jagger, Mick; born Michael Philip Jagger (singer)	July 26, 1943
Jamal, Ahmad (music)	July 2, 1930
James, Arthur Horace (politician)	July 14, 1883
James, Dennis (TV host)	August 24, 1917
James, Dick; born Richard James (football)	May 22, 1934
James, Etta; born Etta James Hawkins (singer)	———1938
James, Harry; born Henry Haag James (music)	March 15, 1916
James, Henry (author)	April 15, 1843
James, Jesse Woodson (outlaw)	September 5, 1847
James, Joni; born Joan Carmella Babbo (singer)	September 22, 1930
James, Ollie Murray (politician)	July 27, 1871
James, Sonny; born James Loden (singer)	May 1, 1929
Jameson, Betty; born Elizabeth Jameson (golf)	May 9, 1919

Jameson, Joyce Beverly (actress)	September 26, 1932
Jamieson, Charlie; born Charles Devine Jamieson (baseball)	February 7, 1893
Jamieson, Jim (golf)	April 21, 1943
Janick, Bobby; born Robert L. Janick (football)	February 9, 1940
Janik, Tom; born Thomas A. Janik (football)	September 6, 1940
Janis, Byron; born Byron Yanks (music)	March 24, 1928
Janis, Conrad (music/actor)	February 11, 1928
Jannings, Emil; born Theodor Friedrich Emil Janenz (actor)	July 23, 1884
Jansen, Larry; born Lawrence Joseph Jansen (baseball)	July 16, 1920
Janssen, David; born David Harold Meyer (actor)	March 27, 1930
January, Don; born Donald January (golf)	November 20, 1929
Jardine, William M. (agronomist/government)	January 16, 1879
Jarman, Claude, Jr. (actor)	September 27, 1934
Jarrett, Douglas (hockey)	April 22, 1944
Jarrett, Gary Walter (hockey)	September 3, 1942
Jarrett, Ned Miller (auto racing)	October 12, 1932
Jarriel, Tom; born Thomas Edwin Jarriel (newscaster)	December 29, 1934
Jarvis, Pat; born Robert Patrick Jarvis (baseball)	March 18, 1941
Jarvis, Ray; born Leon Rafmington Jarvis (football)	February 2, 1949
Jason, Rick (actor)	May 21, 1926
Jason, Sybil; born Sybil Jacobs (actress)	November 23, 1929
Javier, Julian; born Manuel Julian Liranzo Javier (baseball)	August 9, 1936
Javits, Jacob Koppel (politician)	May 18, 1904
Jaworski, Leon (attorney)	September 19, 1905
Jaworski, Ron; born Ronald V. Jaworski (football)	March 23, 1951
Jay, Joey; born Joseph Richard Jay (baseball)	August 15, 1935
Jay, John (statesman/jurist)	December 12, 1745
Jean, Gloria; born Gloria Jean Schoonover (actress)	April 14, 1926
Jean, Norma; born Norma Jean Beasler (singer)	January 30, 1938
Jeanmaire, Renée (dancer/actress)	April 29, 1924
Jeffcoat, Hal; born Harold Bentley Jeffcoat (baseball)	September 6, 1924
Jefferies, Richard Manning (politician)	February 27, 1888
Jefferson, Martha Wayles; born Martha Wayles (First Lady)	October 19, 1748
Jefferson, Roy Lee (football)	November 9, 1943
Jefferson, Thomas (President)	April 13, 1743
Jeffrey, Lawrence Joseph (hockey)	October 12, 1940
Jeffreys, Anne; born Anne Jeffreys Carmichael (actress)	January 26, 1923
Jeffries, Fran (singer/actress)	———1939
Jeffries, Lionel (actor/director)	———1926
Jelks, William Dorsey (politician)	November 7, 1855
Jenkins, Ferguson Arthur (baseball)	December 13, 1943
Jenner, Bruce (olympic athlete/sportscaster)	October 28, 1949
Jenner, Edward (medicine)	May 17, 1749
Jenner, William Ezra (politician)	July 21, 1908
Jennings, Hughie; born Hugh Ambrose Jennings (baseball)	April 2, 1869
Jennings, Peter Charles (newscaster)	July 29, 1938
Jennings, Waylon (singer/music)	June 15, 1937
Jennings, William Sherman (politician)	March 24, 1863
Jens, Salome (actress)	May 8, 1935

Jensen, Jackie; born Jack Eugene Jensen (baseball)	March 9, 1927
Jensen, Leslie (politician)	September 15, 1892
Jergens, Adele Louisa (actress)	November 26, 1917
Jessel, George Albert (comedian/actor)	April 3, 1898
Jessen, Mary Ruth (golf)	November 12, 1936
Jessie, Ron; born Ronald Jessie (football)	February 4, 1948
Jester, Beauford Halbert (politician)	January 12, 1893
Jeter, Bob; born Robert D. Jeter (football)	May 9, 1937
Jethro; born Kenneth C. Burns (singer—Homer & Jethro/ comedian/music)	March 10, 1920
Jewell, Isabel (actress)	July 19, 1909
Jewison, Norman F. (producer/director)	July 21, 1926
Jillson, Joyce (actress)	December 26, 1946
Jimmy The Greek; born Demetrios George Synodinos, changed to James G. Snyder (oddsmaker/sports analyst)	September 9, 1918
Jo, Damita; born Damita Joe DuBlanc (singer)	August 5, 1940
Joan of Arc; born Jeanne D'Arc (French heroine)	January 6, 1412
Joffrey, Robert; born Abdullah Jaffa Bey Khan (choreographer)	December 24, 1930
Johann, Zita (actress)	July 14, 1904
Johansson, Ingemar (boxing)	September 22, 1932
John, Elton; born Reginald Kenneth Dwight (singer)	March 25, 1947
John, Tommy; born Thomas Edward John (baseball)	May 22, 1943
Johncock, Gordon Walter (auto racing)	August 25, 1936
Johns, Charley Eugene (politician)	February 27, 1905
Johns, Glynis (actress)	October 5, 1923
Johns, Jasper (artist)	May 15, 1930
Johnson, Alex; born Alexander Johnson (baseball)	December 7, 1942
Johnson, Andrew (President)	December 29, 1808
Johnson, Arte (actor/comedian/TV host)	January 20, 1934
Johnson, Ben; born Francis Benjamin Johnson (actor)	June 13, 1918
Johnson, Billy; born William Russell Johnson (baseball)	August 30, 1918
Johnson, Billy "White Shoes" (football)	January 21, 1952
Johnson, Bob; born Robert Douglas Johnson (football)	August 19, 1946
Johnson, Bob; born Robert Lee Johnson (baseball)	November 26, 1906
Johnson, Bob; born Robert Wallace Johnson (baseball)	March 4, 1936
Johnson, Celia (actress)	December 18, 1908
Johnson, Charley; born Charles Lane Johnson (football)	November 22, 1938
Johnson, Ching; born Ivan Wilfred Johnson (hockey)	December 7, 1897
Johnson, Curtis (football)	June 22, 1948
Johnson, Darrell Dean (baseball)	August 25, 1927
Johnson, Dave; born David Allen Johnson (baseball)	January 30, 1943
Johnson, Deron Roger (baseball)	July 17, 1938
Johnson, Edwin Carl (politician)	January 1, 1884
Johnson, Edwin Stockton (politician)	February 26, 1857
Johnson, Eliza McCardle; born Eliza McCardle (First Lady)	October 4, 1810
Johnson, Ernie; born Ernest Rudolph Johnson (baseball)	April 29, 1888
Johnson, Essex L. (football)	October 14, 1946
Johnson, Gus (basketball)	December 13, 1938
Johnson, Hiram Warren (politician)	September 2, 1866
Johnson, J. Bennett, Jr. (politician)	June 10, 1932

Johnson, Jack; born John Arthur Johnson (boxing)	March 31, 1878
Johnson, Jimmy; born James Earl Johnson (football)	March 31, 1938
Johnson, John Albert (politician)	July 28, 1861
Johnson, John Henry (football)	November 24, 1929
Johnson, Joseph Blaine (politician)	August 29, 1893
Johnson, Josephine Winslow (author)	June 20, 1910
Johnson, Junior (auto racing)	————1932
Johnson, Kay (actress)	November 29, 1904
Johnson, Keen (politician)	January 12, 1896
Johnson, Ken; born Kenneth Johnson (football)	February 12, 1947
Johnson, Ken; born Kenneth Travis Johnson (baseball)	June 16, 1933
Johnson, Lady Bird; born Claudia Alta Taylor (First Lady)	December 22, 1912
Johnson, Levi (football)	October 30, 1950
Johnson, Luci Baines; born Lucy Baines Johnson	July 2, 1947
(First family)	
Johnson, Lynda Bird (First family)	March 19, 1944
Johnson, Lyndon Baines (President)	August 27, 1908
Johnson, Neil Albert (basketball)	April 17, 1943
Johnson, Paul Burney, Sr. (politician)	March 23, 1880
Johnson, Paul Burney Jr. (politician)	January 23, 1916
Johnson, Rafer Lewis (olympic athlete/actor)	August 18, 1935
Johnson, Randy; born Randolph K. Johnson (football)	June 17, 1944
Johnson, Richard Mentor (Vice President)	October 17, 1781
Johnson, Rita; born Rita McSean (actress)	August 13, 1912
Johnson, Ron; born Ronald Adolphus Johnson (football)	October 17, 1947
Johnson, Roy Cleveland (baseball)	February 23, 1903
Johnson, Samuel (writer)	September 18, 1709
Johnson, Si; born Silas Kenneth Johnson (baseball)	October 5, 1906
Johnson, Syl; born Sylvester W. Johnson (baseball)	December 31, 1900
Johnson, Tom; born Thomas Christian Johnson (hockey)	February 18, 1928
Johnson, Van; born Charles Van Johnson (actor)	August 25, 1916
Johnson, Walter (football)	November 13, 1942
Johnson, Walter Perry (baseball)	November 6, 1887
Johnson, Walter Warren (politician)	April 16, 1904
Johnston, Henry Simpson (politician)	December 30, 1867
Johnston, Jimmy; born James Harle Johnston (baseball)	December 10, 1889
Johnston, Neil (basketball)	February 4, 1929
Johnston, Olin Dewitt (politician)	November 18, 1896
Johnstone, Jay; born John William Johnstone (baseball)	November 20, 1945
Joiner, Charlie; born Charles Joiner (football)	October 14, 1947
Joliat, Aurel (hockey)	August 29, 1901
Jolson, Al; born Asa Yoelson (singer/actor)	May 26, 1886
Jones, Allan (singer/actor)	October 14, 1907
Jones, Andrieus Aristieus (politician)	May 16, 1862
Jones, Bert; born Bertram Hays Jones (football)	September 7, 1951
Jones, Bobby; born Robert Tyre Jones (golf)	March 17, 1902
Jones, Buck; born Charles Frederick Gebhart (actor)	December 4, 1889
Jones, Carolyn Sue (actress)	April 28, 1929
Jones, Charlie; born Charles Norris Jones	November 9, 1930
(sportscaster/actor/attorney)	
Jones, Christopher (actor)	August 18, 1941

Jones, Cleon Joseph (baseball)	August 4, 1942
Jones, Clinton (football)	May 24, 1945
Jones, Deacon; born David Jones (football)	December 9, 1938
Jones, Dean Carroll (actor)	January 25, 1930
Jones, Ed "Too Tall"; born Edward Lee Jones (football)	February 23, 1951
Jones, George Glen (singer/music)	September 12, 1931
Jones, Grandpa; born Louis Marshall Jones (singer/music/comedian)	October 20, 1913
Jones, Grier (golf)	May 6, 1946
Jones, Henry Burk (actor)	August 1, 1912
Jones, Homer C. (football)	February 18, 1941
Jones, Horace (football)	July 31, 1949
Jones, Jack (singer/actor)	January 14, 1938
Jones, James (author)	November 6, 1921
Jones, James Earl (actor)	January 17, 1931
Jones, Jennifer; born Phyllis Lee Isley (actress)	March 2, 1919
Jones, Jesse Holman (government)	April 5, 1874
Jones, Jimmy; born James Jones (basketball)	January 1, 1945
Jones, Joe Willie (football)	January 7, 1948
Jones, John Paul (naval officer)	July 6, 1747
Jones, Jonah; born Robert Elliott Jones (music)	December 31, 1909
Jones, K.C. (basketball)	May 25, 1932
Jones, L.Q. (actor)	———1936
Jones, Mack (baseball)	November 6, 1938
Jones, Marcia Mae (actress)	August 1, 1924
Jones, Parnelli; born Rufus Parnell Jones (auto racing)	August 12, 1933
Jones, Phil; born Phillip Howard Jones (newscaster)	April 27, 1937
Jones, Preston St. Vrain (playwright/actor)	April 7, 1936
Jones, Quincy Delight, Jr. (music)	March 14, 1933
Jones, Rich (basketball)	December 27, 1946
Jones, Robert Taylor (politician)	February 8, 1884
Jones, Robert Trent (golf)	June 20, 1906
Jones, Sad Sam; born Samuel Pond Jones (baseball)	June 26, 1892
Jones, Sam; born Samuel Jones (baseball)	December 14, 1925
Jones, Sam; born Samuel Jones (basketball)	June 24, 1933
Jones, Shirley Mae (actress/singer)	March 31, 1933
Jones, Spike; born Lindley Armstrong Jones (music)	December 14, 1911
Jones, Spike; born John A. Jones (football)	July 9, 1946
Jones, Stan; born Stanley P. Jones (football)	November 24, 1931
Jones, Tom; born Thomas Jones Woodward (singer)	June 7, 1940
Jones, Wesley Livsey (politician)	October 9, 1863
Jones, Wil; born Wilbur Jones (basketball)	February 27, 1947
Jones, Willie Edward (baseball)	August 16, 1925
Jong, Erica; born Erica Mann (writer)	March 26, 1942
Jonson, Ben; born Benjamin Jonson (playwright/poet)	June 11, 1572
Joost, Eddie; born Edwin David Joost (baseball)	June 5, 1916
Joplin, Janis Lyn (singer)	January 19, 1943
Joplin, Scott (music)	November 24, 1868
Jordan, Barbara Charline (politician)	February 21, 1936
Jordan, Benjamin Everett (politician)	September 8, 1896
Jordan, Buck; born Baxter Byerly Jordan (baseball)	January 16, 1907

Jordan, Chester Bradley (politician)	October 15, 1839
Jordan, Dorothy (actress)	August 9, 1908
Jordan, Hamilton; born William Hamilton McWhorter Jordan	September 21, 1944
(government)	
Jordan, Henry Wendell (football)	January 26, 1935
Jordan, Lee Roy (football)	April 27, 1941
Jordan, Leonard Beck (politician)	May 15, 1899
Jordan, Phil (basketball)	September 12, 1933
Jordan, Richard (actor)	July 19, 1938
Jory, Victor (actor)	November 23, 1902
Josephine de Beauharnis; born Marie Josephine Rose	June 23, 1763
Tascher de la Pagerie (French Empress)	
Josephson, Les; born Lester Josephson (football/actor)	July 29, 1942
Joslyn, Allyn (actor)	July 21, 1901
Jourdan, Louis; born Louis Gendre (actor)	June 19, 1920
Joy, Leatrice; born Leatrice Joy Ziedler (actress)	November 7, 1896
Joyal, Edward Abel (hockey)	May 8, 1940
Joyce, Brenda; born Betty Graftina Leabo (actress)	February 25, 1916
Joyce, Elaine (actress/singer)	December 19, 1945
Joyce, James Augustine (poet/author)	February 2, 1882
Joyce, Stephen (actor)	March 7, 1931
Juárez, Benito Pablo (Mexican statesman)	March 21, 1806
Judge, Arline (actress)	February 21, 1912
Judge, Joe; born Joseph Ignatius Judge (baseball)	May 25, 1894
Judge, Thomas Lee (politician)	October 12, 1934
Juliana; born Juliana Louise Emma Marie Wilhelmina	April 30, 1909
(Queen of The Netherlands)	
Jung, Carl Gustav (psychoanalyst/author)	July 26, 1875
Jurado, Katy; born Maria Christina Jurado Garcia	January 16, 1927
(actress)	
Jürgens, Curd (or Curt) (actor/director)	December 13, 1912
Jurgensen, Sonny; born Christian Adolph Jurgensen, III	August 23, 1934
(football/sportscaster)	
Jurges, Bill; born William Frederick Jurges (baseball)	May 9, 1908
Juzda, William (hockey)	October 29, 1920

K

Kaat, Jim; born James Lee Kaat (baseball)	November 7, 1938
Kabalevsky, Dmitri (music)	December 30, 1904
Kabibble, Ish; born Merwyn A. Bogue (singer/comedian)	January 19, 1908
Kaempfert, Bert (music)	October 16, 1923
Kahan, Judy (actress)	May 24, 1948
Kahn, Madeline Gail (actress/singer)	September 29, 1942
Kaiser, Henry John (industrialist)	May 9, 1882
Kalb, Bernard (newscaster)	February 5, 1922
Kalb, Marvin Leonard (newscaster/author)	June 9, 1930
Kalber, Floyd (newscaster)	December 23, 1924
Kaleta, Alexander (hockey)	November 29, 1919
Kaline, Al; born Albert William Kaline (baseball)	December 19, 1934
Kallen, Kitty (singer)	May 25, 1926

Kalmbach, Herbert Warren (government)	October 19, 1921
Kamen, Milt; born Milton Kaiman (comedian/actor)	———1924
Kaminska, Ida; born Ida Kaminski (actress)	September 4, 1899
Kamm, Willie; born William Edward Kamm (baseball)	February 2, 1900
Kampouris, Alex William (baseball)	November 13, 1912
Kander, John Harold (music)	March 18, 1927
Kane, Helen; born Helen Schroeder (actress/singer)	August 4, 1903
Kanicki, Jim; born James Kanicki (football)	December 17, 1942
Kanin, Garson; born Gershon Labe (producer/director/writer)	November 24, 1912
Kant, Immanuel (philosopher)	April 22, 1724
Kantor, MacKinlay (author)	February 4, 1904
Kaplan, Gabriel (comedian/actor)	March 31, 1945
Kaplow, Herb; born Herbert Elias Kaplow (newscaster)	February 2, 1927
Kapp, Joe; born Joseph Robert Kapp (football/actor)	March 19, 1938
Karajan, Herbert von (music)	April 5, 1908
Karakas, Mike; born Michael Karakas (hockey)	December 12, 1911
Karloff, Boris; born William Henry Pratt (actor)	November 23, 1887
Karns, Roscoe (actor)	September 7, 1893
Karras, Alex; born Alexander G. Karras (football/sportscaster/actor)	July 15, 1935
Kasko, Eddie; born Edward Michael Kasko (baseball)	June 27, 1932
Kastner, Peter Bernard Joshua (actor)	October 1, 1943
Kaznar, Kurt; born Kurt Serwischer (actor)	August 12, 1913
Katcavage, Jim; born James R. Katcavage (football)	October 28, 1934
Katzenbach, Nicholas deBelleville (government)	January 17, 1922
Kaufman, George S.; born George Simon Kaufman (playwright/director)	November 14, 1889
Kaufmann, Christine (actress)	January 11, 1945
Kavanaugh, Ken; born Kenneth W. Kavanaugh (football)	November 23, 1916
Kavner, Julie Deborah (actress)	September 7, 1951
Kaye, Danny; born David Daniel Kominski (actor/comedian)	January 18, 1913
Kaye, Sammy (music)	March 13, 1913
Kaye, Stubby (actor)	November 11, 1918
Kazan, Elia; born Elia Kazanjoglous (director/actor)	September 7, 1909
Kazan, Lainie; born Lainie Levine (singer/actress)	May 16, 1940
Kazmierski, Joyce (golf)	August 14, 1945
Keach, Stacy, Sr. (actor/producer/director/writer)	May 29, 1914
Keach, Stacy, Jr. (actor)	June 2, 1941
Kean, Hamilton Fish (politician)	February 27, 1862
Kean, Jane Dawn (actress)	April 10, 1928
Kean, John (politician)	December 4, 1852
Kearney, Jim; born James L. Kearney (football)	January 21, 1943
Kearns, Thomas (politician)	April 11, 1862
Keating, Kenneth Barnard (politician)	May 18, 1900
Keating, Tom; born Thomas Arthur Keating (football)	September 2, 1942
Keaton, Buster; born Joseph Francis Keaton (actor/comedian)	October 4, 1895
Keaton, Diane; born Diane Hall (actress)	January 5, 1946
Keats, John (poet)	October 31, 1795
Keel, Howard; born Harold Clifford Leek (actor/singer)	April 13, 1917
Keeler, Ruby; born Ethel Hilda Keeler (actress/dancer)	August 25, 1909

Keeler, Willie; born William Henry Keeler (baseball)	March 3, 1872
Keeling, Butch; born Melville Sidney Keeling (hockey)	August 1, 1905
Keeshan, Bob; born Robert James Keeshan "Captain Kangaroo" (actor)	June 27, 1927
Kefauver, Estes; born Carey Estes Kefauver (politician)	July 26, 1903
Keiser, Herman (golf)	October 7, 1914
Keith, Brian; born Robert Keith, Jr. (actor)	November 14, 1921
Kell, George Clyde (baseball)	August 23, 1922
Kellaway, Cecil (actor)	August 22, 1891
Keller, Billy (basketball)	August 30, 1947
Keller, Charlie; born Charles Ernest Keller (baseball)	September 12, 1916
Keller, Helen Adams (author/educator)	June 27, 1880
Kellerman, Sally Claire (actress/singer)	June 2, 1937
Kelley, Clarence Marion (government)	October 24, 1911
Kelley, Joe; born Joseph James Kelley (baseball)	December 9, 1871
Kellner, Alex; born Alexander Raymond Kellner (baseball)	August 26, 1924
Kellogg, Frank Billings (politics/government)	December 22, 1856
Kellogg, Lynn (singer/actress)	———1945
Kelly, Emmett Leo, Sr. (clown)	December 9, 1898
Kelly, Gene; born Eugene Curran Kelly (actor/dancer/singer/director)	August 23, 1912
Kelly, George Edward (playwright)	January 16, 1887
Kelly, George Lange (baseball)	September 10, 1895
Kelly, Grace Patricia (actress/Princess Grace of Monaco)	November 12, 1929
Kelly, Harry Francis (politician)	April 19, 1895
Kelly, Jack (actor)	September 16, 1927
Kelly, King; born Michael Joseph Kelly (baseball)	December 31, 1857
Kelly, Leroy (football)	May 20, 1942
Kelly, Nancy (actress)	March 25, 1921
Kelly, Pat; born Harold Patrick Kelly (baseball)	July 30, 1944
Kelly, Patsy; born Sarah Veronica Rose Kelly (actress)	January 12, 1910
Kelly, Paul Michael (actor)	August 9, 1899
Kelly, Paula (actress/dancer/singer)	———1942
Kelly, Pep; born Régis J. Kelly (hockey)	January 17, 1914
Kelly, Red; born Leonard Patrick Kelly (hockey)	July 9, 1927
Kelly, Roz (actress/photographer)	July 29———
Kelly, Walt; born Walter Crawford Kelly (cartoonist)	August 25, 1913
Kelsey, Linda (actress)	July 28, ———
Keltner, Ken; born Kenneth Frederick Keltner (baseball)	October 31, 1916
Kelton, Pert Lizzette (actress)	October 14, 1907
Kem, James Preston (politician)	April 2, 1890
Kemp, Jackie; born John French Kemp (football/politics)	July 13, 1935
Kemp, Jeremy; born Edmund Walker (actor)	February 3, 1935
Kendall, Fred Lyn (baseball)	January 31, 1949
Kendall, Kay; born Justine Kay Kendall McCarthy (actress)	May 21, 1926
Kendall, Nathan Edward (politician)	March 17, 1868
Kendall, Suzy; born Frieda Harrison (actress)	———1944
Kendrick, John Benjamin (politician)	September 6, 1857
Kennedy, Arthur; born John Arthur Kennedy (actor)	February 17, 1914
Kennedy, Bob; born Robert Daniel Kennedy (baseball)	August 18, 1920
Kennedy, Caroline Bouvier (First family)	November 27, 1957

Kennedy, David Matthew (government)   July 21, 1905
Kennedy, Edgar (actor)   April 26, 1890
Kennedy, Ethel; born Ethel Skakel (socialite)   April 11, 1928
Kennedy, George (actor)   February 18, 1925
Kennedy, Jayne; born Jayne Harrison (actress/sportscaster)   October 27, 1951
Kennedy, Joan Bennett; born Joan Bennett (socialite)   September 5, 1936
Kennedy, John Edward (baseball)   May 29, 1941
Kennedy, John Fitzgerald (President)   May 29, 1917
Kennedy, John Fitzgerald, Jr. (First family)   November 25, 1960
Kennedy, Joseph Patrick (President's father)   September 6, 1888
Kennedy, Robert Francis (government/politics)   November 20, 1925
Kennedy, Rose; born Rose Fitzgerald (President's mother)   July 22, 1890
Kennedy, Ted; born Edward Moore Kennedy (politician)   February 22, 1932
Kennedy, Teeder; born Theodore S. Kennedy (hockey)   December 12, 1925
Kennedy, Tom (TV host)   February 16———
Kennedy, Vern; born Lloyd Vernon Kennedy (baseball)   March 20, 1907
Kennon, Robert Floyd (politician)   August 21, 1902
Kent, Barbara; born Barbara Clowtman (actress)   December 16, 1906
Kent, Jean; born Joan Summerfield (actress)   June 29, 1921
Kent, Rockwell (artist)   June 21, 1882
Kenton, Stan; born Stanley Newcomb Kenton (music)   February 19, 1912
Kenyon, Doris (actress)   September 5, 1897
Kenyon, Mel (auto racing)   April 15, 1933
Keon, Dave; born David Michael Keon (hockey)   March 22, 1940
Keough, Marty; born Richard Martin Keough (baseball)   April 14, 1935
Kercheval, Ken (actor)   July 15, 1935
Kerenski, Aleksandr Feodorovich (Russian government)   April 22, 1881
Kermoyan, Michael; born Kalem Missak Kermoyan (actor)   November 29, 1925
Kern, Jerome David (music)   January 27, 1885
Kern, John Worth (politician)   December 20, 1849
Kerner, Otto (politician)   August 15, 1908
Kerr, Anita (singer/music)   October 13, 1927
Kerr, Buddy; born John Joseph Kerr (baseball)   November 6, 1922
Kerr, Davey; born David Alexander Kerr (hockey)   January 11, 1910
Kerr, Deborah; born Deborah Jane Kerr-Trimmer (actress)   September 30, 1921
Kerr, Jean; born Bridget Jean Collins (playwright)   July 10, 1923
Kerr, John (basketball)   August 17, 1932
Kerr, John Grinham (actor)   November 15, 1931
Kerr, Robert Samuel (politician)   September 11, 1896
Kerr, Walter Francis (journalist)   July 8, 1913
Kershaw, Doug; born Douglas James Kershaw (music)   January 24, 1936
Kert, Larry; born Frederick Lawrence Kert (actor/singer/dancer)   December 5, 1934
Kesey, Ken Elton (author)   September 17, 1935
Kessinger, Don; born Donald Eulon Kessinger (baseball)   July 17, 1942
Ketcham, Hank; born Henry King Ketcham (cartoonist)   March 14, 1920
Key, Francis Scott (music/law)   August 1, 1779
Key, Wade; born Allan Wade Key (football)   October 14, 1946
Keyes, Evelyn Louise (actress)   November 20, 1919
Keyes, Frances Parkinson; born Frances Parkinson Wheeler (author)   July 21, 1885

Keyes, Henry Wilder (politician)	May 23, 1863
Keyes, Leroy; born Marvin Leroy Huggins (football)	February 18, 1947
Keyser, Frank Ray, Jr. (politician)	August 17, 1927
Keyworth, Jon; born Jonathan K. Keyworth (football)	December 15, 1950
Khachaturian, Aram Ilich (music)	June 6, 1903
Khayat, Eddie; born Edward Khayat (football)	September 14, 1935
Khomeini, Ayatollah Ruholla Mussavi (Iranian religious & political leader)	May 17, 1900
Khruschchev, Nikita Sergeyevich (Russian government)	April 17, 1894
Kibbee, Guy Bridges (actor)	March 6, 1882
Kidd, Michael; born Milton Greenwald (choreographer/director)	August 12, 1919
Kidder, Margot (actress)	October 17, 1948
Kieran, John Francis (journalist/author/editor)	August 2, 1892
Kiesinger, Kurt Georg (German government)	April 6, 1904
Kiick, Jim; born James Forrest Kiick (football)	August 9, 1946
Kiker, Douglas; born Ralph Douglas Kiker, Jr. (newscaster)	January 7, 1930
Kilbride, Percy (actor)	July 16, 1888
Kilby, Thomas Erby (politician)	July 9, 1865
Kiley, Richard Paul (actor/singer)	March 31, 1922
Kilgallen, Dorothy Mae (journalist)	July 3, 1913
Kilgore, Harley Martin (politician)	January 11, 1893
Kilian, Victor Arthur (actor)	March 6, 1891
Killebrew, Harmon Clayton, Jr. (baseball)	June 29, 1936
Killy, Jean Claude (skiing)	August 30, 1943
Kilmer, Bill; born William Orland Kilmer (football)	September 5, 1939
Kilmer, Joyce; born Alfred Joyce Kilmer (poet)	December 6, 1886
Kilpatrick, James J. "Jack"; born James Jackson Kilpatrick, Jr. (journalist/author)	November 1, 1920
Kilpatrick, Lincoln (actor)	February 12, 1936
Kilrea, Hector J. (hockey)	June 11, 1907
Kimball, Charles Dean (politician)	September 13, 1859
Kimball, Judy (golf)	June 17, 1938
Kimbrough, Emily (author)	October 23, 1899
Kinard, Bruiser; born Frank M. Kinard (football)	October 23, 1914
Kindall, Jerry; born Gerald Donald Kindall (baseball)	May 27, 1935
Kinder, Ellis Raymond (baseball)	July 26, 1914
Kiner, Ralph McPherran (baseball)	October 27, 1922
Kiner, Steve; born Steven Kiner (football)	June 12, 1947
King, Alan; born Irwin Alan Kniberg (comedian/actor)	December 26, 1927
King, Andrea; born Georgetta Barry (actress)	February 1, 1915
King, B.B.; born Riley B. King (singer/music)	September 16, 1925
King, Ben E.; born Benjamin Nelson (singer/music)	September 28, 1938
King, Billie Jean; born Billie Jean Moffitt (tennis)	November 22, 1943
King, Bruce (politician)	April 6, 1924
King, Carole; born Carole Klein (singer/music)	February 9, 1941
King, Coretta Scott; born Coretta Scott (civil rights leader)	April 27, 1927
King, George (basketball)	August 16, 1928
King, James (basketball)	February 7, 1941
King, Jim; born James Hubert King (baseball)	August 27, 1932

King, John William (politician)	October 10, 1918
King, Martin Luther, Jr.; born Michael King (civil rights leader)	January 15, 1929
King, Morgana (singer/actress)	June 4, 1930
King, Perry (actor)	April 30, 1948
King, William Henry (politician)	June 3, 1863
King, William Rufus Devane (Vice President)	April 7, 1786
Kingman; Dong; born Tsang King-man (artist)	April 1, 1911
Kingrea, Rick; born Richard Kingrea (football)	July 18, 1949
Kingsley, Sidney; born Sidney Kirschner (playwright)	October 22, 1906
Kinskey, Leonid (actor)	April 18, 1903
Kipling, Rudyard (author)	December 30, 1865
Kirby, Clay; born Clayton Laws Kirby, Jr. (baseball)	June 25, 1948
Kirby, Durward (announcer/actor)	August 24, 1912
Kirby, George (comedian/impressionist)	June 8, 1924
Kirby, William Fosgate (politician)	November 16, 1867
Kirk, Claude Roy, Jr. (politician)	January 7, 1926
Kirk, Lisa; born Elsie Marie Kirk (actress/singer)	February 25, 1925
Kirk, Phyllis; born Phyllis Kirkegaard (actress)	September 18, 1926
Kirk, Tommy (actor)	December 10, 1941
Kirkland, Gelsey (dancer)	December 29, 1952
Kirkland, Willie Charles (baseball)	February 17, 1934
Kirkpatrick, Ed; born Edgar Leon Kirkpatrick (baseball)	October 8, 1944
Kirkwood, Joseph (golf)	March 22, 1897
Kirman, Richard (politician)	January 14, 1877
Kirsten, Dorothy (singer)	July 6, 1919
Kissinger, Henry; born Heinz Alfred Kissinger (government)	May 27, 1923
Kitchin, William Walton (politician)	October 9, 1866
Kite, Tom; born Thomas O. Kite, Jr. (golf)	December 9, 1949
Kitt, Eartha Mae (singer/actress)	January 26, 1928
Kittredge, Alfred Beard (politician)	March 28, 1861
Kjellin, Alf (actor/director)	February 28, 1920
Klaus, Billy; born William Joseph Klaus (baseball)	December 9, 1928
Klee, Paul (artist)	December 18, 1879
Klein, Bob; born Robert Klein (football)	July 27, 1947
Klein, Calvin Richard (fashion designer)	November 19, 1942
Klein, Chuck; born Charles Herbert Klein (baseball)	October 7, 1904
Klein, Herbert George (government/journalism)	April 1, 1918
Klein, Robert (comedian/actor)	February 8, 1942
Kleindienst, Richard Gordon (government)	August 5, 1923
Klemperer, Otto (music)	May 14, 1885
Klemperer, Werner (actor)	March 22, 1920
Kleppe, Thomas Savig (government)	July 1, 1919
Kline, Ron; born Ronald Lee Kline (baseball)	March 9, 1932
Klippstein, Johnny; born John Calvin Klippstein (baseball)	October 17, 1927
Klugman, Jack (actor)	April 27, 1922
Klukay, Joseph Francis (hockey)	November 6, 1922
Kluszewski, Ted; born Theodore Bernard Kluszewski (baseball)	September 10, 1924
Knapp, Evalyn (actress)	June 17, 1908
Knef, Hildegarde (actress/singer/author)	December 28, 1925

Kneip, Richard Francis (politician)	January 7, 1933
Knickerbocker, Bill; born William Hart Knickerbocker (baseball)	December 29, 1911
Knievel, Evel; born Robert Craig Knievel (daredevil/actor)	October 17, 1938
Knight, Curt (football)	April 14, 1943
Knight, Esmond (actor)	May 4, 1905
Knight, Fuzzy; born John Forrest Knight (actor)	May 9, 1901
Knight, Gladys Maria (singer)	May 28, 1944
Knight, Goodwin Jess (politician)	December 9, 1896
Knight, John Shively (publisher)	October 26, 1894
Knight, Shirley (actress)	July 5, 1936
Knight, Ted; born Tadeus Wladyslaw Konopka (actor)	December 7, 1925
Knoop, Bobby; born Robert Frank Knoop (baseball)	October 18, 1938
Knopf, Alfred A. (publisher)	September 12, 1892
Knott, Jack; born John Henry Knott (baseball)	March 2, 1907
Knotts, Don (comedian/actor)	July 21, 1924
Knous, William Lee (politician)	February 2, 1889
Knowland, William Fife (politician)	June 26, 1908
Knowles, Darold Duane (baseball)	December 9, 1941
Knowles, John (author)	September 16, 1926
Knowles, Patric; born Reginald Lawrence Knowles (actor)	November 11, 1911
Knowles, Warren Perley (politician)	August 19, 1908
Knox, Alexander (actor)	January 16, 1907
Knox, Chuck; born Charles Robert Knox (football)	April 27, 1932
Knox, Elyse (actress)	December 14, 1917
Knox, Philander Chase (government/politics)	May 6, 1853
Knudson, George (golf)	June 28, 1937
Koch, Edward Irving (politician)	December 12, 1924
Kocourek, Dave; born David A. Kocourek (football)	August 20, 1937
Koenig, Mark Anthony (baseball)	July 19, 1902
Koestler, Arthur (author)	September 5, 1905
Kohler, Walter Jodok, Sr. (politician)	March 3, 1875
Kohler, Walter Jodok, Jr. (politician)	April 4, 1904
Kohner, Susan; born Susanna Kohner (actress)	November 11, 1936
Kojis, Don (basketball)	January 15, 1939
Kolb, Jon Paul (football)	August 30, 1947
Kolen, Mike; born John Michael Kolen (football)	January 31, 1948
Kolloway, Don; born Donald Martin Kolloway (baseball)	August 4, 1918
Koosman, Jerry; born Jerome Martin Koosman (baseball)	December 23, 1942
Korbut, Olga (gymnast)	May 16, 1956
Korman, Harvey Herschel (actor/comedian/director)	February 15, 1927
Korvin, Charles; born Geza Korvin Karpathi (actor)	November 21, 1907
Koscina, Sylva (actress)	August 22, 1934
Kosco, Andy; born Andrew John Kosco (baseball)	October 5, 1941
Kosleck, Martin; born Nicolai Yoshkin (actor)	March 24, 1907
Koslo, Dave; born George Bernard Koslowski (baseball)	March 31, 1920
Kostelanetz, Andre (music)	December 22, 1901
Kosygin, Aleksei Nikolayevich (Russian government)	February 20, 1904
Kotar, Doug; born Douglas Allan Kotar (football)	June 11, 1951
Kotto, Yaphet (actor)	November 15, 1937
Koufax, Sandy; born Sanford Koufax (baseball)	December 30, 1935

Koussevitzky, Serge Alexandrovitch (music) — July 26, 1874
Kovack, Nancy Diane (actress) — March 11, 1935
Kovacs, Ernie (actor/comedian) — January 23, 1919
Kowalkowski, Bob; born Robert Kowalkowski (football) — November 5, 1943
Krake, Skip; born Philip Gordon Krake (hockey) — October 14, 1943
Kramer, Jack; born John Albert Kramer, Jr. (tennis) — August 1, 1921
Kramer, Jack; born John Henry Kramer (baseball) — January 5, 1918
Kramer, Jerry; born Gerald L. Kramer (football) — January 23, 1936
Kramer, Ron; born Ronald John Kramer (football) — June 24, 1935
Kramer, Stanley E. (producer/director) — September 29, 1913
Kramm, Joseph (playwright/director/actor) — September 30, 1907
Kranepool, Ed; born Edward Emil Kranepool (baseball) — November 8, 1944
Kraschel, Nelson George (politician) — October 27, 1889
Kratzert, Bill (golf) — June 29, 1952
Kraus, Lili (music) — March 4, 1905
Krause, Paul James (football) — February 19, 1942
Krausse, Lew; born Lewis Bernard Krausse, Jr. (baseball) — April 25, 1943
Kreevich, Mike; born Michael Andreas Kreevich (baseball) — June 10, 1908
Kreisler, Fritz (music) — February 2, 1875
Kremer, Ray; born Remy Peter Kremer (baseball) — March 23, 1893
Kreps, Juanita Morris; born Juanita Morris (government) — January 11, 1921
Kresge, S.S.; born Sebastian Spering Kresge (merchant) — July 31, 1867
Kress, Red; born Ralph Kress (baseball) — January 2, 1907
Kreuger, Charlie; born Charles A. Kreuger (football) — January 28, 1937
Kreuger, Kurt (actor) — July 23, 1916
Kristofferson, Kris (singer/actor/music) — June 22, 1936
Kroll, Ted; born Theodore Kroll (golf) — August 4, 1919
Krug, Julius Albert (government) — November 23, 1907
Kruger, Alma (actress) — September 13, 1868
Kruger, Hardy (actor) — April 12, 1928
Kruger, Otto (actor) — September 6, 1885
Krupa, Gene; born Eugene Bertram Krupa (music) — January 15, 1909
Kruschen, Jack (actor) — March 20, 1922
Kubek, Tony; born Anthony Christopher Kubek, Jr. (baseball/sportscaster) — October 12, 1935
Kubelik, Rafael; born Jeronym Rafael Kubelik (music) — June 29, 1914
Kuberski, Steve (basketball) — November 6, 1947
Kubiak, Ted; born Theodore Rodger Kubiak (baseball) — May 12, 1942
Kubrick, Stanley (producer/director) — July 26, 1928
Kuchel, Thomas Henry (politician) — August 10, 1910
Kuechenberg, Bob; born Robert John Kuechenberg (football) — October 14, 1947
Kuenn, Harvey Edward (baseball) — December 4, 1930
Kuhel, Joe; born Joseph Anthony Kuhel (baseball) — June 25, 1906
Kuhn, Bowie Kent (baseball) — October 28, 1926
Kullman, Edward George (hockey) — December 12, 1923
Kulp, Nancy Jane (actress) — August 28, 1921
Kuluva, Will (actor) — May 2, 1917
Kump, Herman Guy (politician) — October 31, 1877
Kunstler, William Moses (attorney/author) — July 7, 1919
Kunz, George James (football) — July 5, 1947
Kupp, Jake; born Jacob Kupp (football) — March 12, 1941

Kuralt, Charles Bishop (newscaster)   September 10, 1934
Kurtenbach, Orland John (hockey)   September 7, 1936
Kurtz, Efrem (music)   November 7, 1900
Kwalick, Ted; born Thaddeus John Kwalick (football)   April 15, 1947
Kwan, Nancy Ka Shen (actress)   May 19, 1939
Ky, Nguyen Cao (South Vietnamese government)   September 8, 1930
Kyser, Kay; born James Kern Kyser (music)   June 18, 1905

L

Laabs, Chet; born Chester Peter Laabs (baseball)   April 30, 1912
Laaveg, Paul Martin (football)   October 1, 1948
Labine, Clem; born Clement Walter Labine (baseball)   August 6, 1926
Labine, Leo Gerald (hockey)   July 22, 1931
Lacey, Sam (basketball)   March 28, 1948
Lach, Elmer James (hockey)   January 22, 1918
Lacoste, Rene; born Jean-Rene Lacoste (tennis)   July 2, 1905
Lacroix, Andre (hockey)   June 5, 1945
Ladd, Alan Wallbridge (actor)   September 3, 1913
Ladd, Cheryl; born Cheryl Jean Stoppelmoor (actress/singer/dancer) July 12, 1951
Ladd, Diane; born Rose Diane Ladnier (actress)   November 29, 1932
Ladd, Edwin Freemont (politician)   December 13, 1859
La Farge, Oliver Hazard Perry (author)   December 19, 1901
Lafayette, Marquis de; born Marie Joseph Paul Yves Roch   September 6, 1757
    Gilbert Du Motier (French soldier & statesman)
Laffoon, Ruby (politician)   January 15, 1869
Lafleur, Guy Damien (hockey)   September 20, 1951
LaFollette, Philip Fox (politician)   May 8, 1897
LaFollette, Robert Marion (politician)   June 14, 1855
LaFollette, Robert Marion, Jr. (politician)   February 6, 1895
La Guardia, Fiorello Henry (politician)   December 11, 1882
Lahr, Bert; born Irving Lahrheim (actor/comedian)   August 13, 1895
Lahr, Warren (football)   September 5, 1923
Laine, Cleo (singer/actress)   October 27, 1927
Laine, Frankie; born Frank Paul LoVecchio (singer)   March 30, 1913
Laird, Melvin Robert (government)   September 1, 1922
Lajoie, Nap; born Napoleon Lajoie (baseball)   September 5, 1875
Lake, Arthur; born Arthur Silverlake (actor)   April 17, 1905
Lake, Eddie; born Edward Erving Lake (baseball)   March 18, 1916
Lake, Everett John (politician)   February 8, 1871
Lake, Veronica; born Constance Frances Marie Ockelman   November 14, 1919
    (actress)
LaLanne, Jack (physical fitness expert)   September 26, 1914
Lalonde, Newsy; born Edouard Lalonde (hockey)   October 31, 1887
Lamar, Bill; born William Harmong Lamar (baseball)   March 21, 1897
Lamar, Joseph Rucker (jurist)   October 14, 1857
Lamarr, Hedy; born Hedwig Eva Maria Kiesler (actress)   November 9, 1913
Lamas, Fernando Alvaro (actor/director)   January 9, 1915
Lamb, Charles (writer)   February 10, 1775
Lamb, Gil (actor/comedian)   June 14, 1906
Lamb, Joseph Gordon (hockey)   June 18, 1906

Lambeau, Curly; born Earl L. Lambeau (football)	April 9, 1898
Lambert, Jack; born John Harold Lambert (football)	July 8, 1952
Lamm, Richard Douglas (politician)	August 3, 1935
Lammons, Pete; born Peter S. Lammons, Jr. (football)	October 20, 1943
Lamonica, Daryle P. (football)	July 17, 1941
Lamont, Robert Patterson (government)	December 1, 1867
LaMotta, Jake; born Jacob LaMotta (boxing)	July 10, 1921
Lamour, Dorothy; born Mary Leta Dorothy Kaumeyer (actress)	December 10, 1914
Lampert, Zohra (actress)	May 13, 1936
Lancaster, Burt; born Burton Stephen Lancaster (actor)	November 2, 1913
Lanchester, Elsa; born Elizabeth Sullivan (actress)	October 28, 1902
Landau, Martin (actor)	June 30, 1925
Landers, Ann; born Esther Pauline Friedman (journalist)	July 4, 1918
Landi, Elissa; born Elizabeth-Marie-Christine Kuhnelt (actress)	December 6, 1904
Landis, Carole; born Frances Lillian Mary Ridste (actress)	January 1, 1919
Landis, Jessie Royce; born Jessie Royse Medbury (actress)	November 25, 1904
Landis, Jim; born James Henry Landis (baseball)	March 9, 1934
Landon, Alf; born Alfred Mossman Landon (politician)	September 9, 1887
Landon, Michael; born Eugene Maurice Orowitz (actor/producer/director/writer)	October 31, 1936
Landrith, Hobie; born Hobert Neal Landrith (baseball)	March 16, 1930
Landry, Greg; born Gregory Paul Landry (football)	December 18, 1946
Landry, Tom; born Thomas Wade Landry (football)	September 11, 1924
Lane, Abe; born Abigail Francine Lassman (singer/actress)	December 14, 1932
Lane, Burton; born Burton Levy (music)	February 2, 1912
Lane, Franklin Knight (government)	July 15, 1864
Lane, Harry (politician)	August 28, 1855
Lane, Lola; born Dorothy Mullican (actress)	May 21, 1906
Lane, MacArthur (football)	March 16, 1942
Lane, Mark (attorney/author)	February 24, 1927
Lane, Night Train; born Richard Lane (football)	April 16, 1928
Lane, Priscilla; born Priscilla Mullican (actress)	June 12, 1917
Lane, Rosemary; born Rosemary Mullican (actress)	April 4, 1913
Lane, William Preston, Jr. (politician)	May 12, 1892
Laney, Benjamin Travis (politician)	November 25, 1896
Lang, Fritz (director)	December 5, 1890
Lang, June; born Winifred June Vlasek (actress)	May 5, 1915
Langan, Glenn (actor)	July 8, 1917
Langdon, Sue Ane; born Sue Ane Lookhoff (actress)	March 8, 1940
Lange, Hope Elise Ross (actress)	November 28, 1931
Langella, Frank (actor)	January 1, 1940
Langer, Jim; born James John Langer (football)	May 16, 1948
Langer, William (politician)	September 30, 1886
Langford, Frances (actress/singer)	April 4, 1913
Langley, Elmo Harrell (auto racing)	August 22, 1929
Langlie, Arthur Bernard (politician)	July 25, 1900
Langlois, Junior; born Albert Langlois (hockey)	November 6, 1934
Langtry, Lily; born Emily Le Breton (actress)	October 13, 1853
Lanham, Samuel Willis Tucker (politician)	July 4, 1846
Lanier, Bob; born Robert Jerry Lanier, Jr. (basketball)	September 10, 1948

Lanier, Hal; born Harold Clifton Lanier (baseball)	July 4, 1942
Lanier, Max; born Hubert Max Lanier (baseball)	August 18, 1915
Lanier, Sidney (poet)	February 3, 1842
Lanier, Willie Edward (football)	August 21, 1945
Lansbury, Angela Brigid (actress/singer)	October 16, 1925
Lansing, Joi; born Joyce Wassmansdoff (actress)	April 6, 1928
Lansing, Robert (government)	October 17, 1864
Lansing, Robert; born Robert Howell Brown (actor)	June 5, 1929
Lanson, Snooky; born Roy Landman (singer)	March 27, 1914
Lantz, Stu; born Stuart Lantz (basketball)	July 13, 1946
Lanza, Mario; born Alfred Arnold Cocozza (singer/actor)	January 31, 1921
Laperriere, Jacques (hockey)	November 22, 1941
La Plante, Laura (actress)	November 1, 1904
LaPointe, Guy Gerard (hockey)	March 18, 1948
Laprade, Edgar Louis (hockey)	October 10, 1919
Lardner, Ring; born Ringgold Wilmer Lardner (author/playwright/humorist)	March 6, 1885
Larken, Sheila; born Sheila Ann Diamond (actress)	February 24, 1944
Larochelle, Wildor (hockey)	September 3, 1906
La Rosa, Julius (singer)	January 2, 1930
Larose, Claude David (hockey)	March 2, 1942
Larrazolo, Octaviano Ambrosio (politician)	December 7, 1859
Larsen, Don; born Donald James Larsen (baseball)	August 7, 1929
Larson, Morgan Foster (politician)	June 15, 1882
La Rue, Jack; born Gaspare Biondolillo (actor)	May 3, 1900
La Rue, Lash; born Alfred La Rue (actor)	June 14, 1917
LaRusso, Rudy (basketball)	November 11, 1937
Lary, Frank Strong (baseball)	April 10, 1931
Lary, Lyn; born Lynford Hobart Lary (baseball)	January 28, 1906
La Salle, René Robert Cavlier Sieur de (explorer)	November 21, 1643
Lasorda, Tom; born Thomas Charles Lasorda (baseball)	September 22, 1927
Lasser, Louise Jane (actress)	————1937
Latimer, Asbury Churchwell (politician)	July 31, 1851
Latimore, Frank; born Frank Kline (actor)	September 28, 1925
Lau, Charlie; born Charles Richard Lau (baseball)	April 12, 1933
Lauda, Niki; born Andress Nicholas von Lauda (auto racing)	February 22, 1949
Laughton, Charles (actor)	July 1, 1899
Laughton, Michael Frederic (hockey)	February 21, 1944
Laurel, Stan; born Arthur Stanley Jefferson (comedian/actor)	June 16, 1890
Lauren, Ralph; born Ralph Lifshitz (fashion designer)	October 14, 1939
Laurents, Arthur (playwright/director)	July 14, 1918
Laurie, Piper; born Rosetta Jacobs (actress)	January 22, 1932
Lausche, Frank John (politician)	November 14, 1895
Lavagetto, Cookie; born Harry Arthur Lavagetto (baseball)	December 1, 1912
Lavelli, Dante (football)	February 23, 1923
Lavender, Joe; born Joseph Lavender (football)	February 10, 1949
Laver, Rod; born Rodney George Laver (tennis)	August 9, 1938
Lavin, Linda (actress/singer)	October 15, 1937
Law, John Phillip (actor)	September 7, 1937
Law, Vern; born Vernon Law (baseball)	March 12, 1930

Lawford, Peter Aylen (actor)	September 7, 1923
Lawrence, Carol; born Carol Maria Laraia (actress/dancer/singer)	September 5, 1932
Lawrence, D.H. born David Herbert Lawrence (author)	September 11, 1885
Lawrence, David Leo (politician)	June 18, 1889
Lawrence, Gertrude; born Gertrude Alexandra Dagmar Lawrence-Klasen (actress/singer/dancer)	July 4, 1898
Lawrence, Jerome; born Jerome Schwartz (playwright/music)	July 14, 1915
Lawrence, Marjorie (singer)	February 17, 1909
Lawrence, Steve; born Sidney Liebowitz (singer/actor)	July 8, 1935
Lawrence, Sir Thomas (artist)	May 4, 1769
Lawrence, Vicki Ann (actress/dancer/singer)	March 26, 1949
Lawrence of Arabia; born Thomas Edward Lawrence (soldier/archaeologist/author)	August 15, 1888
Lawson, Steve; born Stephen Lawson (football)	January 4, 1949
Laxalt, Paul Dominique (politician)	August 2, 1922
Laycoe, Harold Richardson (hockey)	June 23, 1922
Laye, Evelyn (actress/singer)	July 10, 1900
Layne, Bobby; born Robert Lawrence Layne (football)	December 10, 1926
Layton, Joe; born Joseph Lichtman (director/choreographer)	May 3, 1931
Lazzeri, Tony; born Anthony Michael Lazzeri (baseball)	December 6, 1903
Lea, Preston (politician)	November 12, 1841
Leach, Freddy; born Frederick M. Leach (baseball)	November 23, 1897
Leachman, Cloris (actress)	April 30, 1926
Leadbelly, born Huddie Ledbetter (singer/music)	January 20, 1889
Leader, George Michael (politician)	January 17, 1918
Leahy, Patrick Joseph (politician)	March 31, 1940
Lean, David (director)	March 25, 1908
Lear, Norman Milton (producer)	July 27, 1922
Learned, Michael (actress)	April 9, 1939
LeBaron, Eddie; born Edward Wayne LeBaron, Jr. (football)	January 7, 1930
LeBeau, Dick; born Charles Richard LeBeau (football)	September 9, 1937
Le Carré, John; born David John Moore Cornwell (author)	October 19, 1931
Leche, Richard Webster (politician)	May 17, 1898
Lederer, Frances; born Frantisek Lederer (actress)	November 6, 1902
Leduc, Albert (hockey)	July 31, 1901
Lee, Bill; born William Cruther Lee (baseball)	October 21, 1909
Lee, Bill; born William Francis Lee, III (baseball)	December 28, 1946
Lee, Bivian (football)	August 3, 1948
Lee, Blair (politician)	August 9, 1857
Lee, Bob; born Robert Melville Lee (football)	August 7, 1945
Lee, Brenda; born Brenda Mae Tarpley (singer)	December 11, 1942
Lee, Bruce; born Liu Yuen Kam (Kung-Fu artist/actor)	November 27, 1940
Lee, Canada; born Leonard Lionel Cornelius Canegata (actor)	May 3, 1907
Lee, Christopher Frank Caradini (actor)	May 27, 1922
Lee, David Allen (football)	November 8, 1943
Lee, Dixie; born Wilma Winifred Wyatt (singer/actress)	November 4, 1911
Lee, Dorothy; born Marjorie Millsap (actress)	May 23, 1911
Lee, Gwen; born Gwendolyn LePinski (actress)	November 12, 1904
Lee, Gypsy Rose; born Rose Louise Hovick (actress/dancer)	January 9, 1914
Lee, Harper; born Nelle Harper Lee (author)	April 28, 1926

Lee, J. Bracken; born Joseph Bracken Lee (politician)	January 7, 1899
Lee, Lila; born Augusta Appel (actress)	July 25, 1901
Lee, Michele; born Michele Lee Dusick (actress/singer)	June 24, 1942
Lee, Peggy; born Norma Delores Engstrom (singer/actress)	May 26, 1920
Lee, Pinky; born Pincus Leff (entertainer)	———1916
Lee, Robert E.; born Robert Edward Lee (confederate officer)	January 19, 1807
Lee, Robert E.; born Robert Edwin Lee (playwright/music)	October 15, 1918
Lee, Ruta; born Ruta Mary Kilmonis (actress/singer)	May 30———
Lee, Thornton Starr (baseball)	September 13, 1906
Leeds, Andrea; born Antoinette Lees (actress)	August 18, 1914
Leemans, Tuffy; born Alphonse Leemans (football)	November 12, 1912
Lefebvre, Jim; born James Kenneth Lefebvre (baseball)	January 7, 1943
Le Gallienne, Eva (actress/director/producer)	January 11, 1899
Leggett, Earl (football)	March 5, 1935
Legrand, Michel Jean (music)	February 24, 1931
Le Guin, Ursula Kroeber (author)	October 21, 1929
Lehár, Franz (music)	April 30, 1870
Lehman, Herbert Henry (politician)	March 28, 1878
Lehmann, Lotte (singer)	February 27, 1888
Leiber, Hank; born Henry Edward Leiber (baseball)	January 17, 1911
Leibman, Ron (actor)	October 11, 1937
Leigh, Dorian; born Dorian Parker (actress)	———1919
Leigh, Janet; born Jeanette Helen Morrison (actress)	July 6, 1927
Leigh, Vivien; born Vivian Mary Hartley (actress)	November 5, 1913
Leighton, Margaret (actress)	February 26, 1922
Leinsdorf, Erich (music)	February 4, 1912
Lelouch, Claude (director)	October 30, 1937
Lema, Tony; born Anthony David Lema (golf)	February 25, 1934
Lemaster, Denny; born Denver Clayton Lemaster (baseball)	February 25, 1939
Le May, Curtis Emerson (air force officer)	November 15, 1906
Lembeck, Harvey (actor)	April 15, 1923
Lemmon, Jack; born John Uhler Lemmon, III (actor)	February 8, 1925
Lemon, Bob; born Robert Granville Lemon (baseball)	September 22, 1920
Lemon, Jim; born James Robert Lemon (baseball)	March 23, 1928
Lemon, Meadowlark; born Meadow George Lemon, III (basketball)	April 25, 1932
L'Enfant, Pierre Charles (engineer)	August 2, 1754
Lenglen, Suzanne (tennis)	May 24, 1899
Lenin, Nikolai; born Vladimir Ilyitch Ulyanov (Russian government)	April 10, 1870
Lenkaitis, Bill; born William Lenkaitis (football)	June 30, 1946
Lennon, Dianne Barbara (singer—Lennon Sisters)	December 1, 1939
Lennon, Janet Elizabeth (singer—Lennon Sisters)	June 15, 1946
Lennon, John Winston (singer/music)	October 9, 1940
Lennon, Kathy; born Kathleen Mary Lennon (singer—Lennon Sisters)	August 2, 1943
Lennon, Peggy; born Margaret Ann Lennon (singer—Lennon Sisters)	April 8, 1941
Lenroot, Irvine Luther (politician)	January 31, 1869
Lenya, Lotte; born Karoline Blamauer (singer/actress)	October 18, 1898

Lenz, Kay (actress)	March 4, 1953
Leon, Eddie; born Eduardo Antonio Leon (baseball)	August 11, 1946
Leonard, Bob; born Robert Leonard (basketball)	July 17, 1932
Leonard, Dutch; born Emil John Leonard (baseball)	March 25, 1909
Leonard, Jack E. (comedian)	April 24, 1911
Leonard, Joe; born Joseph Paul Leonard (auto racing)	August 4, 1934
Leonard, Sheldon; born Sheldon Leonard Bershad (actor/producer/director)	February 22, 1907
Leonard, Stan; born Stanley Leonard (golf)	February 2, 1915
Lepcio, Ted; born Thaddeus Stanley Lepcio (baseball)	July 28, 1930
Lepine, Alfred (hockey)	July 31, 1901
Lerner, Alan Jay (music/playwright)	August 31, 1918
Lerner, Max (writer)	December 20, 1902
LeRoy, Mervyn (producer/director)	October 15, 1900
Lescoulie, Jack (actor/announcer)	November 17, 1917
Leslie, Bethel (actress)	August 3, 1929
Leslie, Harry Guyer (politician)	April 6, 1878
Leslie, Joan; born Agnes Theresa Sadie Brodell (actress)	January 26, 1925
Leslie, Sam; born Samuel Andrew Leslie (baseball)	July 26, 1905
Lessing, Doris; born Doris May Taylor (author)	October 22, 1919
Leswick, Tony; born Anthony Joseph Leswick (hockey)	March 17, 1923
Le Vander, Harold L. (politician)	October 10, 1910
Levant, Oscar (music)	December 27, 1906
Levene, Sam; born Samuel Levine (actor)	August 28, 1905
Levenson, Sam (author/humorist)	December 28, 1911
Levi, Edward Hirsch (government)	June 26, 1911
Lévi-Strauss, Claude Gustave (anthropologist/philosopher)	November 28, 1908
Levin, Ira (author)	August 27, 1929
Levine, Joseph E. (producer)	September 9, 1905
Levinsky, Alexander (hockey)	February 2, 1910
Lewicki, Daniel (hockey)	March 12, 1931
Lewis, Al; born Al Meister (actor)	April 30, 1923
Lewis, Buddy; born John Kelly Lewis (baseball)	August 10, 1916
Lewis, C.S. ; born Clive Staples Lewis (author)	November 29, 1898
Lewis, D.D.; born Dwight Douglas Lewis (football)	October 16, 1945
Lewis, Frank Doug (football)	July 7, 1947
Lewis, Freddie (basketball)	July 1, 1943
Lewis, Herbert A. (hockey)	April 17, 1906
Lewis, Jerry; born Joseph Levitch (comedian/actor/singer)	March 16, 1926
Lewis, Jerry Lee (singer/music)	September 29, 1935
Lewis, Joe E.; born Joe Klewan (comedian)	January 12, 1902
Lewis, John L.; born John Llewellyn Lewis (labor leader)	February 12, 1880
Lewis, Meriwether (explorer)	August 18, 1774
Lewis, Mike; born Michael Henry Lewis (football)	July 14, 1949
Lewis, Ramsey Emanuel, Jr. (music)	May 27, 1935
Lewis, Robert Q. (actor)	April 5, 1924
Lewis, Shari; born Shari (or Phyllis) Hurwitz (puppeteer/actress)	January 17, 1934
Lewis, Sinclair; born Harry Sinclair Lewis (author)	February 7, 1885
Lewis, Ted; born Theodore Leopold Friedman (entertainer)	June 6, 1891
Ley, Willy; born Robert Willey Ley (writer)	October 2, 1906

Leypoldt, John H. (football)	March 31, 1946
Liberace; born Wladziu Valentino Liberace (music)	May 16, 1919
Liberace, George J. (music)	July 31, 1911
Licht, Frank (politician)	March 3, 1916
Lichtenstein, Roy (artist)	October 27, 1923
Liddy, G. Gordon; born George Gordon Liddy (government)	November 30, 1930
Lie, Trygve Halvdan (United Nations)	July 16, 1896
Lietzke, Bruce (golf)	July 18, 1951
Lightfoot, Gordon Meredith (singer/music)	November 17, 1938
Lightner, Winnie; born Winifred Josephine Reeves	September 17, 1899
(or Hanson) (actress/comedienne/singer/dancer)	
Lillie, Beatrice Gladys; born Constance Sylvia Munston	May 29, 1898
(actress)	
Lillis, Bob; born Robert Perry Lillis (baseball)	June 2, 1930
Lilly, Bob; born Robert Lewis Lilly (football)	July 26, 1939
Lincoln, Abbey; born Anna Marie Wooldridge (actress/singer)	August 6, 1930
Lincoln, Abraham (President)	February 12, 1809
Lincoln, Elmo; born Otto Elmo Linkenhetter (actor)	———1889
Lincoln, Keith Payson (football)	May 8, 1939
Lincoln, Mary Todd; born Mary Ann Todd (First Lady)	December 13, 1818
Lind, Jenny; born Johanna Maria Lind (singer)	October 6, 1820
Lindbergh, Anne Morrow; born Anne Spencer Morrow (author)	June 22, 1906
Lindbergh, Charles Augustus (aviator)	February 4, 1902
Lindblad, Paul Aaron (baseball)	August 9, 1941
Lindell, Johnny; born John Harlan Lindell (baseball)	August 30, 1916
Linden, Hal; born Harold Lipshitz (actor/singer)	March 20, 1931
Lindfors, Viveca; born Elsa Viveca Torstensdotter	December 29, 1920
Lindfors (actress)	
Lindley, Audra (actress)	September 24, 1918
Lindsay, Howard (playwright/producer/director/actor)	March 29, 1888
Lindsay, John Vliet (politician)	November 24, 1921
Lindsay, Margaret; born Margaret Kies (actress)	September 19, 1910
Lindsay, Ted; born Robert Blake Theodore Lindsay (hockey)	July 29, 1925
Lindsey, Mort (music)	March 21, 1923
Lindsey, Washington Ellsworth (politician)	December 20, 1862
Lindstrom, Fred; born Frederick Charles Lindstrom (baseball)	November 21, 1905
Lindstrom, Pia (actress/newscaster)	September 20, 1938
Link, Arthur A. (politician)	May 24, 1914
Linkletter, Art; born Arthur Gordon Kelley Linkletter	July 17, 1912
(TV host/producer/author)	
Linn, Bambi; born Bambina Aennchen Linnemier	April 26, 1926
(dancer/actress)	
Linville, Larry; born Lawrence Lavon Linville (actor)	September 29, 1939
Lipon, Johnny; born John Joseph Lipon (baseball)	November 10, 1922
Lippmann, Walter (writer)	September 23, 1889
Lipscomb, Big Daddy; born Eugene Alan Lipscomb (football)	November 9, 1931
Lipton, Peggy (actress/singer)	August 30, 1947
Liscombe, Carl; born Harry Carlyle Liscombe (hockey)	May 17, 1915
Lisi, Virna; born Virna Pieralisi (actress)	August 11, 1937
Lister, Ernest (politician)	June 15, 1870
Lister, Joseph (medicine)	April 5, 1827

Liston, Sonny; born Charles Liston (boxing)	May 8, 1932
Liszt, Franz (music)	October 22, 1811
Little, Cleavon Jake (actor)	June 1, 1939
Little, Floyd Douglas (football)	July 4, 1942
Little, John D. (football)	May 3, 1947
Little, Larry; born Lawrence Chatmon Little (football)	November 2, 1945
Little, Lawson; born William Lawson Little (golf)	June 23, 1910
Little, Rich; born Richard Caruthers Little (impressionist/actor/singer)	November 26, 1938
Little, Sally (golf)	October 12, 1951
Little Anthony; born Anthony Gourdine (singer)	January 8, 1940
Little Richard; born Richard Pennimann (singer/music)	December 25, 1932
Littler, Gene; born Eugene Alex Littler (golf)	July 21, 1930
Litwhiler, Danny; born Daniel Webster Litwhiler (baseball)	August 31, 1916
Litzenberger, Eddie; born Edward C.J. Litzenberger (hockey)	July 15, 1932
Livingston, Barry (actor)	December 17, 1953
Livingston, Jay Harold (music)	March 28, 1915
Livingston, Margaret (actress)	November 25, 1900
Livingston, Mike; born Michael Livingston (football)	November 14, 1945
Livingston, Stanley (actor)	November 24, 1950
Livingstone, David (explorer)	March 19, 1813
Livingstone, Mary; born Sadie Marks (actress)	June 22, 1909
Lloyd, Doris (actress)	July 3, 1899
Lloyd, Earl (basketball)	April 3, 1928
Lloyd, Harold Clayton (comedian/actor)	April 20, 1889
LoBianco, Tony (actor)	October 19, 1936
Lock, Don Wilson (baseball)	July 27, 1936
Locke, Bobby; born Arthur D'Arcy Locke (golf)	November 20, 1917
Locke, John (philosopher)	August 29, 1632
Locke, Sondra (actress)	May 28, 1948
Lockhart, Calvin (actor)	———1934
Lockhart, Carl Ford (football)	April 6, 1943
Lockhart, Gene; born Eugene Lockhart (actor)	July 18, 1891
Lockhart, June Kathleen (actress)	June 25, 1925
Locklin, Hank; born Lawrence Hankins Locklin (singer)	February 15, 1918
Lockman, Whitey; born Carroll Walter Lockman (baseball)	July 25, 1926
Lockwood, Gary; born John Gary Yusolfsky (or Yurasek) (actor)	February 21, 1937
Lockwood, Margaret; born Margaret Day (actress)	September 15, 1916
Loden, Barbara Ann (actress)	July 8, 1937
Loder, John; born John Lowe (actor)	March 1, 1898
Lodge, Henry Cabot, Sr. (politician)	May 12, 1850
Lodge, Henry Cabot, Jr. (politics/government)	July 5, 1902
Lodge, John Davis (actor/politician)	October 20, 1903
Loes, Billy; born William Loes (baseball)	December 13, 1929
Loesser, Frank Henry (music/producer)	June 29, 1910
Loewe, Frederick (music)	June 10, 1904
Logan, Ella; born Ella Allan (actress/singer)	March 6, 1913
Logan, Jacqueline (actress)	November 30, 1901
Logan, Jerry Don (football)	August 27, 1941

Logan, Johnny; born John Logan (baseball)	March 23, 1927
Logan, Joshua Lockwood, Jr. (playwright/director)	October 5, 1908
Loggia, Robert (actor)	January 3, 1930
Lolich, Mickey; born Michael Stephen Lolich (baseball)	September 12, 1940
Lollar, Sherm; born John Sherman Lollar (baseball)	August 23, 1924
Lollobrigida, Gina (actress)	July 4, 1927
Lom, Herbert; born Herbert Charles Angelo Kuchacevich ze	————1917
Schluderpacheru (actor)	
Lombard, Carole; born Jane Alice Peters (actress)	October 6, 1908
Lombardi, Ernie; born Ernesto Natali Lombardi (baseball)	April 6, 1908
Lombardi, Vince; born Vincent Thomas Lombardi (football)	June 11, 1913
Lombardo, Carmen (music)	July 16, 1903
Lombardo, Guy; born Gaetano Alberto Lombardo (music)	June 19, 1902
Lonborg, Jim; born James Reynold Lonborg (baseball)	April 16, 1942
London, Jack; born John Griffith Chaney (author)	January 12, 1876
London, Julie; born Julie Peck (actress/singer)	September 26, 1926
Lonergan, Augustine (politician)	May 20, 1874
Long, Dale; born Richard Dale Long (baseball)	February 6, 1926
Long, Earl Kemp (politician)	August 26, 1895
Long, Edward Vaughan (politician)	July 18, 1908
Long, Huey Pierce, Jr. (politician)	August 30, 1893
Long, Oren Ethelbirt (politician)	March 4, 1889
Long, Richard (actor)	December 17, 1927
Long, Russell Billiu (politician)	November 3, 1918
Longden, Johnny; born John E. Longden (jockey)	February 14, 1910
Longet, Claudine Georgette (actress/singer)	January 29, 1942
Longfellow, Henry Wadsworth (poet)	February 27, 1807
Longhurst, Henry Carpenter (sportscaster/journalist/author)	March 18, 1909
Longino, Andrew Houston (politician)	May 16, 1855
Longley, James Bernard (politician)	April 22, 1924
Longworth, Alice Roosevelt; born Alice Lee Roosevelt	February 12, 1884
(First family)	
Longworth, Nicholas (politician)	November 5, 1869
Looney, Joe Don (football)	October 10, 1942
Loos, Anita (playwright/author)	April 26, 1893
Lopat, Ed; born Edmund Walter Lopatynski (baseball)	June 21, 1918
Lopata, Stan; born Stanley Edward Lopata (baseball)	September 12, 1925
Lopes, Davey; born David Earl Lopes (baseball)	May 3, 1946
Lopez, Al; born Alfonso Ramon Lopez (baseball)	August 20, 1905
Lopez, Hector Headley (baseball)	July 8, 1932
Lopez, Nancy Marie (golf)	January 6, 1957
Lopez, Trini; born Trinidad Lopez, III (singer/actor)	May 15, 1937
Lopez, Vincent (music)	December 30, 1895
Lord, Barbara; born Barbara Jeanette Gratz (actress)	November 21, 1937
Lord, Jack; born John John Joseph Patrick Ryan (actor/artist)	December 30, 1928
Lord, Marjorie (actress)	July 26, 1921
Loren, Sophia; born Sofia Villani Scicolone (actress)	September 20, 1934
Lorenzen, Fred (auto racing)	December 30, 1934
Loring, Gloria Jean; born Gloria Jean Goff (singer)	December 10, 1946
Loring, Lynn (actress)	July 13, 1944
Lorne, Marion; born Marion Lorne MacDougall (actress)	August 12, 1885

Lumley, Harry (hockey)	November 11, 1926
Lumpe, Jerry Dean (baseball)	June 2, 1933
Luna, Barbara (actress)	March 2, 1937
Lund, Art; born Arthur Earl Lund, Jr. (singer/actor)	April 1, 1920
Lund, John (actor)	February 6, 1913
Lund, Tiny; born DeWayne Louis Lund (auto racing)	November 14, 1929
Lunde, Leonard Melvin (hockey)	November 13, 1936
Lundeen, Ernest (politician)	August 4, 1878
Lundigan, William (actor)	June 12, 1914
Lundy, Lamar (football)	April 17, 1935
Lunn, Bob; born Robert Lunn (golf)	April 24, 1945
Lunt, Alfred (actor)	August 19, 1892
Lupino, Ida (actress/director)	February 4, 1918
Lupton, John (actor)	August 22————
Lupus, Peter (actor/Mr. Hercules)	June 17————
Luque, Dolf; born Adolfo Luque (baseball)	August 4, 1890
Lurton, Horace Harmon (jurist)	February 26, 1844
Lurtsema, Bob; born Robert Ross Lurtsema (football)	March 29, 1942
Luther, Martin (religious leader)	November 10, 1483
Lutz, Bob; born Robert Charles Lutz (tennis)	August 29, 1947
Luzinski, Greg; born Gregory Michael Luzinski (baseball)	November 22, 1950
Lydon, Jimmy; born James Lydon (actor/producer)	May 30, 1923
Lyle, Sparky; born Albert Walter Lyle (baseball)	July 22, 1944
Lynch, Fran; born Francis Lynch (football)	December 13, 1945
Lynch, Jerry; born Gerald Thomas Lynch (baseball)	July 17, 1930
Lynch, Jim; born James E. Lynch (football)	August 28, 1945
Lynde, Paul Edward (actor/comedian/singer)	June 13, 1926
Lynley, Carol; born Carolyn Lee Jones (actress)	February 13, 1942
Lynn, Diana; born Dolores "Dolly" Loehr (actress)	October 7, 1926
Lynn, Fred; born Frederic Michael Lynn (baseball)	February 23, 1952
Lynn, James Thomas (government)	February 27, 1927
Lynn, Janet; born Janet Lynn Nowicki (ice skating)	April 6, 1953
Lynn, Jeffrey; born Ragnar Godfrey Lind (actor)	February 16, 1909
Lynn, Loretta; born Loretta Webb (singer)	April 14, 1932
Lynn, Sharon E.; born D'Auvergne Sharon Lindsay (actress)	April 9, 1904
Lynn, Victor Ivan (hockey)	January 26, 1925
Lyon, Ben (actor)	February 6, 1901
Lyon, Sue (actress)	July 10, 1946
Lyons, Ted; born Theodore Amar Lyons (baseball)	December 28, 1900
Lyons, Tom; born Thomas Lewis Lyons (football)	August 7, 1948

M

Maas, Duke; born Duane Frederick Maas (baseball)	January 31, 1929
Maazel, Lorin (music)	March 5, 1930
Mabey, Charles Rendell (politician)	October 4, 1877
Mabley, Moms "Jackie"; born Loretta Mary Aiken (comedienne)	March 19, 1894
Mabry, Thomas Jewett (politician)	October 17, 1884
MacArthur, Douglas (army officer)	January 26, 1880
MacArthur, James Gordon (actor)	December 8, 1937
Macauley, Ed; born Edward Macauley (basketball)	March 22, 1928

MacDermot, Galt (music)	December 19, 1928
MacDonald, Jeanette Anna (actress/singer)	June 18, 1901
MacDonald, John Dann (author)	July 24, 1916
MacDonald, John Ross; born Kenneth Millar (author)	December 13, 1915
MacDowell, Edward Alexander (music)	December 18, 1861
MacFarland, Spanky; born George Emmett MacFarland (actor)	October 2, 1928
Macfarlane, Willie; born William Macfarlane (golf)	June 29, 1890
MacGinnis, Niall (actor)	March 29, 1913
MacGraw, Ali (actress)	April 1, 1938
MacGregor, Bruce Cameron (hockey)	April 26, 1941
Machiavelli, Niccolo (political philosopher)	May 3, 1469
MacInnes, Helen Clark (author)	October 7, 1907
Mack, Connie; born Cornelius McGillicuddy (baseball)	December 22, 1862
Mack, Helen; born Helen McDougall (actress)	November 13, 1913
Mack, Ted; born William E. Maguiness (TV host)	February 12, 1904
Mack, Tom; born Thomas Lee Mack (football)	November 1, 1943
Mackaill, Dorothy (actress)	March 4, 1903
MacKell, Fleming David (hockey)	April 30, 1929
MacKenzie, Giselle; born Marie Marguerite Louise Gisele La Fleche (singer/actress)	January 10, 1927
MacKenzie, Joyce (actress)	October 16———
Mackey, John (football)	September 24, 1941
MacLaine, Shirley; born Shirley MacLean Beaty (actress/singer/dancer)	April 24, 1934
MacLane, Barton (actor)	December 25, 1902
MacLaren, Mary; born Mary MacDonald (actress)	January 19, 1896
MacLean, Alistair (author)	———1922
MacLeish, Archibald (poet/playwright)	May 7, 1892
MacLeod, Gavin (actor)	February 28, 1931
MacMahon, Aline Laveen (actress)	May 3, 1899
Macmillan, Harold; born Maurice Harold Macmillan (British government)	February 10, 1894
MacMurray, Fred; born Frederick Martin MacMurray (actor)	August 30, 1908
MacNee, Patrick (actor)	February 6, 1922
MacNeil, Allister Wences (hockey)	September 27, 1935
MacRae, Gordon (singer/actor)	March 12, 1921
MacRae, Meredith (actress/singer)	May 30, 1945
MacRae, Shelia; born Sheila Margot Stephens (actress/singer)	September 24, 1924
Macready, George (actor)	August 29, 1900
MacVeagh, Franklin (government)	November 22, 1837
Macy, Bill; born William M. Garber (actor)	May 18, 1922
Madden, John Earl (football)	April 10, 1936
Maddox, Eillott (baseball)	December 21, 1947
Maddox, Garry Lee (baseball)	September 1, 1949
Maddox, Lester Garfield (politician)	September 30, 1915
Madison, Dolly; born Dorothy Payne (First Lady)	May 12, 1768
Madison, Guy; born Robert Moseley (actor)	January 19, 1922
Madison, James (President)	March 16, 1751
Madlock, Bill; born William Madlock, Jr. (baseball)	January 2, 1951
Magellan, Ferdinand; born Fernando de Magalhaes (navigator)	circa 1480

Maglie, Sal; born Salvatore Anthony Maglie (baseball)	April 26, 1917
Magnani, Anna (actress)	March 7, 1908
Magnuson, Warren Grant (politician)	April 12, 1905
Maguire, Paul L. (football)	August 22, 1933
Mahaffey, John (golf)	May 9, 1948
Mahal, Taj (singer/music)	May 17, 1942
Maharis, George (actor)	September 1, 1928
Mahler, Gustav (music)	July 7, 1860
Mahoney, Jock; born Jacques O'Mahoney (actor)	February 7, 1919
Mahovlich, Frank; born Francis William Mahovlich (hockey)	January 10, 1938
Mailer, Norman (author)	January 31, 1923
Main, Marjorie; born Mary Tomlinson (actress)	February 24, 1890
Mainbocher; born Main Rousseau Bocher (fashion designer)	October 24, 1890
Major, Elliot Woolfolk (politician)	October 20, 1864
Majors, Lee; born Harvey Lee Yeary (actor)	April 23, 1939
Makarova, Natalia (dancer)	November 21, 1940
Makeba, Miriam; born Zensi Miriam Makeba (singer)	March 4, 1932
Maki, Chico; born Ronald Patrick Maki (hockey)	August 17, 1939
Mako, C. Gene (tennis)	January 24, 1916
Malamud, Bernard (author)	April 26, 1914
Malcolm X; born Malcolm Little (Black Muslim leader)	May 19, 1925
Malden, Karl; born Mladen Sekulovich (actor)	March 22, 1913
Malinchak, Bill; born William Malinchak (football)	April 2, 1944
Mallory, Boots; born Patricia Mallory (actress)	October 22, 1913
Malone, Art; born Arthur Lee Malone (football)	March 20, 1948
Malone, Benny (football)	February 3, 1952
Malone, Dorothy; born Dorothy Eloise Maloney (actress)	January 30, 1925
Malone, George Wilson (politician)	August 7, 1890
Malone, Moses (basketball)	March 23, 1954
Malone, Nancy (actress)	March 19, 1935
Maloney, Francis Thomas (politician)	March 31, 1894
Maloney, Jim; born James William Maloney (baseball)	June 2, 1940
Malraux, André; born Georges André Malraux (author)	November 3, 1901
Maltbie, Roger (golf)	June 30, 1951
Malzone, Frank James (baseball)	February 28, 1930
Manchester, Melissa Toni (singer/music)	February 15, 1951
Manchester, William (writer)	April 1, 1922
Mancini, Henry Nicole (music)	April 16, 1924
Mandan, Robert (actor)	February 2, 1932
Mandel, Marvin (politician)	April 19, 1920
Mandich, Jim; born James M. Mandich (football)	July 30, 1948
Mandrell, Barbara Ann (singer/music)	December 25, 1948
Manet, Edouard (artist)	January 23, 1832
Mangano, Silvana (actress)	April 21, 1930
Mangione, Chuck; born Charles Frank Mangione (music)	November 29, 1940
Mangrum, Lloyd Eugene (golf)	August 1, 1914
Manigo, Cesare (hockey)	January 13, 1939
Manilow, Barry (singer/music)	June 17, 1946
Mankiewicz, Frank Fabian (journalist)	May 16, 1924
Mankiewicz, Joseph Leo (producer/director/writer)	February 11, 1909
Mann, Carol Ann (golf/sportscaster)	February 3, 1941

Mann, Daniel; born Daniel Chugerman (director)	August 8, 1912
Mann, Errol Dennis (football)	June 27, 1941
Mann, Herbie; born Herbert Jay Solomon (music)	April 16, 1930
Mann, Horace (educator)	May 4, 1796
Mann, Thomas (author)	June 6, 1875
Mann, William Hodges (politician)	July 30, 1843
Manne, Shelly; born Sheldon Manne (music)	June 11, 1920
Manners, David; born Rauff de Ryther Duan Acklom (actor)	April 30, 1900
Mannes, Marya (author/journalist)	November 14, 1904
Manning, Archie; born Elisha Archie Manning (football)	May 19, 1949
Manning, Richard Irvine (politician)	August 15, 1859
Mansfield, Jayne; born Vera Jayne Palmer (actress)	April 19, 1932
Mansfield, Katherine; born Kathleen Beauchamp (author)	October 14, 1888
Mansfield, Mike; born Michael Joseph Mansfield (politician)	March 16, 1903
Mansfield, Ray; born James Raymond Mansfield (football)	January 21, 1941
Manson, Charles (cult murderer)	November 12, 1934
Mantha, Georges (hockey)	November 29, 1908
Mantha, Sylvio (hockey)	April 14, 1902
Mantilla, Felix Lamela (baseball)	July 29, 1934
Mantle, Mickey Charles (baseball)	October 20, 1931
Mantooth, Randolph (actor)	September 19———
Mantovani, Annunzlo Paolo (music)	November 5, 1905
Manush, Heinie; born Henry Emmett Manush (baseball)	July 20, 1901
Manville, Tommy (playboy heir)	April 9, 1894
Mao Tse-Tung (Chinese government)	December 26, 1893
Maples, Bob; born Bobby Ray Maples (football)	December 28, 1942
Mara, Adele; born Adelaida Delgado (actress)	April 28, 1923
Marais, Jean; born Jean Marais-Villain (actor)	December 11, 1913
Marangi, Gary Angelo (football)	July 29, 1952
Maranville, Rabbit; born Walter James Vincent Maranville (baseball)	November 11, 1891
Maravich, Pete; born Peter Maravich (basketball)	June 22, 1948
Marble, Alice (tennis)	September 28, 1913
Marceau, Marcel; born Marcel Mangel (mime/actor)	March 22, 1923
March, Frederic; born Ernest Frederick McIntyre Bickel (actor)	August 31, 1897
March, Hal; born Harold (or Howard) Mendelson (actor)	April 22, 1920
March, Little Peggy (singer)	March 8, 1948
March, Mush; born Harold C. March (hockey)	October 18, 1908
Marchand, Nancy (actress)	June 19, 1928
Marchetti, Gino John (football)	January 2, 1927
Marchibroda, Ted; born Theodore Marchibroda (football)	March 15, 1931
Marciano, Rocky; born Rocco Francis Marchegiano (boxing)	September 1, 1923
Marcis, Dave; born David A. Marcis (auto racing)	March 1, 1941
Marcol, Chester; born Czelslaw C. Marcol (football)	October 24, 1949
Marconi, Guglielmo (inventor)	April 25, 1874
Margaret, Princess; born Margaret Rose (British Royalty)	August 21, 1930
Margo; born Maria Marguerita Gudalupe Teresa Estela Bolado Castilla y O'Donnell (actress)	May 10, 1917
Margolin, Janet (actress)	July 25, 1943
Margolin, Stuart (actor/director)	January 31———

Margrethe II; born Margrethe Alexandrine Thorhildur Ingrid   April 16, 1940
    (Queen of Denmark)
Marichal, Juan Antonio (baseball)   October 20, 1937
Marie Antoinette; born Josephe Jeanne Marie Antoinette   November 2, 1755
    (Queen of France)
Marin, Jack (basketball)   October 12, 1944
Marinaro, Ed; born Edward F. Marinaro (football)   March 31, 1950
Marion, Marty; born Martin Whitford Marion (baseball)   December 1, 1917
Maris, Roger Eugene (baseball)   September 10, 1934
Marker, Gus; born August Solberg Marker (hockey)   August 1, 1907
Markey, Enid Virginia (actress)   February 22, 1896
Markham, Monte (actor)   June 21, 1935
Markova, Dame Alicia (dancer)   December 1, 1910
Marland, Ernest Whitford (politician)   May 8, 1874
Marland, William Casey (politician)   March 26, 1918
Marley, John (actor)   October 17, 1914
Marlin, Coo Coo; born Clifton Burton Marlin (auto racing)   January 3, 1932
Marlowe, Christopher (dramatist/poet)   February 6, 1564
Marlowe, Hugh; born Hugh Herbert Hipple (actor)   January 30, 1911
Marlowe, Julia; born Sarah Frances Frost (actress)   August 17, 1866
Marotte, Jean Gilles (hockey)   June 7, 1945
Marquand, J.P.; born John Phillips Marquand (author)   November 10, 1893
Marquard, Rube; born Richard William Marquard (baseball)   October 9, 1889
Marquette, Jacques (explorer/missionary)   June 1, 1637
Marr, Dave; born David Marr (golf/sportscaster)   December 27, 1933
Marriott, J. Willard; born John Willard Marriott   September 17, 1900
    (hotel & restaurant magnate)
Marsalis, Jim; born James Marsalis (football)   October 10, 1945
Marsh, Graham (golf)   January 14, 1944
Marsh, Jean Lyndsey Torren (actress/writer)   July 1, 1934
Marsh, Joan; born Dorothy Rosher (actress)   July 10, 1913
Marsh, Linda (actress)   February 8————
Marsh, Mae; born Mary Warne Marsh (actress)   November 9, 1895
Marsh, Marian; born Violet Krauth (actress)   October 17, 1913
Marshall, Bert; born Albert Leroy Marshall (hockey)   November 22, 1943
Marshall, Brenda; born Ardis Anderson Gaines   September 29, 1915
    (or Ardis Ankerson) (actress)
Marshall, Donald Robert (hockey)   March 23, 1932
Marshall, E.G.; born Everett G. Marshall (actor)   June 18, 1910
Marshall, F. Ray; born Freddie Ray Marshall (government)   August 22, 1928
Marshall, George (director)   December 29, 1891
Marshall, George Catlett (military/government)   December 31, 1880
Marshall, Herbert (actor)   May 23, 1890
Marshall, Jim; born James Lawrence Marshall (football)   December 30, 1937
Marshall, Jim; born Rufus James Marshall (baseball)   May 25, 1932
Marshall, John (jurist)   September 24, 1755
Marshall, Mike; born Michael Grant Marshall (baseball)   January 15, 1943
Marshall, Penny; born Carole Penny Marshall (actress)   October 15, 1942
Marshall, Peter; born Ralph Pierre La Cock, Sr.   March 30, 1930
    (actor/singer/TV host)
Marshall, Thomas Riley (Vice President)   March 14, 1854

Marshall, Thurgood; born Thoroughgood Marshall (jurist)	July 2, 1908
Marti, Fred; born Frederick Marti, Jr. (golf)	November 15, 1940
Martin, Billy; born Alfred Manuel Martin (baseball)	May 16, 1928
Martin, Charles Henry (politician)	October 1, 1863
Martin, Clarence Daniel (politician)	June 29, 1886
Martin, Dean; born Dino Paul Crocetti (actor/singer)	June 17, 1917
Martin, Dewey (actor)	December 8, 1923
Martin, Dick; born Thomas Richard Martin (comedian/actor)	January 30, 1922
Martin, Edward (politician)	September 18, 1879
Martin, Ernest; born Ernest Harold Markowitz (producer)	August 28, 1919
Martin, Freddy (music)	December 9, 1906
Martin, Harvey Banks (football)	November 16, 1950
Martin, Jared (actor)	December 21, 1943
Martin, Jim; born James R. Martin (football)	February 14, 1919
Martin, John Wellborn (politician)	June 21, 1884
Martin, Joseph William, Jr. (politician)	November 3, 1884
Martin, Mary Virginia (actress/singer)	December 1, 1913
Martin, Millicent (actress/singer)	June 8, 1934
Martin, Nan Clow (actress)	July 15, 1927
Martin, Pamela Sue (actress)	January 5, 1953
Martin, Pepper; born Johnny Leonard Roosevelt Martin (baseball)	February 29, 1904
Martin, Pit; born Hubert Jacques Martin (hockey)	December 9, 1943
Martin, Quinn (producer/writer)	May 22, 1922
Martin, Richard Lionel (hockey)	July 26, 1951
Martin, Ross; born Martin Rosenblatt (actor)	March 22, 1920
Martin, Slater (basketball)	October 22, 1925
Martin, Steve (comedian/singer/music)	———1945
Martin, Strother (actor)	March 26, 1919
Martin, Thomas Ellsworth (politician)	January 18, 1893
Martin, Thomas Staples (politician)	July 29, 1847
Martin, Tony; born Alfred Norris, Jr. (singer/actor)	December 25, 1912
Martindale, Win (or Wink); born Winston Conrad Martindale (TV host)	December 4, 1934
Martineau, John Ellis (politician)	December 2, 1873
Martinelli, Elsa (actress)	August 3, 1933
Martinelli, Giovanni (singer)	October 22, 1885
Martino, Al; born Alfred Cini (singer)	October 7, 1927
Marvin, Lee (actor)	February 19, 1924
Marx, Chico; born Leonard Marx (comedian/actor —Marx Brothers)	March 22, 1887
Marx, Groucho; born Julius Henry Marx (comedian/actor/ TV host—Marx Brothers)	October 2, 1890
Marx, Gummo; born Milton Marx (singer/dancer/comedian —Marx Brothers	———1893
Marx, Harpo; born Adolph Arthur Marx (comedian/actor —Marx Brothers)	November 23, 1888
Marx, Karl (socialist writer)	May 5, 1818
Marx, Zeppo; born Herbert Marx (comedian/actor —Marx Brothers)	February 25, 1901
Masefield, John Edward (poet)	June 1, 1878

Masekela, Hugh Ramapolo (music)	April 4, 1939
Mason, James Neville (actor)	May 15, 1909
Mason, Marlyn (actress/singer)	August 7, 1940
Mason, Marsha (actress)	April 3, 1942
Mason, Pamela; born Pamela Helen Ostrer (actress/singer)	March 10, 1918
Mason, Tommy; born Thomas Cyril Mason (football)	July 8, 1939
Massenet, Jules-Emile-Frédéric (music)	May 12, 1842
Massengale, Don; born Donald Massengale (golf)	April 23, 1937
Massengale, Rik (golf)	February 6, 1947
Massey, Ilona; born Ilona Hajmassy (actress)	July 5, 1912
Massey, Raymond Hart (actor)	August 30, 1896
Masters, Billy; born William Masters (football)	March 15, 1944
Masters, Edgar Lee (poet/author)	August 23, 1869
Masters, Margee; born Margaret Ann Masters (golf)	October 24, 1934
Masterson, Walt; born Walter Edward Masterson (baseball)	June 22, 1920
Mastroianni, Marcello (actor)	September 28, 1923
Mata Hari; born Gertrud Margarete Zelle (dancer/spy)	August 7, 1876
Mathers, Jerry (actor)	June 2, 1948
Matheson, Bob; born Robert Matheson (football)	November 25, 1944
Matheson, Murray; born Sidney Murray Matheson (actor)	July 1, 1912
Matheson, Scott Milne (politician)	January 9, 1929
Matheson, Tim (actor)	December 31, 1947
Mathews, Eddie; born Edwin Lee Mathews (baseball)	October 13, 1931
Mathews, F. David; born Forrest David Mathews (government)	December 6, 1935
Mathewson, Christy; born Christopher Mathewson (baseball)	August 12, 1878
Mathias, Bob; born Robert Bruce Mathias (olympic athlete/politician/actor)	November 17, 1930
Mathias, Charles McCurdy, Jr. (politician)	July 24, 1922
Mathis, Johnny; born John Royce Mathis (singer)	September 30, 1935
Matisse, Henri Emile Benoit (artist)	December 31, 1869
Matlack, Jon; born Jonathan Trumpour Matlack (baseball)	January 19, 1950
Matson, Ollie; born Oliver Genoa Matson (football)	May 1, 1930
Matson, Pat; born Patrick Matson (football)	July 22, 1944
Matsunaga, Spark Masayuki (politician)	October 8, 1916
Matte, Tom; born Thomas Roland Matte (football/sportscaster)	June 14, 1939
Matthau, Walter; born Walter Matuschanskayasky (actor)	October 1, 1920
Matthews, Gary Nathaniel (baseball)	July 5, 1950
Matthews, Jessie (singer/dancer/actress)	March 11, 1907
Mature, Victor John (actor)	January 29, 1916
Matuszak, John (football)	December 24, 1950
Mauch, Gene William (baseball)	November 18, 1925
Mauck, Carl Frey (football)	July 7, 1947
Maugham, W. Somerset; born William Somerset Maugham (author)	January 25, 1874
Mauldin, Bill; born William Henry Mauldin (cartoonist)	October 29, 1921
Maunder, Wayne (actor)	December 19, 1942
Maurer, Andy; born Andrew Lee Maurer (football)	September 30, 1948
Maw, Herbert Brown (politician)	March 11, 1893
Max, Peter; born with surname Finkelstein (artist)	October 19, 1937
Maximilian; born Ferdinand Maximilian Joseph (Mexican Emperor)	July 6, 1832

Maxvill, Dal; born Charles Dallan Maxvill (baseball)	February 18, 1939
Maxwell, Billy; born William J. Maxwell (golf)	July 23, 1929
Maxwell, Charlie; born Charles Richard Maxwell (baseball)	April 28, 1927
Maxwell, Elsa (actress/writer)	May 24, 1883
Maxwell, Lois; born Lois Hooker (actress)	————1927
Maxwell, Marilyn; born Marvel Marilyn Maxwell (actress)	August 3, 1921
May, Carlos (baseball)	May 17, 1948
May, Elaine; born Elaine Berlin (comedienne/actress/writer)	April 21, 1932
May, Lee Andrew (baseball)	May 23, 1943
May, Ray; born Raymond May (football)	June 4, 1945
May, Rollo Reese (psychologist)	April 21, 1909
May, Rudy; born Rudolph May (baseball)	July 18, 1944
Maybank, Burnet Rhett (politician)	March 7, 1899
Mayberry, John Claiborn (baseball)	February 18, 1950
Maye, Lee; born Arthur Lee Maye (baseball)	December 11, 1934
Mayehoff, Eddie (music/actor/comedian)	July 7, 1911
Mayer, Dick; born Alvin Richard Mayer (golf)	August 29, 1924
Mayer, Louis Burt (producer)	July 4, 1885
Mayes, Rufus Lee (football)	December 5, 1947
Mayfield, Curtis Lee (singer/music)	June 3, 1942
Mayfield, Shelley (golf)	June 19, 1924
Maynard, Don; born Donald Rogers Maynard (football)	January 25, 1937
Maynard, Ken (actor)	July 21, 1895
Maynor, Dorothy; born Dorothy Leigh Mainor (singer)	September 3, 1910
Mayo, Charles Horace (medicine)	July 19, 1865
Mayo, Virginia; born Virginia Jones (actress)	November 30, 1920
Mayo, Whitman (actor)	November 15, 1930
Mayo, William James (medicine)	June 29, 1861
Mays, Rex (auto racing)	————1913
Mays, Willie Howard, Jr. (baseball)	May 6, 1931
Mazeroski, Bill; born William Stanley Mazeroski (baseball)	September 5, 1936
Mazurki, Mike; born Mikhail Mazurwski (actor)	December 25, 1909
McAdoo, Bob; born Robert McAdoo (basketball)	September 25, 1951
McAdoo, William Gibbs (government/politics)	October 31, 1863
McAfee, George Anderson (football)	March 13, 1918
McAlister, Hill (politician)	July 15, 1875
McAllister, Susie; born Mary H. McAllister (golf)	August 27, 1947
McAuliffe, Dick; born Richard John McAuliffe (baseball)	November 29, 1939
McAvoy, May (actress)	September 8, 1901
McBain, Diane Jean (actress)	————1941
McBride, Bake; born Arnold Ray McBride (baseball)	February 3, 1949
McBride, Henry (politician)	February 7, 1856
McBride, Mary Margaret (author/broadcasting)	November 16, 1899
McBride, Patricia (dancer)	August 23, 1942
McCall, Samuel Walker (politician)	February 28, 1851
McCall, Thomas Lawson (politician)	March 22, 1913
McCalla, Irish (actress/artist)	December 25, 1929
McCallister, Lon; born Herbert Alonzo McCallister, Jr. (actor)	April 17, 1923
McCallum, David (actor)	September 19, 1933
McCambridge, Mercedes; born Carlotta Mercedes Agnes McCambridge (actress)	March 17, 1918

McCarran, Patrick Anthony (politician)	August 8, 1876
McCarthy, Eugene Joseph (politician)	March 29, 1916
McCarthy, Joe; born Joseph Raymond McCarthy (politician)	November 14, 1908
McCarthy, Joe; born Joseph Vincent McCarthy (baseball)	April 21, 1887
McCarthy, Johnny; born John Joseph McCarthy (baseball)	January 7, 1910
McCarthy, Kevin (actor)	February 15, 1914
McCarthy, Mary Therese (author)	June 21, 1912
McCartney, Paul; born James Paul McCartney (singer/music)	June 18, 1942
McCarver, Tim; born James Timothy McCarver (baseball)	October 16, 1941
McCauley, Don; born Donald McCauley (football)	May 12, 1949
McCay, Peggy (actress)	November 3, 1931
McClanahan, Brent Anthony (football)	September 21, 1950
McClanahan, Rue; born Eddie-Rue McClanahan (actress)	February 21———
McClellan, George Brinton (army officer)	November 23, 1865
McClellan, John Little (politician)	February 25, 1896
McClinton, Curtis R. (football)	July 25, 1939
McClory, Sean (actor/director)	March 8, 1924
McCloskey, Paul Norton, Jr. (politician)	September 29, 1927
McClure, Doug (actor)	May 11, 1935
McClure, James A. (politician)	December 27, 1924
McCluskey, Roger Frank (auto racing)	August 24, 1930
McConaughy, James Lukens (politician)	October 21, 1887
McCoo, Marilyn (singer)	September 30, 1943
McCord, Darris (football)	January 4, 1933
McCord, James Nance (politician)	March 17, 1879
McCord, Kent; born Kent McWhirter (actor)	September 26, 1942
McCormack, John William (politician)	December 21, 1891
McCormack, Mike; born Michael McCormack (football)	June 21, 1930
McCormack, Patty; born Patricia Ellen Russo (actress)	August 21, 1945
McCormick, Cyrus Hall (inventor)	May 13, 1884
McCormick, Joseph Medill (politician)	May 16, 1877
McCormick, Maureen (actress/singer)	August 5, 1956
McCormick, Mike; born Michael Francis McCormick (baseball)	September 29, 1938
McCormick, Myron; born Walter Myron McCormick (actor)	February 8, 1907
McCosky, Barney; born William Barney McCosky (baseball)	April 11, 1918
McCovey, Willie Lee (baseball)	January 10, 1938
McCowen, Alec; born Alexander Duncan McCowen (actor)	May 26, 1925
McCoy, Mike; born Michael McCoy (football)	September 6, 1948
McCoy, Tim; born Timothy John Fitzgerald McCoy (actor)	April 10, 1891
McCraw, Tommy Lee (baseball)	November 21, 1940
McCray, Warren T. (politician)	February 4, 1865
McCrea, Joel (actor)	November 5, 1905
McCreary, James Bennett (politician)	July 8, 1838
McCreary, Vernon Keith (hockey)	June 19, 1940
McCreary, William Edward (hockey)	December 2, 1934
McCullers, Carson; born Lula Carson Smith (author)	February 19, 1917
McCulloch, Earl (football)	January 10, 1936
McCullough, Clyde Edward (baseball)	March 4, 1917
McCullough, John Griffith (politician)	September 16, 1835
McCutcheon, Lawrence (football)	June 2, 1950
McDaniel, Hattie (actress)	June 10, 1895

McDaniel, Lindy; born Lyndall Dale McDaniel (baseball)	December 13, 1935
McDaniels, Gene; born Eugene B. McDaniels (singer/music)	February 12, 1935
McDermott, John J. (golf)	August 12, 1891
McDermott, Mickey; born Maurice Joseph McDermott (baseball)	August 29, 1928
McDevitt, Ruth; born Ruth Thane Shoecraft (actress)	September 13, 1895
McDivitt, James Alton (astronaut)	June 10, 1929
McDole, Ron; born Roland McDole (football)	September 9, 1939
McDonald, Ab; born Alvin Brian McDonald (hockey)	February 18, 1936
McDonald, Bucko; born Wilfred Kennedy McDonald (hockey)	October 31, 1911
McDonald, Marie; born Cora Marie Frye (actress/singer)	————1923
McDonald, Tommy; born Thomas McDonald (football)	July 26, 1934
McDonald, William C. (politician)	July 25, 1858
McDougald, Gil; born Gilbert James McDougald (baseball)	May 19, 1928
McDowall, Roddy; born Roderick Andrew McDowall (actor)	September 17, 1928
McDowell, Malcolm (actor)	June 19, 1943
McDowell, Sam; born Samuel Edward Thomas McDowell (baseball)	September 21, 1942
McDuffie, J.D.; born John Delphus McDuffie, Jr. (auto racing)	December 5, 1938
McEachin, James Elton (actor)	May 20, 1930
McElhenny, Hugh Edward (football)	December 31, 1928
McElreath, Jim (auto racing)	February 18, 1928
McElroy, Neil Hosler (government)	October 30, 1904
McEnery, Peter (actor)	February 21, 1940
McEnroe, John Patrick, Jr. (tennis)	February 16, 1959
McFadden, James Alexander (hockey)	April 15, 1920
McFadin, Bud; born Lewis B. McFadin (football)	August 21, 1928
McFarland, Ernest William (politician)	October 9, 1894
McGavin, Darren (actor/director/producer)	May 7, 1922
McGee, Fiber; born James Jordan (actor)	November 16, 1896
McGee, Frank (newscaster)	September 12, 1921
McGee, Gale William (politician)	March 17, 1915
McGee, Jerry (golf)	July 21, 1943
McGee, Max; born William M. McGee (football)	July 16, 1932
McGeorge, Rick; born Richard McGeorge (football)	September 14, 1948
McGinley, Phyllis (poet)	March 21, 1905
McGinnis, George (basketball)	August 12, 1950
McGinnity, Joe; born Joseph Jerome McGinnity(baseball)	March 19, 1871
McGiver, John (actor)	November 5, 1913
McGlocklin, Jon Paul (basketball)	June 10, 1943
McGoohan, Patrick (actor)	March 19, 1928
McGovern, Francis Edward (politician)	January 21, 1866
McGovern, George Stanley (politician)	July 19, 1922
McGovern, Maureen Therese (singer)	July 27, 1949
McGrath, J. Howard; born James Howard McGrath (politics/government)	November 28, 1903
McGrath, Jack; born John James McGrath (auto racing)	October 8, 1919
McGraw, Charles Francis (actor)	May 10, 1914
McGraw, John Joseph (baseball)	April 7, 1873
McGraw, Tug; born Frank Edwin McGraw, Jr. (baseball)	August 30, 1944
McGregor Ken; born Kenneth McGregor (tennis)	June 2, 1929

McGuire, Biff; born William Joseph McGuire, (actor)	October 25, 1926
McGuire, Chris; born Christine McGuire	July 30, 1928
(singer—McGuire Sisters)	
McGuire, Dick; born Richard McGuire (basketball)	January 25, 1926
McGuire, Dorothy Hackett (actress)	June 14, 1918
McGuire, Dotty; born Dorothy McGuire	February 13, 1930
(singer—McGuire Sisters)	
McGuire, Phyllis (singer—McGuire Sisters)	February 14, 1931
McHugh, Frank; born Francis Curray McHugh (actor)	May 23, 1898
McIntire, John (actor)	June 27, 1907
McIntrye, John Archibald (hockey)	September 8, 1930
McIntyre, Thomas James (politician)	February 20, 1915
McKay, Douglas (politics/government)	June 24, 1893
McKay, Gardner; born George Cadogan Gardner McKay (actor)	June 10, 1932
McKay, Jim; born James Kenneth McManus (sportscaster)	September 24, 1921
McKay, John H. (football)	July 5, 1923
McKechnie, Bill; born William Boyd McKechnie (baseball)	August 7, 1886
McKeever, Marlin (football)	January 1, 1940
McKeithen, John Julian (politician)	May 28, 1918
McKeldin, Theodore Roosevelt (politician)	November 20, 1900
McKellar, Kenneth Douglas (politician)	January 29, 1869
McKelvie, Samuel Roy (politician)	April 15, 1881
McKenna, Joseph (government/jurist)	August 10, 1843
McKenna, Siobhan; born Siobhan Giollamhuire Nic Cionnaith	May 24, 1922
(actress)	
McKenna, Virginia (actress)	June 7, 1931
McKenney, Don; born Donald Hamilton McKenney (hockey)	April 30, 1934
McKenzie, John Albert (hockey)	December 12, 1937
McKenzie, Reggie; born Reginald McKenzie (football)	July 27, 1950
McKiernan, John Sammon (politician)	October 15, 1911
McKinley, Chuck; born Charles R. McKinley (tennis)	January 5, 1941
McKinley, Ida Saxton; born Ida Saxton (First Lady)	June 8, 1847
McKinley, William (President)	January 29, 1843
McKinley, William Brown (politician)	September 5, 1856
McKinney, Bones; born Horace McKinney (basketball)	January 1, 1919
McKuen, Rod Marvin (poet/music/singer)	April 29, 1933
McLaglen, Victor (actor)	December 11, 1883
McLain, Denny; born Dennis Dale McLain (baseball)	March 24, 1944
McLane, John (politician)	February 27, 1852
McLaren, Bruce (auto racing)	August 30, 1937
McLean, Angus Wilton (politician)	April 20, 1870
McLean, Don (singer)	October 2, 1945
McLean, George Payne (politician)	October 7, 1857
McLendon, Mac; born Benson Rayfield McLendon (golf)	August 10, 1945
McLeod, Fred; born Frederick Robertson McLeod (golf)	April 25, 1882
McLeod, Thomas Gordon (politician)	December 17, 1868
McLerie, Allyn Ann (actress/dancer/singer)	December 1, 1926
McLinton, Harold Lucious (football)	July 1, 1947
McLish, Cal; born Calvin Coolidge Julius Caesar Tushahoma	December 1, 1925
McLish (baseball)	
McLuhan, Marshall; born Herbert Marshall McLuhan	July 21, 1911
(communications expert/writer)	

McMahon, Brien; born James O'Brien McMahon (politician)	October 6, 1903
McMahon, Don; born Donald John McMahon (baseball)	January 4, 1930
McMahon, Ed; born Edward Leo Peter McMahon, Jr. (announcer/actor)	March 6, 1923
McMahon, Horace Thomas (actor)	May 17, 1907
McMahon, Jack (basketball)	December 3, 1928
McManus, Marty; born Martin Joseph McManus (baseball)	March 14, 1900
McMaster, William Henry (politician)	May 10, 1877
McMath, Sidney Sanders (politician)	June 14, 1912
McMillan, Ernie; born Ernest C. McMillan (football)	February 21, 1938
McMillan, Roy David (baseball)	July 17, 1930
McMullen, Adam (politician)	June 12, 1874
McMullen, Kathy (golf)	November 4, 1949
McMullen, Ken; born Kenneth Lee McMullen (baseball)	June 1, 1942
McMullen, Richard Cann (politician)	January 2, 1868
McNair, Barbara J. (singer/actress)	March 4, 1939
McNair, Eric; born Donald Eric McNair (baseball)	April 12, 1909
McNair, Robert Evander (politician)	December 14, 1923
McNally, Dave; born David Arthur McNally (baseball)	October 31, 1942
McNally, John Victor (football)	November 27, 1904
McNally, Stephen; born Horace McNally (actor)	July 29, 1913
McNally, Terrence (playwright)	November 3, 1939
MacNamara, Maggie (actress)	June 18, 1928
McNamara, Patrick Vincent (politician)	October 4, 1894
McNamara, Robert Strange (government)	June 9, 1916
McNary, Charles Linza (politician)	June 12, 1874
McNeil, Claudia Mae (actress)	August 13, 1917
McNeil, Clifton (football)	May 25, 1940
McNeil, Don; born W. Donald McNeil (tennis)	April 30, 1918
McNeil, Gerard George (hockey)	April 17, 1926
McNichol, Jimmy; born James Vincent McNichol (actor)	July 2, 1961
McNichol, Kristy; born Christina Ann McNichol (actress)	September 9, 1962
McNichols, Stephen L. R. (politician)	March 7, 1914
McNutt, Paul Vories (politician)	July 19, 1891
McPeak, Bill; born William McPeak (football)	July 24, 1926
McPhatter, Clyde (singer/music)	November 15, 1933
McQueen, Butterfly; born Thelma McQueen (actress/dancer)	January 8, 1911
McQueen, Steve; born Terence Stephen McQueen (actor)	March 24, 1930
McQuinn, George Hartley (baseball)	May 29, 1909
McRae, Bennie; born Benjamin P. McRae (football)	December 8, 1939
McRae, Carmen (singer)	April 8, 1922
McRae, Hal; born Harold Abraham McRae (baseball)	July 10, 1946
McRae, Thomas Chipman (politician)	December 21, 1851
McReynolds, James Clark (government/jurist)	February 3, 1862
McShane, Ian (actor)	September 29, 1942
McSpaden, Jug; born Harold McSpaden (golf)	May 21, 1908
Mead, Albert Edward (politician)	December 14, 1861
Mead, James Michael (politician)	December 27, 1885
Mead, John Abner (politician)	April 20, 1841
Mead, Margaret (anthropologist)	December 16, 1901
Meade, Julia; born Julia Kunze (actress)	December 17, 1928

Meadows, Audrey; born Audrey Cotter (actress)	————1925
Meadows, Clarence Watson (politician)	February 11, 1904
Meadows, Jayne; born Jane Cotter (actress)	September 27, 1923
Meara, Anne (comedienne/actress)	September 20, 1929
Meany, George (labor leader)	August 16, 1894
Mechem, Edwin Leard (politician)	July 2, 1912
Mechem, Merritt Cramer (politician)	October 10, 1870
Medford, Kay; born Kathleen Patricia Regan	September 14, 1920
(or Maggie O'Regin) (actress)	
Medich, Doc; born George Francis Medich (baseball)	December 9, 1948
Medina, Patricia (actress)	July 19, 1919
Medwick, Joe "Ducky"; born Joseph Michael Medwick	November 24, 1911
(baseball)	
Meek, Donald (actor)	July 14, 1880
Meeker, Howie; born Howard William Meeker (hockey)	November 4, 1924
Meeker, Ralph; born Ralph Rathgeber (actor)	November 21, 1920
Mehta, Zubin (music)	April 29, 1936
Meier, Julius L. (politician)	December 31, 1874
Meir, Golda; born Golda Mabovitz (Israeli government)	May 3, 1898
MeKechnie, Donna (dancer/actress)	November ————— 1940
Melanie; born Melanie Safka (singer/actress/music)	February 3, 1947
Melcher, John (politician)	September 6, 1924
Melchionni, Bill (basketball)	October 19, 1944
Melchior, Lauritz; born Lebrecht Hommel (singer)	March 20, 1890
Mele, Sam; born Sabath Anthony Mele (baseball)	January 21, 1923
Mellon, Andrew William (industrialist/government)	March 24, 1855
Mellon, Paul (philanthropist/art collector)	June 11, 1907
Melnyk, Steve; born Steven Nicholas Melnyk (golf)	February 26, 1947
Melton, James (singer)	January 2, 1904
Melton, Sid; born Sid Meltzer (actor)	May 23, 1920
Melville, Herman (author)	August 1, 1819
Melville, Sam (actor)	August 20————
Mencken, H.L.; born Henry Louis Mencken	September 12, 1880
(journalist/editor/author)	
Mendel, Gregor Johann (botanist)	July 22, 1822
Mendelssohn; born Jakob Ludwig Felix Mendelssohn-Bartholdy	February 5, 1809
(music)	
Mendenhall, John Rufus (football)	December 3, 1948
Mendenhall, Ken; born Kenneth Mendenhall (football)	August 11, 1948
Mendes, Sergio (music)	February 11, 1941
Menjou, Adolphe Jean (actor)	February 18, 1890
Menke, Denis John (baseball)	July 21, 1940
Menne, Bob; born Robert Menne (golf)	February 19, 1942
Mennin, Peter; born Peter Mennini (music)	May 17, 1923
Menninger, Karl Augustus (psychiatrist/author)	July 22, 1893
Menotti, Gian-Carlo (music)	July 7, 1911
Menuhin, Yehudi (music)	April 22, 1916
Menzies, Heather Margaret (actress)	December 3, 1949
Mercer, Beryl (actress)	August 13, 1882
Mercer, Johnny; born John H. Mercer (music)	November 18, 1909
Mercer, Mabel (singer)	January ————— 1900

Mercer, Marian E. (actress/singer)   November 26, 1935
Mercer, Mike; born Michael Mercer (football)   November 21, 1935
Merchant, Larry (sportscaster/journalist/author)   February 11, 1931
Mercouri, Melina; born Maria Amalia Mercouri (actress)   October 18, 1915
Meredith, Burgess George (actor/director/producer)   November 16, 1908
Meredith, Don; born Joseph Donald Meredith   April 10, 1938
    (football/sportscaster/actor)
Meriwether, Lee Ann (Miss America/actress)   May 27, 1935
Merkel, Una (actress)   December 10, 1903
Merman, Ethel; born Ethel Agnes Zimmermann (singer/actress)   January 16, 1908
Merriam, Frank Finley (politician)   December 22, 1865
Merrick, David; born David Margulois (producer)   November 27, 1912
Merrill, Dina; born Nedenia Hutton (actress)   December 9, 1925
Merrill, Gary Franklin (actor)   August 2, 1914
Merrill, Robert; born Morris Miller (singer)   June 4, 1919
Merrow, Jane (actress)   August 26, 1941
Meschery, Tom (basketball)   October 26, 1938
Meskill, Thomas J. (politician)   January 30, 1928
Mesmer, Franz Anton (medicine)   May 23, 1734
Messersmith, Andy; born John Alexander Messersmith   August 6, 1945
    (baseball)
Mesta, Perle; born Perle Skirvin (socialite)   October 12, 1891
Metcalf, Jesse Houghton (politician)   November 16, 1860
Metcalf, Lee (politician)   January 28, 1911
Metcalf, Terry; born Terrance Randolph Metcalf (football)   September 24, 1951
Metcalf, Victor Howard (government)   October 10, 1853
Methot, Mayo (actress)   March 3, 1904
Metro, Charlie; born Charles Moreskonich (baseball)   April 28, 1919
Metz, Dick; born Richard Metz (golf)   May 29, 1908
Metz, Nicholas J. (hockey)   February 16, 1914
Metzenbaum, Howard Morton (politician)   June 4, 1917
Meyer, George von Lengerke (government)   June 24, 1858
Meyer, Louis (auto racing)   ————1904
Meyner, Robert Baumle (politician)   July 3, 1908
Michael, Gene; born Eugene Richard Michael (baseball)   June 2, 1938
Michael, Gertrude (actress)   June 1, 1910
Michaels, Cass; born Casimir Eugene Kwietniewski   March 4, 1926
    (baseball)
Michaels, Walt; born Wladek Majka (football)   October 16, 1929
Michelangelo; born Michelagnolo di Ludovico di Buonarroti-   March 6, 1475
    Simoni (artist)
Michell, Keith Joseph (actor/singer)   December 1, 1926
Michener, James Albert (author)   February 3, 1907
Mickelson, George Theodore (politician)   July 23, 1903
Mickey, John Hopwood (politician)   September 20, 1845
Mickoski, Nicholas (hockey)   December 7, 1927
Middlecoff, Cary; born Emmett Cary Middlecoff   January 6, 1921
    (golf/sportscaster)
Middleton, Ray; born Raymond E. Middleton (actor)   February 8, 1907
Middleton, Robert; born Samuel G. Messer (actor)   May 13, 1911
Midler, Bette (singer/actress)   December 1, 1945

Mielziner, Jo (designer)	March 19, 1901
Mifune, Toshiro (actor/director)	April 1, 1920
Migay, Rudolph Joseph (hockey)	November 18, 1928
Mikan, George (basketball)	June 18, 1924
Mike-Mayer, Nick; born Nicholas Mike-Mayer (football)	March 1, 1950
Mike-Mayer, Steve (football)	September 8, 1947
Mikita, Stan; born Stanley Mikita (hockey)	May 20, 1940
Mikkelsen, Vern; born Arild Verner Agerskov Mikkelsen (basketball)	October 21, 1928
Miksis, Eddie; born Edward Thomas Miksis (baseball)	September 11, 1926
Milanov, Zinka; born Zinka Kunc (singer)	May 17, 1906
Miles, Eddie (basketball)	July 5, 1940
Miles, Joanna; born Joanna Miles Schiefer (actress)	March 6, 1940
Miles, John Esten (politician)	July 28, 1884
Miles, Sarah (actress)	December 31, 1941
Miles, Sylvia (actress)	September 9, 1932
Miles, Vera; born Vera May Ralston (actress)	August 23, 1929
Milhaud, Darius (music)	September 4, 1892
Mill, John Stuart (political economist/philosopher)	May 20, 1806
Millan, Felix Bernardo (baseball)	August 21, 1943
Milland, Ray; born Reginald Truscott-Jones (actor)	January 3, 1905
Millay, Edna St. Vincent (poet)	February 22, 1892
Miller, Allen L., III (golf)	August 10, 1948
Miller, Ann; born Lucille Ann Collier (actress/dancer)	April 12, 1919
Miller, Arthur (playwright)	October 17, 1915
Miller, Benjamin Meek (politician)	March 13, 1864
Miller, Bing; born Edmund John Miller (baseball)	August 30, 1894
Miller, Bob; born Robert Lane Gmeinweisser (baseball)	February 18, 1939
Miller, Caroline (author)	August 26, 1903
Miller, Charles R. (politician)	September 30, 1857
Miller, Cheryl (actress)	February 4, 1943
Miller, Eddie; born Edward Robert Miller (baseball)	November 26, 1916
Miller, Fred; born Frederick D. Miller (football)	August 8, 1940
Miller, Glenn (music)	March 1, 1904
Miller, Henry Valentine (author)	December 26, 1891
Miller, Jack Richard (politician)	June 6, 1916
Miller, Jason; born John Miller (playwright/actor)	April 22, 1939
Miller, Jody (singer)	November 29, 1941
Miller, Johnny; born John Lawrence Miller (golf)	April 29, 1947
Miller, Keith Harvey (politician)	March 1, 1925
Miller, Leslie Andrew (politician)	January 29, 1866
Miller, Marilyn; born Mary Ellen Reynolds (singer/dancer/actress)	September 1, 1898
Miller, Marvin; born Marvin Mueller (actor)	July 18, 1913
Miller, Mitch; born Mitchell William Miller (music)	July 4, 1911
Miller, Nathan Lewis (politician)	October 10, 1868
Miller, Patsy Ruth (actress/writer)	June 22, 1905
Miller, Roger Dean (singer/music)	January 2, 1936
Miller, Sharon Kay (golf)	January 13, 1941
Miller, Stu; born Stuart Leonard Miller (baseball)	December 26, 1927
Millet, Jean Francois (artist)	October 4, 1814

Millett, Kate; born Katherine Murray Millett (feminist)	September 14, 1934
Milliken, Carl Elias (politician)	July 13, 1877
Milliken, William Grawn (politician)	March 26, 1922
Millikin, Eugene Donald (politician)	February 12, 1891
Millner, Wayne (football)	January 13, 1913
Mills, Buster (baseball)	September 16, 1908
Mills, Donald F. (singer—Mills Brothers)	April 29, 1915
Mills, Donna (actress)	December 11, 1943
Mills, Harry F. (singer—Mills Brothers)	August 9, 1913
Mills, Hayley Catherine Rose Vivian (actress/singer)	April 18, 1946
Mills, Herbert (singer—Mills Brothers)	April 2, 1912
Mills, John, Jr. (singer—Mills Brothers)	February 11, 1889
Mills, John Lewis Ernest Watts (actor/singer/dancer/ producer)	February 22, 1908
Mills, Juliet Maryon (actress)	November 21, 1941
Mills, Mary (golf)	January 19, 1940
Mills, Wilbur Daigh (politician)	May 24, 1909
Milne, A.A.; born Alan Alexander Milne (author)	January 18, 1882
Milner, Martin Sam (actor)	December 28, 1927
Milsap, Ronnie (singer/music)	January 16, 1944
Milstein, Nathan (music)	December 31, 1904
Milton, John (poet)	December 9, 1608
Milton, Tommy (auto racing)	———1893
Mimieux, Yvette Carmen M. (actress/music/writer)	January 8, 1939
Mincher, Don; born Donald Ray Mincher (baseball)	June 24, 1938
Mineo, Sal; born Salvadore Mineo (actor/singer)	January 10, 1939
Mingus, Charles (music)	April 22, 1922
Mink, Patsy; born Patsy Takemoto (politician)	December 6, 1927
Minnelli, Liza May (actress/singer)	March 12, 1946
Minnelli, Vincente (director)	February 28, 1910
Minoso, Minnie; born Saturnino Orestes Armas Minoso (baseball)	November 29, 1922
Minton, Sherman (jurist)	October 20, 1890
Mira, George Ignacio (football)	January 11, 1942
Miranda, Carmen; born Marie de Carmo Miranda de Cunha (singer)	February 9, 1914
Miranda, Isa; born Inès Isabella Sampietro (actress)	July 5, 1909
Miranda, Willie; born Guillermo Miranda (baseball)	May 24, 1926
Mirisch, Walter Mortimer (producer)	November 8, 1921
Miró, Joan (artist)	April 20, 1893
Miszuk, John (hockey)	September 29, 1940
Mitchell, Bobby; born Robert Cornelius Mitchell (football)	June 6, 1935
Mitchell, Bobby; born Robert Mitchell (golf)	February 23, 1943
Mitchell, Cameron; born Cameron M. Mitzell (actor)	November 4, 1918
Mitchell, Chad (singer)	———1939
Mitchell, Clarence Elmer (baseball)	February 22, 1891
Mitchell, Dale; born Loren Dale Mitchell (baseball)	August 23, 1921
Mitchell, Guy; born Al Cernick (singer/actor)	February ——— 1925
Mitchell, James Paul (government)	November 12, 1900
Mitchell, John Newton (government)	September 5, 1913
Mitchell, Joni; born Roberta Joan Anderson (singer/music)	November 7, 1943

Mitchell, Lydell Douglas (football)	May 30, 1949
Mitchell, Margaret (author)	November 8, 1900
Mitchell, Martha; born Martha Elizabeth Beall (socialite)	September 2, 1918
Mitchell, Thomas (actor)	July 11, 1892
Mitchell, Tom; born Thomas G. Mitchell (football)	August 22, 1944
Mitchell, William DeWitt (government)	September 9, 1874
Mitchum, James (actor)	May 8, 1941
Mitchum, Robert Charles Duran (actor)	August 6, 1917
Mitford, Jessica Lucy (author)	September 11, 1917
Mitterwald, George Eugene (baseball)	June 7, 1945
Mix, Steve (basketball)	December 30, 1947
Mix, Tom; born Thomas Edwin Mix (actor)	January 6, 1880
Mize, Johnny; born John Robert Mize (baseball)	January 7, 1913
Mizell, Vinegar Bend; born Wilmer David Mizell (baseball/politics)	August 13, 1930
Mobley, Mary Ann (Miss America/actress/singer)	———1937
Modzelewski, Dick; born Richard Modzelewski (football)	February 16, 1931
Moeur, Benjamin Baker (politician)	December 22, 1869
Moffat, Donald (actor/director)	December 26, 1930
Moffo, Anna (singer)	June 26, 1935
Mohns, Douglas Allen (hockey)	December 13, 1933
Mohr, Gerald (actor)	May 11, 1914
Molière; born Jean Baptiste Poquelin (playwright)	January 15, 1622
Molina, Jose (dancer)	November 19, 1937
Molotov, Vyacheslav Mikhailovich (Russian government)	March 9, 1890
Momaday, N. Scott; born Navarre Scott Momaday (author)	February 27, 1934
Monbouquette, Bill; born William Charles Monbouquette (baseball)	August 11, 1936
Mondale, Joan Adams; born Joan Adams (Vice President's wife)	August 8, 1930
Mondale, Walter Frederick "Fritz" (Vice President)	January 5, 1928
Monday, Rick; born Robert James Monday (baseball)	November 20, 1945
Mondou, Armand (hockey)	June 27, 1905
Monet, Claude (artist)	November 14, 1840
Money, Don; born Donald Wayne Money (baseball)	June 7, 1947
Monk, Thelonious Sphere (music)	October 10, 1918
Monroe, Bill; born William Smith Monroe (singer/music)	September 13, 1911
Monroe, Earl; born Vernon Earl Monroe (basketball)	November 21, 1944
Monroe, Elizabeth Kortright; born Elizabeth Kortright (First Lady)	June 30, 1768
Monroe, James (President)	April 28, 1758
Monroe, Marilyn; born Norma Jean Mortensen (actress)	June 1, 1926
Monroe, Vaughn Wilton (music)	October 7, 1911
Monroney, Mike; born Almer Stilwell Monroney (politician)	March 2, 1902
Monsarrat, Nicholas John Turney (author)	March 22, 1910
Montagu, Ashley (anthropologist/author)	June 28, 1905
Montague, Andrew Jackson (politician)	October 3, 1862
Montalban, Ricardo; born Ricardo Gonzalo Pedro Montalban Merino (actor)	November 25, 1920
Montand, Yves; born Yvo (or Ivo) Livi (actor)	October 13, 1921
Montanez, Willie; born Guillermo Montanez (baseball)	April 1, 1948

Monteverdi, Claudio (music) — May 15, 1567
Montez, Maria; born Maria Africa Vidal de Santo Silas (actress) — June 6, 1918
Montgomery, Belinda J. (actress) — July 23, 1950
Montgomery, Douglass; born Robert Douglass Montgomery (actor) — October 29, 1907
Montgomery, Elizabeth (actress) — April 15, 1933
Montgomery, George; born George Montgomery Letz (actor) — August 29, 1916
Montgomery, Melba (singer) — October 14, 1938
Montgomery, Robert; born Henry Montgomery, Jr. (actor/director/producer) — May 21, 1904
Montler, Mike; born Michael R. Montler (football) — January 11, 1944
Montoya, Carlos (music) — December 13, 1903
Montoya, Joseph Manuel (politician) — September 24, 1915
Moody, Dan (politician) — June 1, 1893
Moody, Orville (golf) — December 9, 1933
Moody, Ron; born Ronald Moodnick (actor/singer) — January 8, 1924
Moody, William Henry (government/jurist) — December 23, 1853
Moon, Wally; born Wallace Wade Moon (baseball) — April 3, 1930
Moore, A. Harry; born Arthur Harry Moore (politician) — July 3, 1879
Moore, Arch Alfred, Jr. (politician) — April 16, 1923
Moore, Archie; born Archibald Lee Moore (boxing) — December 13, 1916
Moore, Charles Calvin (politician) — February 26, 1866
Moore, Clayton (actor) — September 14, 1914
Moore, Clement Clarke (poet/author) — July 15, 1779
Moore, Cleo (actress) — October 31, 1928
Moore, Colleen; born Kathleen Morrison (actress) — August 19, 1900
Moore, Constance (actress/singer) — January 18, 1919
Moore, Dan Killian (politician) — April 2, 1906
Moore, Dickie; born John Richard Moore, Jr. (actor/producer/director/writer) — September 12, 1925
Moore, Dickie; born Richard Winston Moore (hockey) — January 6, 1931
Moore, Dudley (music/comedian/actor) — April 19, 1935
Moore, Eddie; born Graham Edward Moore (baseball) — January 18, 1899
Moore, Gary; born Thomas Garrison Morfit (TV host) — January 31, 1915
Moore, Gene; born Eugene Moore, Jr. (baseball) — August 26, 1909
Moore, Grace; born Mary Willie Grace Moore (singer/actress) — December 5, 1898
Moore, Joanna (actress) — November 9———
Moore, Johnny; born John Francis Moore (baseball) — March 23, 1902
Moore, Jo Jo; born Joseph Gregg Moore (baseball) — December 25, 1908
Moore, Lenny; born Leonard Edward Moore (football) — November 25, 1933
Moore, Marianne Craig (poet) — November 15, 1887
Moore, Mary Tyler (actress/singer/dancer/producer) — December 29, 1937
Moore, Maulty (football) — August 12, 1946
Moore, Melba; born Beatrice Hill (singer/actress) — October 29, 1945
Moore, Randy; born Randolph Edward Moore (baseball) — June 21, 1905
Moore, Roger George (actor) — October 14, 1927
Moore, Terry; born Helen Koford (actress) — January 7, 1929
Moore, Terry Bluford (baseball) — May 27, 1912
Moore, Thomas (poet) — May 28, 1779
Moore, Victor Frederick (actor) — February 24, 1876

Moore, Zeke; born Ezekiel Moore (football)	December 2, 1943
Moorehead, Agnes Robertson (actress)	December 6, 1906
Moose, Bob; born Robert Ralph Moose (baseball)	October 9, 1947
Moran, Erin (actress)	October 18, 1961
Moran, Lois; born Lois Darlington Dowling (actress)	March 1, 1907
Moran, Polly; born Pauline Therese Moran (actress)	June 28, 1883
Morath, Max Edward (music)	October 1, 1926
More, Kenneth (actor)	September 20, 1914
More, Sir Thomas (statesman/author/humanist)	February 7, 1478
Moreau, Jeanne (actress)	January 23, 1928
Morehead, John Henry (politician)	December 3, 1861
Moreno, Rita; born Rosita Dolores Alverio (actress/ singer/dancer)	December 11, 1931
Morenz, Howie; born Howarth William Morenz (hockey)	September 21, 1902
Morgan, Dennis; born Stanley Morner (actor/singer)	Deember 10, 1910
Morgan, Ephraim Franklin (politician)	January 16, 1869
Morgan, Frank; born Francis Philip Wuppermann (actor)	June 1, 1890
Morgan, George (singer/music)	June 28, 1925
Morgan, Gil (golf)	September 25, 1946
Morgan, Harry; born Harry Bratsburg (actor)	April 10, 1915
Morgan, Helen; born Helen Riggins (singer/actress)	August 2, 1900
Morgan, Henry; born Henry Lerner von Ost. Jr. (actor)	March 31, 1915
Morgan, J.P.; born John Pierpont Morgan (financier)	April 17, 1837
Morgan, J.P., Jr.; born John Pierpont Morgan, Jr. (financier)	September 7, 1867
Morgan, Jane; born Florence Currier (actress/singer)	—————1920
Morgan, Jaye P.; born Mary Margaret Morgan (singer/actress)	December 3, 1931
Morgan, Joe Leonard (baseball)	September 19, 1943
Morgan, Michèle; born Simone Roussel (actress)	February 29, 1920
Morgan, Ralph; born Raphael Kuhner Wuppermann (actor)	July 6, 1882
Morgan, Robert Burren (politician)	October 5, 1925
Morgan, Terence (actor)	December 8, 1921
Morgenthau, Henry, Jr. (government)	May 11, 1891
Moriarty, Michael (actor)	April 5, 1941
Morin, Milt; born Milton Morin (football)	October 15, 1942
Morini, Erica (music)	January 5, 1908
Morison, Patricia; born Eileen Patricia Augusta Fraser Morison (actress/singer)	March 19, 1914
Morley, Christopher Darlington (author)	May 5, 1890
Morley, Clarence Joseph (politician)	February 9, 1869
Morley, Karen; born Mabel (or Mildred) Linton (actress)	December 12, 1905
Morley, Robert Adolph Wilton (actor/producer)	May 26, 1908
Morrall, Earl Edwin (football)	May 17, 1934
Morris, Chester; born John Chester Brooks Morris (actor)	February 16, 1901
Morris, Garrett (actor/comedian/singer)	February 1, 1937
Morris, Gouverneur (statesman)	January 31, 1752
Morris, Greg (actor)	September 27, 1934
Morris, Howard (actor/director)	September 4, 1919
Morris, Jon Nicholson (football)	April 5, 1942
Morris, Larry; born Lawrence Morris (football)	December 10, 1933
Morris, Mercury; born Eugene Morris (football)	January 5, 1947

Morris, Wayne; born Bertram DeWayne Morris (actor)	February 17, 1914
Morris, William (poet/artist)	March 24, 1834
Morris, Willie (author/editor)	November 29, 1934
Morrison, Cameron (politician)	October 5, 1869
Morrison, Frank Brenner (politician)	May 20, 1905
Morrison, James Steward Hunter (hockey)	October 11, 1931
Morrison, John Tracy (politician)	December 25, 1860
Morrow, Don (TV host)	January 29————
Morrow, Edwin Porch (politician)	November 28, 1878
Morrow, Jeff (actor)	January 13, 1913
Morrow, Jo (actress)	————1940
Morrow, Karen (actress/singer)	December 15, 1936
Morrow, Vic (actor)	February 14, 1932
Morse, Barry Herbert (actor)	June 10, 1919
Morse, Ella Mae (singer)	September 12, 1924
Morse, Robert Alan (actor/singer)	May 18, 1931
Morse, Samuel Finley Breese (inventor)	April 27, 1791
Morse, Wayne Lyman (politician)	October 20, 1900
Morton, Bruce Alexander (newscaster)	October 28, 1930
Morton, Craig; born Larry Craig Morton (football)	February 5, 1943
Morton, Jelly Roll; born Ferdinand Joseph La Menthe (music)	September 20, 1885
Morton, Levi Parsons (Vice President)	May 16, 1824
Morton, Rogers C.B.; born Rogers Clark Ballard Morton (politics/government)	September 19, 1914
Morton, Thruston Ballard (politician)	August 19, 1907
Mortson, Gus; born James Angus Gerald Mortson (hockey)	January 24, 1925
Moryn, Walt; born Walter Joseph Moryn (baseball)	April 12, 1926
Mosdell, Ken; born Kenneth Mosdell (hockey)	July 13, 1922
Mosel, Tad; born George Ault Mosel, Jr. (playwright)	May 1, 1922
Moser-Proell, Annemarie (skiing)	March 27, 1953
Moses, George Higgins (politician)	February 9, 1869
Moses, Grandma; born Ann Mary Robertson (artist)	September 7, 1860
Moses, Haven Christopher (football)	July 27, 1946
Moses, John (politician)	June 12, 1885
Moses, Wally; born Wallace Moses (baseball)	October 8, 1910
Mosienko, Bill; born William Mosienko (hockey)	November 2, 1921
Mosley, Mark (football)	March 12, 1948
Mosley, Mike; born Michael Dean Mosley (auto racing)	December 13, 1944
Moss, Arnold (actor/director)	January 28, 1910
Moss, Frank Edward (politician)	September 23, 1911
Moss, Les; born John Lester Moss (baseball)	May 14, 1925
Moss, Stirling Craufurd (auto racing)	September 17, 1929
Mossi, Don; born Donald Louis Mossi (baseball)	January 11, 1929
Most, Donny (actor/singer)	August 8, 1953
Mostel, Zero; born Samuel Joel Mostel (actor)	February 28, 1915
Mostil, Johnny; born John Anthony Mostil (baseball)	June 6, 1896
Mota, Manny; born Manuel Rafael Mota (baseball)	February 18, 1938
Motley, Marion (football)	June 5, 1920
Motta, Dick; born John Richard Motta (basketball)	September 3, 1931
Motter, Alexander Everett (hockey)	June 20, 1913
Mowbray, Alan (actor)	August 18, 1893

Moyers, Bill; born Billy Don Moyers (journalism/government)	June 5, 1934
Moynihan, Daniel Patrick (government/politics)	March 16, 1927
Mozart, Wolfgang Amadeus; born Johannes Chrysostomus Wolfgangus Theophilus (music)	January 27, 1756
Mudd, Roger Harrison (newscaster)	February 9, 1928
Mueller, Don; born Donald Frederick Mueller (baseball)	April 14, 1927
Mueller, Frederick Henry (government)	November 22, 1893
Mueller, Ray Coleman (baseball)	March 8, 1912
Muggeridge, Malcolm Thomas (writer)	March 24, 1903
Muhammad, Elijah; born Elijah Poole (religious leader)	October 7, 1897
Muhlmann, Horst (football)	January 2, 1940
Muir, Jean; born Jean Muir Fullarton (actress)	February 13, 1911
Muldaur, Diana Charlton (actress)	August 19, 1938
Muldaur, Maria; born Maria Grazia Rose Domenica d'Amato (singer)	September 12, 1942
Mulford, Ralph (auto racing)	———1885
Mulgrew, Kate; born Katherine Mulgrew (actress)	April 29, 1955
Mulhall, Jack; born John Joseph Francis Mulhall (actor)	October 7, 1887
Mulhare, Edward (actor)	April 8, 1923
Mulligan, Gerry; born Gerald Joseph Mulligan (music)	April 6, 1927
Mulligan, Richard (actor)	November 13, 1932
Mullin, Pat; born Patrick Joseph Mullin (baseball)	November 1, 1917
Mullins, Jeff (basketball)	March 18, 1942
Mulloy, Gardnar (tennis)	November 22, 1914
Mumphord, Lloyd N. (football)	December 20, 1946
Mundt, Karl Earl (politician)	June 3, 1900
Mungo, Van Lingle (baseball)	June 8, 1911
Muni, Paul; born Frederich Weisenfreund (actor)	September 22, 1895
Munsel, Patrice Beverly (singer/actress)	May 14, 1925
Munson, Bill; born William A. Munson (football)	August 11, 1941
Munson, Ona; born Ona Wolcott (actress)	June 16, 1903
Munson, Thurman Lee (baseball)	June 7, 1947
Murcer, Bobby Ray (baseball)	May 20, 1946
Murcrief, Bob; born Robert Cleveland Murcrief (baseball)	January 28, 1916
Murdock, John Murray (hockey)	May 19, 1904
Murillo, Bartolomé Esteban (artist)	January 1, 1618
Murphree, Dennis; born Herron Dennis Murphree (politician)	January 6, 1886
Murphy, Audie Leon (actor)	June 20, 1924
Murphy, Ben; born Benjamin Edward Murphy (actor)	March 6, 1942
Murphy, Bob; born Robert Joseph Murphy, Jr. (golf)	February 14, 1943
Murphy, Calvin J. (basketball)	May 9, 1948
Murphy, Francis Parnell (politician)	August 16, 1877
Murphy, Frank (politician/jurist)	April 13, 1890
Murphy, Franklin (politician)	January 3, 1846
Murphy, George Lloyd (actor/dancer/politician)	July 4, 1902
Murphy, Jimmy; born James Anthony Murphy (auto racing)	———1894
Murphy, Johnny; born John Joseph Murphy (baseball)	July 14, 1908
Murphy, Mary (actress)	January 26, 1931
Murphy, Ron; born Robert Ronald Murphy (hockey)	April 10, 1933
Murphy, Rosemary (actress)	January 13, 1927
Murray, Anne (singer)	June 20, 1946

Murray, Arthur; born Arthur Murray Teichman (dancer)	April 4, 1895
Murray, Bill (actor/comedian/singer)	September 21, 1950
Murray, Don; born Donald Patrick Murray (actor/director/writer)	July 31, 1929
Murray, James Edward (politician)	May 3, 1876
Murray, Jan; born Murray Janowitz (comedian/actor/TV host)	October 4, 1917
Murray, Johnston (politician)	July 21, 1902
Murray, Kathryn; born Kathryn Hazel Kohnfelder (dancer)	September 15, 1906
Murray, Ken; born Don Court (actor/producer/author)	July 14, 1903
Murray, Mae; born Marie Adrienne Koening (actress)	May 7, 1889
Murray, William Henry (politician)	November 21, 1869
Murrow, Edward R.; born Edward Roscoe Murrow (newscaster)	April 25, 1908
Murtaugh, Danny; born Daniel Edward Murtaugh (baseball)	October 8, 1917
Musante, Tony (actor)	June 30, 1936
Musburger, Brent Woody (sportscaster)	May 26, 1939
Muse, Clarence (actor)	October 7, 1889
Musial, Stan; born Stanley Frank Musial (baseball)	November 21, 1920
Muskie, Edmund Sixtus (politician)	March 28, 1914
Mussolini, Benito (Italian government)	July 29, 1883
Mustin, Burt (actor)	February 8, 1882
Mutscheller, Jim; born James Mutscheller (football)	March 31, 1930
Myer, Buddy; born Charles Solomon Myer (baseball)	March 16, 1904
Myers, Carmel (actress)	April 9, 1899
Myers, Chip; born Philip Leon Myers (football)	July 9, 1945
Myers, Francis John (politician)	December 18, 1901
Myers, Henry Lee (politician)	October 9, 1862
Myerson, Bess (Miss America/actress/consumer advocate)	July 16, 1924

N

Nabokov, Vladimir (author)	April 23, 1899
Nabors, Jim (actor/singer)	June 12, 1932
Nader, George (actor)	October 19, 1921
Nader, Ralph (consumer crusader)	February 27, 1934
Nagel, Anne; born Ann Dolan (actress)	September 30, 1912
Nagel, Charles (government)	August 9, 1849
Nagel, Conrad (actor)	March 16, 1896
Nagle, Kel; born Kelvin David George Nagle (golf)	December 21, 1920
Nagurski, Bronko; born Bronislaw Nagurski (football)	November 3, 1908
Naish, J. Carrol; born Joseph Patrick Carrol Naish (actor)	January 21, 1897
Naismith, Laurence; born Laurence Bernard Johnson (actor)	December 14, 1908
Namath, Joe; born Joseph William Namath (football/actor)	May 31, 1943
Nance, Jim; born James Solomon Nance (football)	December 30, 1942
Napier, Alan (actor)	January 7, 1903
Nash, George Kilbon (politician)	August 14, 1842
Nash, Johnny (singer)	August 19, 1940
Nash, Odgen; born Frederick Ogden Nash (poet)	August 19, 1902
Nasser, Gamal Abd el-(Egyptian government)	January 15, 1918
Nastase, Ilie (tennis)	July 19, 1946
Nation, Carry; born Carry Amelia Moore (temperance leader)	November 25, 1846
Natwick, Mildred (actress)	June 19, 1908

Naughton, James (actor)	December 6, 1945
Naulls, Willie (basketball)	October 7, 1934
Naumoff, Paul Pete (football)	July 3, 1945
Navratilova, Martina (tennis)	October 18, 1956
Neagle, Anna; born Florence Marjorie Robertson (actress)	October 20, 1904
Neal, Charlie; born Charles Lenard Neal (baseball)	January 30, 1931
Neal, Patricia Louise (actress)	January 20, 1926
Neely, Matthew Mansfield (politician)	November 9, 1874
Neely, Ralph Eugene (football)	September 12, 1943
Neeman, Cal; born Calvin Amandus Neeman (baseball)	February 18, 1929
Neff, Hildegarde; born Hildegarde Knef (actress/singer /author)	December 28, 1925
Neff, Pat Morris (politician)	November 26, 1871
Negri, Pola; born Barbara Appolonia Chalupec (actress)	December 31, 1894
Neft, Art; born Arthur Neukom Nehf (baseball)	July 31, 1892
Nehru, Jawaharlal (Indian government)	November 14, 1889
Neilson, Chief; born James Anthony Neilson (hockey)	November 28, 1940
Nelsen, Bill; born William K. Nelsen (football)	January 29, 1941
Nelson, Al; born Albert Nelson (football)	October 27, 1943
Nelson, Barry; born Robert Haakon Nielsen (actor)	April 16, 1920
Nelson, Byron; born John Byron Nelson, Jr. (golf/sportscaster)	February 4, 1912
Nelson, Dave; born David Earl Nelson (baseball)	June 20, 1944
Nelson, David (actor)	October 24, 1936
Nelson, Don (basketball)	May 15, 1940
Nelson, Ed; born Edwin Stafford Nelson (actor)	December 21, 1928
Nelson, Gaylord Anton (politician)	June 4, 1916
Nelson, Gene; born Gene Berg (actor/dancer/director)	March 24, 1920
Nelson, Harriet Hilliard; born Peggy Lou Snyder (singer/actress)	July 18, 1911
Nelson, Horatio, (English naval officer)	September 29, 1758
Nelson, Jimmy (ventriloquist)	December 15, 1928
Nelson, Knute (politician)	February 2, 1843
Nelson, Larry (golf)	September 10, 1947
Nelson, Lindsey (sportscaster)	May 25, 1919
Nelson, Lori; born Dixie Kay Nelson (actress)	August 15, 1933
Nelson, Ozzie; born Oswald George Nelson (music/actor)	March 20, 1906
Nelson, Rick; born Eric Hilliard Nelson (singer/actor)	May 8, 1940
Nelson, Rocky; born Glenn Richard Nelson (baseball)	November 18, 1924
Nelson, Willie (singer/music)	April 30, 1933
Nero, Franco (actor)	————1942
Nero, Peter; born Peter Bernard Nierow (music)	May 22, 1934
Nesbitt, Cathleen Mary (actress)	November 24, 1888
Nessen, Ron; born Ronald Harold Nessen (newscaster/government)	May 25, 1934
Nesterenko, Eric Paul (hockey)	October 31, 1933
Nestos, Regnvald Anderson (politician)	April 12, 1877
Nettles, Graig (baseball)	August 20, 1944
Nettleton, Lois June (actress)	August 16, 1929
Neuberger, Maurine Brown (politician)	January 9, 1907
Neuberger, Richard Lewis (politician)	December 26, 1912

Neumann, Paul (basketball)	January 30, 1938
Nevers, Ernie; born Ernest A. Nevers (football)	June 11, 1903
Nevil, Dwight D. (golf)	August 25, 1944
Neville, Keith (politician)	February 25, 1884
Neville, Tom; born Thomas Neville (football)	August 12, 1943
Nevin, Robert Frank (hockey)	March 18, 1938
New, Harry Stewart (politics/government)	December 31, 1858
Newcombe, Don; born Donald Newcombe (baseball)	June 14, 1926
Newcombe, John David (tennis)	May 23, 1943
Newhart, Bob; born George Robert Newhart (comedian/actor)	September 5, 1929
Newhouse, Robert Fulton (football)	January 9, 1950
Newhouse, Samuel Irving (publisher)	May 24, 1895
Newhouser, Hal; born Harold Newhouser (baseball)	May 20, 1921
Newlands, Francis Griffith (politician)	August 28, 1848
Newley, Anthony George (actor/singer/music)	September 24, 1931
Newman, Barry Foster (actor)	November 7, 1938
Newman, Edwin Harold (newscaster/author)	January 25, 1919
Newman, Laraine (actress/comedienne/singer)	March 2, 1952
Newman, Paul (actor/director)	January 26, 1925
Newman, Phyllis (actress/singer)	March 19, 1935
Newmar, Julie; born Julia Charlene Newmeyer (actress)	August 16, 1935
Newsom, Bobo; born Louis Norman Newsom (baseball)	August 11, 1907
Newson, Tommy; born Thomas Penn Newsom (music)	February 25, 1929
Newton, Sir Isaac (mathematician)	December 25, 1642
Newton, Robert (actor)	June 1, 1905
Newton, Wayne (singer/actor)	April 3, 1942
Newton-John, Olivia (singer/actress)	September 26, 1947
Nice, Harry Whinna (politician)	December 5, 1877
Nicholas II; born Nikolai Aleksandrovich (Russian Czar)	May 18, 1868
Nicholas, Denise (actress)	July 12, 1944
Nichols, Barbara; born Barbara Nickerauer (actress)	December 30, 1929
Nichols, Bobby; born Robert Nichols (golf)	April 14, 1936
Nichols, Jack (basketball)	April 9, 1926
Nichols, Kid; born Charles Augustus Nichols (baseball)	September 14, 1869
Nichols, Mike; born Michael Igor Peschkowsky (comedian/director)	November 6, 1931
Nicholson, Jack; born John Nicholson Rose (actor/director)	April 22, 1937
Nicklaus, Jack William (golf)	January 21, 1940
Nicol, Alex; born Alexander Livingston Nicol, Jr. (actor/director)	January 20, 1919
Niekro, Joe; born Joseph Franklin Niekro (baseball)	November 7, 1944
Niekro, Phil; born Philip Henry Niekro (baseball)	April 1, 1939
Nielsen, Leslie (actor)	February 11, 1925
Nieman, Bob; born Robert Charles Nieman (baseball)	January 26, 1927
Niesen, Gertrude (actress/singer)	July 8, 1910
Nietzsche, Friedrich Wilhelm (philosopher)	October 15, 1844
Nightingale, Florence (nurse)	May 12, 1820
Niland, John H. (football)	February 29, 1944
Nilsson, Anna Q.; born Anna Qyerentia Nilsson (actress)	March 30, 1889
Nilsson, Birgit (singer)	May 17, 1918
Nimitz, Chester William (naval officer)	February 24, 1885

Nimoy, Leonard (actor)	March 26, 1931
Nissen, Greta; born Grethe Ruzt-Nissen (actress)	January 30, 1906
Nitschke, Ray; born Raymond E. Nitschke (football)	December 29, 1936
Niven, David; born James David Graham Niven (actor/author)	March 1, 1910
Nixon, George Stuart (politician)	April 2, 1860
Nixon, Julie (First family)	July 5, 1948
Nixon, Marian (actress)	October 20, 1904
Nixon, Pat; born Thelma Catherine Patricia Ryan (First Lady)	March 16, 1912
Nixon, Richard Milhous (President)	January 9, 1913
Nixon, Russ; born Russell Eugene Nixon (baseball)	February 19, 1935
Nixon, Tricia; born Patricia Nixon (First family)	February 21, 1946
Nizer, Louis (attorney/author)	February 6, 1902
Nobel, Alfred Bernhard (inventor/industrialist/ philanthropist)	October 21, 1883
Nobis, Tommy; born Thomas Henry Nobis (football)	September 20, 1943
Noble, Chuck (basketball)	July 24, 1931
Noble, Reginald (hockey)	June 23 1895
Noble, Trisha (actress)	February 3, 1944
Noel, Edmund Favor (politician)	March 4, 1856
Noel, Philip William (politician)	June 6, 1931
Nolan, Dick; born Richard C. Nolan (football)	March 26, 1932
Nolan, Doris (actress)	July 14, 1916
Nolan, Gary Lynn (baseball)	May 27, 1948
Nolan, Jeanette (actress)	December 30, 1911
Nolan, Kathleen (actress)	September 27, 1933
Nolan, Lloyd (actor)	August 11, 1902
Noll, Chuck; born Charles H. Noll (football)	January 5, 1932
Nolte, Nick (actor)	February 8, 1941
Nomellini, Leo Joseph (football)	June 19, 1924
Noonan, Tommy; born Thomas Patrick Noon (comedian/actor)	April 29, 1922
Norbeck, Peter (politician)	August 27, 1870
Norblad, Albin Walter, Sr. (politician)	March 19, 1881
Norell, Norman; born Norman Levinson (fashion designer)	April 20, 1900
Noren, Irv; born Irving Arnold Noren (baseball)	November 29, 1924
Norman, Fred; born Fredie Hubert Norman (baseball)	August 20, 1942
Norris, Edward (actor)	March 10, 1910
Norris, Edwin Lee (politician)	August 15, 1865
Norris, George William (politician)	July 11, 1861
Norstad, Lauris (army officer)	March 24, 1907
North, Andy; born Andrew Stewart North (golf)	March 9, 1950
North, Billy; born William Alexander North (baseball)	May 15, 1948
North, Jay; born Jay Hopper (actor)	August 3, 1952
North, John Ringling (circus)	August 14, 1903
North, Sheree; born Dawn Bethel (actress)	January 17, 1933
Northcott, Baldy; born Laurence Northcott (hockey)	September 7, 1907
Northey, Ron; born Ronald James Northey (baseball)	April 26, 1920
Northrup, Jim; born James Thomas Northrup (baseball)	November 24, 1939
Norton, Ken; born Kenneth Howard Norton (boxing/actor)	August 9, 1945
Norvo, Red; born Kenneth Norville (music)	March 31, 1908
Nostradamus; born Michael de Notredame (astrologer)	December 14, 1503
Notte, John Anthony, Jr. (politician)	May 3, 1909

Nottingham, Don; born Donald Nottingham (football)   June 28, 1949
Novack, Shelly (actor)   January 10————
Novak, Eva (actress)   February 14, 1898
Novak, Jane (actress)   January 12, 1896
Novak, Kim; born Marilyn Pauline Novak (actress)   February 13, 1933
Novarro, Ramon; born Ramon Samaniegoes (actor)   February 6, 1899
Novello, Ivor; born David Ivor Davies (actor/writer/music) January 15, 1893
Nugent, Elliott (director/actor/writer)   September 20, 1900
Nunley, Frank (football)   October 1, 1945
Nunn, Louis B. (politician)   March 8, 1924
Nunn, Sam; born Samuel Augustus Nunn (politician)   September 8, 1938
Nureyev, Rudolf; born Rudolf Hametovich (dancer/actor)   March 17, 1938
Nutter, Donald Grant (politician)   November 28, 1915
Nuxhall, Joe; born Joseph Henry Nuxhall (baseball)   July 30, 1928
Nuyen, France; born France Denise Nguyen Vannga (actress) July 31, 1939
Nye, Blaine Francis (football)   March 29, 1946
Nye, Gerald Prentice (politician)   December 19, 1892
Nyro, Laura (singer/music)   October 18, 1947

O

Oakie, Jack; born Lewis Delaney Offield (actor)   November 12, 1903
Oakland, Simon (actor)   August 28, 1918
Oakley, Annie; born Phoebe Anne Oakley Mozee (markswoman) August 13, 1859
Oates, Joyce Carol (author/poet)   June 16, 1938
Oates, Warren (actor)   July 5, 1928
Oberon, Merle; born Estelle Merle O'Brien Thompson   February 19, 1911
  (actress)
O'Brian, Hugh; born Hugh Charles Krampe (or Krampke)   April 19, 1925
  (actor)
O'Brien, Edmond (actor)   September 10, 1915
O'Brien, George (actor)   April 19, 1900
O'Brien, Joan (singer/actress)   February 14, 1936
O'Brien, Lawrence Francis (government/basketball)   July 7, 1917
O'Brien, Margaret; born Angela Maxine O'Brien (actress) January 15, 1937
O'Brien, Pat; born William Joseph Patrick O'Brien, Jr.   November 11, 1899
  (actor)
O'Brien, Virginia (singer/comedienne/actress)   April 18, 1921
O'Brien-Moore, Erin; born Annette Erin O'Brien-Moore   May 2, 1908
  (actress)
O'Callaghan, Mike Donal N. (politician)   September 10, 1929
O'Casey, Sean; born Sean O'Cathasaigh (playwright)   March 31, 1880
Ochs, Phil; born Philip David Ochs (singer/music)   December 19, 1940
O'Connell, Arthur Joseph (actor)   March 29, 1908
O'Connell, Danny; born Daniel Francis O'Connell (baseball) January 21, 1927
O'Connell, Helen (singer/TV host)   May 23, 1920
O'Connor, Buddy; born Herbert William O'Connor (hockey) June 21, 1916
O'Connor, Carroll (actor)   August 2, 1924
O'Connor, Donald David Dixon Ronald (actor/dancer/singer) August 28, 1925
O'Connor, Edwin Greene (author)   July 29, 1918
O'Connor, Glynnis (actress)   November 19, 1956

O'Connor, Una; born Agnes Teresa McGlade (actress)	October 23, 1880
O'Conor, Herbert Romulus (politician)	November 17, 1896
O'Daniel, W. Lee; born Wilbert Lee O'Daniel (politician)	March 11, 1890
O'Day, Anita (singer)	December 18, 1919
Oddie, Tasker Lowndes (politician)	October 24, 1870
Odell, Benjamin Barker, Jr. (politician)	January 14, 1854
O'Dell, Billy; born William Oliver O'Dell (baseball)	February 10, 1933
Odets, Clifford (playwright)	July 18, 1903
Odetta; born Odetta Holmes (singer/music)	December 31, 1930
Odom, Blue Moon; born Johnny Lee Odom (baseball)	May 29, 1945
Odoms, Riley Mackey (football)	March 1, 1950
O'Driscoll, Martha (actress)	March 4, 1922
Offenbach, Jacques; born Jacob Eberscht (music)	June 21, 1819
Ogilvie, Richard Buell (politician)	February 22, 1923
O'Gorman, James Aloysius (politician)	May 5, 1860
O'Hanlon, George; born George Rice (actor)	November 23, 1917
O'Hara, Jill (actress/singer)	August 23, 1947
O'Hara, John Henry (author)	January 31, 1905
O'Hara, Maureen; born Maureen FitzSimons (or Fitzsimmons) (actress)	August 17, 1920
O'Herlihy, Dan; born Daniel O'Herlihy (actor)	May 1, 1919
Ohl, Don (basketball)	August 18, 1936
Ohmart, Carol (actress)	June 3, 1928
O'Keefe, Dennis; born Edward James Flanagan (actor)	March 29, 1908
O'Keeffe, Georgia (artist)	November 15, 1887
Okker, Tom S. (tennis)	February 22, 1944
Oland, Warner; born Johan Warner Oland (actor)	October 3, 1880
Olav V; born Alexander Edward Christian Frederick (King of Norway)	July 2, 1903
Olcott, Ben Wilson (politician)	October 15, 1872
Oldfield, Barney; born Bernd Eli Oldfield (auto racing)	June 3, 1878
Oliva, Tony; born Pedro Oliva (baseball)	July 20, 1940
Oliver; born William Oliver Swofford (singer/music)	February 22, 1945
Oliver, Al; born Albert Oliver (baseball)	October 14, 1946
Oliver, Bob; born Robert Lee Oliver (baseball)	February 8, 1943
Oliver, Edna May; born Edna May Cox-Oliver (actress)	November 9, 1883
Oliver, Gene; born Eugene George Oliver (baseball)	March 22, 1936
Oliver, Murray Clifford (hockey)	November 14, 1937
Oliver, Susan; born Charlotte Gercke (actress)	February 13, 1936
Olivier, Sir Laurence Kerr (actor)	May 22, 1907
Olmstead, Murray Bert (hockey)	September 4, 1926
O'Loughlin, Gerald S.; born Gerald Stuart O'Loughlin (actor)	December 23, 1921
Olsen, Merlin Jay (football/sportscaster/actor)	September 15, 1940
Olsen, Ole; born John Sigvard Olsen (comedian/actor)	November 6, 1892
Olson, Bobo; born Carl Olson (boxing)	July 11, 1928
Olson, Culbert Levy (politician)	November 7, 1876
Olson, Floyd Bjerstjerne (politician)	November 13, 1891
Olson, James (actor)	October 8, 1930
Olson, Nancy Ann (actress)	July 14, 1928
O'Mahoney, Joseph Christopher (politician)	November 5, 1884
O'Malley, J. Pat; born James Patrick O'Malley (actor)	March 15, 1904

O'Malley, Walter (baseball)	October 9, 1903
Onassis, Aristotle Socrates (shipping magnate)	January 20, 1906
Onassis, Jacqueline; born Jacqueline Lee Bouvier (wife of President Kennedy/First Lady)	July 28, 1929
O'Neal, Emmet (politician)	September 23, 1853
O'Neal, Patrick Wisdom (actor)	September 26, 1927
O'Neal, Ryan; born Patrick Ryan O'Neal (actor)	April 20, 1941
O'Neal, Tatum Beatrice (actress)	November 5, 1963
O'Neil, Barbara (actress)	July 10, 1909
O'Neil, Sally; born Virginia Louise Concepta Noonan (actress)	October 23, 1908
O'Neil, Tricia (actress)	March 11, 1945
O'Neill, C. William (politician)	February 14, 1916
O'Neill, Eugene Gladstone (playwright)	October 16, 1888
O'Neill, Jennifer (actress)	February 20, 1948
O'Neill, Tip; born Thomas Philip O'Neill (politician)	December 9, 1912
Ono, Yoko (artist/poet/singer)	February 18, 1933
Oosterhuis, Peter A. (golf)	May 3, 1948
Opatoshu, David Opatovsky (actor)	January 30, 1918
Oppenheimer, J. Robert; born Julius Robert Oppenheimer (nuclear physicist)	April 22, 1904
Orantes, Manuel (tennis)	February 6, 1949
Orbach, Jerry; born Jerome Orbach (actor/singer)	October 20, 1935
Orbison, Roy (singer/music)	April 23, 1936
Orff, Carl (music)	July 10, 1895
Orlando, Tony; born Michael Anthony Orlando Cassevitis (singer)	April 3, 1944
Orman, James Bradley (politician)	November 4, 1849
Ormandy, Eugene (music)	November 18, 1899
O'Rourke, Jim; born James Henry O'Rourke (baseball)	August 24, 1852
Orr, Bobby; born Robert Gordon Orr (hockey)	March 20, 1948
Orr, Jimmy; born James E. Orr, Jr. (football)	October 4, 1935
Orwell, George; born Eric Arthur Blair (author)	June 25, 1903
Osborn, Chase Salmon (politician)	January 22, 1860
Osborn, Dave; born David Osborn (football)	March 18, 1943
Osborn, Paul (playwright)	September 4, 1901
Osborn, Sidney Preston (politician)	May 17, 1884
Osborne, John James (playwright)	December 12, 1929
Osborne, Vivienne (actress)	December 10, 1896
O'Shea, Tessie (actress/singer)	March 13, 1918
Osmond, Alan Ralph (singer/music—Osmond Family)	June 22, 1949
Osmond, Donny; born Donald Clark Osmond (singer/music —Osmond Family)	December 9, 1957
Osmond, Jay Westley (singer/music—Osmond Family)	March 2, 1955
Osmond, Jimmy; born James Arthur Osmond (singer/music —Osmond Family)	April 16, 1963
Osmond, Marie; born Olive Marie Osmond (singer—Osmond Family)	October 13, 1959
Osmond, Merrill Davis (singer/music—Osmond Family	April 30, 1953
Osmond, Wayne; born M. Wayne Osmond (singer/music —Osmond Family)	August 28, 1951
Osteen, Claude Wilson (baseball)	August 9, 1939

Ostermueller, Fritz; born Frederick Raymond Ostermueller (baseball)	September 15, 1907
Osterwald, Bibi; born Margaret Virginia Osterwald (actress)	February 3, 1920
O'Sullivan, Gilbert; born Raymond Edward O'Sullivan (singer/music)	December 1, 1946
O'Sullivan, Maureen Paula (actress)	May 17, 1911
Oswald, Lee Harvey (accused assassin)	October 18, 1939
Otis, Amos Joseph (baseball)	April 26, 1947
Otis, Jim; born James Lloyd Otis (football)	April 29, 1948
Otis, Johnny (singer/music)	December 28, 1921
O'Toole, Peter; born Seamus O'Toole (actor)	August 2, 1932
Ott, Mel; born Melvin Thomas Ott (baseball)	March 2, 1909
Otten, Don (basketball)	April 18, 1921
Ottiano, Rafaela (actress)	March 4, 1894
Otto, Gus; born August J. Otto (football)	December 8, 1943
Otto, Jim; born James Edwin Otto (football)	January 5, 1938
Ouimet, Francis DeSales (golf)	May 8, 1893
Ouspenskaya, Maria (actress)	July 29, 1876
Overman, Lee Slater (politician)	January 3, 1854
Overton, John Holmes (politician)	September 17, 1875
Owen, Catherine Dale (actress)	July 28, 1900
Owen, Reginald; born John Reginald Owen (actor)	August 5, 1887
Owen, Robert Latham (politician)	February 3, 1856
Owen, Steve; born Stephen Joseph Owen (football)	April 21, 1898
Owens, Brig; born Brigman Owens (football)	February 16, 1943
Owens, Buck; born Alvis Edgar Owens, Jr. (singer/music)	August 12, 1929
Owens, Gary (TV host)	May 10, 1936
Owens, Jesse; born James Cleveland Owens (olympic athlete)	September 12, 1913
Owens, R.C.; born Raleigh C. Owens (football)	November 12, 1933
Owens, Steve E. (football)	December 9, 1947

P

Paar, Jack Harold (TV host)	May 1, 1918
Pacino, Al; born Alfredo James Pacino (actor)	April 25, 1939
Packard, Vance Oakley (author)	May 22, 1914
Packwood, Robert William (politician)	September 11, 1932
Paderewski, Ignace Jan (music/Polish government)	November 6, 1860
Pafko, Andy; born Andrew Pafko (baseball)	February 25, 1921
Pagan, Jose Antonio (baseball)	May 5, 1935
Page, Alan Cedric (football)	August 7, 1945
Page, Anita; born Anita Pomares (actress)	August 4, 1910
Page, Carroll Smalley (politician)	January 10, 1843
Page, Gale; born Sally Perkins Rutter (singer/actress)	July 23, 1913
Page, Geraldine Sue (actress)	November 22, 1924
Page, Patti; born Clara Ann Fowler (singer/actress)	November 8, 1927
Paget, Debra; born Debralee Griffin (actress)	August 19, 1933
Pagliaroni, Jim; born James Vincent Pagliaroni (baseball)	December 8, 1937
Paige, Janis; born Donna Mae Jaden (or Tjaden) (actress/singer)	September 16, 1922

Paige, Robert; born John Anthony (or Arthur) Paige (aetor)	December 21, 1910
Paige, Satchel; born Leroy Robert Paige (baseball)	July 7, 1906
Paine, Thomas (political philosopher)	January 29, 1737
Palance, Jack; born Vladimir (or Walter Jack) Palahnuik (actor)	February 18, 1919
Palillo, Ron; born Ronald G. Palillo (actor)	April 2, 1954
Pallette, Eugene (actor)	July 8, 1889
Palmer, Arnold Daniel (golf)	September 10, 1929
Palmer, Betsy; born Patricia Betsy Hrunek (or Brumek) (actress)	November 1, 1926
Palmer, Bud; born John S. Palmer (basketball/sportscaster)	September 14, 1923
Palmer, Jim; born James Alvin Palmer (baseball)	October 15, 1945
Palmer, Johnny; born John Palmer (golf)	July 3, 1918
Palmer, Leland (actress/singer/dancer)	June 16, 1945
Palmer, Lilli; born Lilli Marie Peiser (actress)	May 24, 1914
Palmer, Maria (actress)	September 5, 1924
Palmer, Peter Webster (actor/singer)	September 20, 1931
Palmer, Sandy; born Sandra Jean Palmer (golf)	March 10, 1941
Paluzzi, Luciana (actress)	June 11, 1939
Panch, Marvin (auto racing)	May 28, 1926
Pangborn, Franklin (actor)	January 23, 1893
Papas, Irene (actress)	September 3, 1926
Papp, Joseph; born Joseph Papirofsky (producer/director)	June 22, 1921
Pappas, Ike; born Icarus Nestor Pappas (newscaster)	April 16, 1933
Pappas, Milt; born Milton Edward Pappas (baseball)	May 11, 1939
Pappin, James Joseph (hockey)	September 10, 1939
Pardee, George Cooper (politician)	July 25, 1857
Pardee, Jack; born John Perry Pardee (football)	April 19, 1936
Parent, Bernie; born Bernard Marcel Parent (hockey)	April 3, 1945
Parilli, Babe; born Vito Parilli (football)	May 7, 1929
Park, Brad; born Bradford Douglas Park (hockey)	July 6, 1948
Park, Chung Hee (South Korean government)	September 30, 1917
Park, Guy Brasfield (politician)	June 10, 1872
Parker, Cecilia (actress)	April 26, 1905
Parker, Clarence (football)	May 17, 1913
Parker, Dave; born David Gene Parker (baseball)	June 9, 1951
Parker, Dorothy; born Dorothy Rothschild (author/poet)	August 22, 1893
Parker, Eleanor (actress)	June 26, 1922
Parker, Fess Elijah (actor/singer)	August 16, 1925
Parker, Frank; born Franciszek Andzej Paikowski (tennis)	January 31, 1916
Parker, Jean; born Lois Mae Greene (or Luis Stephanie Zelinska (actress)	August 11, 1912
Parker, Jim; born James Thomas Parker (football)	April 3, 1934
Parker, John Milliken (politician)	March 16, 1863
Parker, Lara (actress)	October 27, 1942
Parker, Suzy; born Cecelia Anne Renee Parker (actress)	October 28, 1932
Parker, Wes; born Maurice Wesley Parker (baseball/actor)	November 13, 1939
Parker, Willard; born Worster Van Eps (actor)	February 5, 1912
Parkes, Mike; born Michael Johnson Parkes (auto racing)	December 24, 1931
Parkins, Barbara (actress)	May 22, 1942
Parks, Bert; born Bert Jacobson (actor/singer/TV host)	December 30, 1914

Parks, Dave; born David Wayne Parks (football)	December 25, 1941
Parks, Gordon Alexander (director/author/music)	November 30, 1912
Parks, Hildy de Forrest (actress)	March 12, 1924
Parks, Larry; born Samuel Lawrence Klausman (actor)	December 13, 1914
Parks, Michael (actor)	April 4, 1938
Parnell, Harvey (politician)	February 28, 1880
Parnell, Mel; born Melvin Lloyd Parnell (baseball)	June 13, 1922
Parnis, Mollie (fashion designer)	March 18, 1905
Parrish, Helen (actress)	March 12, 1922
Parrish, Lemar (football)	December 13, 1947
Parrish, Leslie Maria; born Leslie Maria Fleck (actress)	March 18, 1935
Parseghian, Ara Roul (football/sportscaster)	May 21, 1923
Parsons, Benny (auto racing)	July 12, 1941
Parsons, Estelle (actress)	November 20, 1927
Parsons, Johnnie (auto racing)	July 4, 1918
Parsons, Louella; born Louella Oettinger (journalist)	August 6, 1881
Partee, Dennis (football)	September 1, 1946
Parton, Dolly Rebecca (singer/music)	January 19, 1946
Pascal, Blaise (scientist/mathematician/philosopher/author)	June 19, 1623
Paschal, Jim; born James Roy Paschal (auto racing)	December 5, 1926
Pasqual, Camilo Alberto (baseball)	January 20, 1934
Pasternak, Boris Leonidovich (poet/author)	February 10, 1890
Pasternak, Joseph (producer)	September 19, 1901
Pasteur, Louis (chemist)	December 27, 1822
Pastore, John Orlando (politician)	March 17, 1907
Pastorini, Dan; born Dante Anthony Pastorini, Jr. (football)	May 26, 1949
Pastrano, Willie; born Wilfred Anthony Raleigh Pastrano (boxing)	November 27, 1935
Pate, Jerry; born Jerome Kendrick Pate (golf)	September 16, 1953
Patek, Freddie; born Frederick Joseph Patek (baseball)	October 9, 1944
Paterno, Joe; born Joseph Vincent Paterno (football)	December 21, 1926
Paterson, Pat (actress)	April 7, 1911
Patman, Wright; born John William Wright Patman (politician)	August 6, 1893
Patrick, Dennis (actor)	March 14, 1918
Patrick, Gail; born Margaret LaVelle Fitzpatrick (actress/producer)	June 20, 1911
Patrick, John; born John Patrick Goggan (playwright)	May 17, 1905
Patrick, Lee Salome (actress)	November 22, 1906
Patrick, Lynn (hockey)	February 3, 1912
Patrick, Nigel; born Nigel Dennis Wemyss (actor/director)	May 2, 1913
Patterson, Elizabeth; born Mary Elizabeth Patterson (actress)	November 22, 1874
Patterson, Floyd (boxing)	January 4, 1935
Patterson, Isaac Lee (politician)	September 17, 1859
Patterson, John Malcolm (politician)	September 27, 1921
Patterson, Lee (actor)	March 31, 1929
Patterson, Malcolm Rice (politician)	June 7, 1861
Patterson, Neva Louise (actress)	February 10, 1922
Patterson, Paul Linton (politician)	July 18, 1900
Patterson, Thomas MacDonald (politician)	November 4, 1839
Patteson, Okey Leonidas (politician)	September 14, 1898
Pattin, Marty; born Martin William Pattin (baseball)	April 6, 1943

Patton, George Smith, Jr. (army officer)	November 11, 1885
Patton, Jimmy; born James R. Patton, Jr. (football)	September 29, 1933
Paul, Don; born Donald Paul (football)	March 18, 1925
Paul, Les; born Lester William Polfus (singer/music)	June 9, 1915
Paulen, Ben Sanford (politician)	July 14, 1869
Pauley, Jane ; born Margaret Jane Pauley (newscaster/TV host)	October 31, 1950
Pauling, Linus Carl (scientist)	February 28, 1901
Paulsen, Albert (actor)	December 13, 1927
Paulsen, Pat; born Patrick Laton Paulsen (comedian/actor)	July 6, 1927
Pavan, Marisa; born Maria Luisa Pierangeli (actress)	June 19, 1932
Pavarotti, Luciano (singer)	October 12, 1935
Pavelich, Martin Nicholas (hockey)	November 6, 1927
Pavletich, Don; born Donald Stephen Pavletich (baseball)	July 13, 1938
Pavlov, Ivan Petrovich (physiologist)	September 14, 1849
Pavlova, Anna (dancer)	January 3, 1885
Paycheck, Johnny; born Don Lytle (singer/music)	May 31, 1941
Payne, Freda (singer)	September 19, 1945
Payne, Frederick George (politician)	July 24, 1900
Payne, John (actor)	May 23, 1912
Paynter, Thomas Hanson (politician)	December 9, 1851
Payton, Walter Jerry (football)	July 25, 1954
Payton-Wright, Pamela (actress)	November 1, 1941
Peabody, Endicott (politician)	February 15, 1920
Peabody, James Hamilton (politician)	August 21, 1852
Peaker, E.J.; born Edra Jeanne Peaker (actress/singer/ dancer)	February 22———
Peaks, Clarence E. (football)	September 23, 1935
Peale, Norman Vincent (clergyman/author)	May 31, 1898
Peale, Rembrandt (artist/author)	February 22, 1778
Pearl, Minnie; born Sarah Ophelia Colley (comedienne/singer)	October 25, 1912
Pearson, Albie; born Albert Gregory Pearson (baseball)	September 12, 1934
Pearson, David Gene (auto racing)	December 22, 1934
Pearson, Drew; born Andrew Russell Pearson (journalist)	December 13, 1897
Pearson, Drew (football)	January 12, 1951
Pearson, James Blackwood (politician)	May 7, 1920
Pearson, Lester Bowles (Canadian Government)	April 23, 1897
Pearson, Preston James (football)	January 17, 1945
Peary, Robert Edwin (naval officer/explorer)	May 6, 1856
Peay, Austin (politician)	June 1, 1876
Peck, Gregory; born Eldred Gregory Peck (actor/producer)	April 5, 1916
Peckinpah, Sam; born David Samuel Peckinpah (director/writer)	February 21, 1925
Peerce, Jan; born Jacob Pinkus Perelmuth (singer)	June 3, 1904
Peery, George Campbell (politician)	October 28, 1873
Pegler, Westbrook; born James Westbrook Pegler (journalist)	August 2, 1894
Pelé; born Edson Arantes do Nascimento (soccer)	October 23, 1940
Pell, Claiborne deBorda (politician)	November 22, 1918
Pellington, Bill; born William A. Pellington (football)	September 25, 1927
Penn, Arthur Hiller (director)	September 27, 1922

Penn, William (colonist)   October 14, 1644
Pennewill, Simeon Selby (politician)   July 23, 1867
Penny, J.C.; born James Cash Penney (merchant)   September 16, 1875
Pennock, Herb; born Herbert Jefferis Pennock (baseball)   February 2, 1894
Pennypacker, Samuel Whitaker (politician)   April 9, 1843
Penrose, Boies (politician)   November 1, 1860
Penske, Roger (auto racing)   February 20, 1937
Peoples, Woody; born Woodrow Peoples (football)   August 16, 1943
Pepitone, Joe; born Joseph Anthony Pepitone (baseball)   October 9, 1940
Peppard, George (actor)   October 1, 1928
Pepper, Barbara (actress)   May 31, 1912
Pepper, Claude Denson (politician)   September 8, 1900
Percy, Charles Harting (politician)   September 27, 1919
Percy, Eileen (actress)   August 1, 1899
Percy, Walker (author)   May 28, 1916
Perelman, S.J. born Sidney Joseph Perelman (humorist)   February 1, 1904
Perez, Marty; born Martin Roman Perez, Jr. (baseball)   February 28, 1947
Perez, Tony; born Atanasio Rigal Perez (baseball)   May 14, 1942
Pergine, John (football)   April 19, 1946
Perkins, Anthony (actor)   April 14, 1932
Perkins, Carl (singer/music)   April 9, 1932
Perkins, Don; born Donald Anthony Perkins (football)   March 4, 1938
Perkins, Frances (government)   April 10, 1880
Perkins, George Clement (politician)   August 23, 1839
Perkins, Millie (actress)   May 12, 1938
Perlman, Itzhak (music)   August 31, 1945
Perón, Isabel; born Maria Estela Martinez Cartas   February 4, 1931
      (Argentine government)
Perón, Juan Domingo; born Juan Domingo Perón Sosa   October 8, 1895
      (Argentine government)
Perranoski, Ron; born Ronald Peter Perranoski (baseball)   April 1, 1936
Perreau, Gigi; born Ghislaine Elizabeth Marie Therese   February 6, 1941
      Perreau-Saussine (actress)
Perrine, Valerie (actress/dancer)   September 3, 1943
Perry, Fred; born Frederick John Perry (tennis)   May 18, 1909
Perry, Gaylord Jackson (baseball)   September 15, 1938
Perry, Jim; born James Evan Perry, Jr. (baseball)   October 30, 1935
Perry, Joe; born Fletcher Joseph Perry (football)   January 27, 1927
Perry, Oliver Hazard (naval officer)   August 23, 1785
Perry, Roger L. (actor)   May 7, 1933
Pershing, John Joseph (army officer)   September 13, 1860
Persoff, Nehemiah (actor)   August 14, 1920
Persons, Gordon; born Seth Gordon Persons (politician)   February 5, 1902
Pescarolo, Henri (auto racing)   September 25, 1942
Pescow, Donna Gail (actress)   March 24, 1954
Pesky, Johnny; born John Michael Paveskovich (baseball)   September 27, 1919
Peterkin, Julia Mood (author)   October 31, 1880
Peter the Great; born Pëtr Alekseyevich (Russian Emperor)   June 9, 1672
Peters, Bernadette; born Bernadette Lazzara   February 28, 1948
      (actress/singer)
Peters, Brock; born Brock Fisher (actor)   July 2, 1927

Peters, Garry Lorne (hockey)	October 9, 1942
Peters, Gary Charles (baseball)	April 21, 1937
Peters, Jean, born Elizabeth Jean Peters (actress)	October 15, 1926
Peters, Roberta; born Roberta Peterman (singer)	May 4, 1930
Peters, Susan; born Suzanne Carnahan (actress)	July 3, 1921
Petersen, Hjalmar (politician)	January 2, 1890
Petersen, Paul (actor/singer)	September 23, 1944
Peterson, Fritz Fred (baseball)	February 8, 1942
Peterson, Oscar Emmanuel (music)	August 15, 1925
Peterson, Ronnie; born Bengt Ronald Peterson (auto racing)	February 14, 1944
Peterson, Russell Wilbur (politician)	October 3, 1916
Peterson, Val; born Frederick Valdemar Erastus Peterson (politician)	July 18, 1903
Peterson, Walter Rutherford (politician)	September 19, 1922
Petitbon, Richie; born Richard A. Petitbon (football)	April 18, 1938
Petrocelli, Rico; born Americo Peter Petrocelli (baseball)	June 27, 1943
Pettet, Joanna (actress)	November 16, 1944
Pettit, Bob; born Robert E. Lee Pettit (basketball)	December 12, 1932
Petty, Lee (auto racing)	March 14, 1914
Petty, Richard Lee (auto racing)	July 2, 1937
Philbin, Gerry; born Gerald J. Philbin (football)	July 31, 1941
Philip, Prince; born Philip Mountbatten (Duke of Edinburgh)	June 10, 1921
Philipp, Emanuel Lorenz (politician)	March 25, 1861
Philley, Dave; born David Earl Philley (baseball)	May 16, 1920
Phillip, Andy (basketball)	March 7, 1922
Phillips, Bubba; born John Melvin Phillips (baseball)	February 24, 1930
Phillips, Bum; born Oail Andrew Phillips (football)	September 29, 1923
Phillips, Jim; born James P. Phillips (football)	February 5, 1936
Phillips, John Clayton (politician)	November 13, 1870
Phillips, Leon Chase (politician)	December 9, 1890
Phillips, Mackenzie; born Laura Mackenzie Phillips (actress)	November 10, 1959
Phillips, Mel; born Melvin Phillips (football)	January 6, 1942
Phillips, Michelle; born Holly Michelle Gilliam (singer/actress)	April 6, 1944
Phipps, Lawrence Cowle (politician)	August 30, 1862
Phipps, Mike; born Michael E. Phipps (football)	November 19, 1947
Piaf, Edith Gassion (singer/actress)	December 19, 1915
Piatigorsky, Gregor (music)	April 17, 1903
Piazza, Ben; born Benito Daniel Piazza (actor)	July 30, 1934
Piazza, Marguerite; born Marguerite Piazza Luft (singer)	May 6, 1926
Picard, Henry G. (golf)	November 28, 1907
Picard, Noel; born Jean Noel Yves Picard (hockey)	December 25, 1938
Picasso, Pablo; born Pablo Ruiz y Picasso (artist)	October 25, 1881
Piccinni, Niccolo (music)	January 16, 1728
Piccolo, Brian; born Louis Brian Piccolo (football)	October 21, 1943
Picerni, Paul (actor)	December 1, 1922
Pickens, Slim; born Louis Bert Lindley, Jr. (actor)	June 29, 1919
Pickett, Wilson (singer/music)	March 18, 1941
Pickford, Mary; born Gladys Mary Smith (actress/producer)	April 8, 1893
Picon, Molly; born Molly Pyekoon (actress)	June 1, 1898

Pidgeon, Walter David (actor)	September 23, 1897
Pierce, Billy; born Walter William Pierce (baseball)	April 2, 1927
Pierce, Franklin (President)	November 23, 1804
Pierce, Jane Means Appleton; born Jane Means Appleton (First Lady)	March 12, 1806
Pierce, Walter Marcus (politician)	May 30, 1861
Pierce, Webb (singer/music)	August 8, 1926
Pierpoint, Robert Charles (newscaster)	May 16, 1925
Piersall, Jim; born James Anthony Piersall (baseball)	November 14, 1929
Pierson, John Frederick (hockey)	July 21, 1925
Pietrosante, Nick; born Nicholas Vincent Pietrosante (football)	September 10, 1937
Pihos, Pete; born Peter Louis Pihos (football)	October 22, 1923
Pike, Alfred (hockey)	September 15, 1917
Pilbeam, Nova (actress)	November 15, 1919
Piles, Samuel Henry (politician)	December 28, 1858
Pilote, Pierre Paul (hockey)	December 11, 1931
Pincay, Laffit, Jr. (jockey)	December 29, 1946
Pinchot, Gifford (politician)	August 11, 1865
Pindall, Xenophon Overton (politician)	August 21, 1873
Pine, William Bliss (politician)	December 30, 1877
Piniella, Lou; born Louis Victor Piniella (baseball)	August 28, 1943
Pinson, Vada Edward (baseball)	August 11, 1938
Pinter, Harold (playwright)	October 10, 1930
Pinza, Ezio; born Fortunato Ezio Pinza (singer/actor)	May 18, 1892
Pirandello, Luigi (dramatist/author)	June 28, 1867
Piston, Walter Hamor, Jr. (music)	January 20, 1894
Pitcher, Molly; born Mary Ludwig (revolutionary heroine)	October 13, 1754
Pitney, Gene (singer/music)	February 17, 1941
Pitney, Mahlon (jurist)	February 5 ,1858
Pittman, Key (politician)	September 19, 1872
Pittman, Vail Montgomery (politician)	September 17, 1883
Pitts, Elijah (football)	February 3, 1938
Pitts, Frank (football)	November 12, 1943
Pitts, Zasu; born Eliza Susan Pitts (actress)	January 3, 1898
Pizarro, Francisco (explorer)	circa 1470
Pizarro, Juan Ramon (baseball)	February 7, 1937
Plager, Barclay Graham (hockey)	March 25, 1941
Plager, Robert Bryan (hockey)	March 11, 1943
Plager, William Ronald (hockey)	July 6, 1945
Plaisted, Frederick William (politician)	July 26, 1865
Plank, Eddie; born Edward Stewart Plank (baseball)	August 31, 1875
Plante, Jacques (hockey)	January 17, 1929
Platt, Edward (actor/singer)	February 16, 1916
Platt, Louise (actress)	August 3, 1914
Player, Gary Jim (golf)	November 1, 1935
Pleasant, Ruffin Golson (politician)	June 2, 1871
Pleasence, Donald (actor)	October 5, 1919
Pleshette, Suzanne (actress/textile designer)	January 31, 1937
Plimpton, George Ames (author)	March 18, 1927
Plisetskaya, Maya Mikhailovna (dancer)	November 20, 1925

Plowright, Joan Anne (actress)	October 28, 1929
Plum, Milt; born Milton R.	January 20, 1935
Plummer, Christopher; born Arthur Christopher Orme (actor)	December 13, 1927
Plunkett, Jim; born James William Plunkett, Jr. (football)	December 5, 1947
Plunkett, Sherm; born Sherman Plunkett (football)	April 17, 1933
Pocahontas; born Princess Matoaka (Indian Princess)	circa 1595
Podesta, Rossana (actress)	June 20, 1934
Podhoretz, Norman (author/editor)	January 16, 1930
Podolak, Ed; born Edward Joseph Podolak (football)	September 1, 1947
Podres, Johnny; born John Joseph Podres (baseball)	September 30, 1932
Poe, Edgar Allan (poet/author)	January 19, 1809
Poile, Bud; born Norman Robert Poile (hockey)	February 10, 1924
Poindexter, Miles (politician)	April 22, 1868
Poitier, Sidney (actor/director)	February 20, 1924
Polanski, Roman (director)	August 18, 1933
Polk, James Knox (President)	November 2, 1795
Polk, Sarah Childress; born Sarah Childress (First Lady)	September 4, 1803
Pollard, Jim (basketball)	July 9, 1922
Pollard, John Garland (politician)	August 4, 1871
Pollard, Michael J.; born Michael J. Pollack (actor)	May 30, 1939
Pollet, Howie; born Howard Joseph Pollet (baseball)	June 26, 1921
Polo, Marco (traveler)	circa 1254
Pompidou, Georges Jean Raymond (French government)	July 5, 1911
Ponce de Leon, Juan (explorer)	circa 1460
Pond, Lennie (auto racing)	August 11, 1940
Pons, Lily; born Alice Josephine Pons (singer/actress)	April 12, 1895
Ponselle, Rosa; born Rosa Melba Ponzillo (singer)	January 23, 1897
Ponti, Carlo (producer)	December 11, 1913
Poole, Roy Neil (actor)	March 31, 1924
Pope, Alexander (poet)	May 21, 1688
Pope Benedict XV; born Giacomo della Chiesa	November 21, 1854
Pope John XXIII; born Angelo Giuseppe Roncalli	November 25, 1881
Pope John Paul I; born Albino Luciani	October 17, 1912
Pope John Paul II; born Karol Wojtyla	May 18, 1920
Pope Paul VI; born Giovanni Battista Montoni	September 26, 1897
Pope Pius X; born Giuseppe Melchiorre Sarto	June 2, 1835
Pope Pius XI; born Ambrogio Damiano Achille Ratti	May 31, 1857
Pope Pius XII; born Eugenio Maria Giuseppe Giovanni Pacelli	March 2, 1876
Popein, Lawrence Thomas (hockey)	August 11, 1930
Porsche, Ferdinand (auto designer)	September 3, 1875
Porter, Cole Albert (music)	June 9, 1891
Porter, Don (actor)	September 24, 1912
Porter, Eric (actor)	April 8, 1928
Porter, Katherine Ann (author)	May 15, 1890
Porter, Nyree Dawn (actress)	———1940
Porter, Sylvia Field; born Sylvia Feldman (journalist)	June 18, 1913
Porterfield, Bob; born Erwin Coolidge Porterfield (baseball)	August 10, 1923

Posey, Sam; born Samuel Felton Posey (auto racing)	May 26, 1944
Post, Emily; born Emily Price (etiquette authority)	October 3, 1873
Post, Marjorie Merriweather (heiress/financier) philanthropist)	March 15, 1887
Post, Sandra (golf)	June 4, 1948
Post, Wally; born Walter Charles Post (baseball)	July 9, 1929
Post, Wiley (aviator)	November 22, 1899
Poston, Tom (actor)	October 17, 1921
Pothier, Aram J. (politician)	July 26, 1854
Potok, Chaim (author)	February 17, 1929
Pott, Johnny; born John Pott (golf)	November 6, 1935
Potter, Beatrix (author)	July 28, 1866
Potter, Charles Edward (politician)	October 30, 1916
Pottios, Myron J. (football)	January 18, 1939
Potts, Cliff (actor)	January 5———
Pound, Ezra Loomis (poet)	October 30, 1885
Powell, Adam Clayton, Jr. (politician)	November 29, 1908
Powell, Boog; born John Wesley Powell (baseball)	August 17, 1941
Powell, Dick; born Richard Ewing Powell (actor/producer/ director)	November 14, 1904
Powell, Eleanor Torrey (actress/dancer)	November 21, 1910
Powell, Jane; born Suzanne Burce (actress/singer)	April 1, 1929
Powell, Jody; born Joseph Lester Powell, Jr. (government)	September 30, 1943
Powell, Lewis Franklin, Jr. (jurist)	September 19, 1907
Powell, Wesley (politician)	October 13, 1915
Powell, William Horatio (actor)	July 29, 1892
Power, Tyrone Edmund (actor)	May 5, 1913
Power, Vic; born Victor Pellot Power (baseball)	November 1, 1931
Powers, Mala; born Mary Ellen Powers (actress)	December 29, 1921
Powers, Stefanie; born Stefania Zofia Ferderkievicz (or Federkiewicz) (actress)	November 2, 1942
Pratt, Babe; born Walter Pratt (hockey)	January 7, 1916
Preminger, Otto Ludwig (producer/director)	December 5, 1906
Prentice, Dean Sutherland (hockey)	October 5, 1932
Prentice, Jo Ann (golf)	February 9, 1933
Prentiss, Paula; born Paula Ragusa (actress)	March 4, 1938
Presle, Micheline; born Micheline Chassagne (actress)	August 22, 1922
Presley, Elvis Aaron (singer/actor)	January 8, 1935
Presnell, Harve; born George Harve Presnell, II (actor/singer)	September 14, 1933
Pressman, Lawrence (actor)	July 10, 1939
Preston, Billy; born William Everett Preston (singer/music)	September 9, 1946
Preston, Robert; born Robert Preston Meservey (actor/singer)	June 8, 1913
Preus, Jacob Avail Ottesen (politician)	August 28, 1883
Previn, André George (music)	April 6, 1929
Previn, Dory; born Dory Langdon (music)	October 22, 1929
Prevost, Marie; born Marie Bickford Dunn (or Gunn) (actress)	November 8, 1893
Price, Eddie; born Edward J. Price, (football)	September 2, 1929

Price, James Hubert (politician)   September 7, 1878
Price, Leontyne; born Mary Leontyne Price (singer)   February 10, 1929
Price, Ray Noble (singer/music)   January 12, 1926
Price, Vincent (actor/art expert)   May 27, 1911
Priddy, Jerry; born Gerald Edward Priddy (baseball)   November 9, 1919
Pride, Charley Frank (singer)   March 18, 1934
Priest, Ivy Baker; born Ivy Maude Baker (government)   September 7, 1905
Priestley, J.B.; born John Boynton Priestley (writer)   September 13, 1894
Priestley, Joseph (chemist)   March 13, 1733
Prima, Louis (music)   December 7, 1912
Primeau, Joe; born Joseph Primeau (hockey)   January 29, 1906
Primrose, William (music)   August 23, 1904
Primus, Barry (actor)   February 16, 1938
Prince, Hal; born Harold Smith Prince (producer/director)   January 30, 1928
Prince, William LeRoy (actor)   January 26, 1913
Principal, Victoria (actress)   January 3, 1945
Prine, Andrew Louis (actor)   February 14, 1936
Pringle, Aileen; born Aileen Bisbee (actress)   July 23, 1895
Prinze, Freddie; born Freddie Preutzel (comedian/actor)   June 22, 1954
Pritchard, Ron; born Ronald Pritchard (football)   April 2, 1947
Pritchett, V.S.; born Victor Sawdon Pritchett   December 16, 1900
     (literary critic)
Proctor, Fletcher Dutton (politician)   November 7, 1860
Proctor, Mortimer Robinson (politician)   May 30, 1899
Proctor, Redfield (politician)   June 1, 1831
Promuto, Vince; born Vincent Promuto (football)   June 8, 1938
Pronovost, Joseph Armand Andrew (hockey)   July 9, 1936
Pronovost, Joseph Jean Denis (hockey)   December 18, 1945
Pronovost, Marcel; born Rene Marcel Pronovost (hockey)   June 15, 1930
Prothro, Tommy; born James Thompson Prothro, Jr. (football)   July 20, 1920
Prouty, George Herbert (politician)   March 4, 1862
Prouty, Winston Lewis (politician)   September 1, 1906
Provine, Dorothy Michele (actress)   January 20, 1937
Provost, Claude (hockey)   September 17, 1933
Prowse, Juliet (dancer/actress)   September 25, 1936
Proxmire, William; born Edward William Proxmire   November 11, 1915
     (politician)
Pruitt, Greg; born Gregory Donald Pruitt (football)   August 18, 1951
Pryor, David Hampton (politician)   August 29, 1934
Pryor, Richard (comedian/actor)   December 1, 1940
Pryor, Roger (actor)   August 27, 1900
Prystai, Metro (hockey)   November 7, 1927
Pucci, Emilio; born Emilio Pucci di Barsento   November 20, 1914
     (fashion designer)
Puccini, Giacomo (music)   December 22, 1858
Puckett, Gary (singer/music)   October 17, 1942
Pugh, Jethro, Jr. (football)   July 3, 1944
Pulford, Robert (hockey)   March 31, 1936
Pulitzer, Joseph (publisher)   April 10, 1847
Pullman, George Mortimer (inventor)   March 3, 1831
Purcell, Lee Junior Williams (actress)   June 15, 1947

Purcell, Noel (actor)	December 23, 1900
Purdom, Edmund (actor)	December 19, 1924
Purkey, Bob; born Robert Thomas Purkey (baseball)	July 14, 1929
Purl, Linda (actress)	September 2, 1955
Purtell, William Arthur (politician)	May 6, 1897
Putnam, Duane (football)	September 5, 1928
Puzo, Mario (author)	October 15, 1920
Pyle, Denver (actor)	May 11, 1920
Pyle, J. Howard; born John Howard Pyle (politician)	March 25, 1906
Pynchon, Thomas (author)	May 8, 1937

Q

Quackenbush, Bill; born Hubert George Quackenbush (hockey)	March 2, 1922
Qualen, John; born John Oleson (actor)	December 8, 1899
Quarry, Jerry (boxing)	May 15, 1945
Quatro, Suzie (singer/actress)	June 3, 1950
Quayle, Anthony; born John Anthony Quayle (actor)	September 7, 1913
Quigley, Juanita (actress)	June 24, 1931
Quilici, Frank Ralph (baseball)	May 11, 1939
Quillan, Eddie (comedian/actor)	March 31, 1907
Quinby, Henry Brewer (politician)	June 10, 1846
Quine, Richard (actor/producer/director)	November 12, 1920
Quinn, Anthony Rudolph Oaxaca (actor)	April 21, 1915
Quinn, Robert Emmett (politician) ·	April 2, 1894
Quinn, William Francis (politician)	July 13, 1919
Quintero, Jose Benjamin (director/producer)	October 15, 1924

R

Rabe, David William (playwright)	March 10, 1940
Rachmaninoff, Sergei Vassilievich (music)	April 23, 1873
Racine, Jean Baptiste (dramatist)	December 21, 1639
Radcliff, Rip; born Raymond Allen Radcliff (baseball)	January 19, 1906
Rader, Doug; born Douglas Lee Rader (baseball)	July 30, 1944
Radner, Gilda (actress/comedienne/singer)	June 28, 1946
Radziwill, Lee; born Caroline Lee Bouvier (actress)	March 3, 1933
Rae, Charlotte; born Charlotte Rae Lubotsky (actress/ comedienne/singer)	April 22, 1926
Raeburn, Sir Henry (artist)	March 4, 1756
Raffensberger, Ken; born Kenneth David Raffensberger (baseball)	August 8, 1917
Rafferty, Chips; born John Goffage (actor)	March 26, 1909
Rafferty, Frances (actress)	June 26, 1922
Raffin, Deborah (actress)	March 13, 1953
Raft, George; born George Ranft (actor/dancer)	September 26, 1895
Ragan, Dave; born David William Ragan (golf)	August 7, 1935
Rainer, Luise (actress)	January 12, 1909
Raines, Ella; born Ella Wallace Raubes (actress)	August 6, 1921
Rainey, Ford (actor)	August 8, 1908
Rainey, Henry Thomas (politician)	August 20, 1860

Rainier, Prince; born Rainier Louis Henri Maxence Bertrand de Grimaldi (Ruler of Monaco) — May 31, 1923
Rains, Claude; born William Claude Rains (actor) — November 10, 1889
Rainwater, Marvin; born Marvin Percy (singer/music) — July 2, 1925
Raitt, Bonnie Lynn (singer) — November 8, 1949
Raitt, John Emmett (actor/singer) — January 29, 1917
Raleigh, Bones; born James Donald Raleigh (hockey) — June 27, 1926
Raleigh, Sir Walter (explorer/author) — ————1522
Ralston, Dennis; born Richard Dennis Ralston (tennis) — July 27, 1942
Ralston, Esther (actress) — September 17, 1902
Ralston, John (football) — April 26, 1927
Ralston, Samuel Moffett (politician) — December 1, 1857
Ralston, Vera; born Vera Helena Hruba (actress) — July 12, 1919
Rambeau, Marjorie (actress) — July 15, 1889
Rambo, Dack; born Norman Rambo (actor) — November 13, 1941
Ramirez, Raul (tennis) — June 20, 1953
Ramos, Pete; born Pedro Ramos (baseball) — April 28, 1935
Rampling, Charlotte (actress) — February 5, 1946
Rampton, Calvin Lewellyn (politician) — November 6, 1913
Ramsay, Jack (basketball) — February 21, 1925
Ramsey, Frank (basketball) — July 13, 1931
Ramsey, Logan Carlisle, Jr. (actor) — March 21, 1921
Ramsey, Steve; born Stephen W. Ramsey (football) — April 22, 1948
Rand, Ayn (writer) — February 2, 1905
Rand, Sally; born Helen Gould Beck (dancer/actress) — April 12, 1903
Randall, Tony; born Anthony L. Randall (actor) — February 26, 1920
Randell, Ron; born Ronald Egan Randell (actor) — October 8, 1918
Randle, Sonny; born Ulmo Randle (football) — January 6, 1936
Randolph, Asa Philip (labor leader) — April 15, 1889
Randolph, Edmund Jennings (statesman) — August 10, 1753
Randolph, Jay; born Jennings Randolph, Jr. (sportscaster) — September 19, 1934
Randolph, Jennings (politician) — March 8, 1902
Randolph, John (statesman) — June 2, 1773
Randolph, John; born Emanuel Hirsch Cohen (actor) — June 1, 1915
Rankin, Jeannette (politician/pacifist/suffragist) — June 11, 1880
Rankin, Judy; born Judith Torluemke (golf) — February 18, 1945
Ransdell, Joseph Eugene (politician) — October 7, 1858
Ransom, John Crowe (poet) — April 30, 1888
Raphael Santi (artist) — March 28, 1483
Raschi, Vic; born Victor John Angelo Raschi (baseball) — March 28, 1919
Rashad, Ahmad; born Robert Earl "Bobby" Moore (football) — November 19, 1949
Rasmussen, Randy; born Randall Lee Rasmussen (football) — May 10, 1945
Rasulala, Thalmus; born Jack Crowder (actor) — November 15, 1939
Ratelle, Jean (hockey) — October 3, 1940
Rathbone, Basil; born Philip St. John Basil Rathbone (actor) — June 13, 1892
Rather, Bo; born David Elmer Rather (football) — October 7, 1950
Rather, Dan (newscaster/author) — October 31, 1931
Rathmann, Jim; born Richard R. Rathmann (auto racing) — July 16, 1928
Ratner, Payne Harry (politician) — October 3, 1896
Ratoff, Gregory (director) — April 20, 1893
Ratterman, George (football) — November 12, 1926

Rattigan, Terence Mervyn (playwright)   June 10, 1911
Ravel, Maurice Joseph (music)   March 7, 1875
Ravlich, Mathew Joseph (hockey)   July 12, 1938
Rawlings, Marjorie Kinnan (author)   August 8, 1896
Rawls, Betsy; born Elizabeth Earle Rawls (golf)   May 4, 1928
Rawls, Eugenia; born Mary Eugenia Rawls (actress)   September 11, 1916
Rawls, Lou; born Louis Allen Rawls (singer)   December 1, 1935
Ray, Aldo; born Aldo daRe (actor)   September 25, 1926
Ray, Clifford (basketball)   January 21, 1949
Ray, Dixie Lee (politician)   September 3, 1914
Ray, James Earl (accused assassin)   March 10, 1928
Ray, Johnnie; born John Alvin Ray (singer)   January 10, 1927
Ray, Man; born Emmanuel Rudnitsky (artist/filmmaker)   August 27, 1890
Ray, Robert D. (politician)   September 26, 1928
Ray, Satyajat (director)   May 2, 1921
Rayburn, Gene; born Gene Rubessa (TV host/actor)   December 22, 1917
Rayburn, Sam; born Samuel Taliaferro Rayburn (politician)   January 6, 1882
Raye, Martha; born Margaret Theresa Yvonne O'Reed   August 27, 1916
   (actress/comedienne/singer)
Raymond, Gene; born Raymond Guion (actor)   August 13, 1908
Raymond, Paula; born Paula Romona Wright (actress)   ———1923
Rayner, Chuck; born Claude Earl Rayner (hockey)   August 11, 1920
Rayner, Isidor (politician)   April 11, 1850
Reagan, Ronald Wilson (actor/politician)   February 6, 1911
Reardon, Kenny; born Kenneth Joseph Reardon (hockey)   April 1, 1921
Reason, Rex (actor)   November 30, 1928
Reason, Rhodes (actor)   ———1930
Reasoner, Harry (newscaster)   April 17, 1923
Reaume, Marc Avellin (hockey)   February 7, 1934
Reaves, Ken; born Kenneth M. Reaves (football)   October 29, 1944
Reay, William (hockey)   August 21, 1918
Redding, Otis (singer/music)   September 9, 1941
Reddy, Helen (singer/actress/music)   October 25, 1941
Redfield, William Cox (government)   June 18, 1858
Redford, Robert; born Charles Robert Redford, Jr. (actor)   August 18, 1937
Redgrave, Corin (actor)   July 16, 1939
Redgrave, Lynn Rachel (actress)   March 8, 1943
Redgrave, Sir Michael (actor)   March 20, 1908
Redgrave, Vanessa (actress)   January 30, 1937
Redman, Rick; born Richard C. Redman (football)   March 7, 1943
Redmond, Mickey; born Michael Edward Redmond (hockey)   December 27, 1947
Reed, Alvin (football)   August 1, 1944
Reed, Clyde Martin (politician)   October 19, 1871
Reed, Donna; born Donna Belle Mullenger (actress)   January 27, 1921
Reed, James Alexander (politician)   November 9, 1861
Reed, Jerry; born Jerry Reed Hubbard (singer/actor/music)   March 20, 1937
Reed, Joe; born Joseph Butler Reed (football)   January 8, 1948
Reed, John Hathaway (politician)   January 5, 1921
Reed, Oliver; born Robert Oliver Reed (actor)   February 13, 1938
Reed, Oscar L. (football)   March 24, 1944
Reed, Rex Taylor (journalist/actor)   October 2, 1938

Reed, Robert (actor) — October 19, 1932
Reed, Ron; born Ronald Lee Reed (baseball/basketball) — November 2, 1942
Reed, Stanley Forman (jurist) — December 31, 1884
Reed, Tracy (actress) — August 21, 1941
Reed, Walter (medicine) — September 13, 1851
Reed, Willis (basketball) — August 25, 1942
Reese, Della; born Deloreese Patricia Early (singer/actress) — July 6, 1932
Reese, Pee Wee; born Harold Henry Reese (baseball/sportscaster) — July 23, 1918
Reese, Rich; born Richard Benjamin Reese (baseball) — September 29, 1941
Reeves, Dan; born Daniel Edward Reeves (football) — January 19, 1944
Reeves, Del; born Franklin Delano Reeves (singer/music) — July 14, 1933
Reeves, Jim; born James Travis Reeves (singer/music) — August 20, 1923
Reeves, Steve (actor/Mr. World/Mr. Universe) — January 21, 1926
Regalado, Victor (golf) — April 15, 1948
Regan, Lawrence Emmett (hockey) — August 9, 1930
Regan, Phil; born Phillip Raymond Regan (baseball) — April 6, 1937
Regazzoni, Clay; born Gian-claudio Guiseppe Regazzoni (auto racing) — September 5, 1939
Regner, Tom; born Thomas E. Regner (football) — April 19, 1944
Rehnquist, William Hubbs (jurist) — October 1, 1924
Reibel, Dutch; born Earl Reibel (hockey) — July 21, 1930
Reichardt, Rick; born Frederick Carl Reichardt (baseball) — March 16, 1943
Reid, Elliot; born Edgeworth Blair Reid (actor) — January 16, 1920
Reid, Wallace; born William Wallace Reid (actor) — April 15, 1890
Reilly, Charles Nelson (actor/director) — January 13, 1931
Reiner, Carl (actor/producer/director/writer) — March 20, 1922
Reiner, Fritz (music) — December 19, 1888
Reiner, Rob; born Robert Reiner (actor) — March 6, 1945
Reinhardt, Max; born Max Goldman (producer/director) — September 9, 1873
Reise, Leo Charles, Jr. (hockey) — June 7, 1922
Reiser, Pete; born Harold Patrick Reiser (baseball) — March 17, 1919
Remarque, Erich Maria (author/playwright) — June 22, 1898
Rembrandt, Van Rijn; born Van Rijn Rembrandt Harmenszoon (artist) — July 15, 1606
Remick, Lee Ann (actress) — December 14, 1935
Renaldo, Duncan; born Renault Renaldo Duncan (actor/producer/writer/artist) — April 23, 1904
Renfro, Mel; born Melvin Lacy Renfro (football) — December 30, 1941
Renfro, Ray; born Raymond Renfro (football) — November 7, 1930
Rennebohm, Oscar (politician) — May 25, 1889
Rennie, Michael; born Eric Alexander Rennie (actor) — August 25, 1909
Renoir, Jean (director/writer) — September 15, 1894
Renoir, Pierre Auguste (artist) — February 25, 1841
Rentzel, Lance; born Thomas Lance Rentzel (football) — October 14, 1943
Repoz, Roger Allen (baseball) — August 3, 1940
Repulski, Rip; born Eldon John Repulski (baseball) — October 4, 1927
Resnais, Alain (director) — June 3, 1922
Resnick, Regina (singer) — August 30, 1922
Ressler, Glenn Emanuel (football) — May 21, 1943
Reston, James Barrett (journalist) — November 3, 1909

Rettenmund, Merv; born Mervin Weldon Rettenmund (baseball)	June 6, 1943
Rettig, Tommy; born Thomas Noel Rettig (actor)	December 10, 1941
Retzlaff, Pete; born Palmer Edward Retzlaff (football)	August 21, 1931
Reuss, Jerry (baseball)	June 19, 1949
Reutemann, Carlos Alberto (auto racing)	April 12, 1942
Reuther, Walter Philip (labor leader)	September 1, 1907
Reventlow, Lance (auto racing)	February 24, 1936
Revercomb, William Chapman (politician)	July 20, 1895
Revere, Anne (actress)	June 25, 1903
Revere, Paul (patriot)	January 1, 1735
Revier, Dorothy; born Doris Velegra (actress)	April 18, 1904
Revill, Clive Selsby (actor/singer)	April 18, 1930
Revolta, Johnny; born John Revolta (golf)	April 5, 1911
Revson, Charles (cosmetics)	October 11, 1906
Revson, Peter Jeffrey (auto racing)	February 27, 1939
Rexford, Bill; born William J. Rexford (auto racing)	March 14, 1927
Rey, Alejandro (actor)	February 8, 1930
Rey, Fernando; born Fernando Casado Arambillet (actor)	September 20, 1915
Reynolds, Allie Pierce (baseball)	February 10, 1915
Reynolds, Burt (actor/director)	February 11, 1936
Reynolds, Debbie; born Mary Frances Reynolds (actress/singer/dancer)	April 1, 1932
Reynolds, Frank (newscaster)	November 29, 1923
Reynolds, Jack Sumner (football)	November 22, 1947
Reynolds, John W. (politician)	April 4, 1921
Reynolds, Sir Joshua (artist)	July 16, 1723
Reynolds, Joyce (actress)	October 7, 1924
Reynolds, Marjorie; born Marjorie Goodspeed (actress)	August 12, 1921
Reynolds, Robert Rice (politician)	June 18, 1884
Reynolds, William (actor)	December 9, 1931
Rhem, Flint; born Charles Flint Rhem (baseball)	January 24, 1901
Rhoades, Barbara Jean (actress/dancer)	March 23, 1946
Rhodes, Cecil John (South African financier & statesman)	July 5, 1853
Rhodes, Hari (actor)	April 10, 1932
Rhodes, James Allen (politician)	September 13, 1909
Rhodes, John Jacob, 2nd (politician)	September 18, 1916
Rhome, Jerry; born Gerald B. Rhome (football)	March 6, 1942
Rhue, Madlyn (actress)	October 3, 1934
Ribicoff, Abraham Alexander (government/politics)	April 9, 1910
Rice, Del; born Delbert W. Rice (baseball)	October 27, 1922
Rice, Elmer Leopold; born Elmer Leopold Reizenstein (playwright/author/producer)	September 28, 1892
Rice, Florence (actress)	February 14, 1907
Rice, Grantland (journalist/sportscaster/author)	November 1, 1880
Rice, Jim; born James Edward Rice (baseball)	March 8, 1953
Rice, Sam; born Edgar Charles Rice (baseball)	February 20, 1890
Rich, Buddy; born Bernard Rich (music)	June 30, 1917
Rich, Charlie; born Charles Allan Rich (singer/music)	December 14, 1932
Rich, Irene; born Irene Luther (actress)	October 13, 1891
Richard, Henri (hockey)	February 29, 1936
Richard, Maurice; born Joseph Henri Maurice Richard (hockey)	August 4, 1921

Richards, Ann; born Shirley Ann Richards (actress)	December 20, 1918
Richards, Golden; born John Golden Richards (football)	December 31, 1950
Richards, John Gardiner (politician)	September 11, 1864
Richards, Paul (baseball)	November 21, 1908
Richardson, Bobby; born Robert Clinton Richardson (baseball)	August 19, 1935
Richardson, Elliot Lee (government)	July 20, 1920
Richardson, Friend William (politician)	—————1865
Richardson, Gloster V. (football)	July 18, 1941
Richardson, Harry Alden (politican)	January 1, 1853
Richardson, Sir Ralph David (actor)	December 19, 1902
Richardson, Samuel (author)	July 31, 1689
Richardson, Tony; born Cecil Antonio Richardson (director)	June 5, 1928
Richelieu, Cardinal; born Armand Jean du Plessis de Richelieu (French prelate & statesman)	September 9, 1585
Richert, Pete; born Peter Gerard Richert (baseball)	October 29, 1939
Richey, Cliff; born George Clifford Richey, Jr. (tennis)	December 31, 1946
Richman, Harry; born Harry Reichman (actor/singer)	August 10, 1895
Richman, Peter Mark; born Marvin Jack Richman (actor)	April 16, 1927
Richter, Charles Francis (seismologist)	April 26, 1900
Richter, Conrad Michael (author)	October 13, 1890
Richter, Les; born Leslie A. Richter (football)	October 6, 1930
Rickenbacker, Eddie; born Edward Vernon Rickenbacker (aviator)	October 8, 1890
Rickey, Branch Wesley (baseball)	December 20, 1881
Rickles, Don (comedian/actor)	May 8, 1926
Rickover, Hyman George (naval officer/nuclear power expert)	January 27, 1900
Riddle, Nelson Smock (music)	June 1, 1921
Ridgway, Matthew Bunker (army officer)	March 3, 1895
Riegle, Donald Wayne, Jr. (politician)	February 4, 1938
Riessen, Marty; born Martin Clare Riessen (tennis)	December 4, 1941
Rigby, Cathy (gymnast/actress)	December 12, 1952
Rigg, Diana (actress)	July 20, 1938
Riggins, John (football)	August 4, 1949
Riggs, Bobby; born Robert Larimore Riggs (tennis)	February 25, 1918
Rigney, Bill; born William Joseph Rigney (baseball)	January 29, 1918
Riley, James Whitcomb (poet)	October 7, 1853
Riley, Jeannie C.; born Jeannie Carolyn Stephenson (singer)	October 19, 1945
Riley, Ken; born Kenneth Riley (football)	August 6, 1947
Riley, Pat (basketball)	March 20, 1945
Rimski-Korsakov, Nikolai Andreyevich (music)	March 18, 1844
Rindt, Jochen; born Karl Jochen Rindt (auto racing)	April 18, 1942
Ringo, Jim; born James Ringo (football)	November 21, 1932
Riordan, Mike (basketball)	July 9, 1945
Risdon, Elizabeth (actress)	April 26, 1887
Risen, Arnold (basketball)	October 9, 1924
Ritchard, Cyril; born Cyril Trimnell-Richard (actor/singer/director)	December 1, 1893
Ritchie, Albert Cabell (politician)	August 29, 1876
Ritter, John; born Jonathan Southworth Ritter (actor)	September 17, 1948
Ritter, Tex; born Woodward Maurice Nederland Ritter (actor/singer)	January 12, 1906

Ritter, Thelma Adele (actress)	February 14, 1905
Rivera, Chita; born Dolores Conchita Figueroa del Rivero (actress/singer/dancer)	January 23, 1933
Rivera, Geraldo Miguel (TV host/newscaster)	July 3, 1943
Rivera, Jim; born Manuel Joseph Rivera (baseball)	July 22, 1922
Rivers, Eurith Dickinson (politician)	December 1, 1895
Rivers, Joan; born Joan Molinsky (comedienne/writer)	October 12, 1935
Rivers, Johnny; born John Ramistella (singer/music)	November 7, 1942
Rivers, Larry; born Yitzroch Loiza Grossberg (artist)	August 17, 1923
Rivers, L. Mendel; born Lucius Mendel Rivers (politician)	September 28, 1905
Rivers, Mickey; born John Milton Rivers (baseball)	October 31, 1948
Rixey, Eppa (baseball)	May 3, 1891
Rizzo, Frank Lazarro (politician)	October 23, 1920
Rizzuto, Phil; born Philip Francis Rizzuto (baseball)	September 25, 1917
Roach, Hal (producer/director/writer)	January 14, 1892
Roach, John Ross (hockey)	June 23, 1900
Robards, Jason Nelson, Jr. (actor)	July 26, 1922
Robb, Joe; born Alvis Joe Robb (football)	March 15, 1937
Robbins, Austin (basketball)	September 30, 1944
Robbins, Gale (actress/singer)	May 7, 1924
Robbins, Harold; born Francis Kane (author)	May 21, 1916
Robbins, Jerome; born Jerome Rabinowitz (director/choreographer/dancer)	October 11, 1918
Robbins, Marty; born Martin David Robinson (singer/auto racing)	September 26, 1925
Roberts, Albert Houston (politician)	July 4, 1868
Roberts, Beverly Louise (actress)	May 19, 1914
Roberts, Dennis Joseph (politician)	April 8, 1903
Roberts, Douglas William (hockey)	October 28, 1942
Roberts, Fireball; born Edward Glenn Roberts, Jr. (auto racing)	January 20, 1931
Roberts, Henry (politician)	January 22, 1853
Roberts, James Wilfred (hockey)	April 9, 1940
Roberts, Oral; born Granville Oral Roberts (evangelist)	January 24, 1918
Roberts, Owen Josephus (jurist)	May 2, 1875
Roberts, Pernell (actor)	May 18, 1930
Roberts, Rachel (actress/singer)	September 20, 1927
Roberts, Robin Evan (baseball)	September 30, 1926
Roberts, Sue; born Susan Roberts (golf)	June 22, 1948
Roberts, Tony; born David Anthony Roberts (actor)	October 22, 1939
Robertson, A. Willis (politician)	May 27, 1887
Robertson, Bob; born Robert Eugene Robertson (baseball)	October 2, 1946
Robertson, Cliff; born Clifford Parker Robertson, III (actor)	September 9, 1925
Robertson, Dale; born Dayle LaMoine Robertson (actor)	July 14, 1923
Robertson, Edward Vivian (politician)	May 27, 1881
Robertson, Isiah (football)	August 17, 1949
Robertson, James Brooks Ayers (politician)	March 15, 1871
Robertson, Oscar Palmer (basketball)	November 24, 1938
Robeson, Paul Bustill (singer/actor)	April 9, 1898
Robespierre, Maximilien Francois Marie Isidore de (French revolutionist)	May 6, 1758
Robins, Charles A. (politician)	December 8, 1884

Robinson, Bill "Bojangles" (dancer/actor)	May 25, 1878
Robinson, Brooks Calbert, Jr. (baseball)	May 18, 1937
Robinson, Chris (actor)	November 5, 1938
Robinson, Dave; born Richard David Robinson (football)	May 3, 1941
Robinson, Eddie; born William Edward Robinson (baseball)	December 15, 1920
Robinson, Edward G.; born Emmanuel Goldberg (actor)	December 12, 1893
Robinson, Edwin Arlington (poet)	December 22, 1869
Robinson, Floyd Andrew (baseball)	May 9, 1936
Robinson, Frank (baseball)	August 31, 1935
Robinson, Jackie; born Jack Roosevelt Robinson (baseball)	January 31, 1919
Robinson, Johnny; born John Nolan Robinson (football)	September 9, 1938
Robinson, Joseph Taylor (politician)	August 26, 1872
Robinson, Robert P. (politician)	March 28, 1869
Robinson, Smokey; born William Robinson (singer)	February 19, 1940
Robinson, Sugar Ray; born Walker Smith (boxing/actor)	May 3, 1920
Robinson, Wilbert (baseball)	June 2, 1863
Robson, Dame Flora (actress)	March 28, 1902
Robson, May; born Mary Jeanette Robison (actress)	April 19, 1858
Robustelli, Andy; born Andrew Robustelli (football)	December 6, 1930
Rocco, Alex (actor)	February 29———
Rochambeau, Jean Baptiste Donatien de Vimeur (French marshall)	July 1, 1725
Roche, Alden (football)	April 9, 1945
Roche, Eugene (actor)	September 22, 1928
Roche, Tony; born Anthony Dalton Roche (tennis)	May 17, 1945
Rochefort, Leon (hockey)	May 4, 1939
Rochester; born Eddie Anderson (actor)	September 18, 1905
Rock, Walter (football)	November 4, 1941
Rockefeller, David (banker)	June 12, 1915
Rockefeller, Happy; born Margaretta Large Fitler (Vice President's wife)	June 9, 1926
Rockefeller, John Davidson (industrialist/philanthropist)	July 8,1839
Rockefeller John Davidson, Jr. (industrialist/philanthropist)	January 29, 1874
Rockefeller, John Davidson, III (philanthropist)	March 21, 1906
Rockefeller, John Davidson, IV (politician)	June 18, 1937
Rockefeller, Laurance Spelman (conservationist)	May 26, 1910
Rockefeller, Nelson Aldrich (Vice President)	July 8, 1908
Rockefeller, William (industrialist/financier)	May 31, 1841
Rockefeller, Winthrop (politician)	May 1, 1912
Rockne, Knute Kenneth (football)	March 4, 1888
Rockwell, Norman Percival (artist)	February 3, 1894
Rodd, Marcia (actress/singer)	July 8, 1941
Rodgers, Andre; born Kenneth Andre Ian Rodgers (baseball)	December 2, 1934
Rodgers, Bob; born Robert Leroy Rodgers (baseball)	August 16, 1938
Rodgers, Guy (basketball)	September 1, 1935
Rodgers, Jimmie; born James Charles Rodgers (singer)	September 8, 1897
Rodgers, Jimmie; born James Frederick Rodgers (singer)	September 18, 1933
Rodgers, Mary (music)	January 11, 1931
Rodgers, Pepper; born Franklin C. Rodgers (football)	October 8, 1931
Rodgers, Phil; born Philamon Webster Rodgers (golf)	April 3, 1938

Rodgers, Richard Charles (music/playwright/producer)	June 28, 1902
Rodgers, Wayne (actor)	April 7, 1933
Rodino, Peter Wallace, Jr. (politician)	June 7, 1909
Rodrigues, Percy (actor)	————1924
Rodriguez, Aurelio (baseball)	December 28, 1947
Rodriguez, Chi Chi; born Juan A. Rodriguez Vila (golf)	October 23, 1935
Rodriguez, Ellie; born Eliseo Rodriguez (baseball)	May 24, 1946
Rodriguez, Pedro (auto racing)	January 18, 1940
Rodriguez, Richardo; born Richardo Valentine Rodriguez de la Vega (auto racing)	February 14, 1942
Roe, Preacher; born Elwin Charles Roe (baseball)	February 26, 1915
Roe, Tommy; born Thomas David Roe (singer/music)	May 9, 1943
Rogers, Buddy; born Charles Rogers (actor)	August 13, 1904
Rogers, C.J. "Doc" (politician)	December 20, 1897
Rogers, Ginger; born Virginia Katherine McMath (actress/dancer/singer)	July 16, 1911
Rogers, Kenny; born Kenneth Ray Rogers (singer/music)	August 21, 1938
Rogers, Roy; born Leonard Slye (actor/singer)	November 5, 1911
Rogers, Will; born William Penn Adair Rogers (humorist)	November 4, 1879
Rogers, Will, Jr. (actor)	October 20, 1911
Rogers, William Pierce (government)	June 23, 1913
Rojas, Cookie, born Octavio Victor Rojas (baseball)	March 6, 1939
Roland, Gilbert; born Luis Antonio Damaso De Alonso (actor)	December 11, 1905
Roland, Johnny; born John Earl Roland (football)	May 21, 1943
Rolland, Romain (author)	January 29, 1866
Rolle, Esther (actress)	November 8———
Rollins, Al; born Elwin Ira Rollins (hockey)	October 9, 1926
Rollins, Rich; born Richard John Rollins (baseball)	April 16, 1938
Rollins, Sonny; born Theodore Walter Rollins (music)	September 7, 1929
Rolph, James, Jr. (politician)	August 23, 1869
Rolvaag, Karl Fritjok (politician)	July 18, 1913
Roman, Ruth (actress)	December 23, 1924
Romano, Johnny; born John Anthony Romano (baseball)	August 23, 1934
Romberg, Sigmund (music)	July 29, 1887
Rome, Harold Jacob (music)	May 27, 1908
Romero, Cesar; born Caesar Julius Romero (actor)	February 15, 1907
Rommel, Eddie; born Edwin Americus Rommel (baseball)	September 13, 1897
Rommel, Erwin Johannes Eugen (German army officer)	November 15, 1891
Romney, George Wilcken (politics/government)	July 8, 1907
Ronstadt, Linda Maria (singer)	July 15, 1946
Ronty, Paul (hockey)	June 12, 1928
Roof, Phil; born Phillip Anthony Roof (baseball)	March 5, 1941
Rooney, Mickey; born Joe Yule, Jr. (actor)	September 23, 1920
Roosevelt, Anna Eleanor (First family)	May 3, 1906
Roosevelt, Edith Kermit Carow; born Edith Kermit Carow (second wife of Theodore Roosevelt/First Lady)	August 6, 1861
Roosevelt, Eleanor; born Anna Eleanor Roosevelt (First Lady)	October 11, 1884
Roosevelt, Elliot (First family)	September 23, 1910
Roosevelt, Franklin Delano (President)	January 30, 1882
Roosevelt, Franklin Delano, Jr. (First family)	August 17, 1914

Roosevelt, James (First family)	December 23, 1907
Roosevelt, John Aspinwall (First family)	March 13, 1916
Roosevelt, Theodore (President)	October 27, 1858
Roosevelt, Theodore, Jr. (First family/politics/ government/author)	September 13, 1887
Root, Charlie; born Charles Henry Root (baseball)	March 17, 1899
Root, Elihu (government/politics)	February 15, 1845
Roper, Daniel Calhoun (government)	April 1, 1867
Rosburg, Bob; born Robert Rosburg (golf/sportscaster)	October 21, 1926
Rose, Billy; born William Samuel Rosenberg (music/producer)	September 6, 1899
Rose, David (music)	June 24, 1910
Rose, Mauri (auto racing)	———1906
Rose, Mervyn G. (tennis)	January 23, 1930
Rose, Pete; born Peter Edward Rose (baseball)	April 14, 1942
Rose, Tokyo; born Iva Ikuko Toguri d'Aquino (broadcasting)	July 4, 1916
Rose Marie; born Rose Marie Mazzatta (actress)	August 15———
Roseboro, John (baseball)	May 13, 1933
Rosellini, Albert Dean (politician)	January 21, 1910
Rosen, Al; born Albert Leonard Rosen (baseball)	February 29, 1924
Rosenbloom, Maxie (boxing/actor)	September 6, 1904
Rosewall, Ken; born Kenneth Robert Rosewall (tennis)	November 2, 1934
Ross, Betsy; born Elizabeth Griscom Ross (flag maker)	January 1, 1752
Ross, Charles Benjamin (politician)	December 27, 1876
Ross, Diana (singer/actress)	March 26, 1944
Ross, Katharine (actress)	January 29, 1943
Ross, Marion (actress)	October 25, 1928
Ross, Nellie Tayloe (politics/government)	November 29, 1876
Ross, Shirley; born Bernice Gaunt (actress/singer)	January 7, 1909
Ross, William Bradford (politician)	December 4, 1873
Rossellini, Roberto (director)	May 8, 1906
Rossetti, Dante Gabriel (poet/artist)	May 12, 1828
Rossini, Gioacchino Antonio (music)	February 29, 1792
Rostropovich, Mstislav Leopoldovich (music)	August 12, 1927
Rote, Kyle W. (football/sportscaster)	October 27, 1928
Roth, Lillian; born Lillian Rutstein (actress)	December 13, 1910
Roth, Philip Milton (author)	March 19, 1933
Roth, William, V. Jr. (politician)	July 22, 1921
Roundtree, Richard (actor)	September 7, 1942
Roush, Edd J. (baseball)	May 8, 1893
Rousseau, Bobby; born Robert Rousseau (hockey)	July 26, 1940
Rousseau, Jean-Jacques (French philosopher/writer)	June 28, 1712
Rowan, Carl Thomas (journalism/government)	August 11, 1925
Rowan, Dan Hale (comedian/actor)	July 2, 1922
Rowe, Bob; born Robert Rowe (football)	May 23, 1945
Rowe, Curtis (basketball)	July 2, 1949
Rowe, Dave; born David Rowe (football)	June 20, 1945
Rowe, Schoolboy; born Lynwood Thomas Rowe (baseball)	January 11, 1910
Rowlands, Gena; born Virginia Cathryn Rowlands (actress)	June 19, 1936
Rowser, John (football)	April 24, 1944
Royall, Darrell K. (football)	July 6, 1924
Royle, Selena (actress)	November 6, 1904

Rozelle, Pete; born Alvin Ray Rozelle (football)	March 1, 1926
Rubens, Peter Paul (artist)	June 29, 1577
Rubinstein, Artur (music)	January 28, 1889
Rubinstein, Helena (cosmetics)	————1871
Rubinstein, John Arthur (actor/singer/music)	December 8, 1946
Ruby, Harry; born Harry Rubinstein (music)	January 27, 1895
Ruby, Lloyd; born Richard Lloyd Ruby (auto racing)	January 12, 1928
Ruckelshaus, William Doyle (government)	July 24, 1932
Rucker, Reggie; born Reginald Joseph Rucker (football)	September 21, 1947
Rudd, Hughes Day (newscaster)	September 14, 1921
Rudel, Julius (music)	March 6, 1921
Rudi, Joe; born Joseph Oden Rudi (baseball)	September 7, 1946
Rudolph, Council (football)	January 18, 1950
Rudolph, Mason (golf)	May 23, 1934
Rudolph, Mendy; born Marvin Rudolph (referee/sportscaster)	March 8, 1928
Ruel, Muddy; born Harold Dominic Ruel (baseball)	February 20, 1896
Ruffing, Red; born Charles Herbert Ruffing (baseball)	May 3, 1904
Ruggles, Charles Sherman (actor)	February 8, 1886
Rugolo, Peter (music)	December 25, 1915
Rule, Janice; born Mary Janice Rule (actress)	August 15, 1931
Rumsfeld, Donald (government)	July 9, 1932
Runnels, Pete; born James Edward Runnels (baseball)	January 28, 1928
Runyan, Damon; born Alfred Damon Runyan (journalist/author)	October 4, 1884
Runyan, Paul Scott (golf)	July 12, 1908
Rupp, Duane Edward Franklin (hockey)	March 29, 1938
Rush, Barbara (actress)	January 4, 1927
Rush, Bob; born Robert Ransom Rush (baseball)	December 21, 1925
Rusie, Amos Wilson (baseball)	May 30, 1871
Rusk, Dean; born David Dean Rusk (government)	February 9, 1909
Russell, Andy; born Charles Andrew Russell (football)	October 29, 1941
Russell, Lord Bertrand Arthur William (mathematician/philosopher)	May 18, 1872
Russell, Bill; born William Ellis Russell (baseball)	October 21, 1948
Russell, Bill; born William Felton Russell (basketball)	February 12, 1934
Russell, Cazzie (basketball)	June 7, 1944
Russell, Charles Hinton (politician)	December 27, 1903
Russell, Donald Stuart (politician)	February 22, 1906
Russell, Gail (actress)	September 23, 1924
Russell, Jane; born Ernestine Jane Geraldine Russell (actress)	June 21, 1921
Russell, Jim; born James William Russell (baseball)	October 1, 1918
Russell, John (actor)	January 3, 1921
Russell, Kurt Von Vogel (actor)	March 17, 1951
Russell, Lee Maurice (politician)	November 16, 1875
Russell, Lillian; born Helen Louise Leonard (singer/actress)	December 4, 1861
Russell, Nipsey (comedian/actor/poet)	October 13, 1924
Russell, Richard Brevard, Jr. (politician)	November 2, 1897
Russell, Rosalind (actress)	June 4, 1907
Ruth, Babe; born George Herman Ehrhardt (baseball)	February 6, 1895
Rutherford, Ann; born Therese Ann Rutherford (actress)	November 2, 1917

Rutherford, Johnny; born John Sherman Rutherford, III   March 12, 1938
    (auto racing)
Rutherford, Dame Margaret Taylor (actress)   May 11, 1892
Rutledge, Wiley Blount Jr. (jurist)   July 20, 1894
Ruttman, Troy (auto racing)   March 11, 1930
Ruymen, Ayn (actress)   July 18, 1947
Ryan, Connie; born Cornelius Joseph Ryan (baseball)   February 27, 1920
Ryan, Elizabeth (tennis)   February 5, 1892
Ryan, Frank Beall (football)   July 12, 1936
Ryan, Irene; born Irene Noblette (actress)   October 17, 1902
Ryan, Mitchell (actor)   January 11, 1928
Ryan, Nolan; born Lynn Nolan Ryan (baseball)   January 31, 1947
Ryan, Peggy; born Margaret Orene (or O'Rene) Ryan (actress)   August 28, 1924
Ryan, Robert Bushnell (actor)   November 11, 1909
Ryan, Sheila; born Katherine Elizabeth McLaughlin (actress)   June 8, 1921
Rydell, Bobby; born Robert Lewis Ridarelli (singer/actor)   April 26, 1942
Ryder, Alfred; born Alfred Jacob Corn (actor)   January 5, 1919
Rye, Thomas Clark (politician)   June 2, 1863
Rysanek, Leonie (singer)   November 14, 1928

S

Saban, Lou; born Louis H. Saban (football)   October 13, 1921
Sabatini, Rafael (author)   April 29, 1875
Sabin, Albert Bruce (medicine)   August 26, 1906
Sabu; born Sabu Dastagir (actor)   March 15, 1924
Sackett, Frederick Mosley (politician)   December 17, 1868
Sackler, Howard (playwright)   December 19, 1929
Sadat, Anwar (Egyptian government)   December 25, 1918
Sadecki, Ray; born Raymond Michael Sadecki (baseball)   December 26, 1940
Safer, Morley (newscaster)   November 8, 1931
Sagan, Francoise, born Francoise Quoirez (author)   June 21, 1935
Sahl, Mort; born Morton Lyon Sahl (comedian)   May 11, 1927
Saimes, George (football)   September 1, 1941
Saint, Eva Marie (actress)   July 4, 1924
St. Clair, Bob; born Robert B. St. Clair (football)   February 18, 1931
St. Cyr, Lili; born Marie Van Schaak (actress)   June 3, 1917
St. Jacques, Raymond; born James Arthur Johnson (actor)   March 1, 1932
Saint James, Susan; born Susan Jane Miller (actress)   August 14, 1946
St. John, Betta; born Betty Streidler (actress)   November 26, 1929
St. John, Howard Sidney (actor)   October 9, 1905
St. John, Jill; born Jill Oppenheim (actress)   August 19, 1940
St. Johns, Adela Rogers; born Adela Rogers   May 20, 1894
    (journalist/author)
St. Laurent, Yves; born Henri Donat Mathieu   August 1, 1936
    (fashion designer)
Saint-Subber, Arnold (producer)   February 18, 1918
Sainte-Marie, Buffy; born Beverly Sainte-Marie (singer)   February 20, 1941
Saki; born Hector Hugh Munro (author)   December 18, 1870
Saks, Gene; born Jean Michael Saks (actor/director)   November 8, 1921
Salazar, Antonio de Oliveria (Portuguese government)   April 28, 1889

Sales, Soupy; born Milton Hines (comedian/actor)	January 8, 1926
Salinger, J.D.; born Jerome David Salinger (author)	January 1, 1919
Salinger, Pierre Emil George (journalism/government)	June 14, 1925
Salisbury, Harrison Evans (journalist)	November 14, 1908
Salk, Jonas Edward (medicine)	October 28, 1914
Salmi, Albert (actor)	————1925
Salmon, Thomas Paul (politician)	August 19, 1932
Salt, Jennifer (actress)	September 4, 1944
Salter, Bryant (football)	January 22, 1950
Saltonstall, Leverett (politician)	September 1, 1892
Salvadori, Roy Francesco (auto racing)	May 12, 1922
Sample, John B. (football)	June 15, 1937
Samples, Junior (comedian)	August 10, 1926
Sampson, Flemon Davis (politician)	January 23, 1873
Samuelson, Donald William (politician)	July 27, 1913
Sand, George; born Lucile-Amandine-Aurore Dupin (author)	July 1, 1804
Sandburg, Carl August (poet)	January 6, 1878
Sanders, Carl Edward (politician)	May 15, 1925
Sanders, Charlie; born Charles Alvin Sanders (football)	August 25, 1946
Sanders, Doug; born George Douglas Sanders (golf)	July 24, 1933
Sanders, George (actor)	July 3, 1906
Sanders, Harland "Colonel" (fast foods magnate)	September 9, 1890
Sanders, Jared Young (politician)	January 29, 1869
Sanders, Ken; born Kenneth R. Sanders (football)	August 22, 1950
Sanders, Thomas (basketball)	November 8, 1938
Sanderson, Derek Michael (hockey)	June 16, 1946
Sands, Diana Patricia (actress)	August 22, 1934
Sands, Tommy; born Thomas Adrian Sands (singer/actor)	August 27, 1937
Sandusky, Alex; born Alexander B. Sandusky (football)	August 17, 1932
Sanford, Edward Terry (jurist)	July 23, 1865
Sanford, Isabel Gwendolyn (actress)	August 29————
Sanford, Jack; born John Stanley Sanford (baseball)	May 18, 1929
Sanford, Terry; born James Terry Sanford (politician)	August 20, 1917
Sanger, Margaret; born Margaret Higgins (birth control propagandist)	September 14, 1883
Sanguillen, Manny; born Manuel DeJesus Sanguillen (baseball)	March 21, 1944
San Juan, Olga (actress)	March 16, 1927
San Souci, Emery John (politician)	July 24, 1857
Santamaria, Mongo; born Ramon Santamaria (music)	April 7, 1922
Santana, Manuel; born Manuel Santana Martinez (tennis)	May 10, 1938
Santayana, George (philosopher/poet)	December 16, 1863
Santo, Ron; born Ronald Edward Santo (baseball)	February 25, 1940
Santos, Joe; born Joseph Minieri (actor)	June 9, 1931
Sanudo, Cesar (golf)	October 26, 1943
Sarandon, Chris (actor)	July 24, 1942
Sarandon, Susan; born Susan Tomaling (actress)	October 4, 1946
Sarazen, Gene; born Eugene Saraceni (golf)	February 27, 1902
Sarbanes, Paul Spyros (politician)	February 3, 1933
Sardi, Vincent, Sr.; born Melchiorre Pio Vincenzo Sardi (restaurateur)	December 23, 1885
Sardi, Vincent, Jr. (restaurateur)	July 23, 1915

Sargent, Dick; born Richard Cox (actor)	April 19, 1933
Sargent, Francis Williams (politician)	July 29, 1915
Sargent, John Garibaldi (government)	October 13, 1860
Sargent, John Singer (artist)	January 12, 1856
Sarles, Elmore Yocum (politician)	January 15, 1859
Saroyan, William (playwright)	August 31, 1908
Sarrazin, Michael; born Jacques Michel Andre Sarrazin (actor)	May 22, 1940
Sarto, Andrea del; born Andrea Domenico d-Agnolo di Francesco (artist)	July 6, 1486
Sartre, Jean-Paul (existentialist writer)	June 21, 1905
Sasser, James Ralph (politician)	September 30, 1936
Sato, Eisaku (Japanese government)	March 27, 1901
Saul, Rich; born Richard R. Saul (football)	February 5, 1948
Saul, Ron; born Ronald Saul (football)	February 5, 1948
Sauldsberry, Woody (basketball)	July 11, 1934
Saulsbury, Willard, Jr. (politician)	April 17, 1861
Saunders, Lori; born with surname Hines (actress)	October 4, 1941
Saur, Hank; born Henry John Saur (baseball)	March 17, 1919
Savage, Ezra Perin (politician)	April 3, 1842
Savage, Swede; born David Earle Savage, Jr. (auto racing)	August 26, 1946
Savalas, George Demosthenes (actor)	December 5———
Savalas, Telly; born Aristotle Savalas (actor)	January 21, 1924
Savard, Serge (hockey)	January 22, 1946
Sawatski, Carl Ernest (baseball)	November 4, 1927
Sawchuk, Terry; born Terrance Gordon Sawchuk (hockey)	December 28, 1929
Sawyer, Charles (government)	February 10, 1887
Sawyer, Grant (politician)	December 14, 1918
Saxbe, William Bart (politics/government)	June 24, 1916
Saxon, John; born Carmen Orrico (actor)	August 5, 1935
Sayer, Leo; born Gerard Sayer (singer/music)	May 21, 1948
Sayers, Gale Eugene (football)	May 30, 1943
Scaggs, Boz; born William Royce Scaggs (singer/music)	June 8, 1944
Scala, Gia; born Giovanna Scoglio (actress)	March 3, 1934
Scarlatti, Alessandro (music)	May 2, 1660
Scarlatti, Domenico (music)	October 26, 1685
Scassi, Arnold Martin; born Arnold Martin Isaacs (fashion designer)	———1930
Schaal, Paul (baseball)	March 3, 1943
Schaefer, George Louis (producer/director)	December 16, 1920
Schaefer, Natalie (actress)	November 5, 1912
Schalk, Ray; born Raymond William Schalk (baseball)	August 12, 1892
Schall, Thomas David (politician)	June 4, 1878
Schallert, William Joseph (actor)	July 6, 1922
Schang, Wally; born Walter Henry Schang (baseball)	August 22, 1889
Schary, Dore; born Isidore Schary (actor/producer/director/writer)	August 31, 1905
Schayes, Dolph (basketball)	May 19, 1928
Scheckter, Jody (auto racing)	January 29, 1950
Scheffing, Bob; born Robert Boden Scheffing (baseball)	August 11, 1915
Scheider, Roy Richard (actor)	November 10, 1935
Schell, Harry; born Henry O'Reilly Schell (auto racing)	June 29, 1921

Schell, Maria Margarethe Anna (actress)	January 15, 1926
Schell, Maxmilian Konrad (actor)	December 8, 1930
Schembechler, Bo; born Glenn Edward Schembechler (football)	April 1, 1929
Schenkel, Chris; born Christopher Eugene Schenkel (sportscaster)	August 21, 1923
Schenken, Tim (auto racing)	September 26, 1943
Scherer, Ray; born Raymond Lewis Scherer (newscaster)	June 7, 1919
Schiaparelli, Elsa (fashion designer)	————1890
Schieffer, Bob Lloyd (newscaster)	February 25, 1937
Schifrin, Lalo Boris (music)	June 21, 1932
Schildkraut, Joseph (actor)	March 22, 1895
Schiller, Johann Christoph Friedrich von (dramatist/poet)	November 10, 1759
Schinkel, Kenneth Calvin (hockey)	November 27, 1932
Schirra, Wally; born Walter Marty Schirra, Jr. (astronaut)	March 12, 1923
Schisgal, Murray Joseph (playwright)	November 25, 1926
Schlee, John (golf)	June 2, 1939
Schlesinger, Arthur Meier, Jr. (historian)	October 15, 1917
Schlesinger, James Rodney (government)	February 15, 1929
Schlesinger, John Richard (director)	February 16, 1926
Schmedeman, Albert George (politician)	November 25, 1864
Schmeling, Max; born Maximilian Schmeling (boxing)	September 28, 1905
Schmidt, Harvey Lester (music)	September 12, 1929
Schmidt, Helmut Heinrich Waldemar (German government)	December 23, 1918
Schmidt, Joe; born Joseph Paul Schmidt (football)	January 18, 1932
Schmidt, Milt; born Milton Conrad Schmidt (hockey)	March 5, 1918
Schmitt, Harrison Hagan (astronaut/politician)	July 3, 1935
Schneider, Romy; born Rosemarie Allbach-Retty (actress)	September 23, 1938
Schnelker, Bob; born Robert Schnelker (football)	October 17, 1928
Schnittker, Richard (basketball)	May 27, 1928
Schock, Ronald L. (hockey)	December 19, 1943
Schoendienst, Red; born Albert Frederick Schoendienst (baseball)	February 2, 1923
Schoenke, Ray; born Raymond Schoenke, Jr. (football)	September 10, 1941
Schoeppel, Andrew Frank (politician)	November 23, 1894
Schofield, Dick; born John Richard Schofield (baseball)	January 7, 1935
Schönberg, Arnold (music)	September 13, 1874
Schopenhauer, Arthur (philosopher)	February 22, 1788
Schorr, Daniel Louis (newscaster/author)	August 31, 1916
Schreiber, Avery (comedian/actor)	April 9, 1935
Schreiber, Martin James (politician)	April 8, 1939
Schricker, Henry Frederick (politician)	August 30, 1883
Schriner, Sweeney; born David Schriner (hockey)	November 30, 1911
Schroeder, John (golf)	November 12, 1945
Schroeder, Ted; born Frederick Rudolph Schroeder, Jr. (tennis)	July 20, 1921
Schubert, Franz Peter (music)	January 31, 1797
Schuh, Harry F. (football)	September 25, 1942
Schulberg, Budd Wilson (author)	March 27, 1914
Schuller, Gunther (music)	November 22, 1925
Schultz, Charles Monroe (cartoonist)	November 22, 1922
Schumacher, Hal; born Harold Henry Schumacher (baseball)	November 23, 1910

Schuman, William Howard (music)	August 4, 1910
Schumann, Robert Alexander (music)	June 8, 1810
Schumann-Heink, Ernestine; born Ernestine Rössler (singer)	June 15, 1861
Schwartz, Henry Herman (politician)	May 18, 1869
Schwartz, Stephen Lawrence (music)	March 6, 1948
Schwarzenegger, Arnold (body builder/actor)	July 30, 1947
Schwarzkopf, Elizabeth (singer)	December 9, 1915
Schweikart, Russell Louis (astronaut)	October 25, 1935
Schweiker, Richard Schultz (politician)	June 1, 1926
Schweitzer, Albert (humanitarian)	January 14, 1875
Schwellenbach, Lewis Baxter (politics/government)	September 20, 1894
Scibelli, Joe; born Joseph Scibelli (football)	April 19, 1939
Scofield, Paul; born David Paul Scofield (actor)	January 21, 1922
Scolari, Fred (basketball)	March 1, 1922
Scott, Clarence (football)	April 9, 1949
Scott, David Randolph (astronaut)	June 6, 1932
Scott, Debralee (actress)	April 2, 1953
Scott, George C.; born George Campbell Scott (actor)	October 18, 1927
Scott, George Charles (baseball)	February 23, 1944
Scott, Gordon; born Gordon M. Werschkul (actor)	August 3, 1927
Scott, Hugh Doggett, Jr. (politician)	November 11, 1900
Scott, Jake; born Jacob E. Scott, III (football)	July 20, 1945
Scott, Lizabeth Virginia; born Emma Matzo (actress)	September 29, 1922
Scott, Martha Ellen (actress)	September 22, 1914
Scott, Nathan Bay (politician)	December 18, 1842
Scott, Pippa; born Phillippa Scott (actress)	November 10, 1935
Scott, Randolph Crane (actor)	January 23, 1903
Scott, Ray; (basketball)	July 12, 1938
Scott, Robert Walter (politician)	June 13, 1929
Scott, Sir Walter (author)	August 15, 1771
Scott, Wendell (auto racing)	August 29, 1921
Scott, William Kerr (politician)	April 17, 1896
Scott, William Lloyd (politician)	July 1, 1915
Scott, Zachary Thomson (or Thompson) (actor)	February 21, 1914
Scourby, Alexander (actor)	November 13, 1913
Scranton, William Warren (politician)	July 19, 1917
Scribner, Rob; born Robert Scribner (football)	April 9, 1951
Scruggs, Earl Eugene (music)	January 6, 1924
Scrugham, James Graves (politician)	January 19, 1880
Scully, Vin; born Vincent Edward Scully (sportscaster)	November 29, 1927
Seaman, Dick; born Richard John Beattie-Seaman (auto racing)	February 4, 1913
Sears, Ken (basketball)	August 17, 1933
Sears, Vic; born Victor W. Sears (football)	March 4, 1918
Seaton, Frederick Andrew (government)	December 11, 1909
Seaver, Tom; born George Thomas Seaver (baseball/sportscaster)	November 17, 1944
Sebastian, Dorothy (actress)	April 26, 1903
Sebastian, John B. (music)	March 17, 1944
Seberg, Jean Dorothy (actress)	November 13, 1938
Secombe, Harry (actor/comedian/singer)	September 8, 1921
Sedaka, Neil (singer/music)	March 13, 1939
Sedgman, Frank; born Francis Arthur Sedgman (tennis)	October 29, 1927

Seeger, Pete; born Peter R. Seeger (singer/music)	May 3, 1919
Segal, Erich Wolf (author)	June 16, 1937
Segal, George (actor)	February 13, 1934
Segal, Vivienne Sonia (actress/singer)	April 19, 1897
Segovia, Andrés (music)	February 17, 1893
Segura, Pancho; born Francisco Segura Cano (tennis)	June 20, 1921
Seibert, Earl Walter (hockey)	December 7, 1911
Seiling, Rodney Albert (hockey)	November 14, 1944
Seiple, Larry; born Lawrence Seiple (football)	February 14, 1945
Seixas, Vic; born Elias Victor Seixas (tennis)	August 30, 1923
Selby, Briton (hockey)	March 27, 1945
Seligman, Arthur (politician)	June 14, 1873
Selkirk, George Alexander (baseball)	January 4, 1908
Sellars, Elizabeth (actress)	May 6, 1923
Sellers, Peter (actor/director/producer)	September 8, 1925
Sellers, Ron; born Ronald Sellers (football)	February 5, 1947
Selvy, Frank; born Franklin Delano Selvy (basketball)	November 9, 1932
Selwart, Tonio; born Antonio Franz Thaeus Selmair-Selwart (actor)	June 9, 1896
Selznick, David O.; born David Oliver Selznick (producer)	May 10, 1902
Seminick, Andy; born Andrew Wasil Seminick (baseball)	September 12, 1920
Sendak, Maurice Bernard (author)	June 10, 1928
Senesky, George (basketball)	April 4, 1922
Sennett, Mack; born Michael Sinnott (director/producer)	January 17, 1884
Sensibaugh, Mike; born J. Michael Sensibaugh (football)	November 3, 1949
Sequi, Diego Pablo (baseball)	August 17, 1937
Serafin, Barry Duane (newscaster)	June 22, 1941
Serkin, Rudolph (music)	March 28, 1903
Serling, Rod (author)	December 25, 1924
Sernas, Jacques (actor/producer)	July 30, 1925
Sessions, Roger Huntington (music)	December 28, 1896
Seurat, Georges (artist)	December 2, 1859
Seuss, Dr.; born Theodor Seuss Geisel (author)	March 4, 1904
Sevareid, Eric; born Arnold Eric Sevareid (newscaster/journalist/author)	November 26, 1912
Severinsen, Doc; born Carl H. Severinsen (music)	July 7, 1927
Severson, Jeff; born Jeffrey Severson (football)	September 16, 1949
Sewall, Sumner (politician)	June 17, 1897
Sewell, Harley (football)	April 18, 1931
Sewell, Joe; born Joseph Wheeler Sewell (baseball)	October 9, 1898
Sewell, Luke; born James Luther Sewell (baseball)	January 5, 1901
Sewell, Rip; born Truett Banks Sewell (baseball)	April 7, 1921
Seyler, Athene; born Athene Hannen (actress)	May 31, 1889
Seymour, Anne; born Anne Seymour Eckert (actress)	September 11, 1909
Seymour, Dan (actor)	February 22, 1915
Seymour, Jane; born Joyce Frankenberg (actress)	February 15, 1951
Seymour, Paul (basketball)	January 30, 1928
Seymour, Paul (football)	February 6, 1950
Shaara, Michael Joseph, Jr. (author)	June 23, 1929
Shack, Edward (hockey)	February 11, 1937
Shafer, George F. (politician)	November 23, 1888

Shafer, Raymond Philip (politician)	March 5, 1917
Shafroth, John Franklin (politician)	June 9, 1854
Shah of Iran; born Mohammad Reza Pahlavi	October 26, 1919
Shakespeare, William (author/playwright)	———1564
Shalit, Gene (critic/TV host)	———1932
Shallenberger, Ashton Cokayne (politician)	December 23, 1862
Shamsky, Art; born Arthur Louis Shamsky (baseball)	October 14, 1941
Shankar, Ravi (music)	April 7, 1920
Shannon, Del; born Charles Westover (singer/music)	December 30, 1939
Shannon, James Coughlin (politician)	July 21, 1896
Shannon, Mike; born Thomas Michael Shannon (baseball)	July 15, 1939
Shannon, Peggy; (actress)	January 10, 1907
Shantz, Bobby; born Robert Clayton Shantz (baseball)	September 26, 1925
Shapiro, Karl Jay (poet)	November 10, 1913
Shapiro, Samuel Harvey (politician)	April 25, 1907
Shapp, Milton Jerrold (politician)	June 25, 1912
Share, Chuck; born Charlie Share (basketball)	March 14, 1927
Sharif, Omar; born Michael Shalhoub (actor)	April 10, 1932
Sharkey, Jack; born Josef Paul Zukauskas (or Cuckoschay) (boxing)	October 6, 1902
Sharma, Barbara (actress/singer/dancer)	September 14, 1942
Sharman, Bill (basketball)	May 25, 1926
Sharpe, Merrell Quentin (politician)	January 11, 1883
Shatner, William (actor)	March 22, 1931
Shaughnessy, Mickey (actor)	———1920
Shaute, Joe; born Joseph Benjamin Shaute (baseball)	August 1, 1899
Shaw, Artie; born Abraham Isaac Arshawsy (music)	May 23, 1910
Shaw, Billy; born William L. Shaw (football)	December 15, 1938
Shaw, Bob; born Robert John Shaw (baseball)	June 29, 1933
Shaw, George Bernard (playwright)	July 26, 1856
Shaw, Irwin (author)	February 27, 1913
Shaw, Leslie Mortier (politics/government)	November 2, 1848
Shaw, Reta (actress)	September 13, 1912
Shaw, Robert (actor/author)	August 9, 1925
Shaw, Robert Lawson (music)	April 30, 1916
Shaw, Sebastian (actor)	May 29, 1905
Shaw, Tom; born Thomas Shaw (golf)	December 13, 1942
Shaw, Wilbur; born Warren Wilbur Shaw (auto racing)	October 13, 1902
Shaw, Wini; born Winifred Lei Momi (singer/actress)	February 25, 1910
Shawkey, Bob; born James Robert Shawkey (baseball)	December 4, 1890
Shawlee, Joan (actress)	March 5, 1929
Shawn, Dick; born Richard Schulefand (comedian/actor)	December 1, 1929
Shay, Dorothy; born Dorothy Nell Sims (singer/actress)	April 11, 1921
Shearer, Moira; born Moira Shearer King (dancer/actress)	January 17, 1926
Shearer, Norma; born Edith Norma Shearer (actress)	August 10, 1900
Shearing, George Albert (music)	August 13, 1919
Sheely, Earl Homer (baseball)	February 12, 1893
Sheen, Bishop Fulton John (clergyman)	May 8, 1895
Sheen, Martin; born Ramon Estevez (actor)	August 3, 1940
Sheffield, Johnny; born John Sheffield (actor)	April 11, 1931
Shelby, Carroll (auto racing & manufacturer)	January 11, 1923

Sheldon, George Lawson (politician)   May 31, 1870
Shell, Art; born Arthur Shell (football)   November 26, 1946
Shelley, Barbara (actress)   ————1933
Shelley, Carole Augusta (actress)   August 16, 1939
Shelley, Percy Bysshe (poet)   August 4, 1792
Shepard, Alan Bartlett, Jr. (astronaut)   November 18, 1923
Shepard, Jean (singer)   November 21, 1933
Shepard, Sam (playwright/actor/music)   November 5, 1943
Shepherd, Cybill (actress/singer)   February 18, 1950
Sheppard, Morris (politician)   May 28, 1875
Shera, Mark (actor)   July 10, 1949
Sherdel, Bill; born William Henry Sherdel (baseball)   August 15, 1896
Sheridan, Ann; born Clara Lou Sheridan (actress)   February 21, 1915
Sheridan, Philip Henry (army officer)   March 6, 1831
Sheridan, Richard Brinsley (playwright)   October 30, 1751
Sherk, Jerry (football)   July 7, 1948
Sherman, Allan; born Allan Copelon (comedian/singer)   November 30, 1924
Sherman, Allie; born Alex Sherman (football)   February 10, 1923
Sherman, Bobby (singer/actor/music)   July 22, 1945
Sherman, James Schoolcraft (Vice President)   October 24, 1855
Sherman, John (statesman)   May 10, 1823
Sherman, Richard Morton (music)   June 12, 1921
Sherman, Robert Bernard (music)   December 19, 1925
Sherman, Roger (legislator)   April 19, 1721
Sherman, William Tecumseh (army officer)   February 8, 1820
Shero, Fred Alexander (hockey)   October 23, 1925
Sherriff, R.C.; born Robert Cedric Sherriff   June 6, 1896
    (playwright/author)
Sherwood, Madeleine; born Madeleine Thorton (actress)   November 13, 1926
Sherwood, Robert Emmet (playwright)   April 4, 1896
Sherwood, Roberta (singer/actress)   July 1, 1912
Shields, Brooke (actress)   May 31, 1965
Shields, John Knight (politician)   August 15, 1858
Shiegeta, James (actor)   ————1933
Shimkus, Joanna (actress)   October 10, 1944
Shinners, John Joseph (football)   March 1, 1947
Shinnick, Don; born Donald Shinnick (football)   May 15, 1935
Shipstead, Henrik (politician)   January 8, 1881
Shire, Talia; born Talia Rose Coppola (actress)   April 25, 1946
Shirley, Anne; born Dawn Evelyneen Paris (actress)   April 17, 1918
Shively, Benjamin Franklin (politician)   March 20, 1857
Shivers, Allan (politician)   October 5, 1907
Shoemaker, Ann Dorothea (actress)   January 10, 1891
Shoemaker, Willie; born William Lee Shoemaker (hockey)   August 19, 1931
Shofner, Del; born Delbert M. Shofner (football)   December 11, 1934
Sholtz, David (politician)   October 6, 1891
Shor, Toots; born Bernard Shor (restaurateur)   May 6, 1905
Shore, Dinah; born Frances Rose Shore (singer/TV host)   March 1, 1917
Shore, Eddie; born Edward William Shore (hockey)   November 25, 1902
Short, Bobby; born Robert Waltrip Short (singer/music)   September 15, 1926
Short, Chris; born Christopher Joseph Short (baseball)   September 19, 1937

Shortridge, Samuel Morgan (politician)	August 3, 1861
Shostakovich, Dmitri Dmitrievitch (music)	September 25, 1906
Shoup, Oliver Henry (politician)	December 13, 1869
Showalter, Max G. (actor/music)	June 2, 1917
Shrimpton, Jean (actress)	November 6, 1942
Shriver, Sargent; born Robert Sargent Shriver	November 9, 1915
(government/attorney)	
Shubert, J.J.; born Jacob Szemanski (producer)	August 15, 1878
Shubert, Lee; born Levi Szemanski (producer)	March 15, 1873
Shue, Gene (basketball)	December 18, 1931
Shula, Don; born Donald Francis Shula (football)	January 4, 1930
Shulman, Max (author)	March 14, 1919
Shull, Richard B. (actor)	February 24, 1929
Shultz, George Pratt (government)	December 13, 1920
Shute, Denny; born Herman Densmore Shute (golf)	October 25, 1904
Siani, Mike; born Michael Joseph Siani (football)	May 27, 1950
Sibelius, Jean Julius Christian (music)	December 8, 1865
Sidney, Sylvia; born Sophia Kosow (actress)	August 8, 1910
Siebern, Norm; born Norman Leroy Siebern (baseball)	July 26, 1933
Siebert, Babe; born Albert Charles Siebert (hockey)	January 14, 1904
Siebert, Dick; born Richard Walther Siebert (baseball)	February 19, 1912
Siebert, Sonny; born Wilfred Charles Siebert (baseball)	January 14, 1937
Siegfried, Larry (basketball)	May 22, 1939
Siemon, Jeff; born Jeffrey G. Siemon (football)	June 2, 1950
Sievers, Roy Edward (baseball)	November 18, 1926
Siffert, Jo (auto racing)	July 7, 1936
Sifford, Charles Luther (golf)	June 3, 1923
Sigler, Kim (politician)	May 2, 1894
Signoret, Simone; born Simone-Henriette-Charlotte Kaminker	March 25, 1921
(actress)	
Sikes, Dan; born Daniel D. Sikes (golf)	December 7, 1930
Sikes, R.H.; born Richard H. Sikes (golf)	March 6, 1940
Silas, Paul T. (basketball)	July 12, 1943
Sills, Beverly; born Belle Silverman (singer)	May 25, 1929
Silva, Henry (actor)	————1928
Silvera, Frank Alvin (actor)	July 24, 1914
Silverheels, Jay; born Harold J. Smith (actor)	May 26, 1919
Silvers, Phil; born Philip Silversmith (comedian/actor)	May 11, 1911
Silzer, George S. (politician)	April 14, 1870
Sim, Alastair (actor)	October 9, 1900
Simenon, Georges Joseph Christian (author)	February 13, 1903
Simmons, Al; born Aloysius Harry Szymanski (baseball)	May 22, 1902
Simmons, Connie (basketball)	March 15, 1925
Simmons, Curt; born Curtis Thomas Simmons (baseball)	May 19, 1929
Simmons, Donald (hockey)	September 13, 1931
Simmons, Furnifold McLendel (politician)	January 20, 1854
Simmons, Jean Merilyn (actress)	January 31, 1929
Simmons, Ted Lyle (baseball)	August 9, 1949
Simms, John F. (politician)	December 18, 1916
Simon, Carly (singer/music)	June 25, 1945
Simon, Neil; born Marvin Neil Simon (playwright)	July 4, 1927

Simon, Norton Winfred (business executive)	February 5, 1907
Simon, Paul Frederick (singer/music)	November 5, 1942
Simon, Simone (actress)	April 23, 1910
Simon, William Edward (government)	November 27, 1927
Simone, Nina; born Eunice Kathleen Waymon (singer)	February 21, 1933
Simpson, Adele; born Adele Smithline (fashion designer)	December 8, 1903
Simpson, Harry Leon "Suitcase" (baseball)	December 3, 1925
Simpson, Jim; born James Shores Simpson (sportscaster)	December 20, 1927
Simpson, Milward Lee (politician)	November 12, 1897
Simpson, O.J.; born Orenthal James Simpson	July 9, 1947
(football/sportscaster/actor)	
Simpson, Oramel Hinckley (politician)	March 20, 1870
Simpson, Ralph (basketball)	August 10, 1949
Sims, Duke; born Duane B. Sims (baseball)	June 5, 1941
Sims, Ginny; born Virginia Sims (singer)	May 25, 1916
Sinatra, Frank; born Francis Albert Sinatra (singer/actor)	December 12, 1915
Sinatra, Frank, Jr.; born Francis Wayne Sinatra	January 10, 1944
(singer/actor)	
Sinatra, Nancy, Jr.; born Nancy Sandra Sinatra	June 8, 1940
(singer/actress)	
Sinatra, Tina; born Christina Sinatra (actress)	June 20, 1948
Sinclair, Upton Beall (author)	September 20, 1878
Sinden, Donald (actor)	October 9, 1923
Singer, Bill; born William Robert Singer (baseball)	April 24, 1944
Singer, Isaac Bashevis (author)	July 14, 1904
Singleton, Ken; born Kenneth Wayne Singleton (baseball)	June 10, 1947
Singleton, Penny; born Mariana Dorothy Agnes Letitia McNulty	September 15, 1908
(actress)	
Sipe, Brian Winfield (football)	August 8, 1949
Sirica, John Joseph (jurist)	March 19, 1904
Sisler, Dick; born Richard Allen Sisler (baseball)	November 2, 1920
Sisler, George Harold (baseball)	March 24, 1893
Sisti, Sibby; born Sebastian Daniel Sisti (baseball)	July 26, 1920
Sistrunk, Manny; born Manuel Sistrunk (football)	June 16, 1947
Sistrunk, Otis (football)	September 18, 1947
Sitting Bull; born Tatanka Yotanka (Prairie Sioux	circa 1834
Indian Chief)	
Sizemore, Ted; born Theodore Crawford Sizemore (baseball)	April 15, 1945
Skala, Carole Jo; born Carole Jo Kabler (golf)	June 13, 1938
Skelton, Red; born Richard Bernard Skelton (comedian/actor)	July 18, 1913
Skinner, B.F.; born Burrhus Frederic Skinner	March 20, 1904
(psychologist)	
Skinner, Bob; born Robert Ralph Skinner (baseball)	October 3, 1931
Skinner, Cornelia Otis (actress)	May 30, 1901
Skinner, Otis (actor)	June 28, 1857
Skorich, Nick; born Nicholas L. Skorich (football)	June 26, 1921
Skov, Glen Frederick (hockey)	January 26, 1931
Skowron, Bill "Moose"; born William Joseph Skowron	December 18, 1930
(baseball)	
Slate, Jeremy (actor)	———1925
Slaton, John Marshall (politician)	December 25, 1866

Slaughter, Enos Bradsher (baseball)	April 27, 1916
Slaughter, Frank Giel (author)	February 25, 1908
Slayton, Deke; born Donald Kent Slayton (astronaut)	March 1, 1924
Sledge, Percy (singer)	———1940
Sleeper, Albert E. (politician)	December 31, 1862
Slezak, Walter Leo (actor/singer)	May 3, 1902
Slick, Grace Wing; born Grace Wing (singer)	October 30, 1939
Sloan, John (artist)	August 2, 1871
Sloan, Tod; born Aloysius Martin Sloan (hockey)	November 30, 1927
Sloane, Everett H. (actor)	October 1, 1909
Small, Len; born Lennington Small (politician)	June 16, 1862
Smalley, Roy Frederick, Jr. (baseball)	June 9, 1926
Smathers, George Armistead (politician)	November 14, 1913
Smetana, Bedrich Frederick (music)	March 2, 1824
Smith, Adrian (basketball)	October 5, 1936
Smith, Al; born Alfred John Smith (baseball)	October 12, 1907
Smith, Al; born Alphonse Eugene Smith (baseball)	February 7, 1928
Smith, Alexis; born Gladys Smith (actress)	June 8, 1921
Smith, Alfred Emanuel (politician)	December 30, 1873
Smith, Bessie (singer)	April 15, 1894
Smith, Billy Ray (football)	January 27, 1935
Smith, Bingo; born Bobby Smith (basketball)	February 26, 1946
Smith, Bob; born Robert Eldridge Smith (baseball)	April 22, 1898
Smith, Bubba; born Charles Aaron Smith (football)	February 28, 1945
Smith, Buffalo Bob; born Robert E. Smith (TV host)	November 27, 1917
Smith, C. Aubrey (actor)	July 21, 1863
Smith, Carl (singer/music)	March 15, 1927
Smith, Charles Manley (politician)	August 3, 1868
Smith, Charley; born Charles William Smith (baseball)	September 15, 1937
Smith, Clint; born Clinton James Smith (hockey)	December 12, 1913
Smith, Connie; born Constance Smith (singer)	August 14, 1941
Smith, Dallas (hockey)	October 10, 1941
Smith, Earl Sutton (baseball)	February 14, 1897
Smith, Ellison DuRant (politician)	August 1, 1864
Smith, Elmer John (baseball)	September 21, 1892
Smith, Elmo E. (politician)	November 19, 1909
Smith, Forrest (politician)	February 14, 1886
Smith, Gary Edward (hockey)	February 4, 1944
Smith, H. Alexander (politician)	January 30, 1880
Smith, Hal; born Harold Wayne Smith (baseball)	December 7, 1930
Smith, Hoke (politician)	September 2, 1855
Smith, Hooley; born Reginald Joseph Smith (hockey)	January 7, 1905
Smith, Horton (golf)	May 22, 1908
Smith, Howard K.; born Howard Kingsbury Smith (newscaster)	May 12, 1914
Smith, Hulett Carlson (politician)	October 21, 1918
Smith, J.D. (football)	July 19, 1932
Smith, Jack; born John Smadt (baseball)	June 23, 1895
Smith, Jackie Larue (football)	February 23, 1940
Smith, Jaclyn Ellen (actress)	October 26, 1947
Smith, Jerry T. (football)	July 19, 1943
Smith, John (colonist)	———1580

Smith, John; born Robert E. Van Orden (actor)	March 6, 1931
Smith, John Walter (politician)	February 5, 1845
Smith, Kate; born Kathryn Elizabeth Smith (singer)	May 1, 1909
Smith, Keely; born Dorothy Jacqueline Keely (singer)	March 9, 1931
Smith, Kenneth Alvin (hockey)	May 8, 1924
Smith, Kent; born Frank Kent Smith (actor)	March 19, 1907
Smith, Maggie; born Margaret Smith (actress/singer)	December 28, 1934
Smith, Marcus Aurelius (politician)	January 24, 1851
Smith, Margaret (golf)	September 28, 1936
Smith, Margaret Chase; born Margaret Chase (politician)	December 14, 1897
Smith, Marilynn Louise (golf)	April 13, 1929
Smith, Nels Hansen (politician)	August 27, 1884
Smith, Norman (hockey)	March 18, 1908
Smith, O.C.; born Ocie Lee Smith (singer)	June 21, 1932
Smith, Oliver (producer/designer)	February 13, 1918
Smith, Patricia Harlan (actress)	February 20, 1930
Smith, Paul (football)	August 13, 1945
Smith, Preston Earnest (politician)	March 8, 1912
Smith, Randy (basketball)	December 12, 1948
Smith, Reggie; born Carl Reginald Smith (baseball)	April 2, 1945
Smith, Roger (actor/producer)	December 18, 1932
Smith, Ron; born Ronald Smith (football)	May 3, 1943
Smith, Ronald Floyd (hockey)	May 16, 1935
Smith, Sandra (actress)	June 27, 1940
Smith, Sherry; born Sherrod Malone Smith (baseball)	February 18, 1891
Smith, Sid; born Sidney James Smith (hockey)	July 11, 1925
Smith, Stan; born Stanley Roger Smith (tennis)	December 19, 1946
Smith, Tody; born Lawrence E. Smith (football)	December 24, 1948
Smith, William Alden (politician)	May 12, 1859
Smith, William Emmett, II (actor)	March 24, 1933
Smith, Willis (politician)	December 19,1887
Smithers, William (actor)	July 10, 1927
Smoot, Reed (politician)	January 10, 1862
Smothers, Dick; born Richard Smothers (comedian/actor)	November 20, 1939
Smothers, Tom; born Thomas Bolyn Smothers, 3rd (comedian/actor)	February 2, 1937
Smylie, Robert E. (politician)	October 31, 1914
Snead, J.C. born Jesse Carlyle Snead (golf)	October 14, 1941
Snead, Norm; born Norman B. Snead (football)	July 31, 1939
Snead, Sam; born Samuel Jackson Snead (golf)	May 27, 1912
Sneed, Ed; born Edgar Sneed (golf)	August 6, 1944
Snell, Earl Wilcox (politician)	July 11, 1895
Snell, Matt; born Mathews Snell (football)	August 18, 1941
Snelling, Richard Arkwright (politician)	February 18, 1927
Sneva, Tom; born Thomas Edsol Sneva (auto racing)	June 1, 1948
Snider, Duke; born Edwin Donald Snider (baseball)	September 19, 1926
Snodgress, Carrie (actress)	October 27, 1946
Snow, C.P.; born Charles Percy Snow (author)	October 15, 1905
Snow, Charles Wilbert (politician)	April 6, 1884
Snow, Hank; born Clarence Eugene Snow (singer/music)	May 9, 1914
Snow, Jack T. (football)	January 25, 1943

Snyder, Dick (basketball)	February 1, 1944
Snyder, Frank Elton (baseball)	May 27, 1893
Snyder, John Wesley (government)	June 21, 1895
Snyder, Russ; born Russell Henry Snyder (baseball)	June 22, 1934
Snyder, Tom (newscaster/TV host)	May 12, 1936
Solomon, Freddie (football)	January 11, 1953
Solomon, Harold Charles (tennis)	September 17, 1952
Solters, Moose; born Julius Joseph Soltesz (baseball)	March 22, 1906
Solzhenitsyn, Aleksandr Isayevich (author)	December 11, 1918
Somers, Brett (actress)	July 11, 1927
Somers, Suzanne; born Suzanne Marie Mahoney (actress)	October 16, 1948
Sommars, Julie Sergie (actress)	April 15, 1942
Sommer, Elke; born Elke Schletz (actress/artist)	November 5, 1941
Sommers, Joanie; born Joanie Drost (singer/actress)	————1941
Sondergaard, Gale; born Edith Holm Sondergaard (actress)	February 15, 1899
Sondheim, Stephen Joshua (music)	March 22, 1930
Sontag, Susan (author)	January 28, 1933
Soo, Jack; born Goro Suzuki (actor/singer/comedian)	October 28, 1915
Sorel, Louis (actress)	————1944
Sorenson, Theodore Chaikin (government/attorney)	May 8, 1928
Sorlie, Arthur Gustav (politician)	April 26, 1874
Sorrell, John Arthur (hockey)	January 16, 1906
Sorvino, Paul (actor)	————1939
Souchak, Mike; born Michael Souchak (golf)	May 10, 1927
Soul, David; born David Solberg (actor/singer)	August 28, 1943
Sousa, John Philip (music)	November 16, 1854
Southern, Ann; born Harriette Lake (actress/singer)	January 22, 1909
Southworth, Billy; born William Harrison Southworth (baseball)	March 9, 1893
Spaak, Catherine (actress)	April 4, 1945
Spacek, Sissy; born Mary Elizabeth Spacek (actress)	December 25, 1949
Spahn, Warren Edward (baseball)	April 23, 1921
Spang, Laurette (actress)	May 16, 1951
Spangler, Al; born Albert Donald Spangler (baseball)	July 8, 1933
Spark, Muriel; born Muriel Sarah Camberg (author)	February 1, 1918
Sparkman, John Jackson (politician)	December 20, 1899
Sparks, Chauncey (politician)	October 8, 1884
Sparks, John (politician)	August 30, 1843
Sparks, Randy (singer/music)	July 29, 1933
Sparv, Camilla (actress)	————1943
Spaulding, Huntley Nowell (politician)	October 30, 1869
Spaulding, Rolland Harty (politician)	March 15, 1873
Speaker, Tris; born Tristam E. Speaker (baseball)	April 4, 1888
Speedie, Mac (football)	January 12, 1920
Speier, Chris Edward (baseball)	June 28, 1950
Spelling, Aaron (producer)	April 22, 1925
Spellman, Cardinal Francis Joseph (clergyman)	May 4, 1889
Spencer, Daryl Dean (baseball)	July 13, 1929
Spencer, Herbert (philosopher)	April 27, 1820
Spencer, Jim; born James Lloyd Spencer (baseball)	July 30, 1947
Spencer, Selden Palmer (politician)	September 16, 1862

Spenser, Edmund (poet)	circa 1522
Spiegel, Sam (producer)	November 11, 1903
Spillane, Mickey; born Frank Morrison Spillane (author)	March 9, 1918
Spinks, Leon (boxing)	July 11, 1953
Spinoza, Baruch (philosopher)	November 24, 1632
Spitz, Mark Andrew (swimming)	February 10, 1950
Spivak, Lawrence Edmund (producer/TV moderator)	June 11, 1900
Spock, Benjamin McLane (medicine)	May 2, 1903
Spong, William Belsen, Jr. (politician)	September 29, 1920
Sprague, Charles Arthur (politician)	November 12, 1887
Springfield, Dusty; born Mary Isobel Catherine O'Brien (singer)	April 16, 1939
Springsteen, Bruce (singer/music)	September 23, 1949
Sprinkle, Ed; born Edward A. Sprinkle (football)	September 3, 1923
Sproul, William Cameron (politician)	September 16, 1870
Spry, William (politician)	January 11, 1864
Spurrier, Steve; born Steven Orr Spurrier (football)	April 20, 1945
Spuzich, Sandra Ann (golf)	April 3, 1937
Stabler, Ken; born Kenneth Michael Stabler (football)	December 25, 1946
Stack, Robert Langford; born Robert Modini (actor)	January 13, 1919
Stacy, Hollis (golf)	March 16, 1954
Stacy, James (actor)	December 23———
Stafford, Jo (singer)	November 12, 1918
Stafford, Robert Theodore (politician)	August 8, 1913
Stafford, Thomas Patton (astronaut)	September 17, 1930
Stagg, Amos Alonzo (football)	August 16, 1862
Staggers, Jon; born Jonathan L. Staggers (football)	December 14, 1948
Stahl, Lesley R. (newscaster)	December 16, 1941
Stainback, Tuck; born George Tucker Stainback (baseball)	August 4, 1910
Staley, Gerry; born Gerald Lee Staley (baseball)	August 21, 1920
Stalin, Joseph Vissarionovich; born Iosif Vissarionovich Dzhugashvili (Russian government)	December 21, 1879
Stallings, Larry; born Lawrence Stallings (football)	December 11, 1941
Stallone, Sylvester Enzio; (or born Michael Sylvester Stallone) (actor/writer/director)	July 6, 1946
Stallworth, John Lee (football)	July 15, 1952
Stamp, Terence (actor)	July 22, 1940
Stanbach, Haskel (football)	March 19, 1952
Stander, Lionel Jay (actor)	January 11, 1908
Standish, Myles (colonist)	circa 1584
Stanfield, Frederic William (hockey)	May 4, 1944
Stanfield, Robert Nelson (politician)	July 9, 1877
Stanfill, Bill; born William T. Stanfill (football)	January 13, 1947
Stanford, Rawghlie Clement (politician)	August 2, 1879
Stang, Arnold (actor)	September 28, 1925
Stanis, BernNadette (actress)	December 22, 1953
Stanislavski; born Konstantin Sergeryevich Alekseyev (actor/producer)	January 17, 1863
Stanky, Eddie; born Edward Raymond Stanky (baseball)	September 3, 1916
Stanley, Allan Herbert (hockey)	March 1, 1926
Stanley, Augustus Owsley (politician)	May 21, 1867

Stanley, Sir Henry Morton; born John Rowlands (explorer)	January 28, 1841
Stanley, Kim; born Patricia Kimberly Reid (actress)	February 11, 1921
Stanley, Mickey; born Mitchell Jack Stanley (baseball)	July 20, 1942
Stanley, Thomas Bahnson (politician)	July 16, 1890
Stanowski, Wally; born Walter Peter Stanowski (hockey)	April 28, 1919
Stans, Maurice Hubert (government)	March 22, 1908
Stanton, Edwin McMasters (statesman/jurist)	December 19, 1814
Stanwyck, Barbara; born Ruby Stevens (actress)	July 16, 1907
Stapleton, Jean; born Jeanne Murray (actress)	January 19, 1923
Stapleton, Maureen; born Lois Maureen Stapleton (actress)	June 21, 1925
Stapleton, Pat; born Patrick James Stapleton (hockey)	July 4, 1940
Starbuck, JoJo; born Alicia Jo Starbuck (ice skating)	February 14, 1951
Stargell, Willie; born Wilver Dornel Stargell (baseball)	March 6, 1940
Stark, Lloyd Crow (politician)	November 23, 1886
Starke, Pauline (actress)	January 10, 1900
Starr, Bart; born Bryan Bartlett Starr (football)	January 9, 1934
Starr, Frances (actress)	June 6, 1886
Starr, Kay; born Kathryn Stark (singer)	July 21, 1922
Starr, Ringo; born Richard Starkey (singer/music)	July 7, 1940
Starrett, Charles (actor)	March 28, 1903
Stasiuk, Victor John (hockey)	May 23, 1929
Stassen, Harold Edward (politics/government)	April 13, 1907
Staub, Rusty; born Daniel Joseph Staub (baseball)	April 4, 1944
Staubach, Roger Thomas (football)	February 5, 1942
Stautner, Ernie; born Ernest Stautner (football)	April 2, 1925
Steber, Eleanor (singer)	July 17, 1916
Steel, Anthony (actor)	May 21, 1920
Steele, Bob; born Robert North Bradbury, Jr. (actor)	January 23, 1906
Steele, Tommy; born Thomas Hicks (singer/actor)	December 17, 1936
Stegner, Wallace Earle (author)	Febuary 18, 1909
Steiger, Rod; born Rodney Stephen Steiger (actor)	April 14, 1925
Stein, Bob; born Robert Stein (football)	January 22, 1948
Stein, Gertrude (author)	February 3, 1874
Stein, Joseph (playwright)	May 30, 1912
Stein, Jules Caesar (corporation executive)	April 26, 1896
Steinbeck, John Ernst (author)	February 27, 1902
Steinberg, David (comedian)	August 9, 1942
Steinem, Gloria Marie (feminist/journalist/editor)	March 25, 1934
Steiwer, Frederick (politician)	October 13, 1883
Stelle, John J. (politician)	August 10, 1891
Stemkowski, Peter David (hockey)	August 25, 1943
Sten, Anna; born Anjuschka Stenski Sujakevitch (actress)	December 3, 1907
Stenerud, Jan (football)	November 26, 1942
Stengel, Casey; born Charles Dillon Stengel (baseball)	July 30, 1891
Stenmark, Ingemar (skiing)	March 18, 1956
Stennett, Rennie; born Renaldo Antonio Stennett (baseball)	April 5, 1951
Stennis, John Cornelius (politician)	August 3, 1901
Stephens, Alexander Hamilton (statesman)	February 11, 1812
Stephens, Gene; born Glen Eugene Stephens (baseball)	January 20, 1933
Stephens, Hubert Durrett (politician)	July 2, 1875
Stephens, Vern; born Vernon Decatur Stephens (baseball)	October 23, 1920

188   THE CELEBRITY BIRTHDAY BOOK

Stephens, William Dennison (politician)	December 26, 1859
Stephenson, Isaac (politician)	June 18, 1829
Stephenson, Jan Lynn (golf)	December 22, 1951
Stephenson, Riggs; born Jackson Riggs Stephenson (baseball)	January 5, 1898
Sterling, Jan; born Jane Sterling Adriance (actress)	April 3, 1923
Sterling, Robert; born William Sterling Hart (actor)	November 13, 1917
Sterling, Ross Shaw (politician)	February 11, 1875
Sterling, Thomas (politician)	February 21, 1851
Sterling, Tisha; born Patricia Ann Sterling (actress)	December 10, 1944
Stern, Isaac (music)	July 21, 1920
Stettinhius, Edward Reilly, Jr. (government)	October 22, 1900
Stevens, Andrew (actor)	June 10, 1955
Stevens, April (singer)	April 29, 1936
Stevens, Cat; born Steven Demetre Georgiou (singer/music)	July 21, 1947
Stevens, Connie; born Concetta Ann Ingolia (singer/actress)	August 8, 1938
Stevens, Craig; born Gail Hughes Shikles, Jr. (actor)	July 8, 1918
Stevens, George Cooper (director)	December 18, 1904
Stevens, Inger; born Inger Stensland (actress)	October 18, 1934
Stevens, John Paul (jurist)	April 20, 1920
Stevens, K.T.; born Gloria Wood (actress)	July 20, 1919
Stevens, Kaye; born Catherine Stevens, (singer/actress)	July 21, 1933
Stevens, Mark; born Richard Stevens (actor)	December 13, 1915
Stevens, Onslow; born Onslow Ford Stevenson (actor)	March 29, 1902
Stevens, Paul; born Paul Steven Gattoni (actor)	June 17, 1924
Stevens, Ray; born Harold Ray Ragsdale (singer/music)	January 24, 1939
Stevens, Risë; born Risë Steenberg (singer/actress)	June 11, 1913
Stevens, Roger L.; born Roger Lacey Stevens (producer)	March 12, 1910
Stevens, Stella; born Estelle Eggleston (actress)	October 1, 1936
Stevens, Ted; born Theodore Fulton Stevens (politician)	November 18, 1923
Stevens, Wallace (poet)	October 2, 1879
Stevens, Warren (actor)	November 2, 1919
Stevenson, Adlai Ewing (Vice President)	October 23, 1835
Stevenson, Adlai Ewing (politics/government)	February 5, 1900
Stevenson, Adlai Ewing, III (politician)	October 10, 1930
Stevenson, Chuck; born Charles Stevenson (auto racing)	October 15, 1919
Stevenson, Coke Robert (politician)	March 20, 1888
Stevenson, McLean (actor)	November 14, 1930
Stevenson, Parker; born Richard Stevenson Parker (actor)	June 4, 1952
Stevenson, Robert Louis Balfour (author)	November 13, 1850
Stewart, Bud; born Edward Perry Stewart (baseball)	June 15, 1916
Stewart, Elaine; born Elsy Steinberg (actress)	May 31, 1929
Stewart, Gaye; born James Gaye Stewart (hockey)	June 28, 1923
Stewart, Jack; born John Sherratt Stewart (hockey)	May 6, 1917
Stewart, Jackie; born John Young Stewart (auto racing/ sportscaster)	June 11, 1939
Stewart, James Maitland "Jimmy" (actor)	May 20, 1908
Stewart, Lefty; born Walter Cleveland Stewart (baseball)	September 23, 1900
Stewart, Martha; born Martha Haworth (singer/actress)	October 7, 1922
Stewart, Michael; born Michael Stewart Rubin (playwright)	August 1, 1929
Stewart, Nelson (hockey)	December 29, 1902
Stewart, Paul; born Paul Sternberg (actor)	March 13, 1908

Stewart, Potter (jurist)   January 23, 1915
Stewart, Rod; born Roderick David Stewart (singer/music)   January 10, 1945
Stewart, Ronald George (hockey)   July 11, 1932
Stewart, Samuel Vernon (politician)   August 2, 1872
Stewart, Tom (politician)   January 11, 1892
Stewart, Trish (actress)   June 14,————
Stickney, Dorothy (actress)   June 21, 1900
Stickney, William Wallace (politician)   March 21, 1853
Stiers, David Odgen (actor)   October 31, 1942
Still, Ken; born Kenneth Alan Still (golf)   February 12, 1935
Stiller, Jerry; born Gerald Stiller (comedian/actor)   June 8, 1928
Stills, Stephen (singer/music)   January 3, 1945
Stimson, Henry Lewis (government)   September 21, 1867
Stirling, Linda; born Louise Schultz (actress)   October 11, 1921
Stirnweiss, Snuffy; born George Henry Stirnweiss (baseball)   October 26, 1918
Stobbs, Chuck; born Charles Klein Stobbs (baseball)   July 2, 1929
Stock, Milt; born Milton Joseph Stock (baseball)   July 11, 1893
Stockton, Dave; born David Knapp Stockton (golf)   November 2, 1941
Stockton, Dick; born Richard LaClede Stockton (tennis)   February 18, 1951
Stockwell, Dean; born Robert Dean Stockwell (actor)   March 5, 1936
Stockwell, Guy (actor)   November 16, 1934
Stokes, Edward Casper (politician)   December 22, 1860
Stokowski, Leopold; born Leopold Boleslawawicz Antoni   April 18, 1882
    Stanislaw Stokowski (music)
Stolle, Fred; born Frederick S. Stolle (tennis)   October 8, 1938
Stone, Beth; born Elizabeth Stone (golf)   May 15, 1940
Stone, Ezra Chaim; born Ezra Chaim Feinstone (actor/producer/   December 2, 1917
    director)
Stone, Harlan Fiske (government/jurist)   October 11, 1872
Stone, Harold J. (actor)   ————1911
Stone, I.F.; born Isidor Feinstein Stone (journalist)   December 24, 1907
Stone, Irving; born Irving Tennenbaum (author)   July 14, 1903
Stone, John Thomas (baseball)   October 10, 1905
Stone, Lewis Shepard (actor)   November 15, 1879
Stone, Milburn; born Hugh Milburn Stone (actor)   July 5, 1904
Stone, Richard Bernard (politician)   September 22, 1928
Stone, Sly; born Sylvester Stewart (music)   March 15, 1943
Stone, William Joel (politician)   May 7, 1848
Stoppard, Tom; born Thomas Straussler (playwright)   July 3, 1937
Storch, Larry; born Lawrence Samuel Storch (actor)   January 8, 1923
Storm, Gale; born Josephine Owaissa Cottle (actress/singer)   April 5, 1921
Stottlemyre, Mel; born Melvin Leon Stottlemyre (baseball)   November 13, 1941
Stout, Rex Todhunter (author)   December 1, 1886
Stovall, Jerry L. (football)   April 30, 1941
Stöve, Betty (tennis)   June 24, 1945
Stowe, Harriet Beecher; born Harriet Elizabeth Beecher   June 14, 1811
    (author)
Straight, Beatrice Whitney (actress)   August 2, 1916
Stram, Hank; born Henry Louis Stram (football/sportscaster)   January 3, 1923
Strasberg, Lee (director/actor)   November 17, 1901
Strasberg, Susan Elizabeth (actress)   May 22, 1938

Strassman, Marcia (actress/singer)	April 28, 1948
Stratton, William Grant (politician)	February 26, 1914
Straub, Robert William (politician)	May 6, 1920
Straus, Oscar (music)	March 6, 1870
Straus, Oscar Solomon (government)	December 23, 1850
Strauss, Johann (music)	October 25, 1825
Strauss, Peter (actor)	February 20, 1947
Strauss, Richard (music)	June 11, 1864
Strauss, Robert; born Henry Robert Strauss (actor)	November 8, 1913
Stravinsky, Igor Fedorovich (music)	June 18, 1882
Streep, Meryl; born Mary Louise Streep (actress)	June 22, 1949
Streisand, Barbra, born Barbara Joan Streisand (singer/actress)	April 24, 1942
Stribling, T.S.; born Thomas Sigismund Stribling (author)	March 4, 1881
Strickland, George Bevan (baseball)	January 10, 1926
Strinberg, August (playwright)	January 22, 1849
Stringbean; born David Akeman (singer/comedian/music)	June 17, 1915
Stripp, Joe; born Joseph Valentine Stripp (baseball)	February 3, 1903
Stritch, Elaine (actress/singer)	February 2, 1925
Strock, Don; born Donald J. Strock (football)	November 27, 1950
Strode, Woody; born Woodrow Wilson Strode (actor)	July 25, 1914
Strong, Ken; born Elmer Kenneth Strong (football)	August 6, 1906
Strong, Michael (actor)	February 8, 1918
Stroud, Don (actor)	—————1937
Strouse, Charles Louis (music)	June 7, 1928
Strudwick, Shepperd (actor)	September 22, 1907
Struthers, Sally Ann (actress)	July 28, 1948
Stuart, Dick; born Richard Lee Stuart (baseball)	November 7, 1932
Stuart, Edwin Sydney (politician)	December 28, 1853
Stuart, Gilbert Charles (artist)	December 3, 1755
Stuart, Gloria; born Gloria Stuart Finch (actress)	July 14, 1909
Stuart, Henry Carter (politician)	January 18, 1855
Stuart, Jeb; born James Ewell Brown Stuart (confederate officer)	February 6, 1833
Stubbs, Walter Roscoe (politician)	November 7, 1858
Studstill, Pat; born Patrick L. Studstill (football)	June 4, 1938
Stukes, Charlie; born Charles Stukes (football)	September 13, 1943
Stydahar, Joe; born Joseph Leo Stydahar (football)	March 17, 1912
Styne, Jule; born Julius Kerwin Stein (music/producer)	December 31, 1905
Styron, William Clark, Jr. (author)	June 11, 1925
Sudakis, Bill; born William Paul Sudakis (baseball)	March 27, 1946
Suder, Peter (baseball)	April 16, 1916
Suggs, Louise (golf)	September 7, 1923
Suhr, Gus; born August Richard Suhr (baseball)	January 3, 1906
Sullavan, Margaret Brooke (actress)	May 16, 1909
Sullivan, Sir Arthur Seymour (music)	May 13, 1842
Sullivan, Barry; born Patrick Francis Barry (actor)	August 29, 1912
Sullivan, Billy; born William Joseph Sullivan, Jr. (baseball)	October 23, 1910
Sullivan, Ed; born Edward Vincent Sullivan (TV host/journalist)	September 28, 1902

Sullivan, Francis L.; born Francis Loftus Sullivan (actor)	January 6, 1903
Sullivan, Frank; born Francis John Sullivan (humorist)	September 22, 1892
Sullivan, Frank; born Franklin Leal Sullivan (baseball)	January 23, 1930
Sullivan, John L.; born John Lawrence Sullivan (boxing)	October 15, 1858
Sullivan, Pat; born Patrick J. Sullivan (football)	January 18, 1950
Sullivan, Red; born George James Sullivan (hockey)	December 24, 1929
Sullivan, Silky; born Cynthia Jan Sullivan (golf)	September 15, 1937
Sullivan, Susan (actress)	November 18———
Sullivan, Tom; born Thomas Sullivan (football)	March 5, 1950
Sulzberger, Arthur Ochs (publisher)	February 5, 1926
Sumac, Yma; born Emperatriz Chavarri (singer)	September 10, 1922
Summa, Homer Wayne (baseball)	November 3, 1898
Summer, Donna; born LaDonna Andrea Gaines (singer)	December 31, 1948
Summerall, Pat; born George Summerall (football/sportscaster)	May 10, 1930
Summerfield, Arthur Ellsworth (government)	March 17, 1899
Summerville, Slim; born George J. Summerville (actor)	July 10, 1892
Sumner, Charles (statesman)	January 6, 1811
Surtees, John (auto racing)	February 11, 1934
Susann, Jacqueline (author)	August 20, 1921
Susskind, David Howard (TV host/producer)	December 19, 1920
Sutherland, Donald (actor)	July 17, 1934
Sutherland, Doug; born Douglas Sutherland (football)	April 1, 1948
Sutherland, Gary Lynn (baseball)	September 27, 1944
Sutherland, George (jurist)	March 25, 1862
Sutherland, Joan (singer)	November 7, 1926
Sutorius, James (actor)	December 14, 1944
Sutton, Don; born Donald Howard Sutton (baseball)	April 2, 1945
Sutton, Len (auto racing)	August 9, 1925
Suzman, Janet (actress)	February 9, 1939
Suzuki, Pat; born Chiyoko Suzuki (actress)	September 23, 1931
Suzy; born Aileen Elder (journalist)	———1919
Svare, Harland (football)	November 15, 1930
Svenson, Bo (actor)	February 13, 1941
Swain, Mack (actor)	February 16, 1876
Swainson, John Burley (politician)	July 30, 1925
Swann, Lynn Curtis (football)	March 7, 1952
Swanson, Claude Augustus (politics/government)	March 31, 1862
Swanson, Gloria; born Gloria Josephine May Swenson (actress)	March 27, 1897
Swarthout, Gladys (singer/actress)	December 25, 1904
Swayze, John Cameron (newscaster)	April 4, 1906
Sweeney, Walt; born Walter Francis Sweeney (football)	April 18, 1941
Sweet, Blanche; born Sarah Blanche Sweet (or Daphne Wayne) (actress)	June 18, 1896
Sweet, Dolph; born Adolphus Jean Sweet (actor/director)	July 18, 1920
Sweet, Joe; born Joseph Sweet (football)	July 5, 1948
Sweet, William Ellery (politician)	January 27, 1869
Sweikert, Bob; born Robert Sweikert (auto racing)	May 20, 1926
Swenson, Inga (actress/singer)	December 29, 1932
Swenson, Karl (actor)	July 23, 1908

Swenson, Swen (actor)	January 23, 1932
Swift, Bob; born Robert Virgil Swift (baseball)	March 6, 1915
Swift, Doug; born Douglas Swift (football)	October 24, 1948
Swift, Jonathan (clergyman/writer)	November 30, 1667
Swigert, John Leonard, Jr. (astronaut)	August 30, 1931
Swinburne, Algernon Charles (poet)	April 5, 1837
Swinburne, Nora (actress)	July 24, 1902
Swit, Loretta (actress)	November 4, 1939
Swoboda, Ron; born Ronald Alan Swoboda (baseball)	June 30, 1944
Sykes, Brenda (actress)	June 25————
Sylvester, William (actor)	January 31, 1922
Symington, Stuart; born William Stuart Symington (politician)	June 26, 1901
Syms, Sylvia (actress)	January 6, 1934
Synge, John Millington (playwright)	April 16, 1871
Syzmanski, Dick; born Richard Syzmanski (football)	November 7, 1932

T

Tabor, Jim; born James Reubin Tabor (baseball)	November 5, 1913
Tabori, Kristoffer; born Christopher Donald Siegel (actor)	August 4, 1952
Taft, Nellie; born Helen Herron (First Lady)	June 2, 1861
Taft, Robert Alphonso (First family/politician)	September 8, 1889
Taft, Robert Alphonso, Jr. (politician)	February 26, 1917
Taft, William Howard (President)	September 15, 1857
Talbert, Billy; born William Franklin Talbert, III (tennis)	September 4, 1918
Talbert, Diron (football)	July 1, 1944
Talbot, Jean Guy (hockey)	July 11, 1932
Talbot, Lyle; born Lysle Henderson (actor)	February 8, 1904
Talbot, Nita; born Nita Sokol (actress)	August 8, 1930
Taliaferro, James Piper (politician)	September 30, 1847
Taliaferro, Mike; born Myron E. Taliaferro (football)	July 26, 1941
Tallchief, Maria; born Elizabeth Marie Tallchief (dancer)	January 24, 1925
Talleyrand-Perigord, Charles Maurice de (French diplomatist)	February 13, 1754
Talmadge, Constance (comedienne/actress)	April 19, 1899
Talmadge, Eugene (politician)	September 23, 1884
Talmadge, Herman Eugene (politician)	August 9, 1913
Talmadge, Natalie (actress)	April 29, 1898
Talmadge, Norma (actress)	May 26, 1897
Talman, William Whitney (actor)	February 4, 1915
Tamblyn, Russ (actor)	December 30, 1934
Tamiroff, Akim (actor)	October 29, 1899
Tanana, Frank Daryl (baseball)	July 3, 1953
Tandy, Jessica (actress)	June 7, 1909
Taney, Roger Brooke (jurist)	March 17, 1777
Tanner, Chuck; born Charles William Tanner (baseball)	July 4, 1929
Tanner, Roscoe; born Leonard Roscoe Tanner, III (tennis)	October 15, 1951
Tanner, Tony (actor)	July 27, 1932
Tarasovic, George K. (football)	May 6, 1930
Tarkenton, Fran; born Francis Asbury Tarkenton (football/sportscaster)	February 3, 1940

Tarkington, Booth; born Newton Booth Tarkington (author)	July 29, 1869
Tashman, Lilyan; born Lillian Tashman (actress)	October 23, 1899
Tasso, Torquato (poet)	March 11, 1544
Tate, Sharon (actress)	———1943
Tatum, Jack; born John David Tatum (football)	November 18, 1948
Tawes, J. Millard; born John Millard Tawes (politician)	April 8, 1894
Tayback, Vic; born Victor Tabback (actor)	January 6, 1930
Taylor, Alfred Alexander (politician)	August 6, 1848
Taylor, Altie (football)	September 29, 1947
Taylor, Bruce L. (football)	May 28, 1948
Taylor, Charley; born Charles Robert Taylor (football)	September 28, 1941
Taylor, Danny; born Daniel Turney Taylor (baseball)	December 23, 1900
Taylor, Deems; born Joseph Deems Taylor (music)	December 22, 1885
Taylor, Don (actor/director)	December 13, 1920
Taylor, Dub; born Walter C. Taylor, Jr. (actor)	———1907
Taylor, Elizabeth Rosemond (actress)	February 27, 1932
Taylor, Estelle; born Estelle Boyland (actress)	May 20, 1899
Taylor, Glen Hearst (politician)	April 12, 1904
Taylor, Hugh (football)	July 6, 1923
Taylor, James Vernon (singer/music)	March 12, 1948
Taylor, Jim; born James Charles Taylor (football)	September 20, 1935
Taylor, June (dancer/choreographer)	———1918
Taylor, Kent; born Louis William John Henry Von Weiss (actor)	May 11, 1906
Taylor, Lionel Thomas (football)	August 15, 1936
Taylor, Margaret Mackall Smith; born Margaret Mackall Smith (First Lady)	September 21, 1788
Taylor, Maxwell Davenport (army officer)	August 26, 1901
Taylor, Otis (football)	August 11, 1942
Taylor, Paul Belville, Jr. (dancer/choreographer)	July 29, 1930
Taylor, Robert; born Spangler Arlington Brugh (actor)	August 5, 1911
Taylor, Robert Lewis (author/journalist)	September 24, 1912
Taylor, Robert Love (politician)	July 31, 1850
Taylor, Rod; born Robert Stuart Taylor (actor)	January 11, 1929
Taylor, Roosevelt (football)	July 4, 1938
Taylor, Ruth (comedienne/actress)	January 13———
Taylor, Samuel Albert (playwright)	June 13, 1912
Taylor, Tony; born Antonio Nemesio Taylor (baseball)	December 19, 1935
Taylor, Trevor Patrick (auto racing)	December 26, 1936
Taylor, William James (hockey)	May 3, 1919
Taylor, Zachary (President)	November 24, 1784
Taylor, Zack; born James Wren Taylor (baseball)	July 27, 1898
Taylor-Young, Leigh (actress)	January 25, 1944
Tchaikovsky, Peter; born Pëtr Ilich Tchaikovksy (music)	May 7, 1840
Teagarden, Jack; born Weldon John Teagarden (music)	August 20, 1905
Teague, Marshall (auto racing)	May 22, 1921
Teasdale, Joseph Patrick (politician)	March 29, 1936
Teasdale, Sara (poet)	August 8, 1884
Teasdale, Verree (actress)	March 15, 1904
Tebbetts, Birdie; born George Robert Tebbetts (baseball)	November 10, 1909
Teicher, Louis (music—Ferrante and Teicher)	August 24, 1924
Temple, Johnny; born John Ellis Temple (baseball)	August 8, 1928

Temple, Shirley Jane (actress/government)	April 23, 1928
Templeton, Charles Augustus (politician)	March 4, 1871
Tempo, Nino (singer)	January 6, 1937
Tenace, Gene; born Fiore Gino Tennaci (baseball)	October 10, 1946
Tener, John Kinley (politician)	July 25, 1863
Tennille, Toni; born Cathryn Antoinette Tennille	May 8, 1943
(singer/music/actress)	
Tennyson, Alfred (poet)	August 6, 1809
Terral, Thomas Jefferson (politician)	December 21, 1882
Terrell, Ernie (boxing)	April 4, 1939
Terrell, Joseph Meriwether (politician)	June 6, 1861
Terry, Bill; born William Harold Terry (baseball)	October 30, 1898
Terry, Charles Laymen, Jr. (politician)	September 17, 1900
Terry, Ralph Willard (baseball)	January 9, 1936
Terry-Thomas; born Thomas Terry Hoar-Stevens (actor)	July 14, 1911
Terwilliger, Wayne; born Willard Wayne Terwilliger	June 27, 1925
(baseball)	
Tex, Joe; born Joseph Arrington, Jr. (singer)	August 8, 1933
Thackeray, William Makepeace (author)	July 18, 1811
Thalberg, Irving Grant (producer)	May 30, 1899
Thant, U. (United Nations)	January 22, 1909
Tharp, Twyla (dancer/choreographer)	July 1, 1941
Thatcher, Margaret; born Margaret Hilda Roberts	October 13, 1925
(British government)	
Thatcher, Torin Herbert Erskine (actor)	January 15, 1905
Thaxter, Phyllis St. Felix (actress)	November 20, 1921
Thebom, Blanche (singer)	September 19, 1919
Theismann, Joe; born Joseph R. Theismann (football)	September 9, 1949
Theodore, Donna (singer/actress)	July 25, 1945
Thevenow, Tommy; born Thomas Joseph Thevenow (baseball)	September 6, 1903
Thieu, Nguyen Van (South Vietnamese government)	April 5, 1923
Thinnes, Roy (actor)	April 6, 1938
Thomas, B.J.; born Billy Joe Thomas (singer)	August 7, 1942
Thomas, Charles Spalding (politician)	December 6, 1849
Thomas, Clendon; born Robert Clendon Thomas (football)	December 28, 1935
Thomas, Danny; born Amos Joseph Alphonsus Jacobs	January 6, 1914
(or Amos Muzyad Jacobs) (or Jahoob) (comedian/actor/singer/producer)	
Thomas, Duane (football)	June 21, 1947
Thomas, Dylan Marlais (poet)	October 27, 1914
Thomas, Earl (football)	October 4, 1948
Thomas, Earlie (football)	December 11, 1945
Thomas, Elbert Duncan (politician)	June 17, 1883
Thomas, Elmer; born John William Elmer Thomas (politician)	September 8, 1876
Thomas, Emmitt Earl (football)	June 3, 1943
Thomas, Frank Joseph (baseball)	June 11, 1929
Thomas, George Edward (baseball)	November 29, 1937
Thomas, Herb; born Herbert Watson Thomas (auto racing)	April 6, 1923
Thomas, John W. (politician)	January 4, 1874
Thomas, Lee; born James Leroy Thomas (baseball)	February 5, 1936
Thomas, Lowell Jackson (newscaster/author/explorer)	April 6, 1892
Thomas, Marlo; born Margaret Julia Thomas	November 21, 1937
(actress/producer)	

Thomas, Mike; born Malcolm Thomas (football)	July 17, 1953
Thomas, Richard Earl (actor)	June 13, 1951
Thomas, Rufus (singer)	March 28, 1917
Thomas, Tommy; born Alphonse Thomas (baseball)	December 23, 1899
Thompson, Bill; born William A. Thompson (football)	October 10, 1946
Thompson, Cecil (hockey)	May 31, 1905
Thompson, Dorothy (journalist/author)	July 9, 1894
Thompson, Fresco; born LaFayette Fresco Thompson (baseball)	June 6, 1902
Thompson, Hank; born Henry Curtis Thompson (baseball)	December 8, 1925
Thompson, Hank; born Henry William Thompson (music)	September 3, 1925
Thompson, James Robert, Jr. (politician)	May 8, 1936
Thompson, Leonard (golf)	January 1, 1947
Thompson, Marshall; born James Marshall Thompson (actor)	November 27, 1925
Thompson, Norm; born Norman Thompson (football)	March 5, 1945
Thompson, Paul Ivan (hockey)	November 2, 1906
Thompson, Sada Carolyn (actress)	September 27, 1929
Thompson, Sam; born Samuel Luther Thompson (baseball)	May 5, 1860
Thompson, Speedy; born Alfred Thompson (auto racing)	April 3, 1926
Thoms, Art; born Arthur William Thoms (football)	October 20, 1946
Thoms, William D. (hockey)	March 5, 1910
Thomson, Bobby; born Robert Brown Thomson (baseball)	October 25, 1923
Thomson, Jim; born James Richard Thomson (hockey)	February 23, 1927
Thomson, Meldrim, Jr. (politician)	March 8, 1912
Thomson, Vernon Wallace (politician)	November 5, 1905
Thoreau, Henry David (naturalist/author)	July 12, 1817
Thorn, Rod; born Rodney King Thorn (basketball)	May 23, 1941
Thorndike, Dame Sybil (actress)	October 24, 1882
Thornton, Dan (politician)	January 31, 1911
Thorpe, Jim; born James Francis Thorpe (olympic athlete/ football)	May 28, 1888
Thorson, Linda (actress)	June 18, 1947
Throne, Malachi (actor)	December 1———
Throneberry, Faye; born Maynard Faye Throneberry (baseball)	June 22, 1931
Throneberry, Marv; born Marvin Eugene Throneberry (baseball)	September 2, 1933
Thulin, Ingrid (actress)	January 27, 1929
Thurber, James Grover (author)	December 8, 1894
Thurmond, J. Strom; born James Strom Thurmond (politician)	December 5, 1902
Thurmond, Nate (basketball)	July 25, 1941
Thurston, Fuzzy; born Frederick C. Thurston (football)	November 29, 1933
Thye, Edward John (politician)	April 26, 1896
Tiant, Luis Clemente (baseball)	November 23, 1940
Tibbett, Lawrence Mervil (singer/actor)	November 16, 1896
Tiemann, Norbert Theodore (politician)	July 18, 1924
Tierney, Gene Eliza Taylor (actress)	November 20, 1920
Tierney, Lawrence (actor)	March 15, 1919
Tiffany, Charles Lewis (jeweler)	February 15, 1812
Tiffany, Louis Comfort (artist)	February 18, 1848
Tiffin, Pamela; born Pamela Kimberley Tiffin Wonso (actress)	October 13, 1942
Tiger, Dick; born Richard Ihetu (boxing)	August 14, 1929
Tighe, Kevin (actor)	August 13, 1944

Tilden, Bill; born William Tatem Tilden, Jr. (tennis)	February 10, 1893
Tilleman, Mike; born Michael Tilleman (football)	March 30, 1944
Tillis, Mel (singer/music)	August 8, 1932
Tillman, Benjamin Ryan (politician)	August 11, 1847
Tillman, Bob; born John Robert Tillman (baseball)	March 24, 1937
Tillman, Rusty; born Russell Tillman (football)	February 27, 1946
Tillotson, Johnny (singer/music)	April 20, 1939
Tillstrom, Burr (puppeteer)	October 13, 1917
Tilton, Charlene (actress)	December 1, 1959
Tilton, Martha (singer/actress)	November 14, 1915
Timmerman, George Bell, Jr. (politician)	August 11, 1912
Tingelhoff, Mick; born Henry Michael Tingelhoff (football)	May 22, 1940
Tingley, Clyde (politician)	January 5, 1883
Tinker, Joe; born Joseph Bert Tinker (baseball)	July 27, 1880
Tintoretto; born Jacopo Robusti (artist)	———1518
Tiny Tim; born Herbert Khaury (singer)	April 12, 1930
Tiomkin, Dimitri (music)	May 10, 1899
Titian, born Tiziano Vecelli (artist)	———1477
Tito; born Josip Brozovich (Yugoslavian government)	May 25, 1892
Tittle, Y.A.; born Yelberton Abraham Tittle (football)	October 24, 1926
Tobey, Charles William (politician)	July 22, 1880
Tobias, George (actor)	July 14, 1901
Tobin, Genevieve (actress)	November 29, 1901
Tobin, Jack; born John Thomas Tobin (baseball)	May 4, 1892
Tobin, Jim; born James Anthony Tobin (baseball)	December 27, 1912
Tobin, Maurice Joseph (politics/government)	May 22, 1901
Todd, Al; born Alfred Chester Todd (baseball)	January 7, 1904
Todd, Ann (actress)	January 24, 1909
Todd, Michael; born Avrom Hirsch Goldenborgen (producer)	June 22, 1907
Todd, Richard; born Richard Andrew Palethorpe-Todd (actor)	June 11, 1919
Todd, Richard (football)	November 19, 1953
Todd, Thelma (actress)	July 29, 1905
Todman, William Selden (producer)	July 31, 1916
Todt, Phil; born Philip Julius Todt (baseball)	August 9, 1901
Tolan, Bobby; born Robert Tolan (baseball)	November 19, 1945
Tolan, Michael; born Michael Tuchow (actor)	———1925
Tolar, Charley; born Charles Guy Tolar (football)	September 5, 1937
Tolbert, Jim; born Love James Tolbert (football)	March 12, 1944
Toler, Sidney (actor)	April 28, 1874
Tolstoy, Leo; born Lyof Nikolaievitch Tolstoy (author)	September 9, 1828
Tomjanovich, Rudy (basketball)	November 24, 1948
Tomlin, Lili; born Mary Jean Tomlin (comedienne/actress/ singer)	September 1, 1936
Tomlin, Pinky (singer/comedian/actor/music)	September 9, 1907
Tomlinson, David (actor)	May 17, 1917
Tompkins, Angel (actress)	December 20, 1943
Tompkins, Daniel D. (Vice President)	June 21, 1774
Tone, Franchot; born Stanislas Pascal Franchot Tone (actor)	February 27, 1905
Toneff, Bob; born Robert Toneff (football)	June 23, 1930
Toole, Joseph Kemp (politician)	May 12, 1851
Toomay, Pat; born Patrick Jay Toomay (football)	May 17, 1948

Toomey, Regis (actor)	August 13, 1902
Topol, born Chaim Topol (actor)	September 9, 1935
Toppazzini, Gerald (hockey)	July 29, 1931
Torgeson, Earl; born Clifford Earl Torgeson (baseball)	January 1, 1924
Torgeson, Torgy; born LaVern Torgeson (football)	February 28, 1929
Tormé, Mel; born Melvin Howard Tormé (singer/actor)	September 13, 1923
Torn, Rip; born Elmore Rual Torn (actor)	February 6, 1931
Torre, Joe; born Joseph Paul Torre (baseball)	July 18, 1940
Torres, Hector Epitacio (baseball)	September 16, 1945
Torres, Jose (boxing)	May 3, 1936
Torrez, Mike; born Michael Augustine Torrez (baseball)	August 28, 1946
Tors, Ivan Lawrence (producer/director/writer)	June 12, 1916
Toscanini, Arturo (music)	March 25, 1867
Toski, Bob; born Robert Toski (golf)	September 18, 1927
Totter, Audrey (actress)	December 20, 1918
Toulouse-Lautrec-Monfa, Henri-Marie-Raymond de (artist)	November 24, 1864
Tovar, Cesar Lenardo (baseball)	July 3, 1940
Tower, John Goodwin (politician)	September 29, 1925
Towers, Constance (actress/singer)	May 20, 1933
Towler, Dan; born Daniel Lee Towler (football)	March 6, 1928
Townes, Harry (actor)	September 18, 1918
Townsend, Charles Elroy (politician)	August 15, 1856
Townsend, John Gillis, Jr. (politician)	May 31, 1871
Townsend, Maurice Clifford (politician)	August 11, 1884
Toynbee, Arnold Joseph (historian)	April 14, 1889
Trabert, Tony; born Marion Anthony Trabert (tennis/sportscaster)	August 16, 1930
Tracy, Lee; born William Lee Tracy (actor)	April 14, 1898
Tracy, Spencer Bonaventure (actor)	April 5, 1900
Tracy, Tom; born John Thomas Tracy (football)	February 21, 1933
Trammell, Park (politician)	April 9, 1876
Trapp, Martin Edwin (politician)	April 18, 1877
Trask, Diana Roselyn (singer)	June 23, 1940
Traubel, Helen (singer/actress)	June 16, 1899
Travers, Bill (actor)	January 3, 1922
Travers, Jerry; born Jerome Dunston Travers (golf)	May 19, 1887
Travers, Mary Allin (singer)	November 9, 1936
Travis, Cecil Howell (baseball)	August 8, 1913
Travis, Richard; born William Justice (actor)	April 17, 1913
Travis, Walter J. (golf)	January 10, 1862
Travolta, John Joseph (actor/singer)	February 18, 1954
Traynor, Pie; born Harold Joseph Traynor (baseball)	November 11, 1899
Treacher, Arthur; born Arthur Veary (actor)	July 23, 1894
Tremayne, Les; born Les Henning (actor)	April 16, 1913
Tremblay, Gilles (hockey)	December 18, 1938
Tremblay, J.C.; born Jean Claude Tremblay (hockey)	January 22, 1939
Tresh, Mike; born Michael Tresh (baseball)	February 23, 1914
Tresh, Tom; born Thomas Michael Tresh (baseball)	September 20, 1937
Trevino, Lee Buck (golf)	December 1, 1939
Trevor, Claire; born Claire Wemlinger (actress)	March 8, 1908
Triandos, Gus (baseball)	July 30, 1930

Tribbitt, Sherman Willard (politician)	November 9, 1922
Trigère, Pauline (fashion designer)	November 4, 1912
Trilling, Lionel (author)	July 4, 1905
Frinkle, Elbert Lee (politician)	March 12, 1876
Trintignant, Jean-Louis (actor)	December 11, 1930
Trintignant, Maurice (auto racing)	October 30, 1917
Triplett, Mel; born Melvin Triplett (football)	December 24, 1931
Trippi, Charlie; born Charles Lou Trippi (football)	December 14, 1922
Trips, Wolfgang Graf Berghe von (auto racing)	May 4, 1928
Trosky, Hal; born Harold Arthur Troyavesky, Sr. (baseball)	November 11, 1912
Trotsky (or Trotski), Leon; born Leib (or Liv) Davydovich Bronstein (Russian government)	October 26, 1879
Trottier, David T. (hockey)	June 25, 1906
Troup, Bobby; born Robert William Troup (actor/singer/music)	October 18, 1918
Trout, Dizzy; born Paul Howard Trout (baseball)	June 29, 1915
Trout, Robert (newscaster)	October 15, 1908
Truax, Bill; born William Frederick Truax, III (football)	July 15, 1943
Trucks, Virgil Oliver (baseball)	April 26, 1919
Trudeau, Margaret; born Margaret Joan Sinclair (First Lady of Canada/photographer/author)	September 10, 1948
Trudeau, Pierre Elliott (Canadian government)	October 18, 1919
Trudel, Louis Napoleon (hockey)	July 21, 1913
Truex, Ernest (actor)	September 19, 1899
Truffaut, Francois (director)	February 6, 1932
Trujillo Molina, Rafael Leonidas (Dominican Republic government)	October 24, 1891
Truman, Bess; born Elizabeth Virginia Wallace (First Lady)	February 13, 1885
Truman, Harry S. (President)	May 8, 1884
Truman, Margaret; born Mary Margaret Truman (First family)	February 17, 1924
Trumbull, John (artist)	June 6, 1756
Trumbull, John H. (politician)	March 4, 1873
Trumpy, Bob; born Robert T. Trumpy, Jr. (football)	March 6, 1945
Tryon, Tom; born Thomas Tryon (actor/author)	January 14, 1926
Tubb, Ernest Dale (singer/music)	February 9, 1914
Tubbs, Jerry; born Gerald Tubbs (football)	January 23, 1935
Tuck, William Munford (politician)	September 28, 1896
Tucker, Bob; born Robert Louis Tucker (football)	June 8, 1945
Tucker, Forrest Meredith (actor)	February 12, 1919
Tucker, Sophie; born Sophia Abuza (or Sonia Kalish) (singer/actress)	January 13, 1884
Tucker, Tanya Denise (singer)	October 10, 1958
Tucker, Thurman Lowell (baseball)	September 26, 1917
Tufts, Sonny; born Bowen Charleston Tufts, III (actor)	July 16, 1911
Tully, Tom (actor)	August 21, 1896
Tune, Tommy (dancer/actor)	February 28, 1939
Tunnell, Emlen (football)	March 29, 1925
Tunney, Gene; born James Joseph Tunney (boxing)	May 25, 1898
Tunney, John Varick (politician)	June 26, 1934
Turcotte, Ron; born Ronald Turcotte (jockey)	July 22, 1941
Turgenev, Ivan Sergeevich (author/playwright)	November 9, 1818
Turley, Bob; born Robert Lee Turley (baseball)	September 19, 1930

Turnbull, Wendy (tennis)	November 26, 1952
Turner, Curtis (auto racing)	April 12, 1924
Turner, Daniel Webster (politician)	March 17, 1877
Turner, Ike (music)	November 5, 1931
Turner, Jim; born James A. Turner (football)	March 28, 1941
Turner, Joseph Mallord William (artist)	April 23, 1775
Turner, Lana; born Julia Jean Mildred Frances Turner (actress)	February 8, 1920
Turner, Robert George (hockey)	January 31, 1943
Turner, Roy Joseph (politician)	November 6, 1894
Turner, Tina; born Annie Mae Bullock (singer)	November 26, 1938
Turnesa, Jim; born James Turnesa (golf)	December 9, 1912
Turpin, Ben (actor)	September 17, 1874
Tushingham, Rita (actress)	March 14, 1942
Tutin, Dorothy (actress)	April 8, 1930
Tuttle, Bill; born William Robert Tuttle (baseball)	July 4, 1929
Tuttle, Lurene (actress)	August 20, 1906
Twain, Mark; born Samuel Langhorne Clemens (author)	November 30, 1835
Tweed, William Marcy (politician)	April 3, 1823
Twelvetrees, Helen; born Helen Marie Jurgens (actress)	December 25, 1907
Twiggy; born Leslie Hornby (model/actress)	September 19, 1949
Twilley, Howard (football)	December 25, 1943
Twining, Nathan Farragut (air force officer)	October 11, 1897
Twitty, Conway; born Harold Lloyd Jenkins (singer/music)	September 1, 1933
Twyman, Jack (basketball)	May 11, 1934
Tydings, Joseph Davies (politician)	May 4, 1928
Tydings, Millard Evelyn (politician)	April 6, 1890
Tyler, Beverly; born Beverly Jean Saul (actress)	July 5, 1928
Tyler, John (President)	March 29, 1790
Tyler, Julia Gardiner; born Julia Gardiner (second wife of John Tyler/First Lady)	May 4, 1820
Tyler, Letitia Christian; born Letitia Christian (second wife of John Tyler/First Lady)	November 12, 1790
Tyler, Royall (playwright)	July 18, 1757
Tyrer, Jim; born James E. Tyrer (football)	February 25, 1939
Tyson, Cicely (actress)	December 19, 1939

U

Udall, Morris King (politician)	June 15, 1922
Udall, Stewart Lee (government)	January 31, 1920
Uggams, Leslie Marian (singer/actress)	May 25, 1943
Uhlaender, Ted; born Theodore Otto Uhlaender (baseball)	October 21, 1939
Uhle, George Ernest (baseball)	September 18, 1898
Ulanova, Galina Sergeyevna (dancer)	January 10, 1910
Ullman, Al; born Albert Conrad Ullman (politician)	March 9, 1914
Ullman, Norm; born Norman Victor Alexander Ullman (hockey)	December 26, 1935
Ullmann, Liv Johanne (actress)	December 16, 1939
Ulric, Lenore; born Lenore Ulrich (actress)	July 21, 1892
Umeki, Miyoski (actress)	April 3, 1929
Umstead, William Bradley (politician)	May 13, 1895

Underwood, Cecil Harland (politician)	November 5, 1922
Underwood, Oscar Wilder (politician)	May 6, 1862
Unger, Gary Douglas (hockey)	December 7, 1947
Unitas, Johnny; born John Constantine Unitas (football/sportscaster)	May 7, 1933
Unseld, Wes; born Westley Unseld (basketball)	March 4, 1946
Unser, Al (auto racing)	May 29, 1939
Unser, Bobby; born Robert William Unser (auto racing)	February 20, 1934
Unser, Del; born Delbert Bernard Unser (baseball)	December 9, 1944
Untermeyer, Louis (anthologist)	October 1, 1885
Updike, John Hoyer (author)	March 18, 1932
Upshaw, Gene; born Eugene Upshaw (football)	August 15, 1945
Upshaw, Marvin Allen (football)	November 22, 1946
Urbanski, Billy; born William Michael Urbanski (baseball)	June 5, 1903
Ure, Mary (actress)	February 18, 1933
Urich, Robert (actor)	December 19, 1946
Uris, Leon Marcus (author)	August 3, 1924
Usher, Bob; born Robert Royce Usher (baseball)	March 1, 1925
Ussery, Bob; born Bobby Nelson Ussery (jockey)	September 3, 1935
Ustinov, Peter Alexander (actor/director/writer)	April 16, 1921
Utley, Garrick; born Clifton Garrick Utley (newscaster)	November 19, 1939
Utter, George Herbert (politician)	July 24, 1854

V

Vaccaro, Brenda Buell (actress)	November 18, 1939
Vachon, Rogatien Rosaire (hockey)	September 8, 1945
Vactor, Ted; born Theodore Vactor (football)	May 27, 1944
Vadim, Roger; born Roger Vadim Plemiannikow (director)	January 26, 1928
Vadnais, Carol (hockey)	September 25, 1945
Vale, Jerry; born Genaro Louis Vitaliano (singer)	July 8, 1932
Valens, Ritchie; born Richard Valenzuela (singer/music)	May 13, 1941
Valente, Caterina (singer)	January 14, 1931
Valenti, Jack Joseph (motion picture executive)	September 5, 1921
Valentine, Karen (actress)	May 25, 1947
Valentino; born Valentino Garavani (fashion designer)	May 11, 1932
Valentino, Rudolph; born Rodolpho Alfonso Raffaello Pierre Filibert Guglielmi de Valentina d'Antonguolla (actor)	May 6, 1895
Vallee, Rudy; born Hubert Prior Vallee (singer/actor)	July 28, 1901
Valli, Alida; born Alida Maria Altenburger (actress)	May 31, 1921
Valli, Frankie; born·Frank Castelluccio (singer)	May 3, 1937
Valli, June (singer)	June 30, 1930
Vallone, Raf (actor)	February 17, 1916
Valo, Elmer William (baseball)	March 5, 1921
Van, Bobby; born Robert Van Stein (actor/dancer/singer)	December 6, 1930
Van Ark, Joan (actress)	June 16, 1943
Van Arsdale, Dick; born Richard Albert Van Arsdale (basketball)	February 22, 1943
Van Arsdale, Tom (basketball)	February 22, 1943
Van Brocklin, Norm; born Norman Mack Van Brocklin (football)	March 15, 1926

Van Buren, Abigail; born Pauline Esther Friedman (journalist)	July 4, 1918
Van Buren, Hannah; born Hannah Hoes (First Lady)	March 8, 1783
Van Buren, Martin (President)	December 5, 1782
Van Buren, Steve; born Stephen W. Van Buren (football)	December 28, 1920
Vance, Cyrus Roberts (government)	March 27, 1917
Vance, Dazzy; born Charles Arthur Vance (baseball)	March 4, 1891
Vance, Vivian; born Vivian Jones (actress)	July 26, 1903
Van Cleef, Lee (actor)	January 9, 1925
Vandenberg, Arthur Hendrick (politician)	March 22, 1884
Vanderbilt, Alfred Gwynne (capitalist)	October 20, 1877
Vanderbilt, Alfred Gwynne (sportsman)	September 22, 1912
Vanderbilt, Amy (journalist/author)	July 22, 1908
Vanderbilt, Cornelius (capitalist)	May 27, 1794
Vanderbilt, Cornelius (capitalist/financier)	November 27, 1843
Vanderbilt, Cornelius, III (capitalist)	September 5, 1873
Vanderbilt, Cornelius, Jr. (writer/lecturer)	April 30, 1898
Vanderbilt, Frederick William (capitalist)	————1856
Vanderbilt, George Washington (capitalist)	November 14, 1862
Vanderbilt, Gloria Laura Morgan (artist/heiress)	February 20, 1924
Vanderbilt, Harold Stirling (capitalist/sportsman)	July 6, 1884
Vanderbilt, Reginald Claypoole (investor)	December 19, 1880
Vanderbilt, William H. (politician)	November 24, 1901
Vanderbilt, William Henry (railroad magnate/financier)	May 8, 1821
Vanderbilt, William Kissam (capitalist)	December 12, 1849
Vanderbilt, William Kissam (capitalist)	October 26, 1878
Vanderbundt, Skip; born William Vanderbundt (football)	December 4, 1946
Vander Meer, Johnny; born John Samuel Vander Meer (baseball)	November 2, 1914
Van Der Vlis, Diana (actress)	June 9, 1935
Van Devanter, Willis (jurist)	April 17, 1859
Van Devere, Trish; born Patricia Dressel (actress)	March 9, 1943
Vandis, Titos (actor)	November 7, 1917
Vandiver, Samuel Ernest, Jr. (politician)	July 3, 1918
Van Doren, Mamie; born Joan Lucille Olander (actress)	February 6, 1933
Van Dreelan, John (actor)	May 5, 1922
Van Dyck, Sir Anthony (artist)	March 22, 1599
Van Dyke, Bruce (football)	August 6, 1944
Van Dyke, Dick (comedian/actor)	December 13, 1925
Van Dyke, Jerry (comedian/actor)	————1932
Van Dyke, Leroy Frank (singer/music)	October 4, 1929
van Eeghen, Mark (football)	April 19, 1952
Van Eyck, Peter (actor)	July 16, 1911
Van Fleet, Jo (actress)	December 30, 1919
Vangilder, Elam Russell (baseball)	April 23, 1896
Van Heusen, Bill; born William Van Heusen (football)	August 27, 1946
Van Heusen, Jimmy; born Edward Chester Babcock (music)	January 26, 1913
Van Horn, Doug; born Douglas Van Horn (football)	June 24, 1944
Van Impe, Edward Charles (hockey)	May 27, 1940
Van Lier, Norm (basketball)	April 1, 1947
Van Note, Jeff; born Jeffrey Van Note (football)	February 7, 1946

Van Nuys, Frederick (politician)	April 16, 1874
Vanocur, Sander; born Sander Vinocur (newscaster/ journalist)	January 8, 1928
Van Patten, Dick; born Richard Vincent Van Patten (actor)	December 9, 1928
Van Patten, Joyce Benigna (actress)	March 9, 1934
Van Peebles, Melvin (producer/director/writer/actor/music)	September 21, 1932
Van Pelt, Brad Alan (football)	April 5, 1951
Van Sant, Samuel Rinnah (politician)	May 11, 1844
Van Vooren, Monique (actress/singer)	March 23, 1933
Van Wagoner, Murray Delos (politician)	March 18, 1898
Vardaman, James Kimble (politician)	July 26, 1861
Vardon, Harry (golf)	May 9, 1870
Varrichione, Frank (football)	January 14, 1932
Varsi, Diane Marie Antonia (actress)	February 23, 1938
Vasko, Moose; born Elmer Vasko (hockey)	December 11, 1935
Vataha, Randy; born Randel E. Vataha (football)	December 4, 1948
Vaughan, Arky; born Joseph Floyd Vaughan (baseball)	March 9, 1912
Vaughan, Frankie; born Frank Abelsohn (actor/singer)	February 3, 1928
Vaughan, Sarah Lois (singer)	March 27, 1924
Vaughn, Billy (music)	April 12, 1919
Vaughn, Heidi (actress)	October 12———
Vaughn, Robert Francis (actor/author)	November 22, 1932
Veale, Bob; born Robert Andrew Veale (baseball)	October 28, 1935
Vee, Bobby; born Robert Thomas Velline (singer/music)	April 30, 1943
Veeck, Bill; born William Louis Veeck, Jr. (baseball)	February 9, 1914
Velasquez, Jorge (jockey)	December 28, 1948
Velázquez, Diego Rodriguez de Silva y (artist)	———1599
Velez, Lupe; born Guadeloupe Velez de Villalobos (actress)	July 18, 1908
Venable, Evelyn (actress)	October 18, 1913
Venturi, Ken; born Kenneth Venturi (golf/sportscaster)	May 15, 1931
Venuta, Benay; born Venuta Rose Crooke (singer/actress)	January 27, 1911
Vera; born Vera Salaff (textile designer/artist)	July 24, 1910
Vera-Ellen; born Vera-Ellen Westmeyr Rohe (actress/ dancer/singer)	February 16, 1926
Verdi, Giuseppe Fortunino Francisco (music)	October 10, 1813
Verdon, Gwen; born Gwyneth Evelyn Verdon (actress/dancer singer)	January 13, 1925
Verdugo, Elena (actress)	April 20, 1926
Vereen, Ben Augustus (actor/dancer/singer)	October 10, 1946
Vermeer, Jan; born Jan Van Der Meer Van Delft (artist)	October 31, 1632
Verne, Jules (author)	February 8, 1828
Vernon, Jackie (comedian)	———1928
Vernon, John (actor)	February 24, 1932
Vernon, Mickey; born James Barton Vernon (baseball)	April 22, 1918
Verrett, Shirley (singer)	May 31, 1933
Versalles, Zorro; born Zoilo Casanova Versalles (baseball)	December 18, 1939
Vespucci, Amerigo (navigator)	March 18, 1452
Vessey, Robert Scadden (politician)	May 16, 1858
Victoria, Queen of England; born Alexandrina Victoria	May 24, 1819
Vidal, Gore (author)	October 3, 1925

Vidor, King Wallis (director)	February 8, 1895
Vigoda, Abe (actor)	February 24, 1921
Vilas, Guillermo (tennis)	August 17, 1952
Villa, Pancho; born Doroteo Arango (Mexican bandit)	June 5, 1878
Villapiano, Phil; born Philip James Villapiano (football)	February 26, 1949
Villechaize, Hervé (actor)	April 23, 1943
Villella, Edward Joseph (dancer)	October 1, 1936
Vincent, Jan-Michael (actor)	July 15, 1944
Vinci, Leonardo da (artist)	April 15, 1452
Vines, H. Ellsworth (tennis/golf)	September 29, 1911
Vinson, Frederick Moore (government/jurist)	January 22, 1890
Vinson, Helen; born Helen Rulfs (actress)	September 17, 1907
Vinton, Bobby; born Stanley Robert Vinton (or Vintulla) (singer/music)	April 16, 1935
Virdon, Bill; born William Charles Virdon (baseball)	June 9, 1931
Virgil, Ozzie; born Osvaldo Jose Virgil (baseball)	May 17, 1933
Vitti, Monica; born Maria Luisa Ceciarelli (actress)	November 3, 1933
Vivian, John Charles (politician)	June 30, 1887
Vogel, Bob; born Robert L. Vogel (football)	September 23, 1941
Voight, Jon (actor)	December 29, 1938
Voigt, Stu; born Stuart Alan Voigt (football)	August 12, 1948
Volk, Rick; born Richard Robert Volk (football)	March 15, 1945
Vollmer, Clyde Frederick (baseball)	September 24, 1921
Volpe, John Anthony (politics/government)	December 8, 1908
Voltaire, Jean Francois Marie Arouet (author)	November 21, 1694
Von Braun, Wernher (rocketeer)	March 23, 1912
von Furstenberg, Betsy; born Elizabeth Caroline Maria Agatha Felicitas Therese von Furstenberg-Hedringen (actress)	August 16, 1931
Von Stroheim, Erich, Sr.; born Erich Oswald Hans Carl Maris Von Nordenwall (actor/director)	September 22, 1885
von Sydow, Max; born Carl Adolf von Sydow (actor)	April 10, 1929
Von Zell, Harry R. (announcer/actor)	July 11, 1906
Vonnegut, Kurt, Jr. (author)	November 11, 1922
Voorhees, Donald (music)	July 26, 1903
Voskovec, George (actor)	June 19, 1905
Vosmik, Joe; born Joseph Franklin Vosmik (baseball)	April 4, 1910
Vukovich, Bill; born William Vucerovich (auto racing)	————1919
Vukovich, Billy (auto racing)	March 29, 1944

W

Waddell, Rube; born George Edward Waddell (baseball)	October 13, 1876
Wade, Billy; born William J. Wade, Jr. (football)	October 4, 1930
Wade, Virginia; born Sarah Virginia Wade (tennis)	July 10, 1945
Wadkins, Lanny; born Jerry L. Wadkins (golf)	December 5, 1949
Wadsworth, James Wolcott, Jr. (politician)	August 12, 1877
Waggoner, Lyle Wesley (actor)	April 13, 1935
Wagner, Hal; born Harold Edward Wagner (baseball)	July 2, 1915
Wagner, Honus; born John Peter Wagner (baseball)	February 24, 1874
Wagner, Leon Lamar (baseball)	May 13, 1934
Wagner, Lindsay Jean (actress)	June 22, 1949

Wagner, Mike; born Michael Robert Wagner (football)	June 22, 1949
Wagner, Robert Ferdinand, Sr. (politician)	June 8, 1877
Wagner, Robert Ferdinand, Jr. (politician)	April 20, 1910
Wagner, Robert John (actor)	February 10, 1930
Wagner, Wilhelm Richard (music)	May 22, 1813
Wagoner, Porter (singer/music)	August 12, 1927
Wainwright, James (actor)	March 5, 1938
Waite, Morison Remick (jurist)	November 29, 1816
Waite, Ralph (actor)	June 22, 1928
Waitkus, Eddie; born Edward Stephen Waitkus (baseball)	September 4, 1919
Wakefield, Dick; born Richard Cummings Wakefield (baseball)	May 6, 1921
Wakely, Jimmy; born James Clarence Wakely (actor/singer)	February 16, 1914
Walberg, Rube; born George Elvin Walberg (baseball)	July 27, 1899
Walcott, Jersey Joe; born Arnold Raymond Cream (boxing)	January 31, 1914
Walden, Bobby; born Robert Earl Walden (football)	March 9, 1938
Walden, Robert (actor)	September 25, 1943
Waldheim, Kurt (United Nations)	December 21, 1918
Walker, Chet (basketball)	February 22, 1940
Walker, Chuck; born Charles Walker (football)	August 10, 1941
Walker, Clifford Mitchell (politician)	July 4, 1877
Walker, Clint (actor)	May 30, 1927
Walker, Curt; born William Curtis Walker (baseball)	July 3, 1896
Walker, Daniel (politician)	August 6, 1922
Walker, Dixie; born Fred Walker (baseball)	September 24, 1910
Walker, Doak; born Ewell Doak Walker (football)	January 1, 1927
Walker, Frank Comerford (government)	May 30, 1886
Walker, Gee; born Gerald Holmes Walker (baseball)	March 19, 1908
Walker, Harry William (baseball)	October 22, 1916
Walker, Jimmie; born James Carter Walker (comedian/actor)	June 25, 1949
Walker, Jimmy; born James John Walker (politician)	June 19, 1881
Walker, Jimmy (basketball)	April 8, 1944
Walker, Mickey (boxing)	July 13, 1901
Walker, Mort (cartoonist)	September 3, 1923
Walker, Nancy; born Anna Myrtle Swoyer (actress)	May 10, 1921
Walker, Robert Hudson (actor)	October 13, 1914
Walker, Robert Jr. (actor)	April 15, 1940
Walker, Rube; born Albert Bluford Walker (baseball)	May 16, 1926
Wall, Art; born Arthur Jonathan Wall, Jr. (golf)	November 25, 1923
Wall, Robert James Albert (hockey)	December 1, 1942
Wallace, Bobby; born Roderick John Wallace (baseball)	November 4, 1873
Wallace, DeWitt (publisher)	November 12, 1889
Wallace, George Corley (politician)	August 25, 1919
Wallace, Henry Agard (Vice President)	October 7, 1888
Wallace, Henry Cantwell (government)	May 11, 1866
Wallace, Irving (author)	March 19, 1916
Wallace, Lurleen Burns; born Lurleen Burns (politician)	September 19, 1926
Wallace, Marcia (actress)	November 1, 1942
Wallace, Mike; born Myron Leon Wallace (newscaster)	May 9, 1918
Wallach, Eli (actor)	December 7, 1915
Waller, Fats; born Thomas Waller (music)	May 21, 1904
Waller, William L. (politician)	October 21, 1926

Walley, Deborah E. (actress)	August 13———
Wallgren, Monrad Charles (politician)	April 17, 1891
Wallis, Hal Brent (producer)	September 14, 1898
Wallis, Shani (singer/actress)	April 16, 1933
Wallop, Malcolm (politician)	February 27, 1933
Walls, Lee; born Ray Lee Walls (baseball)	January 6, 1933
Walsh, David Ignatius (politician)	November 11, 1872
Walsh, Ed; born Edward Augustine Walsh (baseball)	May 14, 1881
Walsh, Thomas James (politician)	June 12, 1859
Walston, Bobby; born Robert Walston (football)	October 17, 1928
Walston, Ray (actor/director)	November 2, 1914
Walter, Bruno; born Bruno Walter Schlesinger (music)	September 15, 1876
Walter, Jessica (actress/singer)	January 31, 1944
Walters, Barbara (newscaster/TV host)	September 25, 1931
Walters, Bucky; born William Henry Walters (baseball)	April 19, 1909
Walton, Bill; born William Theodore Walton (basketball)	November 5, 1952
Walton, Chuck; born Charles R. Walton (football)	July 7, 1941
Walton, Izaak (author)	August 9, 1593
Walton, Joe; born Joseph Walton (football)	December 15, 1935
Walton, Larry; born Lawrence James Walton (football)	February 8, 1947
Walton, Michael Robert (hockey)	January 3, 1945
Waltrip, Darrell (auto racing)	February 5, 1947
Wambaugh, Joseph (author)	January 22, 1937
Wambsganss, Bill; born William Adolph Wambsganss (baseball)	March 19, 1894
Wanamaker, John (merchant)	July 11, 1838
Wanamaker, Sam (actor/producer/director)	June 14, 1919
Waner, Lloyd James (baseball)	March 16, 1906
Waner, Paul Glee (baseball)	April 16, 1903
Wanzer, Bobby; born Robert Wanzer (basketball)	June 4, 1921
Ward, Aaron Lee (baseball)	August 28, 1896
Ward, Burt; born Bert John Gervais, Jr. (actor)	July 6, 1945
Ward, Clara (singer)	April 21, 1924
Ward, James (hockey)	September 1, 1906
Ward, Montgomery; born Aaron Montgomery Ward (merchant)	February 17, 1843
Ward, Pete; born Peter Thomas Ward (baseball)	July 26, 1939
Ward, Preston Meyer (baseball)	July 24, 1927
Ward, Rodger (auto racing)	January 10, 1921
Ward, Simon (actor)	October 19, 1941
Warden, Jack (actor)	September 18, 1920
Wares, Edward (hockey)	March 19, 1915
Warfield, Edwin (politician)	May 7, 1848
Warfield, Paul Dryden (football)	November 28, 1942
Warhol, Andy; born Andrew Warhola (artist/filmmaker)	August 6, 1927
Waring, Fred; born Frederic Malcolm Waring (music)	June 9, 1900
Warneke, Lon; born Lonnie Warneke (baseball)	March 28, 1909
Warner, Albert (producer—Warner Brothers)	July 23, 1884
Warner, Fred Maltby (politician)	July 21, 1865
Warner, H.B.; born Henry Bryon Warner (actor)	October 26, 1876
Warner, Harry Morris (producer—Warner Brothers)	December 12, 1881
Warner, Jack Leonard (producer—Warner Brothers)	August 2, 1892
Warner, Sam (producer—Warner Brothers)	———1888

Warner, William (politician)	June 11, 1840
Warren, Earl (politician/jurist)	March 19, 1891
Warren, Francis Emroy (politician)	June 20, 1844
Warren, Fuller (politician)	October 3, 1905
Warren, Harry Salvatore (music)	December 24, 1893
Warren, Jennifer (actress)	August 12, 1941
Warren, Lesley Ann (actress/singer/dancer)	August 16, 1946
Warren, Robert Penn (author)	April 24, 1905
Warrick, Ruth (actress/singer)	June 29, 1915
Warstler, Rabbit; born Harold Burton Warstler (baseball)	September 13, 1903
Warwick, Knobby; born Grant David Warwick (hockey)	October 11, 1921
Warwick, Lonnie Preston (football)	February 26, 1942
Warwicke, Dionne; born Marie Dionne Warwick (singer/actress)	December 12, 1940
Wasdell, Jimmy; born James Charles Wasdell (baseball)	May 15, 1914
Washam, Jo Ann (golf)	May 24, 1950
Washbourne, Mona (actress)	November 27, 1903
Washington, Booker T.; born Booker Taliaferro Washington (educator)	April 5, 1856
Washington, Dave; born David Washington (football)	September 12, 1948
Washington, Dinah; born Ruth Jones (singer)	August 29, 1924
Washington, Eugene (football)	November 23, 1944
Washington, Fredi (actress/dancer)	————1903
Washington, Gene Alden (football)	January 14, 1947
Washington, George (President)	February 22, 1732
Washington, Mark Henry (football)	December 25, 1947
Washington, Martha Dandridge; born Martha Dandridge (First Lady)	June 21, 1731
Washington, Russ; born Russell Washington (football)	December 17, 1946
Washington, Vic; born Victor A. Washington (football)	March 23, 1946
Washington, Walter Edward (politician)	April 15, 1915
Wasserman, Dale (writer/producer)	November 2, 1917
Waterfield, Bob; born Robert Staton Waterfield (football)	July 26, 1920
Waterman, Charles Winfield (politician)	November 2, 1861
Waters, Charlie; born Charles T. Waters (football)	September 10, 1948
Waters, Ethel (actress/singer)	October 31, 1896
Waters, Muddy; born McKinley Morganfield (singer/music)	April 4, 1915
Watkins, Arthur Vivian (politician)	December 18, 1886
Watkins, George Archibald (baseball)	June 4, 1900
Watkins, Larry; born Lawrence Watkins (football)	October 5, 1946
Watson, Bob; born Robert Jose Watson (baseball)	April 10, 1946
Watson, Bobs; born Robert Watson (actor)	November 16, 1930
Watson, Bryan Joseph (hockey)	November 14, 1942
Watson, Harry Percival (hockey)	May 6, 1923
Watson, James Eli (politician)	November 2, 1863
Watson, John (football)	January 11, 1949
Watson, Joseph John (hockey)	July 6, 1943
Watson, Lucille (actress)	May 27, 1879
Watson, Phil; born Phillipe Henri Watson (hockey)	October 24, 1914
Watson, Susan Elizabeth (actress/singer)	December 17, 1938
Watson, Tom; born Thomas Sturges Watson (golf)	September 4, 1949
Watt, James (inventor)	January 19, 1736
Watteau, Jean-Antoine (artist)	October 10, 1684
Watts, André (music)	June 20, 1946

Watwood, Johnny; born John Clifford Watwood (baseball)	August 17, 1906
Waugh, Alex; born Alexander Raban Waugh (author)	July 8, 1898
Wayne, Anthony (military officer)	January 1, 1745
Wayne, David; born Wayne James McMeekan (actor)	January 30, 1914
Wayne, John; born Marion Michael Morrison (actor/producer director)	May 26, 1907
Wayne, Patrick (actor)	July 15, 1939
Weatherly, Joe; born Joseph Herbert Weatherly (auto racing)	May 29, 1922
Weatherly, Roy; born Cyril Roy Weatherly (baseball)	Feburary 25, 1915
Weaver, Arthur J. (politician)	November 18, 1873.
Weaver, Charley; born Cliff Arquette (entertainer)	December 28, 1905
Weaver, Charlie; born Charles E. Weaver (football)	July 12, 1949
Weaver, Dennis (actor)	June 4, 1924
Weaver, De Witt (golf)	September 14, 1939
Weaver, Doodles; born Winstead Sheffield Glendening Dixon Weaver (actor)	May 11, 1914
Weaver, Earl Sidney (baseball)	August 14, 1930
Weaver, Fritz William (actor)	January 19, 1926
Weaver, Herman; born William Herman Weaver (football)	November 17, 1948
Weaver, Marjorie (actress)	March 2, 1913
Weaver, Robert Clifton (government)	December 29, 1907
Webb, Clifton; born Webb Parmalle Hollenbeck (actor/dancer singer)	November 19, 1891
Webb, Earl; born William Earl Webb (baseball)	September 17, 1898
Webb, Jack Randolph (actor/producer/director)	April 2, 1920
Webb, Jimmy Layne (singer/music)	August 15, 1946
Webb, Skeeter; born James Laverne Webb (baseball)	November 4, 1909
Webber, Robert L. (actor)	October 14, 1928
Weber, Baron Karl Maria Friedrich Ernst von (music)	December 18, 1786
Webster, Alex; born Alexander Webster (football)	April 19, 1931
Webster, Daniel (statesman)	January 18, 1782
Webster, George (football)	November 25, 1945
Webster, Noah (lexicographer/author)	October 16, 1758
Weede, Robert (actor/singer)	February 22, 1903
Weeks, Frank Bentley (politician)	January 20, 1854
Weeks, John Eliakim (politician)	June 14, 1853
Weeks, John Wingate (politics/government)	April 11, 1860
Weeks, Sinclair (government)	June 15, 1893
Weger, Mike; born Michael Roy Weger (football)	October 2, 1945
Wehmeier, Herm; born Herman Ralph Wehmeier (baseball)	February 18, 1927
Wehrli, Roger Russell (football)	November 26, 1947
Weicker, Lowell Palmer, Jr. (politician)	May 16, 1931
Weidler, Virginia (actress)	March 21, 1927
Weiland, Cooney; born Ralph Weiland (hockey)	November 5, 1904
Weill, Kurt (music)	March 2, 1900
Weinberger, Casper Willard (government)	August 18, 1917
Weintraub, Phil; born Philip Weintraub (baseball)	October 12, 1907
Weiskopf, Tom; born Thomas Daniel Weiskopf (golf)	November 9, 1942
Weiss, Bob (basketball)	May 7, 1942
Weissmuller, Johnny; born Peter John Weissmuller (swimmer/actor)	June 2, 1903
Weitz, John (fashion designer)	May 25, 1923

Welch, Frank Tiguer (baseball)	August 10, 1897
Welch, Raquel; born Raquel Tejada (actress)	September 5, 1940
Weld, Tuesday; born Susan Ker Weld (actress)	August 27, 1943
Weldon, Joan (singer/actress)	August 5, 1933
Welford, Walter (politician)	May 21, 1869
Welk, Lawrence (music)	March 11, 1903
Welker, Herman (politician)	December 11, 1906
Welles, Orson; born George Orson Welles (actor/producer/ director/writer)	May 6, 1915
Wellington, Duke of; born Arthur Wellesley (statesman)	May 1, 1769
Wells, H.G.; born Herbert George Wells (author)	September 21, 1866
Wells, Kitty; born Muriel Deason (singer/music)	August 30, 1918
Wells, Mary (singer/music)	May 13, 1943
Welsh, Jim; born James Daniel Welsh (baseball)	October 9, 1902
Welsh, Matthew Empson (politician)	September 15, 1912
Welty, Eudora (author)	April 13, 1909
Wentworth, Cy; born Marvin Wentworth (hockey)	January 24, 1905
Werber, Bill; born William Murray Werber (baseball)	June 20, 1908
Werner, Oskar; born Joseph Bschliessmayer (actor/producer director)	November 13, 1922
Wert, Don; born Donald Ralph Wert (baseball)	July 29, 1938
Wertz, Vic; born Victor Woodrow Wertz (baseball)	February 9, 1925
Wesley, John (religious leader)	June 17, 1703
West, Adam; born William West Anderson (actor)	September 19, 1929
West, Charlie; born Charles West (football)	August 31, 1946
West, Dottie; born Dorothy Marie Marsh (singer/music)	October 11, 1932
West, Jerry (basketball)	May 28, 1938
West, Jessamyn; born Mary Jessamyn West (author)	July 18, 1902
West, John Carl (politician)	August 27, 1922
West, Mae (actress)	August 17, 1892
West, Max Edward (baseball)	November 28, 1916
West, Oswald (politician)	May 20, 1873
West, Dame Rebecca; born Cicily Isabel Fairfield (author)	December 25, 1892
West, Sammy; born Samuel Filmore West (baseball)	October 5, 1904
Westfall, Ed; born Vernon Edwin Westfall (hockey)	September 19, 1940
Westinghouse, George (inventor)	October 6, 1846
Westlake, Wally; born Walden Thomas Westlake (baseball)	November 8, 1920
Westley, Helen; born Henrietta Remson Meserole Maney Conroy (actress)	March 28, 1875
Westman, Nydia (actress)	February 19, 1902
Westmoreland, William Childs (army officer)	March 26, 1914
Weston, Ellen; born Ellen R. Weinstein (actress)	April 19, 1939
Weston, Jack (actor)	————1915
Weston, Kim (actress/singer)	December 20, 1939
Weston, Paul (music)	March 12, 1912
Westphal, Paul (basketball)	November 30, 1950
Westrum, Wes; born Wesley Noreen Westrum (baseball)	November 28, 1922
Wetherby, Lawrence Winchester (politician)	January 2, 1908
Wetmore, George Peabody (politician)	August 2, 1846
Whalen, Michael; born Joseph Kenneth Shovlin (actor)	June 30, 1899
Wharram, Kenny; born Kenneth Malcolm Wharram (hockey)	July 2, 1933

Wharton, Edith Newbold; born Edith Newbold Jones (author)	January 24, 1862
Wheat, Zack; born Zachariah Davis Wheat (baseball)	May 23, 1886
Wheeler, Bert; born Albert Jerome Wheeler (comedian)	April 7, 1895
Wheeler, Burton Kendall (politician)	February 27, 1882
Wheeler, Earle Gilmore (army officer)	January 13, 1908
Whelan, Arleen (actress)	September 16, 1916
Wherry, Kenneth Spicer (politician)	February 28, 1892
Whistler, James Abbott McNeill (artist)	July 10, 1834
Whitaker, Jack; born John Francis Whitaker (sportscaster)	May 18, 1924
Whitaker, Johnny (actor)	December 13, 1959
Whitcomb, Edgar Doud (politician)	November 6, 1917
White, Albert Blakeslee (politician)	September 22, 1856
White, Barry (singer/music)	September 12, 1944
White, Betty Marion (actress/singer)	January 17, 1922
White, Bill; born William DeKova White (baseball)	January 28, 1934
White, Bill; born William Earl White (hockey)	August 26, 1939
White, Byron Raymond "Whizzer" (football/jurist)	June 8, 1917
White, Dwight Lynn (football)	July 30, 1949
White, E.B.; born Elwyn Brooks White (author)	July 11, 1899
White, Ed; born Edward Alvin White (football)	April 4, 1947
White, Edward Douglass, Jr. (politician/jurist)	November 3, 1845
White, Frank (politics/government)	December 12, 1856
White, George; born George Weitz (producer/director/writer/ dancer/actor)	————1890
White, George (politician)	August 21, 1872
White, Hugh Lawson (politician)	August 19, 1881
White, Jesse; born Jesse Marc Weidenfeld (or Wiedenfeld) (actor)	January 3, 1918
White, Josh; born Joshua Daniel White (singer/music)	February 11, 1908
White, Jo Jo; born Joseph White (basketball)	November 16, 1946
White, Jo Jo; born Joyner Clifford White (baseball)	June 1, 1909
White, Kevin Hagen (politician)	September 25, 1929
White, Roy Hilton (baseball)	December 27, 1943
White, Sammy; born Samuel Charles White (baseball)	July 7, 1928
White, Teddy; born Theodore Harold White (author/historian)	May 6, 1915
White, Wallace Humphrey, Jr. (politician)	August 6, 1877
Whitehead, Alfred North (mathematician/philosopher)	February 15, 1861
Whitehead, Burgess Urquhard (baseball)	June 29, 1910
Whitehill, Earl Oliver (baseball)	February 7, 1900
Whitelaw, Billie (actress)	June 6, 1932
Whiteman, Paul (music)	March 28, 1890
Whitfield, Fred Dwight (baseball)	January 7, 1938
Whitfield, Henry Lewis (politician)	June 20, 1868
Whiting, Margaret (singer)	July 22, 1924
Whitman, Charles Seymour (politician)	August 28, 1868
Whitman, Stuart Maxwell (actor)	February 1, 1926
Whitman, Walt; born Walter Whitman (poet)	May 13, 1819
Whitmore, James Allen, Jr. (actor)	October 1, 1921
Whitney, Eleanore (dancer/actress)	April 21, 1914
Whitney, Eli (inventor)	December 8, 1765
Whitney, Pinky; born Arthur Carter Whitney (baseball)	January 2, 1905

Whittaker, Charles Evans (jurist)	February 22, 1901
Whittenton, Jess; born Urshell Whittenton (football)	May 9, 1934
Whittier, John Greenleaf (poet)	December 17, 1807
Whitty, Dame May (actress)	June 19, 1865
Whitworth, Kathy; born Kathrynne Ann Whitworth (golf)	September 27, 1939
Wickard, Claude Raymond (government)	February 28, 1893
Wickersham, George Woodward (government)	September 19, 1858
Wickes, Mary; born Mary Isabelle Wickenhauser (actress)	June 13, 1916
Wicks, Sidney (basketball)	September 19, 1949
Widby, Ron; born George Ronald Widby (football)	March 9, 1945
Widdoes, Kathleen Effie (actress)	March 21, 1939
Widmark, Richard (actor)	December 26, 1914
Wiebe, Arthur Walter Ronald (hockey)	September 28, 1913
Wiechers, Jim; born James L. Wiechers (golf)	August 7, 1944
Wietelmann, Whitey; born William Frederick Wietelmann (baseball)	March 15, 1919
Wiggin, Paul (football)	November 8, 1934
Wilbur, Curtis Dwight (government)	May 10, 1867
Wilbur, John (football)	May 21, 1943
Wilbur, Ray Lyman (government)	April 13, 1875
Wilcox, David (football)	September 29, 1942
Wilcox, Larry (actor)	August 8, 1948
Wilcox-Horne, Collin; born Collin Wilcox (actress)	February 4, 1935
Wilcoxen, Henry (actor)	September 8, 1905
Wilde, Cornel Louis (actor/producer/director)	October 13, 1915
Wilde, Oscar Fingal O'Flahertie Wills (poet/playwright)	October 16, 1854
Wilder, Billy; born Samuel Wilder (producer/director)	June 22, 1906
Wilder, Gene; born Jerome Silberman (actor/director)	June 11, 1934
Wilder, Thornton Niven (playwright)	April 17, 1897
Wilding, Michael (actor)	July 23, 1912
Wiley, Alexander (politician)	May 26, 1884
Wilhelm, Hoyt; born James Hoyt Wilhelm (baseball)	July 26, 1923
Wilkerson, Doug; born Douglas Wilkerson (football)	March 27, 1947
Wilkins, Lenny; born Leonard Wilkins (basketball)	October 28, 1937
Wilkins, Roy (civil rights leader)	August 30, 1901
Wilkinson, Bud; born Charles Burnham Wilkinson (football/sportscaster)	April 23, 1916
Willard, Ken; born Kenneth Henderson Willard (football)	July 14, 1943
William, Warren; born Warren William Krech (actor)	December 2, 1895
Williams, Andy; born Howard Andrew Williams (singer)	December 3, 1928
Williams, Anson; born Anson William Heimlick (actor/singer)	September 25, 1949
Williams, Arnold (politician)	May 21, 1898
Williams, Bill; born William Katt (actor)	————1916
Williams, Billy Dee (actor)	April 6, 1937
Williams, Billy Leo (baseball)	June 15, 1938
Williams, Cara; born Bernice Kamiat (actress)	June 29, 1925
Williams, Chuck (basketball)	June 6, 1946
Williams, Cindy; born Cynthia Jane Williams (actress)	August 22, 1948
Williams, Clancy; born Clarence Williams (football)	September 24, 1942
Williams, Clarence (football)	September 3, 1946
Williams, Clarence, III (actor)	August 21, 1939

Williams, Cy; born Fred Williams (baseball) — December 21, 1887
Williams, Dick; born Richard Hirschfeld Williams (baseball) — May 7, 1929
Williams, Earl Craig, Jr. (baseball) — July 14, 1948
Williams, Emlyn; born George Emlyn Williams (actor/writer/ producer) — November 26, 1905
Williams, Esther Jane (swimmer/actress) — August 8, 1923
Williams, G. Mennen; born Gerhard Mennen Williams (politician) — February 23, 1911
Williams, Grant (actor) — August 18, 1930
Williams, Guy (actor) — January 14, 1924
Williams, Hank, Sr.; born Hiram King Williams (singer) — September 17, 1923
Williams, Hank, Jr.; born Randall Hank Williams (singer) — May 26, 1949
Williams, Harrison Arlington, Jr. (politician) — December 10, 1919
Williams, Jack; born John Richard Williams (politician) — October 29, 1909
Williams, Joe; born Joseph Goreed (singer) — December 12, 1918
Williams, John; born Hugh Ernest Leo Williams (actor) — April 15, 1903
Williams, John (football) — October 27, 1945
Williams, John Bell (politician) — December 4, 1918
Williams, John James (politician) — May 17, 1904
Williams, John Sharp (politician) — July 30, 1854
Williams, Ken; born Kenneth Roy Williams (baseball) — June 28, 1890
Williams, Mason (music) — August 24, 1938
Williams, Nate (basketball) — June 2, 1950
Williams, Paul Hamilton (singer/actor/music) — September 19, 1940
Williams, Ransome Judson (politician) — January 4, 1892
Williams, Robert Lee (politician) — December 20, 1868
Williams, Robin (comedian/actor) — July 21, 1952
Williams, Roger (clergyman) — ———1607
Williams, Roger; born Louis Weertz (music) — October 1, 1926
Williams, Stan; born Stanley Wilson Williams (baseball) — September 14, 1936
Williams, Ted; born Theodore Samuel Williams (baseball) — August 30, 1918
Williams, Tennessee; born Thomas Lanter Williams (playwright) — March 26, 1911
Williams, Thomas Mark (hockey) — April 17, 1940
Williams, Travis (football) — January 14, 1946
Williams, Van (actor) — February 27, 1934
Williams, Walt; born Walter Allen Williams (baseball) — December 19, 1943
Williamson, Fred; born Frederick R. Williamson (football/sportscaster/actor) — March 5, 1937
Williamson, Nicol (actor) — September 14, 1938
Willis, Frank Bartlette (politician) — December 28, 1871
Willis, Simeon Slavens (politician) — December 1, 1879
Willkie, Wendell Lewis (politician) — February 18, 1892
Wills, Bob; born James Robert Wills (music) — March 6, 1905
Wills, Chill (actor) — July 18, 1903
Wills, Helen Newington (tennis) — October 6, 1906
Wills, Maury; born Maurice Morning Wills (baseball/ sportscaster) — October 2, 1932
Wills, William Henry (politician) — October 26, 1882
Willson, Augustus Everett (politician) — October 13, 1846
Willson, Meredith; born Robert Meredith Reiniger (music) — May 18, 1902

Wilson, Charles Erwin (government)	July 18, 1890
Wilson, Demond (actor)	October 13, 1946
Wilson, Don; born Donald Edward Wilson (baseball)	February 12, 1945
Wilson, Don; born Donald Harlow Wilson (announcer/actor)	September 1, 1900
Wilson, Dorothy (actress)	November 14, 1909
Wilson, Earl (journalist)	May 3, 1907
Wilson, Earl; born Robert Earl Wilson (baseball)	October 2, 1934
Wilson, Edith Bolling; born Edith Bolling	October 15, 1872
(second wife of Woodrow Wilson/First Lady)	
Wilson, Ellen Louise Axson; born Ellen Louise Axson	May 15, 1860
(first wife of Woodrow Wilson/First Lady)	
Wilson, Flip; born Clerow Wilson (comedian/actor)	December 8, 1933
Wilson, George (basketball)	May 9, 1942
Wilson, George Allison (politician)	April 1, 1884
Wilson, Hack; born Lewis Robert Wilson (baseball)	June 26, 1900
Wilson, Harold; born James Harold Wilson (British	March 11, 1916
government)	
Wilson, Henry (Vice President)	February 16, 1812
Wilson, Jackie (singer)	June 9, 1932
Wilson, James (government)	August 16, 1835
Wilson, Jerrel D. (football)	October 4, 1941
Wilson, Jim; born James Alger Wilson (baseball)	February 20, 1922
Wilson, Jimmie; born James Wilson (baseball)	July 23, 1900
Wilson, John Edward (hockey)	June 14, 1929
Wilson, Joyce Vincent; born Joyce Elaine Vincent (singer)	December 14, 1946
Wilson, Julie (actress/singer)	—————1925
Wilson, Larry; born Lawrence Frank Wilson (football)	March 24, 1938
Wilson, Lois (actress)	June 28, 1895
Wilson, Margaret (author)	January 16, 1882
Wilson, Marie; born Katherine Elizabeth White (actress)	December 30, 1916
Wilson, Nancy (singer)	February 20, 1937
Wilson, Peggy; born Margaret Joyce Wilson (golf)	December 28, 1934
Wilson, Red; born Robert James Wilson (baseball)	March 7, 1929
Wilson, Sloan (author)	May 8, 1920
Wilson, Stanley Calef (politician)	September 10, 1879
Wilson, Teddy; born Theodore Wilson (music)	November 24, 1912
Wilson, William Bauchop (government)	April 2, 1862
Wilson, Woodrow; born Thomas Woodrow Wilson (President)	December 28, 1856
Winant, John Gilbert (politician)	February 23, 1889
Winchell, Paul (ventriloquist/actor)	December 21, 1922
Winchell, Walter; born Walter Winchel (journalist)	April 7, 1897
Windom, William (actor)	September 28, 1923
Windsor, Bob; born Robert Edward Windsor (football)	December 19, 1942
Windsor, Claire; born Clara Viola Cronk (actress)	April 14, 1897
Windsor, Duchess of; born Bessie Wallis Warfield	June 19, 1896
Windsor, Duke of; born Edward Albert Christian George	June 23, 1894
Andrew Patrick David	
Windsor, Marie; born Emily Marie Bertelson (actress)	December 11, 1922
Wine, Bobby; born Robert Paul Wine (baseball)	September 17, 1938
Winfield, Dave; born David Mark Winfield (baseball)	October 3, 1951
Winfield, Paul Edward (actor)	May 22, 1941
Wing, Toby; born Martha Virginia Wing (actress)	July 14, 1913

Wingo, Al; born Absalom Holbrook Wingo (baseball)   May 6, 1898
Winkler, Henry Franklin (actor)   October 30, 1945
Winston, Roy C. (football)   July 15, 1940
Winter, Johnny; born John Dawson Winter, III (singer)   February 23, 1944
Winterhalter, Hugo (music)   August 15, 1910
Winters, Jonathan Harshman (comedian/actor)   November 11, 1925
Winters, Roland; born Roland Winternitz (actor)   November 22, 1904
Winters, Shelly; born Shirley Schrift (actress)   August 18, 1922
Winwood, Estelle; born Estelle Goodwin (actress)   January 24, 1883
Wirtz, W. Willard; born William Willard Wirtz (government)   March 14, 1912
Wisdom, Norman (comedian/actor/singer)   February 4, 1918
Wise, Rick; born Richard Charles Wise (baseball)   September 13, 1945
Wise, Robert (director/producer)   September 10, 1914
Wiseman, Edward Randall (hockey)   December 28, 1912
Wiseman, Joseph (actor)   May 15, 1918
Witek, Mickey; born Nicholas Joseph Witek (baseball)   December 19, 1915
Withers, Bill (singer/music)   July 4, 1938
Withers, Googie; born Georgette Lizette Withers (actress)   March 12, 1917
Withers, Grant (actor)   June 17, 1904
Withers, Jane (actress)   April 12, 1926
Witherspoon, Cora (comedienne/actress)   January 5, 1890
Withycombe, James (politician)   March 21, 1854
Witt, Whitey; born Ladislaw Waldemar Wittkowski (baseball)   September 28, 1895
Wodehouse, P.G.; born Pelham Grenville Wodehouse (author)   October 15, 1881
Woit, Benedict Francis (hockey)   January 7, 1928
Wojciechowicz, Alex; born Alexander Wojciechowicz   August 12, 1915
     (football)
Wolf, Hugo (music)   March 13, 1860
Wolf, Thomas Clayton (author)   October 3, 1900
Wolfe, Tom; born Thomas Kennerly Wolfe (journalist)   March 2, 1931
Wonder, Stevie; born Steveland Morris Hardaway (singer)   May 13, 1950
Wong, Anna May; born Lu Tsong Wong (or Wong Liu Tsong)   January 3, 1907
     (actress)
Wood, Craig Ralph (golf)   November 18, 1901
Wood, Lana (actress)   ———1946
Wood, Natalie; born Natasha Nicholas Gurdin (actress)   July 20, 1938
Wood, Peggy; born Margaret Wood (actress/singer)   February 9, 1892
Wood, Wilbur Forrester, Jr. (baseball)   October 22, 1941
Wood, Willie; born William V. Wood (football)   December 23, 1936
Woodall, Al; born Frank Alley Woodall (football)   December 7, 1945
Woodbury, Joan (actress)   December 17, 1915
Woodcock, Leonard Freel (labor leader)   February 15, 1911
Woodling, Gene; born Eugene Richard Woodling (baseball)   August 16, 1922
Woodring, Harry Hines (politics/government)   May 31, 1890
Woodruff, Rollin Simmons (politician)   July 14, 1854
Woodson, Abe; born Abraham Woodson (football)   February 15, 1934
Woodward, Joanne Gignilliat (actress)   February 27, 1930
Woodward, Morgan; born Thomas Morgan Woodward (actor)   September 16, 1925
Woodward, Woody; born William Frederick Woodward (baseball)   September 23, 1942
Woolf, Virginia; born Adeline Virginia Stephens (author)   January 25, 1882
Woollcott, Alexander Humphreys (journalist/writer)   January 19, 1887
Woolley, Monty; born Edgar Montillion Woolley (actor)   August 17, 1888

Woolworth, F.W.; born Frank W. Woolworth (merchant)	April 13, 1852
Wordsworth, William (poet)	April 7, 1770
Work, Hubert (government)	July 3, 1860
Works, John Downey (politician)	March 29, 1847
Worley, Jo Anne (comedienne/actress)	September 6, 1937
Worsham, Lew; born Lewis Elmer Worsham (golf)	October 5, 1917
Worsley, Gump; born Lorne Worsley (hockey)	May 14, 1929
Worters, Roy (hockey)	October 19, 1900
Worth, Irene (actress)	June 23, 1916
Worthington, Al; born Allan Fulton Worthington (baseball)	February 5, 1929
Wouk, Herman (author)	May 27, 1915
Woytowich, Robert Ivan (hockey)	August 18, 1941
Wray, Fay (actress)	September 15, 1907
Wren, Sir Christopher (architect)	October 20, 1632
Wright, Bill; born William Robert Wright (baseball)	April 12, 1922
Wright, Clyde (baseball)	February 20, 1941
Wright, Cobina Caroline, Jr. (actress)	August 14, 1921
Wright, Ernie; born Ernest H. Wright (football)	November 6, 1939
Wright, Fielding Lewis (politician)	May 16, 1895
Wright, Frank Lloyd (architect)	June 8, 1869
Wright, Glenn; born Forrest Glenn Wright (baseball)	February 6, 1901
Wright, Jeff; born Jeffrey Ralph Wright (football)	June 13, 1949
Wright, Jim; born James Claud Wright, Jr. (politician)	December 22, 1922
Wright, Martha; born Martha Lucile Wiederrecht (actress)	March 23, 1926
Wright, Mickey; born Mary Kathryn Wright (golf)	February 14, 1935
Wright, Nate (football)	December 21, 1947
Wright, Orville (aviator/inventor)	August 19, 1871
Wright, Rayfield; born Larry Rayfield Wright (football)	August 23, 1945
Wright, Taffy; born Taft Shedron Wright (baseball)	August 10, 1911
Wright, Teresa; born Muriel Teresa Wright (actress)	October 27, 1918
Wright, Wilbur (aviator)	April 16, 1867
Wrightson, Earl (singer/actor)	January 1, 1916
Wrightstone, Russ; born Russell Guy Wrightstone (baseball)	March 18, 1893
Wrigley, Philip Knight (corporation executive)	December 5, 1894
Wyatt, Jane Waddington (actress)	August 12, 1912
Wyatt, Whit; born John Whitlow Wyatt (baseball)	September 27, 1907
Wyeth, Andrew Newell (artist)	July 12, 1917
Wyeth, James Browning (artist)	July 6, 1946
Wyeth, N.C.; born Newell Convers Wyeth (artist)	Octoer 22, 1882
Wyler, Gretchen; born Gretchen Patricia Wienecke (actress)	February 16, 1932
Wyler, William (producer/director)	July 1, 1902
Wyman, Jane; born Sarah Jane Fulks (actress)	January 4, 1914
Wyman, Louis Crosby (politician)	March 16, 1917
Wymore, Patrice (actress)	December 17, 1926
Wynette, Tammy; born Wynette Pugh (singer/music)	May 5, 1942
Wynn, Early (baseball)	January 6, 1920
Wynn, Ed; born Isaiah Edwin Leopold (actor)	November 9, 1886
Wynn, Jim; born James Sherman Wynn (baseball)	March 12, 1942
Wynn, Keenan; born Francis Xavier Alousius Keenan Wynn (actor)	July 27, 1916
Wynter, Dana; born Dagmar Winter (actress)	June 8, 1930
Wynyard, Diana; born Dorothy Isobel Cox (actress)	January 16, 1906

Wyrostek, Johnny; born John Barney Wyrostek (baseball)   July 12, 1919
Wysong, Dudley, Jr. (golf)   May 15, 1939

Y

Yancey, Bert; born Albert Winsborough Yancey (golf)   August 6, 1938
Yankowski, Ron; born Ronald William Yankowski (football)   October 23, 1946
Yarborough, Cale; born William Caleb Yarborough (auto racing)   March 27, 1939
Yarborough, Ralph Webster (politician)   June 8, 1903
Yarbrough, Glenn (singer/music)   January 12, 1930
Yarbrough, Jim; born James Kelley Yarbrough (football)   October 28, 1946
Yarbrough, Lee Roy (auto racing)   September 17, 1938
Yardley, George (basketball)   November 3, 1928
Yarnell, Bruce (actor/singer)   December 28,.1935
Yary, Ron; born Anthony Ronald Yary (football)   August 16, 1946
Yastrzemski, Carl Michael (baseball)   August 22, 1939
Yates, Richard (politician)   December 12, 1860
Ycaza, Manuel (jockey)   January 24, 1935
Yeager, Steve; born Stephen Wayne Yeager (baseball)   November 24, 1948
Yeats, William Butler (poet)   June 13, 1865
Yepremian, Garo; born Garabed Sarkis Yepremian (football)   June 2, 1944
Yerby, Frank Garvin (author)   September 5, 1916
York, Dick; born Richard Allen York (actor)   September 4, 1928
York, Michael; born Michael York-Johnson (actor)   March 27, 1942
York, Rudy; born Rudolph Preston York (baseball)   August 17, 1913
York, Susannah Fletcher (actress)   January 9, 1941
Yorkin, Bud; born Alan David Yorkin (producer/director)   February 22, 1926
Yorty, Sam; born Samuel William Yorty (politician)   October 1, 1909
Yost, Eddie; born Edward Frederick Joseph Yost (baseball)   October 13, 1926
Youmans, Vincent Millie (music)   September 27, 1898
Young, Alan; born Angus Young (actor)   November 19, 1919
Young, Andrew Jackson, Jr. (politics/government)   March 12, 1932
Young, Babe; born Norman Robert Young (baseball)   July 1, 1915
Young, Bob; born Robert Allen Young (football)   September 3, 1942
Young, Bobby; born Robert George Young (baseball)   November 22, 1925
Young, Brigham (religious leader)   June 1, 1801
Young, Buddy; born Claude H. Young (football)   January 5, 1926
Young, Chic; born Murat Bernard Young (cartoonist)   January 9, 1901
Young, Clara Kimball (actress)   September————1890
Young, Clement Calhoun (politician)   April 28,1869
Young, Coleman Alexander (politician)   May 24, 1918
Young, Cy; born Denton True Young (baseball)   March 29, 1867
Young, Donna Caponi; born Donna Maria Caponi (golf)   January 29, 1945
Young, Douglas (hockey)   October 1, 1908
Young, Faron (singer/music)   February 25, 1932
Young, Gig; born Byron Ellsworth Barr (actor)   November 4, 1917
Young, Howard John Edward (hockey)   August 2, 1937
Young, Jesse Colin (singer)   November 11, 1944
Young, John Watts (astronaut)   September 24, 1930
Young, Loretta; born Gretchen Michaela Young (actress)   January 6, 1911
Young, Milton Ruben (politician)   December 6, 1897
Young, Pep; born Lemuel Floyd Young (baseball)   August 29, 1907

Young, Robert George (actor)	February 22, 1907
Young, Roland (actor)	November 11, 1887
Young, Stephen; born Stephen Levy (actor)	May 19, 1939
Young, Stephen Marvin (politician)	May 4, 1889
Young, Wilbur Eugene (football)	April 20, 1949
Young, Willie; born William Lull Young (football)	June 27, 1943
Youngblood, Jack; born Herbert Jackson Youngblood, III (football)	January 26, 1950
Youngblood, Jim; born James Lee Youngblood (football)	February 23, 1950
Youngdahl, Luther Wallace Augustinus (politician)	May 29, 1896
Younger, Tank; born Paul Younger (football)	June 25, 1928
Youngman, Henny (comedian)	————1906
Youngs, Ross Middlebrook (baseball)	April 10, 1897
Yulin, Harris (actor)	November 5, 1937
Yurka, Blanche; born Blanche Jurka (actress)	June 19, 1887

Z

Zabel, Steve Gregory (football)	March 20, 1948
Zachary, Tom; born Jonathan Thompson Walton Zachary (baseball)	May 7, 1896
Zaharias, Babe Didrikson; born Mildred Ella Didrikson (olympic athlete/golf)	June 26, 1912
Zanuck, Darryl Francis (producer)	September 5, 1902
Zanuck, Richard Darryl (producer)	December 13, 1934
Zarilla, Al; born Allen Lee Zarilla (baseball)	May 1, 1919
Zarley, Kermit (golf)	September 29, 1941
Zaslofsky, Max (basketball)	December 7, 1925
Zeffirelli, Franco; born Franco Zeffirelli Corisi (director)	February 12, 1922
Zentner, Si; born Simon H. Zentner (music)	June 13, 1917
Zerbe, Anthony (actor)	————1936
Zernial, Gus Edward (baseball)	June 27, 1923
Zetterling, Mai (actress/director/writer)	May 24, 1925
Ziegfeld, Florenz, Jr. (producer)	March 21, 1869
Ziegler, Larry; born Lawrence Ziegler (golf)	August 12, 1939
Ziegler, Ron; born Ronald Lewis Ziegler (government)	May 12, 1939
Zimbalist, Efrem (music)	April 9, 1889
Zimbalist, Efrem Jr.; (actor)	November 30, 1913
Zimmer, Don; born Donald William Zimmer (baseball)	January 17, 1931
Zimmer, Norma; born Norma Beatrice Larsen(singer)	July 13————
Zimmerman, Fred Rudolph (politician)	November 20, 1880
Zindel, Paul (playwright)	May 15, 1936
Zinneman, Fred (director)	April 29, 1907
Zisk, Richie; born Richard Walter Zisk (baseball)	February 6, 1949
Zoeller, Fuzzy; born Frank Urban Zoeller, Jr. (golf)	November 11, 1951
Zola, Emile Edouard Charles Antoine (author)	April 2, 1840
Zook, John Eldon (football)	September 24, 1947
Zorina, Vera; born Eva Brigitta Hartwig (dancer/actress)	January 2, 1917
Zorinsky, Edward (politician)	November 11, 1928
Zukor, Adolph (producer)	January 7, 1873
Zukor, Eugene J. (producer)	October 25, 1897
Zumwalt, Elmo Russell, Jr. (naval officer)	November 29, 1920

Chronological Listing
of Celebrities

JANUARY 1:

Allen, Ethan Nathan (baseball); 1904
Andrews, Dana; born Carver Dana (or Daniel) Andrews (actor); 1909
Armstrong, Murray Alexander (hockey); 1916
Baxley, Barbara (actress); 1925
Bickford,. Charles Ambrose (actor); 1889
Chamberlain, George Earle (politician); 1854
Connor, George (football); 1925
Cortesa, Valentina (actress); 1924
Cugat, Xavier; born Francisco De Asis Javier Cugat Mingall De Bru y
 Deulofeo (music/actor/artist); 1900
Goldwater, Barry Morris (politician); 1909
Graziano, Rocky; born Rocco Barbella (boxing); 1921
Greenberg, Hank; born Henry Benjamin Greenberg (baseball); 1911
Haines, John Michener (politician); 1863
Haines, William (actor); 1900
Hollings, Ernest Frederick (politician); 1922
Hoover, J. Edgar; born John Edgar Hoover (government); 1895
Ickx, Jacky; born Jacques-Bernard Ickx (auto racing); 1945
Johnson, Edwin Carl (politician); 1884
Jones, Jimmy; born James Jones (basketball); 1945
Landis, Carole; born Frances Lillian Mary Ridste (actress); 1919
Langella, Frank (actor); 1940
Lothridge, Billy; born William L. Lothridge (football); 1942
McKeever, Marlin (football); 1940
McKinney, Bones; born Horace McKinney (basketball); 1919
Murillo, Bartolomé Esteban (artist); 1618
Revere, Paul (patriot); 1735
Richardson, Harry Alden (politician); 1853
Ross, Betsy; born Elizabeth Griscom Ross (flag maker); 1752
Salinger, J. D.; born Jerome David Salinger (author); 1919
Thompson, Leonard (golf); 1947
Torgeson, Earl; born Clifford Earl Torgeson (baseball); 1924
Walker, Doak; born Ewell Doak Walker (football); 1927

Wayne, Anthony (military officer); 1745
Wrightson, Earl (singer/actor); 1916

JANUARY 2:

Allott, Gordon Llewellyn (politician); 1907
Asimov, Isaac (author); 1920
Bradley, Bill; born William Bradley (football); 1947
Evers, Jason (actor); 1927
Fischer, Pat; born Patrick Fischer (football); 1940
Fleming, Marv; born Marvin Fleming (football); 1942
Harmon, David Glen (hockey); 1921
Hill, Calvin (football); 1947
Kress, Red; born Ralph Kress (baseball); 1907
La Rosa, Julius (singer); 1930
Madlock, Bill; born William Madlock, Jr. (baseball); 1951
Marchetti, Gino John (football); 1927
McMullen, Richard Cann (politician); 1868
Melton, James (singer); 1904
Miller, Roger Dean (singer/music); 1936
Muhlmann, Horst (football); 1940
Petersen, Hjalmar (politician); 1890
Wetherby, Lawrence Winchester (politician); 1908
Whitney, Pinky; born Arthur Carter Whitney (baseball); 1905
Zorina, Vera; born Eva Brigitta Hartwig (dancer/actress); 1917

JANUARY 3:

Andrews, Maxene (singer—Andrews Sisters); 1918
Attlee, Clement Richard (British government); 1883
Blumenthal, W. Michael; born Werner Michael Blumenthal
    (government); 1926
Borge, Victor; born Borge Rosenbaum (music/comedian/actor); 1908
Cissell, Bill; born Chalmer William Cissell (baseball)); 1904
Coleman, Dabney (actor); ——
Coolidge, Grace Anne Goodhue; born Grace Anne Goodhue (First
    Lady); 1879
Corday, Mara; born Marilyn Watts (actress); 1932
Davies, Marion; born Marion Cecelia Douras (actress); 1897
Dempsey, John Noel (politician); 1915
Flemyng, Robert; born Benjamin Arthur Flemyng (actor); 1912
Furness, Betty; born Elizabeth Mary Furness (actress/consumer
    advocate); 1916
Hills, Carla Anderson; born Carla Anderson (government); 1934
Hudson, Sid; born Sidney Charles Hudson (baseball); 1917
Hull, Bobby; born Robert Marvin Hull, Jr. (hockey); 1939
Hull, Josephine; born Josephine Sherwood (actress); 1884
Loggia, Robert (actor); 1930

Marlin, Coo Coo; born Clifton Burton Marlin (auto racing); 1932
Milland, Ray; born Reginald Truscott-Jones (actor); 1905
Murphy, Franklin (politician); 1846
Overman, Lee Slater (politician); 1854
Pavlova, Anna (dancer); 1885
Pitts, Zasu; born Eliza Susan Pitts (actress); 1898
Principal, Victoria (actress); 1945
Russell, John (actor); 1921
Stills, Stephen (singer/music); 1945
Stram, Hank; born Henry Louis Stram (football/sportscaster); 1923
Suhr, Gus; born August Richard Suhr (baseball); 1906
Travers, Bill (actor); 1922
Walton, Michael Robert (hockey); 1945
White, Jesse; born Jesse Marc Weidenfeld (or Wiedenfeld) (actor); 1918
Wong, Anna May; born Lu Tsong Wong (or Wong Liu Tsong) (actress); 1907

JANUARY 4:

Alexander, Kermit J. (football); 1941
Atkinson, George Henry (football); 1947
Booke, Sorrell (actor); 1926
Braille, Louis C. (teacher of blind); 1809
Bumbry, Grace Ann (singer); 1937
Cannon, Dyan; born Samille Diane Friesen (actress); 1929
Colby, William Egan (government); 1920
Dirksen, Everett McKinley (politician); 1896
Fuentes, Tito; born Rigoberto Peat Fuentes (baseball); 1944
Ginn, Hubert (football); 1947
Glass, Carter (politics/government); 1858
Grimm, Jacob Ludwig Carl (fairy tale author); 1785
Hart, Louis Folwell (politician); 1862
Holloway, Sterling (actor); 1905
Lawson, Steve; born Stephen Lawson (football); 1949
McCord, Darris (football); 1933
McMahon, Don; born Donald John McMahon (baseball); 1930
Patterson, Floyd (boxing); 1935
Rush, Barbara (actress); 1927
Selkirk, George Alexander (baseball); 1908
Shula, Don; born Donald Francis Shula (football); 1930
Thomas, John W. (politician); 1874
Williams, Ransome Judson (politician); 1892
Wyman, Jane; born Sarah Jane Fulks (actress); 1914

JANUARY 5:

Adenauer, Konrad (German government); 1876
Ailey, Alvin (dancer/choreographer); 1931

Aumont, Jean-Pierre; born Jean-Pierre Salomons (actor); 1909
Battey, Earl Jesse (baseball); 1935
Decatur, Stephen (naval officer); 1779
Duvall, Robert Selden (actor); 1931
Keaton, Diane; born Diane Hall (actress); 1946
Kramer, Jack; born John Henry Kramer (baseball); 1918
Martin, Pamela Sue (actress); 1953
McKinley, Chuck; born Charles R. McKinley (tennis); 1941
Mondale, Walter Frederick "Fritz" (Vice President); 1928
Morini, Erica (music); 1908
Morris, Mercury; born Eugene Morris (football); 1947
Noll, Chuck; born Charles H. Noll (football); 1932
Otto, Jim; born James Edwin Otto (football); 1938
Potts, Cliff (actor); ———
Reed, John Hathaway (politician); 1921
Ryder, Alfred; born Alfred Jacob Corn (actor); 1919
Sewell, Luke; born James Luther Sewell (baseball); 1901
Stephenson, Riggs; born Jackson Riggs Stephenson (baseball); 1898
Tingley, Clyde (politician); 1883
Witherspoon, Cora (comedienne/actress); 1890
Young, Buddy; born Claude H. Young (football); 1926

JANUARY 6:

Adams, Joey; born Joseph Abramowitz (comedian); 1911
Amaro, Ruben Mora (baseball); 1936
Bailey, Thomas Lowry (politician); 1888
Branca, Ralph Theodore Joseph (baseball); 1926
Brown, Tom; born Thomas Edward Brown (actor); 1913
Capucine; born Germaine Lefebvre (actress); 1933
Di Salle, Michael Vincent (politician); 1908
Doctorow, E. L.; born Edgar Laurence Doctorow (author); 1931
Ferris, Woodbridge Nathan (politician); 1853
Flaherty, Pat; born George Francis Patrick Flaherty (auto racing); 1926
Fletcher, Duncan Upshaw (politician); 1859
Franklin, Bonnie Gail (actress/singer); 1944
Green, Lenny; born Leonard Charles Green (baseball); 1934
Gullett, Don; born Donald Edward Gullett (baseball); 1951
Hard, Darlene R. (tennis); 1936
Harris, Louis (pollster); 1921
Hockenhull, A. W.; born Andrew Walter Hockenhull (politician); 1877
Jackson, Harold (football); 1946
Joan of Arc; born Jeanne D'Arc (French heroine); 1412
Lopez, Nancy Marie (golf); 1957
Middlecoff, Cary; born Emmett Cary Middlecoff (golf/sportscaster); 1921
Mix, Tom; born Thomas Edwin Mix (actor); 1880

Moore, Dickie; born Richard Winston Moore (hockey); 1931
Murphree, Dennis; born Herron Dennis Murphree (politician); 1886
Phillips, Mel; born Melvin Phillips (football); 1942
Randle, Sonny; born Ulmo Randle (football); 1936
Rayburn, Sam; born Samuel Taliaferro Rayburn (politician); 1882
Sandburg, Carl August (poet); 1878
Scruggs, Earl Eugene (music); 1924
Sullivan, Francis L.; born Francis Loftus Sullivan (actor); 1903
Sumner, Charles (statesman); 1811
Syms, Sylvia (actress); 1934
Tayback, Vic; born Victor Tabback (actor); 1930
Tempo, Nino (singer); 1937
Thomas, Danny; born Amos Joseph Alphonsus Jacobs (or Amos
    Muzyad Jacobs) (or (Jahoob) (comedian/actor/singer/
    producer); 1914
Walls, Lee; born Ray Lee Walls (baseball); 1933
Wynn, Early (baseball); 1920
Young, Loretta; born Gretchen Michaela Young (actress); 1911

JANUARY 7:

Addams, Charles Samuel (cartoonist); 1912
Blatty, Wiilliam Peter (writer/producer); 1928
Brezina, Greg; born Gregory Brezina (football); 1946
Burney, Dwight Willard (politician); 1892
Conigliaro, Tony; born Anthony Richard Conigliaro (baseball); 1945
Dark, Al; born Alvin Ralph Dark (baseball); 1922
Faubus, Orval Eugene (politician); 1910
Fillmore, Millard (President); 1800
Gardenia, Vincent; born Vincenzio Scognamiglio (actor); 1922
Graham, Lou (golf); 1938
Greene, Jack (singer/music); 1930
Grimsley, Ross Albert, II (baseball); 1950
Jones, Joe Willie (football); 1948
Kiker, Douglas; born Ralph Douglas Kiker, Jr. (newscaster); 1930
Kirk, Claude Roy, Jr. (politician); 1926
Kneip, Richard Francis (politician); 1933
LeBaron, Eddie; born Edward Wayne LeBaron, Jr. (football); 1930
Lee, J. Bracken; born Joseph Bracken Lee (politician); 1899
Lefebvre, Jim; born James Kenneth Lefebvre (baseball); 1943
McCarthy, Johnny; born John Joseph McCarthy (baseball); 1910
Mize, Johnny; born John Robert Mize (baseball); 1913
Moore, Terry; born Helen Koford (actress); 1929
Napier, Alan (actor); 1903
Pratt, Babe; born Walter Pratt (hockey); 1916
Ross, Shirley; born Bernice Gaunt (actress/singer); 1909
Schofield, Dick; born John Richard Schofield (baseball); 1935

Smith, Hooley; born Reginald Joseph Smith (hockey); 1905
Todd, Al; born Alfred Chester Todd (baseball); 1904
Whitfield, Fred Dwight (baseball); 1938
Woit, Benedict Francis (hockey); 1928
Zukor, Adolph (producer); 1873

JANUARY 8:

Adams, Sherman; born Llewellyn Sherman Adams (politician); 1899
Arno, Peter (cartoonist); 1904
Bassey, Shirley (singer); 1937
Bertoia, Reno Peter (baseball); 1935
Bowie, David; born David Robert Jones (singer/music); 1947
Busby, Jim; born James Franklin Busby (baseball); 1927
Clark, Bennett Champ (politician); 1890
Colville, Mac; born Mathew Lamont Colville (hockey); 1916
Conley, William Gustavus (politician); 1866
Cooper, Walker; born William Walker Cooper (baseball); 1915
Cromwell, Richard; born Roy M. Radabaugh (actor); 1910
Dixon, Hewritt Frederick, Jr. (football); 1940
Ellis, Ronald John Edward (hockey); 1945
Ferrer, José; born José Vincente Ferrer Otero y Cintron (actor/director);
      1909
Freese, Gene; born Eugene Lewis Freese (baseball); 1934
Gersbach, Carl (football); 1947
Hergesheimer, Walter Edgar (hockey); 1927
Hurley, Patrick Jay (government); 1883
Little Anthony; born Anthony Gourdine (singer); 1940
McQueen, Butterfly; born Thelma McQueen (actress/dancer); 1911
Mimieux, Yvette Carmen M. (actress/music/writer); 1939
Moody, Ron; born Ronald Moodnick (actor/singer); 1924
Presley, Elvis Aaron (singer/actor); 1935
Reed, Joe; born Joseph Butler Reed (football); 1948
Sales, Soupy; born Milton Hines (comedian/actor); 1926
Shipstead, Henrik (politician); 1881
Storch, Larry; born Lawrence Samuel Storch (actor); 1923
Vanocur, Sander; born Sander Vinocur (newscaster/journalist); 1928

JANUARY 9:

Baez, Joan (singer/music); 1941
Balanchine, George; born Gyorgi Melitonovitch Balanchivadze
      (choreographer); 1904
Banky, Vilma; born Vilma Lonchit (actress); 1898
Beauvoir, Simone Lucie Ernestine Marie Bertrand de (author); 1908
Brown, Terry (football); 1947
Catt, Carrie Lane Chapman; born Carrie Lane (suffragist); 1859
Coleman, James Piemon (politician); 1914
Curl, Rod (golf); 1943

Danaher, John Anthony (politician); 1899
Denver, Bob (actor); 1935
Enberg, Dick (sportscaster); ——
Fields, Gracie; born Gracie Stansfield (comedienne/actress/singer);
1898
Gayle, Crystal; born Brenda Gail Webb (singer); 1951
Green, Dwight Herbert (politician); 1897
Lamas, Fernando Alvaro (actor/director); 1915
Lee, Gypsy Rose; born Rose Louise Hovick (actress/dancer); 1914
Louise, Anita; born Anita Louise Fremault (actress); 1915
Matheson, Scott Milne (politician); 1929
Neuberger, Maurine Brown (politician); 1907
Newhouse, Robert Fulton (football); 1950
Nixon, Richard Milhous (President); 1913
Starr, Bart; born Bryan Bartlett Starr (football); 1934
Terry, Ralph Willard (baseball); 1936
Van Cleef, Lee (actor); 1925
York, Susannah Fletcher (actress); 1941
Young, Chic; born Murat Bernard Young (cartoonist); 1901

JANUARY 10:

Allen, Ethan (soldier); 1738
Bolger, Ray; born Raymond Wallace Bolger (actor/dancer); 1904
Bushman, Francis X.; born Francis Xavier Bushman (actor); 1883
Cain, Harry Pulliam (politician); 1906
Castles, Soapy; born Neil Castles (auto racing); 1934
Croce, Jim (singer/music); 1942
Dobson, Chuck; born Charles Thomas Dobson (baseball); 1944
Graves, Teresa (actress); 1938
Hamilton, Bob; born Robert Hamilton (golf); 1916
Henreid, Paul; born Paul Georg Julius von Hernreid Ritter von Wasel-
Waldingau (actor/director); 1908
MacKenzie, Giselle; born Marie Marguerite Louise Gisele La Fleche
(singer/actress); 1927
Mahovlich, Frank; born Francis William Mahovlich (hockey); 1938
McCovey, Willie Lee (baseball); 1938
McCulloch, Earl (football); 1936
Mineo, Sal; born Salvadore Mineo (actor/singer); 1939
Novack, Shelly (actor); ——
Page, Carroll Smalley (politician); 1843
Ray, Johnnie; born John Alvin Ray (singer); 1927
Shannon, Peggy (actress); 1907
Shoemaker, Ann Dorothea (actress); 1891
Sinatra, Frank, Jr.; born Francis Wayne Sinatra (singer/actor); 1944
Smoot, Reed (politician); 1862
Starke, Pauline (actress); 1900
Stewart, Rod; born Roderick David Stewart (singer/music); 1945

Strickland, George Bevan (baseball); 1926
Travis, Walter J. (golf); 1862
Ulanova, Galina Sergeyevna (dancer); 1910
Ward, Rodger (auto racing); 1921

JANUARY 11:

Barry, Don "Red"; born Donald Barry de Acosta (actor); 1912
Blue, Monte (actor); 1890
Borg, Veda Ann (actress); 1915
Calder-Marshall, Anna (actress); 1947
Carey, Max George; born Maximilan Carnarius (baseball); 1890
Cherry, Don; born Donald Cherry (golf/singer); 1924
Conklin, Chester; born Jules Cowles (actor); 1888
Crenshaw, Ben; born Benjamin Daniel Crenshaw (golf); 1952
Crowder, General; born Alvin Floyd Crowder (baseball); 1899
Flick, Elmer Harrison (baseball); 1876
Hamill, Red; born Robert George Hamill (hockey); 1917
Hamilton, Alexander (statesman); 1757
Harrison, Albertis Sydney, Jr. (politician); 1907
Hughes, Roy John (baseball); 1911
Kaufmann, Christine (actress); 1945
Kerr, Davey; born David Alexander Kerr (hockey); 1910
Kilgore, Harley Martin (politician); 1893
Kreps, Juanita Morris; born Juanita Morris (government); 1921
Le Gallienne, Eva (actress/director/producer); 1899
Mira, George Ignacio (football); 1942
Montler, Mike; born Michael R. Montler (football); 1944
Mossi, Don; born Donald Louis Mossi (baseball); 1929
Rodgers, Mary (music); 1931
Rowe, Schoolboy; born Lynwood Thomas Rowe (baseball);
    1910
Ryan, Mitchell (actor); 1928
Sharpe, Merrell Quentin (politician); 1883
Shelby, Carroll (auto racing & manufacturer); 1923
Solomon, Freddie (football); 1953
Spry, William (politician); 1864
Stander, Lionel Jay (actor); 1908
Stewart, Tom (politician); 1892
Taylor, Rod; born Robert Stuart Taylor (actor); 1929
Watson, John (football); 1949

JANUARY 12:

Agronsky, Martin Zama (journalism/broadcasting); 1915
Burke, Edmund (political philosopher/statesman/orator); 1729
Burrud, Bill (actor/producer); 1925
Dempsey, Tom; born Thomas Dempsey (football); 1947
Foster, Murphy James (politician); 1849
Frazier, Joe; born Joseph Frazier (boxing); 1944

Frederickson, Tucker; born Ivan Charles Frederickson (football); 1943
Gates, Charles Winslow (politician); 1856
Gendebien, Olivier (auto racing); 1924
Gurney, Edward John (politician); 1914
Harper, Ron (actor); 1936
Horton, Tim; born Myles Gilbert Horton (hockey); 1930
Jester, Beauford Halbert (politician); 1893
Johnson, Keen (politician); 1896
Kelly, Patsy; born Sarah Veronica Rose Kelly (actress); 1910
Lewis, Joe E.; born Joe Klewan (comedian); 1902
London, Jack; born John Griffith Chaney (author); 1876
Novak, Jane (actress); 1896
Pearson, Drew (football); 1951
Price, Ray Noble (singer/music); 1926
Rainer, Luise (actress); 1909
Ritter, Tex; born Woodward Maurice Nederland Ritter (actor/singer);
    1906
Ruby, Lloyd; born Richard Lloyd Ruby (auto racing); 1928
Sargent, John Singer (artist); 1856
Speedie, Mac (football); 1920
Yarbrough, Glenn (singer/music); 1930

JANUARY 13:

Adams, Brock; born Brockman Adams (politics/government); 1927
Alger, Horatio (author); 1834
Archerd, Army; born Armand Archerd (journalist/actor); 1919
Bulow, William John (politician); 1869
Cargo, David Francis (politician); 1929
Cypher, Jon (actor); 1932
Francis, Kay; born Katherine Edwina Gibbs (actress); 1899
Gage, Jack Robert (politician); 1899
Gola, Tom; born Thomas Joseph Gola (basketball); 1933
Gray, Billy; born William Thomas Gray (actor); 1938
Guthrie, A. B.; born Alfred Bertram Guthrie, Jr. (author); 1901
Manigo, Cesare (hockey); 1939
Miller, Sharon Kay (golf); 1941
Millner, Wayne (football); 1913
Morrow, Jeff (actor); 1913
Murphy, Rosemary (actress); 1927
Reilly, Charles Nelson (actor/director); 1931
Stack, Robert Langford; born Robert Modini (actor); 1919
Stanfill, Bill; born William T. Stanfill (football); 1947
Taylor, Ruth (comedienne/actress); ——
Tucker, Sophie; born Sophia Abuza (or Sonia Kalish) (singer/actress);
    1884
Verdon, Gwen; born Gwyneth Evelyn Verdon (actress/dancer/singer);
    1925
Wheeler, Earle Gilmore (army officer); 1908

JANUARY 14:

Aletter, Frank (actor); 1926
Arbanas, Fred; born Frederick V. Arbanas (football); 1939
Arnold, Benedict (soldier/traitor); 1741
Bavier, Frances; born Franceo Bavier (actress); 1905
Belford, Christine (actress); ——
Bendix, William (actor); 1906
Burgess, Thornton Waldo (author); 1874
Columbo, Russ; born Ruggiero de Rudolpho Columbo (singer/music/
    actor); 1908
Crawford, Coe Isaac (politician); 1858
Daniels, Bebe; born Virginia Daniels (actress); 1901
Dos Passos, John Roderigo (author); 1896
Dunaway, Faye; born Dorothy Faye Dunaway (actress); 1941
Forbes, Brenda; born Brenda Forbes Taylor (actress); 1909
Gilbert, Gibby; born C. L. Gilbert (golf); 1941
Gortner, Marjoe; born Hugh Marjoe Ross Gortner (actor); 1944
Hughes, James Hurd (politician); 1867
Jones, Jack (singer/actor); 1938
Kirman, Richard (politician); 1877
Marsh, Graham (golf); 1944
Odell, Benjamin Barker, Jr. (politician); 1854
Roach, Hal (producer/director/writer); 1892
Schweitzer, Albert (humanitarian); 1875
Siebert, Babe; born Albert Charles Siebert (hockey); 1904
Siebert, Sonny; born Wilfred Charles Siebert (baseball); 1937
Tryon, Tom; born Thomas Tryon (actor/author); 1926
Valente, Caterina (singer); 1931
Varrichione, Frank (football); 1932
Washington, Gene Alden (football); 1947
Williams, Guy (actor); 1924
Williams, Travis (football); 1946

JANUARY 15:

Bridges, Lloyd Vernet, Jr. (actor); 1913
Byrd, Robert Carlyle (politician); 1918
Davies, Bob; born Robert Edris Davies (basketball); 1920
Dever, Paul Andrew (politician); 1903
du Pont, Pierre Samuel (industrialist); 1870
Feuer, Cy; born Seymour Arnold Feuer (producer/director); 1911
Genewich, Joe; born Joseph Edward Genewich (baseball); 1897
Gilchrist, Albert Walker (politician); 1858
Grabowski, Joe (basketball); 1930
Grich, Bobby; born Robert Anthony Grich (baseball); 1949
Grillparzer, Franz (dramatist); 1791
Gromek, Steve; born Stephen Joseph Gromek (baseball); 1920

Ingram, Rex; born Reginald Ingram Montgomery Hitchcock (actor/·
director/producer/writer); 1892
King, Martin Luther, Jr.; born Michael King (civil rights leader); 1929
Kojis, Don (basketball); 1939
Krupa, Gene; born Eugene Bertram Krupa (music); 1909
Laffoon, Ruby (politician); 1869
Marshall, Mike; born Michael Grant Marshall (baseball); 1943
Molière; born Jean Baptiste Poquelin (playwright); 1622
Nasser, Gamal Abd el- (Egyptian government); 1918
Novello, Ivor; born David Ivor Davies (author/writer/music); 1893
O'Brien, Margaret; born Angela Maxine O'Brien (actress); 1937
Sarles, Elmore Yocum (politician); 1859
Schell, Maria Margarethe Anna (actress); 1926
Thatcher, Torin Herbert Erskine (actor); 1905

JANUARY 16:

Angotti, Louis Frederick (hockey); 1938
Batista, Fulgencio; born Fulgencio Batista y Zaldivar (Cuban
government); 1901
Bordoni, Irene (actress/singer); 1895
Carey, Harry; born Henry DeWitt Carey, II (actor); 1878
Collins, Jimmy; born James Joseph Collins (baseball); 1870
Dean, Dizzy; born Jay Hanna Dean (baseball/sportscaster); 1911
Emms, Happy; born Leighton Emms (hockey); 1905
Foyt, A. J.; born Anthony Joseph Foyt (auto racing); 1935
Horne, Marilyn B. (singer); 1934
Jardine, William M. (agronomist/government); 1879
Jordan, Buck; born Baxter Byerly Jordan (baseball); 1907
Jurado, Katy; born Maria Christina Jurado Garcia (actress); 1927
Kelly, George Edward (playwright); 1887
Knox, Alexander (actor); 1907
Merman, Ethel; born Ethel Agnes Zimmermann (singer/actress); 1908
Milsap, Ronnie (singer/music); 1944
Morgan, Ephraim Franklin (politician); 1869
Piccinni, Niccolo (music); 1728
Podhoretz, Norman (author/editor); 1930
Reid, Elliott; born Edgeworth Blair Reid (actor); 1920
Sorrell, John Arthur (hockey); 1906
Wilson, Margaret (author); 1882
Wynyard, Diana; born Dorothy Isobel Cox (actress); 1906

JANUARY 17:

Ali, Muhammad; born Cassius Marcellus Clay, Jr. (boxing/actor); 1942
Asther, Nils (actor); 1897
Beery, Noah, Sr. (actor); 1883
Brontë, Anne (author/poet); 1820

Brown, Dick; born Richard Ernest Brown (baseball); 1935
Capone, Al; born Alfonso (or Alphonse) Capone (gangster); 1899
Chekhov, Anton Pavlovich (playwright); 1860
Denenberg, Gail (golf); 1947
Dutra, Olin (golf); 1901
Franklin, Benjamin (statesman/philosopher/scientist); 1806
Gateson, Marjorie Augusta (actress); 1891
Hawley, James H. (politician); 1847
Jackson, Busher; born Harvey Jackson (hockey); 1911
Jones, James Earl (actor); 1931
Katzenbach, Nicholas deBelleville (government); 1922
Kelly, Pep; born Regis J. Kelly (hockey); 1914
Leader, George Michael (politician); 1918
Leiber, Hank; born Henry Edward Leiber (baseball); 1911
Lewis, Shari; born Shari (or Phyllis) Hurwitz (puppeteer/actress); 1934
North, Sheree; born Dawn Bethel (actress); 1933
Pearson, Preston James (football); 1945
Plante, Jacques (hockey); 1929
Sennett, Mack; born Michael Sinnott (director/producer); 1884
Shearer, Moira, born Moira Shearer King (dancer/actress); 1926
Stanislavski; born Konstantin Sergeryevich Alekseyev (actor/producer);
    1863
White, Betty Marion (actress/singer); 1922
Zimmer, Don; born Donald William Zimmer (baseball); 1931

JANUARY 18:

Apps, Syl; born Joseph Sylvanus Apps (hockey); 1915
Bond, Lilian (actress); 1910
Campbell, Thomas Edward (politician); 1878
Caruthers, Jimmy; born James Douglas Caruthers, Jr. (auto racing);
    1945
Dario, Ruben; born Felix Ruben Garcia-Sarmiento (poet/author); 1867
Evans, John Victor (politician); 1925
Flood, Curt; born Curtis Charles Flood (baseball); 1938
Goldsboro, Bobby (singer/music); 1941
Grant, Cary; born Archibald Alexander Leach (actor); 1904
Hardy, Oliver Norvell (comedian/actor); 1892
Hudson, Brett Stuart Patrick (music/singer/actor/comedian—Hudson
    Brothers); 1953
Kaye, Danny; born David Daniel Kominski (actor/comedian); 1913
Martin, Thomas Ellsworth (politician); 1893
Milne, A. A.; born Alan Alexander Milne (author); 1882
Moore, Constance (actress/singer); 1919
Moore, Eddie; born Graham Edward Moore (baseball); 1899
Pottios, Myron J. (football); 1939
Rodriguez, Pedro (auto racing); 1940
Rudolph, Council (football); 1950

Schmidt, Joe; born Joseph Paul Schmidt (football); 1932
Stuart, Henry Carter (politician); 1855
Sullivan, Pat; born Patrick J. Sullivan (football); 1950
Webster, Daniel (statesman); 1782

JANUARY 19:

Arnaz, Desi, Jr. (actor/singer/music); 1953
Bessemer, Sir Henry (inventor); 1813
Carey, Joseph Maull (politician); 1845
Cézanne, Paul (artist); 1839
Christians, Mady; born Margarethe Marie Christians (actress); 1900
Compton, Ann Woodruff (newscaster); 1947
Dunbar, Dixie; born Christina Elizabeth Dunbar (actress); 1919
Dupree, Minnie (actress); 1873
Everly, Phil (singer—Everly Brothers); 1939
Fabares, Shelley; born Michele Marie Fabares (actress/singer); 1944
Gorman, Tom; born Thomas Warner Gorman (tennis); 1946
Hanratty, Terry; born Terrence H. Hanratty (football); 1948
Harvey, Lilian; born Helene Lilian Muriel Pape (actress); 1906
Hedren, Tippi; born Nathalie Kay Hedren (actress); 1931
Hobby, Oveta Culp; born Oveta Culp (government/journalism); 1905
Joplin, Janis Lyn (singer); 1943
Kabibble, Ish; born Merwyn A. Bogue (singer/comedian); 1908
Lee, Robert E.; born Robert Edward Lee (confederate officer); 1807
MacLaren, Mary; born Mary MacDonald (actress); 1896
Madison, Guy; born Robert Moseley (actor); 1922
Matlack, Jon; born Jonathan Trumpour Matlack (baseball); 1950
Mills, Mary (golf); 1940
Parton, Dolly Rebecca (singer/music); 1946
Poe, Edgar Allan (poet/author); 1809
Radcliff, Rip; born Raymond Allen Radcliff (baseball); 1906
Reeves, Dan; born Daniel Edward Reeves (football); 1944
Scrugham, James Graves (politician); 1880
Stapleton, Jean; born Jeanne Murray (actress); 1923
Watt, James (inventor); 1736
Weaver, Fritz William (actor); 1926
Woollcott, Alexander Humphreys (journalist/writer); 1887

JANUARY 20:

Adamson, Joy; born Joy-Friederike Victoria Gessner (naturalist/writer); 1910
Aldrin, Buzz; born Edwin Eugene Aldrin, Jr. (astronaut); 1930
Ames, Leon; born Leon Waycoff (author); 1903
Anthony, Ray; born Raymond Antonini (music); 1922
Arnovich, Morrie; born Morris Arnovich (baseball); 1910
Bacon, Walter W. (politician); 1880
Breer, Murle Mackenzie; born Murle Mackenzie Lindstrom (golf); 1939

Burns, George; born Nathan Birnbaum (comedian/actor/singer); 1896
Busch, Mae (actress); 1891
Currie, Finlay; born Finlay Jefferson (actor); 1878
Danilova, Alexandra (dancer); 1904
Dobson, Joe; born Joseph Gordon Dobson (baseball); 1917
Donat, Peter; born Pierre Collingwood Donat (actor); 1928
Elman, Mischa (music); 1891
Fellini, Federico (director); 1920
Fontinato, Louis (hockey); 1932
Gray, Harold Lincoln (cartoonist); 1894
Hebert, Lionel Paul (golf); 1928
Heiss, Carol Elizabeth (ice skating); 1940
Howell, Bailey (basketball); 1937
Johnson, Arte (actor/comedian/TV host); 1934
Leadbelly; born Huddie Ledbetter (singer/music); 1889
Neal, Patricia Louise (actress); 1926
Nicol, Alex; born Alexander Livingston Nicol, Jr. (actor/director); 1919
Onassis, Aristotle Socrates (shipping magnate); 1906
Pasqual, Camilo Alberto (baseball); 1934
Piston, Walter Hamor, Jr. (music); 1894
Plum, Milt; born Milton R. Plum (football); 1935
Provine, Dorothy Michele (actress); 1937
Roberts, Fireball; born Edward Glenn Roberts, Jr. (auto racing); 1931
Simmons, Furnifold McLendel (politician); 1854
Stephens, Gene; born Glen Eugene Stephens (baseball); 1933
Weeks, Frank Bentley (politician); 1854

JANUARY 21:

Benson, Robby; born Robert Segal (actor); 1956
Breckinridge, John Cabell (Vice President); 1821
Dalton, Audrey (actress); 1934
Davis, Mac (singer/music); 1942
Dior, Christian (fashion designer); 1905
Domingo, Placido (singer); 1941
Duff, James Henderson (politician); 1883
Falkenburg, Jinx; born Eugenia Lincoln Falkenburg (actress); 1919
Fonseca, Lew; born Lewis Albert Fonseca (baseball); 1899
Garrison, Gary Lynn (football); 1944
Gary, Raymond Daniel (politician); 1908
Harris, Nathaniel Edwin (politician); 1846
Harris, Richard D. (football); 1948
Havens, Richie (singer/music); 1941
Hewitt, Alan Everett (actor); 1915
Jackson, Stonewall; born Thomas Jonathan Jackson (military officer);
     1824
Johnson, Billy "White Shoes" (football); 1952
Kearney, Jim; born James L. Kearney (football); 1943

Mansfield, Ray; born James Raymond Mansfield (football); 1941
McGovern, Francis Edward (politician); 1866
Mele, Sam; born Sabath Anthony Mele (baseball); 1923
Naish, J. Carrol; born Joseph Patrick Carrol Naish (actor); 1897
Nicklaus, Jack William (golf); 1940
O'Connell, Danny; born Daniel Francis O'Connell (baseball); 1927
Ray, Clifford (basketball); 1949
Reeves, Steve (actor/Mr. World/Mr. Universe); 1926
Rosellini, Albert Dean (politician); 1910
Savalas, Telly; born Aristotle Savalas (actor); 1924
Scofield, Paul; born David Paul Scofield (actor); 1922

JANUARY 22:

Ampère, André Marie (physicist/mathematician); 1775
Anderson, Sigurd (politician); 1904
Bacon, Francis (philosopher/writer); 1561
Barnett, Ross Robert (politician); 1898
Bayh, Birch Evans, Jr. (politician); 1928
Bixby, Bill; born Wilfred Bailey Bixby (actor/director); 1934
Blair, Linda Denise (actress); 1959
Byron, Lord; born George Gordon Byron (poet); 1788
Collier, Constance; born Laura Constance Hardie (actress); 1875
Cooke, Sam (singer); 1931
Cristofer, Michael (playwright/actor); 1945
du Pont, Pierre Samuel, IV (politician); 1935
Durnan, Bill; born William Ronald Durnan (hockey); 1915
Foley, Tim; born Thomas Foley (football); 1948
Foreman, George (boxing); 1948
Griffith, D. W.; born David Lewelyn Wark Griffith (producer/director); 1874
Higgins, James Henry (politician); 1876
Lach, Elmer James (hockey); 1918
Laurie, Piper; born Rosetta Jacobs (actress); 1932
Osborn, Chase Salmon (politician); 1860
Roberts, Henry (politician); 1853
Salter, Bryant (football); 1950
Savard, Serge (hockey); 1946
Southern, Ann; born Harriette Lake (actress/singer); 1909
Stein, Bob; born Robert Stein (football); 1948
Strinberg, August (playwright); 1849
Thant, U. (United Nations); 1909
Tremblay, J. C.; born Jean Claude Tremblay (hockey); 1939
Vinson, Frederick Moore (government/jurist); 1890
Wambaugh, Joseph (author); 1937

JANUARY 23:

Amalfitano, Joe; born John Joseph Amalfitano (baseball); 1934

Antonio, Lou; born Louis Demetrious Antonio (actor/director); 1934
Carlson, Frank (politician); 1893
Carrasquel, Chico; born Alfonso Colon Carrasquel (baseball); 1928
Duryea, Dan; born Daniel Edwin Duryea (actor); 1907
Golonka, Arlene Leanore (actress); 1936
Haden, Pat; born Patrick Capper Haden (football); 1953
Hancock, John (statesman); 1737
Johnson, Paul Burney, Jr. (politician); 1916
Kovacs, Ernie (actor/comedian); 1919
Kramer, Jerry; born Gerald L. Kramer (football); 1936
Manet, Edouard (artist); 1832
Moreau, Jeanne (actress); 1928
Pangborn, Franklin (actor); 1893
Ponselle, Rosa; born Rosa Melba Ponzillo (singer); 1897
Rivera, Chita; born Dolores Conchita Figueroa del Rivero (actress/
    singer/dancer); 1933
Rose, Mervyn G. (tennis); 1930
Sampson, Flemon Davis (politician); 1873
Scott, Randolph Crane (actor); 1903
Steele, Bob; born Robert North Bradbury, Jr. (actor); 1906
Stewart, Potter (jurist); 1915
Sullivan, Frank; born Franklin Leal Sullivan (baseball); 1930
Swenson, Swen (actor); 1932
Tubbs, Jerry; born Gerald Tubbs (football); 1935

JANUARY 24:

Belushi, John (actor/comedian/singer); 1950
Borgnine, Ernest; born Ermes Effron Borgnino (actor); 1915
Bryant, Bobby Lee (football); 1944
Clark, Monte (football); 1937
Diamond, Neil Leslie (singer/music); 1941
Dickerson, Denver Sylvester (politician); 1872
Giftos, Elaine (actress); 1945
Goodson, Mark (producer); 1915
Gregg, Julie (actress); 1944
Harreld, John William (politician); 1872
Heathcote, Cliff; born Clifton Earl Heathcote (baseball); 1898
Ives, Irving McNeil (politician); 1896
Kershaw, Doug; born Douglas James Kershaw (music); 1936
Mako, C. Gene (tennis); 1916
Mortson, Gus; born James Angus Gerald Mortson (hockey); 1925
Rhem, Flint; born Charles Flint Rhem (baseball); 1901
Roberts, Oral; born Granville Oral Roberts (evangelist); 1918
Smith, Marcus Aurelius (politician); 1851
Stevens, Ray; born Harold Ray Ragsdale (singer/music); 1939
Tallchief, Maria; born Elizabeth Marie Tallchief (dancer); 1925
Todd, Ann (actress); 1909

Wentworth, Cy; born Marvin Wentworth (hockey); 1905
Wharton, Edith Newbold; born Edith Newbold Jones (author); 1862
Winwood, Estelle; born Estelle Goodwin (actress); 1883
Ycaza, Manuel (jockey); 1935

JANUARY 25:

Allen, Elizabeth; born Elizabeth Ellen Gillease (actress); 1934
Baker, Buddy; born Elzie Wylie Baker, Jr. (auto racing); 1941
Beck, Byron (basketball); 1945
Bell, Bob; born Robert Francis Bell (football); 1948
Burns, Robert (poet); 1759
Curtis, Charles (Vice President); 1860
Davis, Harry Lyman (politician); 1878
Dunnock, Mildred Dorothy (actress); 1906
Eller, Carl (football); 1942
Flaman, Fern; born Ferdinand Charles Flaman (hockey); 1927
Groza, Lou; born Louis Groza (football); 1924
Hyland, Diana; born Joan Diana Gentner (actress); 1936
Jones, Dean Carroll (actor); 1930
Maugham, W. Somerset; born William Somerset Maugham (author);
     1874
Maynard, Don; born Donald Rogers Maynard (football); 1937
McGuire, Dick; born Richard McGuire (basketball); 1926
Newman, Edwin Harold (newscaster/author); 1919
Snow, Jack T. (football); 1943
Taylor-Young, Leigh (actress); 1944
Woolf, Virginia; born Adeline Virginia Stephens (author); 1882

JANUARY 26:

Blaeholder, George Franklin (baseball); 1904
Bond, Derek (actor); 1919
Cannon, Howard Walter (politician); 1912
Daugherty, Harry Micajah (government); 1860
Davis, Angela Yvonne (civil rights leader); 1944
Dodge, Mary Mapes; born Mary Elizabeth Mapes (author); 1831
Feiffer, Jules (cartoonist/writer); 1929
Frederick, Johnny; born John Henry Frederick (baseball); 1901
Gelbert, Charley; born Charles Magnus Gelbert (baseball); 1906
Grant, Julia Boggs Dent; born Julia Boggs Dent (First Lady); 1826
Hopper, William DeWolf (actor); 1915
Jeffreys, Anne; born Anne Jeffreys Carmichael (actress); 1923
Jordan, Henry Wendell (football); 1935
Kitt, Eartha Mae (singer/actress); 1928
Leslie, Joan; born Agnes Theresa Sadie Brodell (actress); 1925
Lowden, Frank Orren (politician); 1861
Lynn, Victor Ivan (hockey); 1925
MacArthur, Douglas (army officer); 1880

Murphy, Mary (actress); 1931
Newman, Paul (actor/director); 1925
Nieman, Bob; born Robert Charles Nieman (baseball); 1927
Prince, William LeRoy (actor); 1913
Skov, Glen Frederick (hockey); 1931
Vadim, Roger; born Roger Vadim Plemiannikow (director); 1928
Van Heusen, Jimmy; born Edward Chester Babcock (music); 1913
Youngblood, Jack; born Herbert Jackson Youngblood, III (football);
    1950

JANUARY 27:

Albert, Frankie; born Frank Culling Albert (football); 1920
Baryshnikov, Mikhail Nikolayevich (dancer); 1948
Carroll, Lewis; born Charles Lutwidge Dodgson (author/
    mathematician); 1832
Compton, Joyce; born Eleanor Hunt (actress); 1907
Dawkins, Joe (football); 1948
Donahue, Troy; born Merle Johnson, Jr. (actor); 1937
Falk, Bibb August (baseball); 1899
Fitzgerald, Frank Dwight (politician); 1885
Follmer, George (auto racing); 1934
Gaston, Milt; born Nathaniel Gaston (baseball); 1896
Gompers, Samuel (labor leader); 1850
Gottfried, Brian Edward (tennis); 1952
Hand, Learned; born Billings Learned Hand (jurist); 1872
Harper, Terrance Victor (hockey); 1940
Hearst, William Randolph, Jr. (publishing); 1908
Henderson, Skitch; born Lyle Russell Cedric Henderson (music); 1918
Hill, Mike; born Michael Hill (golf); 1939
Kern, Jerome David (music); 1885
Lowenstein, John Lee (baseball); 1947
Mozart, Wolfgang Amadeus; born Johannes Chrysostomus Wolfgangus
    Theophilus (music); 1756
Perry, Joe; born Fletcher Joseph Perry (football); 1927
Reed, Donna; born Donna Belle Mullenger (actress); 1921
Rickover, Hyman George (naval officer/nuclear power expert); 1900
Ruby, Harry; born Harry Rubinstein (music); 1895
Smith, Billy Ray (football); 1935
Sweet, William Ellery (politician); 1869
Thulin, Ingrid (actress); 1929
Venuta, Benay; born Venuta Rose Crooke (singer/actress); 1911

JANUARY 28:

Alda, Alan (actor); 1936
Allen Judith; born Marie Elliott (actress); 1913
Benton, Barbi (singer/actress); 1950
Boland, Mary (actress); 1880

Brown, Arnie; born Stewart Arnold Brown (hockey); 1942
Bryan, Jimmy; born James Ernest Bryan (auto racing); 1927
Burke, Martin Alphonsos (hockey); 1903
Cochran, Robert Leroy (politician); 1886
Henderson, Paul Garnet (hockey); 1943
Hoaglin, Fred; born George Frederick Hoaglin (football); 1944
Howard, Susan; born Jeri Lynn Mooney (actress); 1943
Kreuger, Charlie; born Charles A. Kreuger (football); 1937
Lary, Lyn; born Lynford Hobart Lary (baseball); 1906
Metcalf, Lee (politician); 1911
Moss, Arnold (actor/director); 1910
Murcrief, Bob; born Robert Cleveland Murcrief (baseball); 1916
Rubinstein, Artur (music); 1889
Runnels, Pete; born James Edward Runnels (baseball); 1928
Sontag, Susan (author); 1933
Stanley, Sir Henry Morton; born John Rowlands (explorer); 1841
White, Bill; born William DeKova White (baseball); 1934

JANUARY 29:

Blanchard, Newton Crain (politician); 1849
Bolin, Bobby Donald (baseball); 1939
Burke, Jack, Jr. (golf); 1923
Chayefsky, Paddy; born Sidney Chayefsky (playwright); 1923
Davis, Owen (playwright); 1874
Edwards, Hank; born Henry Albert Edwards (baseball); 1919
Fannin, Paul Jones (politician); 1907
Fields, W. C.; born William Claude Dukinfield (comedian/actor); 1879
Forsythe, John; born John Lincoln Freund (actor); 1918
George, Anthony (actor); ——
George, Walter Franklin (politician); 1878
Greer, Germaine (feminist); 1939
Harrison, Noel (actor); 1936
Hayworth, Ray; born Raymond Hall Hayworth (baseball); 1904
Longet, Claudine Georgette (actress/singer); 1942
Mature, Victor John (actor); 1916
McKellar, Kenneth Douglas (politician); 1869
McKinley, William (President); 1843
Miller, Leslie Andrew (politician); 1866
Morrow, Don (TV host); ——
Nelsen, Bill; born William K. Nelsen (football); 1941
Paine, Thomas (political philosopher); 1737
Primeau, Joe; born Joseph Primeau (hockey); 1906
Raitt, John Emmett (actor/singer); 1917
Rigney, Bill; born William Joseph Rigney (baseball); 1918
Rolland, Romain (author); 1866
Rockefeller, John Davidson, Jr. (industrialist/philanthropist); 1874
Ross, Katharine (actress); 1943

Sanders, Jared Young (politician); 1869
Scheckter, Jody (auto racing); 1950
Young, Donna Caponi; born Donna Maria Caponi (golf); 1945

JANUARY 30:

Anderson, Forrest Howard (politician); 1913
Bertolaccini, Silvia (golf); 1950
Boone, Laury; born Laura Gene Boone (singer—Boone Family); 1958
Brown, Ruth (singer); 1928
Caracciola, Rudi; born Rudolph Caracciola (auto racing); 1901
Damrosch, Walter Johannes (music); 1862
Dell, Dorothy; born Dorothy Goff (actress); 1915
Doughty, Glenn Martin (football); 1951
Dropo, Walt; born Walter Dropo (baseball); 1923
Frere, Paul (auto racing); 1917
Grimes, Tammy Lee (actress/singer); 1934
Hackman, Gene; born Eugene Alden Hackman (actor); 1931
Haubiel, Charles Trowbridge (music); 1892
Ireland, John Benjamin (actor); 1914
Jean, Norma; born Norma Jean Beasler (singer); 1938
Johnson, Dave; born David Allen Johnson (baseball); 1943
Malone, Dorothy; born Dorothy Eloise Maloney (actress); 1925
Marlowe, Hugh; born Hugh Herbert Hipple (actor); 1911
Martin, Dick; born Thomas Richard Martin (comedian/actor); 1922
Meskill, Thomas J. (politician); 1928
Neal, Charlie; born Charles Lenard Neal (baseball); 1931
Neumann, Paul (basketball); 1938
Nissen, Greta; born Grethe Ruzt-Nissen (actress); 1906
Opatoshu, David Opatovsky (actor); 1918
Prince, Hal; born Harold Smith Prince (producer/director); 1928
Redgrave, Vanessa (actress); 1937
Roosevelt, Franklin Delano (President); 1882
Seymour, Paul (basketball); 1928
Smith, H. Alexander (politician); 1880
Wayne, David; born Wayne James McMeekan (actor); 1914

JANUARY 31:

Agar, John George (actor); 1921
Aidman, Charles L. (actor); 1925
Bankhead, Tallulah Brockman (actress); 1902
Banks, Ernie; born Ernest Banks (baseball); 1931
Bonnier, Jo (auto racing); 1930
Burns, George Henry (baseball); 1893
Cantor, Eddie; born Edward Israel "Izzie" Iskowitz (actor/singer); 1892
Channing, Carol Elaine (actress/singer); 1921
Chappell, Len (basketball); 1941
Cowles, Gardner (publisher); 1901

Dru, Joanne; born Joanne Letitia La Cock (actress); 1923
Egan, John (basketball); 1939
Franciscus, James Grover (actor); 1934
Frémont, John Charles (explorer/soldier/politician); 1813
Grey, Zane (author); 1875
Hackett, Bobby; born Robert Leo Hackett (music); 1915
Hargrave, Pinky; born William McKinley Hargrave (baseball); 1896
Henry, Camille Wilfrid (hockey); 1933
Hutson, Don; born Donald Montgomery Hutson (football); 1913
Kendall, Fred Lyn (baseball); 1949
Kolen, Mike; born John Michael Kolen (football); 1948
Lanza, Mario; born Alfred Arnold Cocozza (singer/actor); 1921
Lenroot, Irvine Luther (politician); 1869
Maas, Duke; born Duane Frederick Maas (baseball); 1929
Mailer, Norman (author); 1923
Margolin, Stuart (actor/director); ——
Moore, Gary; born Thomas Garrison Morfit (TV host); 1915
Morris, Gouverneur (statesman); 1752
O'Hara, John Henry (author); 1905
Parker, Frank; born Franciszek Andzej Paikowski (tennis); 1916
Pleshette, Suzanne (actress/textile designer); 1937
Robinson, Jackie; born Jack Roosevelt Robinson (baseball); 1919
Ryan, Nolan; born Lynn Nolan Ryan (baseball); 1947
Schubert, Franz Peter (music); 1797
Simmons, Jean Merilyn (actress); 1929
Sylvester, William (actor); 1922
Thornton, Dan (politician); 1911
Turner, Robert George (hockey); 1943
Udall, Stewart Lee (government); 1920
Walcott, Jersey Joe; born Arnold Raymond Cream (boxing); 1914
Walter, Jessica (actress/singer); 1944

FEBRUARY 1:

Anderson, Wendell Richard (politician); 1933
Austin, Debbie; born Deborah E. Austin (golf); 1948
Blair, Paul L. D. (baseball); 1944
Blount, Winton Malcolm (government); 1921
Caraway, Hattie Wyatt (politician); 1878
Chandler, Helen (actress); 1906
Cupit, Jacky (golf); 1938
Everly, Don (singer—Everly Brothers); 1937
Ford, John; born Sean O'Feeney (or O'Fearna) (director); 1895
Gable, Clark; born William Clark Gable (actor); 1901
Hemsley, Sherman (actor); 1938
Herbert, Victor (music); 1859
Hildegarde; born Hildegarde Loretta Sell (singer); 1906
Hughes, Langston; born James Langston Hughes (writer); 1902

Irvine, George (basketball); 1948
King, Andrea; born Georgetta Barry (actress); 1915
Morris, Garrett (actor/comedian/singer); 1937
Perelman, S. J.; born Sidney Joseph Perelman (humorist); 1904
Snyder, Dick (basketball); 1944
Spark, Muriel; born Muriel Sarah Camberg (author); 1918
Whitman, Stuart Maxwell (actor); 1926

FEBRUARY 2:

Alvis, Max; born Roy Maxwell Alvis (baseball); 1938
Andy; born Charles James Correll (actor—Amos n' Andy); 1890
Arroyo, Martina (singer); 1937
Benét, William Rose (poet/author); 1886
Brookhart, Smith Wildman (politician); 1869
Brown, Pete (golf); 1935
Buford, Don; born Donald Alvin Buford (baseball); 1937
Dickey, James (poet); 1923
Eban, Abba (Israeli government); 1915
Fawcett-Majors, Farrah; born Mary Farrah Leni Fawcett (actress); 1947
Ferrell, Wes; born Wesley Cheek Ferrell (baseball); 1908
Getz, Stan; born Stanley Getz (music); 1927
Gilchrist, Connie; born Rose Gilchrist (actress); 1901
Gordon, Gale; born Charles T. Aldrich, Jr. (actor); 1906
Granville, Bonita (actress/producer); 1923
Guild, Curtis, Jr. (politician); 1860
Halas, George Stanley (football); 1895
Heifetz, Jascha (music); 1901
Hopkins, Bo (actor); ——
Jarvis, Ray; born Leon Rafmington Jarvis (football); 1949
Joyce, James Augustine (poet/author); 1882
Kamm, Willie; born William Edward Kamm (baseball); 1900
Kaplow, Herb; born Herbert Elias Kaplow (newscaster); 1927
Knous, William Lee (politician); 1889
Kreisler, Fritz (music); 1875
Lane, Burton; born Burton Levy (music); 1912
Leonard, Stan; born Stanley Leonard (golf); 1915
Levinsky, Alexander (hockey); 1910
Mandan, Robert (actor); 1932
Nelson, Knute (politician); 1843
Pennock, Herb; born Herbert Jefferis Pennock (baseball); 1894
Rand, Ayn (writer); 1905
Schoendienst, Red; born Albert Frederick Schoendienst (baseball); 1923
Smothers, Tom; born Thomas Bolyn Smothers, 3rd (comedian/actor); 1937
Stritch, Elaine (actress/singer); 1925

FEBRUARY 3:

Berman, Shelley; born Sheldon Leonard Berman (comedian/actor);
       1924
Bishop, Joey; born Joseph Abraham Gottlieb (comedian/actor/TV
       host); 1918
Buono, Victor Charles (actor); 1938
Carlisle, Mary (actress); 1912
Coleman, Joe; born Joseph Howard Coleman (baseball); 1947
Fairchild, Morgan; born Patsy Ann McClenny (actress); 1950
Garner, Peggy Ann (actress); 1932
Gillette, Guy Mark (politician); 1879
Gillingham, Gale (football); 1944
Greeley, Horace (journalist/politician); 1811
Griese, Bob; born Robert Allan Griese (football); 1945
Griffith, Emile Alphonse (boxing); 1938
Hanley, Bridget Anne Elizabeth (actress); 1943
Harmon, Judson (politician); 1846
Harris, William Julius (politics/government); 1868
Kemp, Jeremy; born Edmund Walker (actor); 1935
Lanier, Sidney (poet); 1842
Malone, Benny (football); 1952
Mann, Carol Ann (golf/sportscaster); 1941
McBride, Bake; born Arnold Ray McBride (baseball); 1949
McReynolds, James Clark (government/jurist); 1862
Melanie; born Melanie Safka (singer/actress/music); 1947
Michener, James Albert (author); 1907
Noble, Trisha (actress); 1944
Osterwald, Bibi; born Margaret Virginia Osterwald (actress); 1920
Owen, Robert Latham (politician); 1856
Patrick, Lynn (hockey); 1912
Pitts, Elijah (football); 1938
Rockwell, Norman Percival (artist); 1894
Sarbanes, Paul Spyros (politician); 1933
Stein, Gertrude (author); 1874
Stripp, Joe; born Joseph Valentine Stripp (baseball); 1903
Tarkenton, Fran; born Francis Asbury Tarkenton (football/
       sportscaster); 1940
Vaughan, Frankie; born Frank Abelsohn (actor/singer); 1928

FEBRUARY 4:

Ainsmith, Eddie; born Edward Wilbur Ainsmith (baseball); 1890
Bain, Conrad Stafford (actor); 1923
Brenner, David (comedian); 1945
Brown, Adam (hockey); 1920
Bruce, Nigel; born William Nigel Bruce (actor); 1895
Cerrudo, Ron; born Ronald Cerrudo (golf); 1945

Cooper, Alice; born Vincent Furnier (singer); 1948
Coote, Robert (actor); 1909
Craig, James; born James Henry Meador (actor); 1912
Erhard, Ludwig (German government); 1897
Foy, Eddie, Jr.; born Edwin Fitzgerald Foy (actor); 1905
Franklin, Pamela (actress); 1950
Friedan, Betty; born Betty Naomi Goldstein (feminist); 1921
Hagen, Halvor (football); 1947
Jessie, Ron; born Ronald Jessie (football); 1948
Johnston, Neil (basketball); 1929
Kantor, MacKinlay (author); 1904
Leinsdorf, Erich (music); 1912
Lindbergh, Charles Augustus (aviator); 1902
Lupino, Ida (actress/director); 1918
McCray, Warren T. (politician); 1865
Miller, Cheryl (actress); 1943
Nelson, Byron; born John Byron Nelson, Jr. (golf/sportscaster); 1912
Perón, Isabel; born Maria Estela Martinez Cartas (Argentine
    government); 1931
Riegle, Donald Wayne, Jr. (politician); 1938
Seaman, Dick; born Richard John Beattie-Seaman (auto racing); 1913
Smith, Gary Edward (hockey); 1944
Talman, William Whitney (actor); 1915
Wilcox-Horne, Collin; born Collin Wilcox (actress); 1935
Wisdom, Norman (comedian/actor/singer); 1918

FEBRUARY 5:

Aaron, Hank; born Henry Louis Aaron (baseball); 1934
Baldwin, Simeon Eben (politician); 1840
Beasley, John Michael (basketball); 1944
Brooks, Bryant Butler (politician); 1861
Buttons, Red; born Aaron Chwatt (or Schwatt) (actor/comedian/
    singer); 1918
Carradine, John; born Richmond Reed Carradine (actor); 1906
Cutler, John Christopher (politician); 1846
Ehringhaus, John Christoph Blucher (politician); 1882
Hershey, Barbara; born Barbara Herzstein (actress); 1948
Hillman, Larry Morley (hockey); 1937
Hoak, Don; born Donald Albert Hoak (baseball); 1928
Holt, Tim; born John Charles Holt, Jr. (actor); 1918
Kalb, Bernard (newscaster); 1922
Mendelssohn; born Jakob Ludwig Felix Mendelssohn-Bartholdy
    (music); 1809
Morton, Craig; born Larry Craig Morton (football); 1943
Parker, Willard; born Worster Van Eps (actor); 1912
Persons, Gordon; born Seth Gordon Persons (politician); 1902
Phillips, Jim; born James P. Phillips (football); 1936

Pitney, Mahlon (jurist); 1858
Rampling, Charlotte (actress); 1946
Ryan, Elizabeth (tennis); 1892
Saul, Rich; born Richard R. Saul (football); 1948
Saul, Ron; born Ronald Saul (football); 1948
Sellers, Ron; born Ronald Sellers (football); 1947
Simon, Norton Winfred (business executive); 1907
Smith, John Walter (politician); 1845
Staubach, Roger Thomas (football); 1942
Stevenson, Adlai Ewing (politics/government); 1900
Sulzberger, Arthur Ochs (publisher); 1926
Thomas, Lee; born James Leroy Thomas (baseball); 1936
Waltrip, Darrell (auto racing); 1947
Worthington, Al; born Allan Fulton Worthington (baseball); 1929

FEBRUARY 6:

Arrau, Claudio (music); 1903
Brokaw, Tom; born Thomas John Brokaw (newscaster/TV host); 1940
Burgess, Smoky; born Forrest Harrill Burgess (baseball); 1927
Burr, Aaron (Vice President); 1756
Caldwell, Millard Fillmore, Jr. (politician); 1897
Cockroft, Don; born Donald L. Cockroft (football); 1945
Cole, Natalie; born Stephanie Natalie Maria Cole (singer); 1949
Conners, Dan; born Daniel Conners (football); 1941
Dolliver, Jonathan Prentiss (politician); 1858
Fabian; born Fabiano Anthony Forte (singer/actor); 1940
Farrell, Mike (actor); 1939
Gabor, Zsa Zsa; born Sari Gabor (actress); 1919
Gruening, Ernest Henry (politician); 1887
Hodges, George Hartshorn (politician); 1866
Hunnicutt, Gayle (actress); 1943
LaFollette, Robert Marion, Jr. (politician); 1895
Long, Dale; born Richard Dale Long (baseball); 1926
Lund, John (actor); 1913
Lyon, Ben (actor); 1901
MacNee, Patrick (actor); 1922
Marlowe, Christopher (dramatist/poet); 1564
Massengale, Rik (golf); 1947
Nizer, Louis (attorney/author); 1902
Novarro, Ramon; born Ramon Samaniegoes (actor); 1899
Orantes, Manuel (tennis); 1949
Perreau, Gigi; born Ghislaine Elizabeth Marie Therese Perreau-Saussine
    (actress); 1941
Reagan, Ronald Wilson (actor/politician); 1911
Ruth, Babe; born George Herman Ehrhardt (baseball); 1895
Seymour, Paul (football); 1950
Stuart, Jeb; born James Ewell Brown Stuart (confederate officer); 1833

Torn, Rip; born Elmore Rual Torn (actor); 1931
Truffaut, Francois (director); 1932
Van Doren, Mamie; born Joan Lucille Olander (actress); 1933
Wright, Glenn; born Forrest Glenn Wright (baseball); 1901
Zisk, Richie; born Richard Walter Zisk (baseball); 1949

FEBRUARY 7:

Almada, Mel; born Baldomero Melo Almada (baseball); 1913
Blake, Eubie; born James Hubert Blake (music); 1883
Bracken, Eddie; born Edward Vincent Bracken (actor/singer); 1920
Brand, Oscar (music); 1920
Brasselle, Keefe; born Keefe Brusselle (actor/singer); 1923
Crabbe, Buster; born Clarence Linden Crabbe (swimmer/actor); 1907
Dickens, Charles John Huffam (author); 1812
Farr, Derek (actor); 1912
Gamble, Robert Jackson (politician); 1851
Graham, Horace French (politician); 1862
Hall, John Hubert (politician); 1899
Haskell, Floyd Kirk (politician); 1916
Hoffman, Harold Giles (politician); 1896
Hooton, Burt Carlton (baseball); 1950
Jamieson, Charlie; born Charles Devine Jamieson (baseball); 1893
King, James (basketball); 1941
Lewis, Sinclair; born Harry Sinclair Lewis (author); 1885
Mahoney, Jock; born Jacques O'Mahoney (actor); 1919
McBride, Henry (politician); 1856
More, Sir Thomas (statesman/author/humanist); 1478
Pizarro, Juan Ramon (baseball); 1937
Reaume, Marc Avellin (hockey); 1934
Smith, Al; born Alphonse Eugene Smith (baseball); 1928
Van Note, Jeff; born Jeffrey Van Note (football); 1946
Whitehill, Earl Oliver (baseball); 1900

FEBRUARY 8:

Aurie, Harry Lawrence (hockey); 1905
Boyer, Clete; born Cletis Leroy Boyer (baseball); 1937
Buber, Martin (philosopher/theologian); 1878
Coleman, Gary (actor); 1968
Curtis, Kenneth Merwin (politician); 1931
Dean, James Byron (actor); 1931
Dooley, Jim; born James Dooley (football); 1930
Duna, Steffi; born Stephanie Berindey (dancer/actress); 1913
Evans, Dame Edith (actress); 1888
Evers, Hoot; born Walter Arthur Evers (baseball); 1921
Field, Betty (actress); 1918
Haas, Bert; born Berthold John Haas (baseball); 1914
Heffner, Don; born Donald Henry Heffner (baseball); 1911

Jones, Robert Taylor (politician); 1884
Klein, Robert (comedian/actor); 1942
Lake, Everett John (politician); 1871
Lemmon, Jack; born John Uhler Lemmon, III (actor); 1925
Marsh, Linda (actress); ——
McCormick, Myron; born Walter Myron McCormick (actor); 1907
Middleton, Ray; born Raymond E. Middleton (actor); 1907
Mustin, Burt (actor); 1882
Nolte, Nick (actor); 1941
Oliver, Bob; born Robert Lee Oliver (baseball); 1943
Peterson, Fritz Fred (baseball); 1942
Rey, Alejandro (actor); 1930
Ruggles, Charles Sherman (actor); 1886
Sherman, William Tecumseh (army officer); 1820
Strong, Michael (actor); 1918
Talbot, Lyle; born Lysle Henderson (actor); 1904
Turner, Lana; born Julia Jean Mildred Frances Turner (actress); 1920
Verne, Jules (author); 1828
Vidor, King Wallis (director); 1895
Walton, Larry; born Lawrence James Walton (football); 1947

FEBRUARY 9:

Angel, Heather (actress); 1909
Arthur, Harold John (politician); 1904
Bergey, Bill; born William Earl Bergey (football); 1945
Carvel, Elbert Nostrand (politician); 1910
Clapper, Dit; born Aubrey Victor Clapper (hockey); 1907
Colman, Ronald Charles (actor); 1891
Donlevy, Brian; born Grosson Brian Boru Donlevy (actor); 1899
Farrow, Mia; born Maria de Lourdes Villiers Farrow (actress); 1945
Goff, Nathan (politician); 1843
Grayson, Kathryn; born Zelma Kathryn Hedrick (actress); 1923
Harrison, William Henry (President); 1773
Hughson, Tex; born Cecil Carlton Hughson (baseball); 1916
Janick, Bobby; born Robert L. Janick (football); 1940
King, Carole; born Carole Klein (singer/music); 1941
Lowell, Amy (poet/author); 1874
Miranda, Carmen; born Maria de Carmo Miranda de Cunha (singer); 1914
Morley, Clarence Joseph (politician); 1869
Moses, George Higgins (politician); 1869
Mudd, Roger Harrison (newscaster); 1928
Prentice, Jo Ann (golf); 1933
Rusk, Dean; born David Dean Rusk (government); 1909
Suzman, Janet (actress); 1939
Tubb, Ernest Dale (singer/music); 1914
Veeck, Bill; born William Louis Veeck, Jr. (baseball); 1914

Wertz, Vic; born Victor Woodrow Wertz (baseball); 1925
Wood, Peggy; born Margaret Wood (actress/singer); 1892

FEBRUARY 10:

Adler, Larry; born Lawrence Cecil Adler (music); 1914
Anderson, Dick; born Richard Paul Anderson (football); 1946
Anderson, Dame Judith; born Frances Margaret Anderson (actress); 1898
Brecht, Bertolt; born Eugen Berthold Friedrich Brecht (playwright); 1898
Bryan, Charles Wayland (politician); 1867
Chaney, Lon, Jr.; born Creighton Tull Chaney (actor); 1906
Davidson, James Ole (politician); 1854
Davidson, Robert (hockey); 1912
Dudley, Edward Bishop (golf); 1902
Durante, Jimmy; born James Francis Durante (comedian/actor/singer); 1893
Flack, Roberta (singer); 1939
Green, Cornell (football); 1940
Greene, Frank Lester (politician); 1870
Hale, Alan, Sr.; born Rufus Alan McKahan (actor); 1892
Hughes, Harold Everett (politician); 1922
Jackson, Randy; born Ransom Joseph Jackson (baseball); 1926
Lamb, Charles (writer); 1775
Lavender, Joe; born Joseph Lavender (football); 1949
Macmillan, Harold; born Maurice Harold Macmillan (British government); 1894
O'Dell, Billy; born William Oliver O'Dell (baseball); 1933
Pasternak, Boris Leonidovich (poet/author); 1890
Patterson, Neva Louise (actress); 1922
Poile, Bud; born Norman Robert Poile (hockey); 1924
Price, Leontyne; born Mary Leontyne Price (singer); 1929'
Reynolds, Allie Pierce (baseball); 1915
Sawyer, Charles (government); 1887
Sherman, Allie; born Alex Sherman (football); 1923
Spitz, Mark Andrew (swimming); 1950
Tilden, Bill; born William Tatem Tilden, Jr. (tennis); 1893
Wagner, Robert John (actor); 1930

FEBRUARY 11:

Baer, Max, Sr.; born Maximilian Adelbert Baer (boxing); 1909
Bentsen, Lloyd Millard, Jr. (politician); 1921
Brown, Ollie Lee (baseball); 1944
Darden, Colgate Whitehead, Jr. (politician); 1897
Dockery, Alexander Monroe (politician); 1845
Edison, Thomas Alva (inventor); 1847
Farouk I (King of Egypt); 1920

Firkusny, Rudolf (music); 1912
Fuller, Melville Weston (jurist); 1833
Gabor, Eva (actress); 1921
Greene, Bert (golf); 1944
Janis, Conrad (music/actor); 1928
Louise, Tina; born Tina Blacker (actress); 1934
Mankiewicz, Joseph Leo (producer/director/writer); 1909
Meadows, Clarence Watson (politician); 1904
Mendes, Sergio (music); 1941
Merchant, Larry (sportscaster/journalist/author); 1931
Mills, John, Jr. (singer—Mills Brothers); 1889
Nielsen, Leslie (actor); 1925
Reynolds, Burt (actor/director); 1936
Shack, Edward (hockey); 1937
Stanley, Kim; born Patricia Kimberly Reid (actress); 1921
Stephens, Alexander Hamilton (statesman); 1812
Sterling, Ross Shaw (politician); 1875
Surtees, John (auto racing); 1934
White, Josh; born Joshua Daniel White (singer/music); 1908

FEBRUARY 12:

Adams, Louisa Catherine Johnson; born Louisa Catherine Johnson
  (First Lady); 1775
Alioto, Joseph Lawrence (politician); 1916
Baker, Joe Don (actor); 1936
Beneke, Tex; born Gordon Beneke (music); 1914
Bradley, Omar Nelson (army officer); 1893
Darwin, Charles Robert (naturalist); 1809
Di Maggio, Dom; born Dominic Paul Di Maggio (baseball); 1917
Dobson, Pat; born Patrick Edward Dobson, Jr. (baseball); 1942
Ford, Wallace; born Samuel Jones (or Sam Grundy) (actor); 1898
Garagiola, Joe; born Joseph Henry Garagiola (baseball/sportscaster);
  1926
Gillis, Anne; born Alma Mabel O'Connor (actress); 1927
Greene, Lorne (actor); 1915
Hafey, Chick; born Charles James Hafey (baseball); 1903
Harris, Roy Ellsworth (music); 1898
Hughes, Hatcher (playwright); 1881
Johnson, Ken; born Kenneth Johnson (football); 1947
Kilpatrick, Lincoln (actor); 1936
Lewis, John L.; born John Llewellyn Lewis (labor leader); 1880
Lincoln, Abraham (President); 1809
Longworth, Alice Roosevelt; born Alice Lee Roosevelt (First family);
  1884
Mack, Ted; born William E. Maguiness (TV host); 1904
McDaniels, Gene; born Eugene B. McDaniels (singer/music); 1935
Millikin, Eugene Donald (politician); 1891

Russell, Bill; born William Felton Russell (basketball); 1934
Sheely, Earl Homer (baseball); 1893
Still, Ken; born Kenneth Alan Still (golf); 1935
Tucker, Forrest Meredith (actor); 1919
Wilson, Don; born Donald Edward Wilson (baseball); 1945
Zeffirelli, Franco; born Franco Zeffirelli Corsi (director); 1922

FEBRUARY 13:

Ames, Gene (singer—Ames Brothers); 1925
Bando, Sal; born Salvatore Leonard Bando (baseball); 1944
Berg, Patty; born Patricia Jane Berg (golf); 1918
Bettger, Lyle (actor); 1915
Farrell, Eileen (singer); 1920
Ford, Tennessee Ernie; born Ernest Jennings Ford (singer); 1919
Frederick, Pauline (journalist/newscaster/author); 1908
Jackson, Robert Houghwout (government/jurist); 1892
Jacobs, Tommy; born K. Thomas Jacobs (golf); 1935
Lynley, Carol; born Carolyn Lee Jones (actress); 1942
McGuire, Dotty; born Dorothy McGuire (singer—McGuire Sisters);
     1930
Muir, Jean; born Jean Muir Fullarton (actress); 1911
Novak, Kim; born Marilyn Pauline Novak (actress); 1933
Oliver, Susan; born Charlotte Gercke (actress); 1936
Reed, Oliver; born Robert Oliver Reed (actor); 1938
Segal, George (actor); 1934
Simenon, Georges Joseph Christian (author); 1903
Smith, Oliver (producer/designer); 1918
Svenson, Bo (actor); 1941
Talleyrand-Perigord, Charles Maurice de (French diplomatist); 1754
Truman, Bess; born Elizabeth Virginia Wallace (First Lady); 1885

FEBRUARY 14:

Aldridge, Lionel (football); 1941
Allen, Mel; born Melvin Allen Israel (sportscaster); 1913
Atwood, Donna (ice skating); 1923
Benny, Jack; born Benjamin Joseph Kubelsky (or Joseph Benjamin
     Kubelsky) (comedian/actor/music); 1894
Burns, Charles Frederick (hockey); 1936
Carter, Fred (basketball); 1945
Chamberlain, Murph; born Erwin Groves Chamberlain (hockey); 1915
Corrigan, Crash; born Ray Bernard (actor); 1902
Downs, Hugh Malcolm (TV host); 1921
Dragonette, Jessica Valentina (singer); ——
Erwin, Stu; born Stuart Philip Erwin (actor); 1903
Gabrielson, Len; born Leonard Gary Gabrielson (baseball); 1940
Galilei, Galileo (physicist/astronomer); 1564
Geoffrion, Boom-Boom; born Bernard Geoffrion (hockey); 1931

Hayes, Woody; born Wayne Woodrow Hayes (football); 1913
Hebert, Jay; born Junius Joseph Hebert (golf); 1923
Henderson, Florence (actress/singer); 1934
Hoffa, Jimmy; born James Riddle Hoffa (labor leader); 1913
Longden, Johnny; born John E. Longden (jockey); 1910
Martin, Jim; born James R. Martin (football); 1919
McGuire, Phyllis (singer—McGuire Sisters); 1931
Morrow, Vic (actor); 1932
Murphy, Bob; born Robert Joseph Murphy, Jr. (golf); 1943
Novak, Eva (actress); 1898
O'Brien, Joan (singer/actress); 1936
O'Neill, C. William (politician); 1916
Peterson, Ronnie; born Bengt Ronald Peterson (auto racing); 1944
Prine, Andrew Louis (actor); 1936
Rice, Florence (actress); 1907
Ritter, Thelma Adele (actress); 1905
Rodriguez, Richardo; born Richardo Valentine Rodriguez de la Vega
    (auto racing); 1942
Seiple, Larry; born Lawrence Seiple (football); 1945
Smith, Earl Sutton (baseball); 1897
Smith, Forrest (politician); 1886
Starbuck, JoJo; born Alicia Jo Starbuck (ice skating); 1951
Wright, Mickey; born Mary Kathryn Wright (golf); 1935

FEBRUARY 15:

Adams, William Herbert (politician); 1861
Anderson, Ken; born Kenneth A. Anderson (football); 1949
Anthony, Susan B.; born Susan Brownell Anthony (reformer/suffragist);
    1820
Arlen, Harold; born Hyman Arluck (music); 1905
Barrymore, John; born John Sidney Blythe (actor); 1882
Berenson, Marisa (actress); 1947
Bloom, Claire; born Patricia Claire Blume (actress); 1931
Cey, Ron; born Ronald Charles Cey (baseball); 1948
Cummins, Albert Baird (politician); 1850
Curtis, Keene Holbrook (actor); 1923
Earnshaw, George Livingston (baseball); 1900
Forrestal, James Vincent (government); 1892
Grant, Frank (football); 1950
Hadl, John Willard (football); 1940
Hamer, Rusty; born Russell Hamer (actor); 1947
Hill, Graham; born Norman Graham Hill (auto racing); 1929
Hill, John Melvin (hockey); 1914
Jackson, Sherry; born Sharon Diane Jackson (actress); 1947
Korman, Harvey Herschel (actor/comedian/director); 1927
Locklin, Hank; born Lawrence Hankins Locklin (singer); 1918
Manchester, Melissa Toni (singer/music); 1951

McCarthy, Kevin (actor); 1914
Peabody, Endicott (politician); 1920
Romero, Cesar; born Caesar Julius Romero (actor); 1907
Root, Elihu (government/politics); 1845
Schlesinger, James Rodney (government); 1929
Seymour, Jane; born Joyce Frankenberg (actress); 1951
Sondergaard, Gale; born Edith Holm Sondergaard (actress); 1899
Tiffany, Charles Lewis (jeweler); 1812
Whitehead, Alfred North (mathematician/philosopher); 1861
Woodcock, Leonard Freel (labor leader); 1911
Woodson, Abe; born Abraham Woodson (football); 1934

FEBRUARY 16:

Andrews, Patty (singer—Andrews Sisters); 1920
Baker, Tony; born Vernon Baker (football); 1945
Bauer, Bobby; born Robert Theodore Bauer (hockey); 1915
Beaumont, Hugh (actor); 1909
Bedford, Brian Anthony (actor); 1935
Behra, Jean (auto racing); 1921
Bergen, Edgar; born Edgar John Bergren (or Berggren) (ventriloquist); 1903
Bono, Sonny; born Salvatore Phillip Bono (singer/actor); 1935
Burton, LeVar; born Levardis Robert Martyn Burton, Jr. (actor); 1957
Cornell, Katherine (actress); 1893
Darwin, Bobby; born Arthur Bobby Lloyd Darwin (baseball); 1943
Dubenion, Elbert (football); 1933
Hagge, Marlene Bauer; born Marlene Bauer (golf); 1934
Hamilton, Billy; born William Robert Hamilton (baseball); 1866
Huxman, Walter A. (politician); 1887
Kennedy, Tom (TV host); ——
Lynn, Jeffrey; born Ragnar Godfrey Lind (actor); 1909
McEnroe, John Patrick, Jr. (tennis); 1959
Metz, Nicholas J. (hockey); 1914
Modzelewski, Dick; born Richard Modzelewski (football); 1931
Morris, Chester; born John Chester Brooks Morris (actor); 1901
Owens, Brig; born Brigman Owens (football); 1943
Platt, Edward (actor/singer); 1916
Primus, Barry (actor); 1938
Schlesinger, John Richard (director); 1926
Swain, Mack (actor); 1876
Vera-Ellen; born Vera-Ellen Westmeyr Rohe (actress/dancer/singer); 1926
Wakely, Jimmy; born James Clarence Wakely (actor/singer); 1914
Wilson, Henry (Vice President); 1812
Wyler, Gretchen; born Gretchen Patricia Wienecke (actress); 1932

FEBRUARY 17:

Anderson, Marian (singer); 1902
Barber, Red; born Walter Lanier Barber (sportscaster); 1908
Bates, Alan Arthur (actor); 1930
Bethune, Zina (actress/dancer/singer); 1945
Boone, Ike; born Isaac Morgan Boone (baseball); 1897
Bosman, Dick; born Richard Allen Bosman (baseball); 1944
Brandt, Ed; born Edward Arthur Brandt (baseball); 1905
Brian, Mary; born Louise Byrdie Dantzler (actress); 1908
Brown, Jim; born James Nathaniel Brown (football/actor/sportscaster); 1935
Cotsworth, Staats Jennings, Jr. (actor); 1908
Craig, Roger Lee (baseball); 1931
Hannett, Arthur Thomas (politician); 1884
Holbrook, Hal; born Harold Rowe Holbrook, Jr. (actor); 1925
Horton, Henry Hollis (politician); 1866
Houston, David Franklin (government); 1866
Hunnicutt, Arthur (actor); 1911
Hunt, H. L.; born Haroldson Lafayatte Hunt (industrialist); 1889
Kennedy, Arthur; born John Arthur Kennedy (actor); 1914
Kirkland, Willie Charles (baseball); 1934
Lawrence, Marjorie (singer); 1909
Morris, Wayne; born Bertram DeWayne Morris (actor); 1914
Pitney, Gene (singer/music); 1941
Potok, Chaim (author); 1929
Segovia, Andrés (music); 1893
Truman, Margaret; born Mary Margaret Truman (First family); 1924
Vallone, Raf (actor); 1916
Ward, Montgomery; born Aaron Montgomery Ward (merchant); 1843

FEBRUARY 18:

Arnold, Edward; born Guenther Schneider (actor); 1890
Brown, Helen Gurley; born Helen Gurley (author/editor); 1922
Calvert, Phyllis; born Phyllis Bickle (actress); 1915
Clark, Dane; born Bernard Zanville (actor); 1913
Cullen, Bill; born William Lawrence Cullen (actor/TV host); 1920
Denby, Edwin (government); 1870
Denton, Randy (basketball); 1949
de Wolfe, Billy; born William Andrew Jones (actor); 1907
Duff, Richard (hockey); 1936
Ferrari, Enzo (auto racing & manufacturer); 1898
Ford, Len; born Leonard Ford (football); 1926
Foreman, Milos (director); 1932
Goodrich, James Putnam (politician); 1864
Gordon, Joe; born Joseph Lowell Gordon (baseball); 1915

House, Frank; born Henry Franklin House (baseball); 1930
Johnson, Tom; born Thomas Christian Johnson (hockey); 1928
Jones, Homer C. (football); 1941
Kennedy, George (actor); 1925
Keyes, Leroy; born Marvin Leroy Huggins (football); 1947
Maxvill, Dal; born Charles Dallan Maxvill (baseball); 1939
Mayberry, John Claiborn (baseball); 1950
McDonald, Ab; born Alvin Brian McDonald (hockey); 1936
McElreath, Jim (auto racing); 1928
Menjou, Adolphe Jean (actor); 1890
Miller, Bob; born Robert Lane Gmeinweisser (baseball); 1939
Mota, Manny; born Manuel Rafael Mota (baseball); 1938
Neeman, Cal; born Calvin Amandus Neeman (baseball); 1929
Ono, Yoko (artist/poet/singer); 1933
Palance, Jack; born Vladimir (or Walter Jack) Palahnuik (actor); 1919
Rankin, Judy; born Judith Torluemke (golf); 1945
St. Clair, Bob; born Robert B. St. Clair (football); 1931
Saint-Subber, Arnold (producer); 1918
Shepherd, Cybill (actress/singer); 1950
Smith, Sherry; born Sherrod Malone Smith (baseball); 1891
Snelling, Richard Arkwright (politician); 1927
Stegner, Wallace Earle (author); 1909
Stockton, Dick; born Richard LaClede Stockton (tennis); 1951
Tiffany, Louis Comfort (artist); 1848
Travolta, John Joseph (actor/singer); 1954
Ure, Mary (actress); 1933
Wehmeier, Herm; born Herman Ralph Wehmeier (baseball); 1927
Willkie, Wendell Lewis (politician); 1892

FEBRUARY 19:

Arcaro, Eddie; born George Edward Arcaro (jockey/sportscaster); 1916
Bubbles, John; born John William Sublett (actor); 1902
Calhern, Louis; born Carl Henry Vogt (actor); 1895
Copernicus, Nicolaus; born Mikolaj Kopernik (astronomer); 1473
Fairbairn, Bruce (actor); 1947
Fleming, Susan (actress); 1909
Frankenheimer, John Michael (director); 1930
Hardwicke, Sir Cedric Webster (actor); 1893
Kenton, Stan; born Stanley Newcomb Kenton (music); 1912
Krause, Paul James (football); 1942
Lucas, Scott Wike (politician); 1892
Marvin, Lee (actor); 1924
McCullers, Carson; born Lula Carson Smith (author); 1917
Menne, Bob; born Robert Menne (golf); 1942
Nixon, Russ; born Russell Eugene Nixon (baseball); 1935
Oberon, Merle; born Estelle Merle O'Brien Thompson (actress); 1911
Robinson, Smokey; born William Robinson (singer); 1940

Siebert, Dick; born Richard Walther Siebert (baseball); 1912
Westman, Nydia (actress); 1902

FEBRUARY 20:

Albert, Edward (actor); 1951
Altman, Robert (director/producer/writer); 1922
Blake, Amanda; born Beverly Louise Neill (actress); 1929
Brownell, Herbert, Jr. (government); 1904
Crouse, Russel (playwright); 1893
Daly, John Charles, Jr. (newscaster/TV host); 1914
Duncan, Sandy; born Sandra Kay Duncan (actress/singer/dancer); 1946
Dusay, Marj; born Marjorie E. Mahoney (actress); ——
Esposito, Phil; born Philip Anthony Esposito (hockey); 1942
Face, Roy; born Elroy Leon Face (baseball); 1928
Gustine, Frankie; born Frank William Gustine (baseball); 1920
Hadley, Herbert Spencer (politician); 1872
Harbert, Chick; born Melvin R. Harbert (golf); 1915
Hearst, Patty; born Patricia Campbell Hearst (fugitive heiress); 1954
Henrich, Tommy; born Thomas David Henrich (baseball); 1913
Humphrey, Muriel; born Muriel Fay Buck (Vice President's wife); 1912
Kosygin, Aleksei Nikolayevich (Russian government); 1904
McIntyre, Thomas James (politician); 1915
O'Neill, Jennifer (actress); 1948
Penske, Roger (auto racing); 1937
Poitier, Sidney (actor/director); 1924
Rice, Sam; born Edgar Charles Rice (baseball); 1890
Ruel, Muddy; born Harold Dominic Ruel (baseball); 1896
Sainte-Marie, Buffy; born Beverly Sainte-Marie (singer); 1941
Smith, Patricia Harlan (actress); 1930
Strauss, Peter (actor); 1947
Unser, Bobby; born Robert William Unser (auto racing); 1934
Vanderbilt, Gloria Laura Morgan (artist/heiress); 1924
Wilson, Jim; born James Alger Wilson (baseball); 1922
Wilson, Nancy (singer); 1937
Wright, Clyde (baseball); 1941

FEBRUARY 21:

Auden, W. H.; born Wystan Hugh Auden (poet); 1907
Aylmer, Felix; born Felix Edward Aylmer-Jones (actor); 1889
Beymer, Richard; born George Richard Beymer, Jr. (actor); 1939
Billingham, Jack; born John Eugene Billingham (baseball); 1943
Bombeck, Erma; born Erma Louise Fiste (writer); 1927
Bremer, Lucille (actress); 1922
Gethin, Peter Kenneth (auto racing); 1940
Givenchy, Hubert James Taffin de (fashion designer); 1927
Grant, Danny; born Daniel Frederick Grant (hockey); 1946
Hathaway, William Dodd (politician); 1924

Jordan, Barbara Charline (politician); 1936
Judge, Arline (actress); 1912
Laughton, Michael Frederic (hockey); 1944
Lockwood, Gary; born John Gary Yusolfsky (or Yurasek) (actor); 1937
McClanahan, Rue; born Eddie-Rue McClanahan (actress); ——
McEnery, Peter (actor); 1940
McMillan, Ernie; born Ernest C. McMillan (football); 1938
Nixon, Tricia; born Patricia Nixon (First family); 1946
Peckinpah, Sam; born David Samuel Peckinpah (director/writer); 1925
Ramsay, Jack (basketball); 1925
Scott, Zachary Thomson (or Thompson) (actor); 1914
Sheridan, Ann; born Clara Lou Sheridan (actress); 1915
Simone, Nina; born Eunice Kathleen Waymon (singer); 1933
Sterling, Thomas (politician); 1851
Tracy, Tom; born John Thomas Tracy (football); 1933

FEBRUARY 22:

Aaron, Tommy; born Thomas Dean Aaron (golf); 1937
Abel, Sid; born Sidney Gerald Abel (hockey); 1918
Alcott, Amy (golf); 1956
Anderson, Sparky; born George Lee Anderson (baseball); 1934
Awtrey, Dennis (basketball); 1948
Barber, Steve; born Stephen David Barber (baseball); 1939
Brewster, Ralph Owen (politician); 1888
Buñuel, Luis (director); 1900
Charleson, Leslie A. (actress); ——
Chopin, Frederic-Francois (music); 1810
Cody, Lew; born Louis Joseph Coté (actor); 1884
Dubinsky, David; born David Dobniervski (labor leader); 1892
Ely, Joseph Buell (politician); 1881
Erving, Julius Winfield "Dr. J." (basketball); 1950
Finley, Charles Oscar (baseball); 1918
Kennedy, Ted; born Edward Moore Kennedy (politician); 1932
Lauda, Niki; born Andress Nicholas von Lauda (auto racing); 1949
Leonard, Sheldon; born Sheldon Leonard Bershad (actor/producer/
    director); 1907
Lowell, James Russell (poet); 1819
Markey, Enid Virginia (actress); 1896
Millay, Edna St. Vincent (poet); 1892
Mills, John Lewis Ernest Watts (actor/singer/dancer/producer); 1908
Mitchell, Clarence Elmer (baseball); 1891
Ogilivie, Richard Buell (politician); 1923
Okker, Tom S. (tennis); 1944
Oliver; born William Oliver Swofford (singer/music); 1945
Peaker, E. J.; born Edra Jeanne Peaker (actress/singer/dancer); ——
Peale, Rembrandt (artist/author); 1778
Russell, Donald Stuart (politician); 1906

Schopenhauer, Arthur (philosopher); 1788
Seymour, Dan (actor); 1915
Van Arsdale, Dick; born Richard Albert Van Arsdale (basketball); 1943
Van Arsdale, Tom (basketball); 1943
Walker, Chet (basketball); 1940
Washington, George (President); 1732
Weede, Robert (actor/singer); 1903
Whittaker, Charles Evans (jurist); 1901
Yorkin, Bud; born Alan David Yorkin (producer/director); 1926
Young, Robert George (actor); 1907

FEBRUARY 23:

Bilentnikoff, Fred; born Frederick Bilentnikoff (football); 1943
Boswell, Ken; born Kenneth George Boswell (baseball); 1946
Bourne, Jonathan, Jr. (politician); 1855
Brown, Bob; born Robert Eddie Brown (football); 1940
Chase, Sylvia (newscaster); 1938
Dibbs, Eddie; born Edward George Dibbs (tennis); 1951
Dillon, Bobby; born Robert Dillon (football); 1930
Docking, George (politician); 1904
Flanagan, Ed; born Edward Flanagan (football); 1944
Fonda, Peter Henry (actor/producer/director); 1939
Hall, Jon; born Charles Hall Locher (actor); 1913
Handel, George Frideric; born Georg Friedrich Handel (music); 1685
Howard, Elston Gene (baseball); 1929
Hunt, Ron; born Ronald Kenneth Hunt (baseball); 1941
Johnson, Roy Cleveland (baseball); 1903
Jones, Ed "Too Tall"; born Edward Lee Jones (football); 1951
Lavelli, Dante (football); 1923
Lynn, Fred; born Frederic Michael Lynn (baseball); 1952
Mitchell, Bobby; born Robert Mitchell (golf); 1943
Scott, George Charles (baseball); 1944
Smith, Jackie Larue (football); 1940
Thomson, Jim; born James Richard Thomson (hockey); 1927
Tresh, Mike; born Michael Tresh (baseball); 1914
Varsi, Diane Marie Antonia (actress); 1938
Williams, G. Mennen; born Gerhard Mennen Williams (politician); 1911
Winant, John Gilbert (politician); 1889
Winter, Johnny; born John Dawson Winter, III (singer); 1944
Youngblood, Jim; born James Lee Youngblood (football); 1950

FEBRUARY 24:

Abourezk, James G. (politician); 1931
Bostwick, Barry (actor); 1945
Cristal, Linda; born Marta Victoria Moya Burges (actress); 1936
Diener, Joan (actress/singer); 1934
Ellis, Jimmy (boxing); 1940 .

Farentino, James (actor); 1938
Ferrier, James (golf); 1915
Gates, Ralph Fesler (politician); 1893
Grimm, Wilhelm Carl (fairy tale author); 1786
Hill, Steven; born Solomon Berg (actor); 1922
Homer, Winslow (artist); 1836
Lane, Mark (attorney/author); 1927
Larken, Sheila; born Sheila Ann Diamond (actress); 1944
Legrand, Michel Jean (music); 1931
Main, Marjorie; born Mary Tomlinson (actress); 1890
Moore, Victor Frederick (actor); 1876
Nimitz, Chester William (naval officer); 1885
Phillips, Bubba; born John Melvin Phillips (baseball); 1930
Reventlow, Lance (auto racing); 1936
Shull, Richard B. (actor); 1929
Vernon, John (actor); 1932
Vigoda, Abe (actor); 1921
Wagner, Honus; born John Peter Wagner (baseball); 1874

FEBRUARY 25:

Backus, Jim; born James Gilmore Backus (actor); 1913
Baker, Diane (actress); 1938
Brooks, Tony; born Charles Anthony Brooks (auto racing); 1932
Burke, John (politician); 1859
Caruso, Enrico (singer); 1873
Cater, Danny Anderson (baseball); 1940
Cedeno, Cesar Eugenito (baseball); 1951
Cevert, Francois; born Albert Francois Cevert (auto racing); 1944
Chase, Mary Coyle (playwright); 1907
Clancy, King; born Francis Michael Clancy (hockey); 1903
Concannon, Jack; born John J. Concannon, Jr. (football); 1943
Courtenay, Tom; born Thomas Daniel Courtenay (actor); 1937
Dulles, John Foster (government); 1888
Ernst, Richard Pretlow (politician); 1858
Ferguson, Homer (politician); 1889
Fröbe, Gert (actor); 1913
Glick, Fred; born Frederick C. Glick (football); 1937
Goldoni, Carlo (playwright); 1707
Grassle, Karen Gene (actress); ——
Harrison, George (singer/music); 1943
Hollingsworth, Al; born Albert Wayne Hollingsworth (baseball); 1908
Joyce, Brenda; born Betty Graftina Leabo (actress); 1916
Kirk, Lisa; born Elsie Marie Kirk (actress/singer); 1925
Lema, Tony; born Anthony David Lema (golf); 1934
Lemaster, Denny; born Denver Clayton Lemaster (baseball); 1939
Marx, Zeppo; born Herbert Marx (comedian/actor—Marx Brothers); 1901

McClellan, John Little (politician); 1896
Neville, Keith (politician); 1884
Newsom, Tommy; born Thomas Penn Newsom (music); 1929
Pafko, Andy; born Andrew Pafko (baseball); 1921
Renoir, Pierre Auguste (artist); 1841
Riggs, Bobby; born Robert Larimore Riggs (tennis); 1918
Santo, Ron; born Ronald Edward Santo (baseball); 1940
Schieffer, Bob Lloyd (newscaster); 1937
Shaw, Wini; born Winifred Lei Momi (singer/actress); 1910
Slaughter, Frank Giel (author); 1908
Tyrer, Jim; born James E. Tyrer (football); 1939
Weatherly, Roy; born Cyril Roy Weatherly (baseball); 1915
Young, Faron (singer/music); 1932

FEBRUARY 26:

Alda, Robert; born Alphonso Giovanni Guiseppe Roberto D'Abruzzo
    (actor); 1914
Alexander, Grover Cleveland (baseball); 1887
Bertelsen, Jim; born James Bertelsen (football); 1950
Blanchard, Johnny; born John Edwin Blanchard (baseball); 1933
Bowen, Otis Ray (politician); 1918
Buffalo Bill; born William Frederick Cody (frontier scout); 1846
Cambridge, Godfrey MacArthur (comedian/actor); 1933
Carroll, Madeleine; born Marie-Madeleine Bernadette O'Carroll
    (actress); 1906
Cash, Johnny; born John Ray Cash (singer/actor); 1932
Collins, Rip; born Harry Warren Collins (baseball); 1896
Domino, Fats; born Antoine Domino (singer/music); 1928
Fiedler, James Fairman (politician); 1867
Frawley, William (actor); 1887
Gleason, Jackie; born Herbert John Clarence Gleason (comedian/actor/
    music); 1916
Hugo, Victor Marie (author); 1802
Hutton, Betty; born Elizabeth June Thornburg (actress); 1921
Johnson, Edwin Stockton (politician); 1857
Leighton, Margaret (actress); 1922
Lurton, Horace Harmon (jurist); 1844
Melnyk, Steve; born Steven Nicholas Melnyk (golf); 1947
Moore, Charles Calvin (politician); 1866
Randall, Tony; born Anthony L. Randall (actor); 1920
Roe, Preacher; born Elwin Charles Roe (baseball); 1915
Smith, Bingo; born Bobby Smith (basketball); 1946
Stratton, William Grant (politician); 1914
Taft, Robert Alphonso, Jr. (politician); 1917
Villapiano, Phil; born Philip James Villapiano (football); 1949
Warwick, Lonnie Preston (football); 1942

FEBRUARY 27:

Bamberger, Simon (politician); 1847
Bennett, Joan (actress); 1910
Berry, Raymond (football); 1933
Black, Hugo La Fayette (jurist); 1886
Blair, Andrew Dryden (hockey); 1908
Connally, John Bowden, Jr. (politics/government); 1917
Demarest, William (actor); 1892
De Vries, Peter (author/journalist); 1910
Durrell, Lawrence George (author); 1912
Farrell, James Thomas (author); 1904
Fogolin, Lee; born Lidlo John Fogolin (hockey); 1926
Frann, Mary (actress); ——
Fudge, Alan (actor); 1944
Fuller, Alvin Tufts (politician); 1878
Gardiner, Reginald; born William Reginald Gardiner (actor); 1903
Herlihy, James Leo (actor/writer); 1927
Horn, Ted; born Eylard Theodore Horn (auto racing); 1910
Jefferies, Richard Manning (politician); 1888
Johns, Charley Eugene (politician); 1905
Jones, Wil; born Wilbur Jones (basketball); 1947
Kean, Hamilton Fish (politician); 1862
Lehmann, Lotte (singer); 1888
Longfellow, Henry Wadsworth (poet); 1807
Lynn, James Thomas (government); 1927
McLane, John (politician); 1852
Momaday, N. Scott; born Navarre Scott Momaday (author); 1934
Nader, Ralph (consumer crusader); 1934
Revson, Peter Jeffrey (auto racing); 1939
Ryan, Connie; born Cornelius Joseph Ryan (baseball); 1920
Sarazen, Gene; born Eugene Saraceni (golf); 1902
Shaw, Irwin (author); 1913
Steinbeck, John Ernest (author); 1902
Taylor, Elizabeth Rosemond (actress); 1932
Tillman, Rusty; born Russell Tillman (football); 1946
Tone, Franchot; born Stanislas Pascal Franchot Tone (actor); 1905
Wallop, Malcolm (politician); 1933
Wheeler, Burton Kendall (politician); 1882
Williams, Van (actor); 1934
Woodward, Joanne Gignilliat (actress); 1930

FEBRUARY 28:

Ackerman, Bettye Louise (actress); 1928
Andretti, Mario Gabriel (auto racing); 1940
Baker, Stanley (actor); 1927
Bickett, Thomas Walter (politician); 1869

Butler, Hugh Alfred (politician); 1878
Caniff, Milton Arthur (cartoonist); 1907
Colzie, Neal; born Cornelius C. Colzie (football); 1953
Cox, Channing Harris (politician); 1879
Durning, Charles (actor); 1933
Frings, Ketti; born Katharine Hartley (playwright); 1915
Hecht, Ben (writer); 1894
Kjellin, Alf (actor/director); 1920
MacLeod, Gavin (actor); 1931
Malzone, Frank James (baseball); 1930
McCall, Samuel Walker (politician); 1851
Minnelli, Vincente (director); 1910
Mostel, Zero; born Samuel Joel Mostel (actor); 1915
Parnell, Harvey (politician); 1880
Pauling, Linus Carl (scientist); 1901
Perez, Marty; born Martin Roman Perez, Jr. (baseball); 1947
Peters, Bernadette; born Bernadette Lazzara (actress/singer); 1948
Smith, Bubba; born Charles Aaron Smith (football/actor); 1945
Torgeson, Torgy; born LaVern Torgeson (football); 1929
Tune, Tommy (dancer/actor); 1939
Wherry, Kenneth Spicer (politician); 1892
Wickard, Claude Raymond (government); 1893

FEBRUARY 29:

Dorsey, Jimmy; born James Francis Dorsey (music); 1904
Franz, Arthur (actor); 1920
Hardeen, Theodore, Sr. "Theo"; born Theodore Weiss (magician); 1876
Martin, Pepper; born Johnny Leonard Roosevelt Martin (baseball); 1904
Morgan, Michèle; born Simone Roussel (actress); 1920
Niland, John H. (football); 1944
Richard, Henri (hockey); 1936
Rocco, Alex (actor); ——
Rosen, Al; born Albert Leonard Rosen (baseball); 1924
Rossini, Gioacchino Antonio (music); 1792

MARCH 1:

Atwill, Lionel (actor); 1885
Belafonte, Harry; born Harold George Belafonte, Jr. (singer/actor); 1927
Benedict, Dirk; born Dirk Niewoehner (actor); 1946
Bentley, Max; born Maxwell Herbert Lloyd Bentley (hockey); 1920
Bethea, Elvin (football); 1946
Brown, Larry Lesley (baseball); 1940
Clary, Robert; born Robert Widerman (actor); 1926
Conrad, Robert; born Conrad Robert Falk (actor/singer); 1935
Dale, Porter Hinman (politician); 1867

Danova, Cesare Deitinger (actor); 1926
Ellison, Ralph Waldo (author); 1914
Hackett, Joan Ann (actress); 1927
Hartman, Paul William (actor/dancer/comedian); 1904
Haymes, Paul (hockey); 1910
Holt, Homer Adams (politician); 1898
Howard, Ron (actor/director); 1954
Howells, William Dean (author); 1837
Loder, John; born John Lowe (actor); 1898
Lowell, Robert Traill Spence, Jr. (poet); 1917
Marcis, Dave; born David A. Marcis (auto racing); 1941
Mike-Mayer, Nick; born Nicholas Mike-Mayer (football); 1950
Miller, Glenn (music); 1904
Miller, Keith Harvey (politician); 1925
Moran, Lois; born Lois Darlington Dowling (actress); 1907
Niven, David; born James David Graham Niven (actor/author); 1910
Odoms, Riley Mackey (football); 1950
Rozelle, Pete; born Alvin Ray Rozelle (football); 1926
St. Jacques, Raymond; born James Arthur Johnson (actor); 1932
Scolari, Fred (basketball); 1922
Shinners, John Joseph (football); 1947
Shore, Dinah; born Frances Rose Shore (singer/TV host); 1917
Slayton, Deke; born Donald Kent Slayton (astronaut); 1924
Stanley, Allan Herbert (hockey); 1926
Usher, Bob; born Robert Royce Usher (baseball); 1925

MARCH 2:

Arnaz, Desi, Sr.; born Desiderio Alberto Arnaz y de Acha, III (actor/
    singer/music/producer/author); 1917
Barnett, Pam; born Pamela Barnett (golf); 1944
Carpenter, Karen Anne (singer); 1950
Cassady, Howard (football); 1934
Cooper, Mort; born Morton Cecil Cooper (baseball); 1913
Crawford, Katherine; born Katherine Huggins (actress); ——
Cullum, John (actor/singer); 1930
English, Woody; born Elwood George English (baseball); 1907
Houston, Sam (soldier/statesman); 1793
Jones, Jennifer; born Phyllis Lee Isley (actress); 1919
Knott, Jack; born John Henry Knott (baseball); 1907
Larose, Claude David (hockey); 1942
Luna, Barbara (actress); 1937
Monroney, Mike; born Almer Stilwell Monroney (politician); 1902
Newman, Laraine (actress/comedienne/singer); 1952
Osmond, Jay Westley (singer/music—Osmond Family); 1955
Ott, Mel; born Melvin Thomas Ott (baseball); 1909
Pope Pius XII; born Eugenio Maria Giuseppe Giovanni Pacelli; 1876
Quackenbush, Bill; born Hubert George Quackenbush (hockey); 1922

Smetana, Bedrich Frederick (music); 1824
Weaver, Marjorie (actress); 1913
Weill, Kurt (music); 1900
Wolfe, Tom; born Thomas Kennerly Wolfe (journalist); 1931

MARCH 3:

Barrymore, Diana; born Diana Blanche Blythe (actress); 1921
Bell, Alexander Graham (inventor); 1847
Best, Edna (actress); 1900
Boros, Julius Nicholas (golf); 1920
Calder, William Musgrave (politician); 1869
Fernandez, Chico; born Humberto Fernandez (baseball); 1932
Fuller, Johnny; born John Fuller (football); 1946
Gradishar, Randy Charles (football); 1952
Harlow, Jean; born Harlean Carpentier (actress); 1911
Henry, Charlotte (actress); 1913
Keeler, Willie; born William Henry Keeler (baseball); 1872
Kohler, Walter Jodok, Sr. (politician); 1875
Licht, Frank (politician); 1916
Lowe, Edmund (actor); 1890
Methot, Mayo (actress); 1904
Pullman, George Mortimer (inventor); 1831
Radziwill, Lee; born Caroline Lee Bouvier (actress); 1933
Ridgway, Matthew Bunker (army officer); 1895
Scalà, Gia; born Giovanna Scoglio (actress); 1934
Schaal, Paul (baseball); 1943

MARCH 4:

Baker, Buck; born Elzie Wylie Baker, Sr. (auto racing); 1919
Burgess, Dorothy (actress); 1907
Clark, Jim; born James Clark, Jr. (auto racing); 1936
David, Thayer (actor); 1927
du Pont, Margaret Osborne; born Margaret Osborne (tennis); 1918
Fisher, Jack; born John Howard Fisher (baseball); 1939
Garfield, John; born Julius Garfinkle (actor); 1913
Greenwood, Joan (actress); 1919
Johnson, Bob; born Robert Wallace Johnson (baseball); 1936
Kraus, Lili (music); 1905
Lenz, Kay (actress); 1953
Long, Oren Ethelbirt (politician); 1889
MacKaill, Dorothy (actress); 1903
Makeba, Miriam; born Zensi Miriam Makeba (singer); 1932
McCullough, Clyde Edward (baseball); 1917
McNair, Barbara J. (singer/actress); 1939
Michaels, Cass; born Casimir Eugene Kwietniewski (baseball); 1926
Noel, Edmund Favor (politician); 1856
O'Driscoll, Martha (actress); 1922

Ottiano, Rafaela (actress); 1894
Perkins, Don; born Donald Anthony Perkins (football); 1938
Prentiss, Paula; born Paula Ragusa (actress); 1938
Prouty, George Herbert (politician); 1862
Raeburn, Sir Henry (artist); 1756
Rockne, Knute Kenneth (football); 1888
Sears, Vic; born Victor W. Sears (football); 1918
Seuss, Dr.; born Theodore Seuss Geisel (author); 1904
Stribling, T. S.; born Thomas Sigismund Stribling (author); 1881
Templeton, Charles Augustus (politician); 1871
Trumbull, John H. (politician); 1873
Vance, Dazzy; born Charles Arthur Vance (baseball); 1891

MARCH 5:

Bleier, Rocky; born Robert Patrick Bleier (football); 1946
Blue, Lu; born Luzerne Atwell Blue (baseball); 1897
Cassidy, Jack; born John Edward Joseph Cassidy (actor/singer); 1927
Christine, Virginia (actress); 1917
Christman, Paul C. (football/sportscaster); 1918
Crandall, Del; born Delmar Wesley Crandall (baseball); 1930
Douglass, Dale (golf); 1936
Eggar, Samantha; born Victoria Louise Samantha Marie Elizabeth
    Therese Eggar (actress); 1939
Fodor, Eugene Nicholas (music); 1950
Harrison, Rex; born Reginald Carey Harrison (actor); 1908
Hodges, Eddie (actor/singer); 1947
Leggett, Earl (football); 1935
Maazel, Lorin (music); 1930
Roof, Phil; born Phillip Anthony Roof (baseball); 1941
Schmidt, Milt; born Milton Conrad Schmidt (hockey); 1918
Shafer, Raymond Philip (politician); 1917
Shawlee, Joan (actress); 1929
Stockwell, Dean; born Robert Dean Stockwell (actor); 1936
Sullivan, Tom; born Thomas Sullivan (football); 1950
Thompson, Norm; born Norman Thompson (football); 1945
Thoms, William D. (hockey); 1910
Valo, Elmer William (baseball); 1921
Wainwright, James (actor); 1938
Williamson, Fred; born Frederick R. Williamson (football/sportscaster/
    actor); 1937

MARCH 6:

Boll, Buzz; born Frank Thurman Boll (hockey); 1911
Bond, Christopher Samuel (politician); 1939
Boryla, Mike; born Michael J. Boryla (football); 1951
Browning, Elizabeth Barrett; born Elizabeth Moulton (poet); 1806
Cooper, Leroy Gordon, Jr. (astronaut); 1927

Costello, Lou; born Louis Francis Cristillo (comedian/actor); 1906
Cyrano De Bergerac, Savinien de (French soldier/poet); 1619
Donnelly, Phil Matthew (politician); 1891
Du Maurier, George Louis Palmella Busson (author/artist); 1834
Flippen, Jay C. (actor); 1898
Gibson, Ernest William (politician); 1901
Goegan, Peter John (hockey); 1934
Grove, Lefty; born Robert Moses Grove (baseball); 1900
Hudson, Rochelle (actress); 1914
Kibbee, Guy Bridges (actor); 1882
Kilian, Victor Arthur (actor); 1891
Lardner, Ring; born Ringgold Wilmer Lardner (author/playwright/
    humorist); 1885
Logan, Ella; born Ella Allan (actress/singer); 1913
McMahon, Ed; born Edward Leo Peter McMahon, Jr. (announcer/
    actor); 1923
Michelangelo; born Michelagnolo di Ludovico di Buonarroti-Simoni
    (artist); 1475
Miles, Joanna; born Joanna Miles Schiefer (actress); 1940
Murphy, Ben; born Benjamin Edward Murphy (actor); 1942
Reiner, Rob; born Robert Reiner (actor); 1945
Rhome, Jerry; born Gerald B. Rhome (football); 1942
Rojas, Cookie; born Octavio Victor Rojas (baseball); 1939
Rudel, Julius (music); 1921
Schwartz, Stephen Lawrence (music); 1948
Sheridan, Philip Henry (army officer); 1831
Sikes, R. H.; born Richard H. Sikes (golf); 1940
Smith, John; born Robert E. Van Orden (actor); 1931
Stargell, Willie; born Wilver Dornel Stargell (baseball); 1940
Straus, Oscar (music); 1870
Swift, Bob; born Robert Virgil Swift (baseball); 1915
Towler, Dan; born Daniel Lee Towler (football); 1928
Trumpy, Bob; born Robert T. Trumpy, Jr. (football); 1945
Wills, Bob; born James Robert Wills (music); 1905

MARCH 7:

Acker, Tom; born Thomas James Acker (baseball); 1930
Andrews, Charles Oscar (politician); 1877
Avery, Milton Clark (artist); 1893
Beathard, Pete; born Peter F. Beathard (football); 1942
Blancas, Homero (golf); 1938
Broderick, James Joseph (actor); 1927
Burbank, Luther (naturalist/horticulturist); 1849
Burroughs, Jeff; born Jeffrey Allan Burroughs (baseball); 1951
Clark, Champ; born James Beauchamp Clark (politician); 1850
DuPree, Billy Joe (football); 1950
Frear, J. Allen, Jr.; born Joseph Allen Frear, Jr. (politician); 1903

Guthrie, Janet (auto racing); 1938
Harris, Franco (football); 1950
Joyce, Stephen (actor); 1931
Magnani, Anna (actress); 1908
Maybank, Burnet Rhett (politician); 1899
McNichols, Stephen L. R. (politician); 1914
Phillip, Andy (basketball); 1922
Ravel, Maurice Joseph (music); 1875
Redman, Rick; born Richard C. Redman (football); 1943
Swann, Lynn Curtis (football); 1952
Wilson, Red; born Robert James Wilson (baseball); 1929

MARCH 8:

Allen, Richard Anthony "Dick" or "Richie" (baseball); 1942
Bauer, Jaime Lyn (actress); ——
Beavers, Louise (actress); 1898
Bouton, Jim; born James Alan Bouton (baseball/author/actor); 1939
Brooks, C. Wayland; born Charles Wayland Brooks (politician); 1897
Charisse, Cyd; born Tula Ellice Finklea (dancer/actress); 1921
Chase, Stuart (writer); 1888
Clark, Susan Nora Goulding (actress); 1944
Dale, Charles Milby (politician); 1893
Fox, Pete; born Ervin Fox (baseball); 1909
Furillo, Carl Anthony (baseball); 1922
Hale, Alan, Jr. (actor); 1918
Holmes, Oliver Wendell (jurist); 1841
Humphrey, George Magoffin (government); 1890
Jaffe, Sam; born Samuel Jaffe (actor); 1893
Langdon, Sue Ane; born Sue Ane Lookhoff (actress); 1940
March, Little Peggy (singer); 1948
McClory, Sean (actor/director); 1924
Mueller, Ray Coleman (baseball); 1912
Nunn, Louie B. (politician); 1924
Randolph, Jennings (politician); 1902
Redgrave, Lynn Rachel (actress); 1943
Rice, Jim; born James Edward Rice (baseball); 1953
Rudolph, Mendy; born Marvin Rudolph (referee/sportscaster); 1928
Smith, Preston Earnest (politician); 1912
Thomson, Meldrim, Jr. (politician); 1912
Trevor, Claire; born Claire Wemlinger (actress); 1908
Van Buren, Hannah; born Hannah Hoes (First Lady); 1783

MARCH 9:

Barber, Samuel (music); 1910
Betz, Carl (actor); 1920
Buckley, James Lane (politician); 1923

Campaneris, Bert; born Blanco Dagoberto Campaneris (baseball); 1942
Clark, Fred; born Frederic Leonard Clark (actor); 1914
Colbert, Jim; born James Colbert (golf); 1941
Courrèges, André (fashion designer); 1923
Elg, Taina (actress/dancer); 1931
Foy, Eddie, Sr.; born Edward Fitzgerald (actor); 1854
Geer, Will; born William Aughe Ghere (actor); 1902
Hoag, Myril Oliver (baseball); 1908
Hodges, Luther Hartwell (politics/government); 1898
Ingels, Marty; born Marty Ingerman (actor); 1936
Jensen, Jackie; born Jack Eugene Jensen (baseball); 1927
Kline, Ron; born Ronald Lee Kline (baseball); 1932
Landis, Jim; born James Henry Landis (baseball); 1934
Molotov, Vyacheslav Mikhailovich (Russian government); 1890
North, Andy; born Andrew Stewart North (golf); 1950
Smith, Keely; born Dorothy Jacqueline Keely (singer); 1931
Southworth, Billy; born William Harrison Southworth (baseball); 1893
Spillane, Mickey; born Frank Morrison Spillane (author); 1918
Ullman, Al; born Albert Conrad Ullman (politician); 1914
Van Devere, Trish; born Patricia Dressel (actress); 1943
Van Patten, Joyce Benigna (actress); 1934
Vaughan, Arky; born Joseph Floyd Vaughan (baseball); 1912
Walden, Bobby; born Robert Earl Walden (football); 1938
Widby, Ron; born George Ronald Widby (football); 1945

MARCH 10:

Berry, Bob; born Robert Berry (football); 1942
Briggs, Johnny; born John Edward Briggs (baseball); 1944
Broun, Heywood Hale; born Heywood Hale Brown (sportscaster/actor); 1918
Carr, Austin G., Jr. (basketball); 1948
Collins, LeRoy (politician); 1909
Del Sesto, Christopher (politician); 1907
Ellis, Leroy (basketball); 1940
Fitzgerald, Barry; born William Joseph Shields (actor); 1888
Green, Warren Everett (politician); 1870
Harper, Chandler (golf); 1914
Honegger, Arthur (music); 1892
Houghton, Katharine; born Katharine Grant (actress); 1945
Jethro; born Kenneth C. Burns (singer/comedian/music—Homer & Jethro); 1920
Mason, Pamela; born Pamela Helen Ostrer (actress/writer); 1918
Norris, Edward (actor); 1910
Palmer, Sandy; born Sandra Jean Palmer (golf); 1941
Rabe, David William (playwright); 1940
Ray, James Earl (accused assassin); 1928

MARCH 11:

Abernathy, Ralph David (civil rights leader); 1926
Boryla, Vince (basketball); 1921
Brough, Louise; born Althea Louise Brough (tennis); 1923
Donaldson, Sam; born Samuel Andrew Donaldson (newscaster); 1934
Downey, Sheridan (politician); 1884
Ellington, Mercer Kennedy (music); 1919
Ellis, Dock Phillip (baseball); 1945
Ezinicki, William (hockey); 1924
French, Valerie; born Valerie Harrison (actress); 1931
Geronimo, Cesar Francisco (baseball); 1948
Gish, Dorothy; born Dorothy Elizabeth de Guiche (actress); 1898
Kovack, Nancy Diane (actress); 1935
Matthews, Jessie (singer/dancer/actress); 1907
Maw, Herbert Brown (politician); 1893
O'Daniel, W. Lee; born Wilbert Lee O'Daniel (politician); 1890
O'Neil, Tricia (actress); 1945
Plager, Robert Bryan (hockey); 1943
Ruttman, Troy (auto racing); 1930
Tasso, Torquato (poet); 1544
Welk, Lawrence (music); 1903
Wilson, Harold; born James Harold Wilson (British government); 1916

MARCH 12:

Albee, Edward Franklin (playwright); 1928
Andre, Lona; born Laura Anderson (actress); 1915
Ariyoshi, George Ryoichi (politician); 1926
Callison, Johnny; born John Wesley Callison (baseball); 1939
Feldon, Barbara; born Barbara Hall (actress); 1939
Frelinghuysen, Joseph Sherman (politician); 1869
Horvath, Bronco Joseph (hockey); 1930
Kupp, Jake; born Jacob Kupp (football); 1941
Law, Vern; born Vernon Law (baseball); 1930
Lewicki, Daniel (hockey); 1931
MacRae, Gordon (singer/actor); 1921
Minnelli, Liza May (actress/singer); 1946
Mosley, Mark (football); 1948
Parks, Hildy de Forrest (actress); 1924
Parrish, Helen (actress); 1922
Pierce, Jane Means Appleton; born Jane Means Appleton (First Lady);
    1806
Rutherford, Johnny; born John Sherman Rutherford, III (auto racing);
    1938
Schirra, Wally; born Walter Marty Schirra, Jr. (astronaut); 1923
Stevens, Roger L.; born Roger Lacey Stevens (producer); 1910
Taylor, James Vernon (singer/music); 1948

Tolbert, Jim; born Love James Tolbert (football); 1944
Trinkle, Elbert Lee (politician); 1876
Weston, Paul (music); 1912
Withers, Googie; born Georgette Lizette Withers (actress); 1917
Wynn, Jim; born James Sherman Wynn (baseball); 1942
Young, Andrew Jackson, Jr. (politics/government); 1932

MARCH 13:

Anderson, Liz; born Elizabeth Jane Haaby (singer/music); 1930
Baker, Frank; born John Franklin Baker (baseball); 1886
Bean, Andy (golf); 1953
Braase, Ordell (football); 1932
Breck, Peter (actor); 1930
Fillmore, Abigail Powers; born Abigail Powers (First Lady); 1798
Fix, Paul; born Paul Fix Morrison (actor); 1902
Haskell, Charles Nathaniel (politician); 1860
Howard, Jan (singer); 1932
Hutton, Ina Ray (music/singer/dancer); 1916
Kaye, Sammy (music); 1913
McAfee, George Anderson (football); 1918
Miller, Benjamin Meek (politician); 1864
O'Shea, Tessie (actress/singer); 1918
Priestley, Joseph (chemist); 1733
Raffin, Deborah (actress); 1953
Roosevelt, John Aspinwall (First family); 1916
Sedaka, Neil (singer/music); 1939
Stewart, Paul; born Paul Sternberg (actor); 1908
Wolf, Hugo (music); 1860

MARCH 14:

Borman, Frank (astronaut); 1928
Brown, Les; born Lester Raymond Brown (music); 1912
Caine, Michael; born Maurice Joseph Micklewhite (actor); 1933
Cernan, Eugene Andrew (astronaut); 1934
Charles, Bob; born Robert James Charles (golf); 1936
Crystal, Billy (actor/comedian); 1949
Ehrlich, Paul (bateriologist); 1854
Einstein, Albert (theoretical physicist); 1879
Erickson, John Edward (politician); 1863
Ford, Michael Gerald (First family); 1950
Goalby, Bob; born Robert George Goalby (golf/sportscaster); 1929
Gorki (or Gorky), Maxim (or Maksim); born Alexei (or Aleksei)
        Maximovitch (or Maksimovich) Petrov (or Peshkov)
        (playwright); 1868
Jones, Quincy Delight, Jr. (music); 1933
Ketcham, Hank; born Henry King Ketcham (cartoonist); 1920

Marshall, Thomas Riley (Vice President); 1854
McManus, Marty; born Martin Joseph McManus (baseball); 1900
Patrick, Dennis (actor); 1918
Petty, Lee (auto racing); 1914
Rexford, Bill; born William J. Rexford (auto racing); 1927
Share, Chuck; born Charlie Share (basketball); 1927
Shulman, Max (author); 1919
Tushingham, Rita (actress); 1942
Unseld, Wes; born Westley Unseld (basketball); 1946
Wirtz, W. Willard; born William Willard Wirtz (government); 1912

MARCH 15:

Bartlett, John Henry (politician); 1869
Bass, Dick; born Richard Lee Bass (football); 1937
Bean, Alan L. (astronaut); 1932
Blair, James Thomas, Jr. (politician); 1902
Bonds, Bobby Lee (baseball); 1946
Brent, George; born George B. Nolan (actor); 1904
Carey, Macdonald; born Edward Macdonald Carey (actor); 1913
Carroll, Beryl F. (politician); 1860
Chapman, Virgil Munday (politician); 1895
Curtis, Carl Thomas (politician); 1905
Elsom, Isobel; born Isobel Reed (actress); 1893
Hirsch, Judd (actor); 1935
Ickes, Harold LeClaire (government); 1874
Jackson, Andrew (President); 1767
James, Harry; born Henry Haag James (music); 1916
Marchibroda, Ted; born Theodore Marchibroda (football); 1931
Masters, Billy; born William Masters (football); 1944
O'Malley, J. Pat; born James Patrick O'Malley (actor); 1904
Post, Marjorie Merriweather (heiress/financier/philanthropist); 1887
Robb, Joe; born Alvis Joe Robb (football); 1937
Robertson, James Brooks Ayers (politician); 1871
Sabu; born Sabu Dastagir (actor); 1924
Shubert, Lee; born Levi Szemanski (producer); 1873
Simmons, Connie (basketball); 1925
Smith, Carl (singer/music); 1927
Spaulding, Rolland Harty (politician); 1873
Stone, Sly; born Sylvester Stewart (music); 1943
Teasdale, Verree (actress); 1904
Tierney, Lawrence (actor); 1919
Van Brocklin, Norm; born Norman Mack Van Brocklin (football); 1926
Volk, Rick; born Richard Robert Volk (football); 1945
Wietelmann, Whitey; born William Frederick Wietelmann (baseball); 1919

MARCH 16:

Anderson, C. Elmer (politician); 1912
Bell, Charles James (politician); 1845
Biggs, Verlon (football); 1943
Blasingame, Don Lee (baseball); 1932
Borchers, Cornell; born Cornelia Bruch (actress); 1925
Courtney, Clint; born Clinton Dawson Courtney (baseball); 1927
Crozier, Roger Alan (hockey); 1942
Cunningham, R. Walter (astronaut); 1932
DeLamielleure, Joe; born Joseph DeLamielleure (football); 1951
Estrada, Erik; born Enrique Estrada (actor); 1949
Ford, Jack; born John Gardner Ford (First family); 1952
Gillette, Walker (football); 1947
Goodell, Charles Ellsworth, Jr. (politician); 1926
Landrith, Hobie; born Hobert Neal Landrith (baseball); 1930
Lane, MacArthur (football); 1942
Lewis, Jerry; born Joseph Levitch (comedian/actor/singer); 1926
Madison, James (President); 1751
Mansfield, Mike; born Michael Joseph Mansfield (politician); 1903
Moynihan, Daniel Patrick (government/politics); 1927
Myer, Buddy; born Charles Solomon Myer (baseball); 1904
Nagel, Conrad (actor); 1896
Nixon, Pat; born Thelma Catherine Patricia Ryan (First Lady); 1912
Parker, John Milliken (politician); 1863
Reichardt, Rick; born Frederick Carl Reichardt (baseball); 1943
San Juan, Olga (actress); 1927
Stacy, Hollis (golf); 1954
Waner, Lloyd James (baseball); 1906
Wyman, Louis Crosby (politician); 1917

MARCH 17:

Bass, Ross (politician); 1918
Baugh, Sammy; born Samuel Adrian Baugh (football); 1914
Brisson, Frederick; born Carl Frederick Brisson (producer); 1917
Burns, Haydon; born William Haydon Burns (politician); 1912
Butler, Pierce (jurist); 1866
Childs, Marquis William (journalist); 1903
Cole, Nat King; born Nathaniel Adams Coles (singer/actor); 1919
Down, Lesley-Anne (actress); 1954
Duffy, Patrick Garfield (actor); 1949
Edwards, Earl (football); 1946
Gaston, Clarence Edwin (baseball); 1944
Green, Paul Eliot (playwright); 1894
Hall, Jimmie Randolph (baseball); 1938
Hoch, Edward Wallis (politician); 1849
Irwin, James Benson (astronaut); 1930

Jones, Bobby; born Robert Tyre Jones (golf); 1902
Kendall, Nathan Edward (politician); 1868
Leswick, Tony; born Anthony Joseph Leswick (hockey); 1923
McCambridge, Mercedes; born Carlotta Mercedes Agnes McCambridge
    (actress); 1918
McCord, James Nance (politician); 1879
McGee, Gale William (politician); 1915
Nurgeyev, Rudolf; born Rudolf Hametovich (dancer/actor); 1938
Pastore, John Orlando (politician); 1907
Reiser, Pete; born Harold Patrick Reiser (baseball); 1919
Root, Charlie; born Charles Henry Root (baseball); 1899
Russell, Kurt Von Vogel (actor); 1951
Saur, Hank; born Henry John Saur (baseball); 1919
Sebastian, John B. (music); 1944
Stydahar, Joe; born Joseph Leo Stydahar (football); 1912
Summerfield, Arthur Ellsworth (government); 1899
Taney, Roger Brooke (jurist); 1777
Turner, Daniel Webster (politician); 1877

MARCH 18:

Burnette, Smiley; born Lester Alvin Burnette (actor); 1911
Calhoun, John Caldwell (Vice President); 1782
Chamberlain, Neville; born Arthur Neville Chamberlain (British
    government); 1869
Cleveland, Grover; born Stephen Grover Cleveland (President); 1837
Compson, Betty; born Eleanor Lucicime Compson (actress); 1897
Dobson, Kevin (actor); ——
Donat, Robert (actor); 1905
Donohue, Mark Jr. (auto racing); 1937
Fletcher, Elbie; born Elburt Preston Fletcher (baseball); 1916
Granatelli, Andy; born Antonio Granatelli (auto racing); 1923
Graves, Peter; born Peter Aurness (actor/director); 1926
Horton, Edward Everett (actor); 1886
Jarvis, Pat; born Robert Patrick Jarvis (baseball); 1941
Kander, John Harold (music); 1927
Lake, Eddie; born Edward Erving Lake (baseball); 1916
Lapointe, Guy Gerard (hockey); 1948
Longhurst, Henry Carptenter (sportscaster/journalist/author); 1909
Mullins, Jeff (baseball); 1942
Nevin, Robert Frank (hockey); 1938
Osborn, Dave; born David V. Osborn (football); 1943
Parnis, Mollie (fashion designer); 1905
Parrish, Leslie Maria; born Leslie Maria Fleck (actress); 1935
Paul, Don; born Donald Paul (football); 1925
Pickett, Wilson (singer/music); 1941
Plimpton, George Ames (author); 1927
Pride, Charley Frank (singer); 1934

Rimski-Korsakov, Nikolai Andreyevich (music); 1844
Smith, Norman (hockey); 1908
Stenmark, Ingemar (skiing); 1956
Updike, John Hoyer (author); 1932
Van Wagoner, Murray Delos (politician); 1898
Vespucci, Amerigo (navigator); 1452
Wrightstone, Russ; born Russell Guy Wrightstone (baseball); 1893

MARCH 19:

Andress, Ursula (actress); 1936
Andrews, Tige; born Tiger Androwaous (actor); 1923
Ashburn, Richie; born Don Richie Ashburn (baseball); 1927
Brewer, Gay (golf); 1932
Bryan, William Jennings (orator/writer/politics/government); 1860
Earp, Wyatt (frontier marshal & gunfighter); 1848
Eichmann, Adolf; born Otto Adolf Eichmann (Nazi official); 1906
Hayward, Louis; born Seafield Grant (actor); 1909
Johnson, Lynda Bird (First family); 1944
Kapp, Joe; born Joseph Robert Kapp (football/actor); 1938
Livingstone, David (explorer); 1813
Mabley, Moms "Jackie"; born Loretta Mary Aiken (comedienne); 1894
Malone, Nancy (actress); 1935
McGinnity, Joe; born Joseph Jerome McGinnity (baseball); 1871
McGoohan, Patrick (actor); 1928
Mielziner, Jo (designer); 1901
Morison, Patricia; born Eileen Patricia Augusta Fraser Morison (actress
    /singer); 1914
Newman, Phyllis (actress/singer); 1935
Norblad, Albin Walter, Sr. (politician); 1881
Roth, Philip Milton (author); 1933
Sirica, John Joseph (jurist); 1904
Smith, Kent; born Frank Kent Smith (actor); 1907
Stanbach, Haskel (football); 1952
Walker, Gee; born Gerald Holmes Walker (baseball); 1908
Wallace, Irving (author); 1916
Wambsganss, Bill; born William Adolph Wambsganss (baseball); 1894
Wares, Edward (hockey); 1915
Warren, Earl (politician/jurist); 1891

MARCH 20:

Abbott, Philip; born Philip Abbott Alexander (actor); 1924
Altman, George Lee (baseball); 1933
Arnall, Ellis Gibbs (politician); 1907
Barry, Jack (TV host); 1918
Beame, Abraham David (politician); 1906
Benson, Frank Williamson (politician); 1858
Bingham, George Caleb (artist); 1811

Corey, Wendell Reid (actor); 1914
Ehrlichman, John Daniel (government); 1925
Elgart, Larry (music); 1922
Fort, John Franklin (politician); 1852
Goulding, Ray; born Raymond Walter Goulding (comedian); 1922
Ibsen, Henrik Johan (playwright); 1828
Kennedy, Vern; born Lloyd Vernon Kennedy (baseball); 1907
Kruschen, Jack (actor); 1922
Linden, Hal; born Harold Lipshitz (actor/singer); 1931
Malone, Art; born Arthur Lee Malone (football); 1948
Melchior, Lauritz; born Lebrecht Hommel (singer); 1890
Nelson, Ozzie; born Oswald George Nelson (music/actor); 1906
Orr, Bobby; born Robert Gordon Orr (hockey); 1948
Redgrave, Sir Michael (actor); 1908
Reed, Jerry; born Jerry Reed Hubbard (singer/actor/music); 1937
Reiner, Carl (actor/producer/director/writer); 1922
Riley, Pat (basketball); 1945
Shively, Benjamin Franklin (politician); 1857
Simpson, Oramel Hinckley (politician); 1870
Skinner, B. F.; born Burrhus Frederic Skinner (psychologist); 1904
Stevenson, Coke Robert (politician); 1888
Zabel, Steve Gregory (football); 1948

MARCH 21:

Anderson, Gilbert M. "Broncho Billy"; born Max Aronson (actor/
     producer/director); 1882
Bach, Johann Sebastian (music); 1685
Buchanan, Edgar (actor); 1902
Buck, Clayton Douglas (politician); 1890
Carveth, Joseph Gordon (hockey); 1918
Coco, James Emil (actor); 1929
Coffey, Junior Lee (football); 1942
Davis, Tommy; born Herman Thomas Davis (baseball); 1939
Flock, Fonty; born Truman Fontell Flock (auto racing); 1921
Flores, Tom; born Thomas R. Flores (football); 1937
Hilton, Roy (football); 1941
Hofmann, Hans (artist); 1880
Hogan, Shanty; born James Francis Hogan (baseball); 1906
Juárez, Benito Pablo (Mexican statesman); 1806
Lamar, Bill; born William Harmong Lamar (baseball); 1897
Lindsey, Mort (music); 1923
Lucey, Patrick Joseph (politician); 1918
McGinley, Phyllis (poet); 1905
Ramsey, Logan Carlisle, Jr. (actor); 1921
Rockefeller, John Davidson, III (philanthropist); 1906
Sanguillen, Manny; born Manuel DeJesus Sanguillen (baseball); 1944
Stickney, William Wallace (politician); 1853

Weidler, Virginia (actress); 1927
Widdoes, Kathleen Effie (actress); 1939
Withycombe, James (politician); 1854
Ziegfeld, Florenz, Jr. (producer); 1869

MARCH 22:

Benson, George (singer/music); 1943
Britt, May; born Maybritt Wilkens (actress); 1933
Chaney, Don (basketball); 1946
Ellsworth, Dick; born Richard Clark Ellsworth (baseball); 1940
Furgol, Ed; born Edward Furgol (golf); 1917
Gardner, Oliver Max (politician); 1882
Gilligan, John Joyce (politician); 1921
Goodman, Billy; born William Dale Goodman (baseball); 1926
Grey, Virginia (actress); 1917
Hatch, Orrin Grant (politician); 1934
Keon, Dave; born David Michael Keon (hockey); 1940
Kirkwood, Joseph (golf); 1897
Klemperer, Werner (actor); 1920
Macauley, Ed; born Edward Macauley (basketball); 1928
Malden, Karl; born Mladen Sekulovich (actor); 1913
Marceau, Marcel; born Marcel Mangel (mime/actor); 1923
Martin, Ross; born Martin Rosenblatt (actor); 1920
Marx, Chico; born Leonard Marx (comedian/actor—Marx Brothers);
    1887
McCall, Thomas Lawson (politician); 1913
Monsarrat, Nicholas John Turney (author); 1910
Oliver, Gene; born Eugene George Oliver (baseball); 1936
Schildkraut, Joseph (actor); 1895
Shatner, William (actor); 1931
Solters, Moose; born Julius Joseph Soltesz (baseball); 1906
Sondheim, Stephen Joshua (music); 1930
Stans, Maurice Hubert (government); 1908
Vandenberg, Arthur Hendrick (politician); 1884
Van Dyck, Sir Anthony (artist); 1599

MARCH 23:

Breedlove, Craig Norman (auto racing); 1938
Colfax, Schuyler (Vice President); 1823
Crawford, Joan; born Lucille Fay LeSuer (actress); 1904
Dawn, Hazel; born Hazel Dawn La Tout (actress/singer); 1891
Fromm, Erich (psychoanalyst); 1900
Godfrey, Rocky; born Warren Edward Godfrey (hockey); 1931
Green, Ted; born Edward Joseph Green (hockey); 1940
Jackson, Maynard Holbrook, Jr. (politician); 1938
Jaworski, Ron; born Ronald V. Jaworski (football); 1951
Johnson, Paul. Burney, Sr. (politician); 1880

Kremer, Ray; born Remy Peter Kremer (baseball); 1893
Lemon, Jim; born James Robert Lemon (baseball); 1928
Logan, Johnny; born John Logan (baseball); 1927
Malone, Moses (basketball); 1954
Marshall, Donald Robert (hockey); 1932
Moore, Johnny; born John Francis Moore (baseball); 1902
Rhoades, Barbara Jean (actress/dancer); 1946
Van Vooren, Monique (actress/singer); 1933
Von Braun, Wernher (rocketeer); 1912
Washington, Vic; born Victor A. Washington (football); 1946
Wright, Martha; born Martha Lucile Wiederrecht (actress); 1926

MARCH 24:

Alou, Jesus Maria Rojas (baseball); 1943
Arbuckle, Fatty; born Roscoe Conkling Arbuckle (actor/director); 1887
Bradley, Pat; born Patricia Ellen Bradley (golf); 1951
Brown, Vanessa; born Smylla Brind (actress); 1928
Conte, Richard; born Nicholas Peter Conte (actor); 1914
Dewey, Thomas Edmund (politician); 1902
Fell, Norman (actor); 1925
Janis, Byron; born Byron Yanks (music); 1928
Jennings, William Sherman (politician); 1863
Kosleck, Martin; born Nicolai Yoshkin (actor); 1907
McLain, Denny; born Dennis Dale McLain (baseball); 1944
McQueen, Steve; born Terence Stephen McQueen (actor); 1930
Mellon, Andrew William (industrialist/government); 1855
Morris, William (poet/artist); 1834
Muggeridge, Malcolm Thomas (writer); 1903
Nelson, Gene; born Gene Berg (actor/dancer/director); 1920
Norstad, Lauris (army officer); 1907
Pescow, Donna Gail (actress); 1954
Reed, Oscar L. (football); 1944
Sisler, George Harold (baseball); 1893
Smith, William Emmett, II (actor); 1933
Tillman, Bob; born John Robert Tillman (baseball); 1937
Wilson, Larry; born Lawrence Frank Wilson (football); 1938

MARCH 25:

Axton, Hoyt Wayne (singer/music); 1938
Barnes, Binnie; born Gertrude (or Gitelle) Maude Barnes (actress); 1905
Bartók, Belá (music); 1881
Bedelia, Bonnie; born Bonnie Culkin (actress); 1946
Begley, Ed; born Edward James Begley (actor); 1901
Bryant, Anita Jane (singer); 1940
Cagney, Jeanne Carolyn (actress); 1919
Carle, Frankie; born Francis Carlone (music); 1903
Cosell, Howard; born Howard Cohen (sportscaster/attorney); 1920

Franklin, Aretha (singer); 1942
Garrett, Kelly (singer/actress); 1948
Glaser, Paul Michael; born Paul Manfred Glaser (actor); 1943
Held; Woodie; born Woodson George Held (baseball); 1932
John, Elton; born Reginald Kenneth Dwight (singer); 1947
Kelly, Nancy (actress); 1921
Lean, David (director); 1908
Leonard, Dutch; born Emil John Leonard (baseball); 1909
Lovell, James Arthur, Jr. (astronaut); 1928
Philipp, Emanuel Lorenz (politician); 1861
Plager, Barclay Graham (hockey); 1941
Pyle, J. Howard; born John Howard Pyle (politician); 1906
Signoret, Simone; born Simone-Henriette-Charlotte Kaminker (actress);
    1921
Steinem, Gloria Marie (feminist/journalist/editor); 1934
Sutherland, George (jurist); 1862
Toscanini, Arturo (music); 1867

MARCH 26:

Arkin, Alan Wolf (actor/director); 1934
Baeza, Braulio (jockey); 1940
Bianchi, Al; born Alfred Bianchi (basketball); 1932
Boulez, Pierre (music); 1925
Caan, James (actor); 1939
Cappelletti, Gino (football); 1934
Crosby, Robert Berkey (politician); 1911
Elliott, Bob; born Robert B. Elliott (comedian); 1923
Embry, Wayne Richard (basketball); 1937
Frost, Robert Lee (poet); 1875
Harrington, Emerson Columbus (politician); 1864
Hayden, Sterling; born John Hamilton (or Sterling Relyea Walter)
    (actor/author); 1916
Hines, Duncan (author/publisher/traveler); 1880
Hobby, William Pettus (politician); 1878
Housman, A. E.; born Alfred Edward Housman (poet); 1859
Jong, Erica; born Erica Mann (writer); 1942
Lawrence, Vicki Ann (actress/dancer/singer); 1949
Marland, William Casey (politician); 1918
Martin, Strother (actor); 1919
Milliken, William Grawn (politician); 1922
Nimoy, Leonard (actor); 1931
Nolan, Dick; born Richard C. Nolan (football); 1932
Rafferty, Chips; born John Goffage (actor); 1909
Ross, Diana (singer/actress); 1944
Westmoreland, William Childs (army officer); 1914
Williams, Tennessee; born Thomas Lanter Williams (playwright); 1911

MARCH 27:

Callaghan, James; born Leonard James Callaghan (British government);
 1912
Covington, Wes; born John Wesley Covington (baseball); 1932
Currier, Nathaniel (lithographer); 1813
Curtis, Mike; born James Michael Curtis (football); 1943
Denning, Richard; born Louis Albert Denninger (actor); 1914
Hayman, Richard (music); 1920
Huggins, Miller James (baseball); 1879
Janssen, David; born David Harold Meyer (actor); 1930
Lanson, Snooky; born Roy Landman (singer); 1914
Moser-Proell, Annemarie (skiing); 1953
Sato, Eisaku (Japanese government); 1901
Schulberg, Budd Wilson (author); 1914
Selby, Briton (hockey); 1945
Sudakis, Bill; born William Paul Sudakis (baseball); 1946
Swanson, Gloria; born Gloria Josephine May Swenson (actress); 1897
Vance, Cyrus Roberts (government); 1917
Vaughan, Sarah Lois (singer); 1924
Wilkerson, Doug; born Douglas Wilkerson (football); 1947
Yarborough, Cale; born William Caleb Yarborough (auto racing); 1939
York, Michael; born Michael York-Johnson (actor); 1942

MARCH 28:

Algren, Nelson (author); 1909
Barry, Rick; born Richard Francis Barry, III (basketball/sportscaster);
 1944
Bartholomew, Freddie; born Frederick Llewellyn Bartholomew (actor);
 1924
Bartlett, Dewey Follett (politician); 1919
Bogarde, Dirk; born Derek Niven van de Bogaerde (actor); 1920
Brzezinski, Zbigniew Kazimierz (government); 1928
Busch, August Anheuser, Jr. (beer magnate/sportsman); 1899
Douglas, Paul Howard (politician); 1892
Fortunato, Joe; born Joseph F. Fortunato (football); 1931
Herter, Christian Archibald (politics/government); 1895
Howard, Ken; born Kenneth Joseph Howard, Jr. (actor); 1944
Kittredge, Alfred Beard (politician); 1861
Lacey, Sam (basketball); 1948
Lehman, Herbert Henry (politician); 1878
Livingston, Jay Harold (music); 1915
Loughery, Kevin Michael (basketball); 1940
Lovejoy, Frank (actor); 1912
Muskie, Edmund Sixtus (politician); 1914
Raphael Santi (artist); 1483
Raschi, Vic; born Victor John Angelo Raschi (baseball); 1919

Robinson, Robert P. (politician); 1869
Robson, Dame Flora (actress); 1902
Serkin, Rudolph (music); 1903
Starrett, Charles (actor); 1903
Thomas, Rufus (singer); 1917
Turner, Jim; born James A. Turner (football); 1941
Warneke, Lon; born Lonnie Warneke (baseball); 1909
Westley, Helen; born Henrietta Remson Meserole Maney Conroy
     (actress); 1875
Whiteman, Paul (music); 1890

MARCH 29:

Ahn, Philip (actor); 1911
Allred, James V. (politician); 1899
Bailey, Pearl Mae (singer/actress); 1918
Baxter, Warner (actor); 1889
Burrow, Ken; born Kenneth Burrow (football); 1948
Campbell, Earl (football); 1955
Carter, Billy; born William Alton Carter, III (President's brother); 1937
Curtis, Oakley Chester (politician); 1865
Dietrich, Bill; born William John Dietrich (baseball); 1910
Durkin, John Anthony (politician); 1936
Fain, Ferris Roy (baseball); 1921
Foster, Phil; born with surname Feldman (comedian/actor); 1914
Frazier, Walt (basketball); 1945
Harrison, Dutch; born Ernest Joseph Harrison (golf); 1910
Heckart, Eileen; born Anna Eileen Heckart (actress); 1919
Holmes, Tommy; born Thomas Francis Holmes (baseball); 1917
Hoover, Lou Henry; born Lou Henry (First Lady); 1875
Lindsay, Howard (playwright/producer/director/actor); 1888
Lurtsema, Bob; born Robert Ross Lurtsema (football); 1942
MacGinnis, Niall (actor); 1913
McCarthy, Eugene Joseph (politician); 1916
Nye, Blaine Francis (football); 1946
O'Connell, Arthur Joseph (actor); 1908
O'Keefe, Dennis; born Edward James Flanagan (actor); 1908
Rupp, Duane Edward Franklin (hockey); 1938
Stevens, Onslow; born Onslow Ford Stevenson (actor); 1902
Teasdale, Joseph Patrick (politician); 1936
Tunnell, Emlen (football); 1925
Tyler, John (President); 1790
Vukovich, Billy (auto racing); 1944
Works, John Downey (politician); 1847
Young, Cy; born Denton True Young (baseball); 1867

MARCH 30:

Anderson, Victor Emanuel (politician); 1902

Astin, John Allen (actor); 1930
Barnhill, John (basketball); 1938
Beatty, Warren; born Henry Warren Beatty (actor/producer/director); 1937
Bundy, McGeorge (government); 1919
Burns, John Anthony (politician); 1909
Collins, Ripper; born James Anthony Collins (baseball); 1904
Galimore, Willie Lee (football); 1935
Gogh, Vincent van (artist); 1853
Goya y Lucientes, Francisco José de (artist); 1746
Helms, Richard McGarrah (government); 1913
Hoegh, Leo Arthur (politician); 1908
Laine, Frankie; born Frank Paul LoVecchio (singer); 1913
Lucas, Jerry Ray (basketball); 1940
Marshall, Peter; born Ralph Pierre La Cock, Sr. (actor/singer/TV host); 1930
Nilsson, Anna Q.; born Anna Qyerentia Nilsson (actress); 1889
Tilleman, Mike; born Michael Tilleman (football); 1944

MARCH 31:

Alpert, Herb (music); 1935
Barber, Miller (golf); 1931
Bass, Mike; born Michael T. Bass (football); 1945
Bigbee, Carson Lee (baseball); 1895
Bolt, Tommy; born Thomas Bolt (golf); 1918
Chamberlain, Richard; born George Richard Chamberlain (actor); 1935
Chaplin, Sydney Earl (actor/singer); 1926
Chavez, Cesar (labor leader); 1927
Cox, James Middleton (politician); 1870
Daniels, William David (actor); 1927
Denney, William du Hamel (politician); 1873
Descartes, René (philosopher/mathematician); 1596
Dieterich, William Henry (politician); 1876
Grissom, Marv; born Marvin Edward Grissom (baseball); 1918
Hall, Charley; born Charles Val Hall, Jr. (football); 1948
Haydn, Franz Joseph (music); 1732
Hicke, William Lawrence (hockey); 1938
Howe, Gordie; born Gordon Howe (hockey); 1928
Johnson, Jack; born John Arthur Johnson (boxing); 1878
Johnson, Jimmy; born James Earl Johnson (football); 1938
Jones, Shirley Mae (actress/singer); 1933
Kaplan, Gabriel (comedian/actor); 1945
Kiley, Richard Paul (actor/singer); 1922
Koslo, Dave; born George Bernard Koslowski (baseball); 1920
Leahy, Patrick Joseph (politician); 1940
Leypoldt, John H. (football); 1946

Maloney, Francis Thomas (politician); 1894
Marinaro, Ed; born Edward F. Marinaro (football); 1950
Morgan, Henry; born Henry Lerner von Ost, Jr.
  (actor); 1915
Mutscheller, Jim; born James Mutscheller (football); 1930
Norvo, Red; born Kenneth Norville (music); 1908
O'Casey, Sean; born Sean O'Cathasaigh (playwright); 1880
Patterson, Lee (actor); 1929
Poole, Roy Neil (actor); 1924
Pulford, Robert (hockey); 1936
Quillan, Eddie (comedian/actor); 1907
Swanson, Claude Augustus (politics/government); 1862

APRIL 1:

Batchelor, Clarence Daniel (cartoonist); 1888
Beery, Wallace (actor); 1881
Benton, William (politician); 1900
Bismark-Schönhausen, Otto Eduard Leopold von (German statesman);
  1815
Byrne, Brendan Thomas (politician); 1924
Chaney, Lon, Sr.; born Alonso Chaney (actor); 1883
Duchin, Eddy; born Edwin Frank Duchin (music); 1909
Ecton, Zales Nelson (politician); 1898
Farrell, Johnny; born John J. Farrell (golf); 1901
Graves, David Bibb (politician); 1873
Grizzard, George Cooper, Jr. (actor); 1928
Harvey, William (medicine); 1578
Heath, Jeff; born John Geoffrey Heath (baseball); 1915
Isley, Rudolph (singer—Isley Brothers); 1939
Kingman, Dong; born Tsang King-man (artist); 1911
Klein, Herbert George (government/journalism); 1918
Lund, Art; born Arthur Earl Lund, Jr. (singer/actor); 1920
MacGraw, Ali (actress); 1938
Manchester, William (writer); 1922
Mifune, Toshiro (actor/direcctor); 1920
Montanez, Willie; born Guillermo Montanez (baseball); 1948
Niekro, Phil; born Philip Henry Niekro (baseball); 1939
Perranoski, Ron; born Ronald Peter Perranoski (baseball); 1936
Powell, Jane; born Suzanne Burce (actress/singer); 1929
Reardon, Kenny; born Kenneth Joseph Reardon (hockey); 1921
Reynolds, Debbie; born Mary Frances Reynolds (actress/singer/
  dancer); 1932
Roper, Daniel Calhoun (government); 1867
Schembechler, Bo; born Glenn Edward Schembechler (football); 1929
Sutherland, Doug; born Douglas Sutherland (football); 1948
Van Lier, Norm (basketball); 1947
Wilson, George Allison (politician); 1884

APRIL 2:

Acker, Sharon Eileen (actress); 1935
Andersen, Hans Christian (author); 1805
Appling, Luke; born Lucius Benjamin Appling (baseball); 1907
Avila, Bobby; born Roberto Francisco Avila (baseball); 1924
Basilio, Carmen (boxing); 1927
Brabham, Jack; born John Arthur Brabham (auto racing); 1926
Casanova de Seingalt, Giovanni Jacopo (adventurer); 1725
Chrysler, Walter Percy (auto manufacturer); 1875
Clark, David Worth (politician); 1902
Ebsen, Buddy; born Christian Rudolf Ebsen, Jr. (actor/dancer); 1908
Ernst, Max (artist); 1891
Farrar, Frank Leroy (politician); 1929
Floyd, Marlene (golf/sportscaster); 1944
Gam, Rita; born Rita Eleanore Mackay (actress); 1928
Gaye, Marvin (singer/music); 1939
Gerela, Roy (football); 1948
Greer, Dabbs; born Robert William Greer (actor); 1917
Guiness, Sir Alec (actor); 1914
Harris, Emmylou (singer); 1949
Herber, Arnold (football); 1910
Jennings, Hughie; born Hugh Ambrose Jennings (baseball); 1869
Kem, James Preston (politician); 1890
Malinchak, Bill; born William Malinchak (football); 1944
Mills, Herbert (singer—Mills Brothers); 1912
Moore, Dan Killian (politician); 1906
Nixon, George Stuart (politician); 1860
Palillo, Ron; born Ronald G. Palillo (actor); 1954
Pierce, Billy; born Walter William Pierce (baseball); 1927
Pritchard, Ron; born Ronald Pritchard (football); 1947
Quinn, Robert Emmett (politician); 1894
Scott, Debralee (actress); 1953
Smith, Reggie; born Carl Reginald Smith (baseball); 1945
Stautner, Ernie; born Ernest Stautner (football); 1925
Sutton, Don; born Donald Howard Sutton (baseball); 1945
Webb, Jack Randolph (actor/producer/director); 1920
Wilson, William Bauchop (government); 1862
Zola, Emile; born Edouard Charles Antoine (author); 1840

APRIL 3:

Alzado, Lyle Martin (football); 1949
Brando, Marlon (actor); 1924
Chiles, Lawton Mainor (politician); 1930
Day, Doris; born Doris von Kappelhoff (actress/singer); 1924
Dea, William Fraser (hockey); 1933
Ditmar, Art; born Arthur John Ditmar (baseball); 1929

Fernald, Bert Manfred (politician); 1858
Francis, Russ; born Russell R. Francis (football); 1953
Funseth, Rod (golf); 1933
Getliffe, Raymond (hockey); 1914
Gibson, Don (singer/music); 1928
Grammas, Alex; born Alexander Peter Grammas (baseball); 1927
Grissom, Virgil Ivan (astronaut); 1926
Hale, Edward Everett (clergyman/author); 1822
Hughes, William (politician); 1872
Irving, Washington (author); 1783
Jessel, George Albert (comedian/actor); 1898
Lloyd, Earl (basketball); 1928
Luce, Henry Robinson (publisher); 1898
Mason, Marsha (actress); 1942
Moon, Wally; born Wallace Wade Moon (baseball); 1930
Newton, Wayne (singer/actor); 1942
Orlando, Tony; born Michael Anthony Orlando Cassevitis (singer); 1944
Parent, Bernie; born Bernard Marcel Parent (hockey); 1945
Parker, Jim; born James Thomas Parker (football); 1934
Rodgers, Phil; born Philamon Webster Rodgers (golf); 1938
Savage, Ezra Perin (politician); 1842
Spuzich, Sandra Ann (golf); 1937
Sterling, Jan; born Jane Sterling Adriance (actress); 1923
Thompson, Speedy; born Alfred Thompson (auto racing); 1926
Tweed, William Marcy (politician); 1823
Umeki, Miyoski (actress); 1929

APRIL 4:

Benaderet, Bea (actress); 1906
Bernstein, Elmer (music); 1922
Bridges, Bill (basketball); 1939
Carner, JoAnne Gunderson; born JoAnne Gunderson (golf); 1939
Crow, Lindon (football); 1933
Dix, Dorothea Lynde (reformer/philanthropist); 1802
Epstein, Mike; born Michael Peter Epstein (baseball); 1943
Finch, Cliff; born Charles Clifton Finch (politician); 1927
Fosse, Ray; born Raymond Earl Fosse (baseball); 1947
Fregosi, Jim; born James Louis Fregosi (baseball); 1942
Geiger, Gary Merle (baseball); 1937
Hanly, J. Frank; born James Franklin Hanly (politician); 1863
Hodges, Gil; born Gilbert Raymond Hodges (baseball); 1924
Kohler, Walter Jodok, Jr. (politician); 1904
Lane, Rosemary; born Rosemary Mullican (actress); 1913
Langford, Frances (actress/singer); 1913
Lugar, Richard Green (politician); 1932
Masekela, Hugh Ramapolo (music); 1939
Murray, Arthur; born Arthur Murray Teichman (dancer); 1895

Parks, Michael (actor); 1938
Reynolds, John W. (politician); 1921
Senesky, George (basketball); 1922
Sherwood, Robert Emmet (playwright); 1896
Spaak, Catherine (actress); 1945
Speaker, Tris; born Tristam E. Speaker (baseball); 1888
Staub, Rusty; born Daniel Joseph Staub (baseball); 1944
Swayze, John Cameron (newscaster); 1906
Terrell, Ernie (boxing); 1939
Vosmik, Joe; born Joseph Franklin Vosmik (baseball); 1910
Waters, Muddy; born McKinley Morganfield (singer/music); 1915
White, Ed; born Edward Alvin White (football); 1947

APRIL 5:

Asher, Jane (actress); 1946
Barnett, Dick; born Richard Barnett (basketball); 1936
Bateman, Marv (football); 1950
Bowles, Chester Bliss (politics/government); 1901
Costa, Mary (singer/actress); 1930
Davis, Bette; born Ruth Elizabeth Davis (actress); 1908
Douglas, Melvyn; born Melvyn Edouard Hesselberg (actor); 1901
Elam, Cleveland (football); 1952
Fragonard, Jean-Honoré (artist); 1732
Gazzo, Michael V.; born Michael Vincente Gazzo
        (actor/director/playwright); 1923
Glieber, Frank John (sportscaster); 1934
Gorshin, Frank John (impressionist/actor); 1934
Hailey, Arthur (author); 1920
Hansen, Ron; born Ronald Lavern Hansen (baseball); 1938
Hobbes, Thomas (philosopher/writer); 1588
Jones, Jesse Holman (government); 1874
Karajan, Herbert von (music); 1908
Lewis, Robert Q. (actor); 1924
Lister, Joseph (medicine); 1827
Moriarty, Michael (actor); 1941
Morris, Jon Nicholson (football); 1942
Peck, Gregory; born Eldred Gregory Peck (actor/producer); 1916
Revolta, Johnny; born John Revolta (golf); 1911
Stennett, Rennie; born Renaldo Antonio Stennett (baseball); 1951
Storm, Gale; born Josephine Owaissa Cottle (actress/singer); 1921
Swinburne, Algernon Charles (poet); 1837
Thieu, Nguyen Van (South Vietnamese government); 1923
Tracy, Spencer Bonaventure (actor); 1900
Van Pelt, Brad Alan (football); 1951
Washington, Booker T.; born Booker Taliaferro Washington (educator);
        1856

APRIL 6:

Benzell, Mimi; born Miriam Ruth Benzell (singer/actress); 1924
Blyleven, Bert; born Rik Aalbert Blyleven (baseball); 1951
Butterfield, Alexander Porter (government); 1926
Cochrane, Mickey; born Gordon Stanley Cochrane (baseball); 1903
Dixon, Ivan N., III (actor/director); 1931
Haggard, Merle Ronald (singer/music); 1937
Houdini, Harry; born Erik Weisz, changed to Erich Weiss (magician)
       (real birthday) March 24, 1874 (adopted birthday) April 6, 1874
Huston, Walter; born Walter Houghston (actor); 1884
Kiesinger, Kurt Georg (German government); 1904
King, Bruce (politician); 1924
Lansing, Joi; born Joyce Wassmansdoff (actress); 1928
Leslie, Harry Guyer (politician); 1878
Lockhart, Carl Ford (football); 1943
Lombardi, Ernie; born Ernesto Natali Lombardi (baseball); 1908
Lynn, Janet; born Janet Lynn Nowicki (ice skating); 1953
Mulligan, Gerry; born Gerald Joseph Mulligan (music); 1927
Pattin, Marty; born Martin William Pattin (baseball); 1943
Phillips, Michelle; born Holly Michelle Gilliam (singer/actress); 1944
Previn, André George (music); 1929
Regan, Phil; born Phillip Raymond Regan (baseball); 1937
Snow, Charles Wilbert (politician); 1884
Thinnes, Roy (actor); 1938
Thomas, Herb; born Herbert Watson Thomas (auto racing); 1923
Thomas, Lowell Jackson (newscaster/author/explorer); 1892
Tydings, Millard Evelyn (politician); 1890
Williams, Billy Dee (actor); 1937

APRIL 7:

Abdul-Aziz, Zaid; born Donald A. Smith (basketball); 1946
Armstrong, Robert Richard (hockey); 1931
Bare, Bobby (singer/music); 1935
Barthelme, Donald (author); 1931
Brown, Jerry; born Edmund Gerald Brown, Jr. (politician); 1938
Burroughs, John (politician); 1907
Castle, Irene; born Irene Foote (dancer/actress); 1893
Cogdill, Gail R. (football); 1937
Coppola, Francis Ford (producer/director); 1939
Del Greco, Bobby; born Robert George Del Greco (baseball); 1933
Doerr, Bobby; born Robert Pershing Doerr (baseball); 1918
Dorsett, Tony Drew (football); 1954
Dulles, Allen Welsh (government); 1893
Ellsberg, Daniel (government); 1931
Faith, Percy (music); 1908
Fox, Jim (basketball); 1943

Frost, David Paradine (TV host); 1939
Garner, James; born James Scott Baumgarner (actor); 1928
Holiday, Billie; born Eleanor Gough McKay (singer); 1915
Jones, Preston St. Vrain (playwright/actor); 1936
King, William Rufus Devane (Vice President); 1786
Lueck, Bill; born William Lueck (football); 1946
McGraw, John Joseph (baseball); 1873
Paterson, Pat (actress); 1911
Rodgers, Wayne (actor); 1933
Santamaria, Mongo; born Ramon Santamaria (music); 1922
Sewell, Rip; born Truett Banks Sewell (baseball); 1921
Shankar, Ravi (music); 1920
Wheeler, Bert; born Albert Jerome Wheeler (comedian); 1895
Winchell, Walter; born Walter Winchel (journalist); 1897
Wordsworth, William (poet); 1770

APRIL 8:

Barnes, Margaret Ayer; born Margaret Ayer (author); 1886
Brel, Jacques (singer/music); 1929
Chase, Ilka (actress/author); 1903
Chavez, Dennis (politician); 1888
Connolly, Walter (actor); 1887
Corelli, Franco (singer); 1923
Ebb, Fred (music); 1932
Farr, Miller, Jr. (football); 1943
Farrell, Dick; born Richard Joseph Farrell (baseball); 1934
Ford, Betty; born Elizabeth Bloomer (First Lady); 1918
Gavin, John; born John Anthony Golenor (actor); 1928
Greene, Shecky; born Fred Sheldon Greenfield (comedian); 1926
Harburg, E.Y. "Yip"; born Edgar Y. Harburg (music); 1898
Havlicek, John (basketball/sportscaster); 1940
Henie, Sonja (ice skating/actress); 1910
Higbe, Kirby; born Walter Kirby Higbe (baseball); 1915
Hunter, Catfish; born James Augustus Hunter (baseball); 1946
Lennon, Peggy; born Margaret Ann Lennon (singer—Lennon Sisters); 1941
McRae, Carmen (singer); 1922
Mulhare, Edward (actor); 1923
Pickford, Mary; born Gladys Mary Smith (actress/producer); 1893
Porter, Eric (actor); 1928
Roberts, Dennis Joseph (politician); 1903
Schreiber, Martin James (politician); 1939
Tawes, J. Millard; born John Millard Tawes (politician); 1894
Tutin, Dorothy (actress); 1930
Walker, Jimmy (basketball); 1944

APRIL 9:

Aandahl, Fred George (politician); 1897
Allan, Elizabeth (actress); 1908
Arizin, Paul (basketball); 1928
Belmondo, Jean-Paul (actor); 1933
Bond, Ward (actor); 1903
Colbert, Nate; born Nathan Colbert (baseball); 1946
de Wilde, Brandon; born Andre Brandon de Wilde (actor); 1942
Dexter, Brad (actor); 1917
Dorati, Antol (music); 1906
Frankhouse, Fred; born Frederick Meloy Frankhouse (baseball); 1904
Fulbright, J. William; born James William Fulbright (politician); 1905
Goodfellow, Ebbie; born Ebenezer Ralston Goodfellow (hockey); 1907
Heflin, James Thomas (politician); 1869
Hefner, Hugh Marston (publisher); 1926
Hurok, Sol; born Solomon Hurok (producer); 1888
Lambeau, Curly; born Earl L. Lambeau (football); 1898
Learned, Michael (actress); 1939
Lynn, Sharon E.; born D'Auvergne Sharon Lindsay (actress); 1904
Manville, Tommy (playboy heir); 1894
Myers, Carmel (actress); 1899
Nichols, Jack (basketball); 1926
Pennypacker, Samuel Whitaker (politician); 1843
Perkins, Carl (singer/music); 1932
Ribicoff, Abraham Alexander (government/politics); 1910
Roberts, James Wilfred (hockey); 1940
Robeson, Paul Bustill (singer/actor); 1898
Roche, Alden (football); 1945
Schreiber, Avery (comedian/actor); 1935
Scott, Clarence (football); 1949
Scribner, Rob; born Robert Scribner (football); 1951
Trammell, Park (politician); 1876
Zimbalist, Efrem (music); 1889

APRIL 10:

Arliss, George; born George Augustus Andrews (actor); 1868
Blanton, L. Ray; born Leonard Ray Blanton (politician); 1930
Blount, Mel; born Melvin Cornell Blount (football); 1948
Connors, Chuck; born Kevin Joseph Connors (actor); 1921
Cross, Wilbur Lucius (politician); 1862
Darvas, Lili (actress); 1902
Denny, Martin (music); 1911
Fine, John Sidney (politician); 1893
Gates, Thomas Sovereign, Jr. (government); 1906
Gimbel, Bernard Feustman (merchant); 1885
Halberstam, David (journalist/author); 1934

Hawthorn, Mike; born John Michael Hawthorn (auto racing); 1929
Hinkle, Clarke; born William Clarke Hinkle (football); 1910
Kean, Jane Dawn (actress); 1928
Lary, Frank Strong (baseball); 1931
Lenin, Nikolai; born Vladimir Ilyitch Ulyanov (Russian government); 1870
Luce, Clare Boothe; born Anne Clare Booth (writer); 1903
Madden, John Earl (football); 1936
McCoy, Tim; born Timothy John Fitzgerald McCoy (actor); 1891
Meredith, Don; born Joseph Donald Meredith (football/sportscaster/actor); 1938
Morgan, Harry; born Harry Bratsburg (actor); 1915
Murphy, Ron; born Robert Ronald Murphy (hockey); 1933
Perkins, Frances (government); 1880
Pulitzer, Joseph (publisher); 1847
Rhodes, Hari (actor); 1932
Sharif, Omar; born Michael Shalhoub (actor); 1932
von Sydow, Max; born Carl Adolf von Sydow (actor); 1929
Watson, Bob; born Robert Jose Watson (baseball); 1946
Youngs, Ross Middlebrook (baseball); 1897

APRIL 11:

Acheson, Dean Gooderham (government); 1893
Antwine, Houston (football); 1939
Beauchamp, Joe; born Joseph Beauchamp (football); 1944
Carey, Hugh Leo (politician); 1919
Cassini, Oleg; born Oleg Loiewski-Cassini (fashion designer); 1913
Chapman, Sam; born Samuel Blake Chapman (baseball); 1916
Douglas, Paul (actor); 1907
Fortmann, Danny; born Daniel John Fortmann (football); 1916
Grey, Joel; born Joel Katz (actor/singer); 1932
Hearn, Jim; born James Tolbert Hearn (baseball); 1921
Holtz, Lou (comedian/actor); 1893
Hughes, Charles Evans (politician/jurist/government); 1862
Kearns, Thomas (politician); 1862
Kennedy, Ethel; born Ethel Skakel (socialite); 1928
McCosky, Barney; born William Barney McCosky (baseball); 1918
Rayner, Isidor (politician); 1850
Shay, Dorothy; born Dorothy Nell Sims (singer/actress); 1921
Sheffield, Johnny; born John Sheffield (actor); 1931
Weeks, John Wingate (politics/government); 1860

APRIL 12:

Antonelli, Johnny; born John August Antonelli (baseball); 1930
Bankhead, William Brockman (politician); 1874
Brown, Fred Herbert (politician); 1879

Carter, Chip; born James Earl Carter (First family); 1950
Cassidy, David Bruce (singer/actor); 1950
Cherrill, Virginia (actress); 1908
Clay, Henry (statesman); 1777
Dewsbury, Albert Percy (hockey); 1926
Gant, Reuben Charles (football); 1952
Garrett, Mike; born Michael Lockett Garrett (football); 1944
Grosso, Count; born Donald Grosso (hockey); 1915
Hancock, Herbie; born Herbert Jeffrey Hancock (music); 1940
Hoffman, Paul (basketball); 1922
Kruger, Hardy (actor); 1928
Lau, Charlie; born Charles Richard Lau (baseball); 1933
Magnuson, Warren Grant (politician); 1905
MacNair, Eric; born Donald Eric McNair (baseball); 1909
Miller, Ann; born Lucille Ann Collier (actress/dancer); 1919
Moryn, Walt; born Walter Joseph Moryn (baseball); 1926
Nestos, Regnvald Anderson (politician); 1877
Pons, Lily; born Alice Josephine Pons (singer/actress); 1895
Rand, Sally; born Helen Gould Beck (dancer/actress); 1903
Reutemann, Carlos Alberto (auto racing); 1942
Taylor, Glen Hearst (politician); 1904
Tiny Tim; born Herbert Khaury (singer); 1930
Turner, Curtis (auto racing); 1924
Vaughn, Billy (music); 1919
Withers, Jane (actress); 1926
Wright, Bill; born William Robert Wright (baseball); 1922

APRIL 13:

Barnes, Jim (basketball); 1941
Beckett, Samuel Barclay (playwright); 1906
Bibeault, Paul (hockey); 1919
Blanchard, Mari; born Mary Blanchard (actress); 1927
Cantwell, Ben; born Benjamin Caldwell Cantwell (baseball); 1902
Green, Al (singer/music); 1946
Gurney, Dan; born Daniel Sexton Gurney (auto racing); 1931
Himes, Norman (hockey); 1903
Hollett, Bill; born William Frank Hollett (hockey); 1912
Jefferson, Thomas (President); 1743
Keel, Howard; born Harold Clifford Leek (actor/singer); 1917
Murphy, Frank (politician); 1890
Smith, Marilynn Louise (golf); 1929
Stassen, Harold Edward (politics/government); 1907
Waggoner, Lyle Wesley (actor); 1935
Welty, Eudora (author); 1909
Wilbur, Ray Lyman, (government); 1875
Woolworth, F.W.; born Frank W. Woolworth (merchant); 1852

APRIL 14:

Brooks, Dick; born Richard Brooks (auto racing); 1942
Brumbaugh, Martin Grove (politician); 1862
Christie, Julie (actress); 1941
Darling, Joan; born Joan Kugell (actress/director); 1935
DeVicenzo, Roberto (golf); 1923
Dillman, Bradford (actor); 1930
Gielgud, Sir John; born Arthur John Gielgud (actor); 1904
Gilmer, Harry (football); 1926
Hardman, Lamartine Griffin (politician); 1856
Healy, Mary (actress/singer); 1918
Hobson, Valerie (actress); 1917
Howard, John; born John Cox (actor); 1913
Jean, Gloria; born Gloria Jean Schoonover (actress); 1926
Keough, Marty; born Richard Martin Keough (baseball); 1935
Knight, Curt (football); 1943
Lynn, Loretta; born Loretta Webb (singer); 1932
Mantha, Sylvio (hockey); 1902
Mueller, Don; born Donald Frederick Mueller (baseball); 1927
Nichols, Bobby; born Robert Nichols (golf); 1936
Perkins, Anthony (actor); 1932
Rose, Pete; born Peter Edward Rose (baseball); 1942
Silzer, George S. (politician); 1870
Steiger, Rod; born Rodney Stephen Steiger (actor); 1925
Toynbee, Arnold Joseph (historian); 1889
Tracy, Lee; born William Lee Tracy (actor); 1898
Windsor, Claire; born Clara Viola Cronk (actress); 1897

APRIL 15:

Abdul-Rahman, Mahdi; born Walt Hazzard (basketball); 1942
Ansara, Michael George (actor); 1922
Bailey, Ed; born Lonas Edgar Bailey (baseball); 1931
Beeckman, Robert Livingston (politician); 1866
Brady, Michael J. (golf); 1887
Cardinale, Claudia (actress); 1939
Clark, Roy Linwood (singer/music); 1933
Conried, Hans (actor); 1917
Davis, Willie; born William Henry Davis (baseball); 1940
Dickinson, Luren Dudley (politician); 1859
Faulk, Mary Lena (golf); 1926
Fryman, Woodie; born Woodrow Thompson Fryman (baseball); 1940
Huddleston, Walter Darlington (politician); 1926
James, Henry (author); 1843
Kenyon, Mel (auto racing); 1933
Kwalick, Ted; born Thaddeus John Kwalick (football); 1947
Lembeck, Harvey (actor); 1923

McFadden, James Alexander (hockey); 1920
McKelvie, Samuel Roy (politician); 1881
Montgomery, Elizabeth (actress); 1933
Randolph, Asa Philip (labor leader); 1889
Regalado, Victor (golf); 1948
Reid, Wallace; born William Wallace Reid (actor); 1890
Sizemore, Ted; born Theodore Crawford Sizemore (baseball); 1945
Smith, Bessie (singer); 1894
Sommars, Julie Sergie (actress); 1942
Vinci, Leonardo da (artist); 1452
Walker, Robert, Jr. (actor); 1940
Washington, Walter Edward (politician); 1915
Williams, John; born Hugh Ernest Leo Williams (actor): 1903

APRIL 16:
Abdul-Jabbar, Kareem; born Ferdinand Lewis Alcindor, Jr.
   (basketball/actor); 1947
Adams, Edie; born Elizabeth Edith Enke (actress/singer); 1927
Allen, Bernie; born Bernard Keith Allen (baseball); 1939
Amis, Kingsley William (author); 1922
Carroll, Julian Morton (politician); 1931
Case, Clifford Philip (politician); 1904
Chaplin, Sir Charlie; born Charles Spencer Chaplin (actor/director);
   1889
d'Orsay, Fifi; born Yvonne Lussier (actress); 1904
Felker, Samuel Demeritt (politician); 1859
France, Anatole; born Jacques Anatole Francois Thibault (writer); 1844
Gambee, Dave (basketball); 1937
Hamilton, Roy (singer); 1929
Hodiak, John (actor); 1914
Johnson, Walter Warren (politician); 1904
Lane, Night Train; born Richard Lane (football); 1928
Lonborg, Jim; born James Reynold Lonborg (baseball); 1942
Mancini, Henry Nicole (music); 1924
Mann, Herbie; born Herbert Jay Solomon (music); 1930
Margrethe II; born Margrethe Alexandrine Thorhildur Ingrid
   (Queen of Denmark); 1940
Moore, Arch Alfred, Jr. (politician); 1923
Nelson, Barry; born Robert Haakon Nielsen (actor); 1920
Osmond, Jimmy; born James Arthur Osmond (singer/music—Osmond
   Family); 1963
Pappas, Ike; born Icarus Nestor Pappas (newscaster); 1933
Richman, Peter Mark; born Marvin Jack Richman (actor); 1927
Rollins, Rich; born Richard John Rollins (baseball); 1938
Springfield, Dusty; born Mary Isobel Catherine O'Brien (singer); 1939
Suder, Peter (baseball); 1916
Synge, John Millington (playwright); 1871

Tremayne, Les; born Les Henning (actor); 1913
Ustinov, Peter Alexander (actor/director/writer); 1921
Van Nuys, Frederick (politician); 1874
Vinton, Bobby; born Stanley Robert Vinton (or Vintulla) (singer/music); 1935
Wallis, Shani (singer/actress); 1933
Waner, Paul Glee (baseball); 1903
Wright, Wilbur (aviator); 1867

APRIL 17:

Anderson, Lindsay Gordon (director); 1923
Anson, Cap; born Adrian Constantine Anson (baseball); 1851
Chase, Samuel (jurist/revolutionary leader); 1741
Day, William Rufus (government/jurist); 1849
Domres, Marty; born Martin F. Domres (football); 1947
Foss, Joe; born Joseph Jacob Foss (politician); 1915
Genevieve; born Ginette Marguerite Auger (entertainer); 1930
Hemus, Solly; born Solomon Joseph Hemus (baseball); 1923
Holden, William; born William Franklin Beedle, Jr. (actor); 1918
Johnson, Neil Albert (basketball); 1943
Khrushchev, Nikita Sergeyevich (Russian government); 1894
Lake, Arthur; born Arthur Silverlake (actor); 1905
Lewis, Herbert A. (hockey); 1906
Lundy, Lamar (football); 1935
McCallister, Lon; born Herbert Alonzo McCallister, Jr. (actor); 1923
McNeil, Gerard George (hockey); 1926
Morgan, J.P.; born John Pierpont Morgan (financier); 1837
Piatigorsky, Gregor (music); 1903
Plunkett, Sherm; born Sherman Plunkett (football); 1933
Reasoner, Harry (newscaster); 1923
Saulsbury, Willard, Jr. (politician); 1861
Scott, William Kerr (politician); 1896
Shirley, Anne; born Dawn Evelyneen Paris (actress); 1918
Travis, Richard; born William Justice (actor); 1913
Van Devanter, Willis (jurist); 1859
Wallgren, Monrad Charles (politician); 1891
Wilder, Thornton Niven (playwright); 1897
Williams, Thomas Mark (hockey); 1940

APRIL 18:

Archibald, Nate (basketball); 1948
Barrie, Wendy; born Marguerite Wendy Jenkins (actress); 1912
Blass, Steve; born Stephen Robert Blass (baseball); 1942
Crawford, Sam; born Samuel Earl Crawford (baseball); 1880
Darrow, Clarence Seward (attorney); 1857
Davis, John Edward (politician); 1913
Gogolak, Pete; born Peter Gogolak (football); 1942

Hale, Barbara (actress); 1922
Hartford, Huntington; born George Huntington Hartford, II (heir); 1911
Hayes, Tom; born Thomas Hayes (football); 1946
Hooks, Robert Dean (actor); 1937
Kinskey, Leonid (actor); 1903
Mills, Hayley Catherine Rose Vivian (actress/singer); 1946
O'Brien, Virginia (singer/comedienne/actress); 1921
Otten, Don (basketball); 1921
Petitbon, Richie; born Richard A. Petitbon (football); 1938
Revier, Dorothy; born Doris Velegra (actress); 1904
Revill, Clive Selsby (actor/singer); 1930
Rindt, Jochen; born Karl Jochen Rindt (auto racing); 1942
Sewell, Harley (football); 1931
Stokowski, Leopold; born Leopold Boleslawawicz Antoni Stanislaw Stokowski (music); 1882
Sweeney, Walt; born Walter Francis Sweeney (football); 1941
Trapp, Martin Edwin (politician); 1877

APRIL 19:

Adams, Don (actor); 1927
Barker, Sue; born Susan Barker (tennis); 1956
Basquette, Lina; born Lena Baskette (actress); 1907
Broward, Napoleon Bonaparte (politician); 1857
Craft, Harry Francis (baseball); 1915
Donahue, Elinor; born Mary Elinor Donahue (actress); 1937
Erickson, Keith (basketball/sportscaster); 1944
Farmer, George Thaxton (football); 1948
Fontaine, Frank (comedian/actor/singer); 1920
Garfield, Lucretia Rudolph; born Lucretia Rudolph (First Lady); 1832
Kelly, Harry Francis (politician); 1895
Mandel, Marvin (politician); 1920
Mansfield, Jayne; born Vera Jayne Palmer (actress); 1932
Moore, Dudley (music/comedian/actor); 1935
O'Brian, Hugh; born Hugh Charles Krampe (or Krampke) (actor); 1925
O'Brien, George (actor); 1900
Pardee, Jack; born John Perry Pardee (football); 1936
Pergine, John (football); 1946
Regner, Tom; born Thomas E. Regner (football); 1944
Robson, May; born Mary Jeanette Robison (actress); 1858
Sargent, Dick; born Richard Cox (actor); 1933
Scibelli, Joe; born Joseph Scibelli (football); 1939
Segal, Vivienne Sonia (actress/singer); 1897
Sherman, Roger (legislator); 1721
Talmadge, Constance (comedienne/actresss); 1899
van Eeghen, Mark (football); 1952
Walters, Bucky; born William Henry Walters (baseball); 1909

Webster, Alex; born Alexander Webster (football); 1931
Weston, Ellen; born Ellen R. Weinstein (actress); 1939

APRIL 20:

Andrie, George J. (football); 1940
Arnett, Jon Dwane (football); 1935
Bancroft, Dave; born David James Bancroft (baseball); 1891
Bartlett, Edward Louis (politician); 1904
Brandon, Michael (actor); 1945
Cabot, Bruce; born Etienne Pelissier Jacques de Bujac (actor); 1904
Foch, Nina; born Nina Consuelo Maud Fock (actress); 1924
Hampton, Lionel Leo (music); 1913
Hill, Phil; born Philip Toll Hill (auto racing); 1927
Hitler, Adolf (German government); 1889
Howard, Clint (actor); 1959
Lloyd, Harold Clayton (comedian/actor); 1889
McLean, Angus Wilton (politician); 1870
Mead, John Abner (politician); 1841
Miró, Joan (artist); 1893
Norell, Norman; born Norman Levinson (fashion designer); 1900
O'Neal, Ryan; born Patrick Ryan O'Neal (actor); 1941
Ratoff, Gregory (director); 1893
Spurrier, Steve; born Steven Orr Spurrier (football); 1945
Stevens, John Paul (jurist); 1920
Tillotsón, Johnny (singer/music); 1939
Verdugo, Elena (actress); 1926
Wagner, Robert Ferdinand, Jr. (politician); 1910
Young, Wilbur Eugene (football); 1949

APRIL 21:

Boren, David Lyle (politician); 1941
Brontë, Charlotte (author/poet); 1816
Brown, Pat; born Edmund Gerald Brown, Sr. (politician); 1905
Bumbry, Al; born Alonza Benjamin Bumbry (baseball); 1947
Cornell, Don; born Louis F. Varlaro (singer); 1919
Elizabeth II, Queen of England; born Elizabeth Alexandra Mary ; 1926
Evans, Jack; born William John Evans (hockey); 1928
Fleming, Reginald Stephen (hockey); 1936
Green, Dick; born Richard Larry Green (baseball); 1941
Grodin, Charles (actor); 1935
Jamieson, Jim (golf); 1943
Mangano, Silvana (actress); 1930
May, Elaine; born Elaine Berlin (comedienne/actress/writer); 1932
May, Rollo Reese (psychologist); 1909
McCarthy, Joe; born Joseph Vincent McCarthy (baseball); 1887
Owen, Steve; born Stephen Joseph Owen (football); 1898
Peters, Gary Charles (baseball); 1937

Quinn, Anthony Rudolph Oaxaca (actor); 1915
Ward, Clara (singer); 1924
Whitney, Eleanore (dancer/actress); 1914

APRIL 22:

Albert, Eddie; born Edward Albert Heimberger (actor/singer); 1908
Beman, Deane Randolph (golf); 1938
Bottoms, Joseph (actor); 1954
Campbell, Glen Travis (singer/actor/music); 1936
Campbell, Thomas Mitchell (politician); 1856
Cole, George (actor); 1925
Damon, Mark; born Alan Harris (actor); 1933
Douthit, Taylor Lee (baseball); 1901
Fielding, Henry (author); 1707
Frampton, Peter Kenneth (singer/music); 1950
Glasgow, Ellen Anderson Gholson (author); 1874
Haywood, Spencer (basketball); 1949
Isabella I (Queen of Spain); 1451
Jarrett, Douglas (hockey); 1944
Kant, Immanuel (philosopher); 1724
Kerenski, Aleksandr Feodorovich (Russian government); 1881
Longley, James Bernard (politician); 1924
March, Hal; born Harold (or Howard) Mendelson (actor); 1920
Menuhin, Yehudi (music); 1916
Miller, Jason; born John Miller (playwright/actor); 1939
Mingus, Charles (music); 1922
Nicholson, Jack; born John Nicholson Rose (actor/director); 1937
Oppenheimer, J. Robert; born Julius Robert Oppenheimer (nuclear
        physicist); 1904
Poindexter, Miles (politician); 1868
Rae, Charlotte; born Charlotte Rae Lubotsky
        (actress/comedienne/singer); 1926
Ramsey, Steve; born Stephen W. Ramsey (football); 1948
Smith, Bob; born Robert Eldridge Smith (baseball); 1898
Spelling, Aaron (producer); 1925
Vernon, Mickey; born James Barton Vernon (baseball); 1918

APRIL 23:

Berry, Tom (politician); 1879
Bertinelli, Valerie Anne (actress); 1960
Birney, David Edwin (actor); 1939
Blair, Janet; born Martha Janet Lafferty (actress/singer); 1921
Bottomley, Jim; born James LeRoy Bottomley (baseball); 1900
Briscoe, Dolph, Jr. (politician); 1923
Buchanan, James (President); 1791
Camilli, Dolf; born Adolf Louis Camilli (baseball); 1907
Clay, Lucius DuBignon (army officer); 1897

Crane, Winthrop Murray (politician); 1853
Davis, David William (politician); 1873
Dee, Sandra; born Alexandra Zuck (actress); 1942
Devlin, Bernadette Josephine (Irish civil rights leader); 1947
DeWitt, Joyce (actress/singer); 1949
Douglas, Stephen Arnold (politician); 1813
Esposito, Tony; born Anthony James Esposito (hockey); 1943
Ferguson, Joe (football); 1950
Fleckman, Marty; born Martin A. Fleckman (golf); 1944
Goodrich, Gail (basketball); 1943
Halston; born Roy Halston Frowick (fashion designer); 1932
Hillaire, Marcel (actor); 1908
Majors, Lee; born Harvey Lee Yeary (actor); 1939
Massengale, Don; born Donald Massengale (golf); 1937
Nabokov, Vladimir (author); 1899
Orbison, Roy (singer/music); 1936
Pearson, Lester Bowles (Canadian government); 1897
Rachmaninoff, Serge Vassilievich (music); 1873
Renaldo, Duncan; born Renault Renaldo Duncan
     (actor/producer/writer/artist); 1904
Simon, Simone (actress); 1910
Spahn, Warren Edward (baseball); 1921
Temple, Shirley Jane (actress/government); 1928
Turner, Joseph Mallord William (artist); 1775
Vangilder, Elam Russell (baseball); 1896
Villechaize, Hervé (actor); 1943
Wilkinson, Bud; born Charles Burnham Wilkinson
     (football/sportscaster); 1916

APRIL 24:

Boone, Shirley; born Shirley Lee Foley (singer/author—Boone Family);
     1934
Cannon, J.D.; born John Donovan Cannon (actor); 1922
Cordon, Guy (politician); 1890
Dale, Carroll W. (football); 1938
de Kooning, Willem (artist); 1904
Ehmke, Howard Jonathan (baseball); 1894
Howard, Leslie; born Leslie Howard Stainer (actor); 1890
Hunter, Art; born Arthur Hunter (football); 1933
Ireland, Jill Dorothy (actress/singer); 1936
Leonard, Jack E. (comedian); 1911
Lunn, Bob; born Robert Lunn (golf); 1945
MacLaine, Shirley; born Shirley MacLean Beaty
     (actress/singer/dancer); 1934
Rowser, John (football); 1944
Singer, Bill; born William Robert Singer (baseball); 1944

Streisand, Barbra; born Barbara Joan Streisand (singer/actress); 1942
Warren, Robert Penn (author); 1905

APRIL 25:

Barber, Jerry; born Carl Jerome Barber (golf); 1916
Brennan, William Joseph, Jr. (jurist); 1906
Brown, Jimmy; born James Roberson Brown (baseball); 1910
Cromwell, Oliver (lord protector of England); 1599
Egan, Pat; born Martin Joseph Egan (hockey); 1918
Estabella, Bobby; born Robert Estabella (baseball); 1911
Fitzgerald, Ella (singer); 1918
Haney, Fred Girard (baseball); 1898
Hayden, Melissa; born Mildred Herman (dancer); 1928
Hermeling, Terry (football); 1946
Krausse, Lew; born Lewis Bernard Krausse, Jr. (baseball); 1943
Lemon, Meadowlark; born Meadow George Lemon, III (basketball); 1932
Marconi, Guglielmo (inventor); 1874
McLeod, Fred; born Frederick Robertson McLeod (golf); 1882
Murrow, Edward R.; born Edward Roscoe Murrow (newscaster); 1908
Pacino, Al; born Alfredo James Pacino (actor); 1939
Shapiro, Samuel Harvey (politician); 1907
Shire, Talia; born Talia Rose Coppola (actress); 1946

APRIL 26:

Alexander, Dale; born David Dale Alexander (baseball); 1903
Audubon, John James (ornithologist/artist); 1785
Auger, Claudine (actress); 1942
Beltoise, Jean-Pierre (auto racing); 1937
Benenuti, Nino (boxing); 1938
Boozer, Bob; born Robert Boozer (basketball); 1937
Burnett, Carol Creighton (comedienne/actress/singer); 1933
Cuozzo, Gary (football); 1941
Davis, Jonathan McMillan (politician); 1871
Delacroix, Ferdinand Victor Eugene (artist); 1798
Dillon, Cecil Graham (hockey); 1908
Eddy, Duane (music); 1938
Gallatin, Harry (basketball); 1928
Hammer, Granny; born Granville Wilbur Hammer (baseball); 1927
Henderson, Charles (politician); 1860
Hume, David (philosopher); 1711
Kennedy, Edgar (actor); 1890
Linn, Bambi; born Bambina Aennchen Linnemier (dancer/actress); 1926
Loos, Anita (playwright/author); 1893
MacGregor, Bruce Cameron (hockey); 1941
Maglie, Sal; born Salvatore Anthony Maglie (baseball); 1917

Malamud, Bernard (author); 1914
Northey, Ron; born Ronald James Northey (baseball); 1920
Otis, Amos Joseph (baseball); 1947
Parker, Cecilia (actress); 1905
Ralston, John (football); 1927
Richter, Charles Francis (seismologist); 1900
Risdon, Elizabeth (actress); 1887
Rydell, Bobby; born Robert Lewis Ridarelli (singer/actor); 1942
Sebastian, Dorothy (actress); 1903
Sorlie, Arthur Gustav (politician); 1874
Stein, Jules Caesar (corporation executive); 1896
Thye, Edward John (politician); 1896
Trucks, Virgil Oliver (baseball); 1919

APRIL 27:

Aimée, Anouk; born Francoise Sorya (actress); 1932
Alston, Mack (football); 1947
Bel Geddes, Norman; born Norman Geddes
    (producer/director/designer); 1893
Burns, Arthur Frank (government); 1904
Carne, Judy; born Joyce Botterill (actress/singer); 1939
Dennis, Sandy; born Sandra Dale Dennis (actress); 1937
Diegel, Leo (golf); 1899
Foster, Bob (boxing); 1942
Gervin, George (basketball); 1952
Gibbon, Edward (historian); 1737
Grant, Ulysses Simpson; born Hiram Ulysses Grant (President); 1822
Hornsby, Rogers (baseball); 1896
Huff, Gary Earl (football); 1951
Jones, Phil; born Philip Howard Jones (newscaster); 1937
Jordan, Lee Roy (football); 1941
King, Coretta Scott; born Coretta Scott (civil rights leader); 1927
Klugman, Jack (actor); 1922
Knox, Chuck; born Charles Robert Knox (football); 1932
Morse, Samuel Finley Breese (inventor); 1791
Slaughter, Enos Bradsher (baseball); 1916
Spencer, Herbert (philosopher); 1820

APRIL 28:

Anderson, Robert Woodruff (playwright); 1917
Ann-Margret; born Ann Margaret Olsson (actress/singer/dancer);
    1941
Barrymore, Lionel; born Lionel Blythe (actor); 1878
Brandt, Jackie; born John George Brandt (baseball); 1934
Dearie, Blossom (singer); 1926
Heard, William Wright (politician); 1853
Jones, Carolyn Sue (actress); 1929

Lee, Harper; born Nelle Harper Lee (author); 1926
Lucas, Red; born Charles Fred Lucas (baseball); 1902
Mara, Adele; born Adelaida Delgado (actress); 1923
Maxwell, Charlie; born Charles Richard Maxwell (baseball); 1927
Metro, Charlie; born Charles Moreskonich (baseball); 1919
Monroe, James (President); 1758
Ramos, Pete; born Pedro Ramos (baseball); 1935
Salazar, Antonio de Oliveria (Portugese government); 1889
Stanowski, Wally; born Walter Peter Stanowski (hockey); 1919
Strassman, Marcia (actress/singer); 1948
Toler, Sidney (actor); 1874
Young, Clement Calhoun (politician); 1869

APRIL 29:

Allen, George Herbert (football/sportscaster/author); 1922
Aparicio, Luis Ernesto Monteil (baseball); 1934
Carlson, Richard (actor/director/writer); 1912
Davis, Danny; born George Joseph Nowlan (music); 1925
Ellington, Duke; born Edward Kennedy Ellington (music); 1899
Ewell, Tom; born Yewell Tompkins (actor); 1909
Frank, Larry S. (auto racing); 1931
Gauthier, Jean Phillipe (hockey); 1937
Hamilton, Reginald (hockey); 1914
Hart, Jim; born James Warren Hart (football); 1944
Hearst, William Randolph (publishing); 1863
Hirohito (Japanese Emperor); 1901
Holm, Celeste (actress/singer); 1919
Jeanmaire, Renée (dancer/actress); 1924
Johnson, Ernie; born Ernest Rudolph Johnson (baseball); 1888
McKuen, Rod Marvin (poet/music/singer); 1933
Mehta, Zubin (music); 1936
Miller, Johnny; born John Lawrence Miller (golf); 1947
Mills, Donald F. (singer—Mills Brothers); 1915
Mulgrew, Kate; born Katherine Mulgrew (actress); 1955
Noonan, Tommy; born Thomas Patrick Noon (comedian/actor); 1922
Otis, Jim; born James Lloyd Otis (football); 1948
Sabatini, Rafael (author); 1875
Stevens, April (singer); 1936
Talmadge, Natalie (actress); 1898
Zinneman, Fred (director); 1907

APRIL 30:

Arden, Eve; born Eunice Quedens (actress); 1912
Calvet, Corinne born Corinne Dibos (actress); 1925
Clayburgh, Jill (actress); 1944
Collins, Gary (actor); 1938
Cummings, Homer Stillé (government); 1870

Harnick, Sheldon Mayer (music); 1924
Horton, Johnny (singer); 1925
Juliana; born Juliana Louise Emma Marie Wilhelmina (Queen of The Netherlands); 1909
King, Perry (actor); 1948
Laabs, Chet; born Chester Peter Laabs (baseball); 1912
Leachman, Cloris (actress); 1926
Lehár, Franz (music); 1870
Lewis, Al; born Al Meister (actor); 1923
MacKell, Fleming David (hockey); 1929
Manners, David; born Rauff de Ryther Duan Acklom (actor); 1900
McKenney, Don; born Donald Hamilton McKenney (hockey); 1934
McNeil, Don; born W. Donald McNeil (tennis); 1918
Nelson, Willie (singer/music); 1933
Osmond, Merrill Davis (singer/music—Osmond Family); 1953
Ransom John Crowe (poet); 1888
Shaw, Robert Lawson (music); 1916
Stovall, Jerry L. (football); 1941
Vanderbilt, Cornelius Jr. (writer/lecturer); 1898
Vee, Bobby; born Robert Thomas Velline (singer/music); 1943

MAY 1:

Battles, Cliff; born Clifford Franklin Battles (football); 1910
Beard, Frank (golf); 1939
Bednarik, Chuck; born Charles Phillip Bednarik (football); 1925
Berardino, John (baseball/actor); 1917
Brown, Roger L. (football); 1937
Carpenter, Malcolm Scott (astronaut); 1925
Cauthen, Steve; born Stephen Mark Cauthen (jockey); 1960
Clark, Mark Wayne (army officer); 1896
Clemens, Barry (basketball); 1943
Collins, Judy Marjorie (singer/music); 1939
Coolidge, Rita (singer/music); 1944
Darrieux, Danielle (actress); 1917
Dunn, Josephine; born Mary Josephine Dunn (actress); 1906
Elrod, Samuel Harrison (politician); 1856
Ford, Glenn; born Gwyllyn Samuel Newton Ford (actor); 1916
Hale, Sonnie; born John Robert Hale-Monro (actor/comedian/singer/director); 1902
Heard, Jerry Michael (golf); 1947
Heller, Joseph (author); 1923
Hobart, Rose; born Rose Kefer (actress); 1906
Hyams, Leila (actress); 1905
Inness, George (artist); 1825
James, Sonny; born James Loden (singer); 1929
Matson, Ollie; born Oliver Genoa Matson (football); 1930
Mosel, Tad; born George Ault Mosel, Jr. (playwright); 1922

O'Herlihy, Dan; born Daniel O'Herlihy (actor); 1919
Paar, Jack Harold (TV host); 1918
Rockefeller, Winthrop (politician); 1912
Smith, Kate; born Kathyrn Elizabeth Smith (singer); 1909
Wellington, Duke of; born Arthur Wellesley (statesman); 1769
Zarilla, Al; born Allen Lee Zarilla (baseball); 1919

MAY 2:

Aherne, Brian de Lacy (actor); 1902
Bikel, Theodore (actor/singer); 1924
Bressoud, Eddie; born Edward Francis Bressoud (baseball); 1932
Brown, Gates; born William James Brown (baseball); 1939
Byrnes, James Francis (politics/government); 1879
Carroll, Clay Palmer (baseball); 1941
Castle, Vernon; born Vernon Castle Blythe (dancer/actor); 1887
Catharine the Great; born Ekaterina Alekseevna (Russian Empress);
    1729
Chevrefils, Real ((hockey); 1932
Collins, Eddie; born Edward Trowbridge Collins (baseball); 1887
Crosby, Bing; born Harry Lillis Crosby (singer/actor); 1901
Farkas, Andy; born Andrew Farkas (football); 1916
Gatlin, Larry Wayne (singer/music); 1948
Gore, Lesley (singer); 1946
Hart, Lorenz Milton (music); 1895
Irons, Gerald Dwayne (football); 1947
Kuluva, Will (actor); 1917
O'Brien-Moore, Erin; born Annette Erin O'Brien-Moore (actress); 1908
Patrick, Nigel; born Nigel Dennis Wemyss (actor/director); 1913
Ray, Satyajat (director); 1921
Roberts, Owen Josephus (jurist); 1875
Scarlatti, Alessandro (music); 1660
Sigler, Kim (politician); 1894
Spock, Benjamin McLane (medicine); 1903

MAY 3:

Ames, Joe (singer—Ames Brothers); 1924
Astor, Mary; born Lucille Vasconcellos Langhanke (actress); 1906
Bay, Howard (designer/director); 1912
Bondi, Beulah; born Beulah Bondy (actress); 1892
Brown, James (singer/music); 1928
Cannizzaro, Chris; born Christopher John Cannizzaro (baseball); 1938
Comden, Betty; born Betty Cohen (writer); 1919
Cooper, Henry (boxing); 1934
Corwin, Norman Lewis (writer); 1910
Fox, Virgil Keel (music); 1912
Heard, Gar (basketball); 1948
Henning, Doug (magician/actor); 1947

Herring, Clyde LaVerne (politician); 1879
Hinton, Chuck; born Charles Edward Hinton (baseball); 1934
Hopkin, Mary Elizabeth Blowden (singer); 1950
Humperdinck, Engelbert; born Arnold George Dorsey (singer); 1936
Inge, William Motter (playwright); 1913
La Rue, Jack; born Gaspare Biondolillo (actor); 1900
Layton, Joe; born Joseph Lichtman (director/choreographer); 1931
Lee, Canada; born Leonard Lionel Cornelius Canegata (actor); 1907
Little, John D. (football); 1947
Lopes, Davey; born David Earl Lopes (baseball); 1946
Machiavelli, Niccolo (political philosopher); 1469
MacMahon, Aline Leveen (actress); 1899
Meir, Golda; born Golda Mabovitz (Israeli government); 1898
Murray, James Edward (politician); 1876
Notte, John Anthony, Jr. (politician); 1909
Oosterhuis, Peter A. (golf); 1948
Rixey, Eppa (baseball); 1891
Robinson, Dave; born Richard David Robinson (football); 1941
Robinson, Sugar Ray; born Walker Smith (boxing/actor); 1920
Roosevelt, Anna Eleanor (First family); 1906
Ruffing, Red; born Charles Herbert Ruffing (baseball); 1904
Seeger, Pete; born Peter R. Seeger (singer/music); 1919
Slezak, Walter Leo (actor/singer); 1902
Smith, Ron; born Ronald Smith (football); 1943
Taylor, William James (hockey); 1919
Torres, Jose (boxing); 1936
Valli, Frankie; born Frank Castelluccio (singer); 1937
Wilson, Earl (journalist); 1907

MAY 4:

Adler, Luther; born Lutha Adler (actor); 1903
Beard, Butch (basketball); 1947
Blaine, John James (politician); 1875
Da Silva, Howard; born Howard Silverblatt (actor); 1909
Deneen, Charles Samuel (politician); 1863
Durbin, Winfield Taylor (politician); 1847
Ferguson, Maynard (music); 1928
Hepburn, Audrey; born Audrey Hepburn-Ruston (actress); 1929
Hill, Harlon (football); 1932
Knight, Esmond (actor); 1905
Lawrence, Sir Thomas (artist); 1769
Mann, Horace (educator); 1796
Peters, Roberta; born Roberta Peterman (singer); 1930
Rawls, Betsy; born Elizabeth Earle Rawls (golf); 1928
Rochefort, Leon (hockey); 1939
Spellman, Cardinal Francis Joseph (clergyman); 1889
Stanfield, Frederic William (hockey); 1944

Tobin, Jack; born John Thomas Tobin (baseball); 1892
Trips, Wolfgang Graf Berghe von (auto racing); 1928
Tydings, Joseph Davies (politician); 1928
Tyler, Julia Gardiner; born Julia Gardiner (second wife of John Tyler/
    First Lady); 1820
Young, Stephen Marvin (politician); 1889

MAY 5:

Amos; born Freeman Fisher Gosden (actor—Amos n' Andy); 1896
Babich, Bob; born Robert Babich (football); 1947
Baron, Sandy; born Sandy Beresofsky (comedian/actor); 1937
Bender, Chief; born Charles Albert Bender (baseball); 1883
Buddin, Don; born Donald Thomas Buddin (baseball); 1934
Canadeo, Tony; born Anthony Robert Canadeo (football); 1919
Carroll, Pat; born Patricia Ann Carroll (comedienne/actress); 1927
Carter, Duane (auto racing); 1913
Cerv, Bob; born Robert Henry Cerv (baseball); 1926
Conacher, James (hockey); 1921
Davis, Ann B.; born Ann Bradford Davis (actress); 1926
Faye, Alice; born Alice Jeanne Leppert (actress/singer); 1912
Gilliam, Herman (basketball); 1946
Helms, Tommy Van (baseball); 1941
Hisle, Larry Eugene (baseball); 1947
Hummer, John (basketball); 1948
Hutchins, Will (actor); 1932
Lang, June; born Winifred June Vlasek (actress); 1915
Loveless, Herschel Cellel (politician); 1911
Marx, Karl (socialist writer); 1818
Morley, Christopher Darlington (author); 1890
O'Gorman, James Aloysius (politician); 1860
Pagan, Jose Antonio (baseball); 1935
Power, Tyrone Edmund (actor); 1913
Thompson, Sam; born Samuel Luther Thompson (baseball); 1860
Van Dreelan, John (actor); 1922
Wynette, Tammy; born Wynette Pugh (singer/music); 1942

MAY 6:

Cavallaro, Carmen (music); 1913
Celler, Emanuel (politician); 1888
Davis, Jefferson (politician); 1862
Dreyfus, Rene (auto racing); 1905
Ewbank, Weeb; born Wilbur Charles Ewbank (football); 1907
Freud, Sigmund (psychiatry); 1856
Golden, Harry; born Harry Goldhurst (author); 1902
Granger, Stewart; born James Lablache Stewart (actor); 1913
Hands, Bill; born William Alfred Hands, Jr. (baseball); 1940
Harder, Pat; born Marlin M. Harder (football); 1922

Havig, Dennis Eugene (football); 1949
Hunter, Ross; born Martin Fuss (producer/actor); 1921
Jones, Grier (golf); 1946
Knox, Philander Chase (government/politics); 1853
Mays, Willie Howard, Jr. (baseball); 1931
Peary, Robert Edwin (naval officer/explorer); 1856
Piazza, Marguerite; born Marguerite Piazza Luft (singer); 1926
Purtell, William Arthur (politician); 1897
Robespierre, Maximilien Francois Marie Isidore de (French
     revolutionist); 1758
Sellars, Elizabeth (actress); 1923
Shor, Toots; born Bernard Shor (restaurateur); 1905
Stewart, Jack; born John Sherratt Stewart (hockey); 1917
Straub, Robert William (politician); 1920
Tarasovic, George K. (football); 1930
Underwood, Oscar Wilder (politician); 1862
Valentino, Rudolph; born Rodolpho Alfonso Raffaello Pierre Filibert
     Guglielmi de Valentina d'Antonguolla (actor); 1895
Wakefield, Dick; born Richard Cummings Wakefield (baseball); 1921
Watson, Harry Percival (hockey); 1923
Welles, Orson; born George Orson Welles
     (actor/producer/director/writer); 1915
White, Teddy; born Theodore Harold White (author/historian); 1915
Wingo, Al; born Absalom Holbrook Wingo (baseball); 1898

MAY 7:

Ahern, Kathy; born Kathleen Ahern (golf); 1949
Baxter, Anne (actress); 1923
Brahms, Johannes (music); 1833
Brewer, Teresa; born Theresa Breuer (singer); 1931
Browning, Robert (poet); 1812
Cannon, Joseph Gurney (politician); 1836
Collins, Pat; born Patricia Colinaka Allan (performer); 1935
Cooper, Gary; born Frank James Cooper (actor); 1901
Domenici, Pete Vichi (politician); 1932
Fields, Totie; born Sophie Feldman (comedienne); 1930
Green, Bobby Joe; born Robert Joseph Green (football); 1936
Hampton, Dave; born David Hampton (football); 1947
Hayes, Gabby; born George Hayes (actor); 1885
Hegyes, Robert (actor); 1951
Hubbard, Marv; born Marvin Hubbard (football); 1946
Ian, Janis (singer/music); 1950
MacLeish, Archibald (poet/playwright); 1892
McGavin, Darren (actor/director/producer); 1922
Murray, Mae; born Marie Adrienne Koening (actress); 1889
Parilli, Babe; born Vito Parilli (football); 1929
Pearson, James Blackwood (politician); 1920

Perry, Roger L. (actor); 1933
Robbins, Gale (actress/singer); 1924
Stone, William Joel (politician); 1848
Tchaikovsky, Peter; born Pëtr Ilich Tchaikovsky (music); 1840
Unitas, Johnny; born John Constantine Unitas (football/sportscaster); 1933
Warfield, Edwin (politician); 1848
Weiss, Bob (basketball); 1942
Williams, Dick; born Richard Hirschfeld Williams (baseball); 1929
Zachary, Tom; born Jonathan Thompson Walton Zachary (baseball); 1896

MAY 8:

Anderson, John Jr. (politician); 1917
Archer, John; born Ralph Shipwith Bowman (actor); 1915
Atkins, Doug; born Douglas L. Atkins (football); 1930
Barker, Lex; born Alexander Crichlow Barker (actor); 1919
Benchley, Peter Bradford (author); 1940
Braun, Steve; born Stephen Russell Braun (baseball); 1948
Brouthers, Dan; born Dennis Joseph Brouthers (baseball); 1858
Cordero, Angel Tomas, Jr. (jockey); 1942
Cueller, Mike; born Miguel Angel Cueller (baseball); 1937
Deconcini, Dennis (politician); 1937
Fernandel; born Fernand Joseph Désiré Contandin (actor); 1903
Gilbert, Melissa (actress); 1964
Grim, Bob; born Robert Lee Grim (football); 1945
Hammerstein, Oscar (music/playwright/producer); 1847
Jens, Salome (actress); 1935
Joyal, Edward Abel (hockey); 1940
LaFollette, Philip Fox (politician); 1897
Lincoln, Keith Payson (football); 1939
Liston, Sonny; born Charles Liston (boxing); 1932
Marland, Ernest Whitworth (politician); 1874
Mitchum, James (actor); 1941
Nelson, Rick; born Eric Hilliard Nelson (singer/actor); 1940
Ouimet, Francis DeSales (golf); 1893
Pynchon, Thomas (author); 1937
Rickles, Don (comedian/actor); 1926
Rossellini, Roberto (director); 1906
Roush, Edd J. (baseball); 1893
Sheen, Bishop Fulton John (clergyman); 1895
Smith, Kenneth Alvin (hockey); 1924
Sorenson, Theodore Chaikin (government/attorney); 1928
Tennille, Toni; born Cathryn Antoinette Tennille (singer/music/actress); 1943
Thompson, James Robert, Jr. (politician); 1936
Truman, Harry S. (President); 1884

Vanderbilt, William Henry (railroad magnate/financier); 1821
Wilson, Sloan (author); 1920

MAY 9:

Barrie, Sir James Matthew (author/dramatist); 1860
Barthelmess, Richard (actor); 1895
Bergen, Candice (actress/photo-journalist); 1946
Biddle, Francis Beverly (government); 1886
Brown, John (abolitionist); 1800
Finney, Albert (actor); 1936
Freeman, Orville Lothrop (politics/government); 1918
Gonzales, Pancho; born Richard Alonzo Gonzales (tennis); 1928
Jackson, Glenda (actress); 1936
Jameson, Betty; born Elizabeth Jameson (golf); 1919
Jeter, Bob; born Robert D. Jeter (football); 1937
Jurges, Bill; born William Frederick Jurges (baseball); 1908
Kaiser, Henry John (industrialist); 1882
Knight, Fuzzy; born John Forrest Knight (actor); 1901
Mahaffey, John (golf); 1948
Murphy, Calvin J. (basketball); 1948
Robinson, Floyd Andrew (baseball); 1936
Roe, Tommy; born Thomas David Roe (singer/music); 1943
Snow, Hank; born Clarence Eugene Snow (singer/music); 1914
Vardon, Harry (golf); 1870
Wallace, Mike; born Myron Leon Wallace (newscaster); 1918
Whittenton, Jess; born Urshell Whittenton (football); 1934
Wilson, George (basketball); 1942

MAY 10:

Albert, Carl Bert (politician); 1908
Astaire, Fred; born Frederick Austerlitz (dancer/actor/singer); 1899
Berry, Ken; born Allen Kent Berry (baseball); 1941
Carter, Mother Maybelle; born Maybelle Addington (singer); 1909
Demaret, Jimmy; born James Newton Demaret (golf); 1910
Durant, Ariel; born Ariel Kaufman (philosopher/author); 1898
Fabian, Francoise; born Michèle Cortès de Leone y Fabianera (actress); 1935
Grasso, Ella Tambussi (politician); 1919
Hickman, Jim; born James Lucius Hickman (baseball); 1937
Margo; born Maria Marguerita Guadalupe Teresa Estela Bolado Castilla y O'Donnell (actress); 1917
McGraw, Charles Francis (actor); 1914
McMaster, William Henry (politician); 1877
Owens, Gary (TV host); 1936
Rasmussen, Randy; born Randall Lee Rasmussen (football); 1945
Santana, Manuel; born Manuel Santana Martinez (tennis); 1938
Selznick, David O.; born David Oliver Selznick (producer); 1902

Sherman, John (statesman); 1823
Souchak, Mike; born Michael Souchak (golf); 1927
Summerall, Pat; born George Summerall (football/sportscaster); 1930
Tiomkin, Dimitri (music); 1899
Walker, Nancy; born Anna Myrtle Swoyer (actress); 1921
Wilbur, Curtis Dwight (government); 1867

MAY 11:

Berlin, Irving; born Isador Baline (music); 1888
Billings, Franklin Swift (politician); 1862
Brooks, Foster Murrell (comedian/actor); 1912
Bunker, Ellsworth (government); 1894
Cole, Bobby; born Robert Cole (golf); 1948
Cotten, Norris (politician); 1900
Dali, Salvador Felipe Jacinto (artist); 1904
Dent, Jim; born James Dent (golf); 1942
Elkin, Stanley Lawrence (author); 1930
Fairbanks, Charles Warren (Vice President); 1852
Flock, Tim; born Julius Timothy Flock (auto racing); 1924
Gehringer, Charlie; born Charles Leonard Gehringer (baseball); 1903
Graham, Martha (dancer/choreographer); 1894
Hiller, Dutch; born Wilbert Carl Hiller (hockey); 1915
Holmes, Robert Denison (politician); 1909
McClure, Doug (actor); 1935
Mohr, Gerald (actor); 1914
Morgenthau, Henry, Jr. (government); 1891
Pappas, Milt; born Milton Edward Pappas (baseball); 1939
Pyle, Denver (actor); 1920
Quilici, Frank Ralph (baseball); 1939
Rutherford, Dame Margaret Taylor (actress); 1892
Sahl, Mort; born Morton Lyon Sahl (comedian); 1927
Silvers, Phil; born Philip Silversmith (comedian/actor); 1911
Taylor, Kent; born Louis William John Henry Von Weiss (actor); 1906
Twyman, Jack (basketball); 1934
Valentino; born Valentino Garavani (fashion designer); 1932
Van Sant, Samuel Rinnah (politician); 1844
Wallace, Henry Cantwell (government); 1866
Weaver, Doodles; born Winstead Sheffield Glendening Dixon Weaver
    (actor); 1914

MAY 12:

Alou, Felipe Rojas (baseball); 1935
Bacharach, Burt F. (music); 1928
Berra, Yogi; born Lawrence Peter Berra (baseball); 1925
Borowy, Hank; born Henry Ludwig Borowy (baseball); 1916
Bucyk, Johnny; born John Paul Bucyk (hockey); 1935
Carlin, George Denis (comedian/actor); 1938

Dugan, Joe; born Joseph Anthony Dugan (baseball); 1897
Goldham, Bob; born Robert John Goldham (hockey); 1922
Hampshire, Susan (actress); 1938
Hyde-White, Wilfrid (actor); 1903
Kubiak, Ted; born Thedore Rodger Kubiak (baseball); 1942
Lane, William Preston, Jr. (politician); 1892
Lodge, Henry Cabot, Sr. (politician); 1850
Madison, Dolly; born Dorothy Payne (First Lady); 1768
Massenet, Jules-Emile-Frédéric (music); 1842
McCauley, Don; born Donald McCauley (football); 1949
Nightingale, Florence (nurse); 1820
Perkins, Millie (actress); 1938
Rossetti, Dante Gabriel (poet/artist); 1828
Salvadori, Roy Francesco (auto racing); 1922
Smith, Howard K.; born Howard Kingsbury Smith (newscaster); 1914
Smith, William Alden (politician); 1859
Snyder, Tom (newscaster/TV host); 1936
Toole, Joseph Kemp (politician); 1851
Ziegler, Ron; born Ronald Lewis Ziegler (government); 1939

MAY 13:

Arthur, Beatrice; born Bernice Frankel (actress); 1924
Barnes, Clive Alexander (journalist); 1927
Beardsley, William Shane (politician); 1901
Berger, Senta (actress); 1941
Du Maurier, Daphne (writer); 1907
Dye, Babe; born Cecil Dye (hockey); 1898
Gravel, Mike; born Maurice Robert Gravel (politician); 1930
Lampert, Zohra (actress); 1936
Louis, Joe; born Joseph Louis Barrow (boxing); 1914
McCormick, Cyrus Hall (inventor); 1884
Middleton, Robert; born Samuel G. Messer (actor); 1911
Roseboro, John (baseball); 1933
Sullivan, Sir Arthur Seymour (music); 1842
Umstead, William Bradley (politician); 1895
Valens, Ritchie; born Richard Valenzuela (singer/music); 1941
Wagner, Leon Lamar (baseball); 1934
Wells, Mary (singer/music); 1943
Whitman, Walt; born Walter Whitman (poet); 1819
Wonder, Stevie; born Steveland, Morris Hardaway (singer); 1950

MAY 14:

Carville, Edward Peter (politician); 1885
Combs, Earle Bryan (baseball); 1899
Darin, Bobby; born Walden Robert Cassotto (singer/actor); 1936
Deacon, Richard (actor); 1922

Dove, Billie; born Lillian Bohny (actress); 1900
Fahrenheit, Gabriel Daniel (physicist); 1686
Gainsborough, Thomas (artist); 1727
Howser, Dick; born Richard Dalton Howser (baseball); 1937
Klemperer, Otto (music); 1885
Luboff, Norman (music); 1917
Moss, Les; born John Lester Moss (baseball); 1925
Munsel, Patrice Beverly (singer/actress); 1925
Perez, Tony; born Atanasio Rigal Perez (baseball); 1942
Walsh, Ed; born Edward Augustine Walsh (baseball); 1881
Worsley, Gump; born Lorne Worsley (hockey); 1929

MAY 15:

Alberghetti, Anna Maria (actress/singer); 1936
Arnold, Eddy; born Richard Edward Arnold (singer/music); 1918
Boggs, James Caleb (politician); 1909
Brett, George Howard (baseball); 1953
Broda, Turk; born Walter Broda (hockey); 1914
Bush, Prescott Sheldon (politician); 1895
Califano, Joseph Anthony, Jr. (government); 1931
Chambers, Wally; born Wallace Chambers (football); 1951
Cotten, Joseph Chesire (actor); 1905
Cummings, Constance; born Constance Halverstadt (actress); 1910
Daley, Richard Joseph (politician); 1902
Dodd, Thomas Joseph (politician); 1907
Fadiman, Clifton Paul (literary critic); 1904
Frisch, Max Rudolph (playwright); 1911
Johns, Jasper (artist); 1930
Jordan, Leonard Beck (politician); 1899
Lopez, Trini; born Trinidad Lopez, III (singer/actor); 1937
Mason, James Neville (actor); 1909
Monteverdi, Claudio (music); 1567
Nelson, Don (basketball); 1940
North, Billy; born William Alexander North (baseball); 1948
Porter, Katherine Ann (author); 1890
Quarry, Jerry (boxing); 1945
Sanders, Carl Edward (politician); 1925
Shinnick, Don; born Donald Shinnick (football); 1935
Stone, Beth; born Elizabeth Stone (golf); 1940
Venturi, Ken; born Kenneth Venturi (golf/sportscaster); 1931
Wasdell, Jimmy; born James Charles Wasdell (baseball); 1914
Wilson, Ellen Louise Axson; born Ellen Louise Axson
    (first wife of Woodrow Wilson/First Lady); 1860
Wiseman, Joseph (actor); 1918
Wysong, Dudley, Jr. (golf); 1939
Zindel, Paul (playwright); 1936

MAY 16:

Anderson, Donny; born Gary Don Anderson (football); 1943
Carey, Harry, Jr. (actor); 1921
Clark, Watty; born William Watson Clark (baseball); 1902
Craig, Yvonne (actress/dancer); 1941
Fonda, Henry Jaynes (actor); 1905
Herman, Woody; born Woodrow Charles Herman (music); 1913
Hunt, James Baxter, Jr. (politician)
Jones, Andrieus Aristieus (politician); 1862
Kazan, Lainie; born Lainie Levine (singer/actress); 1940
Korbut, Olga (gymnast); 1956
Langer, Jim; born James John Langer (football); 1948
Liberace; born Wladziu Valentino Liberace (music); 1919
Longino, Andrew Houston (politician); 1855
Mankiewicz, Frank Fabian (journalist); 1924
Martin, Billy; born Alfred Manuel Martin (baseball); 1928
McCormick, Joseph Medill (politician); 1877
Morton, Levi Parsons (Vice President); 1824
Philley, Dave; born David Earl Philley (baseball); 1920
Pierpoint, Robert Charles (newscaster); 1925
Smith, Ronald Floyd (hockey); 1935
Spang, Laurette (actress); 1951
Sullavan, Margaret Brooke (actress); 1909
Vessey, Robert Scadden (politician); 1858
Walker, Rube; born Albert Bluford Walker (baseball); 1926
Weicker, Lowell Palmer, Jr. (politician); 1931
Wright, Fielding Lewis (politician); 1895

MAY 17:

Alsop, Stewart Johonnot Oliver (journalist); 1914
Carlson, Hal; born Harold Gust Carlson (baseball); 1894
Cox, Archibald (attorney); 1912
Donnelly, Ruth (actress); 1896
Gabin, Jean; born Alexis Moncourge (actor); 1904
Hoeft, Billy; born William Frederick Hoeft (baseball); 1932
Hopper, Dennis (actor/director); 1936
Jenner, Edward (medicine); 1749
Khomeini, Ayatollah Ruholla Mussavi (Iranian religious & political
        leader); 1900
Leche, Richard Webster (politician); 1898
Liscombe, Carl; born Harry Carlyle Liscombe (hockey); 1915
Mahal, Taj (singer/music); 1942
May, Carlos (baseball); 1948
McMahon, Horace Thomas (actor); 1907
Mennin, Peter; born Peter Mennini (music); 1923
Milanov, Zinka; born Zinka Kunc (singer); 1906
Morrall, Earl Edwin (football); 1934

Nilsson, Birgit (singer); 1918
Osborn, Sidney Preston (politician); 1884
O'Sullivan, Maureen Paula (actress); 1911
Parker, Clarence (football); 1913
Patrick, John; born John Patrick Goggan (playwright); 1905
Roche, Tony; born Anthony Dalton Roche (tennis); 1945
Tomlinson, David (actor); 1917
Toomay, Pat; born Patrick Jay Toomay (football); 1948
Virgil, Ozzie; born Osvaldo Jose Virgil (baseball); 1933
Williams, John James (politician); 1904

MAY 18:

Balmain, Pierre (fashion designer); 1914
Brooks, Richard (writer/director); 1912
Capra, Frank (director/producer); 1897
Coan, Gil; born Gilbert Fitzgerald Coan (baseball); 1922
Como, Perry; born Pierino Roland Como (singer); 1912
Curzon, Clifford (music); 1907
Daniels, Josephus (government/journalism); 1862
Fonteyn, Dame Margot; born Margaret Hookham (dancer); 1919
Gurie, Sigrid; born Sigrid Gurie Haukelid (actress); 1911
Hickman, Dwayne (actor); 1934
Jackson, Reggie; born Reginald Martinez Jackson
        (baseball/sportscaster); 1946
Javits, Jacob Koppel (politician); 1904
Keating, Kenneth Barnard (politician); 1900
Macy, Bill; born William M. Garber (actor); 1922
Morse, Robert Alan (actor/singer); 1931
Nicholas, II; born Nikolai Aleksandrovich (Russian Czar); 1868
Perry, Fred; born Frederick John Perry (tennis); 1909
Pinza, Ezio; born Fortunato Ezio Pinza (singer/actor); 1892
Pope John Paul II; born Karol Wojtyla; 1920
Roberts, Pernell (actor); 1930
Robinson, Brooks Calbert, Jr. (baseball); 1937
Russell, Lord Bertrand Arthur William (mathematician/philosopher);
        1872
Sanford, Jack; born John Stanley Sanford (baseball); 1929
Schwartz, Henry Herman (politician); 1869
Whitaker, Jack; born John Francis Whitaker (sportscaster); 1924
Willson, Meredith; born Robert Meredith Reiniger (music); 1902

MAY 19:

Arn, Edward F. (politician); 1906
Bennett, Bruce; born Herman Brix (actor); 1906
Early, Jake; born Jacob Willard Early (baseball); 1917
Ford, Steve; born Steven Meigs Ford (First family); 1956
Hartman, David Downs (actor/TV host); 1935

Ho Chi Minh (North Vietnamese government); 1890
Kwan, Nancy Ka Shen (actress); 1939
Malcolm X; born Malcolm Little (Black Muslim leader); 1925
Manning, Archie; born Elisha Archie Manning (football); 1949
McDougald, Gil; born Gilbert James McDougald (baseball); 1928
Murdock, John Murray (hockey); 1904
Roberts, Beverly Louise (actress); 1914
Schayes, Dolph (basketball); 1928
Simmons, Curt; born Curtis Thomas Simmons (baseball); 1929
Travers, Jerry; born Jerome Dunston Travers (golf); 1887
Young, Stephen; born Stephen Levy (actor); 1939

MAY 20:

Ames, Vic (singer—Ames Brothers); 1926
Boyer, Ken; born Kenton Lloyd Boyer (baseball); 1931
Bryant, Cullen; born William Cullen Bryant (football); 1951
Cher; born Cherilyn Sarkisian (or Sakisian) (or Cherilyn La Piere)
        (singer/actress); 1946
Cocker, Joe; born John Robert Cocker (singer/music); 1944
Crothers, Austin L. (politician); 1860
Dayan, Moshe (Israeli government); 1915
Ellis, Patricia; born Patricia Gene O'Brien (actress); 1916
Fellows, Edith Marilyn (actress); 1923
Gobel, George Leslie (comedian/actor); 1919
Grant, Bud; born Harry Peter Grant (football); 1927
Grantham, George Farley (baseball); 1900
Harlan, John Marshall (jurist); 1899
Harris, Joe; born Joseph Harris (baseball); 1891
Hedison, David; born Albert David Hedison, Jr. (or Ara Heditsian)
        (actor); 1928
Hill, Dave; born David Hill (golf); 1937
Kelly, Leroy (football); 1942
Lonergan, Augustine (politician); 1874
McEachin, James Elton (actor); 1930
Mikita, Stan; born Stanley Mikita (hockey); 1940
Mill, John Stuart (political economist/philosopher); 1806
Morrison, Frank Brenner (politician); 1905
Murcer, Bobby Ray (baseball); 1946
Newhouser, Hal; born Harold Newhouser (baseball); 1921
St. Johns, Adela Rogers; born Adela Rogers (journalist/author);
        1894
Stewart, James Maitland "Jimmy" (actor); 1908
Sweikert, Bob; born Robert Sweikert (auto racing); 1926
Taylor, Estelle; born Estelle Boylan (actress); 1899
Towers, Constance (actress/singer); 1933
West, Oswald (politician); 1873

MAY 21:

Averill, Earl; born Howard Earl Averill (baseball); 1902
Blane, Marcie (singer); 1944
Burr, Raymond William Stacey (actor); 1917
Cass, Peggy; born Mary Margaret Cass (actress); 1925
Dawson, William Mercer Owens (politician); 1853
Day, Dennis; born Eugene Dennis McNulty (singer/actor); 1917
Dürer, Albrecht (artist); 1471
Fitzgerald, Ed; born Edward Raymond Fitzgerald (baseball); 1924
Groh, David Lawrence (actor); 1939
Gurney, Chan; born John Chandler Gurney (politician); 1896
Hatch, Richard Lawrence (actor); 1946
Heidt, Horace Murray (music); 1901
Isley, Ronald (singer-Isley Brothers); 1941
Jason, Rick (actor); 1926
Kendall, Kay; born Justine Kay Kendall McCarthy (actress); 1926
Lane, Lola; born Dorothy Mullican (actress); 1906
McSpaden, Jug; born Harold McSpaden (golf); 1908
Montgomery, Robert; born Henry Montgomery, Jr.
          (actor/director/producer); 1904
Parseghian, Ara Roul (football/sportscaster); 1923
Pope, Alexander (poet); 1688
Ressler, Glenn Emanuel (football); 1943
Robbins, Harold; born Francis Kane (author); 1916
Roland, Johnny; born John Earl Roland (football); 1943
Sayer, Leo; born Gerard Sayer (singer/music); 1948
Stanley, Augustus Owsley (politician); 1867
Steel, Anthony (actor); 1920
Waller, Fats; born Thomas Waller (music); 1904
Welford, Walter (politician); 1869
Wilbur, John (football); 1943
Williams, Arnold (politician); 1898

MAY 22:

Aznavour, Charles; born Varenagh Aznavourian (singer/actor); 1924
Ball, Kenny (music); 1937
Benjamin, Richard (actor); 1938
Bliss, Aaron Thomas (politician); 1837
Cassatt, Mary (artist); 1845
Constantine, Michael; born Michael Efstration (or Constantine
          Joanides) (actor); 1927
Converse, Frank (actor); 1938
Crist, Judith; born Judith Klein (journalist); 1922
Doyle, Sir Arthur Conan (author); 1859
Hale, Binnie; born Beatrice Mary Hale-Monro
          (actress/comedienne/singer/dancer); 1899

James, Dick; born Richard James (football); 1934
John, Tommy; born Thomas Edward John (baseball); 1943
Martin, Quinn (producer/writer); 1922
Nero, Peter; born Peter Bernard Nierow (music); 1934
Olivier, Sir Laurence Kerr (actor); 1907
Packard, Vance Oakley (author); 1914
Parkins, Barbara (actress); 1942
Sarrazin, Michael; born Jacques Michel Andre Sarrazin (actor); 1940
Siegfried, Larry (basketball); 1939
Simmons, Al; born Aloysius Harry Szymanski (baseball); 1902
Smith, Horton (golf); 1908
Strasberg, Susan Elizabeth (actress); 1938
Teague, Marshall (auto racing); 1921
Tingelhoff, Mick; born Henry Michael Tingelhoff (football); 1940
Tobin, Maurice Joseph (politics/government); 1901
Wagner, Wilhelm Richard (music); 1813
Winfield, Paul Edward (actor); 1941

MAY 23:

Avery, Ken; born Kenneth Avery (football); 1944
Barrie, Barbara; born Barbara Ann Berman (actress); 1931
Bennett, Robert Frederick (politician); 1927
Chapin, Lauren (actress); 1945
Clooney, Rosemary (singer/actress); 1928
Coleman, Jack (basketball); 1924
Collins, Joan (actress); 1933
Crothers, Scatman; born Benjamin Sherman Crothers
    (actor/comedian/singer/music); 1910
Davenport, Nigel (actor); 1928
Fairbanks, Douglas; born Julius Ullman (actor); 1883
Garrett, Betty (actress/singer/dancer); 1919
Garron, Larry; born Lawrence Garron, Jr. (football); 1937
Gleason, James (actor); 1886
Graham, David Anthony (golf); 1946
Heyburn, Weldon Brinton (politician); 1852
Holman, Libby; born Elizabeth Holtzman (actress/singer); 1906
Hudlin, Willis; born George Willis Hudlin (baseball); 1906
Keyes, Henry Wilder (politician); 1863
Lee Dorothy; born Marjorie Millsap (actress); 1911
Marshall, Herbert (actor); 1890
May, Lee Andrew (baseball); 1943
McHugh, Frank; born Francis Curray McHugh (actor); 1898
Melton, Sid; born Sid Meltzer (actor); 1920
Mesmer, Franz Anton (medicine); 1734
Newcombe, John David (tennis); 1943
O'Connell, Helen (singer/TV Host); 1920
Payne, John (actor); 1912

Rowe, Bob; born Robert Rowe (football); 1945
Rudolph, Mason (golf); 1934
Shaw, Artie; born Abraham Isaac Arshawsky (music); 1910
Stasiuk, Victor John (hockey); 1929
Thorn, Rod; born Rodney King Thorn (basketball); 1941
Wheat, Zack; born Zachariah Davis Wheat (baseball); 1886

MAY 24:

Brennan, Peter J. (government); 1918
Brown, Tim; born Thomas Allen Brown (football); 1937
Burghoff, Gary (actor); 1943
Byrne, Jane Margaret; born Jane Margaret Burke (politician); 1934
Cardozo, Benjamin Nathan (jurist); 1870
Conacher, Lionel Pretoria (hockey); 1901
Dylan, Bob; born Robert Allen Zimmerman (singer/music); 1941
Fosdick, Harry Emerson (clergyman); 1878
Gamble, Bruce George (hockey); 1938
Jones, Clinton (football); 1945
Kahan, Judy (actress); 1948
Lenglen, Suzanne (tennis); 1899
Link, Arthur A. (politician); 1914
Maxwell, Elsa (actress/writer); 1883
McKenna, Siobhan; born Siobhan Giollamhuire Nic Cionnaith (actress); 1922
Mills, Wilbur Daigh (politician); 1909
Miranda, Willie; born Guillermo Miranda (baseball); 1926
Newhouse, Samuel Irving (publisher); 1895
Palmer, Lilli; born Lilli Marie Peiser (actress); 1914
Rodriguez, Elli; born Eliseo Rodriguez (baseball); 1946
Victoria, Queen of England; born Alexandrina Victoria; 1819
Washam, Jo Ann (golf); 1950
Young, Coleman Alexander (politician); 1918
Zetterling, Mai (actress/director/writer); 1925

MAY 25:

Akins, Claude (actor); 1918
Cerf, Bennett Alfred (publisher/journalist); 1898
Cochran, Steve; born Robert Alexander Cochran (actor); 1917
Colter, Jessi; born Miriam Johnson (singer/music); 1947
Crain, Jeanne (actress); 1925
David, Hal (music); 1921
Davis, Miles Dewey, Jr. (music); 1926
Emerson, Ralph Waldo (writer/philosopher); 1803
Fisher, John Stuchell (politician); 1867
Galan, Augie; born August John Galan (baseball); 1912
Gilchrist, Cookie; born Carlton Chester Gilchrist (football); 1935
Hall, Tom T. (singer/music); 1936

Himes, Dick; born Richard Dean Himes (football); 1946
Jones, K.C. (basketball); 1932
Judge, Joe; born Joseph Ignatius Judge (baseball); 1894
Kallen, Kitty (singer); 1926
Marshall, Jim; born Rufus James Marshall (baseball); 1932
McNeil, Clifton (football); 1940
Nelson, Lindsey (sportscaster); 1919
Nessen, Ron; born Ronald Harold Nessen (newscaster/government);
    1934
Rennebohm, Oscar (politician); 1889
Robinson, Bill "Bojangles" (dancer/actor); 1878
Sharman, Bill (basketball); 1926
Sills, Beverly; born Belle Silverman (singer); 1929
Sims, Ginny; born Virginia Sims (singer); 1916
Tito; born Josip Brozovich (Yugoslavian government); 1892
Tunney, Gene; born James Joseph Tunney (boxing); 1898
Uggams, Leslie Marian (singer/actress); 1943
Valentine, Karen (actress); 1947
Weitz, John (fashion designer); 1923

MAY 26:

Alexander, Ben; born Nicholas Benton Alexander (actor); 1911
Arness, James King; born James King Aurness (actor); 1923
Bergerac, Jacques (actor); 1927
Cushing, Peter (actor); 1913
Drysdale, Cliff; born E. Clifford Drysdale (tennis); 1941
Evans, Darrell Wayne (baseball); 1947
Ferguson, Lorne Robert (hockey); 1930
Jolson, Al; born Asa Yoelson (singer/actor); 1886
Lee, Peggy; born Norma Delores Engstrom (singer/actress); 1920
Lukas, Paul; born Paul Lugacs (actor); 1894
McCowen, Alec; born Alexander Duncan McCowen (actor); 1925
Morley, Robert Adolph Wilton (actor/producer); 1908
Musburger, Brent Woody (sportscaster); 1939
Pastorini, Dan; born Dante Anthony Pastorini, Jr. (football); 1949
Posey, Sam; born Samuel Felton Posey (auto racing); 1944
Rockefeller, Laurance Spelman (conservationist); 1910
Silverheels, Jay; born Harold J. Smith (actor); 1919
Talmadge, Norma (actress); 1897
Wayne, John; born Marion Michael Morrison
    (actor/producer/director); 1907
Wiley, Alexander (politician); 1884
Williams, Hank, Jr.; born Randall Hank Williams (singer); 1949

MAY 27:

Barth, John Simmons (author); 1930
Bennett, Arnold; born Enoch Arnold Bennett (author/dramatist); 1867

Black, Cilla; born Priscilla Maria Veronica White (singer); 1943
Carson, Rachel Louise (biologist/author); 1907
Cheever, John (author); 1912
Courage, Piers Raymond (auto racing); 1942
Duncan, Isadora (dancer); 1877
Folley, Zora (boxing); 1932
Fong, Kam (actor); ——
Gossett, Lou; born Louis Gossett, Jr. (actor); 1936
Hammett, Dashiell; born Samuel Dashiell Hammett (author); 1894
Harris, Jo Ann (actress); ——
Hickok, Wild Bill; born James Butler Hickok (frontier marshall); 1837
Higgins, Mike "Pinky"; born Michael Franklin Higgins (baseball); 1909
Howe, Julia Ward; born Julia Ward (author/reformer); 1819
Humphrey, Hubert Horatio (Vice President); 1911
Kindall, Jerry; born Gerald Donald Kindall (baseball); 1935
Kissinger, Henry; born Heinz Alfred Kissinger (government); 1923
Lee, Christopher Frank Caradini (actor); 1922
Lewis, Ramsey Emanuel, Jr. (music); 1935
Meriwether, Lee Ann (Miss America/actress); 1935
Moore, Terry Bluford (baseball); 1912
Nolan, Gary Lynn (baseball); 1948
Price, Vincent (actor/art expert); 1911
Robertson, A. Willis (politician); 1887
Robertson, Edward Vivian (politician); 1881
Rome, Harold Jacob (music); 1908
Schnittker, Richard (basketball); 1928
Sinai, Mike; born Michael Joseph Sinai (football); 1950
Snead, Sam; born Samuel Jackson Snead (golf); 1912
Snyder, Frank Elton (baseball); 1893
Vactor, Ted; born Theodore Vactor (football); 1944
Vanderbilt, Cornelius (capitalist); 1794
Van Impe, Edward Charles (hockey); 1940
Watson, Lucille (actress); 1879
Wouk, Herman (author); 1915

MAY 28:

Abel, Taffy; born Clarence John Abel (hockey); 1900
Baker, Carroll (actress); 1931
Blanchard, Tom; born Thomas R. Blanchard (football); 1948
Carson, Jeannie; born Jean Shufflebottom (actress/comedienne/singer);
    1929
Fischer-Dieskau, Dietrich (singer); 1925
Fleming, Ian Lancaster (author); 1908
Giles, Warren Crandall (baseball); 1896
Gombell, Minna (actress); 1892
Hamlin, Shelley (golf); 1949
Howland, Beth; born Elizabeth Howland (actress); 1941

Knight, Gladys Maria (singer); 1944
Locke, Sondra (actress); 1948
McKeithen, John Julian (politician); 1918
Moore, Thomas (poet); 1779
Panch, Marvin (auto racing); 1926
Percy, Walker (author); 1916
Sheppard, Morris (politician); 1875
Taylor, Bruce L. (football); 1948
Thorpe, Jim; born James Francis Thorpe (olympic athlete/football); 1888
West, Jerry (basketball); 1938

MAY 29:

Adrian, Iris; born Iris Adrian Hostetter (actress); 1913
Chapman, Arthur V. (hockey); 1907
Chesterton, Gilbert Keith (journalist/author); 1874
Guerin, Richie (basketball); 1932
Henry, Patrick (patriot); 1736
Hope, Bob; born Leslie Townes Hope (comedian/actor); 1903
Horner, Red; born George Reginald Horner (hockey); 1909
Keach, Stacy Sr. (actor/producer/director/writer); 1914
Kennedy, John Edward (baseball); 1941
Kennedy, John Fitzgerald (President); 1917
Lillie, Beatrice Gladys; born Constance Sylvia Munston (actress); 1898
McQuinn, George Hartley (baseball); 1909
Metz, Dick; born Richard Metz (golf); 1908
Odom, Blue Moon; born Johnny Lee Odom (baseball); 1945
Shaw, Sebastian (actor); 1905
Unser, Al (auto racing); 1939
Weatherly, Joe; born Joseph Herbert Weatherly (auto racing); 1922
Youngdahl, Luther Wallace Augustinus (politician); 1896

MAY 30:

Blair, Frank (newscaster); 1915
Blanc, Mel; born Melvin Jerome Blanc (cartoon voice/actor); 1908
Bourassa, Jocelyn (golf); 1947
Dullea, Keir (actor); 1936
Farley, James Aloysius (government); 1888
Fetchit, Stepin; born Lincoln Theodore Monroe Andrew Perry (actor); 1892
Goodman, Benny; born Benjamin David Goodman (music); 1909
Griffith, Hugh Emrys (actor); 1912
Hawks, Howard Winchester (director/producer); 1896
Lee, Ruta; born Ruta Mary Kilmonis (actress/singer); ——
Lydon, Jimmy; born James Lydon (actor/producer); 1923
McRae, Meredith (actress/singer); 1945
Mitchell, Lydell Douglas (football); 1949

Pierce, Walter Marcus (politician); 1861
Pollard, Michael J.; born Michael J. Pollack (actor); 1939
Proctor, Mortimer Robinson (politician); 1899
Rusie, Amos Wilson (baseball); 1871
Sayers, Gale Eugene (football); 1943
Skinner, Cornelia Otis (actress); 1901
Stein, Joseph (playwright); 1912
Thalberg, Irving Grant (producer); 1899
Walker, Clint (actor); 1927
Walker, Frank Comerford (government); 1886

MAY 31:

Allen, Fred; born John Florence Sullivan (comedian); 1894
Ameche, Don; born Dominic Felix Amici (actor/singer); 1908
Baugh, Laura Zonetta (golf); 1955
Brown, Walter Folger (government); 1869
Burford, Chris; born Christopher W. Burford (football); 1938
Coulter, Art; born Arthur Edmund Coulter (hockey); 1909
Eastwood, Clint; born Clinton Eastwood, Jr. (actor/director); 1930
Elliott, Denholm Mitchell (actor); 1922
Fassbinder, Rainer Werner (director); 1946
Ferry, Bob; born Robert Dean Ferry (basketball); 1937
Gillmore, Margalo (actress); 1897
Gless, Sharon (actress); ——
Hairston, Happy; born Harold Hairston (basketball); 1942
Harris, Patricia Roberts, born Patricia Roberts (government); 1924
Hartke, Vance; born Rupert Vance Hartke (politician); 1919
Hutton, Jim (actor); 1938
Jackson, Henry Martin "Scoop" (politician); 1912
Namath, Joe; born Joseph William Namath (football/actor); 1943
Paycheck, Johnny; born Don Lytle (singer/music); 1941
Peale, Norman Vincent (clergyman/author); 1898
Pepper, Barbara (actress); 1912
Pope Pius XI; born Ambrogio Damiano Achille Ratti; 1857
Rainier, Prince; born Rainier Louis Henri Maxence Bertrand de Grimaldi (Ruler of Monaco); 1923
Rockefeller, William, (industrialist/financier); 1841
Seyler, Athene; born Athene Hannen (actress); 1889
Sheldon, George Lawson (politician); 1870
Shields, Brooke (actress); 1965
Stewart, Elaine; born Elsy Steinberg (actress); 1929
Thompson, Cecil (hockey); 1905
Townsend, John Gillis Jr. (politician); 1871
Valli, Alida; born Alida Maria Altenburger (actress); 1921
Verrett, Shirley (singer); 1933
Woodring, Harry Hines (politics/government); 1890

JUNE 1:

Ameche, Alan D.; born Lino Dante Ameche (football); 1933
Auberjonis, René Murat (actor); 1940
Boone, Pat; born Charles Eugene Boone (singer/actor/author); 1934
Brook, Clive; born Clifford Brook (actor); 1886
Caulfield, Joan; born Beatrice Joan Caulfield (actress); 1922
Chance, Dean; born Wilmer Dean Chance (baseball); 1941
Dieringer, Darel Eugene (auto racing); 1926
Erdman, Richard (actor/director); 1925
Griffith, Andy; born Andrew Samuel Griffith (actor); 1926
Hagaman, Frank Lester (politician); 1894
Hecht, Harold (producer); 1907
Hundley, Randy; born Cecil Randolph Hundley (baseball); 1942
Ike, Reverend; born Frederick Joseph Eikerenkoetter, II (evangelist); 1935
Little, Cleavon Jake (actor); 1939
Marquette, Jacques (explorer/missionary); 1637
Masefield, John Edward (poet); 1878
McMullen, Ken; born Kenneth Lee McMullen (baseball); 1942
Michael, Gertrude (actress); 1910
Monroe, Marilyn; born Norma Jean Mortensen (actress); 1926
Moody, Dan (politician); 1893
Morgan, Frank; born Francis Philip Wuppermann (actor); 1890
Newton, Robert (actor); 1905
Peay, Austin (politician); 1876
Picon, Molly; born Molly Pyekoon (actress); 1898
Proctor, Redfield (politician); 1831
Randolph, John; born Emanuel Hirsch Cohen (actor); 1915
Riddle, Nelson Smock (music); 1921
Schweiker, Richard Schultz (politician); 1926
Sneva, Tom; born Thomas Edsol Sneva (auto racing); 1948
White, Jo Jo; born Joyner Clifford White (baseball); 1909
Young, Brigham (religious leader); 1801

JUNE 2:

Canova, Diana; born Diana Canova Rivero (actress); 1953
Clarke, Horace Meredith (baseball); 1940
Clement, Frank Goad (politician); 1920
Conrad, Pete; born Charles Conrad, Jr. (astronaut); 1930
Elgar, Sir Edward (music); 1857
Ferraris, Jan; born Janis Jean Ferraris (golf); 1947
Grauer, Ben; born Bennett Franklin Grauer (radio & TV announcer); 1908
Grimes, Gary (actor); 1955
Hamlisch, Marvin Frederick (music); 1944
Hardy, Thomas (writer); 1840
Heller, Ott; born Ehrhardt Henry Heller (hockey); 1910

Hopper, Hedda; born Elda Furry (journalist/actress); 1890
Hughes, Pat; born William Patrick Hughes (football); 1947
Jackson, Larry; born Lawrence Curtis Jackson (baseball); 1931
Keach, Stacy, Jr. (actor); 1941
Kellerman, Sally Claire (actress/singer); 1937
Lillis, Bob; born Robert Perry Lillis (baseball); 1930
Lumpe, Jerry Dean (baseball); 1933
Maloney, Jim; born James William Maloney (baseball); 1940
Mathers, Jerry (actor); 1948
McCutcheon, Lawrence (football); 1950
McGregor, Ken; born Kenneth McGregor (tennis); 1929
Michael, Gene; born Eugene Richard Michael (baseball); 1938
Pleasant, Ruffin Golson (politician); 1871
Pope Pius X; born Giuseppe Melchiorre Sarto; 1835
Randolph, John (statesman); 1773
Robinson, Wilbert (baseball); 1863
Rye, Thomas Clark (politician); 1863
Schlee, John (golf); 1939
Showalter, Max G. (actor/music); 1917
Siemon, Jeff; born Jeffrey G. Siemon (football); 1950
Taft, Nellie; born Helen Herron (First Lady); 1861
Weismuller, Johnny; born Peter John Weissmuller (swimmer/actor);
    1903
Williams, Nate (basketball); 1950
Yepremian, Garo; born Garabed Sarkis Yepremian (football); 1944

JUNE 3:

Baker, Josephine (singer/dancer); 1906
Bassler, Johnny; born John Landis Bassler (baseball); 1895
Caffey, Lee Roy (football); 1941
Cunningham, Billy (basketball/sportscaster); 1943
Curtis, Tony; born Bernard Schwartz (actor/author); 1925
Davis, Jefferson (President of the Confederacy); 1808
Dewhurst, Colleen (actress); 1926
Evans, Maurice Herbert (actor); 1901
Gentile, Jim; born James Edward Gentile (baseball); 1934
Ginsberg, Allen (poet); 1926
Goddard, Paulette; born Pauline Marion Levee (actress); 1911
Gorcey, Leo Bernard (actor); 1915
Hayes, Roland (singer); 1887
Hobart, Garret Augustus (Vice President); 1844
Irwin, Hale S., Jr. (golf); 1945
King, William Henry (politician); 1863
Mayfield, Curtis Lee (singer/music); 1942
Mundt, Karl Earl (politician); 1900
Ohmart, Carol (actress); 1928
Oldfield, Barney; born Bernd Eli Oldfield (auto racing); 1878

Peerce, Jan; born Jacob Pinkus Perelmuth (singer); 1904
Quatro, Suzie (singer/actress); 1950
Resnais, Alain (director); 1922
St. Cyr, Lili; born Marie Van Schaak (actress); 1917
Sifford, Charles Luther (golf); 1923
Thomas, Emmitt Earl (football); 1943

JUNE 4:

Anderson, Robert Bernerd (government); 1910
Barrymore, John Blyth "John, Jr.", now John Drew Barrymore (actor);
    1932
Bayard, Thomas Francis (politician); 1868
Blandick, Clara (actress); 1880
Collingwood, Charles Cummings (newscaster); 1917
Dern, Bruce MacLeish (actor); 1936
Fender, Freddy; born Baldemar, G. Huerta (singer/music); 1937
Haynie, Sandra J. (golf); 1943
Hunter, Billy; born Gordon William Hunter (baseball); 1928
King, Morgana (singer/actress); 1930
May, Ray; born Raymond May (football); 1945
Merrill, Robert; born Morris Miller (singer); 1919
Metzenbaum, Howard Morton (politician); 1917
Nelson, Gaylord Anton (politician); 1916
Post, Sandra (golf); 1948
Russell, Rosalind (actress); 1907
Schall, Thomas David (politician); 1878
Stevenson, Parker; born Richard Stevenson Parker (actor); 1952
Studstill, Pat; born Patrick L. Studstill (football); 1938
Wanzer, Bobby; born Robert Wanzer (basketball); 1921
Watkins, George Archibald (baseball); 1900
Weaver, Dennis (actor); 1924

JUNE 5:

Beall, J. Glenn, Sr.; born James Glenn Beall, Sr. (politician); 1894
Boyd, Bill; born William Lawrence Boyd (actor); 1895
Brandon, William Woodward (politician); 1868
Chesbro, Jack; born John Dwight Chesbro (baseball); 1874
Donovan, Art; born Arthur Donovan, Jr. (football); 1925
Floyd, Charles Miller (politician); 1861
Garlington, John (football); 1946
Hayes, Bill; born William Foster Hayes (actor/singer); 1925
Herrmann, Don; born Donald Herrmann (football); 1947
Joost, Eddie; born Edwin David Joost (baseball); 1916
Lacroix, Andre (hockey); 1945
Lansing, Robert; born Robert Howell Brown (actor); 1929
Motley, Marion (football); 1920
Moyers, Bill; born Billy Don Moyers (journalism/government); 1934

Richardson, Tony; born Cecil Antonio Richardson (director); 1928
Sims, Duke; born Duane B. Sims (baseball); 1941
Urbanski, Billy; born William Michael Urbanski (baseball); 1903
Villa, Pancho; born Doroteo Arango (Mexican bandit); 1898

JUNE 6:

Abel, Walter Charles (actor); 1898
Borg, Björn (tennis); 1956
Capehart, Homer Earl (politician); 1897
Dickey, Bill; born William Malcolm Dickey (baseball); 1907
Giacomin, Ed; born Edward Giacomin (hockey); 1939
Grayson, Dave; born David L. Grayson (football); 1939
Hale, Nathan (military officer); 1755
Harrelson, Bud; born Derrel McKinley Harrelson (baseball); 1944
Hutchison, Jock (golf); 1884
Khachaturian, Aram Ilich (music); 1903
Lewis, Ted; born Theodore Leopold Friedman (entertainer); 1891
Mann, Thomas (author); 1875
Miller, Jack Richard (politician); 1916
Mitchell, Bobby; born Robert Cornelius Mitchell (football); 1935
Montez, Maria; born Maria Africa Vidal de Santo Silas (actress); 1918
Mostil, Johnny; born John Anthony Mostil (baseball); 1896
Noel, Philip William (politician); 1931
Rettenmund, Merv; born Mervin Weldon Rettenmund (baseball); 1943
Scott, David Randolph (astronaut); 1932
Sherriff, R.C.; born Robert Cedric Sherriff (playwright/author); 1896
Starr, Frances (actress); 1886
Terrell, Joseph Meriwether (politician); 1861
Thompson, Fresco; born Lafayette Fresco Thompson (baseball); 1902
Trumbull, John (artist); 1756
Whitelaw, Billie (actress); 1932
Williams, Chuck (basketball); 1946

JUNE 7:

Brooks, Gwendolyn (poet); 1917
Burleson, Albert Sidney (government); 1863
Entremont, Philippe (music); 1934
Gauguin, Paul; born Eugène Henri Paul Gauguin (artist); 1848
Giovanni, Nikki; born Yolande Cornelia Giovanni, Jr. (poet); 1943
Gonsoulin, Austin (football); 1938
Gray, Dolores (actress/singer); 1924
Jones, Tom; born Thomas Jones Woodward (singer); 1940
Marotte, Jean Gilles (hockey); 1945
McKenna, Virginia (actress); 1931
Mitterwald, George Eugene (baseball); 1945
Money, Don; born Donald Wayne Money (baseball); 1947
Munson, Thurman Lee (baseball); 1947

Patterson, Malcolm Rice (politician); 1861
Reise, Leo Charles, Jr. (hockey); 1922
Rodino, Peter Wallace, Jr. (politician); 1909
Russell, Cazzie (basketball); 1944
Scherer, Ray; born Raymond Lewis Scherer (newscaster); 1919
Strouse, Charles Louis (music); 1928
Tandy, Jessica (actress); 1909

JUNE 8:

Adderley, Herb; born Herbert Anthony Adderley (football); 1939
Belanger, Mark Henry (baseball); 1944
Casey, Bernie; born Bernard Casey (football/actor); 1939
Darren, James; born James William Ercolani (singer/actor); 1936
Ennis, Del; born Delmer Ennis (baseball); 1925
Gagon, John (hockey); 1905
Grady, Don (actor/singer/music); 1944
Hale, Monte (actor/singer); 1919
Kirby, George (comedian/impressionist); 1924
Martin, Millicent (actress/singer); 1934
McKinley, Ida Saxton; born Ida Saxton (First Lady); 1847
Mungo, Van Lingle (baseball); 1911
Preston, Robert; born Robert Preston Meservey (actor/singer); 1913
Promuto, Vince; born Vincent Promuto (football); 1938
Ryan, Sheila; born Katherine Elizabeth McLaughlin (actress); 1921
Scaggs, Boz; born William Royce Scaggs (singer/music); 1944
Schumann, Robert Alexander (music); 1810
Sinatra, Nancy, Jr.; born Nancy Sandra Sinatra (singer/actress); 1940
Smith, Alexis; born Gladys Smith (actress); 1921
Stiller, Jerry; born Gerald Stiller (comedian/actor); 1928
Tucker, Bob; born Robert Louis Tucker (football); 1945
Wagner, Robert Ferdinand, Sr. (politician); 1877
White, Byron Raymond "Whizzer" (football/jurist); 1917
Wright, Frank Lloyd (architect); 1869
Wynter, Dana; born Dagmar Winter (actress); 1930
Yarborough, Ralph Webster (politician); 1903

JUNE 9:

Axelrod, George (playwright/author); 1922
Bailey, Jim; born James Randall Bailey (football); 1948
Bonaparte, Charles Joseph (government); 1851
Cummings, Bob; born Charles Clarence Robert Orville Cummings (actor); 1908
Elthon, Leo (politician); 1898
Freeman, Mona; born Monica Elizabeth Freeman (actress); 1926
Hobbs, David Wishart (auto racing); 1939
Kalb, Marvin Leonard (newscaster/author); 1930
McNamara, Robert Strange (government); 1916

Parker, Dave; born David Gene Parker (baseball); 1951
Paul, Les; born Lester William Polfus (singer/music); 1915
Peter the Great; born Pëtr Alekseyevich (Russian Emperor); 1672
Porter, Cole Albert (music); 1891
Rockefeller, Happy; born Margaretta Large Fitler (Vice President's wife); 1926
Santos, Joe; born Joseph Minieri (actor); 1931
Selwart, Tonio; born Antonio Franz Thaeus Selmair-Selwart (actor); 1896
Shafroth, John Franklin (politician); 1854
Smalley, Roy Frederick, Jr. (baseball); 1926
Van Der Vlis, Diana (actress); 1935
Virdon, Bill; born William Charles Virdon (baseball); 1931
Waring, Fred; born Frederic Malcolm Waring (music); 1900
Wilson, Jackie (singer); 1932

JUNE 10:

Bailey, F. Lee; born Francis Lee Bailey (attorney); 1933
Beatty, Clyde R. (circus); 1903
Bellow, Saul (writer); 1915
Byrd, Harry Flood, Sr. (politician); 1887
Corcoran, Kevin (actor); 1945
Courbet, Gustave (artist); 1819
Demaree, Frank; born Joseph Franklin Dimaria (baseball); 1910
Derain, André (artist); 1880
Edwards, Johnny; born John Alban Edwards (baseball); 1938
Fairbanks, Chuck; born Charles Leo Fairbanks, (football); 1933
Foiles, Hank; born Henry Lee Foiles (baseball); 1929
Fouts, Dan; born Daniel Francis Fouts (football); 1951
Garland, Judy; born Frances Ethel Milne Gumm (actress/singer); 1922
Haver, June; born June Stovenour (actress); 1926
Hayakawa, Sessue; born Kintaro Hayakawa (actor); 1886
Hayden, Russell; born Hayden Michael Lucid (actor); 1912
Haydon, Julie; born Donella Donaldson (actress); 1910
Johnson, J. Bennett, Jr. (politician); 1932
Kreevich, Mike; born Michael Andreas Kreevich (baseball); 1908
Loewe, Frederick (music); 1904
McDaniel, Hattie (actress); 1895
McDivitt, James Alton (astronaut); 1929
McGlocklin, Jon Paul (basketball); 1943
McKay, Gardner; born George Cadogan Gardner McKay (actor); 1932
Morse, Barry Herbert (actor); 1919
Park, Guy Brasfield (politician); 1872
Philip, Prince; born Philip Mountbatten (Duke of Edinburgh); 1921
Quinby, Henry Brewer (politician); 1846
Rattigan, Terence Mervyn (playwright); 1911
Sendak, Maurice Bernard (author); 1928

Singleton, Ken; born Kenneth Wayne Singleton (baseball); 1947
Stevens, Andrew (actor); 1955

JUNE 11:

Barbeau, Adrienne (actress/singer); 1945
Bresnahan, Robert Philip (baseball); 1879
Bromfield, John; born Farron Bromfield (actor); 1922
Bryan, Jane; born Jane O'Brian (or O'Brien) (actress); 1918
Cash, Dave; born David Cash (baseball); 1948
Constable, John (artist); 1776
Cousteau, Jacques-Yves (marine explorer); 1910
Everett, Chad; born Raymond Lee Cramton (actor); 1936
Hutton, Robert; born Robert Bruce Winne (actor); 1920
Jonson, Ben; born Benjamin Jonson (playwright/poet); 1572
Kilrea, Hector J. (hockey); 1907
Kotar, Doug; born Douglas Allan Kotar (football); 1951
Lombardi, Vince; born Vincent Thomas Lombardi (football); 1913
Manne, Shelly; born Sheldon Manne (music); 1920
Mellon, Paul (philanthropist/art collector); 1907
Nevers, Ernie; born Ernest A. Nevers (football); 1903
Paluzzi, Luciana (actress); 1939
Rankin, Jeannette (politician/pacifist/suffragist); 1880
Spivak, Lawrence Edmund (producer/TV moderator); 1900
Stevens, Risë; born Risë Steenberg (singer/actress); 1913
Stewart, Jackie; born John Young Stewart (auto racing/sportscaster);
    1939
Strauss, Richard (music); 1864
Styron, William Clark, Jr. (author); 1925
Thomas, Frank Joseph (baseball); 1929
Todd, Richard; born Richard Andrew Palethorpe-Todd (actor); 1919
Warner, William (politician); 1840
Wilder, Gene; born Jerome Silberman (actor/director); 1934

JUNE 12:

Allen, Irwin (producer/director); 1916
Brady, James Henry (politician); 1862
Bush, George Herbert Walker (government); 1924
Castro, Raul Hector (politician); 1916
Cooper, Robert Archer (politician); 1874
Cowley, Bill; born William M. Cowley (hockey); 1912
Damone, Vic; born Vito Farinola (singer/actor); 1928
Eden, Sir Anthony; born Robert Anthony Eden (British government);
    1897
Flemming, Arthur Sherwood (government); 1905
Gardiner, William Tudor (politician); 1892
Hagen, Uta Thyra (actress); 1919
Ireland, Innes; born Robert McGregor Innes Ireland (auto racing); 1930

Kiner, Steve; born Steven Kiner (football); 1947
Lane, Priscilla; born Priscilla Mullican (actress); 1917
Lundigan, William (actor); 1914
McMullen, Adam (politician); 1874
McNary, Charles Linza (politician); 1874
Moses, John (politician); 1885
Nabors, Jim (actor/singer); 1932
Rockefeller, David (banker); 1915
Ronty, Paul (hockey); 1928
Sherman, Richard Morton (music); 1921
Tors, Ivan Lawrence (producer/director/writer); 1916
Walsh, Thomas James (politician); 1859

JUNE 13:

Boyd, Fred (basketball); 1950
Budge, Don; born John Donald Budge (tennis); 1915
Chavez, Carlos Antonio de Padua (music); 1899
Conway, Shirl; born Shirley Elizabeth Crosman (actress); 1916
Corby, Ellen Hansen; born Ellen Hansen (actress); 1914
Desautels, Gene; born Eugene Abraham Desautels (baseball); 1907
Edwards, Ralph Livingstone (TV host/producer); 1913
Ferguson, Miriam Amanda (politician); 1875
Grange, Red; born Harold E. Grange (football); 1903
Hunter, Ian (actor); 1900
Johnson, Ben; born Francis Benjamin Johnson (actor); 1918
Lynde, Paul Edward (actor/comedian); 1926
Parnell, Mel; born Melvin Lloyd Parnell (baseball); 1922
Rathbone, Basil; born Philip St. John Basil Rathbone (actor); 1892
Scott, Robert Walter (politician); 1929
Skala, Carole Jo; born Carole Jo Kabler (golf); 1938
Taylor, Samuel Albert (playwright); 1912
Thomas, Richard Earl (actor); 1951
Wickes, Mary; born Mary Isabelle Wickenhauser (actress); 1916
Wright, Jeff; born Jeffrey Ralph Wright (football); 1949
Yeats, William Butler (poet); 1865
Zentner, Si; born Simon H. Zentner (music); 1917

JUNE 14:

Adams, Jack; born John James Adams (hockey); 1895
Andrews, Billy; born William D. Andrews, Jr. (football); 1945
Banks, Henry (auto racing); 1913
Barry, Gene; born Eugene Klass (actor/singer); 1919
Burrough, Ken; born Kenneth O. Burrough (football); 1948
Coleman, Cy; born Seymour Kaufman (music); 1929
Davidson, Ben; born Benjamin Earl Davidson (football/actor); 1940
Day, Happy; born Clarence Henry Day (hockey); 1901
Esmond, Carl (actor); 1906

Guevara, Che; born Ernesto Guevara Serna (Cuban guerrilla leader);
1928
Ives, Burl Icle Ivanhoe (actor/singer); 1909
LaFollette, Robert Marion (politician); 1855
Lamb, Gil (actor/comedian); 1906
La Rue, Lash; born Alfred La Rue (actor); 1917
Matte, Tom; born Thomas Roland Matte (football/sportscaster); 1939
McGuire, Dorothy Hackett (actress); 1918
McMath, Sidney Sanders (politician); 1912
Newcombe, Don; born Donald Newcombe (baseball); 1926
Salinger, Pierre Emil George (journalism/government); 1925
Seligman, Arthur (politician); 1873
Stewart, Trish (actress); ——
Stowe, Harriet Beecher; born Harriet Elizabeth Beecher (author); 1811
Wanamaker, Sam (actor/producer/director); 1919
Weeks, John Eliakim (politician); 1853
Wilson, John Edward (hockey); 1929

JUNE 15:

Almond, James Lindsay, Jr. (politician); 1898
Baker, Dusty; born Johnnie B. Baker, Jr. (baseball); 1949
Balzar, Frederick Bennett (politician); 1880
Bennett, Robert Russell (music); 1894
Cline, Ty; born Tyrone Alexander Cline (baseball); 1939
Dahlgren, Babe; born Ellsworth Tenney Dahlgren (baseball); 1912
De Santis, Joe; born Joseph V. De Santis (actor); 1909
Garner, Erroll Louis (music); 1921
Grieg, Edvard Hagerup (music); 1843
Henderson, Ken; born Kenneth Joseph Henderson (baseball); 1946
Horeck, Peter (hockey); 1923
Jackson, Rachel; born Rachel Donelson (First Lady); 1767
Jennings, Waylon (singer/music); 1937
Larson, Morgan Foster (politician); 1882
Lennon, Janet Elizabeth (singer-Lennon Sisters); 1946
Lister, Ernest (politician); 1870
Pronovost, Marcel; born Rene Marcel Pronovost (hockey); 1930
Purcell, Lee Junior Williams (actress); 1947
Sample, John B. (football); 1937
Schumann-Heink, Ernestine; born Ernestine Rössler (singer); 1861
Stewart, Bud; born Edward Perry Stewart (baseball); 1916
Udall, Morris King (politician); 1922
Weeks, Sinclair (government); 1893
Williams, Billy Leo (baseball); 1938

JUNE 16:

Albertson, Jack (actor); 1910
Atkins, Eileen (actress); 1934

Dine, Jim (artist); 1935
Domergue, Faith (actress); 1925
Flockhart, Ron; born William Ronald Flockhart (auto racing); 1923
Johnson, Ken; born Kenneth Travis Johnson (baseball); 1933
Laurel, Stan; born Arthur Stanley Jefferson (comedian/actor); 1890
Munson, Ona; born Ona Wolcott (actress); 1903
Oates, Joyce Carol (author/poet); 1938
Palmer, Leland (actress/singer/dancer); 1945
Sanderson, Derek Michael (hockey); 1946
Segal, Erich Wolf (author); 1937
Sistrunk, Manny; born Manuel Sistrunk (football); 1947
Small, Len; born Lennington Small (politician); 1862
Traubel, Helen (singer/actress); 1899
Van Ark, Joan (actress); 1943

JUNE 17:

Anderson, Elmer Lee (politician); 1909
Atkinson, Ted; born Theodore Francis Atkinson (hockey); 1916
Bell, Bobby; born Robert Lee Bell (football); 1940
Bellamy, Ralph Rexford (actor); 1904
Bowman, Joe; born Joseph Emil Bowman (baseball); 1910
Concepcion, Dave; born David Ismael Bonitez Concepcion (baseball);
    1948
Draper, Eben Sumner (politician); 1858
Fain, Sammy; born Samuel Feinberg (music); 1902
Fazenda, Louise (comedienne/actress); 1889
Foley, Red; born Clyde Julian Foley (singer); 1910
Gounod, Charles Francois (music); 1818
Hersey, John Richard (author); 1914
Hirsch, Elroy L. (football); 1923
Johnson, Randy; born Randolph K. Johnson (football); 1944
Kimball, Judy (golf); 1938
Knapp, Evalyn (actress); 1908
Lupus, Peter (actor/Mr. Hercules); ——
Manilow, Barry (singer/music); 1946
Martin, Dean; born Dino Paul Crocetti (actor/singer); 1917
Sewall, Sumner (politician); 1897
Stevens, Paul; born Paul Steven Gattoni (actor); 1924
Stringbean; born David Akeman (singer/comedian/music); 1915
Thomas, Elbert Duncan (politician); 1883
Wesley, John (religious leader); 1703
Withers, Grant (actor); 1904

JUNE 18:

Arthur, Robert; born Robert Arthaud (actor); 1925
Bartok, Eva; born Eva Martha Szöke or (Sjoke) (actress); 1926
Boone, Richard Allen (actor); 1916

Brock, Lou; born Louis Clark Brock (baseball); 1936
Cahn, Sammy; born Samuel Cohen (music); 1913
Carmichael, Ian (actor/singer); 1920
Collyer, Bud; born Clayton Collyer (TV host); 1908
Foran, Dick; born John Nicholas Foran (actor); 1910
Hulme, Denis Clive (auto racing); 1936
Kyser, Kay; born James Kern Kyser (music); 1905
Lamb, Joseph Gordon (hockey); 1906
Lawrence, David Leo (politician); 1889
Luke, Keye (actor); 1904
MacDonald, Jeanette Anna (actress/singer); 1901
Marshall E.G.; born Everett G. Marshall (actor); 1910
McCartney, Paul; born James Paul McCartney (singer/music); 1942
McNamara, Maggie (actress); 1928
Mikan, George (basketball); 1924
Porter, Sylvia Field; born Sylvia Feldman (journalist); 1913
Redfield, William Cox (government); 1858
Reynolds, Robert Rice (politician); 1884
Rockefeller, John Davidson, IV (politician); 1937
Stephenson, Isaac (politician); 1829
Stravinsky, Igor Fedorovich (music); 1882
Sweet, Blanche; born Sarah Blanche Sweet (or Daphne Wayne) (actress); 1896
Thorson, Linda (actress); 1947

JUNE 19:

Angeli, Pier; born Anna Maria Pierangeli (actress); 1932
Aspromonte, Bob; born Robert Thomas Aspromonte (baseball); 1938
Beall, J. Glenn, Jr.; born James Glenn Beall, Jr. (politician); 1927
Burdick, Quentin Northrop (politician); 1908
Buttram, Pat (actor/comedian); ——
Coburn, Charles Douville (actor); 1877
Cowan, Charlie; born Charles Cowan (football); 1938
Cranston, Alan MacGregor (politician); 1914
Fortras, Abe (jurist); 1910
Frazier, Willie (football); 1942
Gabel, Martin (actor); 1912
Garvey, Dan E. (politician); 1886
Gehrig, Lou; born Henry Louis Gehrig (baseball); 1903
Glotzbach, Charlie (auto racing); 1938
Gutteridge, Don; born Donald Joseph Gutteridge (baseball); 1912
Jourdan, Louis; born Louis Gendre (actor); 1920
Lombardo, Guy; born Gaetano Alberto Lombardo (music); 1902
Marchand, Nancy (actress); 1928
Mayfield, Shelley (golf); 1924
McCreary, Vernon Keith (hockey); 1940
McDowell, Malcolm (actor); 1943

CHRONOLOGICAL LISTING 329

Natwick, Mildred (actress); 1908
Nomellini, Leo Joseph (football); 1924
Pascal, Blaise (scientist/mathematician/philosopher/author); 1623
Pavan, Marisa; born Maria Luisa Pierangeli (actress); 1932
Reuss, Jerry (baseball); 1949
Rowlands, Gena; born Virginia Cathryn Rowlands (actress); 1936
Voskovec, George (actor); 1905
Walker, Jimmy; born James John Walker (politician); 1881
Whitty, Dame May (actress); 1865
Windsor, Duchess of; born Bessie Wallis Warfield; 1896
Yurka, Blanche; born Blanche Jurka (actress); 1877

JUNE 20:

Atkins, Chet; born Chester Burton Atkins (music); 1924
Dawson, Lenny; born Leonard Ray Dawson (football/sportscaster); 1935
Doucet, Catharine; born Catharine Green (actress); 1875
Elmendorf, Dave; born David C. Elmendorf (football); 1949
Etchebarren, Andy; born Andrew Auguste Etchebarren (baseball); 1943
Flynn, Errol Leslie (actor); 1909
Gordon, Cecil Owen (auto racing); 1941
Gunderson, Carl (politician); 1864
Halsey, Brett (actor); 1933
Hart, Doris J. (tennis); 1925
Hartley, Mariette (actress); 1940
Hellman, Lillian Florence (playwright); 1905
Johnson, Josephine Winslow (author); 1910
Jones, Robert Trent (golf); 1906
Motter, Alexander Everett (hockey); 1913
Murphy, Audie Leon (actor); 1924
Murray, Anne (singer); 1946
Nelson, Dave; born David Earl Nelson (baseball); 1944
Patrick, Gail; born Margaret LaVelle Fitzpatrick (actress/producer); 1911
Podesta, Rossana (actress); 1934
Ramirez, Raul (tennis); 1953
Rowe, Dave; born David Rowe (football); 1945
Segura, Pancho; born Francisco Segura Cano (tennis); 1921
Sinatra, Tina; born Christina Sinatra (actress); 1948
Warren, Francis Emroy (politician); 1844
Watts, André (music); 1946
Werber, Bill; born William Murray Werber (baseball); 1908
Whitfield, Henry Lewis (politician); 1868

JUNE 21:

Birney, Meredith Baxter; born Meredith Baxter (actress); 1947
Costello, Helene (actress); 1903

Ely, Ron; born Ronald Pierce (actor); 1938
Gain, Bob; born Robert Gain (football); 1929
Hirschfeld, Al; born Albert Hirschfeld (cartoonist/artist); 1903
Holliday, Judy; born Judith Tuvin (actress); 1921
Kent, Rockwell (artist); 1882
Lopat, Ed; born Edmund Walter Lopatynski (baseball); 1918
Markham, Monte (actor); 1935
Martin, John Welborn (politician); 1884
McCarthy, Mary Therese (author); 1912
McCormack, Mike; born Michael McCormack (football); 1930
Moore, Randy; born Randolph Edward Moore (baseball); 1905
O'Connor, Buddy; born Herbert William O'Connor (hockey); 1916
Offenbach, Jacques; born Jacob Eberscht (music); 1819
Russell, Jane; born Ernestine Jane Geraldine Russell (actress); 1921
Sagan, Francoise; born Francoise Quoirez (author); 1935
Sartre, Jean-Paul (existentialist writer); 1905
Schifrin, Lalo Boris (music); 1932
Smith, O.C.; born Ocie Lee Smith (singer); 1932
Snyder, John Wesley (government); 1895
Stapleton, Maureen; born Lois Maureen Stapleton (actress); 1925
Stickney, Dorothy (actress); 1900
Thomas, Duane (football); 1947
Tompkins, Daniel D. (Vice President); 1774
Washington, Martha; born Martha Dandridge (First Lady); 1731

JUNE 22:

Anderson, Mike; born Michael Allen Anderson (baseball); 1951
Blass, Bill; (fashion designer); 1922
Bradley, Ed; born Edward R. Bradley, Jr. (newscaster); 1941
Burns, David (actor); 1902
Burton, Harold Hitz (jurist); 1888
Champion, Gower (dancer/actor/choreographer/director); 1920
Dempsey, John Joseph (politician); 1879
Dillinger, John (criminal); 1903
Douglass, Bobby; born Robert G. Douglass (football); 1947
Feinstein, Dianne, born Dianne Goldman (politician); 1933
Hubbell, Carl Owen (baseball); 1903
Johnson, Curtis (football); 1948
Kristofferson, Kris (singer/actor/music); 1936
Lindbergh, Anne Morrow; born Anne Spencer Morrow (author); 1906
Livingstone, Mary; born Sadie Marks (actress); 1909
Maravich, Pete; born Peter Maravich (basketball); 1948
Masterson, Walt; born Walter Edward Masterson (baseball); 1920
Miller, Patsy Ruth (actress/writer); 1905
Osmond, Alan Ralph (singer/music—Osmond Family); 1949
Papp, Joseph; born Joseph Papirofsky (producer/director); 1921
Prinze, Freddie; born Freddie Preutzel (comedian/actor); 1954

Remarque, Erich Maria (author/playwright); 1898
Roberts, Sue; born Susan Roberts (golf); 1948
Serafin, Barry Duane (newscaster); 1941
Snyder, Russ; born Russell Henry Snyder (baseball); 1934
Streep, Meryl; born Mary Louise Streep (actress); 1949
Throneberry, Faye; born Maynard Faye Throneberry (baseball); 1931
Todd, Michael; born Avrom Hirsch Goldenborgen (producer); 1907
Wagner, Lindsay Jean (actress); 1949
Wagner, Mike; born Michael Robert Wagner (football); 1949
Waite, Ralph (actor); 1928
Wilder, Billy; born Samuel Wilder (producer/director); 1906

JUNE 23:

Anouilh, Jean (playwright); 1910
Blyden, Larry; born Ivan Lawrence Blieden (actor/singer/TV host);
        1925
Brucker, Wilber Marion (politician); 1894
Carter, June (singer); 1929
Chennault, Anna Chan; born Anna Chan (author); 1925
Cutting, Bronson Murray (politician); 1888
Dukes, Walter (basketball); 1930
Eberhart, Adolph Olson (politician); 1870
Eisele, Donn Fulton (astronaut); 1930
Faith, Adam; born Terence Neilhams (singer/actor); 1940
Fosse, Bob; born Robert Louis Fosse (director/choreographer/dancer/
        actor); 1927
Haller, Tom; born Thomas Frank Haller (baseball); 1937
Hodge, Ken; born Kenneth Hodge (hockey); 1944
Hunn, John (politician); 1849
Josephine de Beauharnis; born Marie Josephine Rose Tascher de la
        Pagerie (French Empress); 1763
Laycoe, Harold Richardson (hockey); 1922
Little, Lawson; born William Lawson Little (golf); 1910
Noble, Reginald (hockey); 1895
Roach, John Ross (hockey); 1900
Rogers, William Pierce (government); 1913
Shaara, Michael Joseph, Jr. (author); 1929
Smith, Jack; born John Smadt (baseball); 1895
Toneff, Bob; born Robert Toneff (football); 1930
Trask, Diana Roselyn (singer); 1940
Windsor, Duke of; born Edward Albert Christian George Andrew
        Patrick David; 1894
Worth, Irene (actress); 1916

JUNE 24:

Adams, Buster; born Elvin Clark Adams (baseball); 1915
Beecher, Henry Ward (clergyman); 1813

Brown, Georg Stanford (actor/director); 1943
Carter, Jack; born Jack Chakrin (comedian/actor); 1923
Casper, Billy; born William Earl Casper Jr. (golf); 1931
Chabrol, Claude (director); 1930
Cousins, Norman (journalist); 1912
Creighton, David Theodore (hockey); 1930
Dempsey, Jack; born William Harrison Dempsey (boxing); 1895
Dillon, Richard Charles (politician); 1877
Edwards, James Burrows (politician); 1927
Fangio, Jean Manuel (auto racing); 1911
Foust, Larry (basketball); 1928
George, Chief Dan; born Geswanouth Slaholt (actor); 1899
Hamill, Pete; born William Peter Hamill (journalist/author); 1935
Harper, George Washington (baseball); 1892
Harris, Phil (music/comedian/actor); 1906
Hemsley, Rollie; born Ralston Burdett Hemsley (baseball); 1907
Heyward, Duncan Clinch (politician); 1864
Jones, Sam; born Samuel Jones (basketball); 1933
Kramer, Ron; born Ronald John Kramer (football); 1935
Lee, Michele; born Michele Lee Dusick (actress/singer); 1942
McKay, Douglas (politics/government); 1893
Meyer, George von Lengerke (government); 1858
Mincher, Don; born Donald Ray Mincher (baseball); 1938
Quigley, Juanita (actress); 1931
Rose, David (music); 1910
Saxbe, William Bart (politics/government); 1916
Stöve, Betty (tennis); 1945
Van Horn, Doug; born Douglas Van Horn (football); 1944

JUNE 25:

Abbott, George Francis (playwright/producer/director); 1887
Beauchamp, Al; born Alfred Beauchamp (football); 1944
Cahill, William Thomas (politician); 1912
Demeter, Don; born Donald Lee Demeter (baseball); 1935
George, Phyllis Ann (Miss America/sportscaster/TV host); 1949
Gottselig, Johnny; born John P. Gottselig (hockey); 1906
Greenwood, Charlotte; born Frances Charlotte Greenwood (actress/
    dancer); 1893
Hayes, Peter Lind; born Joseph Conrad Lind, Jr. (actor/comedian);
    1915
Hennings, Thomas Carey, Jr. (politician); 1903
Kirby, Clay; born Clayton Laws Kirby, Jr. (baseball); 1948
Kuhel, Joe; born Joseph Anthony Kuhel (baseball); 1906
Lockhart, June Kathleen (actress); 1925
Lumet, Sidney (director); 1924
Orwell, George; born Eric Arthur Blair (author); 1903
Revere, Anne (actress); 1903

Shapp, Milton Jerrold (politician); 1912
Simon, Carly (singer/music); 1945
Sykes, Brenda (actress); ——
Trottier, David T. (hockey); 1906
Walker, Jimmie; born James Carter Walker (comedian/actor); 1949
Younger, Tank; born Paul Younger (football); 1928

JUNE 26:

Buck, Pearl Sydenstricker (author); 1892
Davis, Billy, Jr. (singer); 1940
Doubleday, Abner (inventor of baseball); 1819
Dreier, Alex (newscaster/actor); 1916
Eagles, Jeanne (actress); 1890
Garns, Debs C. (baseball); 1908
Greer, Hal (basketball); 1936
Hainsworth, George (hockey); 1895
Hartley, Roland Hill (politician); 1864
Herman, Babe; born Floyd Caves Herman (baseball); 1903
Howard, Sidney Coe (playwright); 1891
Knowland, William Fife (politician); 1908
Levi, Edward Hirsch (government); 1911
Lorre, Peter; born Laszlo Loewenstein (actor); 1904
Moffo, Anna (singer); 1935
Parker, Eleanor (actress); 1922
Pollet, Howie; born Howard Joseph Pollet (baseball); 1921
Rafferty, Frances (actress); 1922
Skorich, Nick; born Nicholas L. Skorich (football); 1921
Symington, Stuart; born William Stuart Symington (politician); 1901
Tunney, John Varick (politician); 1934
Wilson, Hack; born Lewis Robert Wilson (baseball); 1900
Zaharias, Babe Didrikson; born Mildred Ella Didrikson (olympic athlete
     /golf); 1912

JUNE 27:

Buffone, Doug; born Douglas John Buffone (football); 1944
Christie, Audrey (actress); 1911
Crosby, Gary Evan (actor); 1933
Currie, Dan; born Daniel Currie (football); 1935
Ellington, Buford (politician); 1907
Holland, Vernon (football); 1948
Kasko, Eddie; born Edward Michael Kasko (baseball); 1932
Keeshan, Bob; born Robert James Keeshan "Captain Kangaroo"
     (actor); 1927
Keller, Helen Adams (author/educator); 1880
Mann, Errol Dennis (football); 1941
McIntire, John (actor); 1907
Mondou, Armand (hockey); 1905

Petrocelli, Rico; born Americo Peter Petrocelli (baseball); 1943
Raleigh, Bones; born James Donald Raleigh (hockey); 1926
Smith, Sandra (actress); 1940
Terwilliger, Wayne; born Willard Wayne Terwilliger (baseball); 1925
Young, Willie; born William Lull Young (football); 1943
Zernial, Gus Edward (baseball); 1923

JUNE 28:

Ambler, Eric (author); 1909
Baylor, Don; born Donald Edward Baylor (baseball); 1949
Brooks, Mel; born Melvyn Kaminsky (actor/director/producer/writer);
   1926
Chester, Raymond (football); 1948
Dana, Viola; born Viola Flugrath (actress); 1897
Davis, Clarence Eugene (football); 1949
Downing, Al; born Alphonse Erwin Downing (baseball); 1941
Dubbins, Don (actor); 1929
Flatt, Lester Raymond (singer/music); 1914
Gee, George (hockey); 1922
Gordon, Max; born Mechel Salpeter (producer); 1892
Henry VIII (King of England); 1491
Howley, Chuck; born Charles L. Howley (football); 1936
Inescort, Frieda; born Frieda Wightman (actress); 1901
Knudson, George (golf); 1937
Montagu, Ashley (anthropologist/author); 1905
Moran, Polly; born Pauline Therese Moran (actress); 1883
Morgan, George (singer/music); 1925
Nottingham, Don; born Donald Nottingham (football); 1949
Pirandello, Luigi (dramatist/author); 1867
Radner, Gilda (actress/comedienne/singer); 1946
Rodgers, Richard Charles (music/playwright/producer); 1902
Rousseau, Jean-Jacques (French philosopher/writer); 1712
Skinner, Otis (actor); 1857
Speier, Chris Edward (baseball); 1950
Stewart, Gaye; born James Gaye Stewart (hockey); 1923
Williams, Ken; born Kenneth Roy Williams (baseball); 1890
Wilson, Lois (actress); 1895

JUNE 29:

Bannen, Ian (actor); 1928
Borah, William (politician); 1865
Brown, Bill; born William Dorsey Brown (football); 1938
Browne, Irene (actress); 1891
Carmichael, Stokely (civil rights leader); 1941
Davis, Joan; born Madonna Josephine Davis (actress); 1907
De Mille, Katherine; born Katherine Lester (actress); 1911
Dierdorf, Dan; born Daniel Lee Dierdorf (football); 1949

Eddy, Nelson (singer/actor); 1901
Hoff, Philip Henderson (politician); 1924
Humphrey, Claude B. (football); 1944
Kent, Jean; born Joan Summerfield (actress); 1921
Killebrew, Harmon Clayton, Jr. (baseball); 1936
Kratzert, Bill (golf); 1952
Kubelik, Rafael; born Jeronym Rafael Kubelik (music); 1914
Loesser, Frank Henry (music/producer); 1910
Macfarlane, Willie; born William Macfarlane (golf); 1890
Martin, Clarence Daniel (politician); 1886
Mayo, William James (medicine); 1861
Pickens, Slim; born Louis Bert Lindley, Jr. (actor); 1919
Rubens, Peter Paul (artist); 1577
Schell, Harry; born Henry O'Reilly Schell (auto racing); 1921
Shaw, Bob; born Robert John Shaw (baseball); 1933
Trout, Dizzy; born Paul Howard Trout (baseball); 1915
Warrick, Ruth (actress/singer); 1915
Whitehead, Burgess Urquhard (baseball); 1910
Williams, Cara; born Bernice Kamiat (actress); 1925

JUNE 30:

Bellamy, Madge; born Madge Philpott (actress); 1900
Dussault, Nancy Elizabeth (actress/singer/TV host); 1936
Farrell, Glenda (actress); 1904
Fry, Shirley J. (tennis); 1927
Hampden, Walter Dougherty (actor); 1879
Hannegan, Robert Emmet (government); 1903
Hayward, Susan; born Edythe Marrener (actress); 1918
Horne, Lena Calhoun (singer/actress); 1917
Landau, Martin (actor); 1925
Lenkaitis, Bill; born William Lenkaitis (football); 1946
Maltbie, Roger (golf); 1951
Monroe, Elizabeth Kortright; born Elizabeth Kortright (First Lady);
    1768
Musante, Tony (actor); 1936
Rich, Buddy; born Bernard Rich (music); 1917
Swoboda, Ron; born Ronald Alan Swoboda (baseball); 1944
Valli, June (singer); 1930
Vivian, John Charles (politician); 1887
Whalen, Michael; born Joseph Kenneth Shovlin (actor); 1899

JULY 1:

Aykroyd, Dan; born Daniel Edward Aykroyd (actor/comedian/singer);
    1952
Beveridge, William S. (hockey); 1909
Black, Karen; born Karen Blanche Ziegler (actress); 1942
Bolin, Wesley H. (politician); 1908

Bujold, Geneviève (actress); 1942
Caron, Leslie Claire Margaret (actress/dancer); 1931
Carr, Roger (football); 1952
Cohen, Myron (comedian); 1902
Connor, Roger (baseball); 1857
Costigan, Edward Prentiss (politician); 1874
De Havilland, Olivia Mary (actress); 1916
Donaghey, George W. (politician); 1856
Dunn, Byrant Winfield Culberson (politician); 1927
Evans, Madge; born Margherita Evans (actress); 1909
Farr, Jamie; born Jameel Joseph Farah (actor); 1934
Ford, Constance (actress); 1929
Gilbert, Rod; born Rodrigue Gilbert (hockey); 1941
Glaspell, Susan (playwright/author); 1882
Granger, Farley Earle, II (actor); 1925
Kleppe, Thomas Savig (government); 1919
Laughton, Charles (actor); 1899
Lewis, Freddie (basketball); 1943
Marsh, Jean Lyndsey Torren (actress/writer); 1934
Matheson, Murray; born Sidney Murray Matheson (actor); 1912
McLinton, Harold Lucious (football); 1947
Rochambeau, Jean Baptiste Donatien de Vimeur (French marshall);
    1725
Sand, George; born Lucile-Amandine-Aurore Dupin (author); 1804
Scott, William Lloyd (politician); 1915
Sherwood, Roberta (singer/actress); 1912
Talbert, Diron (football); 1944
Tharp, Twyla (dancer/choreographer); 1941
Wyler, William (producer/director); 1902
Young, Babe; born Norman Robert Young (baseball); 1915

JULY 2:

Carr, Lorne Bell (hockey); 1910
Comstock, William Alfred (politician); 1877
Costello, Larry; born Lawrence Ronald Costello (basketball); 1931
Gluck, Christoph Willibald (music); 1714
Guthrie, Sir Tyrone; born William Tyrone Guthrie (director); 1900
Hawkins, Alex; born Chilton Alex Hawkins (football/sportscaster); 1937
Herseth, Ralph (politician); 1909
Holliday, Polly Dean (actress); 1937
Jamal, Ahmad (music); 1930
Johnson, Luci Baines; born Lucy Baines Johnson (First family); 1947
Lacoste, Rene; born Jean-Rene Lacoste (tennis); 1905
Marshall, Thurgood, born Thoroughgood Marshall (jurist); 1908
McNichol, Jimmy; born James Vincent McNichol (actor); 1961
Mechem, Edwin Leard (politician); 1912

Olav V; born Alexander Edward Christian Frederick (King of Norway);
    1903
Peters, Brock; born Brock Fisher (actor); 1927
Petty, Richard Lee (auto racing); 1937
Rainwater, Marvin; born Marvin Percy (singer/music); 1925
Rowan, Dan Hale (comedian/actor); 1922
Rowe, Curtis (basketball); 1949
Stephens, Hubert Durrett (politician); 1875
Stobbs, Chuck; born Charles Klein Stobbs (baseball); 1929
Wagner, Hal; born Harold Edward Wagner (baseball); 1915
Wharram, Kenny; born Kenneth Malcolm Wharram (hockey); 1933

JULY 3:

Allbritton, Louise (actress); 1920
Bailey, Ace; born Irvine Wallace Bailey (hockey); 1903
Buckley, Betty (actress); 1947
Butz, Earl Lauer (government); 1909
Carter, Jack; born John William Carter (First family); 1947
Cole, Michael (actor); 1945
Copley, John Singleton (artist); 1738
Dahlstrom, Cully; born Carl Dahlstrom (hockey); 1913
Errol, Leon (actor); 1881
Fernandez, Manny; born Manuel J. Fernandez (football); 1946
Fountain, Pete; born Peter Dewey Fountain, Jr. (music); 1930
Garrison, Walt; born Walter Benton Garrison (football); 1944
Gibson, Wynne; born Winifred Gibson (actress); 1899
Hamlin, Luke Daniel (baseball); 1904
Howton, Billy; born William Harris Howton (football); 1930
Kilgallen, Dorothy Mae (journalist); 1913
Lloyd, Doris (actress); 1899
Meyner, Robert Baumle (politician); 1908
Moore, A. Harry; born Arthur Harry Moore (politician);
    1879
Naumoff, Paul Pete (football); 1945
Palmer, Johnny; born John Palmer (golf); 1918
Peters, Susan; born Suzanne Carnahan (actress); 1921
Pugh, Jethro, Jr. (football); 1944
Rivera, Geraldo Miguel (TV host/newscaster); 1943
Sanders, George (actor); 1906
Schmitt, Harrison Hagan (astronaut/politician); 1935
Stoppard, Tom; born Thomas Straussler (playwright); 1937
Tanana, Frank Daryl (baseball); 1953
Tovar, Cesar Lenardo (baseball); 1940
Vandiver, Samuel Ernest, Jr. (politician); 1918
Walker, Curt; born William Curtis Walker (baseball); 1896
Work, Hubert (government); 1860

JULY 4:

Armetta, Henry (actor); 1888
Armstrong, Louis; born Daniel Louis Armstrong (music/singer/actor); 1900
Barnes, Erich (football); 1935
Boozer, Emerson, Jr. (football/sportscaster); 1943
Boyd, Stephen; born William Millar (actor); 1928
Caesar, Irving; born Isidore Irving Caesar (music); 1895
Casares, Rick; born Ricardo Jose Casares (football); 1931
Cohan, George M.; born George Michael Cohan
    (actor/dancer/singer/producer/director/playwright/music)
    (real birthday) July 3, 1878 (adopted birthday) July 4, 1878
Coolidge, Calvin; born John Calvin Coolidge (President); 1872
Cude, Wilfred (hockey); 1910
Davis, Sam; born Samuel Davis (football); 1944
Foster, Stephen Collins (music); 1826
Garibaldi, Giuseppe (Italian patriot); 1807
Graham, Virginia; born Virginia Komiss (TV host/actress); 1912
Hawthorne, Nathaniel (author); 1804
Landers, Ann; born Esther Pauline Friedman (journalist); 1918
Lanham, Samuel Willis Tucker (politician); 1846
Lanier, Hal; born Harold Clifton Lanier (baseball); 1942
Lawrence, Gertrude; born Gertrude Alexandra Dagmar Lawrence-
    Klasen (actress/singer/dancer); 1898
Little, Floyd Douglas (football); 1942
Lollobrigida, Gina (actress); 1927
Mayer, Louis Burt (producer); 1885
Miller, Mitch; born Mitchell William Miller (music); 1911
Murphy, George Lloyd (actor/dancer/politician); 1902
Parsons, Johnnie (auto racing); 1918
Roberts, Albert Houston (politician); 1868
Rose, Tokyo; born Iva Ikuko Toguri d'Aquino (broadcasting); 1916
Saint, Eva Marie (actress); 1924
Simon, Neil; born Marvin Neil Simon (playwright); 1927
Stapleton, Pat; born Patrick James Stapleton (hockey); 1940
Tanner, Chuck; born Charles William Tanner (baseball); 1929
Taylor, Roosevelt (football); 1938
Trilling, Lionel (author); 1905
Tuttle, Bill; born William Robert Tuttle (baseball); 1929
Van Buren, Abigail; born Pauline Esther Friedman (journalist); 1918
Walker, Clifford Mitchell (politician); 1877
Withers, Bill (singer/music); 1938

JULY 5:

Barnum, P.T.; born Phineas Taylor Barnum (showman); 1810
Blefary, Curt; born Curtis LeRoy Blefary (baseball); 1943

Cocteau, Jean (poet/dramatist/author/director/artist); 1889
Coleman, Gordy; born Gordon Calvin Coleman (baseball); 1934
Davis, Dwight Filley (government); 1879
Farragut, David Glasgow; born James Glasgow Farragut (naval officer);
1801
Hadley, Bump; born Irving Darius Hadley (baseball); 1904
Helmond, Katherine (actress); 1933
Knight, Shirley (actress); 1936
Kunz, George James (football); 1947
Lodge, Henry Cabot, Jr. (politics/government); 1902
Massey, Ilona; born Ilona Hajmassy (actress); 1912
Matthews, Gary Nathaniel (baseball); 1950
McKay, John H. (football); 1923
Miles, Eddie (basketball); 1940
Miranda, Isa; born Inès Isabella Sampietro (actress); 1909
Nixon, Julie (First family); 1948
Oates, Warren (actor); 1928
Pompidou, Georges Jean Raymond (French government); 1911
Rhodes, Cecil John (South African financier & statesman); 1853
Stone, Milburn; born Hugh Milburn Stone (actor); 1904
Sweet, Joe; born Joseph Sweet (football); 1948
Tyler, Beverly; born Beverly Jean Saul (actress); 1928

JULY 6:

Andrews, LaVerne (singer—Andrews Sisters); 1915
Armstrong, Chief; born George Edward Armstrong (hockey); 1930
Ballman, Gary J. (football); 1940
Beatty, Ned (actor); 1937
Brooks, Ralph Gilmour (politician); 1898
Cabot, Sebastian (actor); 1918
Cabot, Susan (actress); 1927
Carlton, Doyle Elam (politician); 1885
Davis, Nancy; born Anne Frances Robbins (actress/governor's wife);
1921
Dryer, Fred; born John Fred Dryer (football); 1946
Ford, Susan Elizabeth (First family); 1957
Forsyth, Rosemary (actress); 1944
Graham, Otto Everett (football); 1925
Griffin, Merv; born Mervyn Edward Griffin (TV host/singer); 1925
Gromyko, Andrei Andreyevich (Russian government); 1909
Jones, John Paul (naval officer); 1747
Kirsten, Dorothy (singer); 1919
Leigh, Janet; born Jeanette Helen Morrison (actress); 1927
Maximilian; born Ferdinand Maximilian Joseph (Mexican Emperor);
1832
Morgan, Ralph; born Raphael Kuhner Wuppermann (actor); 1882
Park, Brad; born Bradford Douglas Park (hockey); 1948

Paulsen, Pat; born Patrick Laton Paulsen (comedian/actor); 1927
Plager, William Ronald (hockey); 1945
Resse, Della; born Deloreese Patricia Early (singer/actress); 1932
Royall, Darrel K. (football); 1924
Sarto, Andrea del; born Andrea Domenico d-Agnolo di Francesco
    (artist); 1486
Schallert, William Joseph (actor); 1922
Stallone, Sylvester Enzio (or born Michael Sylvester Stallone)
    (actor/writer/director); 1946
Taylor, Hugh (football); 1923
Vanderbilt, Harold Stirling (capitalist/sportsman); 1884
Ward, Burt; born Bert John Gervais, Jr. (actor); 1945
Watson, Joseph John (hockey); 1943
Wyeth, James Browning (artist); 1946

JULY 7:

Barnett, Jim (basketball); 1944
Boone, Cherry; born Cheryl Lynn Boone (singer—Boone Family); 1954
Brown, Fred (basketball); 1948
Cardin, Pierre (fashion designer); 1922
Chagall, Marc (artist); 1887
Charles, Ezzard; born Charles Ezzard (boxing); 1921
Clement, Percival Wood (politician); 1846
Coleman, William Thaddeus, Jr. (government); 1920
Cukor, George Dewey (director); 1899
De Sica, Vittorio (director/actor); 1902
Dominick, Peter Hoyt (politician); 1915
Donahey, Vic; born Alvin Victor Donahey (politician); 1873
Edwards, Vince; born Vincento Eduardo Zoino (actor); 1928
Ford, Mary; born Irene Colleen Summers (singer); 1924
Ford, Ruth Elizabeth (actress); 1915
Hackbart, Dale L. (football); 1938
Heinlein, Robert Anson (author); 1907
Herman, Billy; born William Jennings Bryan Herman (baseball); 1909
Jacklin, Tony; born Anthony Jacklin (golf); 1944
Kunstler, William Moses (attorney/author); 1919
Lewis, Frank Doug (football); 1947
Mahler, Gustav (music); 1860
Mauck, Carl Frey (football); 1947
Mayehoff, Eddie (music/actor/comedian); 1911
Menotti, Gian-Carlo (music); 1911
O'Brien, Lawrence Francis (government/basketball); 1917
Paige, Satchel; born Leroy Robert Paige (baseball); 1906
Severinsen, Doc; born Carl H. Severinsen (music); 1927
Sherk, Jerry (football); 1948
Siffert, Jo (auto racing); 1936
Starr, Ringo; born Richard Starkey (singer/music); 1940

Walton, Chuck; born Charles R. Walton (football); 1941
White, Sammy; born Samuel Charles White (baseball); 1928

JULY 8:

Arledge, Roone Pickney (broadcasting); 1931
Bankhead, John Hollis, Jr. (politician); 1872
Barrows, Lewis Orin (politician); 1876
Bockhorn, Bucky; born Arlen Bockhorn (baseball); 1933
Branh, Louis Jefferson (politician); 1876
Brown, Clint; born Clinton Harold Brown (baseball); 1903
Brown, Pamela Mary (actress); 1917
Crow, John David (football); 1935
Cruce, Lee (politician); 1863
Darby, Kim; born Deborah Elias Zerby (actress); 1948
Eckstine, Billy; born William Clarence Eckstine (singer); 1914
Emerson, Faye Margaret (actress); 1917
Feldman, Marty (comedian/actor/director); 1933
Grau, Shirley Ann (author); 1929
Hunt, Lester Callaway (politician); 1892
Kerr, Walter Francis (journalist); 1913
Lambert, Jack; born John Harold Lambert (football); 1952
Langan, Glenn (actor); 1917
Lawrence, Steve; born Sidney Liebowitz (singer/actor); 1935
Loden, Barbara Ann (actress); 1937
Lopez, Hector Headley (baseball); 1932
Mason, Tommy; born Thomas Cyril Mason (football); 1939
McCreary, James Bennett (politician); 1838
Niesen, Gertrude (actress/singer); 1910
Pallette, Eugene (actor); 1889
Rockefeller, John Davidson (industrialist/philanthropist); 1839
Rockefeller, Nelson Aldrich (Vice President); 1908
Rodd, Marcia (actress/singer); 1941
Romney, George Wilcken (politics/government); 1907
Spangler, Al; born Albert Donald Spangler (baseball); 1933
Stevens, Craig; born Gail Hughes Shikles, Jr. (actor); 1918
Vale, Jerry; born Genaro Louis Vitaliano (singer); 1932
Waugh, Alex; born Alexander Raban Waugh (author); 1898

JULY 9:

Ames, Ed (singer/actor—Ames Brothers); 1927
Anderson, Cowboy; born Thomas Linton Anderson (hockey); 1911
Andrews, Mike; born; Michael Jay Andrews (baseball); 1943
Brough, Charles Hillman (politician); 1876
Brown, Paul (football); 1908
Brunsdale, Clarence Norman (politician); 1891
Daniels, Clem; born Clemon Daniels (football); 1937
Finnigan, Frank (hockey); 1903

Gresham, Bob; born Robert Gresham (football); 1948
.Hampton, James Wade (actor); 1936
Heath, Edward (British government); 1916
Howe, Elias (inventor); 1819
Jackson, Sonny; born Roland Thomas Jackson (baseball); 1944
Jones, Spike; born John A. Jones (football); 1946
Kelly, Red; born Leonard Patrick Kelly (hockey); 1927
Kilby, Thomas Erby (politician); 1865
Myers, Chip; born Philip Leon Myers (football); 1945
Pollard, Jim (basketball); 1922
Post, Wally; born Walter Charles Post (baseball); 1929
Pronovost, Joseph Armand Andre (hockey); 1936
Riordan, Mike (basketball); 1945
Rumsfeld, Donald (government); 1932
Simpson, O.J.; born Orenthal James Simpson
        (football/sportscaster/actor); 1947
Stanfield, Robert Nelson (politician); 1877
Thompson, Dorothy (journalist/author); 1894

JULY 10:

Adams, Nick; born Nicholas Aloysius Adamshock (actor); 1931
Alley, Gene; born Leonard Eugene Alley (baseball); 1940
Ashe, Arthur Robert, Jr. (tennis); 1943
Brinkley, David McClure (newscaster); 1920
Calvin, John; born Jean Chauvin (religious reformer); 1509
Carpenter, Carleton Upham, II (actor); 1926
Chirico, Giorgio de (artist); 1888
Dallas, George Mifflin (Vice President); 1792
Donnell, Jeff; born Jean Marie Donnell (actress); 1921
Dorsey, Hugh Manson (politician); 1871
Fiss, Galen R. (football); 1931
Gabor, Magda (actress); 1917
Gilbert, John; born John Pringle (actor); 1895
Gomez, Thomas; born Sabino Tomas Gomez, Jr. (actor); 1905
Guthrie, Arlo (singer/music); 1947
Gwynne, Fred (actor); 1926
Hand, Larry; born Lawrence Thomas Hand (football); 1940
Herman, Jerry; born Gerald Herman (music); 1932
Holland, Spessard Lindsey (politician); 1892
Kerr, Jean; born Bridget Jean Collins (playwright); 1923
LaMotta, Jake; born Jacob LaMotta (boxing); 1921
Laye, Evelyn (actress/singer); 1900
Lyon, Sue (actress); 1946
Marsh, Joan; born Dorothy Rosher (actress); 1913
McRae, Hal; born Harold Abraham McRae (baseball); 1946
O'Neil, Barbara (actress); 1909
Orff, Carl (music); 1895

Pressman, Lawrence (actor); 1939
Shera, Mark (actor); 1949
Smithers, William (actor); 1927
Summerville, Slim; born George J. Summerville (actor); 1892
Wade, Virginia; born Sarah Virginia Wade (tennis); 1945
Whistler, James Abbott McNeill (artist); 1834

JULY 11:

Adams, John Quincy (President); 1767
Allison, Bob; born William Robert Allison (baseball); 1934
Barrymore, Georgie; born Georgianna Emma Drew (actress); 1854
Battle, John Stewart (politician); 1890
Blane, Sally; born Elizabeth Jane Young (actress); 1910
Brynner, Yul; born Youl Bryner (or Taidje Khan, Jr.) (actor/singer); 1915
Cornwell, John Jacob (politician); 1867
Dalton, John Nichols (politician); 1931
Evans, Gene (actor); 1922
Harney, Paul (golf); 1929
Hauss, Len; born Leonard Moore Hauss (football); 1942
Hayes, Susan Seaforth; born Susan Seaforth (actress); ——
Hervey, Irene; born Irene Herwick (actress); 1910
Holmes, Ernie; born Ernest Lee Holmes (football); 1948
Hudson, Lou; born Louis Clyde Hudson (basketball); 1944
Hunter, Tab; born Arthur Andrew Kelm (or Arthur Gelien) (actor/singer); 1931
Mitchell, Thomas (actor); 1892
Norris, George William (politician); 1861
Olson, Bobo; born Carl Olson (boxing); 1928
Sauldsberry, Woody (basketball); 1934
Smith, Sid; born Sidney James Smith (hockey); 1925
Snell, Earl Wilcox (politician); 1895
Somers, Brett (actress); 1927
Spinks, Leon (boxing); 1953
Stewart, Ronald George (hockey); 1932
Stock, Milt; born Milton Joseph Stock (baseball); 1893
Talbot, Jean Guy (hockey); 1932
Von Zell, Harry R. (announcer/actor); 1906
Wanamaker, John (merchant); 1838
White, E.B.; born Elwyn Brooks White (author); 1899

JULY 12:

Andes, Keith; born John Charles Andes (actor); 1920
Berle, Milton; born Milton Berlinger (comedian/actor); 1908
Carver, George Washington (botanist); 1861
Cliburn, Van; born Harvey Lavan Cliburn, Jr. (music)
Cosby, Bill; born William Henry Cosby, Jr. (comedian/actor); 1937

Curtis, Ken; born Curtis Gates (actor); 1916
Eastman, George (inventor/philanthropist); 1854
Fairly, Ron; born Ronald Ray Fairly (baseball); 1938
Faye, Joey; born Joseph Anthony Palladino (comedian/actor); 1910
Flagstad, Kirsten Malfred (singer); 1895
Fuller, R. Buckminster; born Richard Buckminster Fuller, Jr.
    (architect/engineer/educator/philosopher/author/poet); 1895
Green, Donnie; born Donald Green (football); 1948
Hammerstein, Oscar, II; born Oscar Greeley Clenndenning
    Hammerstein (music/playwright/producer/director); 1895
Hatfield, Mark Odom (politician); 1922
Hayes, Mark Stephen (golf); 1949
Hersholt, Jean (actor); 1886
Hyde, Arthur Mastick (politics/government); 1877
Ladd, Cheryl; born Cheryl Jean Stoppelmoor (actress/singer/dancer);
    1951
Nicholas, Denise (actress); 1944
Parsons, Benny (auto racing); 1941
Ralston, Vera; born Vera Helena Hruba (actress); 1919
Ravlich, Mathew Joseph (hockey); 1938
Runyan, Paul Scott (golf); 1908
Ryan, Frank Beall (football); 1936
Scott, Ray (basketball); 1938
Silas, Paul T. (basketball); 1943
Thoreau, Henry David (naturalist/author); 1817
Weaver, Charlie; born Charles E. Weaver (football); 1949
Wyeth, Andrew Newell (artist); 1917
Wyrostek, Johnny; born John Barney Wyrostek (baseball); 1919

JULY 13:

Abramowicz, Dan; born Daniel Abramowicz (football); 1945
Ascari, Alberto (auto racing); 1918
Blackmer, Sidney Alderman (actor); 1895
Coody, Charles (golf); 1937
Coveleski, Stanley Anthony "Stan"; born Stanislaus Kowalewski
    (baseball); 1889
Crane, Bob Edward (actor); 1928
Forster, Robert (actor); 1941
Garroway, Dave; born David Cunningham Garroway (TV host); 1913
Gomez, Ruben Colon (baseball); 1927
Hanks, Sam; born Samuel Dwight Hanks (auto racing); 1914
Kemp, Jackie; born John French Kemp (football/politics); 1935
Lantz, Stu; born Stuart Lantz (basketball); 1946
Loring, Lynn (actress); 1944
Milliken, Carl Elias (politician); 1877
Mosdell, Ken; born Kenneth Mosdell (hockey); 1922
Pavletich, Don; born Donald Stephen Pavletich (baseball); 1938

Quinn, William Francis (politician); 1919
Ramsey, Frank (basketball); 1931
Spencer, Daryl Dean (baseball); 1929
Walker, Mickey (boxing); 1901
Zimmer, Norma; born Norma Beatrice Larsen (singer); ——

JULY 14

Annabella; born Suzanne Georgette Charpentier (actress); 1909
Avery, Val (actor); 1924
Bergen, Polly; born Nellie Paulina Burgin (actress/singer/cosmetics); 1929
Bergman, Ingmar; born Ernst Ingmar Bergman (director/writer); 1918
Capper, Arthur (politician); 1865
Chancellor, John William (newscaster); 1927
Chandler, Happy; born Albert Benjamin Chandler (politics/baseball); 1898
Dixon, Jean; born Marie Jacques (actress); 1894
Edwards, Douglas (newscaster); 1917
Elder, Lee; born Robert Lee Elder (golf); 1934
Ford, Gerald Rudolph, Jr.; born Leslie King, Jr. (President); 1913
Grier, Rosey; born Roosevelt Grier (football/actor); 1932
Guthrie, Woody; born Woodrow Wilson Guthrie (singer/music); 1912
Harmon, Claude (golf); 1916
Houser, Jerry (actor); 1952
James, Arthur Horace (politician); 1883
Johann, Zita (actress); 1904
Laurents, Arthur (playwright/director); 1918
Lawrence, Jerome; born Jerome Schwartz (playwright/music); 1915
Lewis, Mike; born Michael Henry Lewis (football); 1949
Meek, Donald (actor); 1880
Murphy, Johnny; born John Joseph Murphy (baseball); 1908
Murray, Ken; born Don Court (actor/producer/author); 1903
Nolan, Doris (actress); 1916
Olson, Nancy Ann (actress); 1928
Paulen, Ben Sanford (politician); 1869
Purkey, Bob; born Robert Thomas Purkey (baseball); 1929
Reeves, Del; born Franklin Delano Reeves (singer/music); 1933
Roberston, Dale; born Dayle LaMoine Robertson (actor); 1923
Singer, Isaac Bashevis (author); 1904
Stone, Irving, born Irving Tennenbaum (author); 1903
Stuart, Gloria; born Gloria Stuart Finch (actress); 1909
Terry-Thomas; born Thomas Terry Hoar-Stevens (actor); 1911
Tobias, George (actor); 1901
Willard, Ken; born Kenneth Henderson Willard (football); 1943
Williams, Earl Craig, Jr. (baseball); 1948
Wing, Toby; born Martha Virginia Wing (actress); 1913
Woodruff, Rollin Simmons (politician); 1854

JULY 15:

Carey, Philip (actor); 1922
Clendenon, Donn Alvin (baseball); 1935
Fields, Dorothy (music); 1905
Hargrave, Bubbles; born Eugene Franklin Hargrave (baseball); 1892
Karras, Alex; born Alexander G. Karras (football/sportscaster/actor);
    1935
Kercheval, Ken (actor); 1935
Lane, Franklin Knight (government); 1864
Litzenberger, Eddie; born Edward C.J. Litzenberger (hockey); 1932
Martin, Nan Clow (actress); 1927
McAlister, Hill (politician); 1875
Moore, Clement Clarke (poet/author); 1779
Rambeau, Marjorie (actress); 1889
Rembrandt, Van Rijn; born Van Rijn Rembrandt Harmenszoon (artist);
    1606
Ronstadt, Linda Maria (singer); 1946
Shannon, Mike; born Thomas Michael Shannon (baseball); 1939
Stallworth, John Lee (football); 1952
Truax, Bill; born William Frederick Truax, III (football); 1943
Vincent, Jan-Michael (actor); 1944
Wayne, Patrick (actor); 1939
Winston, Roy C. (football); 1940

JULY 16:

Anderson, Bill; born Walter W. Anderson (football); 1936
Carson, Mindy (singer); 1926
Clements, Stanley (actor); 1926
Colbert, Robert (actor); ——
Court, Margaret; born Margaret Smith (tennis); 1942
Eddy, Mary Baker; born Mary Morse Baker (religious leader); 1821
Emhardt, Robert (actor); 1901
Fisher, Eddie Gene (baseball); 1936
Giardello, Joey; born Carmine Orlando Tilelli (boxing); 1930
Hughes, Barnard (actor); 1915
Jansen, Larry; born Lawrence Joseph Jansen (baseball); 1920
Kilbride, Percy (actor); 1888
Lie, Trygve Halvdan (United Nations); 1896
Lombardo, Carmen (music); 1903
McGee, Max; born William M. McGee (football); 1932
Myerson, Bess (Miss America/actress/consumer advocate); 1924
Rathmann, Jim; born Richard R. Rathmann (auto racing); 1928
Redgrave, Corin (actor); 1939
Reynolds, Sir Joshua (artist); 1723
Rogers, Ginger; born Virginia Katherine McMath
    (actress/dancer/singer); 1911
Stanley, Thomas Bahnson (politician); 1890

Stanwyck, Barbara; born Ruby Stevens (actress); 1907
Tufts, Sonny; born Bowen Charleston Tufts, III (actor); 1911
Van Eyck, Peter (actor); 1911

JULY 17:

Amies, Hardy; born Edwin Hardy Amies (fashion designer); 1909
Arnaz, Lucie Désirée (actress/singer); 1951
Astor, John Jacob (financier); 1763
Boudreau, Lou; born Louis Boudreau (baseball); 1917
Brown, Eddie; born Edward William Brown (baseball); 1891
Cagney, James Francis, Jr. (actor); 1899
Carroll, Diahann; born Carol Diahann Johnson (singer/actress); 1935
Carroll, John; born Julian la Faye (actor/singer); 1905
Corot, Jean Baptiste Camille (artist); 1796
Daley, Cass; born Catherine Dailey (comedienne/actress); 1915
Diller, Phyllis; born Phyllis Driver (comedienne/actress/author); 1917
Feininger, Lyonel Charles Adrian (artist); 1871
Gardner, Erle Stanley (author); 1889
Gargan, William Dennis (actor); 1905
Gerry, Elbridge (Vice President); 1749
Haile Selassie; born Ras Taffari Makonnen (Ethiopian Emperor); 1891
Hawkins, Connie (basketball); 1942
Hines, Mimi (comedienne/actress/singer); 1933
Hinkle, Lon (golf); 1949
Johnson, Deron Roger (baseball); 1938
Kessinger, Don; born Donald Eulon Kessinger (baseball); 1942
Lamonica, Daryle P. (football); 1941
Leonard, Bob; born Robert Leonard (basketball); 1932
Linkletter, Art; born Arthur Gordon Kelley Linkletter (TV
        host/producer/author); 1912
Lynch, Jerry; born Gerald Thomas Lynch (baseball); 1930
McMillan, Roy David (baseball); 1930
Steber, Eleanor (singer); 1916
Sutherland, Donald (actor); 1934
Thomas, Mike; born Malcolm Thomas (football); 1953

JULY 18:

Albright, Tenley Emma (ice skating); 1935
Awrey, Donald William (hockey); 1943
Barkum, Jerome Phillip (football); 1950
Brolin, James; born James Bruderlin (actor); 1940
Brooks, Phyllis; born Phyllis Weiler (or Seiler) (or Steiller) (actress);
        1914
Brown, Albert Oscar (politician); 1852
Cronyn, Hume; born Hume Blake (actor/director); 1911
Dion; born Dion DiMucci (singer/music); 1939
Dix, Richard; born Ernest Carlton Brimmer (actor); 1894

Evans, Chick; born Charles Evans, Jr. (golf); 1890
Evans, Joan; born Joan Eunson (actress); 1934
Frazee, Jane; born Mary Jane Frashe (or Freshe) (actress); 1918
Freeman, Don (basketball); 1944
Glenn, John Herschel, Jr. (astronaut/politician); 1921
Goudal, Jetta (actress); 1898
Harris, Ted; born Edward Alexander Harris (hockey); 1936
Hayakawa, S.I.; born Samuel Ichiye Hayakawa (educator/politician);
     1906
Hopp, Johnny; born John Leonard Hopp (baseball); 1916
Kingrea, Rick; born Richard Kingrea (football); 1949
Lietzke, Bruce (golf); 1951
Lockhart, Gene; born Eugene Lockhart (actor); 1891
Long, Edward Vaughan (politician); 1908
May, Rudy; born Rudolph May (baseball); 1944
Miller, Marvin; born Marvin Mueller (actor); 1913
Nelson, Harriet Hilliard; born Peggy Lou Snyder (singer/actress); 1911
Odets, Clifford (playwright); 1903
Patterson, Paul Linton (politician); 1900
Peterson, Val; born Frederick Valdemar Erastus Peterson (politician);
     1903
Richardson, Gloster V. (football); 1941
Rolvaag, Karl Fritjok (politician); 1913
Ruymen, Ayn (actress); 1947
Skelton, Red; born Richard Bernard Skelton (comedian/actor); 1913
Sweet, Dolph; born Adolphus Jean Sweet (actor/director); 1920
Thackeray, William Makepeace (author); 1811
Tiemann, Norbert Theodore (politician); 1924
Torre, Joe; born Joseph Paul Torre (baseball); 1940
Tyler, Royall (playwright); 1757
Velez, Lupe; born Guadeloupe Velez de Villalobos (actress); 1908
West, Jessamyn; born Mary Jessamyn West (author); 1902
Wills, Chill (actor); 1903
Wilson, Charles Erwin (government); 1890

JULY 19:

Borden, Lizzie Andrew (alleged murderess); 1860
Carr, Vikki; born Florencia Bisenta De Casillas Martinez Cardona
     (singer); 1942
Cavarretta, Phil; born Philip Joseph Cavaretta (baseball); 1916
Cole, Dennis (actor); 1943
Cronin, A.J.; born Archibald Joseph Cronin (author); 1896
Damita, Lili; born Liliane-Marie-Madeleine Carré (actress); 1901
Degas, Edgar; born Hilaire Germain Edgar Degas (artist); 1834
Gallagher, Helen (actress/dancer/singer); 1926
Gardner, Billy; born William Frederick Gardner (baseball); 1927
Hamilton, George, IV (singer/music); 1937

Hannum, Alex (basketball); 1923
Hathaway, Stanley K. (politics/government); 1924
Hayes, Jackie; born Minter Carney Hayes (baseball); 1906
Hilgenberg, Wally; born Walter Hilgenberg (football); 1942
Hingle, Pat; born Martin Patterson Hingle (actor); 1923
Hollander, Lorin (music); 1944
Jewell, Isabel (actress); 1909
Jordan, Richard (actor); 1938
Koenig Mark Anthony (baseball); 1902
Mayo, Charles Horace (medicine); 1865
McGovern, George Stanley (politician); 1922
McNutt, Paul Vories (politician); 1891
Medina, Patricia (actress); 1919
Nastase, Ilie (tennis); 1946
Scranton, William Warren (politician); 1917
Smith, J.D. (football); 1932
Smith, Jerry T. (football); 1943

JULY 20:

Albright, Lola Jean (actress/singer); 1925
Amon, Chris; born Christopher Arthur Amon (auto racing); 1943
Baird, Butch; born Fred Baird (golf); 1936
Bara, Theda; born Theodosia Goodman (actress); 1890
Boyd, Alan Stephenson (government); 1922
Burfeindt, Betty (golf); 1945
Byrns, Joseph Wellington, Sr. (politician); 1869
Felton, Verna (actress); 1890
Hamilton, Pete; born Peter Goodwill Hamilton (auto racing); 1942
Harris, James L. (football); 1947
Heafner, Clayton (golf); 1914
Hillary, Sir Edmund Percival (apiarist/mountain climber); 1919
Howes, Sally Ann (singer/actress); 1930
Manush, Heinie; born Henry Emmett Manush (baseball); 1901
Oliva, Tony; born Pedro Oliva (baseball); 1940
Prothro, Tommy; born James Thompson Prothro, Jr. (football); 1920
Revercomb, William Chapman (politician); 1895
Richardson, Elliot Lee (government); 1920
Rigg, Diana (actress); 1938
Rutledge, Wiley Blount, Jr. (jurist); 1894
Schroeder, Ted; born Frederick Rudolph Schroeder, Jr. (tennis); 1921
Scott, Jake; born Jacob E. Scott, III (football); 1945
Stanley, Mickey; born Mitchell Jack Stanley (baseball); 1942
Stevens, K.T.; born Gloria Wood (actress); 1919
Wood, Natalie; born Natasha Nicholas Gurdin (actress); 1938

JULY 21:

Banaszak, Pete; born Peter Banaszak (football); 1944

Bateman, John Alvin (baseball); 1942
Burke, Paul (actor); 1926
Burnquist, Joseph Alfred Arner (politician); 1879
Butler, John Marshall (politician); 1897
Chatterton, Fenimore (politician); 1860
Cleveland, Frances Folsom; born Frances Folsom (First Lady); 1864
Clyde, George Dewey (politician); 1898
Drabowsky, Moe; born Myron Walter Drabowsky (baseball); 1935
Fullmer, Gene (boxing); 1931
Hammond, Jay Sterner (politician); 1922
Hart, Christina; born Bonnie Ann Hartzell (actress); ——
Hegan, Mike; born James Michael Hegan (baseball); 1942
Hemingway, Ernest Miller (author); 1898
Herrmann, Edward Kirk (actor); 1943
Hetzel, Fred (basketball); 1942
Hickenlooper, Bourke Blakemore (politician); 1896
Hyland, Bob; born Robert Joseph Hyland (football); 1945
Jenner, William Ezra (politician); 1908
Jewison, Norman F. (producer/director); 1926
Joslyn, Allyn (actor); 1901
Kennedy, David Matthew (government); 1905
Keyes, Frances Parkinson; born Frances Parkinson Wheeler (author);
    1885
Knotts, Don (comedian/actor); 1924
Littler, Gene; born Eugene Alex Littler (golf); 1930
Maynard, Ken (actor); 1895
McGee, Jerry (golf); 1943
McLuhan, Marshall; born Herbert Marshall McLuhan (com-
    munications expert/writer); 1911
Menke, Denis John (baseball); 1940
Murray, Johnston (politician); 1902
Pierson, John Frederick (hockey); 1925
Reibel, Dutch; born Earl Reibel (hockey); 1930
Shannon, James Coughlin (politician); 1896
Smith, C. Aubrey (actor); 1863
Starr, Kay; born Kathryn Stark (singer); 1922
Stern, Isaac (music); 1920
Stevens, Cat; born Steven Demetre Georgiou (singer/music); 1947
Stevens, Kaye; born Catherine Stevens (singer/actress); 1933
Trudel, Louis Napoleon (hockey); 1913
Ulric, Lenore; born Lenore Ulrich (actress); 1892
Warner, Fred Maltby (politician); 1865
Williams, Robin (comedian/actor); 1952

JULY 22:

Albanese, Licia (singer); 1913
Bankston, Warren (football); 1947

Bean, Orson; born Dallas Frederick Burrows (actor); 1928
Benét, Stephen Vincent (poet/author); 1898
Bergland, Robert Selmer (government); 1928
Berning, Susie Maxwell; born Susie Maxwell (golf); 1941
Bristow, Joseph Little (politician); 1861
Cain, J.V.; born James Victor Cain (football); 1951
Cramer, Doc; born Roger Maxwell Cramer (baseball); 1905
De La Renta, Oscar (fashion designer); 1932
Dole, Robert Joseph (politician); 1923
Haines, Jesse Joseph (baseball); 1893
Henderson, Marcia (actress); 1930
Holmes, Phillips (actor); 1907
Jackson, Chuck; born Charles Jackson (singer); 1937
Kennedy, Rose; born Rose Fitzgerald (President's mother); 1890
Labine, Leo Gerald (hockey); 1931
Lyle, Sparky; born Albert Walter Lyle (baseball); 1944
Matson, Pat; born Patrick Matson (football); 1944
Mendel, Gregor Johann (botanist); 1822
Menninger, Karl Augustus (psychiatrist/author); 1893
Rivera, Jim; born Manuel Joseph Rivera (baseball); 1922
Roth, William. V.; Jr. (politician); 1921
Sherman, Bobby (singer/actor/music); 1945
Stamp, Terence (actor); 1940
Tobey, Charles William (politician); 1880
Turcotte, Ron; born Ronald Turcotte (jockey); 1941
Vanderbilt, Amy (journalist/author); 1908
Whiting, Margaret (singer); 1924

JULY 23:

Browne, Coral (actress); 1913
Chandler, Raymond Thornton (author); 1888
Cobb, William Titcomb (politician); 1857
Convy, Bert; born Bernard Whalen Patrick Convy (actor/singer/TV host); 1934
De Haven, Gloria Mildred (actress); 1924
Dietrick, Coby (basketball); 1948
Drysdale, Don; born Donald Scott Drysdale (baseball/sportscaster); 1936
Dutton, Red; born Mervyn Dutton (hockey); 1898
Essex, David; born David Albert Cook (singer/actor); 1947
Ford, Hod; born Horace Hills Ford (baseball); 1897
Goodman, Ival Richard (baseball); 1908
Groth, Johnny; born John Thomas Groth (baseball); 1926
Hearnes, Warren Eastman (politician); 1923
Heinemann, Gustav Walter (German government); 1899
Jannings, Emil; born Theodor Friedrich Emil Janenz (actor); 1884
Kreuger, Kurt (actor); 1916

Maxwell, Billy; born William J. Maxwell (golf); 1929
Mickelson, George Theodore (politician); 1903
Montgomery, Belinda J. (actress); 1950
Page, Gale; born Sally Perkins Rutter (singer/actress); 1913
Pennewill, Simeon Selby (politician); 1867
Pringle, Aileen; born Aileen Bisbee (actress); 1895
Reese, Pee Wee; born Harold Henry Reese (baseball/sportscaster); 1918
Sanford, Edward Terry (jurist); 1865
Sardi, Vincent, Jr. (restaurateur); 1915
Swenson, Karl (actor); 1908
Treacher, Arthur; born Arthur Veary (actor); 1894
Warner, Albert (producer—Warner Brothers); 1884
Wilding, Michael (actor); 1912
Wilson, Jimmie; born James Wilson (baseball); 1900

JULY 24:

Abzug, Bella; born Bella Savitsky (politician); 1920
Bellamy, Walt; born Walter Bellamy (basketball); 1939
Bloch, Ernest (music); 1880
Bolivar, Simón (South American liberator); 1783
Buzzi, Ruth Ann (comedian/actress/singer); 1936
Carter, Lynda (Miss World-USA/actress/singer); 1951
Cohen, Alexander H. (producer); 1920
Davis, Willie; born William D. Davis (football); 1934
Dumas, Alexander (the Elder); born Davy De La Pailleterie (author); 1802
Earhart, Amelia Mary (aviator); 1897
Eberly, Bob (singer); 1915
Grogan, Steve; born Steven James Grogan (football); 1953
Hay, Alexandra Lynn (actress); 1948
Heil, Julius Peter (politician); 1876
MacDonald, John Dann (author); 1916
Mathias, Charles McCurdy, Jr. (politician); 1922
McPeak, Bill; born William McPeak (football); 1926
Noble, Chuck (basketball); 1931
Payne, Frederick George (politician); 1900
Ruckelshaus, William Doyle (government); 1932
Sanders, Doug; born George Douglas Sanders (golf); 1933
San Souci, Emery John (politician); 1857
Sarandon, Chris (actor); 1942
Silvera, Frank Alvin (actor); 1914
Swinburne, Nora (actress); 1902
Utter, George Herbert (politician); 1854
Vera; born Vera Salaff (textile designer/artist); 1910
Ward, Preston Meyer (baseball); 1927

JULY 25:

Belasco, David (playwright/producer/actor); 1854
Bradford, Buddy; born Charles William Bradford (baseball); 1944
Brennan, Walter Andrew (actor); 1894
Church, Frank Forrester (politician); 1924
Cline, Tony; born Anthony Cline (football); 1948
Davey, Martin Luther (politician); 1884
Dixon, Frank Murray (politician); 1892
Eakins, Thomas (artist); 1844
Gilford, Jack; born Jacob Gellman (actor); 1907
Grey, Nan; born Eschol Miller (actress); 1918
Harrison, Anna Tuthill Symmes; born Anna Tuthill Symmes (First
    Lady); 1775
Langlie, Arthur Bernard (politician); 1900
Lee, Lila; born Augusta Appel (actress); 1901
Lockman, Whitey; born Carroll Walter Lockman (baseball); 1926
Margolin, Janet (actress); 1943
McClinton, Curtis R. (football); 1939
McDonald, William C. (politician); 1858
Pardee, George Cooper (politician); 1857
Payton, Walter Jerry (football); 1954
Strode, Woody; born Woodrow Wilson Strode (actor); 1914
Tener, John Kinley (politician); 1863
Theodore, Donna (singer/actress); 1945
Thurmond, Nate (basketball); 1941

JULY 26:

Allen, Gracie; born Grace Ethel Cecile Rosalie Allen
    (comedienne/actress); 1899
Arrington, Buddy (auto racing); 1938
Bellson, Louis; born Louis Balassoni (music); 1924
Best, James (actor); 1926
Bloodworth, Jimmy; born James Henry Bloodworth (baseball); 1917
Boyle, Emmet Derby (politician); 1879
Branigin, Roger Douglas (politician); 1902
Bryant, Farris; born Cecil Farris Bryant (politician); 1914
Clinton, George (Vice President); 1739
Cortelyou, George Bruce (government); 1862
Edwards, Blake; born William Blake McEdwards (director); 1922
Gallico, Paul William (author/journalist); 1897
George, Susan (actress); 1950
Gerulaitis, Vitas Kevin (tennis); 1954
Gilmore, Virginia; born Virginia Sherman Poole (actress); 1919
Hays, Kathryn; born with surname Piper (actress); ——
Huxley, Aldous Leonard (author); 1894
Jagger, Mick; born Michael Philip Jagger (singer); 1943

Jones, Sad Sam; born Samuel Pond Jones (baseball); 1892
Jung, Carl Gustav (psychoanalyst/author); 1875
Kefauver, Estes; born Carey Estes Kefauver (politician); 1903
Kinder, Ellis Raymond (baseball); 1914
Koussevitzky, Serge Alexandrovitch (music); 1874
Kubrick, Stanley (producer/director); 1928
Leslie, Sam; born Samuel Andrew Leslie (baseball); 1905
Lilly, Bob; born Robert Lewis Lilly (football); 1939
Lord, Marjorie (actress); 1921
Martin, Richard Lionel (hockey); 1951
McDonald, Tommy; born Thomas McDonald (football); 1934
Plaisted, Frederick William (politician); 1865
Pothier, Aram J. (politician); 1854
Robards, Jason Nelson, Jr. (actor); 1922
Rousseau, Bobby; born Robert Rousseau (hockey); 1940
Shaw, George Bernard (playwright); 1856
Siebern, Norm; born Norman Leroy Siebern (baseball); 1933
Sisti, Sibby; born Sebastian Daniel Sisti (baseball); 1920
Taliaferro, Mike; born Myron E. Taliaferro (football); 1941
Vance, Vivian; born Vivian Jones (actress); 1903
Vardaman, James Kimble (politician); 1861
Voorhees, Donald (music); 1903
Ward, Pete; born Peter Thomas Ward (baseball); 1939
Waterfield, Bob; born Robert Staton Waterfield (football); 1920
Wilhelm, Hoyt; born James Hoyt Wilhelm (baseball); 1923

JULY 27:

Allen, George Trenholme (hockey); 1914
Boone, Ray; born Raymond Otis Boone (baseball); 1923
Calvin, Mack (basketball); 1949
Celi, Adolfo (actor); 1922
Cook, Marlow Webster (politician); 1926
Crisp, Donald (actor); 1880
Cross, Irv; born Irvin Cross (football/sportscaster); 1939
Dolin, Anton; born Patrick Healey-Kay (dancer/choreographer); 1904
Durocher, Leo; born Leon Ernest Durocher (baseball); 1906
Fleming, Peggy Gale (ice skating); 1948
Galloway, Don (actor); 1937
Gentry, Bobbie; born Roberta Streeter (singer); 1944
Homer; born Henry D. Haynes (singer/comedian/music—
        Homer & Jethro); 1917
James, Ollie Murray (politician); 1871
Klein, Bob; born Robert Klein (football); 1947
Lear, Norman Milton (producer); 1922
Lock, Don Wilson (baseball); 1936
Lowry, Judith (actress); 1890
McGovern, Maureen Therese (singer); 1949

McKenzie, Reggie; born Reginald McKenzie (football); 1950
Moses, Haven Christopher (football); 1946
Ralston, Dennis; born Richard Dennis Ralston (tennis); 1942
Samuelson, Donald William (politician); 1913
Tanner, Tony (actor); 1932
Taylor, Zack; born James Wren Taylor (baseball); 1898
Tinker, Joe; born Joseph Bert Tinker (baseball); 1880
Walberg, Rube; born George Elvin Walberg (baseball); 1899
Wynn, Keenan; born Francis Xavier Alousius Keenan Wynn (actor);
    1916

JULY 28:

Ammons, Elias Milton (politician); 1860
Blue, Vida Rochelle (baseball); 1949
Bradley, Bill; born William Warren Bradley (basketball); 1943
Brown, Joe E.; born Joe Evan Brown (comedian); 1891
d'Amboise, Jacques Joseph (dancer); 1934
Doran, Ann (actress); 1913
Dragon, Carmen (music); 1914
Duchin, Peter Oelrichs (music); 1937
Engel, Georgia Bright (actress); 1948
Fitzsimmons, Freddie; born Frederick Landis Fitzsimmons (baseball);
    1901
Hickman, Darryl Gerard (actor); 1931
Hodge, Charles Edward (hockey); 1933
Johnson, John Albert (politician); 1861
Kelsey, Linda (actress); ——
Lepcio, Ted; born Thaddeus Stanley Lepcio (baseball); 1930
Miles, John Esten (politician); 1884
Onassis, Jacqueline; born Jacqueline Lee Bouvier (wife of President
    Kennedy/First Lady); 1929
Owen, Catherine Dale (actress); 1900
Potter, Beatrix (author); 1866
Struthers, Sally Ann (actress); 1948
Vallee, Rudy; born Hubert Prior Valle (singer/actor); 1901

JULY 29:

Beebe, William; born Charles William Beebe
    (naturalist/explorer/author); 1877
Bochner, Lloyd (actor); 1924
Bow, Clara Gordon (actress); 1904
Burns, George, III (golf); 1949
Casanova, Tom; born Thomas R. Casanova (football); 1950
Corey, Irwin "Professor" (comedian/actor); 1912
Egan, Richard (actor); 1921
Fuller, Robert (actor); 1934
Furcolo, Foster (politician); 1911

Hammarskjold, Dag Hjalmar Agne Carl (United Nations); 1905
Harris, William Edward (hockey); 1935
Himes, Chester Bomar (author); 1909
Horton, Robert; born Meade Howard Horton, Jr. (actor); 1924
Jennings, Peter Charles (newscaster); 1938
Josephson, Les; born Lester Josephson (football/actor); 1942
Kelly, Roz (actress/photographer); ——
Lindsay, Ted; born Robert Blake Theodore Lindsay (hockey); 1925
Mantilla, Felix Lamela (baseball); 1934
Marangi, Gary Angelo (football); 1952
Martin, Thomas Staples (politician); 1847
McNally, Stephen; born Horace McNally (actor); 1913
Mussolini, Benito (Italian government); 1883
O'Connor, Edwin Greene (author); 1918
Ouspenskaya, Maria (actress); 1876
Powell, William Horatio (actor); 1892
Romberg, Sigmund (music); 1887
Sargent, Francis Williams (politician); 1915
Sparks, Randy (singer/music); 1933
Tarkington, Booth; born Newton Booth Tarkington (author); 1869
Taylor, Paul Belville, Jr. (dancer/choreographer); 1930
Todd, Thelma (actress); 1905
Toppazzini, Gerald (hockey); 1931
Wert, Don; born Donald Ralph Wert (baseball); 1938

JULY 30:

Anka, Paul Albert (singer/actor/music); 1941
Atherton, William; born William Atherton Knight (actor); 1947
Bogdanovich, Peter (director/producer/writer/actor); 1939
Brontë, Emily Jane (author/poet); 1818
Byrnes, Edd; born Edward Breitenberger (actor); 1933
Carroll, John Albert (politician); 1901
Ford, Henry (auto manufacturer); 1863
Kelly, Pat; born Harold Patrick Kelly (baseball); 1944
Mandich, Jim; born James M. Mandich (football); 1948
Mann, William Hodges (politician); 1843
McGuire, Chris; born Christine McGuire (singer—
        McGuire Sisters); 1928
Nuxhall, Joe; born Joseph Henry Nuxhall (baseball); 1928
Piazza, Ben; born Benito Daniel Piazza (actor); 1934
Rader, Doug; born Douglas Lee Rader (baseball); 1944
Schwarzenegger, Arnold (body builder/actor); 1947
Sernas, Jacques (actor/producer); 1925
Spencer, Jim; born James Lloyd Spencer (baseball); 1947
Stengel, Casey; born Charles Dillon Stengel (baseball); 1891
Swainson, John Burley (politician); 1925
Triandos, Gus (baseball); 1930

White, Dwight Lynn (football); 1949
Williams, John Sharp (politician); 1854

JULY 31:

Barbour, William Warren (politician); 1888
Bauer, Hank; born Henry Albert Bauer (baseball); 1922
Catts, Sidney Johnston (politician); 1863
Chaplin, Geraldine (actress); 1944
Davalillo, Vic; born Victor Jose Davalillo (baseball); 1936
Dixon, Joseph Moore (politician); 1867
Edwards, Glen (football); 1947
Flannery, Susan (actress); 1943
Goolagong, Evonne Fay (tennis); 1951
Gowdy, Curt; born Curtis Gowdy (sportscaster); 1919
Handley, Lee Elmer (baseball); 1913
Hextall, Bryan Aldwyn, Sr. (hockey); 1913
Hitchcock, Billy; born William Clyde Hitchcock (baseball); 1916
Jones, Horace (football); 1949
Kresge, S.S.; born Sebastian Spering Kresge (merchant); 1867
Latimer, Asbury Churchwell (politician); 1851
Leduc, Albert (hockey); 1901
Lepine, Alfred (hockey); 1901
Liberace, George J. (music); 1911
Murray, Don; born Donald Patrick Murray (actor/director/writer);
    1929
Nehf, Art; born Arthur Neukom Nehf (baseball); 1892
Nuyen, France; born France Denise Nguyen Vannga (actress); 1939
Philbin, Gerry; born Gerald J. Philbin (football); 1941
Richardson, Samuel (author); 1689
Snead, Norm; born Norman B. Snead (football); 1939
Taylor, Robert Love (politician); 1850
Todman, William Selden (producer); 1916

AUGUST 1:

Branch, Cliff; born Clifford Branch (football); 1948
Clark, William (explorer); 1770
Deluise, Dom (comedian/actor); 1933
Hill, Arthur Edward Spence (actor); 1922
Holder, Geoffrey Lamont (dancer/actor/singer/director); 1930
Isaac, Bobby; born Robert Vance Isaac (auto racing); 1934
Jackson, Harold Russell (hockey); 1918
Jones, Henry Burk (actor); 1912
Jones, Marcia Mae (actress); 1924
Keeling, Butch; born Melville Sidney Keeling (hockey); 1905
Key, Francis Scott (music/law); 1779
Kramer, Jack; born John Albert Kramer, Jr. (tennis); 1921
Mangrum, Lloyd Eugene (golf); 1914

Marker, Gus; born August Solberg Marker (hockey); 1907
Melville, Herman (author); 1819
Percy, Eileen (actress); 1899
Reed, Alvin (football); 1944
St. Laurent, Yves; born Henri Donat Mathieu (fashion designer); 1936
Shaute, Joe; born Joseph Benjamin Shaute (baseball); 1899
Smith, Ellison DuRant (politician); 1864
Stewart, Michael; born Michael Stewart Rubin (playwright); 1929

AUGUST 2:

Adams, Charles Francis (government); 1866
Bachman, Nathan Lynn (politician); 1878
Baldwin, James Arthur (writer); 1924
Balon, David Alexander (hockey); 1937
Boivin, Leo Joseph (hockey); 1932
Burns, Bob (comedian/actor); 1893
Cannon, Billy; born William Abb Cannon (football); 1937
Cunningham, Cecil (actress/singer); 1888
Dvorak, Ann; born Ann McKim (actress); 1912
Harnell, Joe; born Joseph Harnell (music); 1924
Hazeltine, Matt; born Matthew Hazeltine (football); 1933
Kieran, John Francis (journalist/author/editor); 1892
Laxalt, Paul Dominique (politician); 1922
L'Enfant, Pierre Charles (engineer); 1754
Lennon, Kathy; born Kathleen Mary Lennon (singer—
        Lennon Sisters); 1943
Loy, Myrna; born Myrna Williams (actress); 1905
Merrill, Gary Franklin (actor); 1914
Morgan, Helen; born Helen Riggins (singer/actress); 1900
O'Connor, Carroll (actor); 1924
O'Toole, Peter; born Seamus O'Toole (actor); 1932
Pegler, Westbrook; born James Westbrook Pegler (journalist); 1894
Sloan, John (artist); 1871
Stanford, Rawghlie Clement (politician); 1879
Stewart, Samuel Vernon (politician); 1872
Straight, Beatrice Whitney (actress); 1916
Warner, Jack Leonard (producer—Warner Brothers); 1892
Wetmore, George Peabody (politician); 1846
Young, Howard John Edward (hockey); 1937

AUGUST 3:

Adler, Richard (music/producer); 1921
Alworth, Lance D. (football); 1940
Ames, Adrienne; born Adrienne Ruth McClure (actress); 1907
Baughan, Maxie C., Jr. (football); 1938
Bennett, Tony; born Antonio Dominick Benedetto (singer); 1926
Bloch, Ray; born Raymond A. Bloch (music); 1902

Burns, James MacGregor (author); 1918
Cord, Alex; born Alexander Viespi (actor); 1931
Del Rio, Dolores; born Lolita Dolores Martinez Asunsolo Lopez
Negrette (actress); 1904
Eisenhower, John Sheldon Doud (First family); 1922
Elgart, Les (music); 1918
Gregory, William (politician); 1849
Gunther, John Joseph (author); 1910
Hagen, Jean; born Jean Shirley VerHagen (actress); 1924
Hegan, Jim; born James Edward Hegan (baseball); 1920
Heilmann, Harry Edwin (baseball); 1894
Howe, Bob; born Robert N. Howe (tennis); 1925
Lamm, Richard Douglas (politician); 1935
Lee, Bivian (football); 1948
Leslie, Bethel (actress); 1929
Martinelli, Elsa (actress); 1933
Maxwell, Marilyn; born Marvel Marilyn Maxwell (actress); 1921
North, Jay; born Jay Hopper (actor); 1952
Platt, Louise (actress); 1914
Repoz, Roger Allen (baseball); 1940
Scott, Gordon; born Gordon M. Werschkul (actor); 1927
Sheen, Martin; born Ramon Estevez (actor); 1940
Shortridge, Samuel Morgan (politician); 1861
Smith, Charles Manley (politician); 1868
Stennis, John Cornelius (politician); 1901
Uris, Leon Marcus (author); 1924

AUGUST 4:

Beckley, Jake; born Jacob Peter Beckley (baseball); 1867
Benson, Ezra Taft (government); 1899
Calleia, Joseph; born Joseph Spurin-Calleja (actor); 1897
Caster, George Jasper (baseball); 1907
Cole, Tina (singer/actress); 1943
Colville, Neil Macneil (hockey); 1914
Cooper, Harry E. (golf); 1904
Fitch, John Cooper (auto racing); 1917
Galloway, Chick; born Clarence Edward Galloway (baseball); 1896
Hallahan, Wild Bill; born William Anthony Hallahan (baseball); 1902
Jones, Cleon Joseph (baseball); 1942
Kane, Helen; born Helen Schroeder (actress/singer); 1903
Kolloway, Don; born Donald Martin Kolloway (baseball); 1918
Kroll, Ted; born Theodore Kroll (golf); 1919
Leonard, Joe; born Joseph Paul Leonard (auto racing); 1934
Lucas, Frank E. (politician); 1876
Lundeen, Ernest (politician); 1878
Luque, Dolf; born Adolfo Luque (baseball); 1890
Page, Anita; born Anita Pomares (actress); 1910

Pollard, John Garland (politician); 1871
Richard, Maurice; born Joseph Henri Maurice Richard (hockey); 1921
Riggins, John (football); 1949
Schuman, William Howard (music); 1910
Shelley, Percy Bysshe (poet); 1792
Stainback, Tuck; born George Tucker Stainback (baseball); 1910
Tabori, Kristoffer, born Christopher Donald Siegel (actor); 1952

AUGUST 5:

Aiken, Conrad Potter (poet/author); 1889
Armstrong, Neil Alden (astronaut); 1930
Beckham, John Crepps Wickliffe (politician); 1869
Benson, Duane (football); 1945
Brian, David (actor); 1914
Briles, Nelson Kelley (baseball); 1943
Carbo, Bernie; born Bernardo Carbo (baseball); 1947
Colby, Anita; born Anita Katherine Counihan (actress); 1914
Drake, Tom; born Alfred Alderdice (or Alderdeiss) (actor); 1918
Gabriel, Roman (football); 1940
Ginther, Richie; born Paul Richard Ginther (auto racing); 1930
Hinson, Larry (golf); 1944
Huston, John (director/actor/writer); 1906
Jo, Damita; born Damita Jo DuBlanc (singer); 1940
Kleindienst, Richard Gordon (government); 1923
McCormick, Maureen (actress/singer); 1956
Owen, Reginald; born John Reginald Owen (actor); 1887
Saxon, John; born Carmen Orrico (actor); 1935
Taylor, Robert; born Spangler Arlington Brugh (actor); 1911
Weldon, Joan (singer/actress); 1933

AUGUST 6:

Ball, Lucille Désirée (comedienne/actress/singer/producer); 1910
Betz, Pauline M. (tennis); 1919
Blades Ray; born Francis Raymond Blades (baseball); 1896
Bonerz, Peter (actor); 1938
Bushfield, Harlan John (politician); 1882
Carrillo, Leo (actor); 1881
Couture, Gerald Joseph Wilfred Arthur (hockey); 1925
Craig, George North (politician); 1909
Culp, Ray; born Raymond Leonard Culp (baseball); 1941
Fleming, Sir Alexander (bateriologist); 1881
Ford, Doug; born Douglas Ford (golf); 1922
Gibson, Hoot; born Edmund Richard Gibson (actor); 1892
Goldsborough, Phillips Lee (politician); 1865
Jacobs, Helen Hull (tennis); 1908
Labine, Clem; born Clement Walter Labine (baseball); 1926
Lincoln, Abbey; born Anna Marie Wooldridge (actress/singer); 1930

Messersmith, Andy; born John Alexander Messersmith (baseball); 1945
Mitchum, Robert Charles Duran (actor); 1917
Parsons, Louella; born Louella Oettinger (journalist); 1881
Patman, Wright; born John William Wright Patman (politician); 1893
Raines, Ella; born Ella Wallace Raubes (actress); 1921
Riley, Ken; born Kenneth Riley (football); 1947
Roosevelt, Edith Kermit Carow; born Edith Kemit Carow (second wife
    of Theodore Roosevelt/First Lady); 1861
Sneed, Ed; born Edgar Sneed (golf); 1944
Strong, Ken; born Elmer Kenneth Strong (football); 1906
Taylor, Alfred Alexander (politician); 1848
Tennyson, Alfred (poet); 1809
Van Dyke, Bruce (football); 1944
Walker, Daniel (politician); 1922
Warhol, Andy; born Andrew Warhola (artist/filmmaker); 1927
White, Wallace Humphrey, Jr. (politician); 1877
Yancey, Bert; born Albert Winsborough Yancey (golf); 1938

AUGUST 7:

Bloom, Verna (actress); ——
Bridges, Rocky; born Everett Lamar Bridges (baseball); 1927
Bunche, Ralph Johnson (government); 1904
Burke, Billie; born Mary William Ethelbert Appleton Burke
    (comedienne/actress); 1884
Busbee, George Dekle (politician); 1927
Cantrell, Lana (singer); 1944
Comer, Anjanette (actress); 1942
Edwards, Edwin Washington (politician); 1927
Fleming, Les; born Leslie Harvey Fleming (baseball); 1915
Freberg, Stan; born Stanley Victor Freberg (comedian); 1926
Gilliam, John Rally (football); 1945
Haines, William T. (politician); 1854
Larsen, Don; born Donald James Larsen (baseball); 1929
Lee, Bob; born Robert Melville Lee (football); 1945
Lyons, Tom; born Thomas Lewis Lyons (football); 1948
Malone, George Wilson (politician); 1890
Mason, Marlyn (actress/singer); 1940
Mata Hari; born Gertrud Margarete Zelle (dancer/spy); 1876
McKechnie, Bill; born William Boyd McKechnie (baseball); 1886
Page, Alan Cedric (football); 1945
Ragan, Dave; born David William Ragan (golf); 1935
Thomas, B.J.; born Billy Joe Thomas (singer); 1942
Wiechers, Jim; born James L. Wiechers (golf); 1944

AUGUST 8:

Allen, Oscar Kelly (politician); 1882
Anderson, Richard Norman (actor); 1926

Bundy, Brooke (actress)——
Calhoun, Rory; born Francis Timothy Durgin (actor); 1922
Carradine, Keith Ian (actor/singer/music); 1949
Cruz, Jose Dilan (baseball); 1947
Culver, John Chester (politician); 1932
De Laurentiis, Dino; born Agostino De Laurentiis (producer); 1919
Dryden, Ken; born Kenneth Wayne Dryden (hockey); 1947
Gadsby, Bill; born William Alexander Gadsby (hockey); 1927
Gernreich, Rudi (fashion designer); 1922
Goddard, Samuel Pearson, Jr. (politician); 1919
Goldberg, Arthur Joseph (government/jurist); 1908
Hillman, Darnell (basketball); 1949
Hoffman, Dustin (actor); 1937
Howard, Frank Oliver (baseball); 1936
Mann, Daniel; born Daniel Chugerman (director); 1912
McCarran, Patrick Anthony (politician); 1876
Miller, Fred; born Frederick D. Miller (football); 1940
Mondale, Joan Adams; born Joan Adams (Vice President's wife); 1930
Most, Donny (actor/singer); 1953
Pierce, Webb (singer/music); 1926
Raffensberger, Ken; born Kenneth David Raffensberger (baseball); 1917
Rainey, Ford (actor); 1908
Rawlings, Marjorie Kinnan (author); 1896
Sidney, Sylvia; born Sophia Kosow (actress); 1910
Sipe, Brian Winfield (football); 1949
Stafford, Robert Theodore (politician); 1913
Stevens, Connie; born Concetta Ann Ingolia (singer/actress); 1938
Talbot, Nita; born Nita Sokol (actress); 1930
Teasdale, Sara (poet); 1884
Temple, Johnny; born John Ellis Temple (baseball); 1928
Tex, Joe; born Joseph Arrington Jr. (singer); 1933
Tillis, Mel (singer/music); 1932
Travis, Cecil Howell (baseball); 1913
Wilcox, Larry (actor); 1948
Williams, Esther Jane (swimmer/actress); 1923

AUGUST 9:

Agee, Tommie Lee (baseball); 1942
Bolling, Milt; born Milton Joseph Bolling, III (baseball); 1930
Cappelletti, John Raymond (football); 1952
Cousy, Bob; born Robert Joseph Cousy (basketball); 1928
Dryden, John (poet); 1631
Exon, John James (politician); 1921
Farrell, Charles (actor); 1901
Francescatti, Zino; born René Francescatti (music); 1905
Genn, Leo (actor); 1905
Hanna, Louis Benjamin (politician); 1861

Houk, Ralph George (baseball); 1919
Javier, Julian; born Manuel Julian Liranzo Javier (baseball); 1936
Jordan, Dorothy (actress); 1908
Kelly, Paul Michael (actor); 1899
Kiick, Jim; born James Forrest Kiick (football); 1946
Laver, Rod; born Rodney George Laver (tennis); 1938
Lee, Blair (politician); 1857
Lindblad, Paul Aaron (baseball); 1941
Mills, Harry F. (singer—Mills Brothers); 1913
Nagel, Charles (government); 1849
Norton, Ken; born Kenneth Howard Norton (boxing/actor); 1945
Osteen, Claude Wilson (baseball); 1939
Regan, Lawrence Emmett (hockey); 1930
Shaw, Robert (actor/author); 1925
Simmons, Ted Lyle (baseball); 1949
Steinberg, David (comedian); 1942
Sutton, Len (auto racing); 1925
Talmadge, Herman Eugene (politician); 1913
Todt, Phil; born Philip Julius Todt (baseball); 1901
Walton, Izaak (author); 1593

AUGUST 10:

Astrologes, Maria (golf); 1951
Beery, Noah, Jr. (actor); 1913
Buehler, George (football); 1947
Colavito, Rocky; born Rocco Demenico Colavito (baseball); 1933
Corey, Jeff (actor/director); 1914
Dean, Jimmy Ray (singer/music); 1928
Duncan, Speedy; born Leslie H. Duncan (football); 1942
Fisher, Eddie; born Edwin Jack Fisher (singer); 1928
Fleming, Rhonda; born Marilyn Louis (actress); 1922
Fromholtz, Dianne Lee (tennis); 1956
Hale, Odell; born Arvel Odell Hale (baseball); 1908
Haley, Jack, Sr.; born John Joseph Haley (actor/comedian/singer);
    1899
Hardy, Joseph (actor); 1918
Holtzman, Red; born William Holtzman (basketball); 1920
Hoover, Herbert Clark (President); 1874
Hughes, Richard Joseph (politician); 1909
Hyer, Martha (actress); 1924
Kuchel, Thomas Henry (politician); 1910
Lewis, Buddy; born John Kelly Lewis (baseball); 1916
McKenna, Joseph (government/jurist); 1843
McLendon, Mac; born Benson Rayfield McLendon (golf); 1945
Miller, Allen L., III (golf); 1948
Porterfield, Bob; born Erwin Coolidge Porterfield (baseball); 1923
Randolph, Edmund Jennings (statesman); 1753

Richman, Harry; born Harry Reichman (actor/singer); 1895
Samples, Junior (comedian); 1926
Shearer, Norma; born Edith Norma Shearer (actress); 1900
Simpson, Ralph (basketball); 1949
Stelle, John H. (politician); 1891
Walker, Chuck; born Charles Walker (football); 1941
Welch, Frank Tiguer (baseball); 1897
Wright, Taffy; born Taft Shedron Wright (baseball); 1911

AUGUST 11:

Avery, William Henry (politician); 1911
Brewer, Earl LeRoy (politician); 1869
Broderick, Helen (actress); 1891
Curry, Busher; born Floyd James Curry (hockey); 1925
Dahl, Arlene Carol (actress); 1924
Douglas, Mike; born Michael Delany Dowd, Jr. (TV host/singer); 1925
Glenn, Robert Brodnax (politician); 1854
Haley, Alex Palmer (author); 1921
Haskins, Clem (basketball); 1944
Hirschhorn, Joseph Herman (financier/art collector); 1899
Leon, Eddie; born Eduardo Antonio Leon (baseball); 1946
Lisi, Virna; born Virna Pieralisi (actress); 1937
Mendenhall, Ken; born Kenneth Mendenhall (football); 1948
Monbouquette, Bill; born William Charles Monbouqette (baseball); 1936
Munson, Bill; born William A. Munson (football); 1941
Newsom, Bobo; born Louis Norman Newsom (baseball); 1907
Nolan, Lloyd (actor); 1902
Parker, Jean; born Lois Mae Greene (or Luis Stephanie Zelinska) (actress); 1912
Pinchot, Gifford (politician); 1865
Pinson, Vada Edward (baseball); 1938
Pond, Lennie (auto racing); 1940
Popein, Lawrence Thomas (hockey); 1930
Rayner, Chuck; born Claude Earl Rayner (hockey); 1920
Rowan, Carl Thomas (journalism/government); 1925
Scheffing, Bob; born Robert Boden Scheffing (baseball); 1915
Taylor, Otis (football); 1942
Tillman, Benjamin Ryan (politician); 1847
Timmerman, George Bell, Jr. (politician); 1912
Townsend, Maurice Clifford (politician); 1884

AUGUST 12:

Bradna, Olympe (actress); 1920
Buhl, Bob; born Robert Ray Buhl (baseball); 1928
Bumpers, Dale Leon (politician); 1925
Cantinflas; born Mario Moreno-Reyes (comedian/actor); 1911

Carey, Robert Davis (politician); 1878
Clift, Harlond Benton (baseball); 1912
De Mille, Cecil B.; born Cecil Blount De Mille (director); 1881
Derek, John; born Derek Harris (actor); 1926
Frazier, Charles Douglas (football); 1939
Frederick, Pauline; born Beatrice Pauline Libbey (actress); 1883
Hamilton, George Stevens, (actor); 1939
Hendrickson, Robert Clymer (politician); 1898
Homolka, Oscar (actor); 1898
Hurst, Don; born Frank O'Donnell Hurst (baseball); 1905
Hutchinson, Fred; born Frederick Charles Hutchinson (baseball); 1919
Jones, Parnelli; born Rufus Parnell Jones (auto racing); 1933
Kasznar, Kurt; born Kurt Serwischer (actor); 1913
Kidd, Michael; born Milton Greenwald (choreogrpaher/director); 1919
Lorne, Marion; born Marion Lorne MacDougall (actress); 1885
Mathewson, Christy; born Christopher Mathewson (baseball); 1878
McDermott, John J. (golf); 1891
McGinnis, George (basketball); 1950
Moore, Maulty (football); 1946
Neville, Tom; born Thomas Neville (football); 1943
Owens, Buck; born Alvis Edgar Owens, Jr. (singer/music); 1929
Reynolds, Marjorie; born Marjorie Goodspeed (actress); 1921
Rostropovich, Mstislav Leopoldovich (music); 1927
Schalk, Ray; born Raymond William Schalk (baseball); 1892
Voigt, Stu; born Stuart Alan Voigt (football); 1948
Wadsworth, James Wolcott, Jr. (politician); 1877
Wagoner, Porter (singer/music); 1927
Warren, Jennifer (actress); 1941
Wojciechowicz, Alex; born Alexander Wojciechowicz (football); 1915
Wyatt, Jane Waddington (actress); 1912
Ziegler, Larry; born Lawrence Ziegler (golf); 1939

AUGUST 13:

Beal, John; born J. Alexander Bleidung (actor); 1909
Brand, Neville (actor); 1920
Castro Ruz, Fidel (Cuban government); 1927
Clark, Alonzo Monroe (politician); 1868
Clarke, Bobby; born Robert Earle Clarke (hockey); 1949
Cloninger, Tony Lee (baseball); 1940
Combs, Bert Thomas (politician); 1911
Corbett, Gretchen (actress); 1947
Cummings, Quinn (actress); 1967
Dickson, Gloria; born Thais Dickerson (actress); 1916
Duncan, Mary (actress); 1903
Finney, Lou; born Louis Klopsche Finney (baseball); 1910
Gordon, Sid born Sidney Gordon (baseball); 1917
Grant, Mudcat; born James Timothy Grant (baseball); 1935

Hanburger, Chris; born Christian Hanburger (football); 1941
Harrington, Pat; born Daniel Patrick Harrington, Jr. (actor); 1929
Hitchcock, Alfred Joseph (producer/director/actor); 1899
Ho, Don (singer/actor); 1930
Hogan, Ben; born William Benjamin Hogan (golf); 1912
Humbard, Rex; born Alpha Rex Emmanuel Humbard (evangelist); 1919
Johnson, Rita; born Rita McSean (actress); 1912
Lahr, Bert; born Irving Lahrheim (actor/comedian); 1895
McNeil, Claudia Mae (actress); 1917
Mercer, Beryl (actress); 1882
Mizell, Vinegar Bend; born Wilmer David Mizell (baseball/politics); 1930
Oakley, Annie; born Phoebe Anne Oakley Mozee (markswoman); 1859
Raymond, Gene; born Raymond Guion (actor); 1908
Rogers, Buddy; born Charles Rogers (actor); 1904
Shearing, George Albert (music); 1919
Smith, Paul (football); 1945
Tighe, Kevin (actor); 1944
Toomey, Regis (actor); 1902
Walley, Deborah E. (actress); ——

AUGUST 14:

Brodie, John Riley (football/sportscaster); 1934
Cullen, Betsy; born Mary Elizabeth Cullen (golf); 1938
Flynn, William Smith (politician); 1885
Futrell, Junius Marion (politician); 1872
Galsworthy, John (author); 1867
Ghostley, Alice Margaret (actress); 1926
Greco, Buddy; born Armando Greco (singer/music); 1926
Horlen, Joe; born Joel Edward Horlen (baseball); 1937
Kazmierski; Joyce (golf); 1945
Nash, George Kilbon (politician); 1842
North, John Ringling (circus); 1903
Persoff, Nehemiah (actor); 1920
Saint James, Susan; born Susan Jane Miller (actress); 1946
Smith, Connie; born Constance Smith (singer); 1941
Tiger, Dick; born Richard Ihetu (boxing); 1929
Weaver, Earl Sidney (baseball); 1930
Wright, Cobina Caroline, Jr. (actress); 1921

AUGUST 15:

Anne, Princess; born Anne Elizabeth Alice Louise Mountbatten (British
    Royalty); 1950
Baird, Bil; born William Britton Baird (puppeteer); 1904
Barrymore, Ethel; born Ethel Mae Blythe (actress); 1879
Benton, Thomas Hart (artist); 1889
Bolt, Robert Oxton (playwright); 1924

Bonaparte, Napoleon (French Emperor); 1769
Bouchet, Barbara; born Barbara Gutscher (actress); 1943
Buzhardt, John William (baseball); 1936
Carter, Lillian; born Bessie Lillian Gordy (President's mother); 1898
Child, Julia; born Julia McWilliams (cook/author/TV personality); 1912
Coleridge-Taylor, Samuel (music); 1875
Comiskey, Charlie; born Charles Comiskey (baseball); 1859
Conigliaro, Billy; born William Michael Conigliaro (baseball); 1947
Connors, Mike; born Krekor Ohanian (actor); 1925
Cunningham, Sam; born Samuel Lewis Cunningham, Jr. (football); 1950
Dalton, Abby (actress); 1935
Dyer, Duffy; born Don Robert Dyer (baseball); 1945
Ferber, Edna (author); 1887
Harding, Florence Kling; born Florence Kling (First Lady); 1860
Hasso, Signe; born Signe Eleonora Cecilia Larsson (actress); 1910
Haworth, Jill (actress/singer); 1945
Hiller, Wendy Margaret (actress); 1912
Hopkins, Albert Jarvis (politician); 1846
Jay, Joey; born Joseph Richard Jay (baseball); 1935
Kerner, Otto (politician); 1908
Lawrence of Arabia; born Thomas Edward Lawrence
    (soldier/archaeologist/author); 1888
Manning, Richard Irvine (politician); 1859
Nelson, Lori; born Dixie Kay Nelson (actress); 1933
Norris, Edwin Lee (politician); 1865
Peterson, Oscar Emmanuel (music); 1925
Rose Marie; born Rose Marie Mazzatta (actress); ——
Rule, Janice; born Mary Janice Rule (actress); 1931
Scott, Sir Walter (author); 1771
Sherdel, Bill; born William Henry Sherdel (baseball); 1896
Shields, John Knight (politician); 1858
Shubert, J.J.; born Jacob Szemanski (producer); 1878
Taylor, Lionel Thomas (football); 1936
Townsend, Charles Elroy (politician); 1856
Upshaw, Gene; born Eugene Upshaw (football); 1945
Webb, Jimmy Layne (singer/music); 1946
Winterhalter, Hugo (music); 1910

AUGUST 16:

Begin, Menachem (Israeli government); 1913
Blyth, Ann Marie (actress/singer); 1928
Bonham, Ernie; born Ernest Edward Bonham (baseball); 1913
Clarke, Mae; born Violet Mary Klotz (actress); 1907
Craig, Locke (politician); 1860
Culp, Robert (actor/director); 1930
Farrell, Suzanne; born Roberta Sue Ficker (dancer); 1945

Fothergil, Bob; born Robert Roy Fothergil (baseball); 1897
Gifford, Frank; born Francis Newton Gifford
    (football/sportscaster/actor); 1930
Gillette, Anita; born Anita Lee Luebben (actress); 1936
Glass, Bill; born William S. Glass (football); 1935
Gormé, Eydie (singer); 1931
Hruska, Roman Lee (politician); 1904
Jacobson, Baby Doll; born William Chester Jacobson (baseball); 1890
Jones, Willie Edward (baseball); 1925
King, George (basketball); 1928
Meany, George (labor leader); 1894
Murphy, Francis Parnell (politician); 1877
Nettleton, Lois June (actress); 1929
Newmar, Julie; born Julia Charlene Newmeyer (actress); 1935
Parker, Fess Elijah (actor/singer); 1925
Peoples, Woody; born Woodrow Peoples (football); 1943
Rodgers, Bob; born Robert Leroy Rodgers (baseball); 1938
Shelley, Carole Augusta (actress); 1939
Stagg, Amos Alonzo (football); 1862
Trabert, Tony; born Marion Anthony Trabert (tennis/sportscaster);
    1930
von Furstenberg, Betsy; born Elizabeth Caroline Maria Agatha Felicitas
    Therese von Furstenberg-Hedringen (actress); 1931
Warren, Lesley Ann (actress/singer/dancer); 1946
Wilson, James (government); 1835
Woodling, Gene; born Eugene Richard Woodling (baseball); 1922
Yary, Ron; born Anthony Ronald Yary (football); 1946

AUGUST 17:

Ankers, Evelyn (actress); 1918
Corbett, Glenn; born Glenn Rothenburg (actor); 1929
Crockett, Davy; born David Crockett (frontiersman); 1786
Davenport, Jim; born James Houston Davenport (baseball); 1933
De Niro, Robert (actor); 1943
Dent, Frederick Baily (government); 1922
Donaldson, Jesse Monroe (government); 1885
Harding, Ann; born Dorothy Walton Gatley (actress); 1901
Hawkes, John Clendennin Burne, Jr. (author); 1925
Howe, Quincy (journalist/newscaster/author); 1900
Kerr, John (basketball); 1932
Keyser, Frank Ray, Jr. (politician); 1927
Maki, Chico; born Ronald Patrick Maki (hockey); 1939
Marlowe, Julia; born Sarah Frances Frost (actress); 1866
O'Hara, Maureen; born Maureen FitzSimons (or Fitzsimmons)
    (actress); 1920
Powell, Boog; born John Wesley Powell (baseball); 1941
Rivers, Larry; born Yitzroch Loiza Grossberg (artist); 1923

Robertson, Isiah (football); 1949
Roosevelt, Franklin Delano, Jr. (First family); 1914
Sandusky, Alex; born Alexander B. Sandusky (football); 1932
Sears, Ken (basketball); 1933
Sequi, Diego Pablo (baseball); 1937
Vilas, Guillermo (tennis); 1952
Watwood, Johnny; born John Clifford Watwood (baseball); 1906
West, Mae (actress); 1892
Woolley, Monty; born Edgar Montillion Woolley (actor); 1888
York, Rudy; born Rudolph Preston York (baseball); 1913

AUGUST 18:

Azcue, Joe; born Jose Joaquin Azcue (baseball); 1939
Bee, Molly; born Molly Beachboard (singer/actress); 1939
Carter, Jeff; born Donnel Jeffrey Carter (First family); 1952
Carter, Rosalynn; born Eleanor Rosalynn Smith (First Lady); 1927
Clemente, Roberto Walker (baseball); 1934
Consolo, Billy; born William Angelo Consolo (baseball); 1934
Factor, Max, Jr. (cosmetics); 1904
Fisher, Gail Ann (actress); 1935
Friberg, Barney; born Augustaf Bernhardt Friberg (baseball); 1899
Gerber, Wally; born Walter Gerber (baseball); 1891
Grimes, Burleigh Arland (baseball); 1893
Hickel, Walter Joseph (politics/government); 1919
Johnson, Rafer Lewis (olympic athlete/actor); 1935
Jones, Christopher (actor); 1941
Kennedy, Bob; born Robert Daniel Kennedy (baseball); 1920
Lanier, Max; born Hubert Max Lanier (baseball); 1915
Leeds, Andrea; born Antoinette Lees (actress); 1914
Lewis, Meriwether (explorer); 1774
Mowbray, Alan (actor); 1893
Ohl, Don (basketball); 1936
Polanski, Roman (director); 1933
Pruitt, Greg; born Gregory Donald Pruitt (football); 1951
Redford, Robert; born Charles Robert Redford, Jr. (actor); 1937
Snell, Matt; born Mathews Snell (football); 1941
Weinberger, Casper Willard (government); 1917
Williams, Grant (actor); 1930
Winters, Shelly; born Shirley Schrift (actress); 1922
Woytowich, Robert Ivan (hockey); 1941

AUGUST 19:

Baclanova, Olga (dancer/actress); 1899
Baruch, Bernard Mannes (financier/statesman); 1870
Boardman, Eleanor (actress); 1898
Carleton, Tex; born James Otto Carleton (baseball); 1906
Chanel, Coco; born Gabrielle Bonheur (fashion designer); 1883

Collyer, June; born Dorothea Heermance (actress); 1907
Connally, Thomas Terry (politician); 1877
Cozzens, James Gould (author); 1903
Dauphin, Claude; born Claude Franc-Nohain (actor); 1903
Enesco, Georges (music); 1881
Forbes, Malcolm Stevenson (publisher/sportsman); 1919
Johnson, Bob; born Robert Douglas Johnson (football); 1946
Knowles, Warren Perley (politician); 1908
Lunt, Alfred (actor); 1892
Moore, Colleen; born Kathleen Morrison (actress); 1900
Morton, Thruston Ballard (politician); 1907
Muldaur, Diana Charlton (actress); 1938
Nash, Johnny (singer); 1940
Nash, Ogden; born Frederick Ogden Nash (poet); 1902
Paget, Debra; born Debralee Griffin (actress); 1933
Richardson, Bobby; born Robert Clinton Richardson (baseball); 1935
St. John, Jill; born Jill Oppenheim (actress); 1940
Salmon, Thomas Paul (politician); 1932
Shoemaker, Willie; born William Lee Shoemaker (jockey); 1931
White, Hugh Lawson (politician); 1881
Wright, Orville (aviator/inventor); 1871

AUGUST 20:

Aiken, George David (politician); 1892
Banks, Tom; born Thomas S. Banks (football); 1948
Collins, Gary J. (football); 1940
Donnell, Forrest C. (politician); 1884
Fracci, Carla (dancer); 1936
Hansen, Don; born Donald Hansen (football); 1944
Harrison, Benjamin (President); 1833
Hayes, Isaac (music/actor); 1942
Kocourek, Dave; born David A. Kocourek (football); 1937
Lopez, Al; born Alfonso Ramon Lopez (baseball); 1905
Melville, Sam (actor); ——
Nettles, Graig (baseball); 1944
Norman, Fred; born Fredie Hubert Norman (baseball); 1942
Rainey, Henry Thomas (politician); 1860
Reeves, Jim; born James Travis Reeves (singer/music); 1923
Sanford, Terry; born James Terry Sanford (politician); 1917
Susann, Jacqueline (author); 1921
Teagarden, Jack; born Weldon John Teagarden (music); 1905
Tuttle, Lurene (actress); 1906

AUGUST 21:

Basie, Count; born William Basie (music); 1904
Blake, Marie; born Blossom MacDonald (actress); 1896
Blake, Toe; born Hector Blake (hockey); 1912

Chamberlain, Wilt; born Wilton Norman Chamberlain (basketball); 1936
Clark, Chase Addison (politician); 1883
Davis, Westmoreland (politician); 1859
DeShannon, Jackie (singer); 1944
Dickson, Murry Monroe (baseball); 1916
Dillon, C. Douglas; born Clarence Douglas Dillon (government); 1909
Kennon, Robert Floyd (politician); 1902
Lanier, Willie Edward (football); 1945
Margaret, Princess; born Margaret Rose (British Royalty); 1930
McCormack, Patty; born Patricia Ellen Russo (actress); 1945
McFadin, Bud; born Lewis B. McFadin (football); 1928
Millan, Felix Bernardo (baseball); 1943
Peabody, James Hamilton (politician); 1852
Pindall, Xenophon Overton (politician); 1873
Reay, William (hockey); 1918
Reed, Tracy (actress); 1941
Retzlaff, Pete; born Palmer Edward Retzlaff (football); 1931
Rogers, Kenny; born Kenneth Ray Rogers (singer/music); 1938
Schenkel, Chris; born Christopher Eugene Schenkel (sportscaster); 1923
Staley, Gerry; born Gerald Lee Staley (baseball); 1920
Tully, Tom (actor); 1896
White, George (politician); 1872
Williams, Clarence, III (actor); 1939

AUGUST 22:

Bergner, Elisabeth; born Elizabeth Ettel (actress); 1898
Blackman, Honor (actress); 1926
Bradbury, Ray Douglas (writer); 1920
Cooley, Denton Arthur (medicine); 1920
Dean, Morton (newscaster); 1935
Debussy, Claude; born Achille Claude Debussy (music); 1862
Halleck, Charles Abraham (politician); 1900
Harper, Valerie Cathryn (actress); 1940
Hein, Mel; born Melvin John Hein (football); 1909
Hickey, John Joseph (politician); 1911
Howell, Delles Ray (football); 1948
Kellaway, Cecil (actor); 1891
Koscina, Sylva (actress); 1934
Langley, Elmo Harrell (auto racing); 1929
Lupton, John (actor); ——
Maguire, Paul L. (football); 1933
Marshall, F. Ray; born Freddie Ray Marshall (government); 1928
Mitchell, Tom; born Thomas G. Mitchell (football); 1944
Parker, Dorothy; born Dorothy Rothschild (author/poet); 1893
Presle, Micheline; born Micheline Chassagne (actress); 1922
Sanders, Ken; born Kenneth R. Sanders (football); 1950

Sands, Diana Patricia (actress); 1934
Schang, Wally; born Walter Henry Schang (baseball); 1889
Williams, Cindy; born Cynthia Jane Williams (actress); 1948
Yastrzemski, Carl Michael (baseball); 1939

AUGUST 23:

Boerwinkle, Tom (basketball); 1945
Brannan, Charles Franklin (government); 1903
Bush, Guy Terrell (baseball); 1901
Bushmiller, Ernie (cartoonist); 1905
Cooper, John Sherman (politician); 1901
Crosby, Bob; born George Robert Crosby (music); 1913
Darling, Jean; born Dorothy Jean LeVake (actress/singer); 1925
Eden, Barbara; born Barbara Moorhead (actress/singer); 1934
Ehret, Gloria Jean (golf); 1941
Frey, Lonny; born Linus Reinhard Frey (baseball); 1910
Gunter, Nancy Richey; born Nancy Richey (tennis); 1942
Hudson, Mark Jeffrey Anthony (music/singer/actor/comedian—
        Hudson Brothers); 1951
Jurgensen, Sonny; born Christian Adolph Jurgensen, III
        (football/sportscaster); 1934
Kell, George Clyde (baseball); 1922
Kelly, Gene; born Eugene Curran Kelly (actor/dancer/singer/director);
        1912
Lollar, Sherm; born John Sherman Lollar (baseball); 1924
Masters, Edgar Lee (poet/author); 1869
McBride, Patricia (dancer); 1942
Miles, Vera; born Vera May Ralston (actress); 1929
Mitchell, Dale; born Loren Dale Mitchell (baseball); 1921
O'Hara, Jill (actress/singer); 1947
Perkins, George Clement (politician); 1839
Perry, Oliver Hazard (naval officer); 1785
Primrose, William (music); 1904
Rolph, James Jr. (politician); 1869
Romano, Johnny; born John Anthony Romano (baseball); 1934
Wright, Rayfield; born Larry Rayfield Wright (football); 1945

AUGUST 24:

Balfour, Murray (hockey); 1936
Beerbohm, Sir Max (author); 1872
Bodnar, Gus; born August Bodnar (hockey); 1925
Edwards, Penny; born Millicent Edwards (actress); 1919
Foster, Preston S. (actor); 1901
Goldsworthy, Bill "Goldy"; born William Alfred Goldsworthy (hockey);
        1944
Halverson, Dean (football); 1946
Hooper, Harry Bartholomew (baseball); 1887

James, Dennis (TV host); 1917
Kirby, Durward (announcer/actor); 1912
McCluskey, Roger Frank (auto racing); 1930
O'Rourke, Jim; born James Henry O'Rourke (baseball); 1852
Teicher, Louis (music—Ferrante & Teicher); 1924
Williams, Mason (music); 1938

AUGUST 25:

Andrus, Cecil Dale (politics/government); 1931
Archer, Anne (actress); 1947
Bates, Blanche (actress); 1873
Bernstein, Leonard (music); 1918
Connery, Sean; born Thomas Connery (actor); 1930
Defore, Don J. (actor); 1917
Ferrer, Mel; born Melchior Gaston Ferrer (actor/director); 1917
Fingers, Rollie; born Roland Glen Fingers (baseball); 1946
Gibson, Althea (tennis/golf); 1927
Greene, Richard (actor); 1918
Hall, Monty; born Morton Halparin (TV host/actor); 1923
Harte, Bret; born Francis Brett Hart (author); 1836
Hurley, Robert Augustine (politician); 1895
Johncock, Gordon Walter (auto racing); 1936
Johnson, Darrell Dean (baseball); 1927
Johnson, Van; born Charles Van Johnson (actor); 1916
Keeler, Ruby; born Ethel Hilda Keeler (actress/dancer); 1909
Kelly, Walt; born Walter Crawford Kelly (cartoonist); 1913
Nevil, Dwight D. (golf); 1944
Reed, Willis (basketball); 1942
Rennie, Michael; born Eric Alexander Rennie (actor); 1909
Sanders, Charlie; born Charles Alvin Sanders (football); 1946
Stemkowski, Peter David (hockey); 1943
Wallace, George Corley (politician); 1919

AUGUST 26:

Adams, Sparky; born Earl John Adams (baseball); 1894
Barnes, Jesse Lawrence (baseball); 1892
Booth, John Wilkes (actor/assassin); 1838
Clayton, Jan; born Jane Byral Clayton (actress/singer); 1917
Couzens, James (politician); 1872
Dana, Vic (dancer/singer); 1942
Davis, Jim (actor); 1915
Farmer, Mike (basketball); 1936
Gale, Zona (playwright/author); 1874
Gibbs, Georgia; born Fredda Lipson (actress); 1926
Graham, Ronny (actor/singer/music); 1919
Heinsohn, Tom; born Thomas William Heinsohn (basketball); 1934
Hylton, James Harvey (auto racing); 1935

Isherwood, Christopher William (author/playwright); 1904
Jackson, Larron (football); 1949
Kellner, Alex; born Alexander Raymond Kellner (baseball); 1924
Long, Earl Kemp (politician); 1895
Merrow, Jane (actress); 1941
Miller, Caroline (author); 1903
Moore, Gene; born Eugene Moore, Jr. (baseball); 1909
Robinson, Joseph Taylor (politician); 1872
Sabin, Albert Bruce (medicine); 1906
Savage, Swede; born David Earle Savage, Jr. (auto racing); 1946
Taylor, Maxwell Davenport (army officer); 1901
White, Bill; born William Earl White (hockey); 1939

AUGUST 27:

Bach, Barbara (actress); 1949
Broglio, Ernie; born Ernest Gilbert Broglio (baseball); 1935
Collins, Phil; born Philip Eugene Collins (baseball); 1901
Cunningham, Joe; born Joseph Robert Cunningham (baseball); 1931
Dawes, Charles Gates (Vice President); 1865
Dragon, Daryl (music); 1942
Goldwyn, Samuel; born Samuel Goldfish (producer); 1882
Hamlin, Hannibal (Vice President); 1809
Herrmann, Ed; born Edward Martin Herrmann (baseball); 1946
Johnson, Lyndon Baines (President); 1908
King, Jim; born James Hubert King (baseball); 1932
Levin, Ira (author); 1929
Logan, Jerry Don (football); 1941
Lowrey, Peanuts; born Harry Lee Lowrey (baseball); 1918
McAllister, Susie; born Mary H. McAllister (golf); 1947
Norbeck, Peter (politician); 1870
Pryor, Roger (actor); 1900
Ray, Man; born Emmanuel Rudnitsky (artist/filmmaker); 1890
Raye, Martha; born Margaret Theresa Yvonne O'Reed
          (actress/comedienne/singer); 1916
Sands, Tommy; born Thomas Adrian Sands (singer/actor); 1937
Smith, Nels Hansen (politician); 1884
Van Heusen, Bill; born William Van Heusen (football); 1946
Weld, Tuesday; born Susan Ker Weld (actress); 1943
West, John Carl (politician); 1922

AUGUST 28:

Avellini, Bob; born Robert H. Avellini (football); 1953
Bathgate, Andy; born Andrew James Bathgate (hockey); 1932
Betjeman, Sir John (poet); 1906
Böhm, Karl (music); 1894
Boyer, Charles (actor); 1899
Cowan, Billy Rolland (baseball); 1938

Demarie, John (football); 1945
Gazzara, Ben; born Biago Anthony Gazzara (actor); 1930
Goethe, Johann Wolfgang von (writer); 1749
Gonzalez, Tony; born Andres Antonio Gonzalez (baseball); 1936
Grimm, Charlie; born Charles John Grimm (baseball); 1898
Hayes, Lucy Ware Webb; born Lucy Ware Webb (First Lady); 1831
Kulp, Nancy Jane (actress); 1921
Lane, Harry (politician); 1855
Levene, Sam; born Samuel Levine (actor); 1905
Lynch, Jim; born James E. Lynch (football); 1945
Martin, Ernest; born Ernest Harold Markowitz (producer); 1919
Newlands, Francis Griffith (politician); 1848
Oakland, Simon (actor); 1918
O'Connor, Donald David Dixon Ronald (actor/dancer/singer); 1925
Osmond, Wayne; born M. Wayne Osmond (singer/music—Osmond
    Family); 1951
Piniella, Lou; born Louis Victor Piniella (baseball); 1943
Preus, Jacob Avail Ottesen (politician); 1883
Ryan, Peggy; born Margaret Orene (or O'Rene) Ryan (actress); 1924
Soul, David; born David Solberg (actor/singer); 1943
Torrez, Mike; born Michael Augustine Torrez (baseball); 1946
Ward, Aaron Lee (baseball); 1896
Whitman, Charles Seymour (politician); 1868

AUGUST 29:

Attenborough, Sir Richard Samuel (actor/director); 1923
Bergman, Ingrid (actress); 1915
Cox, Billy; born William Richard Cox (baseball); 1919
Dworshak, Henry Clarence (politician); 1894
Friedkin, William (director); 1939
Geer, Ellen Ware (actress); 1941
Gould, Elliott; born Elliott Goldstein (actor); 1938
Greene, Tony; born Anthony Greene (football); 1949
Harrison, Pat; born Byron Patton Harrison (politician); 1881
Holmes, Oliver Wendell (author); 1809
Hunt, James (auto racing); 1947
Ingres, Jean Auguste Dominque (artist); 1780
Johnson, Joseph Blaine (politician); 1893
Joliat, Aurel (hockey); 1901
Locke, John (philosopher); 1632
Lutz, Bob; born Robert Charles Lutz (tennis); 1947
Macready, George (actor); 1900
Mayer, Dick; born Alvin Richard Mayer (golf); 1924
McDermott, Mickey; born Maurice Joseph McDermott (baseball); 1928
Montgomery, George; born George Montgomery Letz (actor); 1916
Pryor, David Hampton (politician); 1934
Ritchie, Albert Cabell (politician); 1876

Sanford, Isabel Gwendolyn (actress); ——
Scott, Wendell (auto racing); 1921
Sullivan, Barry; born Patrick Francis Barry (actor); 1912
Washington, Dinah; born Ruth Jones (singer); 1924
Young, Pep; born Lemuel Floyd Young (baseball); 1907

AUGUST 30:

Arthur, Ellen Lewis Herndon; born Ellen Lewis Herndon (First Lady); 1837
Ashley, Elizabeth; born Elizabeth Ann Cole (actress); 1939
Bacon, Coy; born Lander McCoy Bacon (football); 1942
Beene, Geoffrey (fashion designer); 1927
Bishop, Julie; born Jacqueline Wells (actress); 1914
Blondell, Joan (actress); 1909
Booth, Shirley; born Thelma Booth Ford (actress); 1907
Bottoms, Timothy (actor); 1951
Cuyler, Kiki; born Hazen Shirley Cuyler (baseball); 1899
Gendron, Smitty; born Jean Guy Gendron (hockey); 1934
Hall, Luther Egbert (politician); 1869
Johnson, Billy; born William Russell Johnson (baseball); 1918
Keller, Billy (basketball); 1947
Killy, Jean Claude (skiing); 1943
Kolb, Jon Paul (football); 1947
Lindell, Johnny; born John Harlan Lindell (baseball); 1916
Lipton, Peggy (actress/singer); 1947
Long, Huey Pierce, Jr. (politician); 1893
MacMurray, Fred; born Frederick Martin MacMurray (actor); 1908
Massey, Raymond Hart (actor); 1896
McGraw, Tug; born Frank Edwin McGraw, Jr. (baseball); 1944
McLaren, Bruce (auto racing); 1937
Miller, Bing; born Edmund John Miller (baseball); 1894
Phipps, Lawrence Cowle (politician); 1862
Resnik, Regina (singer); 1922
Schricker, Henry Frederick (politician); 1883
Seixas, Vic; born Elias Victor Seixas (tennis); 1923
Sparks, John (politician); 1843
Swigert, John Leonard, Jr. (astronaut); 1931
Wells, Kitty; born Muriel Deason (singer/music); 1918
Wilkins, Roy (civil rights leader); 1901
Williams, Ted; born Theodore Samuel Williams (baseball); 1918

AUGUST 31:

Baldwin, Raymond Earl (politician); 1893
Barnes, Pete; born Peter Barnes (football); 1945
Basehart, Richard (actor); 1914
Beliveau, Jean Marc (hockey); 1931
Berlinger, Warren (actor); 1937

Burns, Jack; born John Irving Burns (baseball); 1907
Cleaver, Eldridge; born Leroy Eldridge Cleaver (civil rights leader); 1935
Coburn, James (actor); 1928
Conner, Martin Sennett (politician); 1891
Ferguson, James Edward (politician); 1871
Garrett, Carl (football); 1947
Godfrey, Arthur Michael (entertainer); 1903
Hackett, Buddy; born Leonard Hacker (comedian/actor); 1924
Haymond, Alvin H. (football); 1942
Lerner, Alan Jay (music/playwright); 1918
Litwhiler, Danny; born Daniel Webster Litwhiler (baseball); 1916
March, Frederic; born Ernest Frederick McIntyre Bickel (actor); 1897
Perlman, Itzhak (music); 1945
Plank, Eddie; born Edward Stewart Plank (baseball); 1875
Robinson, Frank (baseball); 1935
Saroyan, William (playwright); 1908
Schary, Dore; born Isidore Schary (actor/producer/director/writer); 1905
Schorr, Daniel Louis (newscaster/author); 1916
West, Charlie; born Charles West (football); 1946

SEPTEMBER 1:

Arlen, Richard; born Cornelius van Mattemore (actor); 1898
Aronson, John Hugo (politician); 1891
Bass, Robert Perkins (politician); 1873
Blyth, Betty; born Elizabeth Blythe Slaughter (actress); 1893
Brown, Johnny Mack (actor); 1904
Burroughs, Edgar Rice (author); 1875
Carty, Rico; born Ricardo Adolfo Jacobo Carty (baseball); 1939
Crane, Arthur Griswold (politician); 1877
De Carlo, Yvonne; born Peggy Yvonne Middleton (actress); 1922
Gassman, Vittorio (actor); 1922
Geiberger, Al; born Allen L. Geiberger (golf); 1937
Gremminger, Henry (football); 1934
Humperdinck, Engelbert (music); 1854
Laird, Melvin Robert (government); 1922
Maddox, Garry Lee (baseball); 1949
Maharis, George (actor); 1928
Marciano, Rocky; born Rocco Francis Marchegiano (boxing); 1923
Miller, Marilyn; born Mary Ellen Reynolds (singer/dancer/actress); 1898
Partee, Dennis (football); 1946
Podolak, Ed; born Edward Joseph Podolak (football); 1947
Prouty, Winston Lewis (politician); 1906
Reuther, Walter Philip (labor leader); 1907
Rodgers, Guy (basketball); 1935

Saimes, George (football); 1941
Saltonstall, Leverett (politician); 1892
Tomlin, Lili; born Mary Jean Tomlin (comedienne/actress/singer); 1936
Twitty, Conway; born Harold Lloyd Jenkins (singer/music); 1933
Ward, James (hockey); 1906
Wilson, Don; born Donald Harlow Wilson (announcer/actor); 1900

SEPTEMBER 2:

Almeida, Laurindo (music); 1917
Amory, Cleveland (writer/conservationist); 1917
Bradshaw, Terry Paxton (football); 1948
Champion, Marge; born Marjorie Celeste Belcher (dancer/actress); 1919
Connors, Jimmy; born James Scott Connors (tennis); 1952
Crosman, Henrietta (actress); 1861
Drury, Allen Stuart (author/journalist); 1918
Elliott, Lenvil (football); 1951
Fasanella, Ralph (artist); 1914
Field, Eugene (poet/journalist); 1850
Johnson, Hiram Warren (politician); 1866
Keating, Tom; born Thomas Arthur Keating (football); 1942
Mitchell, Martha; born Martha Elizabeth Beall (socialite); 1918
Price, Eddie; born Edward J. Price (football); 1929
Purl, Linda (actress); 1955
Smith, Hoke (politician); 1855
Throneberry, Marv; born Marvin Eugene Throneberry (baseball); 1933

SEPTEMBER 3:

Bellmon, Henry L. (politician); 1921
Bentley, Doug; born Douglas Wagner Bentley (hockey); 1916
Boros, Steve; born Stephen Boros (baseball); 1936
Brennan, Eileen; born Verla Eileen Brennan (actress); 1935
Brewer, Tom; born Thomas Austin Brewer (baseball); 1931
Carlisle, Kitty; born Catherine Conn (or Holzman) (actress/singer);
    1914
Castellano, Richard (actor); 1934
Easterling, Ray; born Charles R. Easterling (football); 1949
Eichelberger, Dave; born Martin Davis Eichelberger, Jr. (golf); 1943
Flemming, Bill; born William Norman Flemming (sportscaster); 1926
Hartness, James (politician); 1861
Jackson, Anne; born Anna June Jackson (actress); 1926
Jarrett, Gary Walter (hockey); 1942
Ladd, Alan Wallbridge (actor); 1913
Larochelle, Wildor (hockey); 1906
Maynor, Dorothy; born Dorothy Leigh Mainor (singer); 1910
Motta, Dick; born John Richard Motta (basketball); 1931
Papas, Irene (actress); 1926
Perrine, Valerie (actress/dancer); 1943

Porsche, Ferdinand (auto designer); 1875
Ray, Dixie Lee (politician); 1914
Sprinkle, Ed; born Edward A. Sprinkle (football); 1923
Stanky, Eddie; born Edward Raymond Stanky (baseball); 1916
Thompson, Hank; born Henry William Thompson (music); 1925
Ussery, Bob; born Bobby Nelson Ussery (jockey); 1935
Walker, Mort (cartoonist); 1923
Williams, Clarence (football); 1946
Young, Bob; born Robert Allen Young (football); 1942

SEPTEMBER 4:

Celebrezze, Anthony J.; born Anthony Giuseppe Cilibrizzi
    (government); 1910
Eagleton, Thomas Francis (politician); 1929
Floyd, Ray; born Raymond Floyd (golf); 1942
Ford, Henry, II (auto manufacturer); 1917
Frey, Leonard (actor); 1938
Gaynor, Mitzi; born Francesca Mitzi Marlene de Charney von Gerber
    (dancer/singer/actress); 1930
Griffin, Samuel Marvin (politician); 1907
Harrelson, Ken; born Kenneth Smith Harrelson (baseball); 1941
Harvey, Paul (newscaster/journalist/author); 1918
Jacobs, Lawrence-Hilton (actor); 1953
Kaminska, Ida; born Ida Kaminski (actress); 1899
Milhaud, Darius (music); 1892
Morris, Howard (actor/director); 1919
Olmstead, Murray Bert (hockey); 1926
Osborn, Paul (playwright); 1901
Polk, Sarah Childress; born Sarah Childress (First Lady); 1803
Salt, Jennifer (actress); 1944
Talbert, Billy; born William Franklin Talbert, III (tennis); 1918
Waitkus, Eddie; born Edward Stephen Waitkus (baseball); 1919
Watson, Tom; born Thomas Sturges Watson (golf); 1949
York, Dick; born Richard Allen York (actor); 1928

SEPTEMBER 5:

Bishop, Max Frederick (baseball); 1899
Carnovsky, Morris (actor); 1897
Cherry, Francis Adams (politician); 1908
Danforth, John Claggett (politician); 1936
Devane, William (actor); 1937
Eldridge, Florence; born Florence McKechnie (actress); 1901
Ferguson, John Bowie (hockey); 1938
Fowler, Henry Hamill (government); 1908
Hassett, Buddy; born John Aloysius Hassett (baseball); 1911
Henderson, Moe; born John Murray Henderson (hockey); 1921
Holden, Gloria (actress); 1908

James, Jesse Woodson (outlaw); 1847
Kennedy, Joan Bennett; born Joan Bennett (socialite); 1936
Kenyon, Doris (actress); 1897
Kilmer, Bill; born William Orland Kilmer (football); 1939
Koestler, Arthur (author); 1905
Lahr, Warren (football); 1923
Lajoie, Nap; born Napoleon Lajoie (baseball); 1875
Lawrence, Carol; born Carol Maria Laraia (actress/dancer/singer);
     1932
Louis XIV (King of France); 1638
Mazeroski, Bill; born William Stanley Mazeroski (baseball); 1936
McKinley, William Brown (politician); 1856
Mitchell, John Newton (government); 1913
Newhart, Bob; born George Robert Newhart (comedian/actor); 1929
Palmer, Maria (actress); 1924
Putnam, Duane (football); 1928
Regazzoni, Clay; born Gian-claudio Guiseppe Regazzoni (auto racing);
     1939
Tolar, Charley; born Charles Guy Tolar (football); 1937
Valenti, Jack Joseph (motion picture executive); 1921
Vanderbilt, Cornelius, III (capitalist); 1873
Welch, Raquel; born Raquel Tejada (actress); 1940
Yerby, Frank Garvin (author); 1916
Zanuck, Darryl Francis (producer); 1902

SEPTEMBER 6:

Addams, Jane (humanitarian/social worker); 1860
Bacon, Irving (actor); 1892
Beatty, Morgan (newscaster); 1902
Boone, Ron (basketball); 1946
Bricker, John William (politician); 1893
Chennault, Claire Lee (army air force officer); 1890
Curtin, Jane Therese (actress/comedienne/singer); 1947
Danning, Harry (baseball); 1911
Di Maggio, Vince; born Vincent Paul Di Maggio (baseball); 1912
Faber, Red; born Urban Clarence Faber (baseball); 1888
Finsterwald, Dow (golf); 1929
Janik, Tom; born Thomas A. Janik (football); 1940
Jeffcoat, Hal; born Harold Bentley Jeffcoat (baseball); 1924
Kendrick, John Benjamin (politician); 1857 ·
Kennedy, Joseph Patrick (President's father); 1888
Kruger, Otto (actor); 1885
Lafayette, Marquis de; born Marie Joseph Paul Yves Roch Gilbert Du
     Motier (French soldier & statesman); 1757
McCoy, Mike; born Michael McCoy (football); 1948
Melcher, John (politician); 1924
Rose, Billy; born William Samuel Rosenberg (music/producer); 1899

Rosenbloom, Maxie (boxing/actor); 1904
Thevenow, Tommy; born Thomas Joseph Thevenow (baseball); 1903
Worley, Jo Anne (comedienne/actress); 1937

SEPTEMBER 7:

Allen, Chuck; born Charles R. Allen (football); 1939
Allison, Donnie Joseph (auto racing); 1939
Basserman, Albert (actor); 1865
Bielski, Dick; born Richard Bielski (football); 1932
Blue, Forrest M. Jr. (football); 1945
Brockington, John Stanley (football); 1948
Caldwell, Taylor; born Janet Taylor Caldwell (author); 1900
Crawford, Willie Murphy (baseball); 1946
Davis, Curt; born Curtis Benton Davis (baseball); 1903
De Bakey, Michael Ellis (medicine); 1908
Elizabeth I, Queen of England; 1533
Freitas, Rockne (football); 1945
Hendricks, Thomas Andrews (Vice President); 1819
Holly, Buddy; born Charles Hardin Holley (singer/music); 1936
Inouye, Daniel Ken (politician); 1924
Jones, Bert; born Bertram Hays Jones (football); 1951
Karns, Roscoe (actor); 1893
Kavner, Julie Deborah (actress); 1951
Kazan, Elia; born Elia Kazanjoglous (director/actor); 1909
Kurtenbach, Orland John (hockey); 1936
Law, John Phillip (actor); 1937
Lawford, Peter Aylen (actor); 1923
Lovellette, Clyde (basketball); 1929
Morgan, J.P., Jr.; born John Pierpont Morgan, Jr. (financier); 1867
Moses, Grandma; born Ann Mary Robertson (artist); 1860
Northcott, Baldy; born Laurence Northcott (hockey); 1907
Price, James Hubert (politician); 1878
Priest, Ivy Baker; born Ivy Maude Baker (government); 1905
Quayle, Anthony; born John Anthony Quayle (actor); 1913
Rollins, Sonny; born Theodore Walter Rollins (music); 1929
Roundtree, Richard (actor); 1942
Rudi, Joe; born Joseph Oden Rudi (baseball); 1946
Suggs, Louise (golf); 1923

SEPTEMBER 8:

Barney, Lem; born Lemuel Jackson Barney (football); 1945
Brooke, Hillary; born Beatrice Sofia Mathilda Peterson (actress); 1914
Caesar, Sid; born Isaac Sidney Caesar (comedian/actor); 1922
Cline, Patsy; born Virginia Patterson Hensley (singer); 1932
Connelly, Christopher (actor); 1941
Darcel, Denise; born Denise Billecard (actress); 1925
Daugherty, Duffy; born Hugh Daugherty (football/sportscaster); 1915

Dern, George Henry (politics/government); 1872
Dietz, Howard (music); 1896
Dvorak, Antonin (music); 1841
Feinstein, Alan (actor); 1941
Ford, Wendell Hampton (politician); 1924
Greenwood, L.C. (football); 1946
Hargan, Steve; born Steven Lowell Hargan (baseball); 1942
Jordan, Benjamin Everett (politician); 1896
Ky, Nguyen Cao (South Vietnamese government); 1930
McAvoy, May (actress); 1901
McIntyre, John Archibald (hockey); 1930
Mike-Mayer, Steve (football); 1947
Nunn, Sam; born Samuel Augustus Nunn (politician); 1938
Pepper, Claude Denson (politician); 1900
Rodgers, Jimmie; born James Charles Rodgers (singer); 1897
Secombe, Harry (actor/comedian/singer); 1921
Sellers, Peter (actor/director/producer); 1925
Taft, Robert Alphonse (First family/politician); 1889
Thomas, Elmer; born John William Elmer Thomas (politician); 1876
Vachon, Rogatien Rosaire (hockey); 1945
Wilcoxen, Henry (actor); 1905

SEPTEMBER 9:

Averill, Earl Douglas (baseball); 1931
Baun, Robert T. (hockey); 1936
Bridges, Henry Styles (politician); 1898
Cartwright, Angela (actress); 1952
Chance, Frank Leroy (baseball); 1877
Chandler, Don; born Donald G. Chandler (football); 1934
Frisch, Frankie; born Frank Francis Frisch (baseball); 1898
Grabowski, Jim; born James S. Grabowski (football); 1944
Greer, Jane; born Bettyjane Greer (actress); 1924
Hamilton, Neil; born James Neil Hamilton (actor); 1899
Hoyt, Waite Charles (baseball); 1899
Jimmy The Greek; born Demetrios George Synodinos, changed to James
     G. Snyder (oddsmaker/sports analyst); 1918
Landon, Alf; born Alfred Mossman Landon (politician); 1887
LeBeau, Dick; born Charles Richard LeBeau (football); 1937
Levine, Joseph E. (producer); 1905
McDole, Ron; born Roland McDole (football); 1939
McNichol, Kristy; born Christina Ann McNichol (actress); 1962
Miles, Sylvia (actress); 1932
Mitchell, William DeWitt (government); 1874
Preston, Billy; born William Everett Preston (singer/music); 1946
Redding, Otis (singer/music); 1941
Reinhardt, Max; born Max Goldman (producer/director);
     1873

Richelieu, Cardinal; born Armand Jean du Plessis de Richelieu (French
    prelate & statesman); 1585
Robertson, Cliff; born Clifford Parker Robertson, III (actor); 1925
Robinson, Johnny; born John Nolan Robinson (football); 1938
Sanders, Harland "Colonel" (fast foods magnate); 1890
Theismann, Joe; born Joseph R. Theismann (football); 1949
Tolstoy, Leo; born Lyof Nikolaievitch Tolstoy (author); 1828
Tomlin, Pinky (singer/comedian/actor/music); 1907
Topol; born Chaim Topol (actor); 1935

SEPTEMBER 10:

Astaire, Adele; born Adele Marie Austerlitz (dancer/actress); 1897
Boe, Nils Andreas (politician); 1913
Briscoe, Marlin O. (football); 1945
Buchanan, Buck; born Junious Buchanan (football); 1940
Campbell, Jack M. (politician); 1916
Doolittle, Hilda "H.D." (poet); 1886
Feliciano, José (singer/music); 1945
Geeson, Judy Amanda (actress); 1948
Hale, Sammy; born Samuel Douglas Hale (baseball); 1896
Kelly, George Lange (baseball); 1895
Kluszewski, Ted; born Theodore Bernard Kluszewski (baseball); 1924
Kuralt, Charles Bishop (newscaster); 1934
Lanier, Bob; born Robert Jerry Lanier, Jr. (basketball); 1948
Love, Bessie; born Juanita Horton (actress); 1891
Maris, Roger Eugene (baseball); 1934
Nelson, Larry (golf); 1947
O'Brien, Edmond (actor); 1915
O'Callaghan, Mike Donal N. (politician); 1929
Palmer, Arnold Daniel (golf); 1929
Pappin, James Joseph (hockey); 1939
Pietrosante, Nick; born Nicholas Vincent Pietrosante (football); 1937
Schoenke, Ray; born Raymond Schoenke, Jr. (football); 1941
Sumac, Yma; born Emperatriz Chavarri (singer); 1922
Trudeau, Margaret; born Margaret Joan Sinclair (First Lady of Canada
    /photographer/author); 1948
Waters, Charlie; born Charles T. Waters (football); 1948
Wilson, Stanley Calef (politician); 1879
Wise, Robert (director/producer); 1914

SEPTEMBER 11:

Allen, Henry Justin (politician); 1868
Askew, Reubin O'Donovan (politician); 1928
Bouchard, Butch; born Emile Joseph Bouchard (hockey); 1920
Bryant, Bear; born Paul William Bryant (football); 1913
Damon, Cathryn (actress); ——
Davis Jimmie; born James Houston Davis (politician/singer); 1902

Drake, Betsy (actress); 1923
Falana, Lola (singer/actress); 1943
Henry, O.; born William Sydney Porter (author); 1862
Holliman, Earl; born Anthony Numkena (actor); 1928
Kerr, Robert Samuel (politician); 1896
Landry, Tom; born Thomas Wade Landry (football); 1924
Lawrence, D.H.; born David Herbert Lawrence (author); 1885
Miksis, Eddie; born Edward Thomas Miksis (baseball); 1926
Mitford, Jessica Lucy (author); 1917
Packwood, Robert William (politician); 1932
Rawls, Eugenia; born Mary Eugenia Rawls (actress); 1916
Richards, John Gardiner (politician); 1864
Seymour, Anne; born Anne Seymour Eckert (actress); 1909

SEPTEMBER 12:

Bettenhausen, Tony; born Melvin Eugene Bettenhausen (auto racing); 1916
Binns, Edward (actor); 1916
Blue, Ben; born Benjamin Bernstein (comedian/actor); 1901
Chandler, Spud; born Spurgeon Ferdinand Chandler (baseball); 1907
Chevalier, Maurice Auguste (actor); 1888
Christianson, Theodore (politician); 1883
Chuvalo, George (boxing); 1937
Dailey, Irene (actress); 1920
Fuqua, John William (football); 1946
Gray, Linda (actress); 1941
Helm, Anne (actress); 1938
Hershey, Lewis Blaine (army officer); 1893
Jones, George Glen (singer/music); 1931
Jordan, Phil (basketball); 1933
Keller, Charlie; born Charles Ernest Keller (baseball); 1916
Knopf, Alfred A. (publisher); 1892
Lolich, Mickey; born Michael Stephen Lolich (baseball); 1940
Lopata, Stan; born Stanley Edward Lopata (baseball); 1925
McGee, Frank (newscaster); 1921
Mencken, H.L.; born Henry Louis Mencken (journalist/editor/author); 1880
Moore, Dickie; born John Richard Moore, Jr. (actor/producer/director/writer); 1925
Morse, Ella Mae (singer); 1924
Muldaur, Maria; born Maria Grazia Rosa Domenica d'Amato (singer); 1942
Neely, Ralph Eugene (football); 1943
Owens, Jesse; born James Cleveland Owens (olympic athlete); 1913
Pearson, Albie; born Albert Gregory Pearson (baseball); 1934
Schmidt, Harvey Lester (music); 1929
Seminick, Andy; born Andrew Wasil Seminick (baseball); 1920

Washington, Dave; born David Washington (football); 1948
White, Barry (singer/music); 1944

SEPTEMBER 13:

Anderson, Sherwood (author); 1876
Ashurst, Henry Fountain (politician); 1874
Bain, Barbara; born Millie Fogel (actress); 1934
Bankhead, John Hollis, Sr. (politician); 1842
Bell, Ed; born Edward Allen Bell (football); 1947
Bisset, Jacqueline Fraser (actress); 1944
Brady, Scott; born Gerard Kenneth Tierney (actor); 1924
Charles, Ray (music); 1918
Cleamons, Jim (basketball); 1949
Colbert, Claudette; born Lily Chauchion (actress); 1905
Francis, Emile Percy (hockey); 1926
Fulton, Eileen; born Margaret Elizabeth McLarty (actress); 1934
George, Gladys; born Gladys Clare (actress); 1900
Haymes, Dick; born Richard Benjamin Haymes (singer/actor); 1916
Hayward, Leland (producer); 1902
Kimball, Charles Dean (politician); 1859
Kruger, Alma (actress); 1868
Lee, Thornton Starr (baseball); 1906
McDevitt, Ruth; born Ruth Thane Shoecraft (actress); 1895
Monroe, Bill; born William Smith Monroe (singer/music); 1911
Pershing, John Joseph (army officer); 1860
Priestley, J.B.; born John Boynton Priestley (writer); 1894
Reed, Walter (medicine); 1851
Rhodes, James Allen (politician); 1909
Rommel, Eddie; born Edwin Americus Rommel (baseball); 1897
Roosevelt, Theodore, Jr. (First family/politics/government/author); 1887
Schönberg, Arnold (music); 1874
Shaw, Reta (actress); 1912
Simmons, Donald (hockey); 1931
Stukes, Charlie; born Charles Stukes (football); 1943
Tormé, Mel; born Melvin Howard Tormé (singer/actor); 1923
Warstler, Rabbit; born Harold Burton Warstler (baseball); 1903
Wise, Rick; born Richard Charles Wise (baseball); 1945

SEPTEMBER 14:

Bailey, Josiah William (politician); 1873
Bentley, Eric Russell (writer); 1916
Caldwell, Zöe Ada (actress); 1933
Cherubini, Maria Luigi Carlo Zenobio Salvatore (music); 1760
Clark, Richard Clarence (politician); 1929
Coleman, Jerry; born Gerald Francis Coleman (baseball); 1924
Compton, Karl Taylor (physicist); 1887

Crosby, Mary Frances (actress); 1959
Harley, Joseph Emile (politician); 1880
Hawkins, Jack (actor); 1910
Heatherton, Joey; born Davenie Johanna Heatherton
   (actress/dancer/singer); 1944
Howell, Jim Lee; born James Lee Howell (football); 1914
Khayat, Eddie; born Edward Khayat (football); 1935
McGeorge, Rick; born Richard McGeorge (football); 1948
Medford, Kay; born Kathleen Patricia Regan (or Maggie O'Regin)
   (actress); 1920
Millett, Kate; born Katherine Murray Millett (feminist); 1934
Moore, Clayton (actor); 1914
Nichols, Kid; born Charles Augustus Nichols (baseball); 1869
Palmer, Bud; born John S. Palmer (basketball/sportscaster); 1923
Patteson, Okey Leonidas (politician); 1898
Pavlov, Ivan Petrovich (physiologist); 1849
Presnell, Harve; born George Harve Presnell, II (actor/singer); 1933
Rudd, Hughes Day (newscaster); 1921
Sanger, Margaret; born Margaret Higgins (birth control propagandist);
   1883
Sharma, Barbara (actress/singer/dancer); 1942
Wallis, Hal Brent (producer); 1898
Weaver, De Witt (golf); 1939
Williams, Stan; born Stanley Wilson Williams (baseball); 1935
Williamson, Nicol (actor); 1938

SEPTEMBER 15:

Abrams, Creighton Williams (army officer); 1914
Acuff, Roy Claxton (singer/music); 1903
Adderley, Cannonball; born Julian Edwin Adderley (music); 1928
Athas, Pete; born Peter G. Athas (football); 1947
Benchley, Robert Charles (humorist); 1889
Bugatti, Ettore (auto manufacturer); 1881
Christie, Agatha; born Agatha Mary Clarissa Miller (author); 1890
Conway, Tom; born Thomas Charles Sanders (actor); 1904
Cooper, Jackie; born John Cooper, Jr. (actor/director); 1921
Cooper, James Fenimore (author); 1789
Crosby, Norm; born Norman Lawrence Crosby (comedian); 1927
Darrow, Henry; born Henry Thomas Delgado (actor); 1933
Eisenhower, Milton Stover (educator); 1899
Hatfield, Henry Drury (politician); 1875
Jensen, Leslie (politician); 1892
Lockwood, Margaret; born Margaret Day (actress); 1916
Murray, Kathryn; born Kathryn Hazel Kohnfelder (dancer); 1906
Olsen, Merlin Jay (football/sportscaster/actor); 1940
Ostermueller, Fritz; born Frederick Raymond Ostermueller (baseball);
   1907

Perry, Gaylord Jackson (baseball); 1938
Pike, Alfred (hockey); 1917
Renoir, Jean (director/writer); 1894
Short, Bobby; born Robert Waltrip Short (singer/music); 1926
Singleton, Penny; born Mariana Dorothy Agnes Letitia McNulty (actress); 1908
Smith, Charley; born Charles William Smith (baseball); 1937
Sullivan, Silky; born Cynthia Jan Sullivan (golf); 1937
Taft, William Howard (President); 1857
Walter, Bruno; born Bruno Walter Schlesinger (music); 1876
Welsh, Matthew Empson (politician); 1912
Wray, Fay (actress); 1907

SEPTEMBER 16:

Bacall, Lauren; born Betty Joan Perske (actress); 1924
Baylor, Elgin Gay (basketball); 1934
Benton, Nelson; born Joseph Nelson Benton, Jr. (newscaster); 1924
Byrd, Charlie; born Charles Lee Byrd (music); 1925
Casals, Rosemary (tennis); 1948
Chakiris, George (actor/dancer); 1933
Dean, Priscilla (actress); 1896
DeMarco, Bob; born Robert A. DeMarco (football); 1938
Falk, Peter Michael (actor); 1927
Francis, Anne (actress); 1930
Funt, Allen (producer/TV host); 1914
Gooding, Frank Robert (politician); 1859
Grantham, Larry; born James Larry Grantham (football); 1938
Henning, Linda Kaye (actress/singer); 1944
Hoskins, Bob; born Robert Juan Hoskins (football); 1945
Kelly, Jack (actor); 1927
King, B.B.; born Riley B. King (singer/music); 1925
Knowles, John (author); 1926
McCullough, John Griffith (politician); 1835
Mills, Buster (baseball); 1908
Paige, Janis; born Donna Mae Jaden (or Tjaden) (actress/singer); 1922
Pate, Jerry; born Jerome Kendrick Pate (golf); 1953
Penney, J.C.; born James Cash Penney (merchant); 1875
Severson, Jeff; born Jeffrey Severson (football); 1949
Spencer, Selden Palmer (politician); 1862
Sproul, William Cameron (politician); 1870
Torres, Hector Epitacio (baseball); 1945
Whelan, Arleen (actress); 1916
Woodward, Morgan; born Thomas Morgan Woodward (actor); 1925

SEPTEMBER 17:

Bancroft, Anne; born Anna Maria Luisa Italiano (actress); 1931
Blake, Sheriff; born John Frederick Blake (baseball); 1899

Blanda, George Frederick (football); 1927
Burger, Warren Earl (jurist); 1907
Cepeda, Orlando Manuel (baseball); 1937
Colonna, Jerry; born Gerard Colonna (comedian/actor/music); 1904
Connolly, Maureen Catherine (tennis); 1934
Costello, Dolores (actress); 1904
Critz, Hughie; born Hugh Melville Critz (baseball); 1900
Crocker, Mary Lou; born Mary Lou Daniel (golf); 1944
Crowley, Pat; born Patricia Crowley (actress); 1929
Current, Mike; born Michael W. Current (football); 1945
Howells, Ursula (actress); 1922
Jackson, Phil (basketball); 1945
Kesey, Ken Elton (author); 1935
Lightner, Winnie; born Winifred Josephine Reeves (or Hanson)
     (actress/comedienne/singer/dancer); 1899
Marriott, J. Willard; born John Willard Marriott (hotel & restaurant
     magnate); 1900
McDowall, Roddy; born Roderick Andrew McDowall (actor); 1928
Moss, Stirling Craufurd (auto racing); 1929
Overton, John Holmes (politician); 1875
Patterson, Isaac Lee (politician); 1859
Pittman, Vail Montgomery (politician); 1883
Provost, Claude (hockey); 1933
Ralston, Esther (actress); 1902
Ritter, John; born Jonathan Southworth Ritter (actor); 1948
Solomon, Harold Charles (tennis); 1952
Stafford, Thomas Patton (astronaut); 1930
Terry, Charles Laymen, Jr. (politician); 1900
Turpin, Ben (actor); 1874
Vinson, Helen; born Helen Rulfs (actress); 1907
Webb, Earl; born William Earl Webb (baseball); 1898
Williams, Hank, Sr.; born Hiram King Williams (singer); 1923
Wine, Bobby; born Robert Paul Wine (baseball); 1938
Yarbrough, Lee Roy (auto racing); 1938

SEPTEMBER 18:

Avalon, Frankie; born Francis Thomas Avallone (actor/singer); 1939
Backstrom, Ralph (hockey); 1937
Bates, John Lewis (politician); 1859
Blake, Robert; born Michael James Vijencio Gubitosi (actor); 1933
Brazzi, Rossano (actor); 1916
Brett, Ken; born Kenneth Alven Brett (baseball); 1948
Clarke, John Hessin (jurist); 1857
Clurman, Harold Edgar (director/author); 1901
Cook, Bun; born Frederick Joseph Cook (hockey); 1903
Diefenbaker, John George (Canadian government); 1895
Garbo, Greta; born Greta Lovisa Gustafsson (actress); 1905

Gerry, Peter Goelet (politician); 1879
Haddix, Harvey (baseball); 1925
Hitchcock, Gilbert Monell (politician); 1859
Howe, Syd; born Sydney Harris Howe (hockey); 1911
Johnson, Samuel (writer); 1709
Kirk, Phyllis; born Phyllis Kirkegaard (actress); 1926
Martin, Edward (politician); 1879
Rhodes, John Jacob, 2nd (politician); 1916
Rochester; born Eddie Anderson (actor); 1905
Rodgers, Jimmie; born James Frederick Rodgers (singer); 1933
Sistrunk, Otis (football); 1947
Toski, Bob; born Robert Toski (golf); 1927
Townes, Harry (actor); 1918
Uhle, George Ernest (baseball); 1898
Warden, Jack (actor); 1920

SEPTEMBER 19:

Ard, Jim (basketball); 1948
Benton, Brook; born Benjamin Franklin Peay (singer); 1931
Blalock, Jane B. (golf); 1945
Brown, Harold (government); 1927
Brown, Larry; born Lawrence Brown, Jr. (football); 1947
Conerly, Charlie; born Charles A. Conerly (football); 1921
Cortez, Ricardo; born Jacob Krantz (actor); 1899
Daniel, Clifton; born Elbert Clifton Daniel, Jr. (journalist); 1912
Danton, Ray (actor/director); 1931
Elliot, Cass "Mama Cass"; born Ellen Naomi Cohen (singer); 1941
Etten, Nick; born Nicholas Raymond Thomas Etten (baseball); 1913
Evans, Bergen Baldwin (writer); 1904
Farmer, Frances (actress); 1910
Ferguson, Joe; born Joseph Vance Ferguson (baseball); 1946
Harris, Rosemary Ann (actress); 1930
Haynes, Abner (football); 1937
Jaworski, Leon (attorney); 1905
Lindsay, Margaret; born Margaret Kies (actress); 1910
Mantooth, Randolph (actor); ——
McCallum, David (actor); 1933
Morgan, Joe Leonard (baseball); 1943
Morton, Rogers C.B.; born Rogers Clark Ballard Morton
    (politics/government); 1914
Pasternak, Joseph (producer); 1901
Payne, Freda (singer); 1945
Peterson, Walter Rutherford (politician); 1922
Pittman, Key (politician); 1872
Powell, Lewis Franklin, Jr. (jurist); 1907
Randolph, Jay; born Jennings Randolph, Jr. (sportscaster); 1934
Short, Chris; born Christopher Joseph Short (baseball); 1937

Snider, Duke; born Edwin Donald Snider (baseball); 1926
Thebom, Blanche (singer); 1919
Truex, Ernest (actor); 1889
Turley, Bob; born Robert Lee Turley (baseball); 1930
Twiggy; born Leslie Hornby (model/actress); 1949
Wallace, Lurleen Burns; born Lurleen Burns (politician); 1926
West, Adam; born William West Anderson (actor); 1929
Westfall, Ed; born Vernon Edwin Westfall (hockey); 1940
Wickersham, George Woodward (government); 1858
Wicks, Sidney (basketball); 1949
Williams, Paul Hamilton (singer/actor/music); 1940

SEPTEMBER 20:

Auerbach, Red; born Arnold Jacob Auerbach (basketball); 1917
Blair, Matt; born Albert Matthew Blair (football); 1951
Bonura, Zeke; born Henry John Bonura (baseball); 1908
Byrd, Butch; born George E. Byrd (football); 1941
Cameron, JoAnna (actress)——
Dankworth, John (music); 1927
Dressen, Chuck; born Charles Walter Dressen (baseball); 1898
Gillett, James Norris (politician); 1860
Grant, Gogi; born Audrey Brown (singer); 1924
Lafleur, Guy Damien (hockey); 1951
Lindstrom, Pia (actress/newscaster); 1938
Loren, Sophia; born Sofia Villani Scicolone (actress); 1934
Meara, Anne (comedienne/actress); 1929
More, Kenneth (actor); 1914
Morton, Jelly Roll; born Ferdinand Joseph Le Menthe (music); 1885
Nobis, Tommy; born Thomas Henry Nobis (football); 1943
Nugent, Elliott (director/actor/writer); 1900
Palmer, Peter Webster (actor/singer); 1931
Rey, Fernando; born Fernando Casado Arambillet (actor); 1915
Roberts, Rachel (actress/singer); 1927
Schwellenbach, Lewis Baxter (politics/government); 1894
Sinclair, Upton Beall (author); 1878
Taylor, Jim; born James Charles Taylor (football); 1935
Tresh, Tom; born Thomas Michael Tresh (baseball); 1937

SEPTEMBER 21:

Addams, Dawn (actress); 1930
Auker, Elden LeRoy (baseball); 1910
Ball, Lewis Heisler (politician); 1861
Bradley, Grace (actress); 1913
Butcher, Max; born Albert Maxwell Butcher (baseball); 1910
Childress, Richard Reed (auto racing); 1945
Curran, Pat; born Patrick M. Curran (football); 1945
Dill, Clarence Cleveland (politician); 1884

Engle, Clair (politician); 1911
Flagg, Fannie; born Frances Carlton Flagg (comedienne/actress); 1944
Gibson, Henry; born Henry Bateman (comedian/actor/poet); 1935
Gilmore, Artis (basketball); 1949
Hagman, Larry Martin (actor); 1931
Holton, Linwood; born Abner Linwood Holton, Jr. (politician); 1923
Jordan, Hamilton; born William Hamilton McWhorter Jordan
    (government); 1944
McClanahan, Brent Anthony (football); 1950
McDowell, Sam; born Samuel Edward Thomas McDowell (baseball);
    1942
Morenz, Howie; born Howarth William Morenz (hockey); 1902
Murray, Bill (actor/comedian/singer); 1950
Rucker, Reggie; born Reginald Joseph Rucker (football); 1947
Smith, Elmer John (baseball); 1892
Stimson, Henry Lewis (government); 1867
Taylor, Margaret Mackall Smith; born Margaret Mackall Smith (First
    Lady); 1788
Van Peebles, Melvin (producer/director/writer/actor/music); 1932
Wells, H.G.; born Herbert George Wells (author); 1866

SEPTEMBER 22:

Alexander, Katherine (actress); 1901
Aspromonte, Ken; born Kenneth Joseph Aspromonte (baseball); 1932
Benson, Elmer Austin (politician); 1895
Boone, Debby; born Deborah Ann Boone (singer—Boone Family); 1956
Carmichael, Harold; born Lee H. Carmichael (football); 1949
Dierker, Larry; born Lawrence Edward Dierker (baseball); 1946
Faraday, Michael (chemist/physicist); 1791
Flagstead, Ira James (baseball); 1893
Gibron, Abe; born Abraham Gibron (football); 1925
Hottelet, Richard C.; born Richard Curt Hottelet (newscaster); 1917
Houseman, John; born Jacques Haussmann
    (actor/producer/director/writer); 1902
James, Joni; born Joan Carmella Babbo (singer); 1930
Johansson, Ingemar (boxing); 1932
Lasorda, Tom; born Thomas Charles Lasorda (baseball); 1927
Lemon, Bob; born Robert Granville Lemon (baseball); 1920
Muni, Paul; born Frederich Weisenfreund (actor); 1895
Roche, Eugene (actor); 1928
Scott, Martha Ellen (actress); 1914
Stone, Richard Bernard (politician); 1928
Strudwick, Shepperd (actor); 1907
Sullivan, Frank; born Francis John Sullivan (humorist); 1892
Vanderbilt, Alfred Gwynne (sportsman); 1912
Von Stroheim, Erich, Sr.; born Erich Oswald Hans Carl Maris Von
    Nordenwall (actor/director); 1885

White, Albert Blakeslee (politician); 1856

SEPTEMBER 23:

Blakely, Colin (actor); 1930
Charles, Ray; born Ray Charles Robinson (singer/music); 1930
Clark, Tom (or Thomas) Campbell (government/jurist); 1899
Collins, Bill; born William Collins (golf); 1928
Coltrane, John William (music); 1926
Creed, Clifford Ann (golf); 1938
Fezler, Forrest (golf); 1949
Hays, George Washington (politician); 1863
Lippmann, Walter (writer); 1889
Moss, Frank Edward (politician); 1911
O'Neal, Emmet (politician); 1853
Peaks, Clarence E. (football); 1935
Petersen, Paul (actor/singer); 1944
Pidgeon, Walter David (actor); 1897
Rooney, Mickey; born Joe Yule, Jr. (actor); 1920
Roosevelt, Elliott (First family); 1910
Russell, Gail (actress); 1924
Schneider, Romy; born Rosemarie Allbach-Retty (actress); 1938
Springsteen, Bruce (singer/music); 1949
Stewart, Lefty; born Walter Cleveland Stewart (baseball); 1900
Suzuki, Pat; born Chiyoko Suzuki (actress); 1931
Talmadge, Eugene (politician); 1884
Vogel, Bob; born Robert L. Vogel (football); 1941
Woodward, Woody; born William Frederick Woodward (baseball); 1942

SEPTEMBER 24:

Armour, Tommy; born Thomas Dickson Armour (golf); 1895
Blue, Robert Donald (politician); 1898
Carey, Bob (auto racing); 1905
Crawford, Cheryl (producer); 1902
Ellender, Allen Joseph (politician); 1891
Fitzgerald, F. Scott; born Francis Scott Key Fitzgerald (author); 1896
Foss, Eugene Noble (politician); 1858
Gates, Larry; born Lawrence Wheaton Gates (actor); 1915
Gonzalez, Mike; born Miguel Angel Cordero Gonzalez (baseball); 1890
Greene, Joe (football); 1946
Henson, Jim; born James Maury Henson (muppeteer); 1936
Hoernschemeyer, Hunchy; born Robert J. Hoernschemeyer (football);
     1925
Lindley, Audra (actress); 1918
Mackey, John (football); 1941
MacRae, Sheila; born Sheila Margot Stephens (actress/singer); 1924
Marshall, John (jurist); 1755
McKay, Jim; born James Kenneth McManus (sportscaster); 1921

Metcalf, Terry; born Terrance Randolph Metcalf (football); 1951
Montoya, Joseph Manuel (politician); 1915
Newley, Anthony George (actor/singer/music); 1931
Porter, Don (actor); 1912
Taylor, Robert Lewis (author/journalist); 1912
Vollmer, Clyde Frederick (baseball); 1921
Walker, Dixie; born Fred Walker (baseball); 1910
Williams, Clancy; born Clarence Williams (football); 1942
Young, John Watts (astronaut); 1930
Zook, John Eldon (football); 1947

SEPTEMBER 25:

Benton, James (football); 1916
Bonavena, Oscar (boxing); 1942
Braun, Carl (basketball); 1927
Burns, Catherine (actress); 1945
Douglas, Michael (actor/producer); 1944
Ericson, John; born Joseph Meibes (actor); 1926
Faulkner, William Harrison; born William Harrison Falkner (author); 1897
Fletcher, Allen Miller (politician); 1853
Gould, Glenn Herbert (music); 1932
Hamill, Mark (actor); 1951
McAdoo, Bob; born Robert McAdoo (basketball); 1951
Morgan, Gil (golf); 1946
Pellington, Bill; born William A. Pellington (football); 1927
Pescarolo, Henri (auto racing); 1942
Prowse, Juliet (dancer/actress); 1936
Ray, Aldo; born Aldo daRe (actor); 1926
Rizzuto, Phil; born Philip Francis Rizzuto (baseball); 1917
Schuh, Harry F. (football); 1942
Shostakovich, Dmitri Dmitrievitch (music); 1906
Vadnais, Carol (hockey); 1945
Walden, Robert (actor); 1943
Walters, Barbara (newscaster/TV host); 1931
White, Kevin Hagen (politician); 1929
Williams, Anson; born Anson William Heimlick (actor/singer); 1949

SEPTEMBER 26:

Allen, Lucius Oliver, Jr. (basketball); 1947
Anderson, Lynn Rene (singer/actress); 1947
Anderson, Melissa Sue (actress); 1962
Bragg, Mike; born Michael E. Bragg (football); 1946
Brimsek, Frank; born Francis Charles Brimsek (hockey); 1915
Britton, Barbara; born Barbara Brantingham (actress); 1919
Casper, Dave; born David John Casper (football); 1951
Cook, Donald (actor); 1901

Douglas, Donna; born Doris Smith (actress); 1939
Duncan, Dave; born David Edwin Duncan (baseball); 1945
Eliot, T.S.; born Thomas Stearns Eliot (poet); 1888
Gericault, Jean Louis André Théodore (artist); 1791
Gershwin, George; born Jacob Gershvin (music); 1898
Gwenn, Edmund (actor); 1875
Holden, Fay; born Dorothy Fay Hammerton (actress); 1894
Jameson, Joyce Beverly (actress); 1932
LaLanne, Jack (physical fitness expert); 1914
London, Julie; born Julie Peck (actress/singer); 1926
McCord, Kent; born Kent McWhirter (actor); 1942
Newton-John, Olivia (singer/actress); 1947
O'Neal, Patrick Wisdom (actor); 1927
Pope Paul VI; born Giovanni Battista Montoni; 1897
Raft, George; born George Ranft (actor/dancer); 1895
Ray, Robert D. (politician); 1928
Robbins, Marty; born Martin David Robinson (singer/auto racing);
    1925
Schenken, Tim (auto racing); 1943
Shantz, Bobby; born Robert Clayton Shantz (baseball); 1925
Tucker, Thurman Lowell (baseball); 1917

SEPTEMBER 27:

Adams, Samuel (statesman/patriot); 1722
Auchincloss, Louis Stanton (author); 1917
Cassidy, Shaun Paul (singer/actor); 1958
Conrad, William (actor/director/producer/singer); 1920
Dickinson, Gardner, Jr. (golf); 1927
Edmondson, James Howard (politician); 1925
Ervin, Sam; born Samuel James Ervin, Jr. (politician); 1896
Glynn, Martin Henry (politician); 1871
Hall, Dick; born Richard Wallace Hall (baseball); 1930
Harris, Labron, Jr. (golf); 1941
Hogan, Robert (actor); ——
Jarman, Claude, Jr. (actor); 1934
Lowe, Paul Edward (football); 1936
MacNeil, Allister Wences (hockey); 1935
Meadows, Jayne; born Jane Cotter (actress); 1923
Morris, Greg (actor); 1934
Nolan, Kathleen (actress); 1933
Patterson, John Malcolm (politician); 1921
Penn, Arthur Hiller (director); 1922
Percy, Charles Harting (politician); 1919
Pesky, Johnny; born John Michael Paveskovich (baseball); 1919
Sutherland, Gary Lynn (baseball); 1944
Thompson, Sada Carolyn (actress); 1929
Whitworth, Kathy; born Kathrynne Ann Whitworth (golf); 1939

Wyatt, Whit; born John Whitlow Wyatt (baseball); 1907
Youmans, Vincent Millie (music); 1898

SEPTEMBER 28:

Bardot, Brigitte; born Camille Javal (actress); 1933
Capp, Al; born Alfred Gerald Caplin (cartoonist); 1909
Caravaggio, Michelangelo Amerighi da; born Michelangelo Merisi
    (artist); 1573
Clemenceau, Georges Eugène Benjamin (French government); 1841
Clower, Jerry (comedian); 1926
Cone, Frederick Preston (politician); 1871
Cooper, Prentice (politician); 1895
Crampton, Bruce Sidney (golf); 1935
Edwards, Turk; born Albert Glen Edwards (football); 1907
Evans, Al; born Alfred Hubert Evans (baseball); 1916
Evans, Norm; born Norman Earl Evans (football); 1942
Finch, Peter; born William Peter Ingle-Finch (actor); 1916
Flanders, Ralph Edward (politician); 1880
Fournier, Jack; born Jacques Frank Fournier (baseball); 1892
Gernert, Dick; born Richard Edward Gernert (baseball); 1928
Gray, Mel; born Melvin Dean Gray (football); 1948
Harmon, Tom; born Thomas Dudley Harmon (football/sportscaster);
    1919
Jackson, Grant Dwight (baseball); 1942
King, Ben E.; born Benjamin Nelson (singer/music); 1938
Latimore, Frank; born Frank Kline (actor); 1925
Marble, Alice (tennis); 1913
Mastroianni, Marcello (actor); 1923
Rice, Elmer Leopold; born Elmer Leopold Reizenstein
    (playwright/author/producer); 1892
Rivers, L. Mendel; born Lucius Mendel Rivers (politician); 1905
Schmeling, Max; born Maximilian Schmeling (boxing); 1905
Smith, Margaret (golf); 1936
Stang, Arnold (actor); 1925
Sullivan, Ed; born Edward Vincent Sullivan (TV host/journalist); 1902
Taylor, Charley; born Charles Robert Taylor (football); 1941
Tuck, William Munford (politician); 1896
Wiebe, Arthur Walter Ronald (hockey); 1913
Windom, William (actor); 1923
Witt, Whitey; born Ladislaw Waldemar Wittkowski (baseball); 1895

SEPTEMBER 29:

Antonioni, Michelangelo (director); 1912
Autry, Gene; born Orvon Gene Autry (actor/singer/business executive);
    1907
Bruce, Virginia; born Helen Virginia Briggs (actress); 1910
Corcoran, Donna (actress); 1942

Eischeid, Mike; born Michael D. Eischeid (football); 1940
Ekberg, Anita (actress/singer); 1931
Fermi, Enrico (physicist); 1901
Forrest, Steve; born William Forrest Andrews (actor); 1924
Gabor, Jolie; born Jancsi Tilleman (actress/mother); 1896
Garson, Greer (actress); 1908
Harkness, Richard Long (newscaster); 1907
Howard, Trevor Wallace (actor); 1916
Kahn, Madeline Gail (actress); 1942
Kramer, Stanley E. (producer/director); 1913
Lewis, Jerry Lee (singer/music); 1935
Linville, Larry; born Lawrence Lavon Linville (actor); 1939
Marshall, Brenda; born Ardis Anderson Gaines (or Ardis Ankerson)
    (actress); 1915
McCloskey, Paul Norton, Jr. (politician); 1927
McCormick, Mike; born Michael Francis McCormick (baseball); 1938
McShane, Ian (actor); 1942
Miszuk, John (hockey); 1940
Nelson, Horatio (English naval officer); 1758
Patton, Jimmy; born James R. Patton, Jr. (football); 1933
Phillips, Bum; born Oail Andrew Phillips (football); 1923
Reese, Rich; born Richard Benjamin Reese (baseball); 1941
Scott, Lizabeth Virginia; born Emma Matzo (actress); 1922
Spong, William Belsen, Jr. (politician); 1920
Taylor, Altie (football); 1947
Tower, John Goodwin (politician); 1925
Vines, H. Ellsworth (tennis/golf); 1911
Wilcox, David (football); 1942
Zarley, Kermit (golf); 1941

SEPTEMBER 30:

Allen, Johnny; born John Thomas Allen (baseball); 1904
Ames, Nancy; born Nancy Hamilton Alfaro (singer/actress); 1937
Baker, Kenny; born Kenneth Lawrence Baker (singer/actor); 1912
Bancroft, George (actor); 1882
Buchtel, Henry Augustus (politician); 1847
Capote, Truman; born Truman Streckfus Persons (author/actor); 1924
Cooper, Ben (actor); 1930
Corey, Jill; born Norma Jean Speranza (singer); 1935
Dickinson, Angie; born Angeline Brown (actress); 1931
Dorn, Philip; born Hein Van Der Niet (or Fritz van Dungen) (actor);
    1901
Guy, William Lewis (politician); 1919
Kerr, Deborah; born Deborah Jane Kerr-Trimmer (actress); 1921
Kramm, Joseph (playwright/director/actor); 1907
Langer, William (politician); 1886
Maddox, Lester Garfield (politician); 1915

Mathis, Johnny; born John Royce Mathis (singer); 1935
Maurer, Andy; born Andrew Lee Maurer (football); 1948
McCoo, Marilyn (singer); 1943
Mickey, John Hopwood (politician); 1845
Miller, Charles R. (politician); 1857
Nagel, Anne; born Ann Dolan (actress); 1912
Park, Chung Hee (South Korean government); 1917
Podres, Johnny; born John Joseph Podres (baseball); 1932
Powell, Jody; born Joseph Lester Powell, Jr. (government); 1943
Robbins, Austin (basketball); 1944
Roberts, Robin Evan (baseball); 1926
Sasser, James Ralph (politician); 1936
Taliaferro, James Piper (politician); 1847

OCTOBER 1:

Andrews, Julie; born Julia Elizabeth Wells (singer/actress); 1935
Archer, George William (golf); 1939
Baldwin, Faith (writer); 1893
Blood, Henry Hooper (politician); 1872
Bosley, Tom; born Thomas Edward Bosley (actor); 1927
Boyd, Bob; born Robert Richard Boyd (baseball); 1925
Carew, Rod; born Rodney Cline Carew (baseball); 1945
Carter, Jimmy; born James Earl Carter, Jr. (President); 1924
Chapman, Lonny; born Lon Leonard Chapman
        (actor/director/playwright); 1920
Dobler, Conrad Francis (football); 1950
Fong, Hiram Leong (politician); 1907
Gardner, Frank (auto racing); 1932
Harris, Richard St. John (actor); 1930
Harrison, Caroline Scott; born Caroline Scott (first wife of Benjamin
        Harrison/First Lady); 1832
Harvey, Laurence; born Larushka Mischa Skikne (actor); 1928
Hiller, Chuck; born Charles Joseph Hiller (baseball); 1935
Holloway, Stanley Augustus (actor); 1890
Horowitz, Vladimir (music); 1904
Kastner, Peter Bernard Joshua (actor); 1943
Laaveg, Paul Martin (football); 1948
Martin, Charles Henry (politician); 1863
Matthau, Walter; born Walter Matuschanskayasky (actor); 1920
Morath, Max Edward (music); 1926
Nunley, Frank (football); 1945
Peppard, George (actor); 1928
Rehnquist, William Hubbs (jurist); 1924
Russell, Jim; born James William Russell (baseball); 1918
Sloane, Everett H. (actor); 1909
Stevens, Stella; born Estelle Eggleston (actress); 1936
Untermeyer, Louis (anthologist); 1885

Villella, Edward Joseph (dancer); 1936
Whitmore, James Allen, Jr. (actor); 1921
Williams, Roger; born Louis Weertz (music); 1926
Yorty, Sam; born Samuel William Yorty (politician); 1909
Young, Douglas (hockey); 1908

OCTOBER 2:

Abbott, Bud; born William Alexander Abbott (actor/comedian); 1895
Drake, Charles; born Charles Ruppert (actor); 1914
Felker, Clay S. (editor/publisher); 1925
Gandhi, Mahatma; born Mohandas Karamchand Gandhi (Hindu
    leader); 1869
Goldsmith, Paul (auto racing); 1927
Green, Theodore Francis (politician); 1867
Greene, Graham; born Henry Graham Greene (author); 1904
Gunn, Moses (actor); 1929
Hayden, Carl Trumbull (politician); 1877
Hindenburg, Paul Ludwig Hans Anton von Beneckendorff und von
    (German military & government); 1847
Hull, Cordell (politics/government); 1871
Ley, Willy; born Robert Willey Ley (writer); 1906
MacFarland, Spanky; born George Emmett MacFarland (actor); 1928
Marx, Groucho; born Julius Henry Marx (comedian/actor/TV host—
    Marx Brothers); 1890
McLean, Don (singer); 1945
Reed, Rex Taylor (journalist/actor); 1938
Robertson, Bob; born Robert Eugene Robertson (baseball); 1946
Stevens, Wallace (poet); 1879
Weger, Mike; born Michael Roy Weger (football); 1945
Wills, Maury; born Maurice Morning Wills (baseball/sportscaster);
    1932
Wilson, Earl; born Robert Earl Wilson (baseball); 1934

OCTOBER 3:

Apodaca, Jerry (politician); 1934
Berg, Gertrude; born Gertrude Edelstein (actress); 1899
Bruhn, Erik Belton Evers (dancer); 1928
Checker, Chubby; born Ernest Evans (singer); 1941
Clarke, Fred Clifford (baseball); 1872
Ferris, Barbara Gillian (actress); 1940
Fraser, Neale Andrew (tennis); 1933
Gregory, Jack; born Earl Gregory (football); 1944
Hall, Glenn Henry (hockey); 1931
Harding, William Lloyd (politician); 1877
Hebenton, Andy; born Andrew Alex Hebenton (hockey); 1929
Hensley, Pamela Gail (actress); 1950
Hunter, Kermit Houston (playwright); 1910

Montague, Andrew Jackson (politician); 1862
Oland, Warner; born Johan Warner Oland (actor); 1880
Peterson, Russell Wilbur (politician); 1916
Post, Emily; born Emily Price (etiquette authority); 1873
Ratelle, Jean (hockey); 1940
Ratner, Payne Harry (politician); 1896
Rhue, Madlyn (actress); 1934
Skinner, Bob; born Robert Ralph Skinner (baseball); 1931
Vidal, Gore (author); 1925
Warren, Fuller (politician); 1905
Winfield, Dave; born David Mark Winfield (baseball); 1951
Wolf, Thomas Clayton (author); 1900

OCTOBER 4:

Brumm, Don; born Donald A. Brumm (football); 1941
Crosetti, Frank Peter Joseph (baseball); 1910
Davis, Clifton D. (actor/singer); 1945
Farr, Felicia (actress); 1932
Fuller, Frances (actress); 1907
Hadfield, Victor Edward (hockey); 1940
Hardman, Cedrick Ward (football); 1948
Hayes, Rutherford Birchard (President); 1822
Heston, Charlton; born Charlton Carter (actor); 1922
Huff, Sam; born Robert Lee Huff (football); 1934
Johnson, Eliza McCardle; born Eliza McCardle (First Lady); 1810
Keaton, Buster; born Joseph Francis Keaton (actor/comedian); 1895
Mabey, Charles Rendell (politician); 1877
McNamara, Patrick Vincent (politician); 1894
Millet, Jean Francois (artist); 1814
Murray, Jan; born Murray Janowitz (comedian/actor/TV host); 1917
Orr, Jimmy; born James E. Orr, Jr. (football); 1935
Repulski, Rip; born Eldon John Repulski (baseball); 1927
Runyan, Damon; born Alfred Damon Runyan (journalist/author); 1884
Sarandon, Susan; born Susan Tomaling (actress); 1946
Saunders, Lori; born with surname Hines (actress); 1941
Thomas, Earl (football); 1948
Van Dyke, Leroy Frank (singer/music); 1929
Wade, Billy; born William J. Wade, Jr. (football); 1930
Wilson, Jerrel D. (football); 1941

OCTOBER 5:

Arthur, Chester Alan (President); 1830
Brown, Peter (actor); ——
Bryant, Bonnie (golf); 1943
Chabot, Lorne (hockey); 1900
Cilento, Diane (actress); 1933
Conacher, Roy Gordon (hockey); 1916

Dana, Bill (comedian/actor); 1924
Davis, Gail; born Betty Jeanne Grayson (actress); 1925
Dresser, Louise; born Louise Kerlin (actress); 1878
Gordon, Richard Francis, Jr. (astronaut); 1929
Hitchcock, Frank Harris (government); 1867
Holmes, Robert (football); 1945
Homeier, Skip; born George Vincent Homeier (actor); 1930
Johns, Glynis (actress); 1923
Johnson, Si; born Silas Kenneth Johnson (baseball); 1906
Kosco, Andy; born Andrew John Kosco (baseball); 1941
Logan, Joshua Lockwood, Jr. (playwright/director); 1908
Ludden, Allan Ellsworth (actor/TV host/producer); 1917
Morgan, Robert Burren (politician); 1925
Morrison, Cameron (politician); 1869
Pleasence, Donald (actor); 1919
Prentice, Dean Sutherland (hockey); 1932
Shivers, Allan (politician); 1907
Smith, Adrian (basketball); 1936
Watkins, Larry; born Lawrence Watkins (football); 1946
West, Sammy; born Samuel Filmore West (baseball); 1904
Worsham, Lew; born Lewis Elmer Worsham (golf); 1917

OCTOBER 6:

Alexander, Shana; born Shana Ager (journalist/author); 1925
Allen, Frank Gilman (politician); 1874
Clines, Gene; born Eugene Anthony Clines (baseball); 1946
Cowan, Jerome Palmer (actor); 1897
Ekland, Britt (actress); 1942
Gaynor, Janet; born Laura Gainor (actress); 1906
Graham, Fred Patterson (newscaster/author/attorney); 1931
Grote, Jerry; born Gerald Wayne Grote (baseball); 1942
Heyerdahl, Thor (ethnologist/explorer); 1914
Lind, Jenny; born Johanna Maria Lind (singer); 1820
Lombard, Carole; born Jane Alice Peters (actress); 1908
McMahon, Brien; born James O'Brien McMahon (politician); 1903
Richter, Les; born Leslie A. Richter (football); 1930
Sharkey, Jack; born Josef Paul Zukauskas (or Cuckoschay) (boxing);
    1902
Sholtz, David (politician); 1891
Westinghouse, George (inventor); 1846
Wills, Helen Newington (tennis); 1906

OCTOBER 7:

Allyson, June; born Ella Geisman (actress); 1917
Baumholtz, Frankie; born Frank Conrad Baumholtz (baseball); 1918
Bergman, Gary Gunnar (hockey); 1938
Bohr, Niels Henrik David (atomic physicist); 1885

Boucher, Frank (hockey); 1901
Cardenal, Jose Rosario Domec (baseball); 1943
Churchill, Sarah (actress); 1914
Dantine, Helmut (actor/director); 1917
Dell, Gabriel; born Gabriel del Vecchio (actor); 1919
Devine, Andy; born Jeremiah Schwartz (actor); 1905
Drake, Alfred; born Alfredo Capurro (actor/singer); 1914
Drivas, Robert Chris; born Robert Choromokos (actor); 1938
Hale, Frederick (politician); 1874
Hatton, Grady Edgebert (baseball); 1922
Keiser, Herman (golf); 1914
Klein, Chuck; born Charles Herbert Klein (baseball); 1904
Lynn, Diana; born Dolores "Dolly" Loehr (actress); 1926
MacInnes, Helen Clark (author); 1907
Martino, Al; born Alfred Cini (singer); 1927
McLean, George Payne (politician); 1857
Monroe, Vaughn Wilton (music); 1911
Muhammad, Elijah; born Elijah Poole (religious leader); 1897
Mulhall, Jack; born John Joseph Francis Mulhall (actor); 1887
Muse, Clarence (actor); 1889
Naulls, Willie (basketball); 1934
Ransdell, Joseph Eugene (politician); 1858
Rather, Bo; born David Elmer Rather (football); 1950
Reynolds, Joyce (actress); 1924
Riley, James Whitcomb (poet); 1853
Stewart, Martha; born Martha Haworth (singer/actress); 1922
Wallace, Henry Agard (Vice President); 1888

OCTOBER 8:

Bailey, Carl Edward (politician); 1894
Barnard, Christiaan N. (medicine); 1922
Barrett, Rona; born Rona Burstein (journalist); 1936
Blease, Coleman Livingston (politician); 1868
Chase, Chevy; born Cornelius Crane Chase (comedian/actor); 1943
Conn, Billy; born William David Conn (boxing); 1917
Egan, William Allen (politician); 1914
Gardner, John William (government); 1912
Hay, John Milton (statesman); 1838
Hewitt, Bill; born William Ernest Hewitt (football); 1909
Holshouser, James Eubert, Jr. (politician); 1934
Jackson, Jesse Louis (civil rights leader); 1941
Kirkpatrick, Ed; born Edgar Leon Kirkpatrick (baseball); 1944
Matsunaga, Spark Masayuki (politician); 1916
McGrath, Jack; born John James McGrath (auto racing); 1919
Moses, Wally; born Wallace Moses (baseball); 1910
Murtaugh, Danny; born Daniel Edward Murtaugh (baseball); 1917
Olson, James (actor); 1930

Perón, Juan Domingo; born Juan Domingo Perón Sosa (Argentine government); 1895
Randell, Ron; born Ronald Egan Randell (actor); 1918
Rickenbacker, Eddie; born Edward Vernon Rickenbacker (aviator); 1890
Rodgers, Pepper; born Franklin C. Rodgers (football); 1931
Sparks, Chauncey (politician); 1884
Stolle, Fred; born Frederick S. Stolle (tennis); 1938

OCTOBER 9:

Andrews, Edward (actor); 1914
Browne, Jackson (singer/music); 1950
Burkemo, Walter (golf); 1918
Catton, Bruce; born Charles Bruce Catton (author); 1899
Cook, Bill; born William Osser Cook (hockey); 1896
Docking, Robert Blackwell (politician); 1925
Finch, Robert Hutchinson (government); 1925
Folsom, James Elisha (politician); 1908
Hardin, Clifford Morris (government); 1915
Herrick, Myron Timothy (politician); 1854
Hershberger, Mike; born Norman Michael Hershberger (baseball); 1939
Hunt, E. Howard; born Everett Howard Hunt, Jr. (government); 1918
Hutchinson, Josephine (actress); 1898
Jones, Wesley Livsey (politician); 1863
Kitchin, William Walton (politician); 1866
Lennon, John Winston (singer/music); 1940
Marquard, Rube; born Richard William Marquard (baseball); 1899
McFarland, Ernest William (politician); 1894
Moose, Bob; born Robert Ralph Moose (baseball); 1947
Myers, Henry Lee (politician); 1862
O'Malley, Walter (baseball); 1903
Patek, Freddie; born Frederick Joseph Patek (baseball); 1944
Pepitone, Joe; born Joseph Anthony Pepitone (baseball); 1940
Peters, Garry Lorne (hockey); 1942
Risen, Arnold (basketball); 1924
Rollins, Al; born Elwin Ira Rollins (hockey); 1926
St. John, Howard Sidney (actor); 1905
Sewell, Joe; born Joseph Wheeler Sewell (baseball); 1898
Sim, Alastair (actor); 1900
Sinden, Donald (actor); 1923
Welsh, Jim; born James Daniel Welsh (baseball); 1902

OCTOBER 10:

Baker, Floyd Wilson (baseball); 1916
Berger, Wally; born Walter Antone Berger (baseball); 1905
Bottolfsen, Clarence A. (politician); 1891
Cavendish, Henry (chemist/physicist); 1731

Culp, Curley (football); 1946
Daniel, Price; born Marion Price Daniel (politician); 1910
Devlin, Bruce (golf/sportscaster); 1937
Downs, Johnny (actor/singer); 1913
Elcar, Dana; born Ibson Dana Elcar (actor); 1927
Friebus, Florida (actress); 1909
Green, Johnny; born John W. Green (music); 1908
Griswold, Morley (politician); 1890
Hayes, Helen; born Helen Hayes Brown (actress); 1900
Jaeckel, Richard Hanley (actor); 1926
King, John William (politician); 1918
Laprade, Edgar Louis (hockey); 1919
Le Vander, Harold L. (politician); 1910
Looney, Joe Don (football); 1942
Marsalis, Jim; born James Marsalis (football); 1945
Mechem, Merritt Cramer (politician); 1870
Metcalf, Victor Howard (government); 1853
Miller, Nathan Lewis (politician); 1868
Monk, Thelonious Sphere (music); 1918
Pinter, Harold (playwright); 1930
Shimkus, Joanna (actress); 1944
Smith, Dallas (hockey); 1941
Stevenson, Adlai Ewing, III (politician); 1930
Stone, John Thomas (baseball); 1905
Tenace, Gene; born Fiore Gino Tennaci (baseball); 1946
Thompson, Bill; born William A. Thompson (football); 1946
Tucker, Tanya Denise (singer); 1958
Verdi, Giuseppe Fortunino Francisco (music); 1813
Vereen, Ben Augustus (actor/dancer/singer); 1946
Watteau, Jean-Antoine (artist); 1684

OCTOBER 11:

Alsop, Joseph Wright, Jr. (journalist); 1910
Boone, Lindy; born Linda Lee Boone (singer—Boone Family); 1955
Bueno, Maria Ester Audion (tennis); 1939
Case, Norman Stanley (politician); 1888
Clark, Dutch; born Earl Clark (football); 1906
Courtney, Chuck; born Charles Courtney (golf); 1940
Day, J. Edward; born James Edward Day (government); 1914
Ginsberg, Joe; born Myron Nathan Ginsberg (baseball); 1926
Groh, Gary (golf); 1944
Guerra, Mike; born Fermin Romero Guerra (baseball); 1912
Leibman, Ron (actor); 1937
Morrison, James Stewart Hunter (hockey); 1931
Revson, Charles (cosmetics); 1906
Robbins, Jerome; born Jerome Rabinowitz
         (director/choreographer/dancer); 1918

Roosevelt, Eleanor; born Anna Eleanor Roosevelt (First Lady); 1884
Stirling, Linda; born Louise Schultz (actress); 1921
Stone, Harlan Fiske (government/jurist); 1872
Twining, Nathan Farragut (air force officer); 1897
Warwick, Knobby; born Grant David Warwick (hockey); 1921
West, Dottie; born Dorothy Marie Marsh (singer/music); 1932

OCTOBER 12:

Anton, Susan (singer/actress); 1950
Bailey, Willis Joshua (politician); 1854
Beckert, Glenn Alfred (baseball); 1940
Cronin, Joe; born Joseph Edward Cronin (baseball); 1906
Dane, Karl; born Karl Daen (actor); 1886
Delaplane, Stan; born Stanton Hill Delaplane (journalist); 1907
Dunne, Edward Fitzsimons (politician); 1853
Ferrell, Rick; born Richard Benjamin Ferrell (baseball); 1905
Garn, Jake; born Edwin Jacob Garn (politician); 1932
Gordone, Charles (playwright); 1925
Gore, Howard Mason (politics/government); 1887
Gregory, Dick; born Richard Claxton Gregory (comedian/civil rights
    leader); 1932
Harrison, Dwight (football); 1948
Hill, Jerry; born Gerald A. Hill (football); 1939
Jarrett, Ned Miller (auto racing); 1932
Jeffrey, Lawrence Joseph (hockey); 1940
Judge, Thomas Lee (politician); 1934
Kubek, Tony; born Anthony Christopher Kubek, Jr.
    (baseball/sportscaster); 1935
Little, Sally (golf); 1951
Marin, Jack (basketball); 1944
Mesta, Perle; born Perle Skirvin (socialite); 1891
Pavarotti, Luciano (singer); 1935
Rivers, Joan; born Joan Molinsky (comedienne/writer); 1935
Smith, Al; born Alfred John Smith (baseball); 1907
Vaughn, Heidi (actress); ——
Weintraub, Phil; born Philip Weintraub (baseball); 1907

OCTOBER 13:

Allin, Brian (golf); 1944
Bailey, Bob; born Robert Sherwood Bailey (baseball); 1942
Bilbo, Theodore Gilmore (politician); 1877
Bruce, Lenny; born Leonard Alfred Schneider (comedian); 1925
Clifton, Nat; born Nathaniel Clifton (basketball); 1922
Davis, Tom; born Thomas R. Davis (football); 1934
Day, Laraine; born La Raine Johnson (actress); 1917
Dumbrille, Douglas (actor); 1889
Gann, Ernest Kellogg (author); 1910

Garfunkel, Art; born Arthur Garfunkel (singer/actor); 1941
Gilroy, Frank Daniel (playwright); 1925
Gorman, Cliff (actor); 1936
Hayes, Frankie; born Franklin Witman Hayes (baseball); 1914
Herblock; born Herbert Lawrence Block (cartoonist); 1909
Hershfield, Harry (humorist/journalist/cartoonist); 1885
Higuchi, Chako; born Hisako Higuchi (golf); 1945
Hooper, Ben Walter (politician); 1870
Kerr, Anita (singer/music); 1927
Langtry, Lily; born Emily Le Breton (actress); 1853
Mathews, Eddie; born Edwin Lee Mathews (baseball); 1931
Montand, Yves; born Yvo (or Ivo) Livi (actor); 1921
Osmond, Marie; born Olive Marie Osmond (singer—Osmond Family);
     1959
Pitcher, Molly; born Mary Ludwig (revolutionary heroine); 1754
Powell, Wesley (politician); 1915
Rich, Irene; born Irene Luther (actress); 1891
Richter, Conrad Michael (author); 1890
Russell, Nipsey (comedian/actor/poet); 1924
Saban, Lou; born Louis H. Saban (football); 1921
Sargent, John Garibaldi (government); 1860
Shaw, Wilbur; born Warren Wilbur Shaw (auto racing); 1902
Steiwer, Frederick (politician); 1883
Thatcher, Margaret; born Margaret Hilda Roberts (British
     government); 1925
Tiffin, Pamela; born Pamela Kimberley Tiffin Wonso (actress); 1942
Tillstrom, Burr (puppeteer); 1917
Waddell, Rube; born George Edward Waddell (baseball); 1876
Walker, Robert Hudson (actor); 1914
Wilde, Cornel Louis (actor/producer/director); 1915
Willson, Augustus Everett (politician); 1846
Wilson, Demond (actor); 1946
Yost, Eddie; born Edward Frederick Joseph Yost (baseball); 1926

OCTOBER 14:

Arendt, Hannah (historian); 1906
Birdwell, Dan; born Daniel L. Birdwell (football); 1940
Brecheen, Harry David (baseball); 1914
Cummings, E.E.; born Edward Estlin Cummings (author); 1894
Dean, John Wesley, III (government); 1938
Eisenhower, Dwight David; born David Dwight Eisenhower (President);
     1890
Evigan, Greg; born Gregory Ralph Evigan (actor); 1953
Gish, Lillian Diana; born Lillian Diana de Guiche (actress); 1896
Hammill, John (politician); 1875
Harper, Tommy (baseball); 1940
Holman, Rufus Cecil (politician); 1877

Holt, W. Elmer; born William Elmer Holt (politician); 1884
Hume, Benita (actress); 1906
Johnson, Essex L. (football); 1946
Joiner, Charlie; born Charles Joiner (football); 1947
Jones, Allan (singer/actor); 1907
Kelton, Pert Lizzette (actress); 1907
Key, Wade; born Allan Wade Key (football); 1946
Krake, Skip; born Philip Gordon Krake (hockey); 1943
Kuechenberg, Bob; born Robert John Kuechenberg (football); 1947
Lamar, Joseph Rucker (jurist); 1857
Lauren, Ralph; born Ralph Lifshitz (fashion designer); 1939
Mansfield, Katherine; born Kathleen Beauchamp (author); 1888
Montgomery, Melba (singer); 1938
Moore, Roger George (actor); 1927
Oliver, Al; born Albert Oliver (baseball); 1946
Penn, William (colonist); 1644
Rentzel, Lance; born Thomas Lance Rentzel (football); 1943
Shamsky, Art; born Arthur Louis Shamsky (baseball); 1941
Snead, J.C.; born Jesse Carlyle Snead (golf); 1941
Webber, Robert L. (actor); 1928

OCTOBER 15:

Adkins, Homer Martin (politician); 1890
Beirne, Jim; born James Beirne (football); 1946
Carpenter, Richard Lynn (singer/music); 1945
Claire, Ina; born Ina Fagan (actress); 1892
Darwell, Jane; born Patti Woodward (actress); 1879
Economaki, Chris; born Christopher Constantine Economaki
        (sportscaster/journalist); 1920
Feld, Fritz (actor); 1900
Galbraith, John Kenneth (economist); 1908
Gray, Sam; born Samuel David Gray (baseball); 1897
Haas, Mule; born George William Haas (baseball); 1903
Harder, Mel; born Melvin LeRoy Harder (baseball); 1909
Haskell, Peter Abraham (actor); 1934
Jordan, Chester Bradley (politician); 1839
Lavin, Linda (actress/singer); 1937
Lee, Robert E.; born Robert Edwin Lee (playwright/music); 1918
LeRoy, Mervyn (producer/director); 1900
Lotz, Dick; born Richard Lotz (golf); 1942
Marshall, Penny; born Carole Penny Marshall (actress); 1942
McKiernan, John Sammon (politician); 1911
Morin, Milt; born Milton Morin (football); 1942
Nietzsche, Friederich Wilhelm (philosopher); 1844
Olcott, Ben Wilson (politician); 1872
Palmer, Jim; born James Alvin Palmer (baseball); 1945
Peters, Jean; born Elizabeth Jean Peters (actress); 1926

Puzo, Mario (author); 1920
Quintero, Jose Benjamin (director/producer); 1924
Schlesinger, Arthur Meier, Jr. (historian); 1917
Snow, C.P.; born Charles Percy Snow (author); 1905
Stevenson, Chuck; born Charles Stevenson (auto racing); 1919
Sullivan, John L.; born John Lawrence Sullivan (boxing); 1858
Tanner, Roscoe; born Leonard Roscoe Tanner, III (tennis); 1951
Trout, Robert (newscaster); 1908
Wilson, Edith Bolling; born Edith Bolling (second wife of Woodrow
     Wilson/First Lady); 1872
Wodehouse, P.G.; born Pelham Grenville Wodehouse (author); 1881

OCTOBER 16:

Anthony, Tony (actor); 1937
Ardrey, Robert (author); 1908
Caster, Richard (football); 1948
Colson, Chuck; born Charles Wendell Colson (government); 1931
Conrad, Michael (actor); ——
Counts, Mel (basketball); 1941
Darnell, Linda; born Monetta (or Manetta) Eloyse (or Eloisa) Darnell
     (actress); 1921
De Busschere, Dave; born David Albert De Busschere (basketball); 1940
Douglas, William Orville (jurist); 1898
Evans, Daniel Jackson (politician); 1925
Gillett, Frederick Huntington (politician); 1851
Goslin, Goose; born Leon Allen Goslin (baseball); 1900
Grass, Günter Wilhelm (author); 1927
Hansen, Clifford Peter (politician); 1912
Kaempfert, Bert (music); 1923
Lansbury, Angela Brigid (actress/singer); 1925
Lewis, D.D.; born Dwight Douglas Lewis (football); 1945
Lott, George M., Jr. (tennis); 1906
MacKenzie, Joyce (actress); ——
McCarver, Tim; born James Timothy McCarver (baseball); 1941
Michaels, Walt; born Wladek Majka (football); 1929
O'Neill, Eugene Gladstone (playwright); 1888
Somers, Suzanne; born Suzanne Marie Mahoney (actress); 1948
Webster, Noah (lexicographer/author); 1758
Wilde, Oscar Fingal O'Flahertie Wills (poet/playwright); 1854

OCTOBER 17:

Abel, Elie (newscaster); 1920
Adams, Julie; born Betty May Adams (actress); 1926
Anders, William Alison (astronaut); 1933
Arthur, Jean; born Gladys Georgianna Greene (actress); 1905
Breslin, Jimmy (journalist/author); 1930
Byington, Spring (actress); 1892

Caraway, Thaddeus Horatius (politician); 1871
Cherry, Robert Gregg (politician); 1891
Clift, Montgomery; born Edward Montgomery Clift (actor); 1920
Cole, Cozy; born William R. Cole (music); 1909
Derringer, Paul; born Samuel Paul Derringer (baseball); 1906
Garland, Beverly Lucy; born Beverly Lucy Fessenden (actress); 1926
Gilliam, Jim "Junior"; born James William Gilliam (baseball); 1928
Hayworth, Rita; born Margarita Carmen Cansino (actress); 1918
Hudson, Bill; born William Louis Hudson, II
        (music/singer/actor/comedian—Hudson Brothers); 1949
Hunt, Marsha; born Marcia Virginia Hunt (actress); 1917
Johnson, Richard Mentor (Vice President); 1781
Johnson, Ron; born Ronald Adolphus Johnson (football); 1947
Kidder, Margot (actress); 1948
Klippstein, Johnny; born John Calvin Klippstein (baseball); 1927
Knievel, Evel; born Robert Craig Knievel (daredevil/actor); 1938
Lansing, Robert (government); 1864
Mabry, Thomas Jewett (politician); 1884
Marley, John (actor); 1914
Marsh, Marian; born Violet Krauth (actress); 1913
Miller, Arthur (playwright); 1915
Pope John Paul I; born Albino Luciani; 1912
Poston, Tom (actor); 1921
Puckett, Gary (singer/music); 1942
Ryan, Irene; born Irene Noblette (actress); 1902
Schnelker, Bob; born Robert Schnelker (football); 1928
Walston, Bobby; born Robert Walston (football); 1928

OCTOBER 18:

Austin, Bill; born William Austin (football); 1928
Berry, Charlie; born Charles Francis Berry (baseball); 1902
Berry, Chuck; born Charles Edward Anderson Berry (singer/music);
        1926
Carey, Andy; born Andrew Arthur Carey (baseball); 1931
Cullenbine, Roy Joseph (baseball); 1915
Davis, Harold Lenoir (author); 1896
Dawber, Pam (actress/singer); 1951
Ditka, Mike; born Michael Keller Dyzcko (football); 1939
Dowler, Boyd H. (football); 1937
Elkins, Hillard (producer); 1929
Frazier, James Beriah, Sr. (politician); 1856
Goldsworthy, Leroy D. (hockey); 1908
Gregg, Forrest; born Alvin Forrest Gregg (football); 1933
Helms, Jesse Alexander, Jr. (politician); 1921
Hopkins, Miriam; born Ellen Miriam Hopkins (actress); 1902
Horton, Willie Wattison (baseball); 1942
Hurst, Fannie (author); 1889

Jackson, Keith MacKenzie (sportscaster); 1928
Knoop, Bobby; born Robert Frank Knoop (baseball); 1938
Lenya, Lotte; born Karoline Blamauer (singer/actress); 1898
March, Mush; born Harold C. March (hockey); 1908
Mercouri, Melina; born Maria Amalia Mercouri (actress); 1915
Moran, Erin (actress); 1961
Navratilova, Martina (tennis); 1956
Nyro, Laura (singer/music); 1947
Oswald, Lee Harvey (accused assassin); 1939
Scott, George C.; born George Campbell Scott (actor); 1927
Stevens, Inger; born Inger Stensland (actress); 1934
Troup, Bobby; born Robert William Troup (actor/singer/music); 1918
Trudeau, Pierre Elliott (Canadian government); 1919
Venable, Evelyn (actress); 1913

OCTOBER 19:

Alomar, Sandy; born Conde Santos Alomar (baseball); 1943
Anderson, Jack Northman (journalist); 1922
Beatty, Robert (actor); 1909
Brazle, Al; born Alpha Eugene Brazle (baseball); 1913
Brown, Three Fingers; born Mordecai Peter Centennial Brown
    (baseball); 1876
Browne, Kathie (actress); ——
Burke, Arleigh Albert (naval officer); 1901
Carter, Amy Lynn (First family); 1967
Dickey, Lynn; born Clifford Lynn Dickey (football); 1949
Garrison, Sean (actor); 1937
Ghezzi, Victor (golf); 1912
Haynes, Lloyd; born Samuel Lloyd Haynes (actor); 1935
Jefferson, Martha Wayles; born Martha Wayles (First Lady); 1748
Kalmbach, Herbert Warren (government); 1921
Le Carré, John; born David John Moore Cornwell (author); 1931
LoBianco, Tony (actor); 1936
Max, Peter; born with surname Finkelstein (artist); 1937
Melchionni, Bill (basketball); 1944
Nader, George (actor); 1921
Reed, Clyde Martin (politician); 1871
Reed, Robert (actor); 1932
Riley, Jeannie C.; born Jeannie Carolyn Stephenson (singer); 1945
Ward, Simon (actor); 1941
Worters, Roy (hockey); 1900

OCTOBER 20:

Ash, Roy Lawrence (government); 1918
Bernardi, Herschel (actor); 1923
Bratkowski, Zeke; born Edmund R. Bratkowski (football); 1931
Brent, Evelyn "Eve"; born Mary Elizabeth Riggs (actress); 1899

Brothers, Joyce; born Joyce Diane Bauer (psychologist); 1928
Brown, Roosevelt (football); 1932
Buchwald, Art; born Arthur Buchwald (journalist/humorist/author);
   1925
Campbell, Bruce Douglas (baseball); 1909
Chase, Barrie (dancer); 1934
Chase, Charlie; born Charles Parrott (comedian/actor); 1893
Corcoran, Noreen (actress); 1943
Curtis, Isaac Fisher (football); 1950
Dumont, Margaret; born Margaret Baker (actress); 1889
Dunn, Michael; born Gary Neil Miller (actor); 1934
Francis, Arlene; born Arlene Francis Kazanjian (actress); 1908
Green, Fred Warren (politician); 1872
Hall, David (politician); 1930
Hart, Dolores; born Dolores Hicks (actress); now Mother Dolores (nun);
   1938
Herreid, Charles N. (politician); 1857
Hinkle, James Fielding (politician); 1864
Ingram, Rex (actor); 1895
Ives, Charles Edward (music); 1874
Jackson, Wanda (singer/music); 1937
Jones, Grandpa; born Louis Marshall Jones (singer/music/comedian);
   1913
Lammons, Pete; born Peter S. Lammons, Jr. (football); 1943
Lodge, John Davis (actor/politician); 1903
Lugosi, Bela; born Bela Lugosi Blasko (actor); 1882
Major, Elliott Woolfolk (politician); 1864
Mantle, Mickey Charles (baseball); 1931
Marichal, Juan Antonio (baseball); 1937
Minton, Sherman (jurist); 1890
Morse, Wayne Lyman (politician); 1900
Neagle, Anna; born Florence Marjorie Robertson (actress); 1904
Nixon, Marian (actress); 1904
Orbach, Jerry; born Jerome Orbach (actor/singer); 1935
Rogers, Will, Jr. (actor); 1911
Thoms, Art; born Arthur William Thoms (football); 1946
Vanderbilt, Alfred Gwynne (capitalist); 1877
Wren, Sir Christopher (architect); 1632

OCTOBER 21:

Beecher, Janet; born Janet B. Meysenburg (actress); 1884
Brewer, Carl Thomas (hockey); 1938
Brown, Georgia; born Lillian Claire Laizer Getel Klot (actress/singer);
   1933
Butler, Skip; born William Foster Butler (football); 1947
Cameron, Ralph Henry (politician); 1863
Christman, Mark; born Marquette Joseph Christman (baseball); 1913

Clark, Joseph Sill, Jr. (politician); 1901
Coleridge, Samuel Taylor (poet); 1772
Dierking, Connie (basketball); 1936
Fisher, Carrie Frances (actress); 1956
Ford, Whitey; born Edward Charles Ford (baseball); 1928
Gillespie, Dizzy; born John Birks Gillespie (music); 1917
Hill, James Webster (football); 1946
Lee, Bill; born William Cruther Lee (baseball); 1909
Le Guin, Ursula Kroeber (author); 1929
McConaughy, James Lukens (politician); 1887
Mikkelsen, Vern; born Arild Verner Agerskov Mikkelsen (basketball); 1928
Nobel, Alfred Bernhard (inventor/industrialist/philanthropist); 1883
Piccolo, Brian; born Louis Brian Piccolo (football); 1943
Rosburg, Bob; born Robert Rosburg (golf/sportscaster); 1926
Russell, Bill; born William Ellis Russell (baseball); 1948
Smith, Hulett Carlson (politician); 1918
Uhlaender, Ted; born Theodore Otto Uhlaender (baseball); 1939
Waller, William L. (politician); 1926

OCTOBER 22:

Bennett, Constance Campbell (actress); 1904
Bernhardt, Sarah; born Henriette Rosine Bernard (actress); 1844
Chafee, John Hubbard (politician); 1922
Chapman, Oscar Littleton (government); 1896
Clements, Earle C. (politician); 1896
Deneuve, Catherine; born Catherine Dorléac (actress); 1943
Drake, Frances; born Frances Dean (actress); 1908
Fontaine, Joan; born Joan de Beauvoir De Havilland (actress); 1917
Foxx, Jimmie; born James Emory Foxx (baseball); 1907
Funicello, Annette (actress); 1942
Green, Mitzi; born Elizabeth Keno (actress); 1920
Hall, James; born James Brown (actor); 1900
Kingsley, Sidney; born Sidney Kirschner (playwright); 1906
Lessing, Doris; born Doris May Taylor (author); 1919
Liszt, Franz (music); 1811
Mallory, Boots; born Patricia Mallory (actress); 1913
Martin, Slater (basketball); 1925
Martinelli, Giovanni (singer); 1885
Pihos, Pete; born Peter Louis Pihos (football); 1923
Previn, Dory; born Dory Langdon (music); 1929
Roberts, Tony; born David Anthony Roberts (actor); 1939
Stettinius, Edward Reilly, Jr. (government); 1900
Walker, Harry William (baseball); 1916
Wood, Wilbur Forrester, Jr. (baseball); 1941
Wyeth, N.C.; born Newell Convers Wyeth (artist); 1882

OCTOBER 23:

Anderson, Clinton Presba (politics/government); 1895
Blackwell, Ewell (baseball); 1922
Bressler, Rube; born Raymond Bloom Bressler (baseball); 1894
Bunning, Jim; born James Paul David Bunning (baseball); 1931
Byrne, Frank M. (politician); 1858
Carlson, George Alfred (politician); 1876
Carson, Johnny; born John William Carson (comedian/TV host); 1925
Crichton, Michael; born John Michael Crichton (author/director); 1942
Daly, James Firman (actor); 1918
Dors, Diana; born Diana Fluck (actress); 1931
Drillon, Gordie; born Gordon Arthur Drillon (hockey); 1914
Gray, Coleen; born Doris Jensen (actress); 1922
Heinz, H. John, III; born Henry John Heinz, III (politician); 1938
Henry, Sugar Jim; born Samuel James Henry (hockey); 1920
Hill, Winston Cordell (football); 1941
Kimbrough, Emily (author); 1899
Kinard, Bruiser; born Frank M. Kinard (football); 1914
O'Connor, Una; born Agnes Teresa McGlade (actress); 1880
O'Neil, Sally; born Virginia Louise Concepta Noonan (actress); 1908
Pelé; born Edson Arantes do Nascimento (soccer); 1940
Rizzo, Frank Lazarro (politician); 1920
Rodriguez, Chi Chi; born Juan A. Rodriguez Vila (golf); 1935
Shero, Fred Alexander (hockey); 1925
Stephens, Vern; born Vernon Decatur Stephens (baseball); 1920
Stevenson, Adlai Ewing (Vice President); 1835
Sullivan, Billy; born William Joseph Sullivan, Jr. (baseball); 1910
Tashman, Lilyan; born Lillian Tashman (actress); 1899
Yankowski, Ron; born Ronald William Yankowski (football); 1946

OCTOBER 24:

Beisler, Randy; born Randall Beisler (football); 1944
Bluege, Ossie; born Oswald Louis Bluege (baseball); 1900
Clarke, George W. (politician); 1852
Hart, Moss (playwright/producer/director); 1904
Kelley, Clarence Marion (government); 1911
Mainbocher; born Main Rousseau Bocher (fashion designer); 1890
Marcol, Chester; born Czelslaw C. Marcol (football); 1949
Masters, Margee; born Margaret Ann Masters (golf); 1934
Nelson, David (actor); 1936
Oddie, Tasker Lowndes (politician); 1870
Sherman, James Schoolcraft, (Vice President); 1855
Swift, Doug; born Douglas Swift (football); 1948
Thorndike, Dame Sybil (actress); 1882
Tittle, Y.A.; born Yelberton Abraham Tittle (football); 1926
Trujillo Molina, Rafael Leonidas (Dominican Republic government);
    1891

Watson, Phil; born Phillippe Henri Watson (hockey); 1914

OCTOBER 25:

Aldridge, Vic; born Victor Eddington Aldridge (baseball); 1893
Beaty, Zelmo (basketball); 1941
Bizet, Georges; born Alexandre César Léopold Bizet (music); 1838
Byrd, Richard Evelyn (naval officer/polar explorer); 1888
Carroll, Leo G. (actor); 1892
Commager, Henry Steele (historian); 1902
Cook, Barbara Nell (actress/singer); 1927
Cowens, Dave; born David William Cowens (basketball); 1948
Driscoll, Alfred Eastlack (politician); 1902
Erbe, Norman Arthur (politician); 1919
Franciosa, Anthony; born Anthony George Papaleo (actor); 1928
Ingarfield, Earl Thompson (hockey); 1934
Issel, Dan (basketball); 1948
McGuire, Biff; born William Joseph McGuire, Jr. (actor); 1926
Pearl, Minnie; born Sarah Ophelia Colley (comedienne/singer); 1912
Picasso, Pablo; born Pablo Ruiz y Picasso (artist); 1881
Reddy, Helen (singer/actress/music); 1941
Ross, Marion (actress); 1928
Schweikart, Russell Louis (astronaut); 1935
Shute, Denny; born Herman Densmore Shute (golf); 1904
Strauss, Johann (music); 1825
Thomson, Bobby; born Robert Brown Thomson (baseball); 1923
Zukor, Eugene J. (producer); 1897

OCTOBER 26:

Barnet, Charlie; born Charles Daly Barnet (music); 1913
Brewer, Albert Preston (politician); 1928
Brooke, Edward William (politician); 1919
Brown, Ed; born Charles Edward Brown (football); 1928
Carnera, Primo (boxing); 1906
Coogan, Jackie; born John Leslie Coogan, Jr. (actor); 1914
Crawford, Jack; born John Shea Crawford (hockey); 1916.
Foreman, Chuck; born Walter Eugene Foreman (football); 1950
Fulks, Joe; born Joseph Fulks (basketball); 1921
Gillman, Sid; born Sidney Gillman (football); 1911
Gronouski, John Austin (government); 1919
Hundley, Rod; born Rodney Hundley (basketball); 1934
Jackson, Mahalia (singer); 1911
Knight, John Shively (publisher); 1894
Meschery, Tom (basketball); 1938
Sanudo, Cesar (golf); 1943
Scarlatti, Domenico (music); 1685
Shah of Iran; born Mohammad Reza Pahlavi; 1919
Smith, Jaclyn Ellen (actress); 1947

Stirnweiss, Snuffy; born George Henry Stirnweiss (baseball); 1918
Trotsky (or Trotski), Leon; born Leib (or Liv) Davydovich Bronstein
    (Russian government); 1879
Vanderbilt, William Kissam (capitalist); 1878
Warner, H.B.; born Henry Bryon Warner (actor); 1876
Wills, William Henry (politician); 1882

OCTOBER 27:

Babcock, Tim (politician); 1919
Bagnold, Enid Algerine (author); 1889
Boles, John (actor); 1895
Carson, Jack; born John Elmer Carson (actor); 1910
Cornelius, Kathy; born Katharine McKinnon (golf); 1932
Costa, Dave; born David J. Costa (football); 1941
Cramer, Floyd (music); 1933
Davis, James John (politics/government); 1873
Dee, Ruby; born Ruth Ann Wallace (actress); 1924
Erickson, Leif; born William Wycliffe Anderson (actor); 1911
Fabray, Nanette; born Ruby Bernadette Nanette Fabares
    (actress/singer); 1920
George, Bill; born William George (football); 1930
Haldeman, H.R. "Bob"; born Harry Robbins Haldeman (government);
    1926
Herschler, Ed C. (politician); 1918
Kennedy, Jayne; born Jayne Harrison (actress/sportscaster); 1951
Kiner, Ralph McPherran (baseball); 1922
Kraschel, Nelson George (politician); 1889
Laine, Cleo (singer/actress); 1927
Lichtenstein, Roy (artist); 1923
Lum, Mike; born Michael Ken-Wai Lum (baseball); 1945
Nelson, Al; born Albert Nelson (football); 1943
Parker, Lara (actress); 1942
Rice, Del; born Delbert W. Rice (baseball); 1922
Roosevelt, Theodore (President); 1858
Rote, Kyle W. (football/sportscaster); 1928
Snodgress, Carrie (actress); 1946
Thomas, Dylan Marlais (poet); 1914
Williams, John (football); 1945
Wright, Teresa; born Muriel Teresa Wright (actress); 1918

OCTOBER 28:

Alexander, Jane; born Jane Quigley (actress); 1939
Cook, James (navigator); 1728
Erasmus, Desiderius; born Gerhard Gerhards (scholar); 1467
Foley, Dave; born David Foley (football); 1947
Folk, Joseph Wingate (politician); 1869
Goodman, Dody; born Dolores Goodman (comedienne/actress); 1929

Hanson, Howard Harold (music); 1896
Head, Edith (costume designer); 1907
Herbert, Thomas John (politician); 1894
Hopkins, Telma Louise (singer); 1948
Iverson, Don; born Donald Iverson (golf); 1945
Jenner, Bruce (olympic athlete/sportscaster); 1949
Katcavage, Jim; born James R. Katcavage (football); 1934
Kuhn, Bowie Kent (baseball); 1926
Lanchester, Elsa; born Elizabeth Sullivan (actress); 1902
Morton, Bruce Alexander (newscaster); 1930
Parker, Suzy; born Cecelia Anne Renee Parker (actress); 1932
Peery, George Campbell (politician); 1873
Plowright, Joan Anne (actress); 1929
Roberts, Douglas William (hockey); 1942
Salk, Jonas Edward (medicine); 1914
Soo, Jack; born Goro Suzuki (actor/singer/comedian); 1915
Veale, Bob; born Robert Andrew Veale (baseball); 1935
Wilkins, Lenny; born Leonard Wilkins (basketball); 1937
Yarbrough, Jim; born James Kelley Yarbrough (football); 1946

OCTOBER 29:

Adams, Alva Blanchard (politician); 1875
Brice, Fanny; born Frances Borach (actress/singer); 1891
Brooks, Geraldine; born Geraldine Stroock (actress); 1925
Dreyfuss, Richard Stephan (actor); 1947
Garmaker, Dick (basketball); 1932
Hill, John Fremont (politician); 1855
Jackson, Kate (actress); 1948
Juzda, William (hockey); 1920
Mauldin, Bill; born William Henry Mauldin (cartoonist); 1921
Montgomery, Douglass; born Robert Douglass Montgomery (actor); 1907
Moore, Melba; born Beatrice Hill (singer/actress); 1945
Reeves, Ken; born Kenneth M. Reaves (football); 1944
Richert, Pete; born Peter Gerard Richert (baseball); 1939
Russell, Andy; born Charles Andrew Russell (football); 1941
Sedgman, Frank; born Francis Arthur Sedgman (tennis); 1927
Tamiroff, Akim (actor); 1899
Williams, Jack; born John Richard Williams (politician); 1909

OCTOBER 30:

Adams, John (President); 1735
Adcock, Joe; born Joseph Wilbur Adcock (baseball); 1927
Akins, Zöe (playwright/poet); 1886
Atlas, Charles (body builder); 1893
Bragan, Bobby; born Robert Randall Bragan (baseball); 1917
Carol Sue; born Evelyn Lederer (actress); 1907

Chenier, Phil (basketball); 1950
Delahanty, Ed; born Edward James Delahanty (baseball); 1867
Farina, Nino; born Giuseppe Farina (auto racing); 1908
Flatt, Ernest Orville (dancer/choreographer); 1918
Gardner, Calvin Pearly (hockey); 1924
Gautier, Dick (actor/singer); 1931
Gordon, Ruth; born Ruth Gordon Jones (actress); 1896
Halsey, William Frederick, Jr. (naval officer); 1882
Hart, Jim Ray; born James Raymond Hart (baseball); 1941
Hill, J.D. (football); 1948
Hussey, Ruth Carol (actress); 1913
Johnson, Levi (football); 1950
Lelouch, Claude (director); 1937
McElroy, Neil Hosler (government); 1904
Perry, Jim; born James Evan Perry, Jr. (baseball); 1935
Potter, Charles Edward (politician); 1916
Pound, Ezra Loomis (poet); 1885
Sheridan, Richard Brinsley (playwright); 1751
Slick, Grace Wing; born Grace Wing (singer); 1939
Spaulding, Huntley Nowell (politician); 1869
Terry, Bill; born William Harold Terry (baseball); 1898
Trintignant, Maurice (auto racing); 1917
Winkler, Henry Franklin (actor); 1945

OCTOBER 31:

Allgood, Sara (actress); 1883
Bel Geddes, Barbara; born Barbara Geddes (actress); 1922
Bell, Griffin Boyette (government); 1918
Bromley, Sheila (actress); 1911
Chiang Kai-shek (Chinese government); 1887
Cioffi, Charles (actor); 1935
Collins, Michael (astronaut); 1930
Evans, Dale; born Frances Octavia Smith (actress); 1912
Fondy, Dee Virgil (baseball); 1924
Franz, Eduard (actor); 1902
Goodfriend, Lynda (actress); 1950
Goyette, Phil; born Philippe Goyette (hockey); 1933
Grant, Lee; born Lyova Haskell Rosenthal (actress); 1929
Gunter, Julius Caldeen (politician); 1858
Jackson, Luke; born Lucious Jackson (basketball); 1941
Keats, John (poet); 1795
Keltner, Ken; born Kenneth Frederick Keltner (baseball); 1916
Kump, Herman Guy (politician); 1877
Lalonde, Newsy; born Edouard Lalonde (hockey); 1887
Landon, Michael; born Eugene Maurice Orowitz
        (actor/producer/director/writer); 1936
McAdoo, William Gibbs (government/politics); 1863

McDonald, Bucko; born Wilfred Kennedy McDonald (hockey); 1911
McNally, Dave; born David Arthur McNally (baseball); 1942
Moore, Cleo (actress); 1928
Nesterenko, Eric Paul (hockey); 1933
Pauley, Jane; born Margaret Jane Pauley (newscaster/TV host); 1950
Peterkin, Julia Mood (author); 1880
Rather, Dan (newscaster/author); 1931
Rivers, Mickey; born John Milton Rivers (baseball); 1948
Smylie, Robert E. (politician); 1914
Stiers, David Ogden (actor); 1942
Vermeer, Jan; born Jan Van Der Meer Van Delft (artist); 1632
Waters, Ethel (actress/singer); 1896

NOVEMBER 1:

Anderson, Bill (singer/music); 1937
Angeles, Victoria de los; born Victoria Gamez Cima (singer); 1924
Arbour, Al; born Alger Arbour (hockey); 1932
Aycock, Charles Brantley (politician); 1859
Barton, James (actor); 1890
Berlin, Jeannie (actress); 1949
Caldwell, Joe (basketball); 1941
Crane, Stephen (writer); 1871
Denison, Michael (actor); 1915
Ellison, Willie; born William H. Ellison (football); 1945
Foxworth, Robert (actor); 1941
French, Larry; born Lawrence Herbert French (baseball); 1907
Hendricks, Ted; born Theodore Paul Hendricks (football); 1947
Hunt, George Wylie Paul (politician); 1859
Kilpatrick, James J. "Jack"; born James Jackson Kilpatrick, Jr.
    (journalist/author); 1920
La Plante, Laura (actress); 1904
Mack, Tom; born Thomas Lee Mack (football); 1943
Mullin, Pat; born Patrick Joseph Mullin (baseball); 1917
Palmer, Betsy; born Patricia Betsy Hrunek (or Brumek) (actress); 1926
Payton-Wright, Pamela (actress); 1941
Penrose, Boies (politician); 1860
Player, Gary Jim (golf); 1935
Power, Vic; born Victor Pellot Power (baseball); 1931
Rice, Grantland (journalist/sportscaster/author); 1880
Wallace, Marcia (actress); 1942

NOVEMBER 2:

Bakken, Jim; born James Leroy Bakken (football); 1940
Boone, Daniel (frontiersman); 1734
Brady, Alice (actress); 1892
Budde, Ed; born Edward Budde (football); 1940
Buncom, Frank J., Jr. (football); 1939

Conklin, Peggy; born Margaret Eleanor Conklin (actress); 1910
Dunn, James Howard (actor); 1901
Flavin, Martin Archer (author/playwright); 1883
Ford, Paul; born Paul Ford Weaver (actor); 1901
Harding, Warren Gamaliel (President); 1865
Jackson, Travis Calvin (baseball); 1903
Lancaster, Burt; born Burton Stephen Lancaster (actor); 1913
Little, Larry; born Lawrence Chatmon Little (football); 1945
Marie Antoinette; born Josephe Jeanne Marie Antoinette (Queen of
    France); 1755
Mosienko, Bill; born William Mosienko (hockey); 1921
Polk, James Knox (President); 1795
Powers, Stefanie; born Stefania Zofia Ferderkievicz (or Federkiewicz)
    (actress); 1942
Reed, Ron; born Ronald Lee Reed (baseball/basketball); 1942
Rosewall, Ken; born Kenneth Robert Rosewall (tennis); 1934
Russell, Richard Brevard, Jr. (politician); 1897
Rutherford, Ann; born Therese·Ann Rutherford (actress); 1917
Shaw, Leslie Mortier (politics/government); 1848
Sisler, Dick; born Richard Allen Sisler (baseball); 1920
Stevens, Warren (actor); 1919
Stockton, Dave; born David Knapp Stockton (golf); 1941
Thompson, Paul Ivan (hockey); 1906
Vander Meer, Johnny; born John Samuel Vander Meer (baseball); 1914
Walston, Ray (actor/director); 1914
Wasserman, Dale (writer/producer); 1917
Waterman, Charles Winfield (politician); 1861
Watson, James Eli (politician); 1863

NOVEMBER 3:

Austin, Stephen F.; born Stephen Fuller Austin (colonizer/statesman);
    1793
Ball, Joseph Hurst (politician); 1905
Berry, Ken (actor/dancer/singer); 1933
Bronson, Charles; born Charles Dennis Buchinsky (actor); 1921
Bryant, William Cullen (poet); 1749
Connor, John Thomas (government); 1914
Dick, Charles William Frederick (politician); 1858
Dukakis, Michael Stanley (politician); 1933
Ehman, Gerald Joseph (hockey); 1932
Emerson, Roy (tennis); 1936
Farr, Mel; born Melvin Farr (football); 1944
Feller, Bob; born Robert William Andrew Feller (baseball); 1918
Freed, Bert (actor); 1919
Hendrix, Wanda; born Dixie Wanda Hendrix (actress); 1928
Holmes, Larry (boxing); 1949
Holtzman, Ken; born Kenneth Dale Holtzman (baseball); 1945

Houston, Jim; born James E. Houston (football); 1937
Long, Russell Billiu (politician); 1918
Lulu; born Marie McDonald McLaughlin Lawrie (singer/actress); 1948
Malraux, André; born Georges André Malraux (author); 1901
Martin, Joseph William Jr. (politician); 1884
McCay, Peggy (actress); 1931
McNally, Terrence (playwright); 1939
Nagurski, Bronko; born Bronislaw Nagurski, (football); 1908
Reston, James Barrett (journalist); 1909
Sensibaugh, Mike; born J. Michael Sensibaugh (football); 1949
Summa, Homer Wayne (baseball); 1898
Vitti, Monica; born Maria Luisa Ceciarelli (actress); 1933
White, Edward Douglass, Jr. (politician/jurist); 1845
Yardley, George (basketball); 1928

NOVEMBER 4:

Balsam, Martin Henry (actor); 1919
Buchanon, Willie James (football); 1950
Carney, Art; born Arthur William Matthew Carney (actor); 1918
Cronkite, Walter Leland, Jr. (newscaster); 1916
Field, Virginia; born Margaret Cynthia St. John Field (actress); 1917
Francona, Tito; born John Patsy Francona (baseball); 1933
Groat, Dick; born Richard Morrow Groat (baseball); 1930
Lee, Dixie; born Wilma Winifred Wyatt (singer/actress); 1911
McMullen, Kathy (golf); 1949
Meeker, Howie; born Howard William Meeker (hockey); 1924
Mitchell, Cameron; born Cameron M. Mitzell (actor); 1918
Orman, James Bradley (politician); 1849
Patterson, Thomas MacDonald (politician); 1839
Rock, Walter (football); 1941
Rogers, Will; born William Penn Adair Rogers (humorist); 1879
Sawatski, Carl Ernest (baseball); 1927
Swit, Loretta (actress); 1939
Trigère, Pauline (fashion designer); 1912
Wallace, Bobby; born Roderick John Wallace (baseball); 1873
Webb, Skeeter; born James Laverne Webb (baseball); 1909
Young, Gig; born Byron Ellsworth Barr (actor); 1917

NOVEMBER 5:

Bosley, Bruce L. (football); 1933
Cotton, Baldy; born Harold Cotton (hockey); 1902
Debs, Eugene Victor (Socialist leader); 1855
Donohue, Pete; born Peter Joseph Donohue (baseball); 1900
Durant, Will; born William James Durant (philosopher/author); 1885
Ebersole, John Joel (football); 1948
Edelman, Herb; born Herbert Edelman (actor); 1933
Floren, Myron (music); ——

420 THE CELEBRITY BIRTHDAY BOOK

Gumbert, Harry Edward (baseball); 1909
Kowalkowski, Bob; born Robert Kowalkowski (football); 1943
Leigh, Vivien; born Vivian Mary Hartley (actress); 1913
Longworth, Nicholas (politician); 1869
Mantovani, Annunzlo Paolo (music); 1905
McCrea, Joel (actor); 1905
McGiver, John (actor); 1913
O'Mahoney, Joseph Christopher (politician); 1884
O'Neal, Tatum Beatrice (actress); 1963
Robinson, Chris (actor); 1938
Rogers, Roy; born Leonard Slye (actor/singer); 1911
Schafer, Natalie (actress); 1912
Shepard, Sam (playwright/actor/music); 1943
Simon, Paul Frederick (singer/music); 1942
Sommer, Elke; born Elke Schletz (actress/artist); 1941
Tabor, Jim; born James Reubin Tabor (baseball); 1913
Thomson, Vernon Wallace (politician); 1905
Turner, Ike (music); 1931
Underwood, Cecil Harland (politician); 1922
Walton, Bill; born William Theodore Walton (basketball); 1952
Weiland, Cooney; born Ralph Weiland (hockey); 1904
Yulin, Harris (actor); 1937

NOVEMBER 6:

Conniff, Ray (music); 1916
Field, Sally Margaret (actress); 1946
Finnie, Roger (football); 1945
Gardner, Frederick Dozier (politician); 1869
Gosger, Jim; born James Charles Gosger (baseball); 1942
Gregory, Thomas Watt (government); 1861
Griffin, Robert Paul (politician); 1923
Hall, Juanita; born Juanita Long (actress/singer); 1901
Jackson, Stonewall (singer/music); 1932
Johnson, Walter Perry (baseball); 1887
Jones, James (author); 1921
Jones, Mack (baseball); 1938
Kerr, Buddy; born John Joseph Kerr (baseball); 1922
Klukay, Joseph Francis (hockey); 1922
Kuberski, Steve (basketball); 1947
Langlois, Junior; born Albert Langlois (hockey); 1934
Lederer, Frances; born Frantisek Lederer (actress); 1902
Nichols, Mike; born Michael Igor Peschkowsky (comedian/director); 1931
Olsen, Ole; born John Sigvard Olsen (comedian/actor); 1892
Paderewski, Ignace Jan (music/Polish government); 1860
Pavelich, Martin Nicholas (hockey); 1927
Pott, Johnny; born John Pott (golf); 1935

Rampton, Calvin Lewellyn (politician); 1913
Royle, Selena (actress); 1904
Shrimpton, Jean (actress); 1942
Turner, Roy Joseph (politician); 1894
Whitcomb, Edgar Doud (politician); 1917
Wright, Ernie; born Ernest H. Wright (football); 1939

NOVEMBER 7:

Attles, Alvin (basketball); 1936
Baker, Samuel Aaron (politician); 1874
Brydson, Glenn (hockey); 1910
Camus, Albert (author); 1913
Clark, Mike; born Michael V. Clark (football); 1940
Collett, Elmer; born Charles Elmer Collett (football); 1944
Comer, Braxton Bragg (politician); 1848
Copeland, Royal Samuel (politician); 1868
Curie, Marie; born Marja Sklodowski (physical chemist); 1867
Davis, Deane Chandler (politician); 1900
Ford, Samuel Clarence (politician); 1882
Graham, Billy; born William Franklin Graham (evangelist); 1918
Groesbeck, Alexander Joseph (politician); 1873
Hart, Tommy; born Thomas Lee Hart (football); 1944
Hirt, Al; born Alois Maxwell Hirt (music); 1922
Jagger, Dean; born Dean Jeffries (actor); 1903
Jelks, William Dorsey (politician); 1855
Joy, Leatrice; born Leatrice Joy Zeidler (actress); 1896
Kaat, Jim; born James Lee Kaat (baseball); 1938
Kurtz, Efrem (music); 1900
Mitchell, Joni; born Roberta Joan Anderson (singer/music); 1943
Newman, Barry Foster (actor); 1938
Niekro, Joe; born Joseph Franklin Niekro (baseball); 1944
Olson, Culbert Levy (politician); 1876
Proctor, Fletcher Dutton (politician); 1860
Prystai, Metro (hockey); 1927
Renfro, Ray; born Raymond Renfro (football); 1930
Rivers, Johnny; born John Ramistella (singer/music); 1942
Stuart, Dick; born Richard Lee Stuart (baseball); 1932
Stubbs, Walter Roscoe (politician); 1858
Sutherland, Joan (singer); 1926
Syzmanski, Dick; born Richard Syzmanski (football); 1932
Vandis, Titos (actor); 1917

NOVEMBER 8:

Bower, Johnny; born John William Bower (hockey); 1924
Brosch, Red; born Alfred Brosch (golf); 1911
Clark, Boobie; born Charles L. Clark (football); 1950
Collins, Peter (auto racing); 1931

Cuccinello, Tony; born Anthony Francis Cuccinello (baseball); 1907
Delon, Alain (actor); 1935
Fleck, Jack (golf); 1921
Flynn, Joe; born Joseph Anthony Flynn (actor); 1924
Fuqua, Henry Luce (politician); 1865
Garrett, Leif (singer/actor); 1961
Gracie, Robert J. (hockey); 1911
Harris, Bucky; born Stanley Raymond Harris (baseball); 1896
Havoc, June; born Ellen Evangeline Hovick (actress); 1916
Hepburn, Katharine Houghton (actress); 1907
Hines, Jerome; born Jerome Heinz (singer); 1921
Kranepool, Ed; born Edward Emil Kranepool (baseball); 1944
Lee, David Allen (football); 1943
Mirisch, Walter Mortimer (producer); 1921
Mitchell, Margaret (author); 1900
Page, Patti; born Clara Ann Fowler (singer/actress); 1927
Prevost, Marie; born Marie Bickford Dunn (or Gunn) (actress); 1893
Raitt, Bonnie Lynn (singer); 1949
Rolle, Esther (actress); ——
Safer, Morley (newscaster); 1931
Saks, Gene; born Jean Michael Saks (actor/director); 1921
Sanders, Thomas (basketball); 1938
Strauss, Robert; born Henry Robert Strauss (actor); 1913
Westlake, Wally; born Walden Thomas Westlake (baseball); 1920
Wiggin, Paul (football); 1934

NOVEMBER 9:

Agnew, Spiro Theodore "Ted" (Vice President); 1918
Ayers, Roy Elmer (politician); 1882
Dalton, John Montgomery (politician); 1900
Dandridge, Dorothy (actress); 1922
Dressler, Marie; born Leila Marie Von Koerber (actress); 1868
Ferrigno, Lou (body builder/actor); 1951
Gibson, Bob; born Robert Gibson (baseball/sportscaster); 1931
Gooch, Johnny; born John Beverly Gooch (baseball); 1897
Gossett, Bruce; born Daniel Bruce Gossett (football); 1941
Hendrick, Harvey Lee (baseball); 1897
Herzog, Whitey; born Dorrell Norman Elvert Herzog (baseball); 1931
Jefferson, Roy Lee (football); 1943
Jones, Charlie; born Charles Norris Jones (sportscaster/actor/attorney);
    1930
Lamarr, Hedy; born Hedwig Eva Maria Kiesler (actress); 1913
Lipscomb, Big Daddy; born Eugene Alan Lipscomb (football); 1931
Marsh, Mae; born Mary Warne Marsh (actress); 1895
Moore, Joanna (actress); ——
Neely, Matthew Mansfield (politician); 1874
Oliver, Edna May; born Edna May Cox-Oliver (actress); 1883

Priddy, Jerry; born Gerald Edward Priddy (baseball); 1919
Reed, James Alexander (politician); 1861
Selvy, Frank; born Franklin Delano Selvy (basketball); 1932
Shriver, Sargent; born Robert Sargent Shriver (government/attorney); 1915
Travers, Mary Allin (singer); 1936
Tribbitt, Sherman Willard (politician); 1922
Turgenev, Ivan Sergeevich (author/playwright); 1818
Weiskopf, Tom; born Thomas Daniel Weiskopf (golf); 1942
Wynn, Ed; born Isaiah Edwin Leopold (actor); 1886

NOVEMBER 10:

Aldrich, Chester Hardy (politician); 1862
Andrews, Harry (actor); 1911
Barrett, Frank A. (politician); 1892
Blocker, Chris (golf); 1939
Blood, Robert Oscar (politician); 1887
Burton, Richard; born Richard Walter Jenkins, Jr. (actor); 1925
Carmichael, Al; born Albert R. Carmichael (football); 1929
Cash, Norm; born Norman Dalton Cash (baseball); 1934
Conley, Gene; born Donald Eugene Conley (baseball/basketball); 1930
Dale, Esther (singer/actress); 1885
Dykes, Jimmy; born James Joseph Dykes (baseball); 1896
Fargo, Donna; born Yvonne Vaughan (singer/music); 1949
Fenneman, George (announcer); 1919
Froman, Jane; born Ellen Jane Froman (singer); 1907
Goldsmith, Oliver (writer); 1728
Hogarth, William (artist); 1697
Lipon, Johnny; born John Joseph Lipon (baseball); 1922
Luther, Martin (religious leader); 1483
Marquand, J.P.; born John Phillips Marquand (author); 1893
Phillips, Mackenzie; born Laura Mackenzie Phillips (actress); 1959
Rains, Claude; born William Claude Rains (actor); 1889
Scheider, Roy Richard (actor); 1935
Schiller, Johann Christoph Friedrich von (dramatist/poet); 1759
Scott, Pippa; born Phillippa Scott (actress); 1935
Shapiro, Karl Jay (poet); 1913
Tebbetts, Birdie; born George Robert Tebbetts (baseball); 1909

NOVEMBER 11:

Adams, Maude; born Maude Kiskadden (actress); 1872
Andersson, Bibi; born Birgitta Andersson (actress); 1935
Case, George Washington (baseball); 1915
Clair, René; born René-Lucien Chomette (director); 1898
Cullen, Brian Joseph (hockey); 1933
Delock, Ike; born Ivan Martin Delock (baseball); 1929
Dostoyevsky, Fyodor Mikhailovich (author); 1821

Fast, Howard Melvin (author); 1914
Hiss, Alger (government/attorney); 1904
Kaye, Stubby (actor); 1918
Knowles, Patric; born Reginald Lawrence Knowles (actor); 1911
Kohner, Susan; born Susanna Kohner (actress); 1936
LaRusso, Rudy (basketball); 1937
Luisi, James (actor); 1928
Lumley, Harry (hockey); 1926
Maranville, Rabbit; born Walter Vincent Maranville (baseball); 1891
O'Brien, Pat; born William Joseph Patrick O'Brien, Jr. (actor); 1899
Patton, George Smith, Jr. (army officer); 1885
Proxmire, William; born Edward William Proxmire (politician); 1915
Ryan, Robert Bushnell (actor); 1909
Scott, Hugh Doggett, Jr. (politician); 1900
Speigel, Sam (producer); 1903
Traynor, Pie; born Harold Joseph Traynor (baseball); 1899
Trosky, Hal; born Harold Arthur Troyavesky, Sr. (baseball); 1912
Vonnegut, Kurt, Jr. (author); 1922
Walsh, David Ignatius (politician); 1872
Winters, Jonathan Harshman (comedian/actor); 1925
Young, Jesse Colin (singer); 1944
Young, Roland (actor); 1887
Zoeller, Fuzzy; born Frank Urban Zoeller, Jr. (golf); 1951
Zorinsky, Edward (politician); 1928

NOVEMBER 12:

Austin, Warren Robinson (politician); 1877
Baker, Sam; born Loris H. Baker (football); 1929
Balin, Ina; born Ina Sandra Rosenberg (actress); 1937
Bartkowski, Steve (football); 1952
Blackmun, Harry Andrew (jurist); 1908
Carson, Sunset; born Michael Harrison (actor); 1922
Comaneci, Nadia (gymnast); 1961
DeJordy, Denis (hockey); 1938
Fairchild, Barbara (singer/music); 1950
Harris, Cliff; born Clifford Allen Harris (football); 1948
Houston, Ken; born Kenneth Ray Houston (football); 1944
Hunter, Kim; born Janet Cole (actress); 1922
Hyland, Brian (singer); 1943
Jessen, Mary Ruth (golf); 1936
Kelly, Grace Patricia (actress/Princess Grace of Monaco); 1929
Lea, Preston (politician); 1841
Lee, Gwen; born Gwendolyn LePinski (actress); 1904
Leemans, Tuffy; born Alphonse Leemans (football); 1912
Manson, Charles (cult murderer); 1934
Mitchell, James Paul (government); 1900
Oakie, Jack; born Lewis Delaney Offield (actor); 1903

Owens R.C.; born Raleigh C. Owens (football); 1933
Pitts, Frank (football); 1943
Quine, Richard (actor/producer/director); 1920
Ratterman, George (football); 1926
Schroeder, John (golf); 1945
Simpson, Milward Lee (politician); 1897
Sprague, Charles Arthur (politician); 1887
Stafford, Jo (singer); 1918
Tyler, Letitia Christian; born Letitia Christian (first wife of John
    Tyler/First Lady); 1790
Wallace, Dewitt (publisher); 1889

NOVEMBER 13:

Alexander, Moses (politician); 1853
Baddeley, Hermione; born Hermione Clinton-Baddeley (actress); 1906
Bennett, Wallace Foster (politician); 1898
Bilko, Steve; born Stephen Bilko (baseball); 1928
Booth, Edwin Thomas (actor); 1833
Brandeis, Louis Dembitz (jurist); 1856
Brickell, Beth (actress); ——
Brundige, Bill; born William G. Brundige (football); 1948
Christian, Linda; born Blanca Rosa Welter (actress); 1923
Corri, Adrienne; born Adrienne Riccoboni (actress); 1930
Delsing, Jim; born James Henry Delsing (baseball); 1925
Elam, Jack (actor); 1916
Garvin, Lucius Fayette Clark (politician); 1841
George, Jack (basketball); 1928
Hardee, Cary Augustus (politician); 1876
Harris, Fred Roy (politician); 1930
Hillman, Wayne James (hockey); 1938
Johnson, Walter (football); 1942
Kampouris, Alex William (baseball); 1912
Lunde, Leonard Melvin (hockey); 1936
Mack, Helen; born Helen McDougall (actress); 1913
Mulligan, Richard (actor); 1932
Olson, Floyd Bjerstjerne (politician); 1891
Parker, Wes; born Maurice Wesley Parker (baseball/actor); 1939
Phillips, John Clayton (politician); 1870
Rambo, Dack; born Norman Rambo (actor); 1941
Scourby, Alexander (actor); 1913
Seberg, Jean Dorothy (actress); 1938
Sherwood, Madeleine; born Madeleine Thorton (actress); 1926
Sterling, Robert; born William Sterling Hart (actor); 1917
Stevenson, Robert Louis Balfour (author); 1850
Stottlemyre, Mel; born Melvin Leon Stottlemyre (baseball); 1941
Werner, Oskar; born Josef Bschliessmayer (actor/producer/director);
    1922

NOVEMBER 14:

Avery, Phyllis (actress); 1924
Bromwich, Jack; born John Edward Bromwich (tennis); 1918
Brooks, Louise (actress); 1900
Charles, Prince; born Charles Philip Arthur George Mountbatten
    (British Royalty); 1948
Copland, Aaron (music); 1900
De Camp, Rosemary (actress); 1914
Desmond, Johnny; born Giovanni Alfredo de Simone (singer/actor);
    1921
Downey, Morton (singer); 1901
Dwinell, Lane (politician); 1906
Eisenhower, Mamie; born Mamie Geneva Doud (First Lady); 1896
Fulton, Robert (inventor); 1765
Haise, Fred Wallace, Jr. (astronaut); 1933
Hughes, Kathleen; born Betty von Gerlean (actress); 1928
Hussein I; born Hussein ibn Talal ibn Abdullah el Hashim (King of
    Jordan); 1935
Hutton, Barbara (heiress); 1912
Kaufman, George S.; born George Simon Kaufman
    (playwright/director); 1889
Keith, Brian; born Robert Keith, Jr. (actor); 1921
Lake, Veronica; born Constance Frances Marie Ockelman (actress);
    1919
Lausche, Frank John (politician); 1895
Livingston, Mike; born Michael Livingston (football); 1945
Lund, Tiny; born DeWayne Louis Lund (auto racing); 1929
Mannes, Marya (author/journalist); 1904
McCarthy, Joe; born Joseph Raymond McCarthy (politician); 1908
Monet, Claude (artist); 1840
Nehru, Jawaharlal (Indian government); 1889
Oliver, Murray Clifford (hockey); 1937
Piersall, Jim; born James Anthony Piersall (baseball); 1929
Powell, Dick; born Richard Ewing Powell (actor/producer/director);
    1904
Rysanek, Leonie (singer); 1928
Salisbury, Harrison Evans (journalist); 1908
Seiling, Rodney Albert (hockey); 1944
Smathers, George Armistead (politician); 1913
Stevenson, McLean (actor); 1930
Tilton, Martha (singer/actress); 1915
Vanderbilt, George Washington (capitalist); 1862
Watson, Bryan Joseph (hockey); 1942
Wilson, Dorothy (actress); 1909

NOVEMBER 15:

Adams, Franklin Pierce (journalist/author); 1881

Armstrong, Otis (football); 1950
Asner, Edward (actor); 1929
Baker, Howard Henry, Jr. (politician); 1925
Barenboim, Daniel (music); 1942
Barnes, Joanna (actress/author); 1934
Bell, Gus; born David Russell Bell (baseball); 1928
Bruce, Carol (actress/singer); 1919
Chapman, Judith (actress); ——
Clark Petula Sally Olwen (singer/actress); 1932
Cole, Larry; born Lawrence R. Cole (football); 1946
Cross, Burton Melvin (politician); 1902
Dandridge, Bob (basketball); 1947
Drinan, Robert Frederick (priest/politician); 1920
Frankfurter, Felix (jurist); 1882
Harriman, W. Averill; born William Averill Harriman
    (politics/government); 1891
Hawes, Harry Bartow (politician); 1869
Kerr, John Grinham (actor); 1931
Kotto, Yaphet (actor); 1937
Le May, Curtis Emerson (air force officer); 1906
Marti, Fred; born Frederick Marti, Jr. (golf); 1940
Mayo, Whitman (actor); 1930
McPhatter, Clyde (singer/music); 1933
Moore, Marianne Craig (poet); 1887
O'Keeffe, Georgia (artist); 1887
Pilbeam, Nova (actress); 1919
Rasulala, Thalmus; born Jack Crowder (actor); 1939
Rommel, Erwin Johannes Eugen (German army officer); 1891
Stone, Lewis Shepard (actor); 1879
Svare, Harland (football); 1930

NOVEMBER 16:

Barry, Patricia (actress); ——
Bolling, Frank Elmore (baseball); 1931
Brown, Aaron L.; Jr. (football); 1943
Chiti, Harry (baseball); 1932
Condon, Eddie; born Albert Edwin Condon (music); 1905
Cruickshank, Bobby; born Robert Allan Cruickshank (golf); 1894
Dano, Royal Edward (actor); 1922
Dobrynin, Anatoly Fedorovich (Russian government); 1919
Drew, Elizabeth Brenner; born Elizabeth Brenner (journalist); 1935
Foytack, Paul Eugene (baseball); 1930
Gulager, Clu (actor); 1935
Handy, W.C.; born William Christopher Handy (music); 1873
Hindemith, Paul (music); 1895
Kirby, William Fosgate (politician); 1867
Martin, Harvey Banks (football); 1950

McBride, Mary Margaret (author/broadcasting); 1899
McGee, Fiber; born James Jordan (actor); 1896
Meredith, Burgess George (actor/director/producer); 1908
Metcalf, Jesse Houghton (politician); 1860
Pettet, Joanna (actress); 1944
Russell, Lee Maurice (politician); 1875
Sousa, John Philip (music); 1854
Stockwell, Guy (actor); 1934
Tibbett, Lawrence Mervil (singer/actor); 1896
Watson, Bobs; born Robert Watson (actor); 1930
White, Jo Jo; born Joseph White (basketball); 1946

NOVEMBER 17:

Auer, Mischa; born Mischa Ounskowsky (actor); 1905
Bell, Gary (baseball); 1936
Brewer, Jim; born James Thomas Brewer (baseball); 1937
Bronson, Betty; born Elizabeth Ada Bronson (actress); 1906
Broughton, Melville; born Joseph Melville Broughton (politician); 1888
Campbell, Archie (singer/comedian); 1914
Conrad, Bobby Joe; born Robert Joseph Conrad (football); 1935
Cook, Peter Edward (comedian/actor/writer); 1937
Fay, Frank; born Francis Anthony Fay (actor); 1894
Garcia, Mike; born Edward Miguel Garcia (baseball); 1923
Haden, Sara (actress); 1897
Harris, Andrew Linter (politician); 1835
Hayes, Elvin (basketball); 1945
Hudson, Rock; born Roy Scherer, adopted name Roy Fitzgerald
    (actor/singer); 1925
Hutchison, Chuck; born Charles Hutchison (football); 1948
Hutton, Lauren; born Mary Hutton (actress); 1943
Lescoulie, Jack (actor/announcer); 1917
Lightfoot, Gordon Meredith (singer/music); 1938
Mathias, Bob; born Robert Bruce Mathias (olympic
    athlete/politician/actor); 1930
O'Conor, Herbert Romulus (politician); 1896
Seaver, Tom; born George Thomas Seaver (baseball/sportscaster); 1944
Strasberg, Lee (director/actor); 1901
Weaver, Herman; born William Herman Weaver (football); 1948

NOVEMBER 18:

Bettenhausen, Gary (auto racing); 1941
Brando, Jocelyn (actress); 1919
Coca, Imogene; born Imogene Fernandez y Coca (comedienne/actress);
    1908
Collins, Dorothy; born Marjorie Chandler (singer); 1926
Dix, Dorothy; born Elizabeth Meriwether (journalist/author); 1861
Evans, Linda (actress); 1942

Gallup, George Horace (pollster); 1901
Gilbert, Sir William Schwenck (dramatist); 1836
Hemmings, David (actor); 1938
Johnston, Olin Dewitt (politician); 1896
Mauch, Gene William (baseball); 1925
Mercer, Johnny; born John H. Mercer (music); 1909
Migay, Rudolph Joseph (hockey); 1928
Nelson, Rocky; born Glenn Richard Nelson (baseball); 1924
Ormandy, Eugene (music); 1899
Shepard, Alan Bartlett, Jr. (astronaut); 1923
Sievers, Roy Edward (baseball); 1926
Stevens, Ted; born Theodore Fulton Stevens, (politician); 1923
Sullivan, Susan (actress)——
Tatum, Jack; born John David Tatum (football); 1948
Vaccaro, Brenda Buell (actress); 1939
Weaver, Arthur J. (politician); 1873
Wood, Craig Ralph (golf); 1901

NOVEMBER 19:

Boone, Bob; born Robert Raymond Boone (baseball); 1947
Campanella, Roy (baseball); 1921
Carroll, Nancy; born Ann Veronica La Hiff (actress); 1904
Cavett, Dick; born Richard Cavett (TV host/actor); 1936
Dorsey, Tommy; born Thomas Francis Dorsey (music); 1905
Foster, Jodie (actress); 1962
Gandhi, Indira; born Indira Priyadarshini Nehru (Indian government); 1917
Garfield, James Abram (President); 1831
Godwin, Mills Edwin, Jr. (politician); 1914
Haggerty, Dan (actor/animal trainer); 1941
Hull, Dennis William (hockey); 1944
Klein, Calvin Richard (fashion designer); 1942
Molina, Jose (dancer); 1937
O'Connor, Glynnis (actress); 1956
Phipps, Mike; born Michael E. Phipps (football); 1947
Rashad, Ahmad; born Robert Earl "Bobby" Moore (football); 1949
Smith, Elmo E. (politician); 1909
Todd, Richard (football); 1953
Tolan, Bobby; born Robert Tolan (baseball); 1945
Utley, Garrick; born Clifton Garrick Utley (newscaster); 1939
Webb, Clifton; born Webb Parmalle Hollenbeck (actor/dancer/singer); 1891
Young, Alan; born Angus Young (actor); 1919

NOVEMBER 20:

Armstrong, Robert (actor); 1890

Ballard, Kaye; born Catherine Gloria Balotta
    (comedienne/actress/singer); 1926
Benton, Larry; born Lawrence James Benton (baseball); 1897
Bible, Alan Harvey (politician); 1909
Biden, Joseph Robinette, Jr. (politician); 1942
Canova, Judy; born Juliet Canova (comedienne/actress/singer); 1916
Christy, June (singer); 1925
Cooke, Alistair; born Alfred Alistair Cooke
    (journalist/broadcaster/author/TV host); 1908
Curley, James Michael (politician); 1874
Dampier, Louie (basketball); 1944
Dawson, Richard (actor/TV host); 1932
Denny, Reginald; born Reginald Leigh Dugmore (or Daymore) (actor);
    1891
Edge, Walter Evans, (politician); 1873
Frazer, Dan (actor); ——
Gould, Chester (cartoonist); 1900
Griffith, Clark Calvin (baseball); 1869
Hawkes, Albert Wahl (politician); 1878
January, Don; born Donald January (golf); 1929
Johnstone, Jay; born John William Johnstone (baseball); 1945
Kennedy, Robert Francis (government/politics); 1925
Keyes, Evelyn Louise (actress); 1919
Locke, Bobby; born Arthur D'Arcy Locke (golf); 1917
McKeldin, Theodore Roosevelt (politician); 1900
Monday, Rick; born Robert James Monday (baseball); 1945
Parsons, Estelle (actress); 1927
Plisetskaya, Maya Mikhailovna (dancer); 1925
Pucci, Emilio; born Emilio Pucci di Barsento (fashion designer); 1914
Smothers, Dick; born Richard Smothers (comedian/actor); 1939
Thaxter, Phyllis St. Felix (actress); 1921
Tierney, Gene Eliza Taylor (actress); 1920
Zimmerman, Fred Rudolph (politician); 1880

NOVEMBER 21:

Bishop, Jim; born James Alonzo Bishop (journalist/author); 1907
Blackwood, Ibra Charles (politician); 1878
Blaine, Vivian; born Vivienne Stapleton (actress/singer); 1921
Campanella, Joseph Mario (actor); 1927
Dischinger, Terry (basketball); 1940
Hawkins, Coleman (music); 1904
Hawn, Goldie; born Goldie Jean Btudlendgehawn
    (actress/comedienne/singer/dancer); 1945
High, Andy; born Andrew Aird High (baseball); 1897
Hiskey, Babe; born Bryant Hiskey (golf); 1938
Korvin, Charles; born Geza Korvin Karpathi (actor); 1907
La Salle, René Robert Cavlier Sieur de (explorer); 1643

Lindstrom, Fred; born Frederick Charles Lindstrom (baseball); 1905
Lord, Barbara; born Barbara Jeanette Gratz (actress); 1937
Luckinbill, Lawrence George (actor); 1934
Luckman, Sid; born Sidney Luckman (football); 1916
Luft, Lorna (singer); 1952
Makarova, Natalia (dancer); 1940
McCraw, Tommy Lee (baseball); 1940
Meeker, Ralph; born Ralph Rathgeber (actor); 1920
Mercer, Mike; born Michael Mercer (football); 1935
Mills, Juliet Maryon (actress); 1941
Monroe, Earl; born Vernon Earl Monroe (basketball); 1944
Murray, William Henry (politician); 1869
Musial, Stan; born Stanley Frank Musial (baseball); 1920
Pope Benedict XV; born Giacomo della Chiesa; 1854
Powell, Eleanor Torrey (actress/dancer); 1910
Richards, Paul (baseball); 1908
Ringo, Jim; born James Ringo (football); 1932
Shepard, Jean (singer); 1933
Thomas, Marlo; born Margaret Julia Thomas (actress/producer); 1937
Voltaire, Jean Francois Marie Arouet (author); 1694

NOVEMBER 22:

Bartell, Dick; born Richard William Bartell (baseball); 1907
Baxter, Percival Proctor (politician); 1876
Bayne, Beverly Pearl (actress); 1895
Blasingame, Wade Allen (baseball); 1943
Britten, Benjamin; born Edward Benjamin Britten (music); 1913
Browning, Gordon (politician); 1889
Burdette, Lou; born Selva Lewis Burdette (baseball); 1926
Callan, Michael; born Martin Calinieff (actor/singer/dancer); 1935
Carmichael, Hoagy; born Hoagland Howard Carmichael (music/actor); 1899
Cournoyer, Yvan Serge (hockey); 1943
Curtis, Jamie Lee (actress); 1958
Dangerfield, Rodney (comedian/actor/author); 1921
De Gaulle, Charles André Joseph Marie (French government); 1890
Eliot, George; born Mary Ann (or Marian) Evans (author); 1819
Garfield, Allen; born Allen Goorwitz (actor); 1939
Garner, John Nance (Vice President); 1868
Gide, André (author); 1869
Guldahl, Ralph (golf); 1912
Hiller, Arthur (director); 1923
Hutchins, Mel (basketball); 1928
Johnson, Charley; born Charles Lane Johnson (football); 1938
King, Billie Jean; born Billie Jean Moffitt (tennis); 1943
Laperriere, Jacques (hockey); 1941
Luzinski, Greg; born Gregory Michael Luzinski (baseball); 1950

MacVeagh, Franklin (government); 1837
Marshall, Bert; born Albert Leroy Marshall (hockey); 1943
Mueller, Frederick Henry (government); 1893
Mulloy, Gardnar (tennis); 1914
Page, Geraldine Sue (actress); 1924
Patrick, Lee Salome (actress); 1906
Patterson, Elizabeth; born Mary Elizabeth Patterson (actress); 1874
Pell, Claiborne deBorda (politician); 1918
Post, Wiley (aviator); 1899
Reynolds, Jack Sumner (football); 1947
Schuller, Gunther (music); 1925
Schultz, Charles Monroe (cartoonist); 1922
Upshaw, Marvin Allen (football); 1946
Vaughn, Robert Francis (actor/author); 1932
Winters, Roland; born Roland Winternitz (actor); 1904
Young, Bobby; born Robert George Young (baseball); 1925

NOVEMBER 23:

Adams, Abigail Smith; born Abigail Smith (First Lady); 1744
Billy The Kid; born William H. Bonney (outlaw); 1859
Bock, Jerry; born Jerrold Lewis Bock (music); 1928
Bolton, Guy; born St. George Guy Reginald Bolton (playwright); 1884
Brewster, Daniel Baugh (politician); 1923
Brock, William Emerson, III (politician); 1930
Cox, John Isaac (politician); 1855
Dehner, John (actor); 1915
Drew, Ellen; born Terry Parker (or Terry Ray) (actress); 1915
Etting, Ruth (singer); 1897
Falla, Manuel de; born Manuel Maria de Falla y Matheu (music); 1876
Folsom, Marion Bayard (government); 1893
Hoad, Lew; born Lewis A. Hoad (tennis); 1934
Jason, Sybil; born Sybil Jacobs (actress); 1929
Jory, Victor (actor); 1902
Karloff, Boris; born William Henry Pratt (actor); 1887
Kavanaugh, Ken; born Kenneth W. Kavanaugh (football); 1916
Krug, Julius Albert (government); 1907
Leach, Freddy; born Frederick M. Leach (baseball); 1897
Marx, Harpo; born Adolph Arthur Marx (comedian/actor—Marx
        Brothers); 1888
McClellan, George Brinton (army officer); 1865
O'Hanlon, George; born George Rice (actor); 1917
Pierce, Franklin (President); 1804
Schoeppel, Andrew Frank (politician); 1894
Schumacher, Hal; born Harold Henry Shumacher (baseball); 1910
Shafer, George F. (politician); 1888
Stark, Lloyd Crow (politician); 1886

Tiant, Luis Clemente (baseball); 1940
Washington, Eugene (football); 1944

NOVEMBER 24:

Baldridge, H. Clarence (politician); 1868
Barkley, Alben William (Vice President); 1877
Bibby, Henry (basketball); 1949
Buckley, William F.; born William Frank Buckley, Jr. (journalist); 1925
Carnegie, Dale (lecturer/author); 1888
Duff, Howard (actor); 1917
Fitzgerald, Geraldine (actress); 1912
Friend, Bob; born Robert Bartmess Friend (baseball); 1930
Grant, Kirby; born Kirby Grant Hoon, Jr. (actor); 1911
Griffith, Corinne (actress); 1896
Hurley, Charles Francis (politician); 1893
Johnson, John Henry (football); 1929
Jones, Stan; born Stanley P. Jones (football); 1931
Joplin, Scott (music); 1868
Kanin, Garson; born Gershon Labe (producer/director/writer); 1912
Lindsay, John Vliet (politician); 1921
Livingston, Stanley (actor); 1950
Medwick, Joe "Ducky"; born Joseph Michael Medwick (baseball); 1911
Nesbitt, Cathleen Mary (actress); 1888
Northrup, Jim; born James Thomas Northrup (baseball); 1939
Robertson, Oscar Palmer (basketball); 1938
Spinoza, Baruch (philosopher); 1632
Taylor, Zachary (President); 1784
Tomjanovich, Rudy (basketball); 1948
Toulouse-Lautrec-Monfa, Henri-Marie-Raymond de (artist); 1864
Vanderbilt, William H. (politician); 1901
Wilson, Teddy; born Theodore Wilson (music); 1912
Yeager, Steve; born Stephen Wayne Yeager (baseball); 1948

NOVEMBER 25:

Brodie, Steve; born Johnny Stevens (actor); 1919
Carnegie, Andrew (industrialist); 1835
Cooper, Myers Young (politician); 1873
Crosby, Kathryn; born Olive Kathryn Grandstaff (actress); 1933
Di Maggio, Joe; born Joseph Paul Di Maggio (baseball); 1914
Douglas, Helen Gahagan; born Helen Mary Gahagan
    (actress/singer/politician); 1900
Hunter, Jeffrey; born Henry Herman McKinnies (actor); 1925
Kennedy, John Fitzgerald, Jr. (First family); 1960
Landis, Jessie Royce; born Jessie Royse Medbury (actress); 1904
Laney, Benjamin Travis (politician); 1896
Livingston, Margaret (actress); 1900

Matheson, Bob; born Robert Matheson (football); 1944
Montalban, Ricardo; born Ricardo Gonzalo Pedro Montalban Merino
    (actor); 1920
Moore, Lenny; born Leonard Edward Moore (football); 1933
Nation, Carry; born Carry Amelia Moore (temperance leader); 1846
Pope John XXIII; born Angelo Giuseppe Roncalli; 1881
Schisgal, Murray Joseph (playwright); 1926
Schmedeman, Albert George (politician); 1864
Shore, Eddie; born Edward William Shore (hockey); 1902
Wall, Art; born Arthur Jonathan Wall, Jr. (golf); 1923
Webster, George (football); 1945

NOVEMBER 26:

Breathitt, Edward Thompson, Jr. (politician); 1924
Cusack, Cyril (actor); 1910
Dee, Frances; born Jean Dee (actress); 1907
Duffy, Hugh (baseball); 1866
Elliot, Bob; born Robert Irving Elliot (baseball); 1916
Fall, Albert Bacon (politics/government); 1861
Garrahy, John Joseph (politician); 1930
Gomez, Lefty; born Vernon Louis Gomez (baseball); 1908
Goulet, Robert Gerard (singer/actor); 1933
Hebner, Richie; born Richard Joseph Hebner (baseball); 1947
Ionesco, Eugene (playwright); 1912
Jacoby, Scott (actor); 1955
Jergens, Adele Louisa (actress); 1917
Johnson, Bob; born Robert Lee Johnson (baseball); 1906
Little, Rich; born Richard Caruthers Little (impressionist/actor/singer);
    1938
Mercer, Marian E. (actress/singer); 1935
Miller, Eddie; born Edward Robert Miller (baseball); 1916
Neff, Pat Morris (politician); 1871
St. John, Betta; born Betty Streidler (actress); 1929
Sevareid, Eric born Arnold Eric Sevareid
    (newscaster/journalist/author); 1912
Shell, Art; born Arthur Shell (football); 1946
Stenerud, Jan (football); 1942
Turnbull, Wendy (tennis); 1952
Turner, Tina; born Annie Mae Bullock (singer); 1938
Wehrli, Roger Russell (football); 1947
Williams, Emlyn; born George Emlyn Williams
    (actor/writer/producer); 1905

NOVEMBER 27:

Adams, Don (basketball); 1947
Agee, James (author); 1909
Allwyn, Astrid (actress); 1909

Bush, Bullet Joe; born Leslie Ambrose Bush (baseball); 1892
Dubcek, Alexander (Czechoslovakian government); 1921
Giusti, Dave; born David John Giusti, Jr. (baseball); 1939
Griswold, Dwight Palmer (politician); 1893
Handley, Harold Willis (politician); 1909
Hatch, Carl Atwood (politician); 1889
Hendrix, Jimi; born James Marshall Hendrix (singer); 1942
Kennedy, Caroline Bouvier (First family); 1957
Lee, Bruce; born Liu Yuen Kam (King-Fu artist/actor); 1940
McNally, John Victor (football); 1904
Merrick, David; born David Margulois (producer); 1912
Pastrano, Willie; born Wilfred Raleigh Pastrano (boxing); 1935
Schinkel, Kenneth Calvin (hockey); 1932
Simon, William Edward (government); 1927
Smith, Buffalo Bob; born Robert E. Smith (TV host); 1917
Strock, Don; born Donald J. Strock (football); 1950
Thompson, Marshall; born James Marshall Thompson (actor);
        1925
Vanderbilt, Cornelius (capitalist/financier); 1843
Washbourne, Mona (actress); 1903

NOVEMBER 28:

Atkinson, Brooks; born Justin Brooks Atkinson (journalist);
        1894
Blake, William (poet/artist); 1757
Bruneteau, Mud; born Modere Bruenteau (hockey); 1914
Burke, Edward Raymond (politician); 1880
Den Herder, Vern; born Vernon W. Den Herder (football); 1948
Eastland, James Oliver (politician); 1904
Engles, Friedrich (socialist writer); 1820
Ennis, Ethel (singer); 1934
Garrison, Lindley Miller (government); 1864
Grahame, Gloria; born Gloria Grahame Hallward (actress); 1924
Hart, Gary Warren (politician); 1937
Holcomb, Marcus Hensey (politician); 1844
Iturbi, José (music); 1895
Lange, Hope Elise Ross (actress); 1931
Lévi-Strauss, Claude Gustave (anthropologist/philosopher); 1908
McGrath, J. Howard; born James Howard McGrath
        (politics/government); 1903
Morrow, Edwin Porch (politician); 1878
Neilson, Chief; born James Anthony Neilson (hockey); 1940
Nutter, Donald Grant (politician); 1915
Picard, Henry G. (golf); 1907
Warfield, Paul Dryden (football); 1942
West, Max Edward (baseball); 1916
Westrum, Wes; born Wesley Noreen Westrum (baseball); 1922

NOVEMBER 29:

Alcott, Louisa May (author); 1832
Berkeley, Busby; born William Berkeley Eno.
    (choreographer/director/actor); 1895
Bing, Dave; (basketball); 1943
Freehan, Bill; born William Ashley Freehan (baseball); 1941
Gary, John; born John Gary Strader (singer); 1932
Inman, Joe (golf); 1947
Johnson, Kay (actress); 1904
Kaleta, Alexander (hockey); 1919
Kermoyan, Michael; born Kalem Missak Kermoyan (actor); 1925
Ladd, Diane; born Rose Diane Ladnier (actress); 1932
Lewis, C.S.; born Clive Staples Lewis (author); 1898
Loughran, Tommy (boxing); 1902
Love, John Arthur (politician); 1916
Mangione, Chuck; born Charles Frank Mangione (music); 1940
Mantha, Georges (hockey); 1908
McAuliffe, Dick; born Richard John McAuliffe (baseball); 1939
Miller, Jody (singer); 1941
Minoso, Minnie; born Saturnino Orestes Armas Minoso (baseball); 1922
Morris, Willie (author/editor); 1934
Noren, Irv; born Irving Arnold Noren (baseball); 1924
Powell, Adam Clayton, Jr. (politician); 1908
Reynolds, Frank (newscaster); 1923
Ross, Nellie Tayloe (politics/government); 1876
Scully, Vin; born Vincent Edward Scully (sportscaster); 1927
Thomas, George Edward (baseball); 1937
Thurston, Fuzzy; born Frederick C. Thurston (football); 1933
Tobin, Genevieve (actress); 1901
Waite, Morrison Remick (jurist); 1816
Zumwalt, Elmo Russell, Jr. (naval officer); 1920

NOVEMBER 30:

Chisholm, Shirley; born Shirley Anita St. Hill (politician); 1924
Churchill, Sir Winston Leonard Spencer (British government); 1874
Clark, Dick; born Richard Wagstaff Clark (TV host/actor/producer);
    1929
Crenna, Richard (actor/director); 1927
Ging, Jack L. (actor); ——
Guillaume, Robert; born Robert Peter Williams (actor); 1937
Hoffman, Abbie; born Abbott Hoffman (political activist); 1936
Horner, Henry (politician); 1878
Hutcherson, Dick; born Richard Leon Hutcherson (auto racing); 1931
Liddy, G. Gordon; born George Gordon Liddy (government); 1930
Logan, Jacqueline (actress); 1901
Mayo, Virginia; born Virginia Jones (actress); 1920
Parks, Gordon Alexander (director/author/music); 1912

Reason, Rex (actor); 1928
Schriner, Sweeney; born David Schriner (hockey); 1911
Sherman, Allan; born Allan Copelon (comedian/singer); 1924
Sloan, Tod; born Aloysius Martin Sloan (hockey); 1927
Swift, Jonathan (clergyman/writer); 1667
Twain, Mark; born Samuel Langhorne Clemens (author); 1835
Westphal, Paul (basketball); 1950
Zimbalist, Efrem, Jr. (actor); 1913

DECEMBER 1:

Allen, Woody; born Allen Stewart Konigsberg (actor/director); 1935
Alston, Walter Emmons (baseball); 1911
Doyle, David Fitzgerald (actor); 1929
Edwards, Edward Irving (politician); 1863
Foster, George Arthur (baseball); 1948
Griffith, Cal; born Calvin Robertson Griffith (baseball); 1911
Lamont, Robert Patterson (government); 1867
Lavagetto, Cookie; born Harry Arthur Lavagetto (baseball); 1912
Lennon, Dianne Barbara (singer—Lennon Sisters); 1939
Marion, Marty; born Martin Whitford Marion (baseball); 1917
Markova, Dame Alicia (dancer); 1910
Martin, Mary Virginia (actress/singer); 1913
McLerie, Allyn Ann (actress/dancer/singer); 1926
McLish, Cal; born Calvin Coolidge Julius Caesar Tushahoma McLish (baseball); 1925
Michell, Keith Joseph (actor/singer); 1926
Midler, Bette (singer/actress); 1945
O'Sullivan, Gilbert; born Raymond Edward O'Sullivan (singer/music); 1946
Picerni, Paul (actor); 1922
Pryor, Richard (comedian/actor); 1940
Ralston, Samuel Moffett (politician); 1857
Rawls, Lou; born Louis Allen Rawls (singer); 1935
Ritchard, Cyril; born Cyril Trimnell-Ritchard (actor/singer/director); 1893
Rivers, Eurith Dickinson (politician); 1895
Shawn, Dick; born Richard Schulefand (comedian/actor); 1929
Stout, Rex Todhunter (author); 1886
Throne, Malachi (actor); ——
Tilton, Charlene (actress); 1959
Trevino, Lee Buck (golf); 1939
Wall, Robert James Albert (hockey); 1942
Willis, Simeon Slavens (politician); 1879

DECEMBER 2:

Austin, Tracy (tennis); 1962
Brown, Willie; born William Ferdie Brown (football); 1940

Cheevers, Gerald (hockey); 1940
Clyde, June (actress); 1909
Delugg, Milton (music); 1918
Fonteyne, Valere Ronald (hockey); 1933
Gardner, Hy (journalist); 1904
Green, Adolph (writer); 1915
Haig, Alexander Meigs, Jr. (military/government); 1924
Hall, Charlie; born Charles Leslie Hall (football); 1948
Harris, Julie; born Julia Ann Harris (actress); 1925
Hearst, David Whitmire (publishing); 1915
Hearst, Randolph Apperson (publishing); 1915
Hildreth, Horace Augustus (politician); 1902
Martineau, John Ellis (politician); 1873
McCreary, William Edward (hockey); 1934
Moore, Zeke; born Ezekiel Moore (football); 1943
Rodgers, Andre; born Kenneth Andre Ian Rodgers (baseball); 1934
Seurat, Georges (artist); 1859
Stone, Ezra Chaim; born Ezra Chaim Feinstone
    (actor/producer/director); 1917
William, Warren; born Warren William Krech (actor); 1895

DECEMBER 3:

Allison, Bobby; born Robert Arthur Allison (auto racing); 1937
Ammons, Teller (politician); 1895
Baker, Newton Diehl (government); 1871
Boswell, Connee (singer/actress); 1907
Boyd, Bob; born Robert D. Boyd (football); 1937
Callas, Maria Meneghini; born Cecilia Sophia Anna Maria
    Kalogeropoulou (singer); 1923
Collins, Joe; born Joseph Edward Kollonige (baseball); 1922
Conrad, Joseph; born Jozef Teodor Konrad Nalecz Korzeniowski
    (author); 1857
Curtin, Phyllis; born Phyllis Smith (singer); 1922
Dalrymple, Clay; born Clayton Errol Dalrymple (baseball); 1936
Fears, Tom; born Thomas Jesse Fears (football); 1923
Garrett, Wayne; born Ronald Wayne Garrett (baseball); 1947
Godard, Jean Luc (director); 1930
Hodgson, James Day (government); 1915
Husky, Ferlin (singer/comedian); 1927
McMahon, Jack (basketball); 1928
Mendenhall, John Rufus (football); 1948
Menzies, Heather Margaret (actress); 1949
Morehead, John Henry (politician); 1861
Morgan, Jaye P.; born Mary Margaret Morgan (singer/actress);
    1931
Simpson, Harry Leon "Suitcase" (baseball); 1925
Sten, Anna; born Anjuschka Stenski Sujakevitch (actress); 1907

Stuart, Gilbert Charles (artist); 1755
Williams, Andy; born Howard Andrew Williams (singer); 1928

DECEMBER 4:

Baer, Max, Jr.; born Maximilian Adelbert Baer, Jr. (actor/producer); 1937
Boyington, Pappy; born Gregory Boyington (aviator); 1912
Bridges, Jeff (actor); 1949
Buchholz, Horst Werner (actor); 1933
Burkett, Jesse Cail (baseball); 1868
Cannon, Freddy; born Frederick Anthony Picariello (singer); 1940
Carlyle, Thomas (writer/historian); 1795
Collins, Shano; born John Francis Collins (baseball); 1885
Delvecchio, Alex; born Alexander Peter Delvecchio (hockey); 1931
Dietrich, Dena (actress); 1928
Durbin, Deanna; born Edna Mae Durbin (actress); 1921
Franco, Francisco; born Francisco Paulino Hermenegildo Teodulo Franco-Bahamonde (Spanish government); 1892
Jones, Buck; born Charles Frederick Gebhart (actor); 1889
Kean, John (politician); 1852
Kuenn, Harvey Edward (baseball); 1930
Martindale, Win (or Wink); born Winston Conrad Martindale (TV host); 1934
Riessen, Marty; born Martin Clare Riessen (tennis); 1941
Ross, William Bradford (politician); 1873
Russell, Lillian; born Helen Louise Leonard (singer/actress); 1861
Shawkey, Bob; born James Robert Shawkey (baseball); 1890
Vanderbundt, Skip; born William Vanderbundt (football); 1946
Vataha, Randy; born Randel E. Vataha (football); 1948
Williams, John Bell (politician); 1918

DECEMBER 5:

Custer, George Armstrong (military officer); 1839
Didion, Joan (author/journalist); 1934
Disney, Walt; born Walter Elias Disney (producer); 1901
Earle, George Howard, III (politician); 1890
French, Victor (actor/director); ——
Hayes, Margaret "Maggie"; born Dana Dale (actress); 1924
Higgins, Pam; born Pamela Sue Higgins (golf); 1945
Kert, Larry; born Frederick Lawrence Kert (actor/singer/dancer); 1934
Lang, Fritz (director); 1890
Mayes, Rufus Lee (football); 1947
McDuffie, J.D.; born John Delphus McDuffie, Jr. (auto racing); 1938
Moore, Grace; born Mary Willie Grace Moore (singer/actress); 1898
Nice, Harry Whinna (politician); 1877
Paschal, Jim; born James Roy Paschal (auto racing); 1926
Plunkett, Jim; born James William Plunkett, Jr. (football); 1947

Preminger, Otto Ludwig (producer/director); 1906
Savalas, George Demosthenes (actor); ——
Thurmond, J. Strom; born James Strom Thurmond (politician); 1902
Van Buren, Martin (President); 1782
Wadkins, Lanny; born Jerry L. Wadkins (golf); 1949
Wrigley, Philip Knight (corporation executive); 1894

DECEMBER 6:

Bassen, Hank; born Henry Bassen (hockey); 1932
Bowa, Larry; born Lawrence Robert Bowa (baseball); 1945
Braddock, Jim; born James J. Braddock (boxing); 1905
Brubeck, David Warren (music); 1920
Cox, Wally; born Wallace Maynard Cox (actor); 1924
Fontanne, Lynn; born Lillie Louise Fontanne (actress); 1887
Foster, Susanna; born Suzanne DeLee Flanders Larson (actress); 1924
Gershwin, Ira; born Israel Gershvin (music); 1896
Hack, Stan; born Stanley Camfield Hack (baseball); 1909
Hart, William S.; born William Surrey Hart (actor/director); 1862
Kilmer, Joyce; born Alfred Joyce Kilmer (poet); 1886
Landi, Elissa; born Elizabeth-Marie-Christine Kuhnelt (actress); 1904
Lazzeri, Tony; born Anthony Michael Lazzeri (baseball); 1903
Mathews, F. David; born Forrest David Mathews (government); 1935
Mink, Patsy; born Pasty Takemoto (politician); 1927
Moorehead, Agnes Robertson (actress); 1906
Naughton, James (actor); 1945
Robustelli, Andy; born Andrew Robustelli (football); 1930
Thomas, Charles Spalding (politician); 1849
Van, Bobby; born Robert Van Stein (actor/dancer/singer); 1930
Young, Milton Ruben (politician); 1897

DECEMBER 7:

Bainter, Fay Okell (actress); 1892
Bench, Johnny Lee (baseball); 1947
Brooks, Leo; born Leonard Leo Brooks (football); 1947
Burstyn, Ellen; born Edna Rae Gillooly (actress); 1932
Cameron, Rod; born Roderick Cox (actor); 1910
Cardwell, Don; born Donald Eugene Cardwell (baseball); 1935
Cary, Joyce; born Arthur Joyce Lunel Cary (author); 1888
Cather, Willa Sibert (author); 1876
Chamberlain, Abiram (politician); 1837
Chapin, Harry Forster (singer/music); 1942
Doeg, John Hope (tennis); 1908
Donovan, Dick; born Richard Edward Donovan (baseball); 1927
Friml, Rudolf; born Charles Rudolf Friml (music); 1879
Galehouse, Denny; born Dennis Ward Galehouse (baseball); 1911
Gifford, Frances; born Mary Frances Gifford (actress); 1920
Hatfield, Hurd; born William Rukard Hurd Hatfield (actor); 1918

Johnson, Alex; born Alexander Johnson (baseball); 1942
Johnson, Ching; born Ivan Wilfred Johnson (hockey); 1897
Knight, Ted; born Tadeus Wladyslaw Konopka (actor); 1925
Larrazolo, Octaviano Ambrosio (politician); 1859
Mickoski, Nicholas (hockey); 1927
Prima, Louis (music); 1912
Seibert, Earl Walter (hockey); 1911
Sikes, Dan; born Daniel D. Sikes (golf); 1930
Smith, Hal; born Harold Wayne Smith (baseball); 1930
Unger, Gary Douglas (hockey); 1947
Wallach, Eli (actor); 1915
Woodall, Al; born Frank Alley Woodall (football); 1945
Zaslofsky, Max (basketball); 1925

DECEMBER 8:

Allison, Wilmer Lawson (tennis); 1902
Barron, William Wallace (politician); 1911
Barry, Martin J. (hockey); 1905
Basinger, Kim (actress); 1953
Berenson, Red; born Gordon Berenson (hockey); 1939
Brinkman, Eddie born Edwin Albert Brinkman (baseball); 1941
Brown, Bob; born Robert Stanford Brown (football); 1941
Carradine, David (actor); 1936
Davis, Sammy, Jr. (singer/actor/dancer); 1925
Green, John (basketball); 1933
Harris, Joel Chandler (author/journalist); 1848
Hay, Red; born William Charles Hay (hockey); 1935
Hoak, Dick; born Richard John Hoak (football); 1939
Irvine, Ted; born Edward Amos Irvine (hockey); 1944
Love, Bob (basketball); 1943
MacArthur, James Gordon (actor); 1937
Martin, Dewey (actor); 1923
McRae, Bennie; born Benjamin P. McRae (football); 1939
Morgan, Terence (actor); 1921
Otto, Gus; born August J. Otto (football); 1943
Pagliaroni, Jim; born James Vincent Pagliaroni (baseball); 1937
Qualen, John; born John Oleson (actor); 1899
Robins, Charles A. (politician); 1884
Rubinstein, John Arthur (actor/singer/music); 1946
Schell, Maxmilian Konrad (actor); 1930
Sibelius, Jean Julius Christian (music); 1865
Simpson, Adele; born Adele Smithline (fashion designer); 1903
Thompson, Hank; born Henry Curtis Thompson (baseball); 1925
Thurber, James Grover (author); 1894
Volpe, John Anthony (politics/government); 1908
Whitney, Eli (inventor); 1765
Wilson, Flip; born Clerow Wilson (comedian/actor); 1933

DECEMBER 9:

Bridges, Beau; born Lloyd Vernet Bridges, III (actor); 1941
Butkus, Dick; born Richard John Butkus (football//actor); 1942
Case, Francis Higbee (politician); 1896
Cassavetes, John (actor/director); 1929
Caulfield, Henry Stewart (politician); 1873
Cobb, Lee J.; born Leo Jacob (or Lee Jacoby) (actor); 1911
Comorosky, Adam Anthony (baseball); 1904
Crawford, Broderick; born William Broderick Crawford (actor); 1911
DeMaestri, Joe; born Joseph Paul DeMaestri (baseball); 1928
Douglas, Kirk; born Issur Danielovitch, changed to Isidore Demsky
        (actor/producer/director); 1916
Fairbanks, Douglas Elton, Jr. (actor); 1909
Foxx, Redd; born John Elroy Sanford (comedian/actor); 1922
Gingold, Hermione Ferdinanda (actress/singer); 1897
Guidolin, Bep; born Armand Guidolin (hockey); 1925
Hagan, Cliff (basketball); 1931
Hamilton, Margaret Brainard (actress); 1902
Hardwick, Thomas William (politician); 1872
Hartack, Willie; born William John Hartack, Jr. (jockey); 1932
Hay, Marion E. (politician); 1865
Houston, David (singer/music); 1938
Jones, Deacon; born David Jones (football); 1938
Kelley, Joe; born Joseph James Kelley (baseball); 1871
Kelly, Emmett Leo, Sr. (clown); 1898
Kite, Tom; born Thomas O. Kite, Jr. (golf); 1949
Klaus, Billy; born William Joseph Klaus (baseball); 1928
Knight, Goodwin Jess (politician); 1896
Knowles, Darold Duane (baseball); 1941
Martin, Freddy (music); 1906
Martin, Pit; born Hubert Jacques Martin (hockey); 1943
Medich, Doc; born George Francis Medich (baseball); 1948
Merrill, Dina; born Nedenia Hutton (actress); 1925
Milton, John (poet); 1608
Moody, Orville (golf); 1933
O'Neill, Tip; born Thomas Philip O'Neill (politician); 1912
Osmond, Donny; born Donald Clark Osmond (singer/music—Osmond
        Family); 1957
Owens, Steve E. (football); 1947
Paynter, Thomas Hanson (politician); 1851
Phillips, Leon Chase (politician); 1890
Reynolds, William (actor); 1931
Schwarzkopf, Elizabeth (singer); 1915
Turnesa, Jim; born James Turnesa (golf); 1912
Unser, Del; born Delbert Bernard Unser (baseball); 1944
Van Patten, Dick; born Richard Vincent Van Patten (actor); 1928

DECEMBER 10:

Alderman, Grady C. (football); 1938
Bies, Don; born Donald Bies (golf); 1937
Colicos, John (actor); 1928
Collins, Ray (actor); 1889
Conacher, Charlie; born Charles William Conacher, Jr. (hockey); 1909
Dey, Susan Hallock (actress); 1952
Dickinson, Emily Elizabeth (poet); 1830
Felix, Ray (basketball); 1930
Flanagan, Fionnula (or Fionnuala) Manon (actress); 1941
Franck, César Auguste (music); 1822
Garrison, William Lloyd (abolitionist/reformer); 1805
Gore, Thomas Pryor (politician); 1870
Gould, Harold (actor); 1923
Gould, Morton (music); 1913
Gronna, Asle Jorgenson (politician); 1858
Gwynne, Anne; born Marguerite Gwynne Trice (actress); 1918
Hart, Philip Aloysius (politician); 1912
Huntley, Chet; born Chester Robert Huntley (newscaster); 1911
Johnston, Jimmy; born James Harle Johnston (baseball); 1889
Kirk, Tommy (actor); 1941
Lamour, Dorothy; born Mary Leta Dorothy Kaumeyer (actress); 1914
Layne, Bobby; born Robert Lawrence Layne (football); 1926
Loring, Gloria Jean; born Gloria Jean Goff (singer); 1946
Merkel, Una (actress); 1903
Morgan, Dennis; born Stanley Morner (actor/singer); 1910
Morris, Larry; born Lawrence Morris (football); 1933
Osborne, Vivienne (actress); 1896
Rettig, Tommy; born Thomas Noel Rettig (actor); 1941
Sterling, Tisha; born Patricia Ann Sterling (actress); 1944
Williams, Harrison Arlington, Jr. (politician); 1919

DECEMBER 11:

Armstrong, Bess; born Elizabeth Armstrong (actress); 1953
Baur, Elizabeth (actress); 1947
Beck, Ernie (basketball); 1931
Berlioz, Hector; born Louis Hector Berlioz (music); 1803
Blair, Betsy; born Elizabeth Boger (actress); 1923
Brown, Hal; born Hector Harold Brown (baseball); 1924
Carr, Ralph L. (politician); 1887
Cox, Fred; born Frederick W. Cox (football); 1938
Dowling, Eddie; born Joseph Nelson Goucher (actor); 1894
Eilers, Sally; born Dorethea Sallye Eilers (actress); 1908
Fess, Simeon Davison (politician); 1861
Firestone, Eddie; born Edward William Firestone (actor); 1920
George, Lynda Day; born Lynda Day (actress); 1946

444   THE CELEBRITY BIRTHDAY BOOK

Hampson, Ted; born Edward George Hampson (hockey); 1936
Harriss, Slim; born William Jennings Bryan Harriss (baseball); 1896
Heywood, Anne; born Violet Pretty (actress); 1931
Hoey, Clyde Roark (politician); 1877
La Guardia, Fiorello Henry (politician); 1882
Lee, Brenda; born Brenda Mae Tarpley (singer); 1942
Marais, Jean; born Jean Marais-Villain (actor); 1913
Maye, Lee; born Arthur Lee Maye (baseball); 1934
McLaglen, Victor (actor); 1883
Mills, Donna (actress); 1943
Moreno, Rita; born Rosita Dolores Alverio (actress/singer/dancer);
    1931
Pilote, Pierre Paul (hockey); 1931
Ponti, Carlo (producer); 1913
Roland, Gilbert; born Luis Antonio Damaso De Alonso (actor); 1905
Seaton, Frederick Andrew (government); 1909
Shofner, Del; born Delbert M. Shofner (football); 1934
Solzhenitsyn, Aleksandr Isayevich (author); 1918
Stallings, Larry; born Lawrence Stallings (football); 1941
Thomas, Earlie (football); 1945
Trintignant, Jean-Louis (actor); 1930
Vasko, Moose; born Elmer Vasko (hockey); 1935
Welker, Herman (politician); 1906
Windsor, Marie; born Emily Marie Bertelson (actress); 1922

DECEMBER 12:

Barker, Bob; born Robert William Barker (TV host); ——
Burdett, Winston M. (newscaster); 1913
Carr, Darlene; born with surname Farnon (actress/singer); ——
Crews, Laura Hope (actress); 1879
Dallenbach, Wally; born Wallace J. Dallenbach (auto racing); 1936
Doak, William Nuckles (government); 1882
Englehorn, Shirley Ruth (golf); 1940
Fittipaldi, Emerson (auto racing); 1946
Flaubert, Gustave (author); 1821
Francis, Connie; born Concetta Franconero (singer/actress); 1938
Garr, Ralph Allen (baseball); 1945
Houx, Frank L. (politician); 1860
Jay, John (statesman/jurist); 1745
Karakas, Mike; born Michael Karakas (hockey); 1911
Kennedy, Teeder; born Theodore S. Kennedy (hockey); 1925
Koch, Edward Irving (politician); 1924
Kullman, Edward George (hockey); 1923
McKenzie, John Albert (hockey); 1937
Morley, Karen; born Mabel (or Mildred) Linton (actress); 1905
Osborne, John James (playwright); 1929
Pettit, Bob; born Robert E. Lee Pettit (basketball); 1932

Rigby, Cathy (gymnast/actress); 1952
Robinson, Edward G.; born Emmanuel Goldberg (actor); 1893
Sinatra, Frank; born Francis Albert Sinatra (singer/actor); 1915
Smith, Clint; born Clinton James Smith (hockey); 1913
Smith, Randy (basketball); 1948
Vanderbilt, William Kissam (capitalist); 1849
Warner, Harry Morris (producer—Warner Brothers); 1881
Warwicke, Dionne; born Marie Dionne Warwick (singer/actress); 1940
White, Frank (politics/government); 1856
Williams, Joe; born Joseph Goreed (singer); 1918
Yates, Richard (politician); 1860

DECEMBER 13:

Connelly, Marc; born Marcus Cook Connelly (playwright); 1890
Davidson, John Hamilton (singer/actor); 1941
Doby, Larry; born Lawence Eugene Doby (baseball); 1923
Dusek, Brad; born John Bradley Dusek (football); 1950
Erskine, Carl Daniel (baseball); 1926
Garver, Kathy; born Kathleen Marie Garver (actress); 1947
Glasscock, William Ellsworth (politician); 1862
Heflin, Van; born Emmet Evan Heflin, Jr. (actor); 1910
Jenkins, Ferguson Arthur (baseball); 1943
Johnson, Gus (basketball); 1938
Jürgens, Curd (or Curt) (actor/director); 1912
Ladd, Edwin Freemont (politician); 1859
Lincoln, Mary Todd; born Mary Ann Todd (First Lady); 1818
Loes, Billy; born William Loes (baseball); 1929
Lynch, Fran; born Francis Lynch (football); 1945
MacDonald, John Ross; born Kenneth Millar (author); 1915
McDaniel, Lindy; born Lyndall Dale McDaniel (baseball); 1935
Mohns, Douglas Allen (hockey); 1933
Montoya, Carlos (music); 1903
Moore, Archie; born Archibald Lee Moore (boxing); 1916
Mosley, Mike; born Michael Dean Mosley (auto racing); 1944
Parks, Larry; born Samuel Lawrence Klausman (actor); 1914
Parrish, Lemar (football); 1947
Paulsen, Albert (actor); 1927
Pearson, Drew; born Andrew Russell Pearson (journalist); 1897
Plummer, Christopher; born Arthur Christopher Orme (actor); 1927
Roth, Lillian; born Lillian Rutstein (actress); 1910
Shaw, Tom; born Thomas Shaw (golf); 1942
Shoup, Oliver Henry (politician); 1869
Shultz, George Pratt (government); 1920
Stevens, Mark; born Richard Stevens (actor); 1915
Taylor, Don (actor/director); 1920
Van Dyke, Dick (comedian/actor); 1925

Whitaker, Johnny (actor); 1959
Zanuck, Richard Darryl (producer); 1934

DECEMBER 14:

Adams, Bobby; born Robert Henry Adams (baseball); 1921
Amsterdam, Morey (comedian/actor/music); 1912
Bell, Les; born Lester Rowland Bell (baseball); 1901
Buckner, Bill; born William Joseph Buckner (baseball); 1949
Burke, Billy; born William Burke (golf); 1902
Cochet, Henri (tennis); 1901
Cooper, Joseph (hockey); 1914
Dailey, Dan (actor/dancer); 1917
Doolittle, James Harold (army air force officer); 1896
Duke, Patty; born Anna Maria Patricia Duke (actress); 1946
Edwards, Dave; born David Edwards (football); 1939
Furth, George (actor); 1932
Jones, Sam; born Samuel Jones (baseball); 1925
Jones, Spike; born Lindley Armstrong Jones (music); 1911
Knox, Elyse, (actress); 1917
Lane, Abbe; born Abigail Francine Lassman (singer/actress); 1932
McNair, Robert Evander (politician); 1923
Mead, Albert Edward (politician); 1861
Naismith, Laurence; born Laurence Bernard Johnson (actor); 1908
Nostradamus; born Michael de Notredame (astrologer); 1503
Remick, Lee Ann (actress); 1935
Rich, Charlie; born Charles Allan Rich (singer/music); 1932
Sawyer, Grant (politician); 1918
Smith, Margaret Chase; born Margaret Chase (politician); 1897
Staggers, Jon; born Jonathan L. Staggers (football); 1948
Sutorius, James (actor); 1944
Trippi, Charlie; born Charles Lou Trippi (football); 1922
Wilson, Joyce Vincent; born Joyce Elaine Vincent (singer); 1946

DECEMBER 15:

Anderson, Maxwell (playwright); 1888
Bahnsen, Stan; born Stanley Raymond Bahnsen (baseball); 1944
Bloomgarden, Kermit (producer); 1904
Bradford, Robert Fiske (politician); 1902
Bukich, Rudy; born Rudolph A. Bukich (football); 1932
Buoniconti, Nick; born Nicholas Anthony Buoniconti
          (football/sportscaster/attorney); 1940
Chandler, Jeff; born Ira Grossel (actor); 1918
Cole, Buddy; born Edwin Le Mar Cole (music); 1916
Conway, Tim; born Thomas Daniel Conway (comedian/actor); 1933
Getty, J. Paul; born Jean Paul Getty (oil magnate); 1892
Herbert, Ray; born Raymond Ernest Herbert (baseball); 1929
Holloway, William Judson (politician); 1888

Jackson, Arthur (hockey); 1915
Keyworth, Jon; born Jonathan K. Keyworth (football); 1950
Morrow, Karen (actress/singer); 1936
Nelson, Jimmy (ventriloquist); 1928
Robinson, Eddie; born William Edward Robinson (baseball); 1920
Shaw, Billy; born William L. Shaw (football); 1938
Walton, Joe; born Joseph Walton (football); 1935

DECEMBER 16:

Albright, Hardie; born Hardy Albrecht (actor); 1903
Austen, Jane (author); 1775
Beethoven, Ludwig van (music); 1770
Ben-Gurion, David; born David Green (Israeli government); 1886
Brezhnev, Leonid Ilyich (Russian government); 1906
Brinegar, Claude Stout (government); 1926
Brookshier, Tom; born Thomas Brookshier (football/sportscaster); 1931
Colquitt, Oscar Branch (politician); 1861
Connelly, Wayne Francis (hockey); 1939
Coward, Sir Noel Pierce (playwright/actor/director/music); 1899
Fugett, Jean S., Jr. (football); 1951
Hunt, Frank W. (politician); 1861
Kent, Barbara; born Barbara Clowtman (actress); 1906
Mead, Margaret (anthropologist); 1901
Pritchett, V.S.; born Victor Sawdon Pritchett (literary critic); 1900
Santayana, George (philosopher/poet); 1863
Schaefer, George Louis (producer/director); 1920
Stahl, Lesley R. (newscaster); 1941
Ullmann, Liv Johanne (actress); 1939

DECEMBER 17:

Adair, Jerry; born Kenneth Jerry Adair (baseball); 1936
Cadmus, Paul (artist); 1904
Caldwell, Erskine Preston (author); 1903
Cardenas, Leo; born Leonardo Lazaro Cardenas (baseball);
    1938
Fiedler, Arthur (music); 1894
Kanicki, Jim; born James Kanicki (football); 1942
Livingston, Barry (actor); 1953
Long, Richard (actor); 1927
McLeod, Thomas Gordon (politician); 1868
Meade, Julia; born Julia Kunze (actress); 1928
Sackett, Frederick Mosley (politician); 1868
Steele, Tommy; born Thomas Hicks (singer/actor); 1936
Washington, Russ; born Russell Washington (football); 1946
Watson, Susan Elizabeth (actress/singer); 1938
Whittier, John Greenleaf (poet); 1807

Woodbury, Joan (actress); 1915
Wymore, Patrice (actress); 1926

DECEMBER 18:

Bari, Lynn; born Marjorie Bitzer (or Marjorie Schuyler Fisher) (actress); 1913
Barrie, Mona; born Mona Smith (actress); 1909
Brandt, Willy; born Herbert Ernst Karl Frahm (German government); 1913
Burrows, Abe; born Abram Solman Borowitz (playwright/director); 1910
Cimoli, Gino Nicholas (baseball); 1929
Clark, Ramsey (government); 1927
Cobb, Ty; born Tyrus Raymond Cobb (baseball); 1886
Coffman, Dick; born Samuel Richard Coffman (baseball); 1906
Cooper, Gladys Constance (actress); 1888
Cummins, Peggy (actress); 1925
Dassin, Jules (director); 1911
Davis, Ossie (actor/director/writer); 1917
Dennison, Doug; born William D. Dennison (football); 1951
Fry, Christopher; born Christopher Fry Harris (dramatist/poet); 1907
Grable, Betty; born Elizabeth Ruth Grasle (actress); 1913
Johnson, Celia (actress); 1908
Klee, Paul (artist); 1879
Landry, Greg; born Gregory Paul Landry (football); 1946
MacDowell, Edward Alexander (music); 1861
Myers, Francis John (politician); 1901
O'Day, Anita (singer); 1919
Pronovost, Joseph Jean Denis (hockey); 1945
Saki, born Hector Hugh Munro (author); 1870
Scott, Nathan Bay (politician); 1842
Shue, Gene (basketball); 1931
Simms, John F. (politician); 1916
Skowron, Bill "Moose"; born William Joseph Skowron (baseball); 1930
Smith, Roger (actor/producer); 1932
Stevens, George Cooper (director); 1904
Tremblay, Gilles (hockey); 1938
Versalles, Zorro; born Zoilo Casanova Versalles (baseball); 1939
Watkins, Arthur Vivian (politician); 1886
Weber, Baron Karl Maria Friedrich Ernst von (music); 1786

DECEMBER 19:

Emerson, Lee Earl (politician); 1898
Fiske, Minnie Maddern; born Marie Augusta Davey (actress); 1865
Frick, Ford Christopher (baseball); 1894
Genet, Jean (playwright); 1910
Harvey, Doug; born Douglas Norman Harvey (hockey); 1924

Joyce, Elaine (actress/singer); 1945
Kaline, Al; born Albert William Kaline (baseball); 1934
La Farge, Oliver Hazard Perry (author); 1901
MacDermot, Galt (music); 1928
Maunder, Wayne (actor); 1942
Nye, Gerald Prentice (politician); 1892
Ochs, Phil; born Philip David Ochs (singer/music); 1940
Piaf, Edith Gassion (singer/actress); 1915
Purdom, Edmund (actor); 1924
Reiner, Fritz (music); 1888
Richardson, Sir Ralph David (actor); 1902
Sackler, Howard (playwright); 1929
Schock, Ronald L. (hockey); 1943
Sherman, Robert Bernard (music); 1925
Smith, Stan; born Stanley Roger Smith (tennis); 1946
Smith, Willis (politician); 1887
Stanton, Edwin McMasters (statesman/jurist); 1814
Susskind, David Howard (TV host/producer); 1920
Taylor, Tony; born Antonio Nemesio Taylor (baseball); 1935
Tyson, Cicely (actress); 1939
Urich, Robert (actor); 1946
Vanderbilt, Reginald Claypoole (investor); 1880
Williams, Walt; born Walter Allen Williams (baseball); 1943
Windsor, Bob; born Robert Edward Windsor (football); 1942
Witek, Mickey; born Nicholas Joseph Witek (baseball); 1915

DECEMBER 20:

Agutter, Jenny (actress); 1952
Aubrey, Skye; born Susan Schuyler Aubrey (actress); 1945
Austin, Pamela (actress); 1941
Byrd, Harry Flood, Jr. (politician); 1914
Calisher, Hortense (author); 1911
Callas, Charlie (comedian/actor/music); ——
Christiansen, Jack L. (football); 1928
Davis, Spud; born Virgil Lawrence Davis (baseball); 1904
Dekker, Albert (actor); 1905
Dunne, Irene Marie (actress/singer); 1901
Ericson, Devon (actress); ——
Gamble, Oscar Charles (baseball); 1949
Hartnett, Gabby; born Charles Leo Hartnett (baseball); 1900
Hayes, Bob; born Robert Lee Hayes (olympic athlete/football); 1942
Henline, Butch; born Walter John Henline (baseball); 1894
Hill, George Roy (director); 1922
Kern, John Worth (politician); 1849
Lerner, Max (writer); 1902
Lindsey, Washington Ellsworth (politician); 1862
Mumphord, Lloyd N. (football); 1946

Richards, Ann; born Shirley Ann Richards (actress); 1918
Rickey, Branch Wesley (baseball); 1881
Rogers, C.J. "Doc" (politician); 1897
Simpson, Jim; born James Shores Simpson (sportscaster); 1927
Sparkman, John Jackson (politician); 1899
Tompkins, Angel (actress); 1943
Totter, Audrey (actress); 1918
Weston, Kim (actress/singer); 1939
Williams, Robert Lee (politician); 1868

DECEMBER 21:

Alonso, Alicia; born Alicia Ernestina de la Caridad del Cobre Martinez
    Hoyo (dancer); 1921
Ball, George Wildman (government); 1909
Disraeli, Benjamin; born Benjamin D'Israeli (statesman/author); 1804
Donahue, Phil; born Phillip John Donahue (TV host); 1935
Eglevsky, André Eugenovitch (dancer); 1917
Evert, Chris; born Christine Marie Evert (tennis); 1954
Fonda, Jane Seymour (actress); 1937
Frazier, Lynn Joseph (politician); 1874
Hagen, Walter Charles (golf); 1892
Love, Phyllis Ann (actress); 1925
Maddox, Elliott (baseball); 1947
Martin, Jared (actor); 1943
McCormack, John William (politician); 1891
McRae, Thomas Chipman (politician); 1851
Nagle, Kel; born Kelvin David George Nagle (golf); 1920
Nelson, Ed; born Edwin Stafford Nelson (actor); 1928
Paige, Robert; born John Anthony (or Arthur) Paige (actor); 1910
Paterno, Joe; born Joseph Vincent Paterno (football); 1926
Racine, Jean Baptiste (dramatist); 1639
Rush, Bob; born Robert Ransom Rush (baseball); 1925
Stalin, Joseph Vissarionovich; born Iosif Vissarionovich Dzhugashvili
    (Russian government); 1879
Terral, Thomas Jefferson (politician); 1882
Waldheim, Kurt (United Nations); 1918
Williams, Cy; born Fred Williams (baseball); 1887
Winchell, Paul (ventriloquist/actor); 1922
Wright, Nate (football); 1947

DECEMBER 22:

Alou, Matty; born Mateo Rojas Alou (baseball); 1938
Bruton, Bill; born William Haron Bruton (baseball); 1929
Carlton, Steve; born Stephen Norman Carlton (baseball); 1944
Castle, Peggie; born Peggie Blair (actress); 1927
Clark, Barzilla Worth (politician); 1881
Darro, Frankie; born Frank Johnson (actor); 1917

Garvey, Steve; born Steven Patrick Garvey (baseball); 1948
Goodland, Walter Samuel (politician); 1862
Guy, Ray; born William Ray Guy (football); 1949
Hart, Freddie (singer); 1928
Hawkins, Tom; born Thomas Jerome Hawkins (basketball); 1936
Hendricks, Elrod Jerome (baseball); 1940
Johnson, Lady Bird; born Claudia Alta Taylor (First Lady); 1912
Kellogg, Frank Billings (politics/government); 1856
Kostelanetz, Andre (music); 1901
Mack, Connie; born Cornelius McGillicuddy (baseball); 1862
Merriam, Frank Finley (politician); 1865
Moeur, Benjamin Baker (politician); 1869
Pearson, David Gene (auto racing); 1934
Puccini, Giacomo (music); 1858
Rayburn, Gene; born Gene Rubessa (TV host/actor); 1917
Robinson, Edwin Arlington (poet); 1869
Stanis, BernNadette (actress); 1953
Stephenson, Jan Lynn (golf); 1951
Stokes, Edward Casper (politician); 1860
Taylor, Deems; born Joseph Deems Taylor (music); 1885
Wright, Jim; born James Claud Wright, Jr. (politician); 1922

DECEMBER 23:

Barron Herman (golf); 1909
Blore, Eric (actor); 1887
Devine, Dan; born Daniel John Devine (football); 1924
Dumart, Woody; born Woodrow Wilson Clarence Dumart (hockey); 1916
Greco, José; born Costanzo Greco (dancer); 1918
Gregory, James (actor); 1911
Guardino, Harry; born Harold Vincent Guardino (actor); 1925
Ham, Jack; born John Raphael Ham (football); 1948
Hartman, Elizabeth (actress); 1941
Hornung, Paul Vernon (football/sportscaster); 1935
Kalber, Floyd (newscaster); 1924
Koosman, Jerry; born Jerome Martin Koosman (baseball); 1942
Moody, William Henry (government/jurist); 1853
O'Loughlin, Gerald S.; born Gerald Stuart O'Loughlin (actor); 1921
Purcell, Noel (actor); 1900
Roman, Ruth (actress); 1924
Roosevelt, James (First family); 1907
Sardi, Vincent, Sr.; born Melchiorre Pio Vincenzo Sardi (restaurateur); 1885
Schmidt, Helmut Heinrich Waldemar (German government); 1918
Shallenberger, Ashton Cokayne (politician); 1862
Stacy, James (actor); ——
Straus, Oscar Solomon (government); 1850

Taylor, Danny; born Daniel Turney Taylor (baseball); 1900
Thomas, Tommy; born Alphonse Thomas (baseball); 1899
Wood, Willie; born William V. Wood (football); 1936

DECEMBER 24:

Adam, Noelle Huguette (actress); 1933
Banaszek, Cas; born Casmir J. Banaszek, II (football); 1945
Bennett, Jill (actress); 1930
Cain, Herbert (hockey); 1913
Carson, Kit; born Christopher Carson (frontiersman); 1809
Chatterton, Ruth (actress/author); 1893
Dudley, Bill; born William M. Dudley (football); 1921
Ganley, Howden; born James Howden Ganley (auto racing); 1941
Gardner, Ava Lavinnia; born Lucy Johnson (actress); 1922
Haney, Carol (dancer/actress/choreographer); 1924
Howard, Bob; born Robert L. Howard (football); 1944
Hughes, Howard Robard, Jr. (industrialist); 1905
Joffrey, Robert; born Abdullah Jaffa Bey Khan (choreographer); 1930
Matuszak, John (football); 1950
Parkes, Mike; born Michael Johnson Parkes (auto racing); 1931
Smith, Tody; born Lawrence E. Smith (football); 1948
Stone, I.F.; born Isidor Feinstein Stone (journalist); 1907
Sullivan, Red; born George James Sullivan (hockey); 1929
Triplett, Mel; born Melvin Triplett (football); 1931
Warren, Harry Salvatore (music); 1893

DECEMBER 25:

Ashley, John; born John Atchley (actor); 1934
Barton, Clara; born Clarissa Harlowe Barton (founder of American Red
    Cross); 1821
Bogart, Humphrey DeForest (actor); 1899
Brown, Lloyd Andrew (baseball); 1904
Buffett, Jimmy (singer/music); 1946
Bulaich, Norm; born Norman B. Bulaich (football); 1946
Cahan, Lawrence Louis (hockey); 1933
Calloway, Cab; born Cabell Calloway, III (music/singer/actor); 1907
Chapman, Ben; born William Benjamin Chapman (baseball); 1908
Chevrolet, Louis Joseph (auto racing & manufacturer); 1878
Churchill, Marguerite (actress); 1909
Clifford, Clark McAdams (government); 1906
Csonka, Larry; born Lawrence Richard Csonka (football); 1946
Dix, John Alden (politician); 1860
Durr, Francois (tennis); 1942
Fletcher, Chris; born Christopher Fletcher (football); 1948
Fox, Nellie; born Jacob Nelson Fox (baseball); 1927
Garver, Ned Franklin (baseball); 1925
Hilton, Conrad Nicholson (hotel magnate); 1887

Holke, Walter Henry (baseball); 1892
Isley, O'Kelly (singer—Isley Brothers); 1937
Jackson, Al; born Alvin Neal Jackson (baseball); 1935
Little Richard; born Richard Pennimann (singer/music); 1932
MacLane, Barton (actor); 1902
Mandrell, Barbara Ann (singer/music); 1948
Martin, Tony; born Alfred Norris, Jr. (singer/actor); 1912
Mazurki, Mike; born Mikhail Mazurwski (actor); 1909
McCalla, Irish (actress/artist); 1929
Moore, Jo Jo; born Joseph Gregg Moore (baseball); 1908
Morrison, John Tracy (politician); 1860
Newton, Sir Isaac (mathematician); 1642
Parks, Dave; born David Wayne Parks (football); 1941
Picard, Noel; born Jean Noel Yves Picard (hockey); 1938
Rugolo, Peter (music); 1915
Sadat, Anwar (Egyptian government); 1918
Serling, Rod (author); 1924
Slaton, John Marshall (politician); 1866
Spacek, Sissy; born Mary Elizabeth Spacek (actress); 1949
Stabler, Ken; born Kenneth Michael Stabler (football); 1946
Swarthout, Gladys (singer/actress); 1904
Twelvetrees, Helen; born Helen Marie Jurgens (actress); 1907
Twilley, Howard (football); 1943
Washington, Mark Henry (football); 1947
West, Dame Rebecca; born Cicily Isabel Fairfield (author); 1892

DECEMBER 26:

Allen, Steve; born Stephen Valentine Patrick William Allen
    (comedian/actor/singer/TV host/music/author); 1921
Broyles, Frank; born John Franklin Broyles (football/sportscaster);
    1924
Causey, Wayne; born James Wayne Causey (baseball); 1936
Chambliss, Chris; born Carroll Christopher Chambliss (baseball); 1948
Cook, Elisha, Jr. (actor); 1902
Dewey, George (naval officer); 1837
Fisk, Carlton Ernest (baseball); 1948
Gore, Albert Arnold (politician); 1907
Gray, Thomas (poet); 1716
Jillson, Joyce (actress); 1946
King, Alan; born Irwin Alan Kniberg (comedian/actor); 1927
Mao Tse-Tung (Chinese government); 1893
Miller, Henry Valentine (author); 1891
Miller, Stu; born Stuart Leonard Miller (baseball); 1927
Moffat, Donald (actor/director); 1930
Neuberger, Richard Lewis (politician); 1912
Sadecki, Ray; born Raymond Michael Sadecki (baseball); 1940
Stephens, William Dennison (politician); 1859

Taylor, Trevor Patrick (auto racing); 1936
Ullman, Norm; born Norman Victor Alexander Ullman (hockey); 1935
Widmark, Richard (actor); 1914

DECEMBER 27:

Amos, John (actor); 1942
Arno, Sig; born Siegfried Aron (actor); 1895
Bromfield, Louis (author); 1896
Courtland, Jerome; born Courtland Jourolman, Jr.
    (actor/singer/producer); 1926
Dietrich, Marlene; born Maria Madgalena Dietrich, adopted Maria
    Magdalena von Losch (actress); 1901
Emmerson, Louis Lincoln (politician); 1863
Feldshuh, Tovah; born Terri Sue Feldshuh (actress); 1951
Gagliano, Phil; born Philip Joseph Gagliano (baseball); 1941
Greenstreet, Sydney Hughes (actor); 1879
Hackel, Stella Bloomberg (politician); 1926
Jackson, Edward L. (politician); 1873
Jones, Rich (basketball); 1946
Levant, Oscar (music); 1906
Marr, Dave; born David Marr (golf/sportscaster); 1933
McClure, James A. (politician); 1924
Mead, James Michael (politician); 1885
Pasteur, Louis (chemist); 1822
Redmond, Mickey; born Michael Edward Redmond (hockey); 1947
Ross, Charles Benjamin (politician); 1876
Russell, Charles Hinton (politician); 1903
Tobin, Jim; born James Anthony Tobin (baseball); 1912
White, Roy Hilton (baseball); 1943

DECEMBER 28:

Allen, James Browning (politician); 1912
Ayres, Lew; born Lewis Frederick Ayer, III (actor); 1908
Bowman, Lee; born Lucien Lee Bowman, Sr. (actor); 1910
Bridges, Tommy; born Thomas Jefferson Davis Bridges (baseball); 1906
Brown, Joseph Mackey (politician); 1851
Duggan, Andrew (actor); 1923
Green, Hubie; born Hubert Myatt Green (golf); 1946
Haber, Joyce (journalist); 1932
Hines, Fatha; born Earl Kenneth Hines (music); 1905
Jacobi, Lou; born Louis Harold Jacobi (actor); 1913
Knef (or Neff), Hildegarde (actress/singer/author); 1925
Lee, Bill; born William Francis Lee, III (baseball); 1946
Levenson, Sam (author/humorist); 1911
Lyons, Ted; born Theodore Amar Lyons (baseball); 1900
Maples, Bob; born Bobby Ray Maples (football); 1942
Milner, Martin Sam (actor); 1927

Otis, Johnny (singer/music); 1921
Piles, Samuel Henry (politician); 1858
Rodriguez, Aurelio (baseball); 1947
Sawchuk, Terry; born Terrance Gordon Sawchuk (hockey); 1929
Sessions, Roger Huntington (music); 1896
Smith, Maggie; born Margaret Smith (actress/singer); 1934
Stuart, Edwin Sydney (politician); 1853
Thomas, Clendon; born Robert Clendon Thomas (football); 1935
Van Buren, Steve; born Stephen W. Van Buren (football); 1920
Velasquez, Jorge (jockey); 1948
Weaver, Charley; born Cliff Arquette (entertainer); 1905
Willis, Frank Bartlette (politician); 1871
Wilson, Peggy; born Margaret Joyce Wilson (golf); 1934
Wilson, Woodrow; born Thomas Woodrow Wilson (President); 1856
Wiseman, Edward Randall (hockey); 1912
Yarnell, Bruce (actor/singer); 1935

DECEMBER 29:

Bradley, Thomas (politician); 1917
Casals, Pablo; born Pablo Pau Carlos Salvador Defillp de Casals
    (music); 1876
Cheyunski, Jim; born James M. Cheyunski (football); 1945
Dodd, Claire (actress); 1908
Elliman, Yvonne (singer/actress); 1953
Fields, William Jason (politician); 1874
Flanders, Ed; born Edward Paul Flanders (actor); 1934
Gibson, Ernest Willard (politician); 1872
Gladstone, William Ewart (statesman/author); 1809
Gogolak, Charley; born Charles Gogolak (football); 1944
Guffey, Joseph Finch (politician); 1870
Hill, Lister (politician); 1894
Howell, Harry; born Henry Vernon Howell (hockey); 1932
Jackson, Freda (actress); 1909
Jarriel, Tom; born Thomas Edwin Jarriel (newscaster); 1934
Johnson, Andrew (President); 1808
Kirkland, Gelsey (dancer); 1952
Knickerbocker, Bill; born William Hart Knickerbocker (baseball); 1911
Lindfors, Viveca; born Elsa Viveca Torstensdotter Lindfors (actress);
    1920
Lucci, Mike; born Michael G. Lucci (football); 1940
Marshall, George (director); 1891
Moore, Mary Tyler (actress/singer/dancer/producer); 1937
Nitschke, Ray; born Raymond E. Nitschke (football); 1936
Pincay, Laffit, Jr. (jockey); 1946
Powers, Mala; born Mary Ellen Powers (actress); 1921
Stewart, Nelson (hockey); 1902
Swenson, Inga (actress/singer); 1932

Voight, Jon (actor); 1938
Weaver, Robert Clifton (government); 1907

DECEMBER 30:

Davis, Skeeter; born Mary Frances Penick (singer); 1931
Diddley, Bo; born Ellas McDaniels (singer/music); 1928
Guggenheim, Simon (philanthropist/financier/politician); 1867
Hoblitzell, John Dempsey, Jr. (politician); 1912
Johnston, Henry Simpson (politician); 1867
Kabalevsky, Dmitri (music); 1904
Kipling, Rudyard (author); 1865
Koufax, Sandy; born Sanford Koufax (baseball); 1935
Lopez, Vincent (music); 1895
Lord, Jack; born John Joseph Patrick Ryan (actor/artist); 1928
Lorenzen, Fred (auto racing); 1934
Marshall, Jim; born James Lawrence Marshall (football); 1937
Mix, Steve (basketball); 1947
Nance, Jim; born James Solomon Nance (football); 1942
Nichols, Barbara; born Barbara Nickerauer (actress); 1929
Nolan, Jeanette (actress); 1911
Parks, Bert; born Bert Jacobson (actor/singer/TV host); 1914
Pine, William Bliss (politician); 1877
Renfro, Mel; born Melvin Lacy Renfro (football); 1941
Shannon, Del; born Charles Westover (singer/music); 1939
Smith, Alfred Emanuel (politician); 1873
Tamblyn, Russ (actor); 1934
Van Fleet, Jo (actress); 1919
Wilson, Marie; born Katherine Elizabeth White (actress); 1916

DECEMBER 31:

Allen, Rex E. (actor/singer); 1920
Arden, Elizabeth; born Florence Nightingale Graham (cosmetics); 1884
Brady, Pat; born Robert Patrick Brady (actor/singer); 1914
Byrne, Tommy; born Thomas Joseph Byrne (baseball); 1919
Cartier, Jacques (explorer); 1491
Cooney, Frank H. (politician); 1872
Cornwallis, Charles (English soldier); 1738
Denver, John; born Henry John Deutschendorf, Jr. (singer/actor); 1943
Gardiner, Chuck; born Charles Robert Gardiner (hockey); 1904
Gilder, Bob; born Robert Gilder (golf); 1950
Gubbrud, Archie M. (politician); 1910
Hopkins, Anthony (actor); 1937
Johnson, Syl; born Sylvester W. Johnson (baseball); 1900
Jones, Jonah; born Robert Elliott Jones (music); 1909
Kelly, King; born Michael Joseph Kelly (baseball); 1857
Marshall, George Catlett (military/government); 1880
Matheson, Tim (actor); 1947

Matisse, Henri Emile Benoit (artist); 1869
McElhenny, Hugh Edward (football); 1928
Meier, Julius L. (politician); 1874
Miles, Sarah (actress); 1941
Milstein, Nathan (music); 1904
Negri, Pola; born Barbara Appolonia Chalupec (actress); 1894
New, Harry Stewart (politics/government); 1858
Odetta; born Odetta Holmes (singer/music); 1930
Reed, Stanley Forman (jurist); 1884
Richards, Golden; born John Golden Richards (football); 1950
Richey, Cliff; born George Clifford Richey, Jr. (tennis); 1946
Sleeper, Albert E. (politician); 1862
Styne, Jule; born Julius Kerwin Stein (music/producer); 1905
Summer, Donna; born LaDonna Andrea Gaines (singer); 1948

Appendix I
ASTROLOGY GUIDE*

ARIES March 21-April 20

Aries, the first sign of the zodiac, is a masculine, cardinal, fire sun sign ruled by the planet Mars and symbolized by the Ram.

The individual born under the sign of the Ram is anything but a sheep in the middle of a flock. He is a born leader, not a follower. He is a courageous trailblazer with a pioneer spirit and sense of adventure. An Aries is an independent, strongwilled, forceful individual who takes the initiative because of his high degree of self-confidence. He is a free-thinker with original, imaginative, creative, and progressive ideas which are enhanced by an active, alert, and highly intelligent mind. The typical Aries is very goal-oriented, ambitious, aggressive, and resourceful, with endless energy and enthusiasm. A true Arien is possessed with an impulsive nature; he is impetuous.

---

*The Astrology Guide, and the Numerology Guide that follows, do not necessarily represent the author's beliefs and convictions. Rather, they are composite capsule narrative personality portraits based on the conclusions of recognized astrologers and numerologists. The author is neither an astrologer nor a numerologist and does not claim to be an authority in these fields. Furthermore, the guides are not intended to be a definitive discourse delving into the complexity of horoscopes and numberscopes. However, on the basis of the highlights provided, it is the author's contention that neither astrology nor numerology are in themselves truly sufficient to be self-supporting. The combination of the two, however, known as astro-numerology, do complement each other, and provide a more accurate description of one's self. It is recommended that after reading the delineation of your particular sign of the zodiac in Appendix I you also read the information for the numerical digit of the day on which you were born, as provided in the Numerology Guide, to determine if your traits and characteristics are intensifed or mitigated.

headstrong, and hates to compromise, as he wants everything his own way.

The normal first sign native is extremely extroverted, with a pleasing and magnetic personality. He is a good conversationalist with a sense of humor. He is a good, dependable, and generous friend. An eternal optimist, he is highly trustworthy himself, but often he places his trust in the wrong people, and finds himself being used by others. An Aries is understanding, sympathetic, and sensitive about the rights of other individuals and can be counted on to champion the cause of the underdog, providing he can justify how the cause can directly relate to him and his rather self-centered nature. He is an idealist, with a well-defined sense of values, who seeks perfection in everything and everybody. The textbook Arien has a large ego, which is intensified by a high degree of impatience, and when his ego is not constantly massaged, and the course of events is not accelerating at his prescribed pace, his explosive temper becomes readily visible. He is a very direct person who more often than not lacks subtlety, tact and diplomacy, since he is unafraid to speak out and says precisely what is on his mind.

The Aries man is neither an economist nor a saver; he will spend his money as quickly as he makes it. Due to his generous, charitable and trustworthy nature, he would be ill-suited to a career as a banker, finance company loan officer, or grant administrator because he would have a strong tendency to give money away quite freely. He is always a soft touch for friends who wish to borrow from him. Although he is honest and would recognize his debts and financial obligations, he usually is somewhat slow in paying his bills. The authoritative Arien would be ideal as a free-lancer or the owner of his own business, since he is efficient and conscientious only when he works free of constant supervision. He works best when he must improvise, and his methods are often considered unorthodox by others.

The Aries person, although basically endowed with good health, is to an extent careless about his health and often abuses his body by overworking and showing up for work when he is ill. Since he is such a hard worker, he often suffers from migraines, high blood pressure, and ulcers. He dislikes seeing members of the medical profession, except socially. An Arien is not a health nut, and would not be found jogging, playing tennis, or adhering to any daily exercise plan. However, he does like sports, especially those with an element of danger, such as skiing, sky-diving, hang-gliding, or auto racing, but usually finds very little time in his busy schedule to participate.

Aries is the perfect astrological sign for the working wife, who can successfully combine a career and motherhood. Many feminists and women's liberation proponents are born under the sign of the Ram.

An Aries individual is very attractive to the opposite sex, craves affection, considers himself a great lover, and seeks the mutual respect of his partner. For an Arien, love and romance are key ingredients for compatibility, and he would not engage in casual affairs where these ingredients are missing. It is uncommon for a typical Aries to have a large family, yet he loves children and makes a good parent, and he is almost always strict when it comes to raising his offspring.

TAURUS April 21-May 21

Taurus, the second sign of the zodiac, is a feminine, fixed, earth sun sign ruled by the planet Venus and symbolized by the Bull.

Like the Bull, which symbolizes the second sign of the zodiac, a Taurus is very down-to-earth, earthy; in fact he's the salt of the earth. He is very practical, sensible, and possesses an abundance of common sense. The typical Taurean is basically cautious, suspicious, and very analytical, too much so for his own good. Because of these earthy qualities, his outlook on life is more pessimistic than optimistic. An individual born under the sign of the Bull is further likened to the animal in that he is rather passive, undemonstrative, gentle and easy going until he is provoked. Once provoked, a violent outrage ensues. The old story about the Bull in the china shop is a classic description of a Taurean. He hates to be confined and needs wide open spaces to roam, greatly preferring suburban living to an urban environment.

A Taurus believes that hard work will bring justified rewards in the end. He is intelligent, and is usually a fast learner with an excellent memory. A patient, methodical, and industrious worker, he can be depended upon under virtually all cirmcumstances and will always cut through the red tape to get things done. The Taurean will never talk about doing something, he simply will do it with great determination. He's a doer, and does things his own way. Stubborn, obstinate, and hardheaded best describe him, and obstacles only make him more persistent. Perseverance and a strong endurance are the key ingredients for the successful Taurus. A Taurus is a good administrator, good organizer, and an excellent money manager. He has a great love of comfort and luxury and above all else needs financial security and emotional security to be truly happy. The Taurean native is driven with a desire to accomplish something which will benefit others and live on after him.

The individual born under the sign of the Bull is kind, generous, thoughtful and helpful to others. He is endowed with the attributes of honesty, loyalty and integrity. A Taurus has good social graces and hates others' bad manners. He appreciates esthetic beauty and loves music. Although a Taurean is gifted with good health, strength, and will power, he is usually a self-indulgent person, who partakes of food and drink in the excess. He does absolutely nothing in moderation.

A Taurean is seldom apt to worry but is paranoid in that he constantly fears rejection and ridicule. He can't stand being criticized and contradicted, finds it very difficult to apologize, and generally has an unforgiving nature. Because of his earthy ways, a Taurus is essentially a traditionalist, with a conventional outlook, and is not receptive to change. Flexibility of thought is not a Taurean strong point.

Both the male and female of this astrological sign are sensuous and affectionate persons with a great capacity for love and with a powerful sex drive. A Taurus is accused of being jealous and possessive, and justly so. A Taurean most often has a large family because of his love for children, and makes a loving and sympathetic parent, but occasionally spoils his offspring with expensive gifts.

GEMINI May 22-June 21

Gemini, the third sign of the zodiac, is a masculine, mutable, air sun sign ruled by the planet Mercury and symbolized by the Twins.

Gemini is probably the most difficult of the twelve signs of the zodiac to understand. Symbolized by the Twins, a person born under this sign automatically possesses a duality to his nature and forever seems to be contradicting himself. A typical Geminian is unpredictable, with a changeable personality. He changes his mind rapidly and is plagued by indecision. For Gemini, variety is the spice of life. A Gemini is easily bored, hates dullness and routine, and considers monotony the end of the world. Hence, he does not like to be part of highly organized or structured environments. The Gemini woman does not enjoy domesticity or the idea of being tied down and restricted. She loves change, and remodeling and redecorating are among her favorite and diversified hobbies. Both the male and female are restless and like to travel. A frequent vacation is essential for the emotional stability of a Gemini. Happiness to a Gemini is doing two or more things at once.

A native of the third astrological sign is intelligent, with a thirst for knowledge, blessed with the ability to interpret, and possessed with outstanding powers of analysis. He is exceptionally curious, with a fine mind and a good memory, but is anything but nostalgic. He has a very intuitive nature and a logical thought process. However, he is not particularly creative or original, but likes to experiment, or at least likes the idea of experimenting. A Gemini is dedicated, ambitious, enthusiastic, and forceful but is impatient and lacks perseverance. He freely asks for advice but rarely ever takes it. The Geminian is obsessed with self-expression, is a good conversationalist with a sense of humor, and is a fast talker, with the innate ability to master foreign languages. He is endowed with tact and diplomacy but often is sarcastic. He likes to argue and expresses himself more emphatically through his speech, and he is very definite about his viewpoint of the moment, which of course could change in the next moment. A Geminian dislikes and criticizes anything not in good taste. Many con-artists are born under the sign of the Twins.

A Geminian is cheerful and witty, with charisma and a bubbly effervescence, which enables him to make friends easily. Keeping these friends is another story, as the Gemini invariably becomes moody, irritable, and lacks continual genuine sincerity. What makes the sophisticated and versatile Gemini a valuable member of society is his ability to adapt to new surroundings and situations with the greatest of ease. He loves surprises. Dependability is not a Geminian asset, as he always gets sidetracked and shows up late.

A Gemini is a sensitive and uncertain individual with a high strung disposition. His life is filled with tension, worry, fear, and emotional upsets, producing a lot of nervous energy and insomnia. In general, he does not necessarily enjoy good health and is often the victim of economic struggle.

The Geminian likes to experiment when it comes to sex. For him, the experience is more important than love and romance, and he is frequently disappointed and disillusioned, partly because he shows rather shallow emotions. Jealousy and possessiveness are not part of his nature. He prefers an intellectual equal in a mate, is quite capable of loving more than one person at a time, and often marries more than once. The Geminian tends to gossip about intimate things.

The average Geminian makes an excellent parent because he is fascinated with the challenge of raising children. Unfortunately, he usually does not produce many offspring.

Inconsistency is the key word in describing the person born under the sign of the Twins. He is always searching for his other self, or the other half of himself.

CANCER June 22-July 23

Cancer, the fourth sign of the zodiac, is a feminine, cardinal, water sun sign ruled by the Moon and symbolized by the Crab.

Akin to the shellfished Crab, which symbolizes his astrological sign, a Cancer is always retreating into a shell to hide his emotional insecurity. The typical Cancerian is unsure of himself and his abilities. He is filled with self-doubt and feelings of inadequacy. He suffers from a pronounced inferiority complex, constantly fears rejection and ridicule, and needs frequent reassurance and praise. In order for this fourth sign native to be happy, he must develop self-confidence. His outlook is somewhat pessimistic.

The shy and timid Cancerian is difficult to get to know, although there is absolutely no affectation about him whatsoever. He is exactly as he appears. A Cancerian has a few select friends, rather than many, and often tries to run their lives. He doesn't like to discuss his personal life, never confides in strangers, and likes to keep secrets. He is a loyal, faithful, and unselfish friend but is sometimes critical of others, even though he can't bear to receive criticism himself.

It is the basic nature of a Cancer to cling to the past and preserve the status quo. He is a sentimental traditionalist, patriotic, conservative, and perhaps even prejudiced. Naturally, a Cancerian's favorite course of study in school is history. He is overly nostalgic and loves to reminisce. A moon child loves to dream, to dream of a perfect and ideal world. He desires progress for humanity, is concerned with public good, and wants to see the world a better place. He is compassionate, and self-sacrificing and frequently is seen volunteering his time in community social service endeavors. A Cancerian is an industrious worker with patience, determination, and tenacity who never leaves anything undone. He finishes what he starts. Even though a Cancerian is highly suspicious, intuitive and endowed with great insight, he is basically a gullible and vulnerable individual.

Utopia for a moon child is the home environment. It is his sanctuary, his shell. He especially likes to spend hours at home reading. An unrequited love of marriage and domesticity abounds an individual born under the sign of the Crab. The female Crab's life goal is to become the best wife and mother imaginable. A Cancerian is extremely family-oriented and makes an excellent, sympathetic, and loving parent who displays infinite patience with his children. He is very protective as a parent, loves for his children to depend on just him, thereby spoiling his children on many occasions.

It is the basic nature of a Cancerian to be economical and frugal. He is adept at managing money, as well as making money. His mind works like a calculator, and he is more interested in saving than spending. When he does spend, it most likely will be for food. He hates starvation, feels sorry for the hungry of the world, and can't tolerate seeing food wasted. Food represents security for a Cancerian, and when he is unhappy or depressed, he eats. As a result of these qualities, he enjoys cooking.

A moon child is inhibited and uptight, experiences intense moods and many emotional highs and lows, thereby leading him to seek solitude. He quite often suffers from psychosomatic illnesses, and it is not uncommon for him to be a hypochondriac. The Cancer native is not very athletic and doesn't exercise much. He particuarly likes water sports, such as swimming, water-skiing, and boating, and invariably prefers to vacation at the beach. A Cancerian loves culture and is habitually blessed with artistic and photographic talent.

The average Cancerian is curious when it comes to sex, covertly relishes attention, and craves love. He is romantic, with a strong sexual urge, and seeks to please and give pleasure to his partner. However, he needs constant assurance and reassurance from his mate. Sex is tied to home and family, and both male and female Crabs tend to mother their lovers and be overly possessive and jealous. For the Cancerian, sex is a form of nourishment.

LEO July 24-August 23

Leo, the fifth sign of the zodiac, is a masculine, fixed, fire sun sign ruled by the Sun and symbolized by the Lion.

That Leo is ruled by the Sun and symbolized by the King of Beasts in itself describes the fifth sign native better thàn all of the available lengthy delineations combined. The Sun is the center of the solar system, and the Lion rules the jungle. Leo possesses a magnetic personality, a commanding presence, and gravitates to the center of attention with powerful energy. He is a gregarious, aggressive, courageous man of action. He is a doer and an achiever. Leo in an idealistic inspirational leader filled with faith, optimism, enthusiasm, and determination. He has an abundant zest for life and charges everything full-speed ahead. This proud and dignifed person lives his life for adventure, challenge, and excitement.

The highly extroverted sun child is very pretentious and tends to be a flamboyant show-off. He is arrogant in nature, with an air of superiority about him. The Leo is immensely egotistical and has a high opinion of himself. Above all else, he wants to be respected and admired by others and to have them depend on him. Leo is a loyal and generous friend, yet he often trusts the wrong people. He frequently exaggerates and makes promises he can't keep, but he has a very forgiving nature and doesn't hold grudges. The average Leo is a very direct person, without tact, who loves to give advice. Unfortunately, he is very good in helping others but never seems to be able to make the right decision regarding his own life. Outwardly Leo exudes self-confidence, but inwardly has doubts, and needs assurance and pampering. The Lion's pitfall is flattery, to which he is highly vulnerable, and becomes a gentle pussycat when he receives it. You can get whatever you want from Leo just by complimenting him.

Leo is ambitious but lacks perseverance. He likes positions of authority and responsibility and works best when he is the boss or is in situations free from direct supervision. The Leo is a good organizer and knows how to delegate duties for mutual advantage. He is bored by repetition, and hates menial tasks. Since the Lion is drawn to the limelight he much prefers to be a big fish in a small pond, rather than a small fish in a big pond.

An individual born under the sign of the Lion loves comfort and luxury. He is excessively extravagant, since he wants to go first-class all the time, and usually spends lavishly on the furnishings for his home. A Leo is a speculator, a gambler, a high-roller, who relishes high-risk monetary investments and business ventures and is quite successful with them. He will always outbid the other astrological signs at auctions.

The mechanically inclined Leo works hard and plays hard. He has tremendous vitality, but often overexerts himself by working beyond his endurance. The fifth sign native usually suffers from exhaustion from overwork, and frequently is the victim of accidents caused by his own negligence. The Lion is a thrill-seeker who loves risking his life. He frequently engages in sports which present an element of danger.

Impulsive Leo is an affectionate, passionate, accomplished lover with a powerful sex drive who needs the feeling of romantic conquest to feed his ego. However, more often than not he falls in love with love itself rather than with his partner. The challenge of the hunt and chase is sometimes more important than the catch because he creates an ideal image of the person he is chasing who once caught, can never live up to the standards the Leo has set forth, thus greatly disappointing the Lion. Leo likes a partner who is physically attractive, and the opposite sex is attracted to him because of his physical appearance. He inevitably becomes involved with the wrong person since he often selects a partner who is intellectually or financially beneath him, because of his need to dominate the relationship. The sentimental and jealous sun child demands respect from his mate and doesn't want his wife to work. However, the Lioness needs a professional career away from the home environment and likes to compete with men on a professional level.

While the hot-blooded Leo makes a good parent, he does not customarily raise a large family. Frequently he is the parent of an only child, and often does not produce offspring.

VIRGO August 24-September 23

Virgo, the sixth sign of the zodiac, is a feminine, mutable, earth sun sign ruled by the planet Mercury and symbolized by the Virgin.

Virgo is probably the most misunderstood sign of the zodiac. Symbolized by the Virgin, purity is represented in the form of perfection in the eyes of Virgo. A Virgo is very discriminating and not at all easily satisfied. He has a strict code of conduct and ethics and is the most self-disciplined individual in the zodiac. Highly intelligent and well educated, the Virginian possess a logical and analytical mind, has a good memory, and is perpetually involved in the art of self-examination. He is critical not only of others, but much more so of himself, yet he abhors receiving critical comments.

A typical Virginian is eminently practical and down to earth. He is modest, unassuming, undemonstrative, and shows little overt enthusiasm. A Virginian is introverted, shy, not at all sociable in nature, and likes to remain in the background. He doesn't get along easily with others and is quite selective in seeking friends, but does manage to establish lasting friendships which withstand the test of time. Virgo does not want to be obligated to others or to be dependent on others. He is the rare individualist who receives more satisfaction in serving others than satisfying himself. A sixth sign native is honest and sincere, says what he means, and means what he says, and rarely, if ever, loses his temper.

A Virginian is a dependable, efficient, industrious worker with a deep sense of responsibility. He likes to follow routines and is a creature of habit. He is fastidious, meticulous, and precise; pays undue attention to detail, and is obsessed with neatness and order. Virgo usually can't see the forest from the trees. Although he is both perceptive and objective in his thinking, his systematic mind forces him unwisely to place labels on everything and everybody. Virgo is always on time and considers punctuality a virtue. For Virgo, truth is beauty, and beauty is truth. He has rather simple but dignified tastes and is far from being extravagant.

Inhibited Virgo is normally a nervous person with a highstrung disposition, who constantly worries, producing mental tension. He even borders on the neurotic, is often a hypochondriac, and makes an appointment to see a doctor for the slightest thing. He is apt to watch his diet closely and frequently becomes a vegetarian. Virgo is not very athletically inclined and does not exercise much.

Because the average Virginian is so cautious, has such high standards, and is so covertly emotional and romantic, he does not score well when it comes to sex and marriage. He admires and desires an intellectual equal as a partner and needs mental compatibility for fulfillment. The Virgo tends to make sex too complicated and sometimes finds it frustrating, yet he makes a loyal and devoted mate. He is not particuarly jealous, but is somewhat possessive. A lot of bachelors and bachelorettes are Virgo natives. Parenthood is not an especially important aspect in the life of a Virginian, yet he loves and wants children, but habitually has small families. While a Virgo neither spoils nor neglects his offspring, he usually does not make a good parent, because he is so overly strict and demanding.

LIBRA September 24-October 23

Libra, the seventh sign of the zodiac, is a masculine, cardinal, air sun sign ruled by the planet Venus and symbolized by the Scales.

The seventh sign of the zodiac is symbolized by the Scales, and that is precisely what a Libra is searching for: a perfect balance in his life. Libra is a calm and peaceful person who lives for tranquility and peace of mind. He is constantly seeking inner stability and serenity. Happiness for a Libran is inner contentment. He is highly intellectual but often lets his emotions rule his intellect. A Libran possesses a great love of justice and has the innate ability to make fair and impartial judgements, which make him an excellent mediator. He is a seeker of truth, endowed with a high degree of concentration, who rationalizes everything by weighing the pros and cons over and over. While he enjoys comparing things and debating people, he sometimes is plagued by indecision, since he can't make up his mind whether the pros outnumber the cons or vice versa. The Libran hates impatience in others, can't stand being pushed or rushed into making a decision, and does not work well under pressure. He is a procrastinator who dislikes saying "no," and his most frequent reply is "I'll think it over". Libra's invented the answer "maybe."

The extroverted Libran is a charming, amiable, tactful, and diplomatic person who has lots of friends and leads an active social life. His favorite form of recreation is party-going, yet he detests large crowds. A Libran is an honest sincere, kind, generous individual who is sympathetic and considerate of other people's feelings. He is gifted with the uncanny knack of sensing the needs of others. However, a Libran is somewhat self-centered, dependent on the approval of others, and associates with people who understand him. He is quite vulnerable to flattery as well as emotional shock. A Libran likes to escape reality when unpleasantness arises and is therefore to a certain extent naive and gullible. Basically, he works well with others, especially in partnerships, and virtually requires a partner to provide the necessary balance for his life's Scales.

A Libran loves comfort and luxury. He has expensive tastes and often overspends. The typical Libran is artistic, with a keen appreciation of the arts. He thrives in a cultured environment and prefers aesthetically pleasing surroundings. The well-mannered Libran is both fastidious and fashion conscious.

A seventh sign native is usually nervous and emotional in nature, has lots of ups and downs, and can sometimes suffer from psychosomatic illnesses. He does suffer from many genuine minor illnesses, but he has the capability of recuperating quickly. Since the Libran's main form of recreation is partying, he tends to overindulge, partake of rich foods, and not get nearly enough physical exercise.

The physically attractive and affectionate Libran is an imaginative and accomplished lover, with a powerful sex drive, who experiences many love affairs and romances. For Librans, love is a basic necessity, just as food, shelter and clothing, and love making becomes an art form. He is romantic as well as sentimental and is in love with love itself. The Libran takes marriage and its accompanying responsibilites seriously, and in marriage he considers togetherness the most important element. A female is inclined to marry young and soon gets a divorce. She desires to work after she is married so that she can afford the extra luxuries which befit her.

A Libran generally makes an excellent parent since he loves children, but his children will always be secondary to his spouse. Even though he always gives his child a logical reason for punishment, he tends to be permissive and let the child get his or her own way, because of his love for a tranquil home environment.

SCORPIO October 24-November 22

Scorpio, the eighth sign of the zodiac, is a feminine, fixed, water sun sign ruled by the planet Mars and/or Pluto and symbolized by the Scorpion, Eagle, or Gray Lizard.

Scorpio is perhaps the most mysterious sign of the zodiac. A Scorpio loves mystery, and there is a certain mystique about him. He is many things to many people. The highly intuitive and perceptive Scorpio is generally quite suspicious of other people and their motives, and is equally deceptive in masking his own motives. He keeps many secrets. He is intelligent, ambitious, persistent, and resourceful, with outstanding powers of concentration and great strength of body and mind. The intense and self-confident Scorpio absolutely abhors failure or the thought of failure. Endowed with great will-power and self-discipline, he has the inborn ability to overcome adversity. Winning is everything to him, and he usually always achieves his aims because of his energetic determination.

The typical tenacious Scorpio is blessed with many fine attributes, like honesty, loyalty and pride. He is gifted with magnificent personal magnetism and outstanding leadship capabilities. Scorpio is drawn to positions of power and has a strong sense of justice. He thrives in the midst of turmoil and works well under pressure. He is independent yet dependable, but rebels against restrictions and close supervision. A Scorpio is a very direct and demanding person who has difficulty distinguishing the difference between an order and a request when he asks something of someone. He is immune to insults as well as to compliments. The courageous Scorpio would risk his own life to save a friend's and would also lend his assistance and aid to the underdog. He is egotistical and arrogant at times, with an explosive temper, and can't stand to be wronged by others. Scorpio has an unforgiving and vindictive nature. He holds grudges, and delights in plotting revenge. Scorpio is very selective in choosing friends, and he is either your best friend or your worst enemy.

The eighth sign native loves comfort and luxury. He is concerned with material possessions and likes to be surrounded by glamour. Shrewd Scorpio enjoys money, but is unpredictable when it comes to saving or spending. He is eloquent in both the spoken and written word. He is deeply philosphical, interested in the concepts of life and death, and intrigued by the occult.

Scorpio enjoys excellent health and is seldom sick. He not only dislikes seeing members of the medical profession, he is very apt to ignore a doctor's advice. A Scorpio normally works hard and plays hard. He is a very active and athletic person who participates in strenuous physical athletic activities. He loves those sports which present an element of danger, and finds most water sports to his liking.

The affectionate, passionate, seductive Scorpio is irresistible to members of the opposite sex. He is possessed with an extremely powerful erotic sex drive, becomes completely uninhibited in romantic situations, and generally overindulges in sex, an area where he craves experimentation and variety. He engages in numerous affairs and romances, most of which are brief, but very intense. Scorpio seeks a balance between intellectual and sexual compatibility in marriage, as well as the respect of his partner. He is naturally jealous and possessive. The female willingly gives up employment after marriage, if that is the wish of her spouse.

A Scorpio makes an excellent parent because of his great love for children. While he is domineering and a stern disciplinarian, he teaches his children respect. Scorpio encourages his children to set and attain goals and will help them achieve their goals in any way he can.

SAGITTARIUS November 23-December 21

Sagittarius, the ninth sign of the zodiac, is a masculine, mutable, fire sun sign ruled by the planet Jupiter and symbolized by the Archer.

Sagittarius in all likelihood is the most personable and carefree individual in the zodiac. He is good-natured, good-humored, sincere, and benevolent, with an enthusiastic zest for living. His cheerful, affable, delightful personality is what distinguishes the extroverted ninth sign native. The independent Sagittarian is basically a nonconformist, a true free-spirit, who has a total disregard for conventional behavior. He is a naive idealist, an eternal optimist, who possesses unyielding blind faith. A Sagittarian is an impetuous, impulsive, energetic innovator, who thinks big, acts big, and tends to exaggerate. He is overconfident, and lacks self-discipline and well as purpose and direction in life. While he is always truthful and completely free of malice, he is not especially responsible or reliable and often does not finish what he starts. The nonchalant Sagittarian fears nothing except being confined and restricted. He is forever restless and loves to travel. Happiness is change and variety.

A typical Sagittarian is highly intelligent, intuitive, and articulate, with a quick mind. Although he has good judgement and wisdom, the quickness with which he thinks often results in inaccuracy. He is gifted with a compelling curiosity and an unbelievable memory for facts, yet he has a tendency to forget where he puts things, and he can't keep secrets whatsoever. Sagittarians are deeply philosophical, and sometimes even clairvoyant.

The outgoing and likeable Sagittarian is highly sociable, makes friends easily, and continually is surrounded by lots of friends. He is a congenial conversationalist with a good sense of humor and is never demanding or critical of others. Conversely though, the Sagittarian is straightforward, blunt and outspoken. He is tactless and unknowingly hurts other people's feelings by what he says. The easily humiliated Sagittarian practically invented giving left-handed compliments.

The Sagittarian is successful because he is ever so lucky, and he likes to gamble. Endowed with versatility and adaptability, he fits into almost any environment. However, he dislikes routine work, is bored by petty details, and does not work well under direct supervision. He has a rather irresponsible and casual attitude when it comes to money. He often overspends and does not pay his bills on time, although he can be practical when he has to.

The high-spirited, high-strung Sagittarian has enduring stamina and is blessed with good health. He generally lives to a ripe old age and almost never is affected by senility. He has many avocational interests and pursuits and loves animals and all outdoor sports and forms of recreation. Active Sagittarians are more apt to be laid up from athletic injuries rather than illnesses or disease.

Sagittarians are definitely appealing to the opposite sex; they seek companionship in romance and partners with mutual interests. They have an innate shyness of marriage and prefer casual romantic relationships that are uncomplicated with future promises. Jealousy and possessiveness are not natural traits. Domesticity is not attractive to a ninth sign native, and bachelorhood is quite common. In fact, the Sagittarian is not generally close to his relatives, or even to his immediate family, as family ties tend to stifle his freedom.

A Sagittarian normally makes a good parent because he can relate to and communicate with his children. He is lax in discipline since he considers his children his friends. The Sagitarrian is more a big brother or big sister to his offspring than a father or mother.

CAPRICORN December 22-January 20

Capricorn, the tenth sign of the zodiac, is a feminine, cardinal, earth sun sign ruled by the planet Saturn and symbolized by the Goat.

The tenth sign of the zodiac is symbolized by an animal who is a natural mountain climber. Like the Goat, the Capricornian is motivated by the obsession of reaching the top of the mountain of success. All of his efforts are directed to the furtherance of his own career. The overly ambitious Capricornian is a social climber who desires public prominence and craves admiration. He is most concerned with prestige, reputation, and image. The self-centered and self-interested Capricornian takes life quite seriously and is the hardest worker of any of the astrological signs. His basic philosophy is that all work and no play will make him a success, and he considers failure the greatest sin of all. He is practical, punctilious, extremely conscientious, and possessed with tremendous initiative, drive, and perseverance. Capricornian's great determination enables him to overcome adversity.

The Capricornian's nature is one of cautiousness and conservatism. He is neither original nor creative. He feels that what was good enough for his father is good enough for him. He is rigid, inflexible, and intolerant and has an affinity for clinging to traditional methods and procedures. Obstinate Capricorn has very definite preconceived notions of right and wrong and finds it difficult to admit his mistakes. He is a self-disciplined moral man with great integrity and self-respect.

Capricorn is shy, introverted, passive, and undemonstrative. He is discriminating in choosing his friends, never interferes in other people's lives, and often is his own best friend. While he is sensitive to other people's feelings and wants to make conditions better for others, he is completely unsympathetic to those who don't share his pointed views. He respects authority and generally never questions the directives of authority figures. The Capricornian is intelligent and is especially interested in cultivating his mind. He requires solitude and time for meditation. Capricorn works best in highly organized, structured, and mental environments. His talent is for management and administration, and he is often drawn to public and government service that does not require travel. Capricorn is generous yet exceptionally thrifty. He likes to involve himself with money, computations, and finance, and makes sound investments in respected and established companies.

The average tenth sign native has great endurance and nerves of steel. He probably experienced sickness during his childhood but has become a healthy adult and can expect to live to a ripe old age. Since his nature is more cerebral than physical, he is not particularly interested in athletic pursuits or strenuous exercise.

A Capricornian is reserved, normally displays no outward signs of affection or emotion, and does not appreciate surprises or overt emotional expressions from others. There is a pronounced detachment in his romantic relationships, and he is quite selective in choosing a spouse. He finds it almost impossible to say the words "I love you" to his partner. For the male, marriage is viewed in terms of emotional security, and for the female marriage represents financial security. Capricorn is a protective, loyal spouse and a good provider, which he considers his duty. The Capricornian can be jealous and possessive, and he believes that divorce is a form of failure.

Capricorn is very family-oriented, with great respect and love for his own parents and relatives. He is a strict and domineering parent who demands respect and obedience from his rebellious children.

AQUARIUS January 21-February 19

Aquarius, the eleventh sign of the zodiac, is a masculine, fixed, air sun sign ruled by the planet Uranus and symbolized by the Water Bearer.

That Aquarius is an air sun sign symbolized by the Water Bearer would seem contradictory, since water drowns one's intake of air. Indeed, an individual born under the sign of Aquarius is inconsistent and unpredictable. An Aquarian is fearful of being drowned, fearful of having his superior intellect and inventive ideas submerged in the present. He lives in the future and is actually ahead of his time. Others think he has his head in the clouds.

An Aquarian is, above all else, an individualist, a non-conformist, who despises tradition in the sense that tradition usually spells imperfection. He is both an idealist and a humanitarian, who wants to rid the traditionally imperfect world of suffering and injustice. The Aquarian is noble and unselfish and has the public welfare at heart; he has long-term solutions to the world's problems. He generally devotes himself to others more than to himself, and often neglects himself completely. Happiness to the Aquarius is an international utopia. He is fascinated by virtually everything and is especially interested in human behavior and philosophy. The Aquarian has been labeled the astrological sign of genius. He is analytical, scientific, imaginative, and unconsciously psychic, with the ability to theorize and with great powers of concentration. An Aquarian is well balanced, open-minded, free from prejudice, and he detests narrow-minded people. However, altruistic Aquarius is opinionated, with a rigid moral code, and his own personal behavior is fairly conservative. He is inspirational and possesses divinatory powers.

A typical Aquarian is calm and peaceful and needs an environment in which he is free to think and express himself. He can't stand restriction of any kind and works best on his own. Although he will usually excel in any chosen field, he is impatient, procrastinating, and lacks perseverance. A person of great integrity, he is always impersonal, yet he has no difficulty making friends. An Aquarian is a good, stimulating conversationalist who leads an active social life. He needs praise, is susceptible to flattery, and is easily taken advantage of by others. He likes to travel and join organizations, but still needs time to be alone.

For the Aquarian, money is a means to an end; he is not really interested in accumulating money. Furthermore, an Aquarian does not like to be obligated to others, and pays his bills almost instantaneously, but on occasion he is absent-minded. He is fortunate in having good health and is sensible in taking good care of himself. An Aquarian is overactive mentally and suffers from nervous tension, in addition to having trouble sleeping. At some point in his life, he is apt to consult either a psychiatrist or clinical psychologist. He is blessed with longevity and normally outlives all other signs of the zodiac.

An Aquarian considers everyone special, not just one particular person. Since he doesn't desire to reveal his true feelings, he finds it difficult to be aggressive and to relax in romantic relationships. He is most attracted to members of the opposite sex who intrigue him. Friendship is the basis of a relationship, and he seeks an intelligent partner with a mutual outlook on life. He is much more platonic than passionate, and his emphasis is directed at pleasing his partner, often denying himself pleasure. An Aquarian must respect and trust his partner, to whom he is loyal but of whom he is never jealous or possessive. He never forgets his first love, and not infrequently wants to avoid marriage as long as possible.

It is the nature of the Aquarian to be a serious parent. As a parent, he is reasonable and understanding and never spoils his children. An Aquarian's primary goal in raising his offspring is to develop them intellectually.

PISCES February 20-March 20

Pisces, the twelfth sign of the zodiac, is a feminine, mutable, water sun sign ruled by the planet Neptune and symbolized by the Fishes.

Pisces is the last sign of the zodiac, and the Piscean's personality is a composite blend of the traits of all of the preceding astrological signs. Pisces is the most compassionate of all signs and is the sympathetic ear to others' problems, as well as the shoulder others cry on. He is the humanitarian of the zodiac, who constantly wants to be of service. The altruistic, self-sacrificing Pisces is highly impressionable and believes just about any hard-luck story. He judges no man, criticizes no man, and expects others to refrain from judging and criticizing him. A Piscean is shocked by nothing that is said to him and has a very forgiving nature. He is endowed with intellectual brilliance, wisdom, insight, an excellent memory, and astute powers of observation. He can visualize the past, present, and future as one entity.

A Piscean is highly trustworthy, honest, and deceptively practical. He is able to achieve success in most any chosen field of endeavor; however, he is lazy and has a tendency to take the path of least resistance. Pisces is adaptable to different surroundings, but does not like to be confined and is bored by routine. Even though he possesses organizational ability, he is not particularly interested in positions of power or leadership. Pisces is completely free of greed, does not tend to make a lot of money, and does not have the best possible credit rating.

The Piscean is extremely emotional, and because of his overly sensitive nature, he fears emotional hurt and rejection. Although he appears outgoing, he is secretly shy and timid and lacks self-confidence. He is frequently moody, with lots of emotional ups and downs, and continually needs solitude. The kind, gentle, unselfish Piscean is a fascinating person. He is modest and unassuming, yet he has a magnetic personality. A Piscean is a loyal and devoted person who will do virtually anything for one of his friends, but usually never asks favors for himself.

The typical Piscean is blessed with good health, although he is not physically strong. Mental and emotional fatigue often weaken his resistance, which is compounded by the fact that he basically does not take the best care of himself. Because of his vivid imagination, he might suffer psychosomatic illnesses. A Piscean leads an active social life, loves to drink plenty of liquids, but has a low tolerance to alcohol. He is gifted with artistic and creative talent, appreciates aesthetic beauty, and finds that music uplifts his emotional despondency. Since Pisces is a water sign, it is only natural for him to like all water sports and prefer to vacation at the beach.

A Piscean is an affectionate, passionate, imaginative and experimenting lover, with a strong sexual drive. Sentimental Pisces is very much of a traditional romantic who experiences many intense, but short-lived romances. He is so fragile and unstable emotionally, he seeks emotional security and contentment in marriage and needs constant emotional reassurance from his partner. Above all else, a Piscean must feel needed by his spouse. The female, who enjoys domesticity, is often regarded as the ultimate wife, and she is the most feminine of all astrological signs.

Pisces is an excellent but emotional parent. He listens intently to his children's problems, yet he may be permissive in their upbringing. A Piscean will almost automatically sacrifice anything so that his child can have what he was denied.

Appendix II
NUMEROLOGY GUIDE

ONES—Persons born on the 1st, 10th, 19th, or 28th of any month

A One is an independent individualist who places himself above everyone else. He is generally self-centered, selfish, conceited, and egotistical. This person projects a positive, aggressive, forceful image. He is headstrong, opinionated, and obstinate and wants his own way all of the time. In most cases, a One has been forced to stand on his own at an early age and believes that he can only rely on himself for success.

The typical One is a courageous leader with creative, original, inventive ideas. He is ambitious, determined, and somewhat overconfident. An impatient One wants to be number one; he wants to be the head one, the boss. He does not function at all well under direct supervision, and can't stand taking orders, as he feels that he should be the person giving the orders. He dislikes being given advice and resents criticism, even though he is critical of others. The One prefers to learn from experience rather than from the teaching of others. He hates handling details and really works best when alone.

The highly ethical One is honest, loyal, and proud, with a great sense of dignity. He is a very domineering and direct person who often lacks tact and diplomacy. The slightly antagonistic One is intelligent, with a clever mind. While he is recognized as a doer, he is lazy and sometimes guilty of procrastination. He doesn't always finish what he starts which he tends to rationalize.

The practical and idealistic One, fearless in nature, is sensitive, easily hurt, and suffers emotional upsets. His instability leads him to lose his temper. He usually doesn't hold grudges for long, and has a forgiving nature. Will power is not a virtue of a One.

A One is especially interested in improving his own immediate environment. He is basically undemonstrative and is not particularly affectionate or passionate. The normal One is not inclined towards domesticity and is never completely happy when married, as he somehow still feels alone.

TWOS—Persons born on the 2nd, 11th, 20th, or 29th of any month.

A two is the complete and total opposite of the One. He is a follower and has no desire to become a leader. He is shy, timid, quiet, and lacks self-confidence. He is self-endowed with an inferiority complex and lives with a misguided feeling of inadequacy. The modest and unassuming Two has a deep-seated tendency to underestimate himself and his capabilities. He is not known for taking the initiative, since he is fearful of making a mistake. The Two's real forte is his love of peace and his ability to recognize different points of view. Gifted with a highly tactful and diplomatic manner, he is an excellent arbitrator, with an unbelievable degree of tolerance and patience.

The cooperative and congenial Two is well-liked by other people and gets along well with almost everyone because of his easygoing, gentle nature. He stands ready to help others, never expecting anything in return. A Two is somewhat gullible and lets people use him. He is always a soft touch for friends and relatives who want to borrow money. For the Two, peace is paramount, and he can't bring himself to say "no". He is overly sensitive, easily hurt, and finds it hard to forgive and forget. Needless to say, the Two is anything but a disciplinarian.

A Two is an efficient and conscientious worker, who pays keen attention to detail, but he lacks ambition and is not particularly goal-oriented. He works best in a partnership, and needs a partner to bring balance into his life. The spiritually inclined Two loves a cultured environment and has an appreciation of the arts.

Two is the number of duality and cannot stand alone. A Two not only needs a partner in his professional life, he needs a partner in his private life as well. He is very adaptive to marriage and makes an ideal spouse. The emotional Two is quite affectionate but has difficulty expressing feelings.

THREES—Persons born on the 3rd, 12th, 21st, or 30th of any month

Some numerologists regard Three as the perfect number because a Three enjoys life so much and has such an enthusiastic zest for living. Nothing ever seems to faze the Three at all; he is easily satisfied, takes life as it comes, and never gives anyone a hard time. He has a very cavalier attitude and never worries or becomes depressed. Happiness to a Three is having a good time.

A Three is endowed with intelligence, wit, imagination and intuition. He is equally blessed with creative and artistic talent. Additionally, he is gifted with a quick and alert mind and finds learning a rather easy experience. Self-expression is the key ingredient to a Three's success, as he is eloquent in both the spoken and written word. While he is ambitious, he is not too serious-minded. A Three dislikes detail and routine, although he is never actually bored with anything. Because he is so versatile, his greatest difficulty is channeling his energies in one positive direction and persevering. Patience and practicality are not his leading attributes. The overly optimistic Three is opinionated and wants his own way. He has a forever youthful attitude and is independent and restless. A Three is somewhat self-indulgent since he loves pleasure, desires all of the comforts of life, and is interested in the material things life has to offer. He can not stand sticking to a budget and spends freely.

The likeable Three is possessed with a good sense of humor, makes wonderful friends very easily, and is quite popular. He leads an active social life, and brings joy and happiness to others. A Three generally likes discipline and order in his life and usually recuperates quickly from illness.

A Three is fickle and is in love with love. He considers marriage as something exciting. The typical Three loves both children and animals. He is a good parent but a strict disciplinarian in raising his offspring.

FOURS—Persons born on the 4th, 13th, 22nd, or 31st of any month

A four is usually quite unconventional and unpredictable. He is very precise in his thinking but changes his mind frequently. He is methodical, logical and analytical. He pays meticulous attention to detail, but his attention span is rather short. The practical Four is a solid citizen who has common sense and his feet planted firmly on the ground. He is not particularly creative or imaginative but has a good mechanical aptitude. A Four is considered narrow-minded, rigid, and conservative in his viewpoints. However, he is a seeker of justice and becomes a rebel when injustices arise. A Four is a patriot at heart.

The dependable and reliable Four is a conscientious worker with good business ability. He is possessed with determination, perseverance, and tenacity of purpose and does his job thoroughly, no matter how routine it may be. A Four is honest, truthful, sincere, and patient, but he is rather forthright and lacks tact. While he is systematic, he is also stubborn and reluctant to change. Endowed with great self-discipline, the Four is also an excellent disciplinarian. He is not so much domineering as he is dictatorial, and others often believe he is unreasonable in his demands. Although a Four is interested in material possessions, he is economical. He works hard for his money, is a good saver and does not overspend.

A Four does not make friends easily, but to those friends he does have he is loyal. He is a good conversationalist and delights in taking the opposite side in an argument. The Four is normally obsessed with neatness and believes in punctuality. He loves both nature and travel.

A typical Four is a supersensitive individual and becomes depressed at times. He is very sports-oriented and athletically inclined, but he has a tendency to be accident prone. A Four is rather undemonstrative and does not generally show much affection. He does not like to live alone, but is quite careful in selecting a marriage partner.

FIVES—Persons born on the 5th, 14th, or 23rd of any month

Freedom is the key word in describing a Five. Free to be himself is his goal in life. He is very independent and quite impulsive, and he likes to do things on the spur of the moment. A Five craves change and is changeable himself. He is attracted to anything new and unusual. The latest thing on the market has a great appeal to him. The restless Five is enthusiastic, eternally youthful, and loves adventure. He wants to try everything once.

The curious, creative Five is endowed with an investigative, inquisitive mind. He is blessed with the dual attributes of intelligence and versatility. A Five is quick-witted and equally quick-tempered. He is quick to form opinions and make decisions. The Five is intolerant of discipline and abhors routine. He lacks concentration and often never finishes what he starts. Never worried about or concerned with the future, the generous Five is a speculator at heart and is not opposed to taking a risk. He has the innate ability to recover quickly from adversity.

The pleasure-loving Five has a charming magnetic personality. He gets along well with everybody and makes friends easily. A Five is a good conversationalist with a great sense of humor, and he leads an active social life. He is an excellent promoter, with the fine qualities of salesmanship, and is adept at dealing with the public.

A Five is attracted to and liked by the opposite sex. Not infrequently he deals better with the opposite sex than with his own sex. He enjoys marriage only with a partner who understands his compulsive need for freedom, since marriage represents confinement in his eyes.

SIXES—Persons born on the 6th, 15th, or 24th or any month

The person who was born a Six is both an idealist and a perfectionist. Since the world is neither ideal nor perfect, he is often disillusioned and disappointed that everybody and everything doesn't match up to his high standards. The obstinate and stubborn Six has preconceived notions of right and wrong. He wants his own way and more often than not attempts to impose his views on others.

A Six possesses an inborn love for his fellow man. He makes friends easily and craves companionship because he hates to be alone. For a Six, loneliness is the worst thing on earth. He works well in close contact with others and has a keen sense of duty to other people. The compassionate, sympathetic Six is invariably drawn to the civic and community service work. While he can't stand criticism of himself, he enjoys counseling and advising others and frequently is guilty of interfering in other people's lives. Although the efficient Six is methodical and meticulous, he is emotional and needs constant reassurance and praise from those around him. Responsibility and dependability are the assets which most distinguish a Six.

It is the basic nature of a Six to be reluctant to, and even fearful, of change. Even though he is often called upon too adjust to new situations during his lifetime, he prefers familiarity and routine. The Six loves beautiful and comfortable surroundings. He is especially interested in achieving financial success. For him, money is an end in itself, and financial security brings contentment. The economical Six is quite conservative in his investments and is rarely in debt. He never gambles and virtually has no use for people who do.

A Six is demonstrative and romantically inclined and believes that the home environment is of supreme importance. He is a kind, tolerant, devoted spouse who needs love and domesticity for total fulfillment. Parenthood is paramount to the Six's happiness, and he is always doing for his children. Without hesitation, he will sacrifce anything and deny himself for the benefit of his offspring.

SEVENS—Persons born on the 7th, 16th, or 25th of any month

Silence is indeed golden for someone who was born a Seven. The intellectual and analytical Seven is a deep thinker whose goal it is to attain knowledge and wisdom. A Seven requires solitude and privacy to meditate. He is a creative, original, independent thinker with a theoretical, scientific mind. Gifted with a highly intuitive and inventive brain, a Seven is spiritually and philosophically inclined and occasionally is psychic. He is a non-conforming idealist who desires perfection.

The cerebral Seven is basically reserved and introverted. Although sensitve and thoughtful, he is neither popular nor concerned with popularity. A Seven is a loner who detests large crowds. He works best by himself and does not take orders well. Endowed with good business ability, a Seven dislikes manual labor and work involving attention to detail. The Seven takes life very seriously and is self-centered as well as self-critical. He is anything but a man of action, and often procrastinates in order to have time to arrive at a careful and well-thought-out course of direction.

The determination to have others regard him as honorable, reliable, and a respected authority in his field of endeavor gives a Seven a sense of pride and accomplishment. He appreciates beauty in all forms, has an acute awareness of nature, and loves plants and animals. A Seven loves to travel and is more at home living in a tranquil suburban atmosphere than in an upsetting urban environment. Although he is generous and charitable, the Seven is thrifty and prefers to save his money, since he is not especially interested in acquiring material possessions.

A Seven is gentle and loving yet undemonstrative. He has considerable difficulty expressing his emotions and is misunderstood much of the time. Finding a marriage partner who will completely understand him and his needs is one of the Seven's most troublesome pursuits.

EIGHTS—Persons born on the 8th, 17th, or 26th of any month

The Eight is probably the most dynamic number in numerology. A person who was born an Eight is invariably destined for the world of big business. The ambitious Eight most likely will score his success in the areas of commerce and finance. His great determination and perseverance, coupled with his executive leadership ability, make him ideally suited for top level corporate positions. The Eight is a leader, not a follower. Luck is inconsequential in the Eight's drive for success, as he achieves only through his dedication to hard work. An Eight is particularly interested in achieving financial success and acquiring material possessions. He is certainly not above putting on a show to impress people, as it is of supreme importance to him to be considered influential.

The persuasive Eight is endowed with superior intellect and good value judgement. He is outspoken yet tactful, and is known for his creative, progressive, original, offbeat ideas. An Eight is both philosophical and analytical and is somewhat set in his ways.

An individual who was born an Eight is generous and compassionate, with a deep love for humanity. He is gifted with self-discipline but often becomes fanatical, as he has a tendency to engage in events and embark on courses of action to the extreme. However, the Eight is efficient, has exceptional organizational ability, and knows how to manage money. It is the Eight's nature to find it much easier to give than to receive.

While the Eight has a magnetic personality, he finds it quite difficult to establish lasting friendships, even though his honesty and loyalty are above reproach. An Eight is usually unstable emotionally, fears rejection, and finds it hard to express his feelings. He could frequently find himself in a state of loneliness, since he is so often misunderstood by others. The exciting Eight makes a truly devoted spouse when he is married to the right partner.

NINES— Persons born on the 9th, 18th or 27th of any month

In numerology, Nine is the number of universality. An individual who was born a Nine is the humanitarian of the universe. The self-sacrificing Nine is dedicated to serving his fellow man. He is spiritually inclined and sees the good in everyone. He is compassionate, sympathetic, and sensitive to the needs and feelings of others. The dutiful and selfless Nine gives freely of himself without expecting anything in return. He is known for both his hospitality and philanthropy.

The typical Nine is independent, courageous, and fearless and relies on intuition rather than logic to guide him. He is optimistc, idealistic, and broadminded and has the ability to make a quick decision. The only thing quicker than the decision made by a Nine is his temper. He likes to argue and quarrel and has a considerably high opinion of himself. Although he displays fairness, honesty, and efficiency, the hard-working Nine has a tendency to push himself and others too hard. While he is lucky, he experiences many disappointments in life. The Nine is generally not regarded as a good business person.

The kind and generous Nine is friendly and is liked by everyone, except for those he has pushed too hard or exploded his temper at. He is nervous, erratic, and subject to many emotional ups and downs. Even though he constantly seeks to help others, he needs periods of solitude to relax and medidate. A Nine is artistic in nature and has an appreciation of the arts. He also loves to travel and is possessed with an aptitude for foreign languages.

A Nine normally takes personal love lightly, yet he wants to be romantic. He is not particularly sentimental and has difficulty saying the words "I love you." The Nine is sometimes so wrapped up in his concern for the welfare of others, he often temporarily and unconsciously neglects his own family.

Appendix III
BIRTHSTONES

JANUARY—Garnet
FEBRUARY—Amethyst
MARCH—Aquamarine or Bloodstone
APRIL—Diamond
MAY—Emerald
JUNE—Agate, Alexandrite, Pearl, or Moonstone
JULY—Ruby or Star Ruby
AUGUST—Peridot or Sardonyx
SEPTEMBER—Sapphire or Star Sapphire
OCTOBER—Opal or Tourmaline
NOVEMBER—Topaz
DECEMBER—Lapis Lazuli, Turquoise, or Zircon

Appendix IV
ZODIAC STONES

ARIES—Amethyst, Bloodstone, Diamond, Fire Opal, and Moonstone
TAURUS—Amethyst, Coral, Emerald, Moss Agate, and Topaz
GEMINI—Beryl, Emerald, Marcasite, Sapphire, and Tourmaline
CANCER—Aquamarine, Crystal, Moonstone, and Sapphire
LEO—Diamond, Emerald, Lodestone, Onyx, and Ruby
VIRGO—Blue Sapphire, Diamond, Lapis Lazuli, and Sardonyx
LIBRA—Carnelian, Diamond, Pink Jasper, and Sapphire
SCORPIO—Beryl, Chrysolite, Malachite, and Topaz
SAGITTARIUS—Amethyst, Carbuncle, Diamond, and Turquoise
CAPRICORN—Emerald, Garnet, Moss Agate, and Onyx
AQUARIUS—Beryl, Carnelian, Jade, Marcasite, and Sapphire
PISCES—Amethyst, Chrysolite, Crystal, and Pearl

Appendix V
ZODIAC METALS

ARIES—Iron or Zinc
TAURUS—Copper
GEMINI—Quicksilver
CANCER—Silver
LEO—Gold
VIRGO—Quicksilver
LIBRA—Copper
SCORPIO—Iron or Zinc and/or Plutonium
SAGITTARIUS—Electrum or Tin
CAPRICORN—Lead
AQUARIUS—Uranium
PISCES—Neptunium

Appendix VI
ZODIAC COLORS

ARIES—Red
TAURUS—Red-Orange or Yellow
GEMINI—Orange
CANCER—Silver or Yellow-Orange
LEO—Gold or Yellow
VIRGO—Yellow-Green
LIBRA—Green or Yellow
SCORPIO—Blue-Green or Red
SAGITARRIUS—Blue or White
CAPRICORN—Deep Blue or Gray
AQUARIUS—Blue-Violet
PISCES—Violet

Appendix VII
BIRTHDAY FLOWERS

JANUARY—Carnations
FEBRUARY—Violets
MARCH—Jonquils
APRIL—Sweetpeas
MAY—Lilies-of-the-Valley
JUNE—Roses
JULY—Larkspurs
AUGUST—Gladioli
SEPTEMBER—Asters
OCTOBER—Calendulas
NOVEMBER—Chrysanthemums
DECEMBER—Narcissus

Appendix VIII
ZODIAC FLOWERS

ARIES—Anemones and Buttercups
TAURUS—Daisies, Jonquils, and Narcissus
GEMINI—Bittersweet (Celastrus & Solanum), Lilies-of-the-Valley, and Myrtle
CANCER—Moonflower (Calonyction) and Wallflower
LEO—Marigolds and Peonies
VIRGO—Azaleas, Bachelor's Buttons, and Lavender
LIBRA—Daisies, Foxgloves, and Violets
SCORPIO—Carnations, Gentians, and Honeysuckles
SAGITTARIUS—Goldenrods
CAPRICORN—Hollies and Poppies
AQUARIUS—Daffodils, Pansies, Primroses, and Tulips
PISCES—Jasmine and Mignonette (Reseda)

Appendix IX
CHINESE LUNAR CALENDAR
ANIMAL DESIGNATIONS
1776-2000

Year of the Rat:
1780, 1792, 1804, 1816, 1828, 1840, 1852, 1864, 1876, 1888, 1900,
1912, 1924, 1936, 1948, 1960, 1972, 1984, 1996

Year of the Ox:
1781, 1793, 1805, 1817, 1829, 1841, 1853, 1865, 1877, 1889, 1901,
1913, 1925, 1937, 1949, 1961, 1973, 1985, 1997

Year of the Tiger:
1782, 1794, 1806, 1818, 1830, 1842, 1854, 1866, 1878, 1890, 1902,
1914, 1926, 1938, 1950, 1962, 1974, 1986, 1998

Year of the Hare (or Rabbit):
1783, 1795, 1807, 1819, 1831, 1843, 1855, 1867, 1879, 1891, 1903,
1915, 1927, 1939, 1951, 1963, 1975, 1987, 1999

Year of the Dragon:
1784, 1796, 1808, 1820, 1832, 1844, 1856, 1868, 1880, 1892, 1904,
1916, 1928, 1940, 1952, 1964, 1976, 1988, 2000

Year of the Snake:
1785, 1797, 1809, 1821, 1833, 1845, 1857, 1869, 1881, 1893, 1905,
1917, 1929, 1941, 1953, 1965, 1977, 1989

Year of the Horse:
1786, 1798, 1810, 1822, 1834, 1846, 1858, 1870, 1882, 1894, 1906,
1918, 1930, 1942, 1954, 1966, 1978, 1990

Year of the Sheep:
1787, 1799, 1811, 1823, 1835, 1847, 1859, 1871, 1883, 1895, 1907,
1919, 1931, 1943, 1955, 1967, 1979, 1991

Year of the Monkey:
1776, 1788, 1800, 1812, 1824, 1836, 1848, 1860, 1872, 1884, 1896,
1908, 1920, 1932, 1944, 1956, 1968, 1980, 1992

Year of the Cock (or Rooster):
1777, 1789, 1801, 1813, 1825, 1837, 1849, 1861, 1873, 1885, 1897, 1909, 1921, 1933, 1945, 1957, 1969, 1981, 1993

Year of the Dog:
1778, 1790, 1802, 1814, 1826, 1838, 1850, 1862, 1874, 1886, 1898, 1910, 1922, 1934, 1946, 1958, 1970, 1982, 1994

Year of the Boar (or Pig):
1779, 1791, 1803, 1815, 1827, 1839, 1851, 1863, 1875, 1887, 1899, 1911, 1923, 1935, 1947, 1959, 1971, 1983, 1995

Appendix X
PERPETUAL CALENDARS
1776-2000*

DIRECTIONS FOR USE Look for the year you want in the Index. The number opposite each year is the number of the calendar to use for that year.

I N D E X

1776.... 9	1801... 5	1826... 1	1851.... 4	1876...14	1901... 3	1926... 6	1951... 2	1976...12
1777.... 4	1802... 6	1827... 2	1852. .12	1877.... 2	1902... 4	1927... 7	1952...10	1977.....7
1778.... 5	1803... 7	1828...10	1853... 7	1878.... 3	1903....5	1928... 8	1953.... 5	1978.... 1
1779.... 6	1804... 8	1829... 5	1854 . 1	1879.... 4	1904...13	1929... 3	1954.... 6	1979.... 2
1780...14	1805... 3	1830...6	1855.... 2	1880...12	1905... 1	1930... 4	1955.... 7	1980...10
1781.... 2	1806... 4	1831... 7	1856...10	1881.... 7	1906... 2	1931... 5	1956.... 8	1981.... 5
1782.... 3	1807... 5	1832... 8	1857... 5	1882.... 1	1907... 3	1932...13	1957.... 3	1982.... 6
1783.... 4	1808...13	1833... 3	1858.... 6	1883.... 2	1908...11	1933... 1	1958.... 4	1983....7
1784...12	1809... 1	1834.... 4	1859... 7	1884...10	1909... 6	1934... 2	1959.... 5	1984....8
1785.... 7	1810... 2	1835... 5	1860... 8	1885.... 5	1910... 7	1935... 3	1960...13	1985.... 3
1786.... 1	1811... 3	1836...13	1861... 3	1886.... 6	1911... 1	1936...11	1961... 1	1986.... 4
1787.... 2	1812...11	1837... 1	1862.... 4	1887.... 7	1912... 9	1937... 6	1962... 2	1987.... 5
1788...10	1813... 6	1838... 2	1863.... 5	1888.... 8	1913... 4	1938... 7	1963... 3	1988...13
1789.... 5	1814... 7	1839... 3	1864...13	1889.... 3	1914... 5	1939... 1	1964...11	1989... 1
1790.... 6	1815... 1	1840...11	1865... 1	1890.... 4	1915... 6	1940... 9	1965... 6	1990... 2
1791.... 7	1816... 9	1841... 6	1866.... 2	1891.... 5	1916...14	1941... 4	1966... 7	1991... 3
1792.... 8	1817... 4	1842... 7	1867... 3	1892...13	1917... 2	1942... 5	1967... 1	1992...11
1793.... 3	1818... 5	1843... 1	1868...11	1893... 1	1918... 3	1943... 6	1968... 9	1993... 6
1794.... 4	1819... 6	1844... 9	1869... 6	1894... 2	1919... 4	1944...14	1969... 4	1994... 7
1795.... 5	1820...14	1845... 4	1870... 7	1895... 3	1920...12	1945... 2	1970... 5	1995... 1
1796...13	1821... 2	1846... 5	1871... 1	1896...11	1921... 7	1946... 3	1971... 6	1996...9
1797... 1	1822... 3	1847... 6	1872... 2	1897... 6	1922... 1	1947... 4	1972...14	1997... 4
1798... 2	1823... 4	1848...14	1873... 4	1898... 7	1923... 2	1948...12	1973... 2	1998... 5
1799... 3	1824...12	1849... 2	1874... 5	1899... 1	1924...10	1949... 7	1974... 3	1999... 6
1800.... 4	1825... 7	1850... 3	1875... 6	1900... 2	1925... 5	1950... 1	1975... 4	2000...14

*The Perpetual Calendars will enable you to determine which day of the week a celebrity was born on, which day of the week you were born on and which days of the week future birthdays will fall on.

3

JANUARY

S	M	T	W	T	F	S
		1	2	3	4	5
6	7	8	9	10	11	12
13	14	15	16	17	18	19
20	21	22	23	24	25	26
27	28	29	30	31		

FEBRUARY

S	M	T	W	T	F	S
					1	2
3	4	5	6	7	8	9
10	11	12	13	14	15	16
17	18	19	20	21	22	23
24	25	26	27	28		

MARCH

S	M	T	W	T	F	S
					1	2
3	4	5	6	7	8	9
10	11	12	13	14	15	16
17	18	19	20	21	22	23
24	25	26	27	28	29	30
31						

APRIL

S	M	T	W	T	F	S
	1	2	3	4	5	6
7	8	9	10	11	12	13
14	15	16	17	18	19	20
21	22	23	24	25	26	27
28	29	30				

MAY

S	M	T	W	T	F	S
			1	2	3	4
5	6	7	8	9	10	11
12	13	14	15	16	17	18
19	20	21	22	23	24	25
26	27	28	29	30	31	

JUNE

S	M	T	W	T	F	S
						1
2	3	4	5	6	7	8
9	10	11	12	13	14	15
16	17	18	19	20	21	22
23	24	25	26	27	28	29
30						

JULY

S	M	T	W	T	F	S
	1	2	3	4	5	6
7	8	9	10	11	12	13
14	15	16	17	18	19	20
21	22	23	24	25	26	27
28	29	30	31			

AUGUST

S	M	T	W	T	F	S
				1	2	3
4	5	6	7	8	9	10
11	12	13	14	15	16	17
18	19	20	21	22	23	24
25	26	27	28	29	30	31

SEPTEMBER

S	M	T	W	T	F	S
1	2	3	4	5	6	7
8	9	10	11	12	13	14
15	16	17	18	19	20	21
22	23	24	25	26	27	28
29	30					

OCTOBER

S	M	T	W	T	F	S
		1	2	3	4	5
6	7	8	9	10	11	12
13	14	15	16	17	18	19
20	21	22	23	24	25	26
27	28	29	30	31		

NOVEMBER

S	M	T	W	T	F	S
					1	2
3	4	5	6	7	8	9
10	11	12	13	14	15	16
17	18	19	20	21	22	23
24	25	26	27	28	29	30

DECEMBER

S	M	T	W	T	F	S
1	2	3	4	5	6	7
8	9	10	11	12	13	14
15	16	17	18	19	20	21
22	23	24	25	26	27	28
29	30	31				

4

JANUARY

S	M	T	W	T	F	S
			1	2	3	4
5	6	7	8	9	10	11
12	13	14	15	16	17	18
19	20	21	22	23	24	25
26	27	28	29	30	31	

FEBRUARY

S	M	T	W	T	F	S
						1
2	3	4	5	6	7	8
9	10	11	12	13	14	15
16	17	18	19	20	21	22
23	24	25	26	27	28	

MARCH

S	M	T	W	T	F	S
						1
2	3	4	5	6	7	8
9	10	11	12	13	14	15
16	17	18	19	20	21	22
23	24	25	26	27	28	29
30	31					

APRIL

S	M	T	W	T	F	S
		1	2	3	4	5
6	7	8	9	10	11	12
13	14	15	16	17	18	19
20	21	22	23	24	25	26
27	28	29	30			

MAY

S	M	T	W	T	F	S
				1	2	3
4	5	6	7	8	9	10
11	12	13	14	15	16	17
18	19	20	21	22	23	24
25	26	27	28	29	30	31

JUNE

S	M	T	W	T	F	S
1	2	3	4	5	6	7
8	9	10	11	12	13	14
15	16	17	18	19	20	21
22	23	24	25	26	27	28
29	30					

JULY

S	M	T	W	T	F	S
		1	2	3	4	5
6	7	8	9	10	11	12
13	14	15	16	17	18	19
20	21	22	23	24	25	26
27	28	29	30	31		

AUGUST

S	M	T	W	T	F	S
					1	2
3	4	5	6	7	8	9
10	11	12	13	14	15	16
17	18	19	20	21	22	23
24	25	26	27	28	29	30
31						

SEPTEMBER

S	M	T	W	T	F	S
	1	2	3	4	5	6
7	8	9	10	11	12	13
14	15	16	17	18	19	20
21	22	23	24	25	26	27
28	29	30				

OCTOBER

S	M	T	W	T	F	S
			1	2	3	4
5	6	7	8	9	10	11
12	13	14	15	16	17	18
19	20	21	22	23	24	25
26	27	28	29	30	31	

NOVEMBER

S	M	T	W	T	F	S
						1
2	3	4	5	6	7	8
9	10	11	12	13	14	15
16	17	18	19	20	21	22
23	24	25	26	27	28	29
30						

DECEMBER

S	M	T	W	T	F	S
	1	2	3	4	5	6
7	8	9	10	11	12	13
14	15	16	17	18	19	20
21	22	23	24	25	26	27
28	29	30	31			

5

JANUARY

S	M	T	W	T	F	S
				1	2	3
4	5	6	7	8	9	10
11	12	13	14	15	16	17
18	19	20	21	22	23	24
25	26	27	28	29	30	31

FEBRUARY

S	M	T	W	T	F	S
1	2	3	4	5	6	7
8	9	10	11	12	13	14
15	16	17	18	19	20	21
22	23	24	25	26	27	28

MARCH

S	M	T	W	T	F	S
1	2	3	4	5	6	7
8	9	10	11	12	13	14
15	16	17	18	19	20	21
22	23	24	25	26	27	28
29	30	31				

APRIL

S	M	T	W	T	F	S
			1	2	3	4
5	6	7	8	9	10	11
12	13	14	15	16	17	18
19	20	21	22	23	24	25
26	27	28	29	30		

MAY

S	M	T	W	T	F	S
					1	2
3	4	5	6	7	8	9
10	11	12	13	14	15	16
17	18	19	20	21	22	23
24	25	26	27	28	29	30
31						

JUNE

S	M	T	W	T	F	S
	1	2	3	4	5	6
7	8	9	10	11	12	13
14	15	16	17	18	19	20
21	22	23	24	25	26	27
28	29	30				

JULY

S	M	T	W	T	F	S
			1	2	3	4
5	6	7	8	9	10	11
12	13	14	15	16	17	18
19	20	21	22	23	24	25
26	27	28	29	30	31	

AUGUST

S	M	T	W	T	F	S
						1
2	3	4	5	6	7	8
9	10	11	12	13	14	15
16	17	18	19	20	21	22
23	24	25	26	27	28	29
30	31					

SEPTEMBER

S	M	T	W	T	F	S
		1	2	3	4	5
6	7	8	9	10	11	12
13	14	15	16	17	18	19
20	21	22	23	24	25	26
27	28	29	30			

OCTOBER

S	M	T	W	T	F	S
				1	2	3
4	5	6	7	8	9	10
11	12	13	14	15	16	17
18	19	20	21	22	23	24
25	26	27	28	29	30	31

NOVEMBER

S	M	T	W	T	F	S
1	2	3	4	5	6	7
8	9	10	11	12	13	14
15	16	17	18	19	20	21
22	23	24	25	26	27	28
29	30					

DECEMBER

S	M	T	W	T	F	S
		1	2	3	4	5
6	7	8	9	10	11	12
13	14	15	16	17	18	19
20	21	22	23	24	25	26
27	28	29	30	31		

6

JANUARY

S	M	T	W	T	F	S
					1	2
3	4	5	6	7	8	9
10	11	12	13	14	15	16
17	18	19	20	21	22	23
24	25	26	27	28	29	30
31						

FEBRUARY

S	M	T	W	T	F	S
	1	2	3	4	5	6
7	8	9	10	11	12	13
14	15	16	17	18	19	20
21	22	23	24	25	26	27
28						

MARCH

S	M	T	W	T	F	S
	1	2	3	4	5	6
7	8	9	10	11	12	13
14	15	16	17	18	19	20
21	22	23	24	25	26	27
28	29	30	31			

APRIL

S	M	T	W	T	F	S
				1	2	3
4	5	6	7	8	9	10
11	12	13	14	15	16	17
18	19	20	21	22	23	24
25	26	27	28	29	30	

MAY

S	M	T	W	T	F	S
						1
2	3	4	5	6	7	8
9	10	11	12	13	14	15
16	17	18	19	20	21	22
23	24	25	26	27	28	29
30	31					

JUNE

S	M	T	W	T	F	S
		1	2	3	4	5
6	7	8	9	10	11	12
13	14	15	16	17	18	19
20	21	22	23	24	25	26
27	28	29	30			

JULY

S	M	T	W	T	F	S
				1	2	3
4	5	6	7	8	9	10
11	12	13	14	15	16	17
18	19	20	21	22	23	24
25	26	27	28	29	30	31

AUGUST

S	M	T	W	T	F	S
1	2	3	4	5	6	7
8	9	10	11	12	13	14
15	16	17	18	19	20	21
22	23	24	25	26	27	28
29	30	31				

SEPTEMBER

S	M	T	W	T	F	S
			1	2	3	4
5	6	7	8	9	10	11
12	13	14	15	16	17	18
19	20	21	22	23	24	25
26	27	28	29	30		

OCTOBER

S	M	T	W	T	F	S
					1	2
3	4	5	6	7	8	9
10	11	12	13	14	15	16
17	18	19	20	21	22	23
24	25	26	27	28	29	30
31						

NOVEMBER

S	M	T	W	T	F	S
	1	2	3	4	5	6
7	8	9	10	11	12	13
14	15	16	17	18	19	20
21	22	23	24	25	26	27
28	29	30				

DECEMBER

S	M	T	W	T	F	S
			1	2	3	4
5	6	7	8	9	10	11
12	13	14	15	16	17	18
19	20	21	22	23	24	25
26	27	28	29	30	31	

7

JANUARY

S	M	T	W	T	F	S
						1
2	3	4	5	6	7	8
9	10	11	12	13	14	15
16	17	18	19	20	21	22
23	24	25	26	27	28	29
30	31					

FEBRUARY

S	M	T	W	T	F	S
		1	2	3	4	5
6	7	8	9	10	11	12
13	14	15	16	17	18	19
20	21	22	23	24	25	26
27	28					

MARCH

S	M	T	W	T	F	S
		1	2	3	4	5
6	7	8	9	10	11	12
13	14	15	16	17	18	19
20	21	22	23	24	25	26
27	28	29	30	31		

APRIL

S	M	T	W	T	F	S
					1	2
3	4	5	6	7	8	9
10	11	12	13	14	15	16
17	18	19	20	21	22	23
24	25	26	27	28	29	30

MAY

S	M	T	W	T	F	S
1	2	3	4	5	6	7
8	9	10	11	12	13	14
15	16	17	18	19	20	21
22	23	24	25	26	27	28
29	30	31				

JUNE

S	M	T	W	T	F	S
			1	2	3	4
5	6	7	8	9	10	11
12	13	14	15	16	17	18
19	20	21	22	23	24	25
26	27	28	29	30		

JULY

S	M	T	W	T	F	S
					1	2
3	4	5	6	7	8	9
10	11	12	13	14	15	16
17	18	19	20	21	22	23
24	25	26	27	28	29	30
31						

AUGUST

S	M	T	W	T	F	S
	1	2	3	4	5	6
7	8	9	10	11	12	13
14	15	16	17	18	19	20
21	22	23	24	25	26	27
28	29	30	31			

SEPTEMBER

S	M	T	W	T	F	S
				1	2	3
4	5	6	7	8	9	10
11	12	13	14	15	16	17
18	19	20	21	22	23	24
25	26	27	28	29	30	

OCTOBER

S	M	T	W	T	F	S
						1
2	3	4	5	6	7	8
9	10	11	12	13	14	15
16	17	18	19	20	21	22
23	24	25	26	27	28	29
30	31					

NOVEMBER

S	M	T	W	T	F	S
		1	2	3	4	5
6	7	8	9	10	11	12
13	14	15	16	17	18	19
20	21	22	23	24	25	26
27	28	29	30			

DECEMBER

S	M	T	W	T	F	S
				1	2	3
4	5	6	7	8	9	10
11	12	13	14	15	16	17
18	19	20	21	22	23	24
25	26	27	28	29	30	31

8

JANUARY

S	M	T	W	T	F	S
1	2	3	4	5	6	7
8	9	10	11	12	13	14
15	16	17	18	19	20	21
22	23	24	25	26	27	28
29	30	31				

FEBRUARY

S	M	T	W	T	F	S
			1	2	3	4
5	6	7	8	9	10	11
12	13	14	15	16	17	18
19	20	21	22	23	24	25
26	27	28	29			

MARCH

S	M	T	W	T	F	S
				1	2	3
4	5	6	7	8	9	10
11	12	13	14	15	16	17
18	19	20	21	22	23	24
25	26	27	28	29	30	31

APRIL

S	M	T	W	T	F	S
1	2	3	4	5	6	7
8	9	10	11	12	13	14
15	16	17	18	19	20	21
22	23	24	25	26	27	28
29	30					

MAY

S	M	T	W	T	F	S
		1	2	3	4	5
6	7	8	9	10	11	12
13	14	15	16	17	18	19
20	21	22	23	24	25	26
27	28	29	30	31		

JUNE

S	M	T	W	T	F	S
					1	2
3	4	5	6	7	8	9
10	11	12	13	14	15	16
17	18	19	20	21	22	23
24	25	26	27	28	29	30

JULY

S	M	T	W	T	F	S
1	2	3	4	5	6	7
8	9	10	11	12	13	14
15	16	17	18	19	20	21
22	23	24	25	26	27	28
29	30	31				

AUGUST

S	M	T	W	T	F	S
			1	2	3	4
5	6	7	8	9	10	11
12	13	14	15	16	17	18
19	20	21	22	23	24	25
26	27	28	29	30	31	

SEPTEMBER

S	M	T	W	T	F	S
						1
2	3	4	5	6	7	8
9	10	11	12	13	14	15
16	17	18	19	20	21	22
23	24	25	26	27	28	29
30						

OCTOBER

S	M	T	W	T	F	S
	1	2	3	4	5	6
7	8	9	10	11	12	13
14	15	16	17	18	19	20
21	22	23	24	25	26	27
28	29	30	31			

NOVEMBER

S	M	T	W	T	F	S
				1	2	3
4	5	6	7	8	9	10
11	12	13	14	15	16	17
18	19	20	21	22	23	24
25	26	27	28	29	30	

DECEMBER

S	M	T	W	T	F	S
						1
2	3	4	5	6	7	8
9	10	11	12	13	14	15
16	17	18	19	20	21	22
23	24	25	26	27	28	29
30	31					

9

JANUARY	MAY	SEPTEMBER
FEBRUARY	JUNE	OCTOBER
MARCH	JULY	NOVEMBER
APRIL	AUGUST	DECEMBER

10

JANUARY	MAY	SEPTEMBER
FEBRUARY	JUNE	OCTOBER
MARCH	JULY	NOVEMBER
APRIL	AUGUST	DECEMBER

11

JANUARY	MAY	SEPTEMBER
FEBRUARY	JUNE	OCTOBER
MARCH	JULY	NOVEMBER
APRIL	AUGUST	DECEMBER

12

JANUARY	MAY	SEPTEMBER
FEBRUARY	JUNE	OCTOBER
MARCH	JULY	NOVEMBER
APRIL	AUGUST	DECEMBER

13

JANUARY	MAY	SEPTEMBER
FEBRUARY	JUNE	OCTOBER
MARCH	JULY	NOVEMBER
APRIL	AUGUST	DECEMBER

14

JANUARY	MAY	SEPTEMBER
FEBRUARY	JUNE	OCTOBER
MARCH	JULY	NOVEMBER
APRIL	AUGUST	DECEMBER